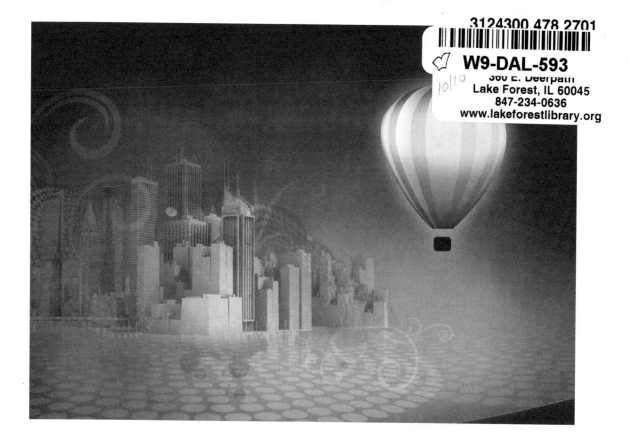

CorelDRAW® X5
The Official Guide

Gary David Bouton

New York   Chicago   San Francisco
Lisbon   London   Madrid   Mexico City
Milan   New Delhi   San Juan
Seoul   Singapore   Sydney   Toronto

Cataloging-in-Publication Data is on file with the Library of Congress

McGraw-Hill books are available at special quantity discounts to use as premiums and sales promotions, or for use in corporate training programs. To contact a representative, please e-mail us at bulksales@mcgraw-hill.com.

CorelDRAW® X5 The Official Guide

1 2 3 4 5 6 7 8 9 0   WFR WFR   1 0 9 8 7 6 5 4 3 2 1 0

ISBN   978-0-07-174517-8
MHID   0-07-174517-3

Sponsoring Editor	**Technical Editor**	**Production Supervisor**
Megg Morin	William Schneider	George Anderson
Editorial Supervisor	**Copy Editor**	**Composition**
Janet Walden	Jan Jue	Glyph International
Project Editor	**Proofreader**	**Illustration**
LeeAnn Pickrell	Paul Tyler	Gary Bouton and
Acquisitions Coordinator	**Indexer**	Glyph International
Meghan Riley	Rebecca Plunkett	**Art Director, Cover**
		Jeff Weeks

Adobe Systems, Corel Corporation, Microsoft, PostScript, and other brand names and trademarked items referenced in this book are the copyrights of their respective owners.

It's hard to have a passion about art without being somewhat of a dreamer.
I dedicate this book to the dream that there will be peace on Earth within our lifetime.

About the Author

Gary David Bouton is a seasoned author and illustrator with over 20 books to his name, covering programs such as CorelDRAW, Adobe Photoshop, and topics such as digital video editing, content creation for the Web, and 3D modeling. Gary has been drawing and painting both traditionally and electronically for close to 40 years and has been writing books and articles on art since 1992. He has received four international awards for design and desktop publishing and was a finalist in the CorelDRAW World Design Contest. In his other life, Gary composes and records music and works on CGI special effects for films.

About the Technical Editor

Having degrees in both engineering and art, William Schneider currently teaches computer graphics and darkroom photography in the School of Visual Communication at Ohio University. He has twice been a finalist in the annual Corel World Design Contest.

He has written 16 magazine articles about photography and computer artwork, and has had his graphic work published in a number of venues. For the textbook *Italian Renaissance Art: A Source Book,* he was responsible for furnishing hundreds of illustrations and photos. When he's not working at the computer or printing in his darkroom, he likes to ice skate and to build unusual loudspeakers in his shop.

CONTENTS AT A GLANCE

CONTENTS

FOREWORD

Having celebrated our 20th anniversary last year, it's our second decade of creating and refining our complete and easy-to-use graphic design suite. Learning resources remains a key element to enable users of CorelDRAW Graphics Suite to get going quickly and create amazing illustrations, layouts, graphics, and more. We are, therefore, including, in addition to our help system, electronic documentation, and video tutorials, a full-color hard-cover book of tips and techniques in the latest boxed version of the suite.

We're excited about the new *CorelDRAW X5 The Official Guide* you hold in your hands, because McGraw-Hill Professional and author Gary Bouton have taken a different approach to grasping and ultimately mastering our suite of programs. Because the team at Corel has covered the basics with our documentation, this has freed *The Official Guide* to focus on methods for perfecting your craft and design ambitions. You'll find expert instruction on illustration techniques, not only how to use CorelDRAW, but also how to get the *results* you have in mind. As you'll see, all the examples in *The Official Guide* are explained in digestible detail in a way that is *relevant* to a goal you have in mind. You'll learn as you create; step-by-step instructions are supported by dozens of example files you can download, and these examples will also provide an idea book you can build upon for inspiration in your own work.

This comprehensive guide is the result of a valued partnership between Corel Corporation and McGraw-Hill Professional. The author has worked closely with the product team at Corel to ensure that professionals and aspiring designers using our product have the information they need to quickly achieve stunning results.

Congratulations to our official guide author, Gary Bouton, for providing such a quality book packed with references, insights, and an accomplished illustrator's perspective on that intangible item that makes artwork attractive to an audience: *insight.* As you go through each chapter, I'm sure you'll find this to be an invaluable resource for both beginners and graphics professionals alike.

Both McGraw-Hill Professional and Corel present you with something truly new in this book and in the X5 Graphics suite, because like any successful communication that has to be open and two-way, you told us what you wanted, we listened, and *The Official Guide* is our reply to you.

Happy CorelDRAWing!
Gérard Métrailler
Sr. Director, Product Management, Graphics
Corel Corporation
Ottawa, Ontario
August 2010

ACKNOWLEDGMENTS

C'mon: you and I both know that no one reads the acknowledgments section in a book when it's much more fun to dive right into the meat of a detective novel, a historical fiction, and even a book on computer software. But if I've by chance caught your eye here, I'd like you to know that if you enjoy this book (the correct answer is yes, you will), the folks who worked together had just as much fun *creating* it. I can't think of a single book I've written in the past when the author, the production and layout people, and the editors just *clicked* as we did with this book. The bonus was that we got to know each other as we worked against deadlines to bring you this hefty piece of documentation. I'd like to introduce my friends to you now and to thank them for making my part in the *CorelDRAW X5 The Official Guide* the best kick one could possibly have without breaking any federal laws:

- To Megg Morin. Once again, Megg has played the gracious asylum keeper. She has freely offered me encouragement, advice, lots and lots of support for the direction in which I wanted to move this book, at times has humored me, and has let me get silly at least once in every chapter. Megg is good therapy for me, and this book will, in turn, be good therapy for you in the way it's written while you learn a very, very deep suite of applications.

- To Meghan Riley, for not only keeping track of an immense amount of data, but also for helping *me s*tay organized, in the kindest, most gracious fashion a freelance writer could hope for. Oh, oh; *look,* Meghan—the figure on page 285 is upside-down!!! *Onnnnnly* kidding! Thank you, Meghan.

- Project Editor LeeAnn Pickrell. Let me make it known that LeeAnn didn't just work on copy for this book; she worked with *me* to bring a sense of organization, worked with my style and not against it, and discussed chapters with me down to a level where at times I felt she was sitting in my office. Unfortunately, I have only one chair here, but I still want to thank you, LeeAnn, for making my mots into *bon* mots.

- Copy Editor Jan Jue. Jan went to extremes to ensure the book you're holding is accurate. I know of no other copy editor who actually installs the program a book is about and works alongside my documentation. Jan, thanks for your thoroughness, and for pointing out that certain thesauruses actually *do* contain synonyms for "thesaurus."

- Technical Editor William Schneider. Bill really should be listed as coauthor on the cover of this book, but that would probably mean making my own name smaller. Nah. Bill flew with me through every chapter, even the online bonus chapters, and he didn't stop at letting me know when I made a (small, insignificant, hardly worth mentioning) mistake in a tutorial step, or accidentally called the Mesh fill tool "that funny looking icon that messes up fills." Bill always offered a different and better way to cast a sentence and put a tutorial step in more reader-friendly terms. Bill, thanks, as always, for being my favorite technical editor for over a decade of books.

- Nicky Elliott, Barbara Bouton, and William Schneider for the use of their photography in this book's tutorials.

- Nick Wilkinson for portions of his original manuscript on VBA.

- Lyssa Wald for once again making the color section look as good on the printed page as it does on my monitor.

- Production Supervisor George Anderson. Thanks to George and his expert team for the layout of this book's interior.

- The folks at Glyph, who allowed me to get in there and work on a few figures to make them look their best in a black-and-white book.

- John Falsetto at Corel Corporation. Thanks for going that extra mile, John, and promptly providing me with answers to technical questions during the beta cycle right up to the release version of X5. The sort of candid backs-and-forths we exchanged in email were productive, refreshing, and ultimately for the better of the book.

- Tony Severenuk at Corel Corporation. Thanks to Tony for his technical support, his speed, and his ability to cut to the chase when I needed frank answers at a moment's notice. I'm sorry you never took me up on putting a cartoon of you in one of the book's illustrations, Tony; I had to make fun of Bill Schneider as a last-minute substitution. Hats off and a big bow of appreciation to you and all the people at Corel Corporation for supporting this book and my efforts. I hope I did you all proud.

INTRODUCTION

Bear with me as you read this book. Like any ongoing piece of literature, *CorelDRAW X5 The Official Guide* is a work in progress. Yes, the book is complete, but I wanted to approach the documentation of a new version of DRAW a little differently—okay, a *lot* differently—than did previous versions of this book. I've tried very hard to put a little of myself into this book, so you know that someone real, who professes to know CorelDRAW in certain ways better than you do, is communicating with you. Let's get real: CorelDRAW is *large.* The application has so many features that you might feel at times as well-oriented as if you were visiting this planet from another planet and a taxi driver dropped you off in the middle of Los Angeles. At 2 A.M.

So I want you to know I'm *here* for you; I want you to feel as though you own a Pocket Author, who talks to you in PlainSpeak, who makes tutorial files not only relevant but also interesting, and who as an artist provides you with what you need to accomplish a task instead of a generic, "This is what you need," or a presumptuous, "This is what we think you need." I'm going to ask you to think about what it is you want to do in CorelDRAW throughout the chapters, because you're probably a goal-oriented sort of fine artist or business professional. Although we have some of the best documentation on these pages concerning where items are, what tools do, and other structural definitions of CorelDRAW, knowing where a tool is, and knowing the steps to create a logo your boss wanted last Tuesday are two entirely different approaches to understanding. One is called "having a bunch of facts memorized" and the other is called Wisdom.

You'll see what I mean as you read through the chapters and work through the dozens of tutorial examples and files. Read this book, but *embrace* what you learn. I've learned through years of working in the field of graphics that when you understand a technique or a principle, you *own* it. You take it everywhere you go, it's part of your own personal craft, and you're all the richer as an artist when you digest the information you're given and turn it into something uniquely your own.

CorelDRAW X5 The Official Guide is divided into nine parts plus two online Bonus Chapters and an online Quick Reference listing keyboard shortcuts that'll speed up your work in CorelDRAW.

Organization is key to explaining things, so the parts follow a progression, from a very basic introduction to later chapters that delve into special effects, and with this edition, we've added two complete chapters on Corel PHOTO-PAINT, because it's an important program you *will* use if you first understand how to edit bitmap images. If you're the type of reader who likes to begin at the beginning and make a linear voyage to finish with the last chapter, you won't be surprised. However, the chapters are structured and fairly compartmentalized to address a specific topic; if you want fast solutions for specific areas within CorelDRAW, you can also "pick and choose." One of the wonderful things about books is that you can skip ahead and rewind—and probably do it faster than using an online search engine.

- **Part I** starts you off with the new features in CorelDRAW X5, a must-read for users who've made the upgrade. In particular, Chapter 1 is a tutorial-based jumpstart into graphics productivity—you'll create new stuff as you learn what's new! Also in this part, you'll be guided through CorelDRAW options, thoroughly pore through the menus and palettes (including CorelDRAW dockers), and you'll learn how to set up the workspace to make you feel right at home. New users are encouraged to set aside some quality time for this part—you'll save a lot of time later when you want to get to the Fun Stuff.

- **Part II** focuses on navigating and measuring the workspace and your document, and how to size things up, from measuring objects to moving and rotating them. You'll also learn how to set up a multi-page document, create brochures and flyers, and you'll see that each page can be a unique size and orientation.

- **Part III** gets you up and running with two of the most important tools used in designing original artwork, the Pen tools and the Shape tool. You'll also get a handle on creating shapes by using various presets CorelDRAW has to offer. Once you have your object created and edited to your liking, it's only natural to make more of them; this part shows you how to arrange, group, duplicate, clone, and perform other tasks in your document to make laying out what you've created an inspired effort.

- **Part IV** dives into typography, working with artistic and paragraph text, spelling and other CorelDRAW proofing tools, and some special effects you can create for fancy headlines. Sometimes it's better to just say it instead of show it; CorelDRAW has the ideal tools for both the text and graphic message, and these parts of the book also show how to blend the two vehicles artistically for what you want to communicate.

- **Part V** puts the meat on the bones of the objects you design; in these chapters, you'll learn everything you need to know about object fills, outline properties, and most importantly, about digital color. Learn how to define and apply uniform fills, bitmap fills, and colors from different *color models* to your work so they'll print exactly as you intend them to. And if you need a map or schematic drawing, check out this part for the lowdown on creating dashed lines, lines with arrowheads, and more.

- **Part VI** is a truly special part; you'll see that 3D object and scene creation doesn't require a megabuck modeling program—you'll find what you need to make scenes in camera-perfect perspective with CorelDRAW's Effects menu. You'll also learn how to extrude objects, letting CorelDRAW perform calculations to create a side view of the front of objects you draw. It's fun and the result can have the visual impact you need to create new worlds and sell your ideas.

- **Part VII** comes with a boatload of CorelDRAW special effects features, and these chapters take you through the steps to distorting, blending, and creating photorealistic effects such as object transparency and soft, lifelike shadows. If you've ever been stuck at a point where your design needs that "special something," look into this special part of the book. Learn how to create shading like you've seen in airbrush illustrations, to design chrome and glass-like objects, and to create a seamless integration between what you draw and the digital photos you can place in your document.

- **Part VIII** (that's "8" if you're tired of reading Roman numerals) moves from vector drawing to bitmap editing; specifically, you'll learn how Corel PHOTO-PAINT can help you resize and retouch photos and help you make near-perfect pictures into outstanding ones. Also in this part, you'll see how to work *between* DRAW and PHOTO-PAINT, to make a seamless composition that contains *both* vector and bitmap art. PHOTO-PAINT is part of the CorelDRAW Graphics Suite; it's sitting there for you on disk or on your hard drive. If you have a brochure or gallery photo you need to get out there and get noticed, you need to get with the program, and the program is Corel PHOTO-PAINT. This is truly an advanced section of the book, but it's accessible to readers of all skill levels, and its contents take you through working with photographs, getting your prints looking their best, and more. You'll also see how to get the best look out of imported bitmaps, beginning right with CorelDRAW's Raw Lab. Learn how to work with image resolutions, and see how to export your vector drawings to bitmap file format. You'll also want to pore through CorelDRAW's HTML publishing features—make that print ad you've designed into a web banner with only a few clicks. Finally…

- **Part IX** (pronounced "icks") introduces you to CorelDRAW's extensive host of print options and features; the techniques for output to paper, film, and transfer materials; and CorelDRAW's preflight options so your time and the expense of professional printing are on your side. Also, you'll learn how to prep your designs for nonprinting purposes. Get all the details on how CorelDRAW X5 can export your work for the Web, how to make a basic web page, and something additional and quite special. On the CorelDRAW installation DVD is a full working copy of SWiSH miniMax. This program can generate Flash animation for the Web; you'll learn step-by-step how to move copies of your CorelDRAW work to SWiSH, animate the objects, add a little audio that's provided for you via our website download, and how about this: you'll make a full-screen animation that loops (plays over and over) that's only 70K! A movie that's smaller than some CorelDRAW files? Yes. And it's all laid out for you in terms that someone who has no previous experience with animation can follow.

- **Online Bonus Chapters** document Visual Basic for Applications (VBA) in a PDF file you can download from www.mhprofessional.com/computingdownload and www.theboutons.com. See how to write simple scripts without actually writing a line of code (it's visual; you record cursor movements), and speed up your work by making common tasks automated through VBA. Also, learn how to design a typeface using CorelDRAW, and export your very own TrueType font. Imagine making and distributing a font that has your company logo to everyone in your department. You'll learn the steps in this online PDF document, and become font savvy in a jiffy.

- **The CorelDRAW Quick Reference**, which you'll also find online, is full of shortcuts you can use in CorelDRAW. Find a task you need to perform faster, and the Quick Reference lists the combinations of keys you can press to get you where you need to go.

Tutorial and Bonus Content: Where to Find It

 You can't miss a Tutorial section: it's marked with the Educated Lightbulb icon. Many of these Tutorials will go better and more smoothly, and better demonstrate a technique or principle, if you have a working file loaded in the drawing window, so we've provided you with several. To get the tutorial files, go to the following URLs:

- **www.mhprofessional.com**   From this page, click the Downloads link and locate this book's title to get to the tutorial files.
- **www.theboutons.com**   This is a mirror site for the files. Go to the top page, and you can't miss the conspicuous, obnoxious, but superbly designed CorelDRAW X5 Official Guide Download icon.

Additionally, www.theboutons.com has some Bonus Content, goodies for our readers that have nothing to do with this book's Tutorials, but *everything* to do with your continuing adventures in CorelDRAW. The Boutons are offering original, seamless tiling textures— perfect for web page backgrounds, custom object fills, and backgrounds in your CorelDRAW documents. You'll also find high-resolution images of indoor and outdoor scenes with blank signage. Because so many CorelDRAW users create billboards, package designs, and vinyl signs for vehicles, we thought it would be nice if you could previsualize a logo or other signage. You can then show your design to clients and coworkers before you go through the expense of commercial printing.

The Boutons also offer original typefaces and some content that we want to remain a surprise for now.

I know I speak for the entire group who helped make this book happen that we were highly motivated to make this *Official Guide* reflect all the creative possibilities that you'll have fun learning, exploring, and building upon. Playtime isn't the only time when a creative person can have fun. Work time can be fun, too. It's how you *approach* it.

So *enough* with introductions! Turn the page and get to the Good Stuff!

—Gary David Bouton

PART I

CorelDRAW X5
Essentials

CHAPTER 1

What's New in CorelDRAW X5?

The dozens of enhancements and improvements to CorelDRAW in version X5 aren't as obvious on paper as you'll *experience*; everything from significantly more precise drawing tools to a comprehensive color management system helps get what you envision down on the printable page. This version boasts something new and welcome to users at all skill levels and professions—both professional graphics designers and entrepreneurs with little artistic experience will be drawn to CorelDRAW.

Whether you're new to CorelDRAW or an old hand, you should take a few moments and review the new features covered in this chapter. Although features are categorized, *everyone* will find something to like in the sections to follow. You'll discover that "working smart" can also be a lot of *fun*.

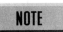 *Download and extract all the files from the Chapter 01.zip archive to follow the tutorials in this chapter.*

Features for the Graphics Designer

CorelDRAW X5 starts you off right with new drawings, with the New Document dialog box. From there, you'll notice several enhancements to DRAW's familiar design tools including new ones. Here's an overview of what's in store in this new version and covered in *The Official Guide*.

The Create a New Document Dialog Box

Unless you choose to override this feature, every time you choose File | New, or click the New button on the standard toolbar, the Create a New Document dialog box appears, as shown next. In the Create a New Document dialog you can choose color mode and color profile options, which alone are lifesavers when you have, for example, a dozen bitmap images to import and you need color consistency between what you draw, the color mode of the bitmaps, and the color profile of your intended output. Whether it's to the screen as a web page, or to a commercial printer—color reproduction and color accuracy are at the heart of every document you begin. Chapters 27 and 28 are your guides to personal and professional printing.

Additionally, document resolution (in dpi, or dots per inch) can be declared before you begin a drawing. The usefulness of this enhancement becomes immediately clear when you need to draw something for commercial presses—the document would be 300 dpi—or for the Web, which usually uses from 72 to 96 dpi screen resolution. You also have the familiar page size and orientation options, and also you can convert an existing document's color profile to a different one of your choosing.

Corel PHOTO-PAINT has the same dialog for new documents as CorelDRAW.

Drawing Tool Enhancements

One of the things you *won't* see in version X5—that you'll *like*—is the smoothness with which the Freehand and Artistic media tools produce paths. Corel Corp. has worked very hard to refine these curve tools, and you'll find you might not even need to use the Reduce Nodes feature while drawing.

Also, arrowheads (and tails!) you apply to paths can now be scaled to suit the proportion you need when designing maps and other diagrams. Suppose you need to convince a friend who's coming to visit you at your loft in SoHo in New York that the taxi will be much cheaper coming into Newark Liberty instead of JFK Airport—a fact only New Yorkers seem to know. Your intricate map needs 10-point outline paths, but the preset Arrowhead 2 is much too large to fit on East Houston Street and would cover part of Hamilton Fish Park. The solution is simple.

Scaling an Arrowhead

1. Select the 10-point path (with Arrowhead 2 applied), and double-click the Outline pen properties (nib) icon on the status bar to display the Outline Pen dialog.

2. Click the Options button below the arrowhead, and then click Attributes from the drop-down list.

3. Set the Length and Width interactively: put your cursor between the arrows to the right of the number field so the cursor becomes a double-headed arrow with the horizontal bar in the center, and then drag down in this example. Dragging up increases the Length or Width. This user interface element is called an *elevator button*; you can also enter values by typing them into the num boxes. At right, you'll see the preview window change the size of the arrowhead. In this example when the Length is about 40 points and the Width is about 34, you can click OK, and then click OK to exit the Outline Pen dialog, and your arrowhead is scaled to your liking.

Double-click
Outline icon.

Original arrowhead

Scaled arrowhead

E. Houston St.

That Italian Ice
and Soft Pretzel
Guy

My Loft

New to version X5 is the B-Spline tool for drawing perfectly smooth curves. B-splines are unlike paths produced with the Bézier and other drawing tools; they don't always have nodes directly on a path to steer a curve segment after or during drawing, and they don't have control handles for the curve's nodes. Figure 1-1 shows a creative example of B-splines—on a locked layer below the drawing is an image of a retro coffee table and chair, and the table is decorated with a design reflecting the art sensibilities of the late 1950s. The pattern was drawn with the B-Spline tool in Float control point mode. When you draw with this tool in Float control point mode, you're best off clicking instead of click-dragging: a faint series of dashed line segments is produced off the curve with control nodes, also off the curve of the path you draw. You simply have to try this tool to appreciate its many uses. To end a path, double-click, and then use the Shape tool to refine the curve. Editing the curve is done by dragging the control nodes. In 3D modeling applications, these dashed lines connecting nodes are called "control hulls"—a hull shapes each path segment. At any time, you can put a control node directly on a path segment by clicking the Make Control Point Clamped button on the property bar. To make the path editable as you'd edit all other paths created with any of the Curve tool group, choose Arrange | Convert To Curves (CTRL+Q). However, unless you have a truly specific need for converting the control hull to nodes along a path, don't do this, because it will destroy the smoothness of the path when you edit it with the Shape tool.

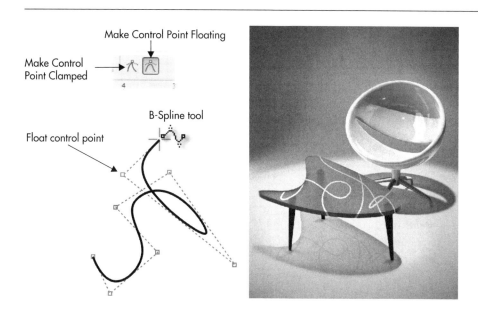

FIGURE 1-1   The new B-Spline drawing tool is like having a traditional French curve at your disposal in CorelDRAW.

New Corner Edits for Rectangles

CorelDRAW X5 has better and easier to use Fillet (rounded corner)/Scallop/Chamfer features on a docker whenever you want to embellish a sharp turn in a path. Now, these same features are available on the property bar whenever you've drawn *a rectangle,* even one you've drawn with the Smart Drawing tool. If you're not familiar with editing corners of rectangles and other shapes, the steps aren't Newtonian or anything:

1. If you've drawn a rectangle, choose the Shape tool for custom editing, and then click either the Fillet, Scallop, or Chamfer button on the property bar. This action sets all four corners of the rectangle to have an equal, predefined amount of corner alteration.

2. To change the amount of corner alteration, drag with the Shape tool on one corner control node, toward or away from the original corner. By default, the Edit Corners Together lock button on the property bar is switched on, and all edits you perform to one corner apply to all corners.

3. Let's say you're an asymmetrical sort of designer and want one corner more deeply cut than the other three. Unlock the Edit Corners Together button by clicking it. Now CTRL-click one of the corner control nodes and drag. You can also click a corner node to select it, and then *release the mouse button,* and *then* click-drag the control node to edit only that corner.

4. If you want to lop off the corners of a polygon created with, for example, the Polygon tool—or any freeform shape you've designed that has a sharp cusp turn along the path—you need to choose Window | Dockers | Fillet/Scallop/Chamfer. Choose one of the operations from the drop-down list, and then use the elevator button to increase or decrease the radius the docker uses to trim the corners. You'll see a live preview in faint blue around the object, and you click Apply when you're satisfied with the preview.

Figure 1-2 shows callouts for the buttons used for rectangles, and there's also an illustration of a severely messed-up polygon or two, perfect for certificates and fancy badges. Corel didn't cut any corners with the Fillet/Scallop/Chamfer feature in X5, but *you* will.

> **NOTE** *The Relative Corner Scaling button is for when you want to change the size of a rectangle, with or without changing the corner work you've done. If the option is enabled, the corners of your rectangle scale proportionately when you use the Pick tool or other method to increase or decrease the rectangle's size. When you turn this feature off, you can get some really weird and visually interesting effects. Imagine making deep corner cuts on a rectangle, and then making the rectangle half its original size...but the corners remain the same cut size.*

Why settle for plain rectangles when you can fancy up the corners with the new rectangle features in X5?

Revamped Mesh Fill Tool

The Mesh fill tool has undergone some refinements, and it's not only easier to work with, but it's also a positive joy to fill an object and then move colors around in it, in a way that makes fountain fills look like kids' stuff. Here's a short example you can work through in less than 2 minutes: try to think of another way to get a feathered drop shadow that you can move anywhere on the drawing page!

1. Open Bowl of fruit.cdr and then choose Tools | Object Manager so you can arrange the object you'll create to go behind the grouped bowl of grapes, but in front of the background rectangle. Click the little + symbol to the left of the Layer 1 entry so you can see the contents of Layer 1.

2. With the Ellipse tool, click-drag an oval that suggests the shape and size of a cast shadow beneath the bowl. Then click a dark shade of black on the Color Palette, and finally, right-click the "None" color well to remove the outline from the object.

3. On the Object Manager list, click-drag the Ellipse entry to below the Group of 137 Objects entry, but above the Rectangle entry.

4. Choose the Mesh fill tool from the toolbox; it's in the group with the Interactive fill tool. With the ellipse selected, you'll see mesh nodes and a dashed outline depicting the default two rows and two columns of mesh areas for the fill within the ellipse.

5. Marquee-select the entire object with the Mesh fill tool, and then on the property bar click the Transparency button to the right of the num box to reveal the slider—drag the slider to 100% transparency.

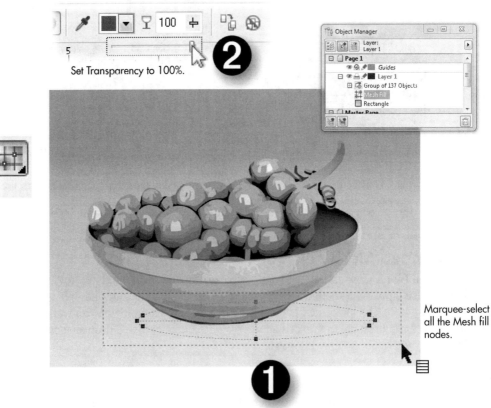

Set Transparency to 100%.

Marquee-select all the Mesh fill nodes.

6. Click the pasteboard area of the workspace, the area *outside* of the page, to deselect everything, and then click the center mesh intersection node.

7. Click-drag the Transparency slider on the property bar to 0% transparency, all the way to the left.

8. Have some fun shaping the ellipse to make it a little more irregular and less like an ellipse. You'll see that the Mesh fill's transparent regions change as you reshape the ellipse, and you can make the fill even more intricate by click-dragging any of the mesh intersection node control handles. You can also recolor and specify a different transparency by clicking a path and then editing it. Figure 1-3 shows some of the editing in progress.

If you'd like to open and examine a complex illustration that demonstrates the creative use of the Mesh fill tool, check out wet.cdr, as shown in Wireframe and Enhanced views in Figure 1-4. On occasion a Linear or Radial fountain fill will complete a graphic idea you have in mind, but it you want to approach painting-like compositions and photorealistic drawing of natural shapes, the enhanced Mesh fill tool in version X5 is your ticket.

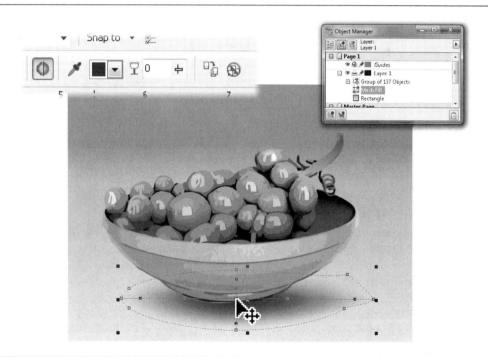

FIGURE 1-3   Work with the Mesh fill tool to make color and transparency transitions in a way that regular fountain fills cannot match.

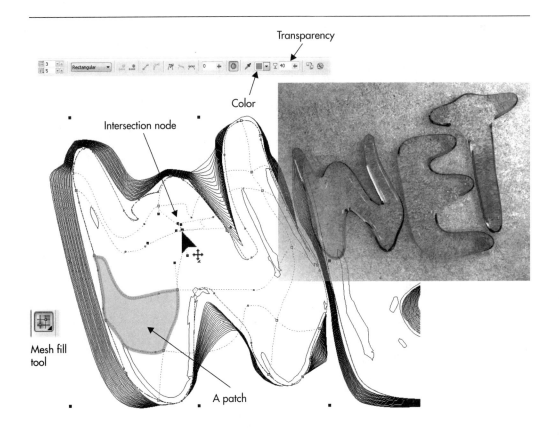

FIGURE 1-4   Use the Mesh fill tool on objects you want to make look reflective, semitransparent, or just less like "computer art."

More Power to PowerTRACE

The auto-trace feature in X5 has been supercharged in this new CorelDRAW version to the point where it rivals—if not exceeds—the smoothness and accuracy of Vector Magic, a favored late entry in the stand-alone bitmap-to-vector application field of software. The feature set will seem familiar, but you'll be pleased at the new results. As an acid test, the author enlarged a single character from a shareware font and deliberately aliased the copy. Figure 1-5 shows the results of a very challenging assignment for PowerTRACE. The result actually was a usable character for a typeface, and as you can see here, even with all the jaggy bitmap aliasing, Corel PowerTRACE maintained smoothness and accuracy in the trace and produced far fewer control points than were in the original typeface!

Aliased bitmap Corel PowerTRACE conversion PowerTRACE character

Original vector character Corel PowerTRACE conversion

FIGURE 1-5 The improved PowerTRACE feature can smoothly trace even poor copies of bitmap images.

If you'd like to try this little experiment, open Tracing.cdr. At right is the bitmap; you select it, click the Trace Bitmap button on the property bar, choose Outline Trace from the drop-down list, and then try the Detailed logo setting. At left in this file is the finished trace—the objects were combined so the trace is one combined path that could be exported as a TrueType character, but the font already exists as shareware, so case closed on this one.

New Pixel View

Under View you have a new entry in X5: the Pixel view of everything on your page. This is a welcome addition to DRAW for everyone who needs to preview a button or other web graphic before exporting it. Pixel view works hand-in-hand with the new graphic resolution settings: you'll clearly see a preview of individual pixels on the page when you zoom in if your document is defined at a screen resolution such as 72 or 96 pixels per inch (ppi).

New Document Palette

Wouldn't it be nice to have a collection of the colors you've used in a document all neatly arranged for future use? Corel thought so, too, and now X5 sports the Document palette, accessed via Window | Color Palettes | Document Palette. You can add a color to the palette by dragging one from an existing palette, you can eyedropper-sample anything in the workspace—including anything on a docker—and you can even move CorelDRAW's application window down to then sample your Windows desktop or other application—and add a sample to the Document palette.

Colors can be deleted, the palette can be saved as a global palette, and other operations are performed through the palette's menu—click the triangle icon to open the menu list.

Eyedroppers All Over the Place

Corel has simplified the task of getting the color you need at a moment's notice by adding eyedropper tools to several of the dockers, tool option palettes, and possibly the front door to Corel's offices in Ottawa. When you need a color, X5 has you covered.

Adobe Application Compatibility

If you have a client or coworker who uses Adobe applications such as Photoshop or Illustrator, file types such as PSD, PDF, and AI seamlessly import and export from and to these programs, to and from CorelDRAW X5. Try starting a new document using sRGB as the color settings. Click the Color Settings double down-arrow in the Create a New Document dialog if sRGB is not apparent as a choice, and then import Hot ideas.psd. As shown in Figure 1-6, this layered bitmap file was originally composed in Photoshop CS 5,

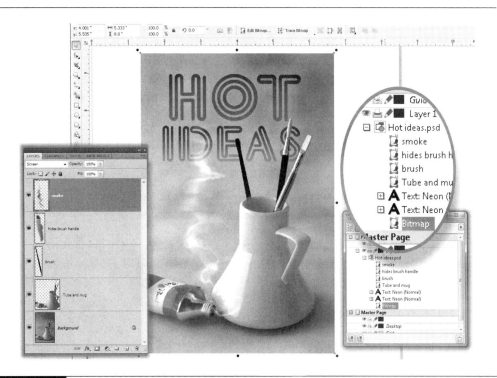

FIGURE 1-6   Work with Photoshop layers in CorelDRAW as easily as done in Adobe programs.

saved in Photoshop with maximum backward compatibility enabled, and it imports to a CorelDRAW page as a bitmap group, with all the user names of the layers preserved.

You can easily do the sort of editing shown in this figure:

1. After importing and placing the layered bitmap on a page, open Tools | Object Manager, right-click the PSD filename entry, and then choose Ungroup All.

2. Add some text. In this figure, the font Neon is used with a small glow applied using the Drop Shadow tool.

3. Drag the text entry down on the Object Manager list to just above the bottom layer in the PSD file. In this example, by doing this, one of the brush handles intrudes on the text, making the composition more integrated and dimensional.

You can also move layer contents around, and when you create a new document you need to export as a PSD bitmap file, every layer you create in CorelDRAW can appear as a separate layer when someone opens the exported file in Photoshop. The same is true of Illustrator—CorelDRAW preserves layers and layer order.

Introducing Corel CONNECT

Ever since Corel stopped direct support of DRAW's Scrapbook, some diehard fans just prefer to connect to drawings—and *also* to fonts, images, and *media on the Web*—by using new Corel CONNECT. Corel CONNECT is a media browser that runs as a stand-alone application and also can be called from inside DRAW and PHOTO-PAINT. Corel CONNECT can be configured in only moments to display the contents of offline media (such as Flickr and your Corel Graphics Suite installation DVD), the contents of any folder on your hard disk, and to create a favorites list for quick access. For even quicker access, CONNECT features a tray where you can drag and drop content you frequently need—you then access the tray's contents from CONNECT, or as a docker from within DRAW and PHOTO-PAINT.

Here's a quick tour of how you set up and use Corel CONNECT in tandem with CorelDRAW to find a piece of artwork you created a year ago and want to use as part of a new composition.

Connecting with Your Content

1. If you can't find Corel CONNECT in Windows' Start application list, launch CorelDRAW and then click the Application Launcher icon on the standard toolbar.

2. If this is the first time you've run Corel CONNECT, you'll see a welcome screen in the main viewing pane, your Favorite Folders list at left is probably empty, and the tray at the bottom of the interface is empty. Display the "expand list" triangles next to the items in the Folders list by moving the mouse to that area. Click the triangle to the left of "Computer" in the Folders list area (bottom left) to expand the tree, and then navigate down until you find a folder that you know contains saved CorelDRAW illustrations. Put a check in the box to the left of the folder, and before you know it, the main preview window is populated with not only CorelDRAW artwork files, but everything Corel CONNECT can recognize as vector art, bitmap images, typeface files, and over 100 other file types, complete with preview thumbnails.

3. Let's limit the search to only CorelDRAW files. In the Search field at top right, type the wildcard ***.CDR** and then press ENTER. Bingo, other vector file types are ignored, and you now see only CorelDRAW preview thumbnails. Hover your cursor over a thumbnail to see a larger version and file info associated with the file. To zoom your view of *all* the main pane's contents, use the slider below the main pane.

4. Let's say you want quick access to these files: you make them a favorites location. Drag the folder from the Folders area into the Favorite Folders area, and then click the newly dragged folder in the Favorite Folders area. Only the Favorite Folders location you've clicked has its contents displayed in the main preview pane.

5. You are bound to have at least one or two favorites that you want immediate access to in DRAW or PHOTO-PAINT. Put these items in the tray—drag a thumbnail from the main pane when you have your favorites folder selected, and then drag it down to the tray. Right-clicking any tray item gives you access to shortcut commands such as opening the media in DRAW or PAINT, and opening the location of the file as it resides on your hard disk. Corel CONNECT organizes your files, but it doesn't move them from their original folder location. At the left side of the tray are launch commands and also the Remove button. Clicking the Remove button removes the item from the tray, but it doesn't delete any of your work from your hard disk. Figure 1-7 shows a labeled layout of Corel CONNECT.

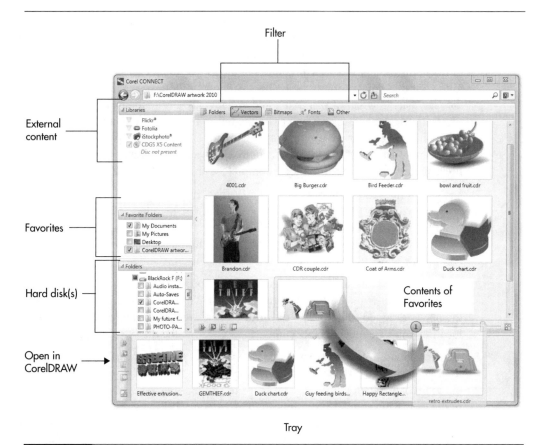

FIGURE 1-7 Use Corel CONNECT to organize your work and access most-used items from within DRAW and PHOTO-PAINT.

6. Once you have even one item in CONNECT's tray, this item is automatically synchronized to show in DRAW and PHOTO-PAINT when you open them and choose to display the application tray; the command is Windows | Dockers | Tray. Open CorelDRAW now, perhaps create a rectangle and apply a texture fill, and then open the tray so you can add a foreground object (or group of objects) to the composition.

7. Drag the thumbnail onto the page. CorelDRAW copies the content, and presto, your composition is hours ahead of any other method for adding content to a composition.

*Corel CONNECT's Search field does more than filter for specific file types. If, for example, you insert your CorelDRAW Graphics Suite DVD into an optical drive, and then choose the disk from the Libraries list, you can type the name of a file in the Search field to hone in on the DVD content you want. Type **flower** as an example, and the main preview window will display all images and vector files whose metadata tags (created for you by Corel) have "flower" as a keyword. A file doesn't have to be named "flower" for CONNECT to locate and display it. This is also why it's a good idea when saving your own files to fill in keywords; choose File | Document Properties and then type anything that will help you recall the file into the Keywords field. Then press CTRL+S.*

For the Business Professional

If you're a new user, or a professional who needs graphics but doesn't illustrate, X5 bundles not only outstanding tools to make complex drawing go very simply, but also a handsome collection of ready-to-use artwork. The following sections describe what's new and what's been fortified in X5.

Clip Art and Photographs

The CorelDRAW Graphics Suite DVD comes with over 10,000 drawings and beautiful digital images to complement a banner, brochure cover, or any other collateral material for a small to medium business. Much of this content is all new, and this is another good reason to learn to use Corel CONNECT— without some organization you'd be like a wealthy tycoon drowning in a vault of gold pieces!

Fonts

Over a thousand new OpenType fonts have been added to the already comprehensive list of typefaces you can install from the DVD. In particular, the complete Helvetica family is at your beck and call, a very classic, clean font family, perfect for sales materials. And there's also Frutiger, a nice alternative to Helvetica, more contemporary, with a sleek and slick look in any graphics use.

Templates

The DVD comes with 2,000 templates for vehicles, and 350 other templates for business use. Use Corel CONNECT to browse these goodies for the template you need, and then choose File | New From Template to get up and running in no time.

X5 Extras

The DVD provides extra media brushstrokes and bitmap fills, which will appeal to both business users and graphics professionals. You'll also want to check out the over 2 hours' worth of training tutorials on the DVD; again, use Corel CONNECT to browse for the tips and tricks you needed yesterday.

For anyone who has enjoyed watching animated Flash banners on the Web and said, "I gotta learn this Flash stuff…someday," your day has come. The install DVD has a copy of SWiSH miniMax, a limited edition of SWiSH miniMax's popular Flash-generating software. SWiSH miniMax takes the mind-boggling details out of Flash animation creation, and you might also want to check out Chapter 28, where *The Official Guide* walks you through, step-by-step, how to produce a vector animation complete with audio.

NOTE
As you travel through this book's examples, you'll be asked to change certain CorelDRAW settings, and as a (happy) consequence, your copy of CorelDRAW X5 will no longer be set at its factory defaults. There's nothing wrong *with using a nonstandard configured copy of DRAW, but if your boss or coworker insists that you undo changes to settings and options, hold* F8 *before you launch CorelDRAW, and continue to hold until you see the splash screen. This action restores CorelDRAW to* all *of its default settings, which is* something you'll want to think about with due deliberation*, without the distraction of playing Lady GaGa on your iPod at 124 decibels, operating heavy machinery, or having a tooth extracted with an "As Seen on TV" device.*

You could call this chapter the tip of the iceberg, if your idea of a fun time is an iceberg (Leonardo DiCaprio didn't). Kidding aside, there are a lot of pages under your right thumb, and it's all good stuff. Bring along some curiosity and a design idea or two, and shift into second gear.

CHAPTER 2

Exploring Your Workspace

Working in CorelDRAW X5, you'll find yourself using an assortment of interface elements that offer control over everything you do. Many areas make up the interface because the program offers an abundance of creative tools that you can use to create compelling graphics and documents. Certain areas of the interface such as the property bar are context sensitive: your available options change as you choose different toolbox tools. Other interface areas, like the toolbox, are always visible in the workspace. And then there are dockers, which are displayed only if you specifically open them. Exactly which—and where—elements appear in the program interface is not a set piece; you have ultimate flexibility and customization control so you can *personalize* CorelDRAW. You can choose a predesigned workspace—CorelDRAW's default—or you can add, remove, and rearrange options to suit your work needs and even make the interface look like Adobe Illustrator. The important thing is that you should *feel at home* working in CorelDRAW; this chapter shows you where everything is, and how you can make it suit your work style.

The CorelDRAW X5 Workspace

CorelDRAW X5 has been carefully revamped from previous versions to make it easier for you to find and work with the tools you need to use, when you need to use them.

CorelDRAW workspace elements can be divided into two categories:

- Global and program control elements, such as measurement scales, backup files, and memory use

- Design or complete document features, such as guidelines, styles, and nudge distances

If you're new to CorelDRAW or just new to this version, you *will* want to take a look at the roadmap to follow, and get a handle on CorelDRAW's interface.

CorelDRAW X5's Application Window

The application window is mainly what you see when CorelDRAW X5 is open. It is the stage that surrounds and contains the drawing windows. *Drawing windows* (sometimes called document windows) contain the drawing page or pages that hold the graphics and other content you create. Even if no drawing windows are open, the application window provides access to certain command menus, toolbars, the toolbox, dockers, status bar, and the Color Palette. Figure 2-1 identifies the application window parts.

You can have more than one drawing window (sometimes called a *document window* in other applications) open in the application window, but only one can be active at a time. The specific settings you see displayed on the toolbar, property bar, dockers, and other application window interface elements are those that are assigned to the currently active drawing window. They change if you make another drawing window active by clicking the desired drawing window.

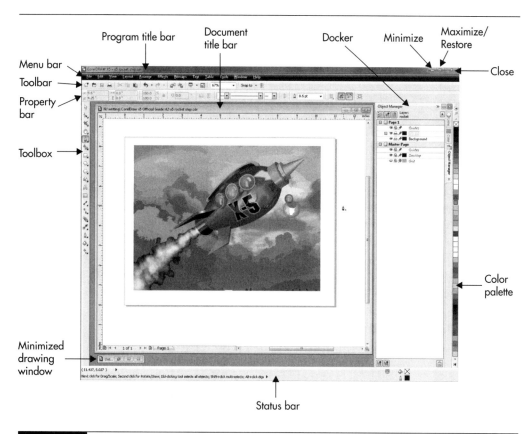

FIGURE 2-1   CorelDRAW X5's application window features these interface areas.

As in all standard Windows applications, clicking the Close button at the top right side of the application window's title bar closes CorelDRAW X5. Clicking the Minimize button shows or hides CorelDRAW X5, and clicking the Maximize/Restore button quickly changes the size of the application window itself. Clicking a drawing window's Close button closes the drawing window, removing it from the application window, while clicking a drawing window's Minimize or Maximize/Restore button minimizes it to a document title bar near the bottom of the application window or restores it to size within the application window.

NOTE   *With CorelDRAW open and all documents closed, you can still perform many necessary tasks. You can use File commands and open suite applications such as Corel CAPTURE, Corel BARCODE WIZARD, Corel PHOTO-PAINT, and even another copy of CorelDRAW with the Application Launcher. You can also use some of Corel's tool managers, work with macros, view help topics, and access Corel's online web resources through the Welcome screen.*

The Application Launcher on the application window's toolbar allows you to open another, unique copy of CorelDRAW, but simply because you can *doesn't mean you* should. *Depending on how your memory preferences are set up in Tools | Options | Workspace | Memory, you could potentially throttle your computer's system RAM and lose valuable work; the only reason you'd do this would be to copy objects between documents. You can achieve the same result much more simply and with less chance of a system halt by copying and moving objects between drawing windows in a* single *session of CorelDRAW.*

Drawing Windows

When a drawing window is fully maximized, it fills the dark gray space in the center of the application window and looks as if it is *part* of the application window. When a drawing window is open but *not* fully maximized, it is easy to see that it's a separate window element with its own interface elements that are unique to that drawing window.

Unlike the menu bar, property bar, toolbar, toolbox, Color Palette, and dockers, a drawing window cannot be dragged outside of the application window and onto the desktop or onto a second monitor's desktop.

Not surprisingly, the interface elements that are contained within a drawing window report on or control that specific drawing window. Like the application window, a drawing window also has standard window controls such as a title bar that identifies the document's file path and name, as well as Minimize, Maximize/Restore, and Close buttons. Drawing windows also have page borders, which (as with other windows) can be dragged to change the size of the window. They also have scroll bars that are used to change your view of the document's contents.

Interface elements special to drawing windows include *rulers;* the *document navigator,* which is used to add, delete, and move between pages in a multi-page drawing window (see Chapter 6); the *drawing page,* which contains what can be printed; and the *Navigator button,* which helps you move around a drawing without having to zoom out.

CorelDRAW X5 is compliant with the Microsoft Windows standard for multiple document interfaces, meaning you can have more than one document (drawing) window open at a time. To switch between drawing windows, choose Window | *document name* (where *document name* is the actual name of your CorelDRAW X4 document). In Figure 2-2, you can see a

Parent and Child Window Buttons

A document's Minimize, Maximize/Restore, and Close buttons are not located in the drawing window frame when a drawing window is maximized in the application window. The Minimize, Maximize/Restore, and Close buttons for the current drawing window are grayscale, smaller in size, and placed just below the Minimize, Maximize/Restore, and Close buttons that belong to the application window.

If you want to close a document window, but your attention is wandering a bit and you are running on autopilot, it's easy to make a mistake and click the larger, more colorful Close button that belongs to the *entire* CorelDRAW application.

So save your work often and try to remember that the big, red button is for the whole application and the smaller one is for the document at hand.

basic and very useful drawing window technique: Suppose you have an object in one document window and want a copy of it in a different one. You choose Window | Tile Vertically (you can do this manually if you're skilled manipulating windows in Windows), and then move the object by just dragging it into the other window using the Pick tool. To copy the object, hold the modifier key CTRL as you drag from one window to the other.

Hold CTRL and click-drag to copy.

FIGURE 2-2   Working between drawing windows is accomplished by click-dragging using the Pick tool.

CorelDRAW uses a default naming system of Untitled-1, Untitled-2, and so on, incrementing the number for each new document you open in the current CorelDRAW session. You are given the chance (and you should take it) to give your drawing a more meaningful name when you save the document by choosing File | Save or pressing CTRL+S.

You can also open more than one document window showing the *same* document, enabling you to work on one document in multiple windows. This is a particularly useful feature when you need to zoom in close to work on a small area of a graphic, but you also need to be able to see how your work on that area affects the whole composition.

Both windows are "live," so you can edit in either of them, and all the changes you make editing in one window will also appear in the other window, because these windows represent different *views* of the same document, *not* two independent files that can be saved as different versions.

To open another view of the active drawing window, choose Window | New Window. To make one of the open views the active window, you can click that window, or you can also use Window | *document name:N* (where *N* is the automatically applied view number). Open as many windows as you need—this feature is limited only by your available system resources.

Specifying Toolbar and Dialog Values

Many times when working in CorelDRAW, you need to enter measurements or numeric values, choose options and states, and control the behavior of interface elements on toolbars, in dialogs, and so on. CorelDRAW uses a wide variety of standard input fields and controls to make it easy for you to enter or tweak the specific kind of data you need. This section guides you through the ways data can be entered and alerts you to some of the extra power and usability Corel engineers have given these interface elements.

- **Num boxes**   To specify values, you'll find *num* boxes—short for *numeric* boxes. Usually a value already is in the box, such as the page width in the following illustration. Just highlight the existing value using a click-drag action, and then type a new value. Alternatively, you can double-click to select the entire value in the num box before typing the value you want. If you insert the cursor at any point in the existing value, you can use your keyboard arrow keys to move within the value and then backspace to remove the number entry, then adding the value you need. Finally, you need to confirm the value you entered by pressing…ENTER. Press TAB to quickly move your cursor from one num box to the next in the group, or press SHIFT+TAB to move to the previous box. In dialogs, clicking the Apply button applies the new options and leaves the dialog open; clicking OK closes the dialog and applies the new values or options. On toolbars, pressing ENTER after typing the value does the same thing, as shown here.

Highlight the existing value; then type in the value you need.

TIP *Here's an unexpected convenience: you can perform calculations in num boxes using simple math equations to arrive at a value you need. Type symbols between values to create the equation sequences. Use your plus (+) and minus (−) keys for adding and subtracting, and your asterisk (*) and forward slash (/) keys for multiplying and dividing. Pressing ENTER performs the calculation. Naturally, you can't enter invalid keystrokes in a value box, such as alphabet letters—you'll just get a system beep after pressing ENTER, and the previous, proper numerical value will reappear.*

- **Combo boxes** *Combo* (short for *combination*) is a num box with a clickable selection button for access to preset values. You can enter a specific value into a combo box either by typing, or by choosing a preset value from the selector. Toolbar and docker combo boxes often require pressing ENTER to apply the new value you type in, while clicking Apply or OK in dialogs does the same thing.

Enter value or click button to select preset value.

- **Flyout option menus** On certain toolbars and dockers, you're going to find flyout menus, which are often accessed by clicking a button that has a small, triangular-shaped, flyout arrow pointing to the right. For example, you can spot a tool on the toolbox that has extended options you access from the tool button by a tick mark on the button's lower right. Flyouts often contain ways to change behavior states, apply commands, and access options. Some apply options immediately, while others require that they be closed first using the small X symbol usually found at the upper-right corner. Examples of each are shown in the following:

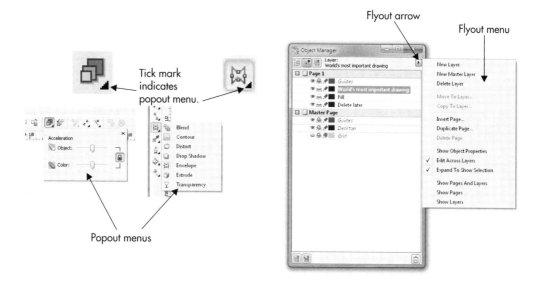

Tick mark indicates popout menu.

Flyout arrow

Flyout menu

Popout menus

- **Color selectors**   *Color selectors* often appear in dialogs or toolbars as a clickable button that has the secondary function of displaying the currently selected color, as shown here. Clicking opens a selector to display the current color palette and requires you to click once to specify a color. Most color selectors also include the Other button, which is a shortcut to color models, mixers, and palettes (covered in Chapter 17).

Click to access a complete set of color mixers and digital color models.

- **List selectors**   *List selectors* differ from combo boxes in that you cannot enter a value, but instead pick from a predefined list of values or graphic samples that show the way that a style or arrow (or similar) will be applied or created, as shown on the next page. Clicking one of the entries in the list chooses and applies a value, size, state, mode, or style to the currently selected object. These lists are occasionally called drop-down lists in other applications and pull-down lists in Apple's OS X.

Click to access preset values.

- **Radio buttons and option boxes** These two interface devices are slightly different, not just in shape, but also in the choices they offer, as shown next. *Radio* buttons are round, come in groups, and only allow you to select one of the options in the group at a time. *Option* boxes are square and let you choose an option or state to be either on (with a check mark) or off (without a check mark). You'll find in many areas of the Options pages that you can choose more than one option (more than one box can be checked) at a time.

Click to activate the option.

Click to choose between options.

- **Buttons** Buttons appear throughout CorelDRAW and can do one of several things. *Command* buttons perform commands instantaneously, but *toggle* buttons control (and indicate) a specific feature's On and Off states, using a pressed or not pressed appearance. Generally, a *pressed* state indicates On, while the *not pressed* state indicates Off. *Shortcut* buttons open dialogs to further options, while *selector* buttons open lists of preset selections.

Off (inactive) ⟶ ⟵ On (active)

2

- **Spinners** *Spinners* (also known as *spin boxes*) are similar to combo boxes, in that they can be used to specify values by typing *or* by using mouse actions. Single clicks on the up and down arrow buttons increase or decrease the values incrementally, but you can also click-drag on the divider between the two arrow buttons—up to increase or down to decrease the value.

Highlight existing value; then type value in the box.

Click-drag to increase/decrease.

Click to increase/decrease.

- **Sliders** You use sliders to specify values within a given range—often between 0 and 100 and often based on percent—by entering values, or by dragging a control slider, which is intuitive and provides the anticipated results. To manipulate a slider value, use a click-drag action to move the slider either right (to increase) or left (to decrease), as shown here on the property bar after the Interactive transparency tool has been used.

Enter value.

Click-drag to increase/decrease.

- **Pop-up menus** To access pop-up menu commands and options, click your right mouse button (instead of the typical left-click) on any given point. The pop-up menu appears at the tip of your cursor (as shown on the next page) and closes automatically after a selection is made or by clicking elsewhere in the interface. Pop-up menus are sometimes called contextual menus, and a right-facing arrow next to a pop-up menu item indicates that there's a submenu with still more options, usually relating to the main menu option.

Pop-up menu

Indicates submenu options

Left-handed artists are not uncommon; if you're a southpaw, the order of your mouse buttons is not defined in CorelDRAW, but instead in the operating system's Control Panel | Mouse. Just mirror the instructions in this chapter: if a step tells you to left-click, it's the right mouse button, and vice versa.

Working with Dockers

Dockers are panels—palettes—where many different commands and controls related to specific tasks are grouped together in one handy location. Dockers put more of Corel's power right at the tip of your cursor without forcing you to dig through lots of dialogs or flit between various toolbars and menus.

These controls can be anchored to the edge of the screen and reduced to tabs or title bars; so you can tear them off and float them right next to where you are working in the interface. You can also resize them to make your own groups of commonly used dockers. And, if you have a multi-monitor setup, you can even drag them out of the application window and stick them on a different monitor so that you have the maximum amount of space for your drawing windows.

If you don't find a docker that fills your needs after looking through the list of 29 dockers on the Window | Dockers menu, dust off your programming skills, and make your own *custom* docker. If you're not a programmer, check the Internet for any third-party developers who are taking advantage of CorelDraw X5's capability to use third-party dockers.

Opening, Moving, and Closing Dockers

Dockers can be opened using shortcut keys or menu commands, or through toolbars. Most dockers are found on the Window | Dockers menu, but some, such as dockers dealing with text formatting, are found on the Text menu and on the text-related property bar. For example, to open the Contour docker, choose Window | Dockers | Contour, or press CTRL +F9. To open the Character Formatting docker, you can choose Text | Character Formatting from the menu, or press CTRL+T; additionally you can click the Character Formatting button on the property bar *after* you've chosen the Text tool on the toolbox. Again, the property bar is contextual.

Dockers open to their last-used screen position and state, either docked or undocked, either open or rolled-up. While *docked,* they are by default attached to the right side of your application window. Alternatively, dockers can be positioned on the left side of the screen or anchored on both sides of the screen with your document window in the middle, if that suits you best.

While *undocked,* dockers float above the document window and can be positioned anywhere on your monitor screen(s). Docked or floating is *not* an all-or-nothing choice; you can have some dockers docked and some floating—at the same time. The only situation you *can't* have is more than one copy of a specific docker open at one time. Figure 2-3 shows examples of docked and floating dockers.

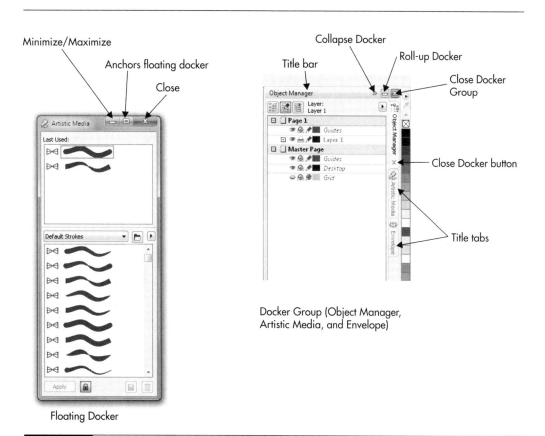

FIGURE 2-3   Examples of a floating docker and an anchored docker group

Dockers feature a common look: each has a title bar; a Close Docker Group button, which closes only that specific docker; and a Roll-up/Roll-down Docker button, which is used to toggle the display between the title bar–only state and a fully open one. While undocked, floating dockers can be resized by click-dragging at the sides or bottom edges.

To move a floating docker, click-drag anywhere on its title bar. Rolled-up (minimized) floating dockers appear only as floating title bars on your screen. Minimized, docked dockers appear as vertical title tabs on the right side of the docker area.

If you're a southpaw or prefer to dock a docker at a location in the interface other than standard right, dockers on the left side of the screen have title tabs on the left side, not on the right.

Nested (Grouped) Dockers

When more than one docker is open, they often appear *nested,* meaning that multiple dockers overlay each other on the right side of your application window. While dockers are nested, clicking their individual title bars or name tabs brings them to the front of the interface. Floating nested dockers, depending on how you've sized the group, might or might not feature a flyout button at bottom right (see Figure 2-4); if you've sized the group so that the tabs cannot show, you can easily access the docker you need through the flyout menu. It's fairly intuitive stuff.

FIGURE 2-4 Nested dockers can float; you can resize them and access individual dockers from the flyout menu.

Although nesting dockers (anchored or floating) are likely the best way to work with multiple dockers, you can quickly separate them—kicking them out of the nest—if you prefer. To do this, click-drag the name tab identifying the docker (or anywhere within the fully open docker pane), and then drag away from the nested docker arrangement. As you do this, you see an outline preview of the frame of your selected docker as you drag, indicating its new screen position when the mouse button is released. You can also float single-anchored dockers by dragging them from their docked position by their title bars. To *nest* multiple dockers together, click-drag the title bar (while it's floating) or the name tab of the docker, and then drag it to a position inside the boundaries of another floating docker.

TIP	*To set whether title bars in floating dockers are visible, open the Tools	Options dialog (press CTRL+J or click the Options button on the standard toolbar) to the General page of the Workspace section, where you'll find an option called "Show titles on floating dockers."*

Finally, if you want to maximize your drawing window area but still keep docked and nested dockers handy, you can click the Collapse Docker arrow on the title bar of the docker group. Collapsing the docker reduces the nested dockers to a thin vertical set of tabs that correspond to the currently open dockers, as shown here in the collapsed state:

Using the Toolbox

All dockers and virtually everything that's a subwindow of an interface, by Microsoft Windows convention, is called a *child window.* Corel leverages this definition of the user interface to make just about everything detachable and capable of floating (if not flying!).

The toolbox is a component of the application window and is where you'll find all the tools in CorelDRAW X5. CorelDRAW offers tons of features, but *tools* are found only on the toolbox. The toolbox itself may be altered in different ways. By default, the toolbox is docked, but you can *un*dock it to float over your document window, which is often a handy way to quickly choose tools if you haven't memorized their shortcut keys. To detach the toolbox from its docked position, first, right-click over a vacant area of the toolbar, and uncheck Lock Toolbars (if it's checked); a single row of dots appears just above the Pick tool. Click-drag directly on the row of dots at the top of the docked toolbox. Your cursor should turn into a four-headed arrow when you are in the correct position. Then move the toolbox away from the edge of your screen, as shown here:

Click-drag here to float the toolbox.

An undocked toolbox, shown next, includes a title bar and a Close button. When it's floating, you can move it around by click-dragging its title bar. Double-clicking the title bar redocks the toolbox. Clicking the Close button hides the toolbox from view. Right-click anywhere in your document window, and choose View | Toolbox from the pop-up menu to make the toolbox reappear.

Click-drag title bar to move.   Double-click to dock.   Close

Drag edge to make more than one row of icons.

TIP *The toolbox can feature larger icons and text labels (which are useful when just learning any program), and the orientation of the toolbox can be vertical or horizontal (as shown in the previous illustration). To customize the toolbox, press CTRL+J to open the Options dialog, and then open the Workspace | Customization | Command Bars section in the tree on the left. Individual tools on the toolbox can be customized by opening the Workspace | Toolbox section on the left and then clicking the tools listed.*

You can access groups of tools by clicking buttons that feature flyout buttons. Single-clicking the tool button selects the visible "top" tool from the group, while clicking-and-holding the button opens the tool's flyout menu. You can also separate individual flyouts from the toolbox and have them float independently. To do this, click-hold to open any group of tools. When your cursor turns into a four-headed arrow as you move it over the dots at the top of the flyout, click-drag the top of the flyout to drag it away from the toolbox. The result is a *duplicate* of the tool flyout (the original flyout group is still on the toolbox) as a floating toolbox group that can be treated like any floating toolbar, as shown here. To hide a duplicate mini-toolbox group, click the Close button. This hides the duplicate toolbar group without affecting the toolbox version of the same group.

NOTE *The toolbox must be unlocked to move the flyouts. You unlock a toolbox by right-clicking over it and then unchecking the Lock Toolbars item on the shortcut menu.*

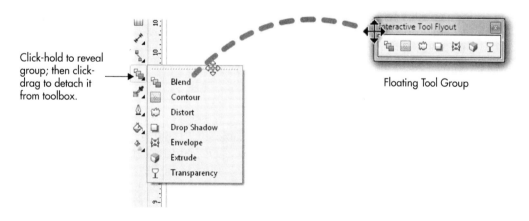

Click-hold to reveal group; then click-drag to detach it from toolbox.

Floating Tool Group

Working with Toolbars

Like other interface devices, toolbars can also appear docked or floating. This doesn't just include standard and custom toolbars, but also the menu toolbar, the standard toolbar, and the property bar. While the toolbars are docked, you'll see a small line of dots on the toolbars themselves. To undock any docked toolbar, first right-click over the toolbar and uncheck the Lock Toolbars option; then click-drag their line of dots away from the edge of the window. Undocked toolbars each feature their own title bar and Close button, as shown next. Usually, it's not a good idea to close the toolbars—instead, return them by double-clicking their title bar. However, if you've closed a toolbar you need, such as the property bar, you can easily retrieve it by right-clicking over any other toolbar, and then choosing the toolbar from the pop-up menu, with any tool chosen.

Click-drag here.

Double-click to return property bar.

Close

Floating Property Bar

Using the Color Palette

The *Color Palette* is, by default, the vertical strip docked to the right of the workspace and is the most convenient place to get colors for filling in your document's objects. By default, a single column of colors is shown; you can change this display, and it has scroll buttons to advance and rewind the colors visible in the column. Like all Windows child windows, the Color Palette comes undocked, you can resize the floating palette, and you can dock it to any side of the application window, in any toolbar location, above or below the status bar, and to either side of the toolbox or a docked docker.

Viewing Palette Colors

The tiny squares of color you see in this palette are referred to as *wells*. Hover over a color well to display a tooltip containing that color's name (by default, tooltips are enabled; if you turned them off, go to Tools | Options | Workspace | Display).To scroll the Color Palette color well collection, click the up or down arrow buttons at the top and bottom of the palette. Single clicks using your left mouse button on these arrow buttons advance and rewind the palette, one color well at a time. Single clicks on these arrow buttons with your right mouse button produce a Page Up and Page Down effect, scrolling the visible color selection a complete column up or down. Clicking the bottom left-arrow button expands the palette to show all the color wells (it retracts after you click to make a color selection). At the top of the palette is the right-arrow Options flyout button for loading different color palettes, saving, renaming, and so on.

Options flyout

Scroll up

Scroll down

Click to expand palette.

You float the Color Palette exactly as you do with other interface child windows: by dragging the palette into the drawing window by its dots. While the Color Palette is floating (shown next), click-drag its title bar to move it around your window, or click the Close button to hide it from view. Choose View | Color Palettes and select any palette to display it in its last used state. Double-click the title bar to return the floating Color Palette to its original docked location in the workspace.

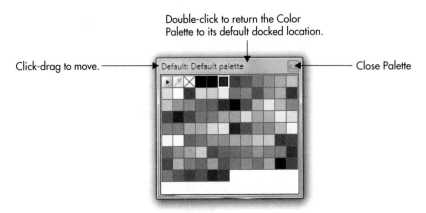

Double-click to return the Color Palette to its default docked location.

Click-drag to move.

Default: Default palette

Close Palette

| TIP | *As with other day-to-day child windows, it's best not to close the Color Palette, particularly if you're new to the program, because it's a hassle to restore it. If you've by chance closed the Color Palette, the quickest way to restore it to the workspace is by right-clicking in the drawing window to get a pop-up menu. Choose View | Color Palettes, choose any palette you like from the submenu, and life is good again.* |

Hovering over any of the Color Palette's scroll buttons or the Expand button produces a tooltip that displays the name of the Color Palette collection you are using, for example, Default: Default Palette.

Changing Palette Options

The Options flyout button (shown next) on the Color Palette features several important commands, letting you apply fill and outline colors (as opposed to using left and right mouse button clicks to apply colors to objects) and control how the palette itself is viewed.

Color Palette Options button

Using the Options flyout provides some, but not all, of the options available to you for getting and using colors. CorelDRAW has an extensive color library including Pantone and Trumatch from onscreen simulations of printing press colors, as well as other colors for web work. However, as mentioned at the beginning of this chapter, some workspace elements in CorelDRAW are tool-specific, while others belong to global elements—and the color library that appears on the Color Palette is a global resource. Therefore, with the Pick tool and nothing selected in the drawing window, you right-click to display the pop-up menu, choose View | Color Palettes, then choose from the submenu, which also features the Color Editor dialog (see following illustration). Displaying the child window called Color Palette and choosing a collection with which you populate the Color Palette are two different things and require different commands: Chapter 17 walks you through all the different ways in which you work with color in CorelDRAW.

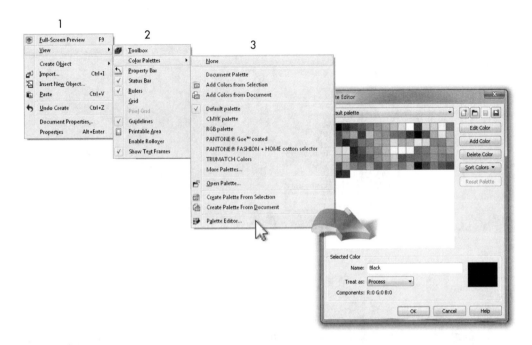

When an artist creates art, the most successful pieces are drawn from a generalization to the specifics, from a coarse outline to filling in the details. Similarly, CorelDRAW deserves a coarse examination, as covered in this chapter, but as you progress to later chapters, the details are filled in. You've got a general idea of how to navigate in this chapter; it's time to move from the interface to the palettes and options you have when building objects, filling them, and changing them. Chapter 3 sits by your side as you cruise the menus and palettes in X5; take a guided tour of CorelDRAW's resources right around the page.

CHAPTER 3

CorelDRAW's Ins and Outs: Importing, Exporting, and Saving Design Work

One of the very first things you learn as a new computer user is how to open and close files and how to use the Clipboard to copy data from one document window to another. To accomplish these basic tasks working with CorelDRAW X5, you have nothing new or exotic to do. But version X5 has *additional* functions and options, such as file handling and data import and export, to make your design experience efficient and the results professional. In this chapter, you'll learn about file-saving options that let coworkers who are using previous versions of CorelDRAW work with your files and learn how to use timesaving templates and other file types. You'll also see how to protect your work with CorelDRAW's automatic backup feature, how to make the Clipboard work overtime for you, as well as how to store and retrieve scrapbook items and symbols and how to import and export graphics, text, and data into and out of CorelDRAW.

NOTE	*Download and extract all the files from the Chapter03.zip archive to follow the tutorials in this chapter.*

CorelDRAW X5's Welcome Screen

When CorelDRAW opens, the Welcome/Quick Start tabbed screen appears, where you can quickly open a new or existing drawing file, access learning tools, check for program updates, and set automatic checks for program updates. You can also view the latest gallery of art created by fellow CorelDRAW designers. This launch pad is shown in Figure 3-1.

The first tab along the right edge, Quick Start, is your jumping-off point for opening a file. Here, in the Open Recent section, you are presented with a list of the last files you opened and closed in CorelDRAW. Hover over the name of one of these files, and a thumbnail preview for that file appears along with the document information. Click the name of the file, and the Welcome dialog closes, and the file you selected opens. If you want to open an existing file that is not among the five most recent files you've opened, click the Open Other button to close the Welcome screen page and to open a standard Open Drawing dialog.

To start a new drawing document from the Quick Start tab, go to the Start New section, and click the New Blank Document link, or click the New From Template link if you want to create a document from one of the special design layouts that ship with CorelDRAW or from a template you previously created.

The other tabs lead you to the following areas of interest:

- From the *What's New* tab, you can click your way through the CorelDRAW New Features Tour slideshow.

- The *Learning Tools* tab contains links to launch documentation from your hard disk such as CorelTUTOR, and Insights From The Experts as well as a link to Corel's online learning resources. If you purchased the DVD of the CorelDRAW install instead of the electronic download version, you can also easily access the tutorial videos from this page.

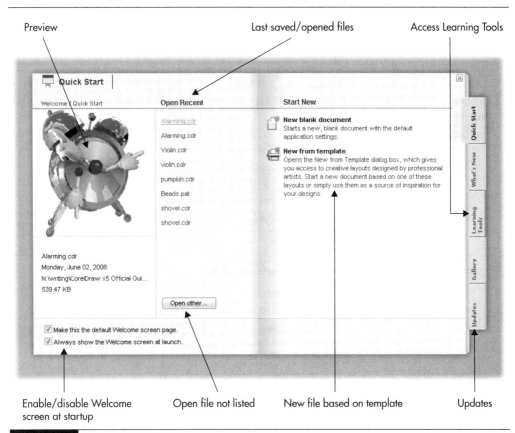

FIGURE 3-1   CorelDRAW welcomes you with a tabbed launch pad after loading.

- The *Gallery* tab displays a changing selection of artwork created in CorelDRAW. It also contains a link to the CorelDRAW.com Community page, where you can create an online gallery of your artwork for the world to see and enjoy, participate in online forums, and download helpful files like custom media strokes, textures, and macros.

- The last tab is the *Updates* tab. At the top of the tab window is the word "Settings." If you click this link, the Update Settings dialog opens. It contains two options that are turned on if the box next to the option is checked, or turned off if it is unchecked. Your choices here are "Notify me of available product updates, news, and tutorials" and "Automatically download product updates and ask me before installing." These are useful and helpful options to keep up to date both your copy of CorelDRAW and your knowledge of things related to CorelDRAW.

If these boxes are checked (they are by default), every time you start CorelDRAW it will access your Internet connection in the background and check in with the Corel website to see if any updates or files should be downloaded for you. So don't be alarmed if your computer's firewall software pops up a notice that CorelDRAW is trying to access the Internet. If CorelDRAW displays a message that it could not find an Internet connection, you will probably have to open your firewall software and give CorelDRAW permission to access the Internet. If you don't want CorelDRAW checking the website every time you start CorelDRAW, uncheck both of these boxes, and then click the close box in the corner of the Update Settings dialog to apply the changed Updates option settings.

If you don't want to use the features offered by the Welcome screen, click the close box. To *never* see the Welcome dialog again, click to uncheck the "Always show the Welcome screen at launch" check box. To open the Welcome screen at any time, choose Help | Welcome Screen, or click the button directly to the left of the zoom percentage field on the standard toolbar.

Opening Your First New Document File

If you are not using the Welcome screen, choosing File | New (CTRL+N) or clicking the New button on the standard toolbar, shown here, opens the Create a New Document dialog, where you choose the settings such as color space and document resolution, and can also choose not to display this dialog in the future. If you check "Do not show this dialog again," new documents are based on the current settings. If you *do* want to see this box again because the default settings aren't right for your type of work, click the Options button on the standard toolbar, and then under Workspace | General, check the "Show New Document dialog box" check box.

Open a new document

3

Create a New Document that Suits You

The Create a New Document dialog, shown next, is new to version X5, and although new users might feel a little intimidated by the number of options, it's really quite straightforward to use and to set up a page that reflects your intended output. Here is a brief explanation of the fields and what you choose depending on your printing and export needs:

- **Name**   You don't have to wait until you save a file to name it. By default, a new document is named "Untitled-1," using a sequential naming pattern—your next document in a session of CorelDRAW is named "Untitled-2," and so on. It's fine to accept the default name, but it's a better idea to name the file now if you know what you're going to create.

- **Preset Destination**   "Destination" refers to where the file is ultimately going: to commercial printing, to the Web as an HTML page or graphic…you have five choices here in addition to Custom. If you want to set up a Rendering Resolution or Color Settings entirely of your own choosing, Preset Destination will automatically call your settings "Custom." If you want to keep and reuse the existing page setup, click the Save button (the diskette icon) to the right of the drop-down list and name the preset. The next time you create a new document, you can choose your preset from the drop-down list and spare yourself defining any other field in this dialog.

- **Size**   Define the page size you need by choosing from the large selection of preset page sizes, or set your own custom size by typing values into the Height and Width fields below it. Also, next to the Height field, click an orientation icon—portrait or landscape—for your new document.

- **Primary Color Mode**   You have your choice of RGB or CMYK. If you choose CMYK, the Color Palette's color wells will look duller than you'd expect, because CMYK color mode is *print legal*—CorelDRAW simulates what the colors you use for object fills will look like when *printed,* because certain colors you see onscreen cannot be faithfully reproduced using printing inks and other pigments. If you are designing for the *Web,* choose RGB from the drop-down list. Also, if you are designing for a personal home inkjet printer, choose RGB. Although inkjet printers use cyan, magenta, yellow, and black pigments, today's inkjets have conversion circuitry that takes—and actually expects—RGB data and automatically converts it to fairly closely matching CMYK-equivalent colors.

- **Rendering Resolution**   Although CorelDRAW is a vector-drawing program, and as such produces *resolution-independent* vector shapes, you will want to choose a Rendering Resolution that is best for any CorelDRAW effect that is rendered as a bitmap when you print or export your file to a format other than CorelDRAW's native CDR file format. For example, if you've created a drop shadow on an object and intend to print your file to a high-resolution image-setting device, image setters at commercial print houses usually expect 266 to 300 ppi (pixels per inch, frequently called dpi, dots per inch)—so you'd specify 300 dpi to ensure a smooth rendered drop shadow. If you're printing to a home inkjet, effects can look good at lower resolution settings such as 225 to 260 dpi. Rendering Resolution has no bearing on files you export to bitmap format via File | Export; the resolution for exporting to JPEG, TIFF, and other image formats is set in their Export dialogs.

- **Preview Mode**   There is little reason to specify anything other than Enhanced for previews. If you choose Draft or Wireframe by accident, this is easily changed by choosing Enhanced from the View menu when your document is open.

- **Color Settings**   If you're concerned about color consistency while you work (hint: you should be!), this is one of the new features in version X5. (By default, this area is "rolled up.") Windows offers color management in the form of ICC profiles that are located in your Windows | System32 | spool | drivers | color folder. *Color profiling* is a method by which you can increase your odds that what you see on your monitor is represented in a color print you make. Three components use color management: your monitor (which you calibrate using third-party software, hardware you can buy, or Windows Control Panel settings for your video card); your application (which is CorelDRAW, and here is where you tell CorelDRAW which color profile to use when it imports and how to tag images when it exports); and your printer (most printers today understand color management and have settings you manage through a proprietary control panel or through Windows Printer options). If you're a home-printing or Web-designer sort of person, note that most users access one or two RGB color profiles. sRGB is used by many home inkjet printers and digital cameras, so sRGB is a safe color setting to ensure consistent color output from what you see onscreen, what your photos look like when you import them to CorelDRAW, and when you print your work. Many designers own more than one application, and as a result, it's hard *not* to accumulate color profiles that other applications installed, perhaps without your realizing it. Scroll down the list of color profiles in the color folder: if you see CIE RGB or Adobe RGB, you might want to use it as your color setting. Adobe RGB is an optimized version of CIE RGB—color profiles "live" in something called a *color space*—an area of the visible spectrum within which certain colors can be expressed while those outside this area cannot. CIE RGB color occupies a greater color space than sRGB. If you deal with delicate shades of color and you need great control of a precise color, such as in fashion design and corporate logos, CIE RGB gives your document a much larger color space than sRGB.

NOTE   *Rendering Intent is used when importing and exporting an image or other bitmap graphic that has been tagged with a color profile: CorelDRAW X5 can both read and write information into the header of a bitmap that tells the application importing it how to handle color data. Often, the color space of a bitmap you import to a page either doesn't have a compatible color profile, or the image is not tagged with a color profile at all. Relative Colorimetric is the default option for reassigning imported images the color space of the file you're working on, and it's probably the best choice for most images. Relative Colorimetric compares the brightest areas in the imported image's color space to those of the destination color space (your document) and shifts all colors to fit within the color space. Out-of-gamut colors, colors that cannot be expressed in your CorelDRAW document's assigned color space, are shifted to the closest color in the destination color space, thus preserving more of the original colors in an image than the Perceptual option, which would be a good second choice if the colors in the imported or exported image look wrong.*

Working with Multiple Documents

Like many graphics applications, CorelDRAW can keep more than one document open in the interface. Each open document, whether it is new or is a previously created document, is listed at the bottom of the Window menu. If you've opened several documents, you might notice that each document window is maximized, but only the most recently opened document appears in view, indicated by the document default name in CorelDRAW's application title bar. This is because while document windows are maximized, only the document in the forefront is visible. Any other opened documents are hidden from view. To navigate between document windows in the maximized state, choose Window | *Filename,* as shown here.

 TIP *To see all open document windows and automatically arrange them in your CorelDRAW application window, choose Cascade, Tile Horizontally, or Tile Vertically from the Window command menu.*

Opening Document Files

To open an existing document, choose from one of these three actions: click the Open Other button from the Welcome screen, click the Open button in the standard toolbar, or choose File | Open (CTRL+O). In any case, the Open Drawing dialog appears, as shown in Figure 3-2. The Open Drawing dialog is mostly a standard Windows 7 configuration with some interesting and useful CorelDRAW additions. You can choose different-sized icon views of documents, and CorelDRAW files do indeed display graphical thumbnails of your saved

FIGURE 3-2 The Open Drawing dialog in CorelDRAW is an enhanced version of the standard Windows Open dialog.

work. Also, an application identifier tick at the bottom right of the icons lets you instantly tell that a folder contains either CorelDRAW files or Corel Presentation Exchange (CMX) documents. Additionally, if you click the All File Formats drop-down arrow, a comprehensive list of all the file types CorelDRAW can open appears; this is a handy way to filter out file types when you've opened a folder containing CorelDRAW files, video, and audio files, for example. To open a file, click its title or icon, and then choose Open. If you've recently opened a CorelDRAW-supported file type, you can click the down arrow to the right of the selected File Name, and you can choose from a list of CorelDRAW files from all over your hard drive.

If you're new to both CorelDRAW and Windows 7, note some areas of interest in the Open dialog, some of which are standard Windows conventions, while others are CorelDRAW enhancements to the Open dialog:

- **Windows View** Click the drop-down list (as was done in Windows XP) to set how a folder you open displays its contents. You can usually get a good view for locating a file you need to open using the Large Icons view. Another useful view configuration is to use Details view in combination with the preview pane (the button directly to the right of the Windows View drop-down list). With the Details view enabled, you can then sort files by date, type, and size.

- **Filter** By default, CorelDRAW will show you all files within a folder. If you're not organizationally fastidious with your hard disk(s), finding the CorelDRAW file you seek can be a nightmare, but not if you choose, for example, CDR-CorelDRAW (*.CDR) from the file formats list. The list of files that can be opened is a comprehensive one in version X5, with over two dozen vector-type files recognized, not simply CorelDRAW native files. See the section later in this chapter about the important differences between *opening* a non-CorelDRAW file and *importing* one to an open file in CorelDRAW's workspace.

NOTE *CorelDRAW X5 can open files that are saved in CorelDRAW 1 or later in the CDR file format, although if you used CorelDRAW version 1's proprietary WFN fonts, the PANOSE Font Substitution box will pop up; Corel doesn't support WFN typefaces today. CorelDRAW X5 can also save as far back as version 7 in case you need to share a file with a coworker who hasn't upgraded to the 21st century.*

- **Recently Opened Files** If you do filter for only CDR files and then click the down arrow at the right of the File Name field, you can access several of the most-recently opened CorelDRAW files that can be located anywhere on your hard drive(s), not just in the current folder's contents. If you click to select a file, its name appears in the File Name area, and if you type in the wildcard characters *.*, the filter list resets to display All File Formats.

TIP *When you're currently working on a page in CorelDRAW, to open your most-recently accessed documents, go to File | Open Recent, where the 15 most-recently opened files are listed.*

- **Code Page** If you are working with files that were created in a version of CorelDRAW that uses a different language than your copy does, you might need to change the code page before you open the file. Code pages control *mapping*: which character in a typeface is used when you press a specific key on your keyboard. If you have a lot of square boxes displayed where you know you should have text (and you have the document's typeface installed), try reopening the file using a different code page. The code page chosen in the drop-down list should match that used when the file was created. For example, if you are using a copy of CorelDRAW that uses US English, the code page that is used by default is 1252 (ANSI – Latin 1). However, if the file you are opening was created in the Korean language edition of CorelDRAW, then you should choose 949 (ANSI/OEM—Korean) from the Select Code Page drop-down when you open that file.

- **Maintain Layers And Pages** CorelDRAW has supported layers and multi-page files for seemingly forever; if you want to preserve the layer order between different versions of saved files, check this box. If you leave this box unchecked, you might create a mess of the document you open—all objects on all pages will be merged to a single, one-layer CDR page.

 In a work environment where users have different versions of CorelDRAW, it's a good idea when you save a file to also save a copy of the file in Corel's CMX (Corel Presentation Exchange) file format. CMX is covered later in this chapter, and it's your gateway to saving copies of files from version X5 that users of almost any version of CorelDRAW can open.

In the Open Drawing dialog, locate and select your document file, and then click the Open button (or double-click the filename) to open it. CorelDRAW supports multiple file–opening using modifier keys. You can open neighboring files on the directory list (in the same folder) by holding SHIFT while selecting your files. Open nonadjacent files in the file list (in the same folder) by holding CTRL while clicking to select the filenames, and then click the Open button. This is a standard Windows convention, as is marquee-dragging to select multiple file icons.

Opening Files from Other Applications

You can open many other files that are not native to CorelDRAW, such as Adobe Illustrator or Microsoft PowerPoint, in CorelDRAW. When a file originally created in a different application is opened, CorelDRAW automatically converts its contents to CorelDRAW format. If you look at the title bar of the drawing window, you will see that CorelDRAW has opened the file, preserved the filename, but has given it a .CDR extension. The original application file remains on the hard disk unchanged. In a way, opening a nonnative CorelDRAW file is similar to importing nonnative graphics data.

When you open nonnative application files supported by CorelDRAW's Import filters, the graphics and text objects contained in the file are converted as closely as possible to compatible equivalents supported in CorelDRAW. Although the Open command is *like* an Import operation, certain file formats might not open flawlessly, depending on their type and contents. You might get better results if you import the files as objects into an open CorelDRAW document by pressing CTRL+I (File | Import). If CorelDRAW is unable to interpret a file's contents while trying to open it, an alert dialog appears.

Warning Messages

When you open files—especially older files or files created on a different system or using a third-party application—warning messages might appear before the file actually opens. For the most part, these messages aren't meant to cause alarm, but instead to advise. Two of the most common messages warn of inappropriate data types and fonts.

If, for example, you try to use the Open dialog to open a GIF bitmap, CorelDRAW alerts you that the file cannot be opened and suggests that you try using the Import command instead. As far as opening a document that was originally created using fonts that you don't have installed, the Font Substitution For Missing Fonts dialog will appear and give you the chance to view a list of the fonts used in the document and to substitute ones you *do* have installed. An alternative measure is to jot down the names of the typefaces used, click Cancel, and then install the needed fonts if you have identical or similar ones. Then reopen the document; if the font you installed is similarly but not identically named, you will need to work through the Font Substitution choices, but after a few moments you can be assured that the file looks mostly like it did when created.

Pantone and Basic Font-Matching

Font-matching sounds good in theory, and in the Font Substitution For Missing Fonts dialog, you have the option to let CorelDRAW try to match a missing font, to locate a compatible font manually (click the Substitute Font With button and then choose from the drop-down list), or choose the Use The Panose Suggested Match. Usually, you're best off noting the name of the missing font, canceling the Open dialog, finding a similar font yourself, installing it, reopening the document, and choosing the font you just installed.

You'll soon notice a problem with letting any computer program try to match a font. It doesn't use its eyes (it doesn't have any), but instead relies on *metadata* (data about data) that is written into the header of a typeface. The problem isn't with CorelDRAW: if someone who created a digital typeface didn't bother to write the correct metadata into the file, you indeed will get suggested matches of Arial for Windsor Condensed. CorelDRAW can't *find* a match, there's no file information listed for the missing font, and it's as simple and as frustrating as that. The good news is that if you point the Font Substitution box to an installed font you want to use, CorelDRAW remembers it for this and all other documents with the missing typeface.

Saving and Closing Documents

Whether you save often (pressing CTRL+S at regular intervals is a good idea) or you're saving your document for the first time, you'll want to define some file information for your saves, and to practice good hard-drive housekeeping by saving to user-defined folders. When you know you'll want to retrieve a document in the near future, setting a save location, applying a name, adding user data, and other options go along with the job.

Saving Your First Document

You can save an *existing* document simply by clicking the Save button on the standard toolbar or by choosing File | Save (CTRL+S), which causes your most recent changes to the page to be saved immediately without opening any dialogs.

CorelDRAW X5's Save Drawing dialog contains more than just options on where to save and what name to use when saving the file. For a practical exercise that explores the additional options you have when saving, follow these steps.

Saving Files with User Info

1. If you've just started a new document and want to save it, click the Save button in the standard toolbar, use the CTRL+S shortcut, or choose File | Save. The Save Drawing dialog appears, as shown in Figure 3-3.

2. With the Save Drawing dialog open, use the dialog options to set a location for your document, and type a unique name in the File Name box. If you're saving your document to a format other than CorelDRAW's native CDR format, choose a file format from the Save As Type menu. Doing this is similar to choosing File | Export. The disadvantage to saving in a non-CorelDRAW file type is that it's usually going to be hard to open this file again and edit it using all of CorelDRAW's features.

3. Saving as a CDR file gives you the option to choose a version from the Version drop-down. Unless you *must* save to an older file format to allow the saved file to be used with legacy software, always choose the most recent (highest number) version. If you choose an older file version, some of the work you did in your file may not save as you expect, because an effect or other feature used may not have existed in the file version you selected.

4. If saving your document in CorelDRAW file or template file (CDT) format, you can enter (optional) Title, Subject, and a star rating as part of the file's metadata. If you take a moment to fill in the Title or Subject field with a word or two about the file you save, it becomes much easier to sort through your saved files a month or a year later, especially with the new CorelCONNECT utility that ships with version X5. You and every CorelDRAW user (so be tasteful with your descriptive text) can use the File | Document Properties dialog to view and edit any information you appended to your file.

Advanced Options

Click from left to right to add star ratings.

Original color profile

Title

Subject

FIGURE 3-3 The Save Drawing dialog can save a file with user information and other options.

5. If you want to save only the object(s) you currently have selected, check the Selected Only check box. Everything that is not selected will not be saved to the file.

6. Decide if you want to check the Embed Fonts Using TrueDoc™ check box. Checking this check box increases the saved file size just a little because the font(s) are rewritten as very small document information when you save. This can be a useful feature when you're working with fonts you don't have loaded every day or if you are giving the file to a coworker who does not have the font. TrueDoc technology originally developed by Bitstream embeds the font data so you or anyone else can make changes and print the file using the correct font. However, TrueDoc does not *install* a typeface embedded in a CDR document on your computer or anyone else's—the typeface stays inside of CorelDRAW.

7. You can choose to embed the color profile you used to create a document by checking the Embed Color Profiles box upon saving. This is usually a good idea, and it adds only marginally to the overall saved file size. Embedding the color profile means that you and anyone else who opens the document will view it as it's intended to be output for the screen and for printing. The only time you wouldn't want to embed the color profile is if the document was created with the wrong profile for a printing job, for example. To change a document's color profile before saving it, choose Tools | Color Management | Document Settings.

Advanced Save Drawing Options

The Save Drawing dialog sports still more refinements you can make when saving a file. Clicking the Advanced button opens the same Options dialog that you can navigate to at any time by choosing Tools | Options (CTRL+J), expanding the tree directory under Document, and then clicking the Save item. In this area you can make choices about File Optimization, Textures, and Blends And Extrudes. These options are set on a document basis, *not* a global one, so you can make different choices for each file you save.

- *Save Presentation Exchange (CMX)*. Check this box if you want to place or edit the file in other applications that accept this file format, such as Corel WordPerfect or Xara Xtreme, and older versions of CorelDRAW. For example, CorelDRAW 5 can't open an X5 CDR file, but version 5 *can* open a CMX file. The CMX file format can hold both bitmap and vector data. It is a subset of the CDR format and as such is not as capable of certain recently added features, but it is a good way to use graphics created in CorelDRAW in other applications and for users of previous versions to open your files in case you saved to version X5.

- *Use Bitmap Compression*. Bitmaps and bitmap effects in a drawing can really plump up the final file size of a document. To save precious hard disk storage space, put a check in this box. The compression used is *lossless,* so you don't have to worry that choosing this option will degrade the quality of your file onscreen or when printed.

- *Use Graphic Object Compression*. Checking this box reduces saved file sizes by compressing the vector elements in the file. This is particularly welcome if you've created a lot of extrude objects in a document whose component objects can number in the 30s, 40s, or even hundreds if you've used complex shading options.

- *Save Textures With The File or Rebuild Textures When Opening The File*. Choose the radio button next to one of these mutually exclusive options. Saving the textures increases the file's size and uses more hard disk space. Rebuilding the textures saves hard disk space, but it then takes longer to open and save a file. Your choice here is between maximizing your hard disk space or your time.

- *Save Blends And Extrudes With The File or Rebuild Blends And Extrudes When Opening The File.* As with saving or rebuilding textures, here your choice is really between maximizing hard disk space or your time. Click the radio button next to the choice that suits you best.

After you've made your selections, click the OK button to be returned to the Save Drawing dialog. With all your options for this file spent, go ahead and click the Save button, or click the Cancel button to abandon the save.

Save As Command

The Save As command (CTRL+SHIFT+S) is useful for saving copies of your document using the same or different Save command settings. The Save As command is often used to save a file at regular intervals throughout the creation of a graphic—so you can go back to an earlier version of the file or see what different color schemes or layouts look like. Using the Save As command in combination with the Selected Only option (available only while objects are selected) is a truly useful option; if you've been working with a lot of objects you won't need later, you don't have to delete them all to tidy up—you simply use Selected Only. Otherwise, the options available in the Save As command dialog are identical to those in the Save dialog.

Although using the Save As command may seem similar to using the Export command in some ways, the two are quite different; in some cases it might be better to use one command instead of the other. Usually the Save As command is the best option to choose when saving native CorelDRAW files.

The Export command (File | Export) is best for saving your document or selected objects as any *other* type of file format, particularly bitmap formats like CPT, GIF, JPEG, PNG, or a wide variety of text formats as well as other specialized vector formats such as EPS and SVG. In CorelDRAW you can save—but not export—files in CorelDRAW (CDR), Corel Pattern file (PAT), and CorelDRAW Template (CDT) format.

Using File Backup Options

Countless hours of work can be saved using CorelDRAW's Backup feature. When it comes to saving and backing up your document files, CorelDRAW lets you take full control over *how, where,* and *when* backup files are created. *Backup files* let you retrieve recent changes made to documents should something unfortunate (such as a power failure) occur while you're working. Backup files created automatically are named auto_backup_of_*filename*.cdr, where *FILENAME* is the name of your original CorelDRAW document. It's best to specify a custom folder for your auto-saves instead of accepting the default location, so you can quickly locate and proceed with your work after a mishap.

If CorelDRAW closes unexpectedly, the next time you open CorelDRAW, the File Recovery dialog prompts you to open the Auto-Backup file that it found. Click OK to open the file. If you click Cancel and do not open the file, the Auto-Backup file will be deleted when you exit CorelDRAW. So open and save the file when you can—you won't be prompted to do so again.

At your command, backup files can be created every time you save a file. The naming convention for these files is in the form of backup_of_*filename*.cdr, and these backup files are stored in the same folder location as the file you saved. You can open backup files the same way as with any CorelDRAW document file, by using the File | Open command (CTRL+O).

To access CorelDRAW's backup controls, use the Workspace | Save page of the Options dialog (shown in Figure 3-4). Choose Tools | Options | Workspace | Save.

FIGURE 3-4 Use these options to control where and when backup files are created.

This list should help you decide which options to choose:

- **Auto-Backup Every**   While this option is selected (the default), your document files are backed up at specified time intervals. The default is 20 minutes and can be set to anywhere between 1 and 60 minutes (or never).

- **Always Back-Up To**   Specify the location of the backups to be saved in your temporary folder (the default), or choose Specific Folder and use the Browse button to specify a drive and folder location.

- **Make Backup On Save**   Activating the Make Backup On Save option (selected by default) causes CorelDRAW to update the backup file to match your original document file each time you use the File | Save command (CTRL+S). This backup system is in addition to the Auto-Backup feature and complements it, because the files are in a more accessible location and *are not* automatically deleted (although they are overwritten each time you save a file), which leaves you with a backup of the most recent version of the file. It is handy to have this kind of backup file because you can revert to the last saved version of the file if you should make a mistake while editing a file—or if you just want to start over.

Working with Templates

Templates are special files that can be saved based on existing settings and/or document content. Templates can be used as starting points to avoid repetitive page setup and document defaults. You can recognize template files by the .CDT file extension.

Opening Templates

To open an existing template file with the aim of creating a new document based on the template, choose File | New From Template to open the New From Template dialog, as shown in Figure 3-5. Here you can choose from a list containing many categories of professionally designed templates that came with CorelDRAW. Additional templates are found on the CorelDRAW DVD and on CorelDRAW.com.

Some of the templates use typefaces you might not have installed from the CorelDRAW CD. If you choose to open a new document based on a template containing text, it's possible you'll get the Font Substitution dialog, discussed earlier in this chapter. If this happens, you can certainly open a new file based on the template, and then replace the typeface used in the document. Alternatively, you can install the fonts listed in this dialog and come back to the document later.

Templates are organized in two general groups: Type and Industry. Choose Type in the View By drop-down to see a list of template categories that is broken down by kind of document produced—a catalog, a flyer, a letterhead, and so on. Choose Industry to see the

FIGURE 3-5 Choose from these template categories to begin your new document.

templates arranged in categories that correspond to various industries such as Hospitality, Retail, or Services. To use any templates you've created and saved, either search the list in the My Templates section on the left side of the dialog, or, if you didn't specify the Type or Industry of your own template, choose All, and then go to Not Specified.

Clicking a category such as Business Cards or Brochures in the list on the left opens (in the center of the dialog) thumbnail views of the templates available. Click once on a thumbnail to load information about the template into the Template Details section at the bottom of the dialog and into Designer Notes on the right of the dialog. To increase the size of the thumbnail for a better view or to decrease the size of the thumbnail to view more thumbnails, click-drag the slider at the bottom of the dialog.

While a template is selected, the preview window displays a thumbnail of the first page of the template. Click Open or double-click the file to open a new (unsaved) document using the template's content and page layout.

The Browse button opens a Windows standard file Open dialog that you can use to locate, select, and open a new document based on a template somewhere on your computer or network other than CorelDRAW's default location for templates.

Opening and Saving Templates

You can open any template file that has a .CDT extension you've saved from X5 or from any previous version for editing, and change its actual template format and/or its content. Use the File | Open command and choose CorelDRAW Template (CDT) as the file type. Before the file opens, a dialog (shown at right) will ask whether you want to open the template as a new document or for editing. If your aim is to open a new document based on the template content and structure, leave New From Template selected in combination with the With Contents option. If your intention is to edit the template file itself, choose Open For Editing.

When saving an edited template file, performing a Save command automatically saves the file as a template without opening any dialogs—and without the need to re-specify the file as a CDT template file in the Save dialog. Additionally, a CDT file you opened will appear on the File | Open Recent list, and if you choose it, it will simply open without the dialog shown in the illustration.

Clipboard Commands

As you probably already know, the Windows *Clipboard* is a temporary "place" that's capable of storing the last objects copied and is a feature of your computer's operating system. While the data you copied or cut is stored in your system's RAM, you can "paste" duplicates of the data into your document. The three most common Clipboard commands you'll likely use are Copy, Cut, and Paste—each of which is accessible either from the Edit menu or from the standard toolbar, as shown here. Cut, Copy, and Paste are also standard Windows commands, so you can use the keyboard shortcuts CTRL+C (Copy), CTRL+V (Paste), and CTRL+X (Cut) to speed up your work.

TIP *To create duplicates of your selected objects immediately, press the + key on your keyboard's numeric keypad. Copies immediately are placed in front of the selected objects in the document and in exactly the same page position. This action does not use Windows' Clipboard, so your current Clipboard contents remain intact.*

Copying vs. Cutting

Each time an object is copied to the Windows Clipboard, the previous Clipboard contents are overwritten. To copy selected objects onto your Clipboard, choose Edit | Copy. Better yet, click the Copy button on the standard toolbar, or use the standard CTRL+C shortcut. The older Windows SHIFT+INSERT shortcut also works. After being copied, the items remain unaltered in your document.

 Windows 7 only supports a Clipboard Viewer under a virtual machine such as one running XP, so Windows 7 users can't see important content that might be on the Clipboard from moment to moment. However, Karen Kenworthy offers a free Clipboard Viewer at http://www.karenware.com/powertools/ptclpvue.asp. It's a good idea to download it and to thank Karen.

The *Cut* command automatically deletes the selected items from your document and puts a copy on the Clipboard. To cut items, click the Cut button in the standard toolbar, choose Edit | Cut, or use the standard CTRL+X shortcut. The older Windows SHIFT+DELETE shortcut also applies.

 If what you've copied to the Clipboard is something that you will use again in this document or that might be useful in future creations, consider saving it to the scrapbook covered later in this chapter, or as a symbol, which is covered in Chapter 13.

Paste vs. Paste Special

Copies of items on your Clipboard can be placed into your current document by using the Paste command. Each time you use the Paste command, another copy is pasted. When an item is pasted into CorelDRAW, it is placed on the very top or front of the active layer. To paste Clipboard contents, perform one of these actions: click the Paste button in the standard toolbar, choose Edit | Paste, or use the CTRL+V shortcut. The older Windows SHIFT+INSERT shortcut also applies.

Paste Special in the Edit menu is used to place "unusual" data into a CorelDRAW document: text that is specially formatted, a graphic that the Clipboard doesn't completely understand, or data that CorelDRAW has no way of clearly understanding as text, vector art, or bitmap data. Windows Clipboard can assign any of 27 data types, frequently more than one type, to media that is copied to it; one of the ways that the mechanism Paste Special operates is to offer you a choice as to how the media on the Clipboard is interpreted by CorelDRAW as it puts a copy of this media on a page.

Paste Special should be used on three occasions (possibly more) when you need something in a CorelDRAW document that wasn't created in CorelDRAW and pressing CTRL+V results in nothing pasted:

- *When you've copied formatted text from WordPerfect, MS Word, or a desktop publishing application, and you do not want the text formatted.* Suppose you've created a table and used fancy bullets and an equally fancy font in your word-processing program, and you want the text imported to CorelDRAW via the Clipboard only. You want to reformat the data in CorelDRAW with different fonts, you don't want bullets, but you also don't want to retype the text. You use Edit | Paste Special, and then choose Rich Text Format, or better still you choose Text, and then click OK.

- *When you've copied data from an application that creates things that are completely inappropriate for CorelDRAW to import.* For example, you own a 3D modeling program and want to use a model you've created in a CorelDRAW page. CorelDRAW has no 3D tools, but it *will* accept a special pasted interpreted bitmap copy of the model. In this case, the Special Paste of the model cannot be edited in CorelDRAW, but the bitmap interpretation of the model program's data can be scaled, moved, rotated, and the document will print with the bitmap and any other CorelDRAW media on the page.

- *When you want to update data you need to paste, especially with text.* By default, CorelDRAW's Paste Special dialog is set to Paste, not to Paste Link, and you really need to think *carefully* and read this section twice before choosing Paste Link and then clicking OK. Paste Link embeds, for example, a section of MS Word text that can be later edited using MS Word, and not CorelDRAW. The data you Paste Special and Paste Link falls into that fuzzy category of data that doesn't actually "belong" to the CorelDRAW document—the data requires both a valid link to its source, and that the application that was used to create the data is still installed on your computer a month from now when it's editing time. A linked pasted object is not directly editable in CorelDRAW, although it can be printed, moved, and scaled as an embedded object. To edit the object, you double-click it with the Pick Tool, and the program you used to generate this media pops up...and you can edit away. When you're finished editing, you save the document in the program, you can close it, and when you come back to CorelDRAW, the media has been updated. If you work extensively with CorelDRAW and a word processor, and your client requests revisions as often as leaves fall from a tree, the Link Paste Special feature can be a charm. However, if you don't save documents regularly or uninstall programs frequently, do not use the link feature. The next time you open the document, the link might not be linked, and there goes part of your design. Figure 3-6 shows the Paste Special dialog and the different options on the list when (at left) a 3D model has been copied to the Clipboard, and when (at right) a word-processing document has been copied.

One of the very first things you learn as a new computer user is how to open and close files and how to use the Clipboard to copy data from one document window to another. There is nothing new or exotic you have to do when working with CorelDRAW X5 to accomplish these basic tasks. But version X5 has *additional* functions and options such as file handling and data import and export, to you're your design experience efficient and the results professional. In this chapter you'll learn about file-saving options that let coworkers who are using previous versions of CorelDRAW work with your files and about how to use timesaving templates and other file types. You'll also see how to protect your work with CorelDRAW's automatic backup feature, how to make the Clipboard work overtime for you, as well as how to store and retrieve scrapbook items and symbols and how to import and export graphics, text, and data into and out of CorelDRAW.

Paste 3D model data as a picture.

Paste Link text as a Word document.

FIGURE 3-6 Paste Special is for data that cannot be imported as regular data, and for when you want to use an editor other than CorelDRAW.

 Paste Special does not have a keyboard shortcut assigned to it by default. It can be handy to assign it one yourself by using the Customization | Commands section of the Options dialog.

Undoing and Redoing Changes

Albert Einstein might have said (under his breath) that for every action, there is an equal and opposite mistake. Then again, Mr. Einstein probably never used CorelDRAW, so he was unaware that you have several ways to undo a mistake. Or to redo something you originally thought was a mistake, and even to back up and undo a mistake you made a dozen steps ago. It's a shame that Life isn't as forgiving as CorelDRAW.

Basic Undo Commands

Choose Edit | Undo or use the standard CTRL+Z shortcut. To reverse an Undo command, choose Edit | Redo or use the CTRL+SHIFT+Z shortcut. CorelDRAW takes both of these commands further by offering Undo and Redo buttons in the standard toolbar; they can be used either to undo or redo single or multiple commands. The buttons even have drop-down menus, as shown next. Clicking the toolbar button applies to the most recent action; clicking the toolbar button's drop-down arrow lets you choose a specific Undo or Redo command. To reverse either an Undo or Redo action using the drop-downs, click one of the listed commands. Doing so takes your composition back or forward to the point you specified in the drop-down. Undo and Redo drop-downs show your most recent actions at the top of the listing.

Click to undo/redo last action.

Most recent action

Click to open drop-down menu.

> **NOTE**   *You can customize the number of Undo levels CorelDRAW performs. The default setting records your 20 most recent actions, but this value can be set as high as 99,999 actions (provided your system has the available resources). To access Undo options, open the Options dialog (click the Options button on the standard toolbar), and then at left click Document | General.*

Using the Undo Docker

For even more control over your most recent actions, you might try the Undo docker opened by choosing Window | Dockers | Undo. The Undo docker, shown in Figure 3-7, provides different views of your drawing as it appeared before certain recent actions. The Undo docker can also be used to save your recent actions as a Visual Basic for Applications (VBA) macro, which is terrific when you want to apply, for example, a dozen complex edits to different objects in different documents (on different days!).

The Undo docker displays your most recent actions in reverse order of the Undo and Redo drop-down menus, with recent actions placed *at the bottom* of the docker list. Selecting a command on the list shows you a view of your document as it appeared before your most recent actions were performed.

Clicking the Clear Undo List icon clears the entire list of actions in the Undo docker list, providing you with a clean slate. You cannot clear or delete *some* of the actions; clearing is an all or nothing decision. By default, an alert dialog, shown in the following illustration, appears, warning you that clearing the Undo list can't be undone. Having a robust Undo list

Save list to a VBA macro

Actions arranged from the oldest action at the top to the most recent at the bottom

Clear Undo list

FIGURE 3-7   The Undo docker features all sorts of ways to undo or redo recent actions.

can be a much-needed safety net, so don't clear the list unless you have so many undos in the list that it is bogging down your system resources.

When you save and then *close* a file, the Undo docker list is automatically cleared—you will be starting fresh when you reopen the document. If you Save the document but don't close it, and continue to work on the file, the actions in the Undo docker remain, and your new actions continue to be added to the list.

The Undo docker is also a great way to create VBA macros. Clicking the Save List To A VBA Macro button in the docker opens the Save Macro dialog, where you provide a name and description for the new macro and store it either with your open document or to CorelDRAW's main Global Macros list. Keep in mind when naming your macros that spaces are not valid characters, but underscores are.

Scrapbooks, An Old Favorite

If you are a longtime user of CorelDRAW, you may also be a fan of the Scrapbook docker, which can be used to store and retrieve drawings, photos, text, or floating photo objects. Many users have found it useful for searching through vast collections of clip art. The Scrapbook docker is still available for you to use, but is no longer installed by default—the Symbol Manager docker is proving to be a better feature for storing work because in X5 all the Corel clip art and your own work can be searched for using XP and Vista's native search engines.

But it's natural to stick with what works for you; if you want to use the Scrapbook, you can use CorelDRAW's customization options to bring the Scrapbook out into the open. Here's how.

Revealing the CorelDRAW Scrapbook

1. Click the Options button on the standard toolbar, and then choose Workspace | Customization | Commands in the tree on the left.

2. Click the Search icon (the one with the binoculars on it) next to the drop-down list in the center of the dialog.

3. In the Find What field of the Find Text dialog, type in **Scrapbook** and then click the Find Next button. The Scrapbook command is highlighted in the list of commands. Click the close box for Find Text.

4. Click-drag the Scrapbook command out of the list, and drop it on the toolbar or menu of your choice. The standard toolbar is a good location if you use the Scrapbook often.

5. Click OK to close the Options dialog.

Drag icon to add it to a toolbar.

Importing and Exporting Files

CorelDRAW's Import and Export filter collection is one of the largest in any graphics application. Here is a list of the document types that version X5 can import and export.
Support for new file formats:

- Microsoft Publisher (versions 2002, 2003, and 2007)

- Microsoft Word 2007

- AutoCAD DXF

- AutoCAD DWG (versions R2.5 to 2007)

- Corel Painter 11

Enhanced export options when working with Adobe products including:

- Adobe Photoshop CS4 and previous versions

- Adobe Illustrator CS4 (you can now choose to export text to Illustrator as Curves or as Text; compressed Illustrator files are not currently supported)

- PDF 1.7, PDF/A (an ISO-approved format for long-term document archiving)

- Adobe Acrobat

Filters are data translators for files created in other applications or in formats not native to CorelDRAW. *Import filters* take the data from other applications and translate that data into information that can be viewed and edited from within CorelDRAW. *Export filters* translate data from your CorelDRAW document to a format recognized by a different program or publishing medium. As with Import filters, Export filters frequently contain dialogs where you set up options to export the precise data you need for the target application or publishing medium.

 When you export a file, the new file format may not support all the features that CorelDRAW's native file format (CDR) supports. For this reason, even when exporting work, you should always save a copy of your work in CorelDRAW's native file format.

Set Up Color Management Before Importing

Earlier, in the "Create a New Document that Suits You" section, the importance of color management was discussed. Enabling and using a color profile is your best bet to ensure color consistency between your monitor, CorelDRAW, and your personal or commercial printer. Because CorelDRAW can import so many different graphics file types, especially documents created with Adobe products, you will want to be alerted when importing a photo that was tagged with a color profile. Go to Tools | Color Management | Default Settings right now. In Figure 3-8 you can see four check boxes toward the right of the dialog: check them. You can always uncheck these alert options if you feel pestered by them in your work, but you really shouldn't. When you import, for example, a coworker's Photoshop PSD file, the chances are very good that this image was saved with a color profile. The chances are also fairly good that this color-profile tagged photo *won't* have the same color profile as the CorelDRAW document you've created. When an imported image has a profile that doesn't match the current CorelDRAW document's color profile, the imported photo might look dull, overly saturated, or too dark or too light. And it will print that way, and then you have an unhappy client, coworker, or most importantly, you have an unhappy *you*. Fortunately, it only takes two seconds to be happier.

Now that the alerts have been checked, here's what happens when you import a PSD, TIFF, JPEG, and even CDR and Corel CMX documents that have been embedded with a color profile: you click to import it (the exact method is covered in the following section), and before anything happens, a dialog appears. In this box, you're told exactly what color

Check to display attention box on opening and pasting.

Enable an alert that gives you the chance to correct a mismatched or missing color profile when you import a document.

profile the incoming document is tagged with, what your current document's color profile is, and you have three options (shown next) to choose from to remedy the mismatch:

- *Ignore the import's color profile and assign it the CorelDRAW document's profile.* This is not the best solution if the imported photo or graphic is really important to the design and your client.

- *Convert the document's color profile to match your CorelDRAW document's color profile.* This is a much better option; see "Create a New Document that Suits You" for the reason why and the color conversion CorelDRAW uses.

- *Convert the CorelDRAW document's colors to accommodate the imported document's color profile.* Don't choose this option if you've worked for hours on other native elements in your CorelDRAW document design, but consider this option if the import is the first element you're working with in a new document.

Click OK with the confidence that you've just accessed one of the most powerful, new features in CorelDRAW X5.

Importing Files and Setting Options

You import a file by clicking File | Import, clicking the Import button on the standard toolbar, or using the CTRL+I shortcut. All of these moves open the Import dialog (see left, Figure 3-9), which can show thumbnails, provide information such as date and file size depending on which Windows view you have the panes set up for, and options for importing

Proprietary media imports might pop up a second dialog.

Generic bitmaps are imported with no subsequent dialog or options boxes.

FIGURE 3-9 The Import dialog might trigger a second options box for additional import features, depending on the type of file you want to import.

in this box, and possibly a subsequent box, depending on the file you choose to import. For example, at right in Figure 3-9, an Acrobat PDF file has been chosen, and after clicking Import in the first dialog, a box with options on which page and whether the import should convert Text to Curves appears. Bitmaps such as BMPs, JPEG photos, PNG files, and TIFFs are imported with no further questions asked (except about color profiles) because these image types are generated by dozens of applications, and CorelDRAW understands these data types. The Import dialog looks similar to the Open Drawing dialog, but it has a few more check boxes and options that are available depending on the kind of file you are importing. Check For Watermark is a common Import option; if you choose this, CorelDRAW informs you that the photo has been tagged by its creator. If you choose a file type not supported by CorelDRAW, such as an MP3 audio file, CorelDRAW lets you know (politely) that the file format is not supported.

If you choose to filter the contents of a folder—exactly the same way as when you choose to Open a file (covered earlier), you not only simplify your search for the file you seek, but you also simplify the number of options for importing a specific media type. For getting various file formats into your document, CorelDRAW's list of file types is pretty comprehensive. Of the importable file types, Corel provides support for all its own formats, including CorelDRAW (CDR), Corel Symbol Library (CSL), Corel Painter (RIFF), CorelDRAW Compressed (CDX), Corel Presentation Exchange (CMX), Corel ArtShow 5 (CPX), Corel R.A.V.E. (CLK), Corel WordPerfect (WPD and WPG), Corel Quattro Pro (WB, WQ), Corel/Micrografx Designer (DES, DSF, and DRW), Corel Picture Publisher (PP5, PP4, and PPF), Corel Paint Shop Pro (PSP), and Corel PHOTO-PAINT (CPT).

You'll also find filter support for importing files from third-party products such as Adobe Photoshop (PSD), Adobe Illustrator (AI), Adobe Acrobat (PDF), Visio (VSD), and other Microsoft Office products. Other filters support popular PostScript, CAD, bitmap, text, and word processor file formats, and a selection of specialty file formats. Certain file types (such as PDF, discussed earlier) might have multiple pages; depending on the file type, you might see additional check boxes in the Import dialog:

- **Do Not Show Filter Dialog**   For a few import file formats, a secondary dialog may appear, offering further options for handling inherent properties in the imported file. Choosing this option kills the display of this secondary dialog and is particularly useful for uninterrupted importing of multiple images. By default, this option is not selected.

- **Maintain Layers And Pages**   If the file you are importing contains multiple pages and/or multiple layers, this option becomes available. By default, this option is selected. As the file is imported, additional pages are automatically added to your current document and/or layers are automatically added. Layers are controlled using the Object Manager docker.

 You can import multiple files if they are stored in the same folder. Click one of the files you want to open, and then hold the CTRL *key while clicking additional files. You can open an entire folder's contents: click the first file, then hold the* SHIFT *key, and finally, click the last file in the folder.*

Exporting Files and Choosing Options

If this is the first chapter you're reading in *The Official Guide,* you're in for a treat—much of the rest of this guide shows you how to create exotic, intricate, and expressive artwork, logos, layouts, and other visuals that communicate your ideas. However, the world doesn't own CorelDRAW (yet), so you need to convert your media by using export filters. Keep in mind (reading the rest of this guide will help you) that choosing the best export options affects your design's appearance, quality, and compatibility with other applications.

From the File menu, CorelDRAW offers a general-purpose Export command that is used to export your work to formats the world can view, plus a special Export For Office command for when your work will be used in a Corel WordPerfect Office application or in a Microsoft Office application. First, let's look at the Export command that offers the greatest variety of export formats.

Export

File | Export (CTRL+E) contains all of the export filters you chose to install during the installation of CorelDRAW. If you installed the recommended set of import/export filters, you'll find over 40 different file formats available in the Export dialog. If you need or just want to, you can always run the CorelDRAW installation program again to install additional export filters—the Secondary Import/Export File types: CUR, EXE, FMV, ICO, PCD, PCX, SCT, VSD, XCF, XPM, and/or the Tertiary Import/Export File types: GEM, HTM, IMG, MET, NAP, PIC, SHW, MOV, and QTM.

The options available to you in the Export dialog vary depending on your document's properties, such as whether you have anything selected, how many pages are in your file, and what type of file format you have chosen in the Save As Type drop-down. Secondary dialogs can also appear depending on the export file format. In Figure 3-10, this logo needs to be shared with a client as an email attachment. The JPG - JPEG Bitmaps file format for email attachments is one of the smallest file size, yet highest quality bitmap, file formats; this is chosen from the Save As Type drop-down list. General options are then displayed in this dialog, and version X5 offers a secondary dialog after you choose a file location, a filename, and then click Export. For JPEG images, you almost *never* want to check the Do Not Show Filter Dialog check box. CorelDRAW X5 has a host of options for writing JPEG copies of your work that you do not want to pass by. A short tutorial provided next explains JPEG options so your work is crisp, hi-fi, and as small in file size as possible.

The following Export dialog options are available:

- **Export This Page Only**   If your document consists of multiple pages, this option becomes available when exporting to EPS or to any file format supporting text as characters (such as text or word processor formats). Choosing this option causes only your current page to be exported.

- **Selected Only**   Choose this option to export only your currently selected object(s) instead of your entire page or document.

- **Do Not Show Filter Dialog**   Choose this option to export your file immediately using the options currently set in some secondary filter dialogs; this can be useful when exporting multiple individual files in identical ways. However, as a rule, skipping the secondary filter dialog is like skipping a meal—you might feel okay at the moment, but you'll regret it in the long run.

To get a good working idea of how to export a CorelDRAW design as a JPEG image, open Famous Elmer's.cdr now. There's an excellent possibility you can draw a better logo than Elmer did, but that's not the point—this happens to be a representative image with colors and the drop shadow effect that you might use in your own work, and you'll see shortly how visible quality and saved file size are affected by the options you use in the secondary filter dialog.

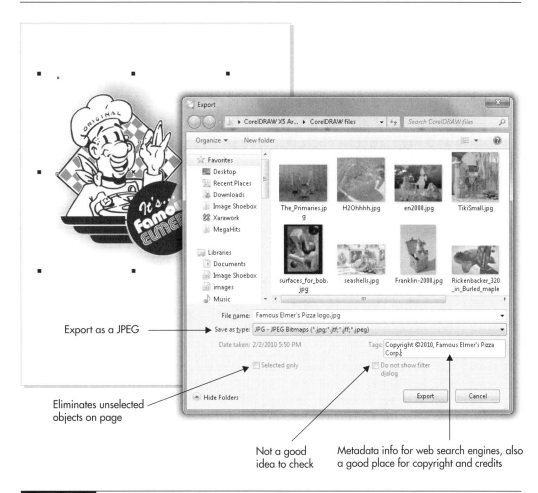

Export as a JPEG

Eliminates unselected
objects on page

Not a good
idea to check

Metadata info for web search engines, also
a good place for copyright and credits

FIGURE 3-10   The Export dialog is the first step to exporting your current document page or
selected objects.

Exporting a Design

1. Let's assume your client (Elmer) doesn't want a sea of white around the logo you're
   presenting—he only wants to see the logo. Select the grouped object using the Pick
   Tool. Always do this *before* proceeding with your Export operation.

2. Choose File | Export (CTRL+E) or click the Export button in the standard toolbar to
   open the Export dialog.

3. Choose a folder and/or location, and enter a unique name for your exported file. **Elmer's Terrific Logo.jpg** seems to fit the bill here.

4. Choose JPEG - JPEG Bitmaps from the Save As Type drop-down menu.

5. Check the Selected Only option.

6. Date Taken is an optional field into which you can enter a date that a photo was taken, but obviously this isn't a photo you're exporting. As a rule, when you send anything to a web page or attach it as an email, fill in as many metadata tags as are offered. Metadata adds very little to a saved file's size, and it really helps web search engines identify and publicize your work. Type keywords or credits and copyright information in the Tags field, too.

7. Click Export to proceed with your export operation.

8. Here's where the action happens: the secondary filter dialog specific to JPEG images, as shown in Figure 3-11. First, click the Two Vertical Previews button near the top left. Now you have two previews and can compare, for example, 100% quality versus 50% quality settings for export. JPEG compression discards some original photo information, but you get to set the level of compression in this dialog, and you can preview an acceptable and an unacceptable amount of visual compression. To use the preview panes, click inside one to select it, and then choose a JPEG setting from the Presets drop-down at right or enter it manually. Then compare what you see onscreen.

9. You can choose a preset from the Presets list; however, this list only provides the most general and basic amount of control over your exported image: Low, Medium, High—you get the picture. Setting quality with JPEGs is inversely proportional to saved file size, and you can do this manually by using the Quality spin box (or by entering a value in the number box). Look at the image in the right pane to see the quality, and then look below it to see the estimated saved file size. As a rule, Medium Quality compression generally provides excellent quality, except when your design has a billion different colors sitting right next to each other, such as in a drawing of confetti. JPEG doesn't work very well for what is called *high-frequency* images, and if this is the case, a GIF file would work better, display better, and have a much smaller file size.

10. In the Advanced section, you can choose to tag the image with a color profile, the profile your document is defined with. You can also check Optimize, which helps compress the image a little more with little cost to the final rendered quality. You probably don't want to check Progressive—doing this causes the JPEG to stream as it is downloaded to the recipient. The streaming image increases its resolution until it's completely downloaded; it appears a little weird to the recipient, and Progressive should be reserved for large JPEGs (over 3 or 4MB) you send to people who only have dial-up connections.

11. You can scale your exported JPEG without scaling your original; use the percentage boxes in the Transformation field. It's not usually a good idea to uncheck Maintain Aspect Ratio unless you deliberately want to stretch or "smoosh" your exported image.

12. Once you've performed all your customization in all the Export areas, check one last time and decide on the quality you see in the preview frame that displays the compression you've decided upon, take a look at the approximate saved file size, and then click OK to export your image to the specified folder on your hard drive.

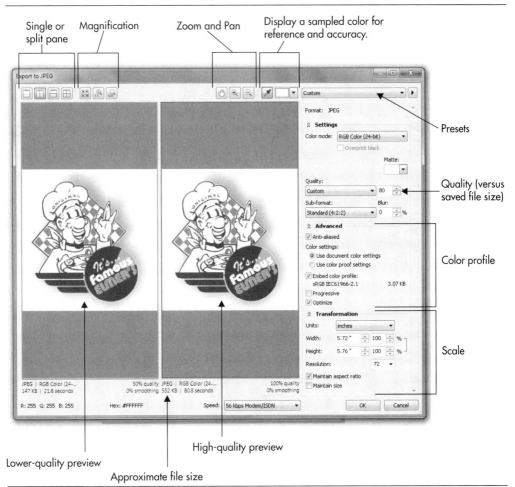

FIGURE 3-11   When an Export displays a secondary dialog, use it to your advantage. Create the right size dimensions and file size for your intended audience.

NOTE	*When you export your design to certain bitmap file formats such as TIFF and PSD, these file types can retain color profiles. Color profiles add to total saved file size, and this is also true when you save CorelDRAW documents. If you absolutely, positively have to conserve hard drive space, you might forego saving color profiles along with a document. As accurately estimated in the Export and Save dialogs, color profiles can "cost" up to 500K of additional file size. Generally, it's worth the price; very few professional designers and commercial printers work without color profiles, but embedding color profiles is one area where you can conserve on saved file sizes.*

Choosing Export File Formats

The preceding tutorial covers you for exporting your CorelDRAW work to one of the most common and popular bitmap file formats used today for email attachments and web graphics. You can also choose third-party application file formats such as Photoshop, Acrobat PDF, and even AutoDesk CAD data. Where you begin your adventures exporting CorelDRAW design work depends completely on who your final audience or target is—a friend, a commercial press house, or a different application to add a finishing touch to a composition. The following is a brief summary of the available export filters:

- **Bitmap formats** Specific bitmap types whose format is openly used and supported by many software vendors—such as BMP (Windows and OS2), CALS, GIF, JPEG (JPG, JP2), PCX, PNG, TGA, TIF, WI—feature their own filter dialogs, custom tailoring your export for the application that receives the work. Third-party bitmap formats such as Photoshop PSD display a secondary dialog so you can set options specific to Photoshop data. Corel programs such as Painter and Paint Shop Pro will accept file formats such as PSD, TIFF, and other types.

- **Metafile formats** Metafile formats such as CGM, EMF, FMV, and WFM *can* contain both vector and bitmap information, but *in practice* they commonly contain only vector *or* bitmap information. It is usually better to choose a dedicated bitmap or vector format.

- **Text formats** When exporting to text formats (such as native word processor or simple text formats), no additional dialogs appear. Choose from ANSI Text (TXT), Rich Text Format (RTF), or virtually any version of Microsoft Word (DOC), WordPerfect (WPD), or WordStar 7 and 2000 (WSD).

- **Font formats** You have the choice of exporting to TTF to create a TrueType Font or to PFB (PostScript Font Binary) to create an Adobe Type 1 font format to create your own font. A secondary dialog opens where you specify the properties for the font and character you are exporting. See "Creating Your Own Font," an online downloadable bonus chapter that covers font creation using CorelDRAW (http://theboutons.com/index.php?option=com_content&view=article&id=21:creating-your-own-font-with-coreldraw-x4&catid=14:font-creation&Itemid=428).

- **Vector formats**   CorelDRAW includes the following vector graphics filters: Frame Vector Metafile (FMV) and a Scalable Vector Graphics filter (SVG and SVGZ compressed), as shown in the SVG Export dialog in Figure 3-12. SVG has become quite popular as an alternative to vector-based Flash media; if you're considering posting a graphic to Wikipedia, the audience will appreciate SVG. Also included in this Export dialog is a preflight tab for correcting incorrect option choices (such as ICC color profiling; note the "1 Issue" remark in this figure) and options to create saved presets.

- **CAD/Plotter formats**   You can now export files to AutoCAD (DXF and DWG) as well as to HPGL 2 Plotter files (PLT). These filters include their own specific dialog filter options.

FIGURE 3-12   The improved Scalable Vector Graphics filter offers property options such as embedding a subset of fonts used and compression schemes for bitmaps in your document.

- **EPS formats**   When you choose to export to Encapsulated PostScript (EPS) format, CorelDRAW's filter offers a comprehensive set of PostScript-related options, organized into General and Advanced tabbed areas in the EPS Export dialog, as shown in Figure 3-13. EPS files are the coin of the realm in desktop publishing, and CorelDRAW can write an EPS graphics file that is Mac and Windows compatible.

- **Third-party application formats**   Export to Adobe Illustrator (AI), Adobe Photoshop (PSD), Macromedia Flash (SWF), or Kodak FlashPix Image (FPX)—each of which opens a dialog filter with specific options. The Macintosh OS native file formats, MACPaint Bitmap (MAC) and Macintosh PICT (PIC), are also available.

FIGURE 3-13   The EPS Export dialog offers full control over all aspects of your exported graphics and images.

- **Corel native formats**   Export to any of Corel's own native formats: Corel WordPerfect Graphic (WPG), Corel PHOTO-PAINT (CPT), Picture Publisher (PPF or PP5), or Corel Presentation Exchange 5.0 (CMX)—each of which features its own filter dialogs.

Export for Office

Corel WordPerfect Office and Microsoft Office are used by tens of millions of people every day to produce letters, reports, charts, and presentations. These people often do not have graphics training or graphics software, but want and need graphics in their documents. To address these needs, Office suites not only accept graphics for placement in documents, but also provide simple tools to create and edit graphics within the suite. The tools are limited and the file formats that work best with office suites are also limited when compared with graphics applications.

CorelDRAW's Export For Office feature makes it easy for you to be sure that any graphics you supply for use in WordPerfect and Microsoft Office are optimized for their use in an Office document. Export For Office also helps you and your client avoid delays, bum documents, and other migraine-inducing issues.

Choose File | Export For Office to display the Export For Office dialog and kick off the process of creating a file for your customer that's Office-suite optimized. The Export For Office dialog has a large preview window in the center that shows what will be exported. You can navigate around the preview window and zoom in and out by clicking on the appropriate Zoom or Hand Tool icon on the side of the dialog, shown next.

Export For Office cannot export multiple pages; it only works with the page you have active at the time you opened the dialog. If you have a multi-page document that you want to export, you'll need to do this page by page. And unlike with the Export dialog, there is no Selected Only check box; however, you can, indeed, export a selected object only. In the Export For Office process, if you have any object(s) selected before you open the dialog, only the objects you had selected appear in the preview window. On the other hand, if you have nothing selected, everything you have on the page and *partially* on the page is what is saved by the Export For Office process.

The gray checkerboard background to the preview area corresponds to areas of transparency. Vector objects and text have no background, but any bitmaps you created from vector objects will have a white background around them unless you explicitly checked the Transparent Background check box in the Convert To Bitmap dialog when converting the object for export. Bitmaps you imported into your original document that contained transparent backgrounds will retain the transparent areas.

The drop-down lists at the top of the dialog are where you make some preparations for the intended use of the exported graphic. To make good choices here, you really need to know what your customer is likely to do with the file. First, you need to know which Office suite they will be using the graphics file with: Corel's or Microsoft's. The answer to this question determines which file format you choose in the Export To drop-down list. Also, ask yourself (and your coworker receiving the file): Will you edit this file using the Office suite's tools, or will you just place it in their document as finished work? You also should know what the final destination for their document will be: an onscreen presentation or on the Web, printing to a low-resolution desktop printer or to a professional, commercial printer.

If your customer is using Corel WordPerfect Office, choose that in the Export To drop-down list, and all other options gray out. Your exported file will be saved as a WordPerfect Graphics (WPG) file. The Estimated File Size of the saved WPG file appears at the bottom of the dialog. Click OK and the now-familiar Save As dialog appears with Corel WordPerfect Graphic already selected in the Save As Type drop-down. Navigate to where you want to save your file, give it a name in the File Name field, click Save, and you are done.

If your customer uses Microsoft Office, choose that in the Export To drop-down. Next, choose either Compatibility or Editing in the Graphic Should Be Best Suited For drop-down. If you choose Compatibility, your exported file will be saved as a bitmap in the PNG file format. As a bitmap your graphic will look just like you see it onscreen, but it can no longer be edited using vector tools.

If you choose Editing, the file will be saved in the Extended Metafile Format (EMF), which can retain some (but not all) vector information and some CorelDRAW effects. EMF files can be easily edited in Microsoft Office, but fancy effects such as Distort may not travel well or at all, so you will want to open the document yourself in Microsoft Office to see how it looks. As a measure to ensure that the export looks like the original does in CorelDRAW, you can make a copy of the graphic, particularly if it has dynamic effects such as envelopes or extrude. Then use Arrange | Break Apart and similar commands on the Arrange menu to "genericize" the vector information, adding to the saved file size, but also adding to your chances that an elegant graphic displays in a Word document as you intend it to.

If you choose Compatibility, which will save your work as a bitmap, the Optimized For drop-down needs your attention. If you choose Editing, the Optimized For drop-down will be grayed out. Here your choices are Presentation, which basically means it will be displayed on a monitor and not printed, or one of the two print options on the list—Desktop Printing or Commercial Printing. The PNG format bitmap file saved with the Presentation setting saves at 96 dpi; the Desktop Printing setting saves at 150 dpi; and Commercial Printing saves at 300 dpi.

As you make your choices, you will notice that the Estimated File Size changes. As when you selected WordPerfect Office as your export option, click OK to open the Save As dialog where the file type is already selected in the Save As Type drop-down. Navigate to where you want to save your file, give it a name in the File Name field, click Save, deliver the goods, and ask for a (large) check!

Saving, importing, and exporting might not be as exciting as the headlines on supermarket tabloids, but they're essential skills that are a prerequisite to reaping your rewards as a CorelDRAW designer. Compare it to the ennui of learning how to use a knife and fork— they're essential to being able to savor the meal that comes after learning Silverware 101! If you've read Chapter 2, you now know where a lot of the Good Stuff is in CorelDRAW's interface, and how to save anything you've created using the Good Stuff. Now it's time to get a handle on navigating this interface in Chapter 4. You know how to bring stuff in and copy stuff out of CorelDRAW; it'd be nice if you first had the best view of these objects, on layers and on multiple pages you're soon going to be cranking out.

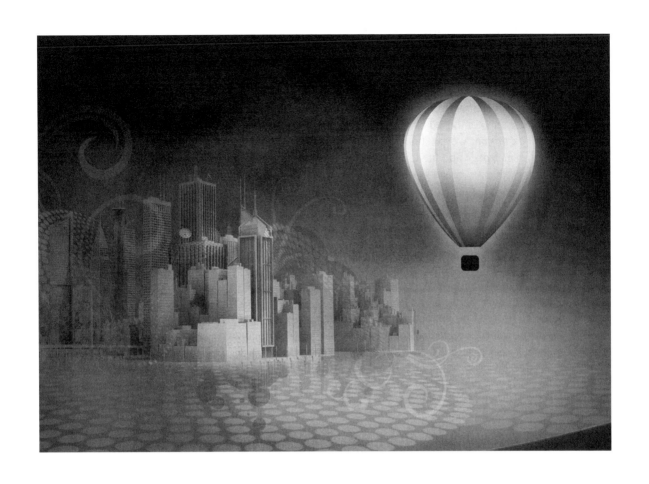

CHAPTER 4

Navigation and Page Setup

A rtists who have embraced digital media enjoy not only new tools, but also new ways to *look* at our artwork. Because your CorelDRAW designs can be extremely large, intricate, and composed on several different layers, now's the time to discover the ways you can look at your work. This chapter covers the different ways you can view dimensions of the drawing page and the level of detail displayed on your screen as you preview and work. You'll work smarter and more efficiently—regardless of your skill level—when you understand how wide, tall, and deep your drawings can be, and how to view the details you need at any given second. Learning the ins and outs of CorelDRAW document navigation might just be your ticket to better artwork in less time!

> **NOTE**   *Download and extract all the files from the Chapter04.zip archive to follow the tutorials in this chapter.*

Setting View Mode

Because the type of artwork you usually design in CorelDRAW is vector artwork, the objects you create need to be written to screen from moment to moment: the process is called *rasterizing*. With today's video cards and computer processors, the response time between changing an element in a file and seeing the change can usually be measured in a fraction of a second. CorelDRAW has always supported different levels of detail with which you view your CorelDRAW work. They're accessed through the View menu, and these view modes can help you find an object and draw an object when your design becomes intricate and the page gets cluttered.

View modes are used to specify how your drawing appears onscreen. Modes offer feedback as to how a design will print or export, and lower-quality view modes can help you locate an object hidden by other objects. You switch between view modes by using the View menu and through keyboard shortcuts. The *View menu* itself indicates the current view using a button indicator to the left of each menu item.

You have the option of choosing from one of six display qualities: Simple Wireframe, Wireframe, Draft, Normal, Enhanced, and Pixels. The default mode is Enhanced, and this is the best proofing quality for working and displaying your work to others. Additionally, you can check or uncheck Simulate Overprints and Rasterize Complex Effects when viewing in Enhanced mode. The following section explains how these display modes render to screen paths and objects that have different fills and effects. Here you can see the list of View commands:

Button indicator ——→   Viewing quality modes

Wireframe and Simple Wireframe

The views listed make a top-to-bottom progression from low to high detail. At the top, Simple Wireframe and Wireframe provide the least detail and refresh onscreen almost immediately when you make edits or change the zoom level of your document. In Simple Wireframe viewing mode, all you see is the silhouette of vector objects: a thin black outline with no fill. This is a very useful view mode for locating a shape on the page when you don't have the time to perform a search in CorelDRAW (covered in Chapter 14). Simple Wireframe mode provides no view of object fills, but it does reveal the structure of effects objects such as extrudes and blends. Figure 4-1 is a visual comparison of Simple Wireframe, Wireframe, Pixels view, and the default viewing mode in CorelDRAW, Enhanced. Clearly, you're not going to apply fills to objects in Wireframe mode while you work; however, these different modes indeed provide user information about objects you don't usually see, and you can edit paths, copy objects, and perform most other necessary design tasks in any of these view modes.

Getting a Draft View

Draft view is the middle-ground of view quality between Wireframe and Enhanced modes. In Draft viewing mode, the objects in your drawing are rendered with color fills, but only Uniform fills are displayed with any accuracy. Outline properties such as dashed lines, width,

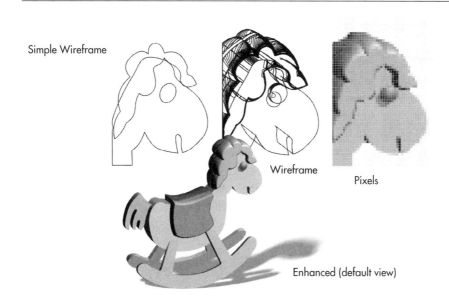

FIGURE 4-1   View modes can help you see the structure of complex objects and provide you with "unseen" clues where editing might be desired.

Enhanced view

Draft view

Fountain fill   Bitmap fill   PostScript fill

FIGURE 4-2   Draft view provides Uniform color fill views and outline colors, but not more elaborate object fills.

and color are displayed. The two greatest visual differences between Draft and Enhanced views are that there is no anti-aliasing in Draft mode (so object edges look harsh and jaggy), and bitmaps and Fountain fills do not display as you'd expect them to. Figure 4-2 shows a Fountain fill, a Bitmap fill, and a PostScript fill viewed in (the default) Enhanced view at the top and then at bottom in Draft mode. There is a subtle visual indication that you can use to tell the difference between a Bitmap fill and a Fountain fill in this mode, but it's hardly worth the challenge. Draft mode is best used to evaluate basic color schemes in a vector drawing and for quickly navigating incredibly dense and complex illustrations such as CAD architecture designs and a single page containing 45,000 Extrude effect objects.

Using Normal View

Normal view displays all object properties—Bitmap fills, Fountain fills, and PostScript fills—correctly, unlike Draft and Wireframe views. The only difference between Enhanced and Normal view modes is that Normal mode does not anti-alias the edges of objects. *Anti-aliasing* is part of the rasterization process because visual data is written to the screen that creates a smooth transition, whereas image areas have very different colors and brightness. This is usually done by adding pixels to the color edge of an object whose color is a blend between the neighboring, contrasting areas. The effect of anti-aliasing is particularly evident along edges of objects that travel diagonally across the page, and in curved areas such as circles and ellipses. Without anti-aliasing, the Normal view might remind you of Microsoft Paint back in 1991, when the best monitor you could buy was a VGA and you ran Windows 3.*x*.

Normal view mode will appeal to users whose video card doesn't have a lot of RAM, and to artists who create thousands of objects on a page. Screen refreshes are quicker, and if you don't mind the stair-steppy edges of aliased object edges, you can pick up some speed using Normal mode.

NOTE *Bitmaps—whether they're imported photos or bitmap fills you define using the Interactive fill tool—do not change their screen appearance if you switch from Normal to Enhanced view mode. Bitmaps do not update or refresh in CorelDRAW because the pixel color definitions are set within the image or fill.*

Using Enhanced View

When you use Enhanced view, all vector objects (text is a vector object, too) are anti-aliased around the edges. It's your best view of your work and is the default setting in CorelDRAW.

Previewing with Pixels View

New to version X5 is a view option that displays both vector and bitmap data onscreen as though the objects all were constructed from pixels. Pixels view quality depends on the resolution of your document, another new X5 feature. When you open a new document, you're presented with the Create A New Document screen; there, you set the Rendering Resolution—the factory default setting is 300 dpi (dots, or pixels, per inch). As an example, suppose you're creating a web graphic. Because CorelDRAW artwork is vector- and resolution-independent in nature, you can't truly preview what a bitmap version of your vector design will look like on the Web, because every zoom level you choose displays the vector graphic smoothly using Enhanced view. The previewing solution is simple—before you draw, set up your document to 96 dpi in the Create A New Document box, and then use Pixels view mode to preview your artwork before delivering it and getting paid handsomely for it.

The higher the resolution of the document, the smoother that Pixels view displays your artwork.

TIP *To change the resolution of a document, double-click the gray page border to bring up the Page Size tab in Options. Change the Rendering Resolution to suit your current need, and go to town.*

Simulate Overprints

Simulate Overprints is a print production preview mode. Overprinting is part of the standard commercial printing process used to simulate how colors actually will print to a physical page and also is used to check for any gaps between printed objects due to any printing registration problems. If you have no need for commercial printing, Simulate Overprints will be a seldom-used view. However, if you use CorelDRAW for physical commercial output, bear in mind two things:

- You need to check in with Window | Dockers | Color Proof Settings and to ensure that your intended output device is chosen from the Simulate Environment list (shown next). If you don't find the printing press of your choice, contact the commercial printer and request the drivers or ICM profile they use. By default, SWOP is the color space when proofing, and chances are good that the simulation of a CMYK color space will display colors as accurately as any monitor can.

- "Simulation" means exactly that. It is physically impossible to proof physical pigments rendered to a physical surface with total accuracy by using a monitor that displays virtual artwork. However, CorelDRAW's color simulation of real-world color output is excellent, and "close" is far better than "none" when it comes to proofing printed material on your screen.

To quickly switch between your current view mode and the last-used view mode, press SHIFT+F9.

Zooming and Panning Pages

There are at least two meanings in CorelDRAW for the term *view,* and the previous sections have covered only one of them: *view quality,* the level of detail with which you see your work. *Zooming*—increasing and decreasing the resolution of a page—and *panning* (sliding your view without zooming, similar to using the scroll bars on the edge of a document window) are the topics of the sections to follow. In the real world, evaluating the progress of a design from different perspectives is a chore when compared to CorelDRAW's workspace: you back into a ladder in your artist's loft, you can't find your favorite magnifying glass, and you wear the carpet thin moving toward and away from your canvas! One way to work faster (and usually smarter) is through a digital design program such as CorelDRAW. Another good way is to master all the features for zooming your view, covered next.

Using the Zoom Tool and Property Bar

The Zoom tool is in the fourth group of tools from the top on the toolbox and is marked by its magnifying glass icon. If you see a hand icon and not the magnifying glass, click-hold on the icon to reveal the group. The tool is used to zoom in and zoom out of a page.

When you've chosen the Zoom tool, the property bar displays buttons plus a drop-down list that provides just about every common degree of magnification you could ask for, as shown in Figure 4-3. You therefore have at least two methods for page navigation when you select the Zoom tool: clicking with the tool in the document workspace, and choosing degrees of magnification from the property bar (not including click or click-drag actions with the cursor).

FIGURE 4-3 Here are all the property bar options you'll need to navigate a magnified CorelDRAW document.

The following list describes the purpose of these options on the property bar:

- **Zoom Levels** To increase your current view by a preset magnification, use the Zoom Levels drop-down selector from the standard property bar when the Zoom tool is not chosen. When the tool is chosen, you'll want to use the Zoom tool property bar. You'll find selections ranging from 10 percent to 1,600 percent, along with some quick views for zooming based on page size. You can also type a value directly in the Zoom Levels combo box and then press ENTER; however, the zoom levels always increase and decrease beginning at the center of the drawing window. The option to "zoom in to 1,600 percent, but zoom toward the lower left of the window" isn't an option. Views saved in the View Manager (discussed later in this chapter) are also included on the drop-down list.

- **Zoom In** Zoom In is the default state while the Zoom tool is selected. Clicking once in the drawing window increases your view magnification by twice the current percentage of zoom—100 percent goes to 200 percent with a click, then to 400 percent with another click in the window. Here's an important point: when you zoom in this way, using the tool and not the Zoom Levels selections, *you zoom in centered relative to the tool's cursor location onscreen.* You direct the final point of your zoom by centering it with your cursor. You can also use the Zoom tool to perform *marquee* zooming, shown in Figure 4-4. You place your cursor at the corner of the area you want to magnify, and then click-drag diagonally to the opposing corner of an imaginary bounding box that defines the area to which you want to zoom. You can target any two opposing corners, but most users tend to diagonally drag from upper left to lower right of an area.

Begin at a corner.   Click-drag to the opposing corner.   Zoomed-in area

FIGURE 4-4   Marquee-dragging is the easy way to pinpoint a location and zoom in.

TIP   *CorelDRAW's zooming extent runs from a minimum of 1 percent to a maximum of 264,583 percent. You'd be hard-pressed to need a greater magnification range. The Royal Observatory in Edinburgh is currently looking into CorelDRAW X5—they downloaded the trial version.*

● **Zoom Out**   To decrease your view magnification using the Zoom tool, click the right mouse button anywhere on or off your document page, or hold SHIFT in combination with the left mouse button (in case your right mouse button is broken). Alternatively, click the Zoom Out button (shown next) on the property bar. Doing so decreases your view to your last-used magnification or by a power of 2, and the center of the zoom out is the center of the drawing window. Just as with zooming in, zooming out while using the Zoom tool is directed by the location of the Zoom tool cursor onscreen. If you want, for example, to zoom out to the upper right of a page, you put the cursor at the upper right of the page and then right-click. To zoom out while any tool is selected, press F3.

Zoom in (normal tool state, click left mouse button)

Zoom out (hold SHIFT while using Zoom tool, or right-click)

- **Zoom One-Shot** The Zoom One-Shot command is for selecting the Zoom tool momentarily for a single Zoom In or Zoom Out command while you are using any tool. Once the zoom has been accomplished, your previous tool reappears. This zoom command is available in CorelDRAW, but you won't find it on any toolbar or on the property bar. Instead, it's an unassigned feature that you can access only through customization using a button. If you prefer to use keyboard shortcuts, F2 is your key. To make the Zoom One-Shot command appear as a button in a logical and convenient place, the property bar is ideal—the Zoom One-Shot button can be seen there whenever the Pick tool is chosen. First, make sure nothing is selected with the Pick tool, or this isn't going to work. Open the Options dialog (CTRL+J), click Workspace | Customization | Commands to display the command customization page, and choose View from the drop-down menu. Then, find the Zoom One-Shot button, drag the button to the property bar (between the Nudge Distance and Duplicate Distance boxes is good), and then release the button, though only after you see an I-beam to confirm that you're adding the button to the desired location.

- **Zoom To Selected** When you have one or more objects selected in the drawing window, choosing this command changes your view magnification and viewing position of the page to show the entire selection in the window. Choose Zoom To Selected from either the Zoom property bar or the Zoom Levels drop-down menu. You can also Zoom to a selected object while *any* tool is selected by pressing SHIFT+F2.

- **Zoom To All Objects**   Zoom To All Objects changes your view magnification to display all objects visible in your document window, regardless of whether the objects are on or off the current document page. Choose Zoom To All Objects from either the Zoom property bar or the Zoom Levels drop-down menu. Alternatively, use the F4 shortcut while any tool is selected.

- **Zoom To Page**   This changes your view to fit your current page size completely within the document window. Choose Zoom To Page from either the Zoom property bar or the Zoom Levels drop-down menu, or press SHIFT+F4 while any tool is selected.

- **Zoom To Page Width/Height**   These two commands enable you to zoom your view to the entire width or height of the current page. You'll find these tool buttons in the Zoom property bar or the Zoom Levels drop-down menu.

Using the Mouse Wheel for Zooming

Affordable, high-quality input devices such as the mouse and even some styli for graphics tablets have had a combo wheel/button between the left and the right since the 1990s. Applications (when the engineers wrote the feature in) can scroll a document window and also zoom a document window. Happily, Corel engineers built in this capability for zooming (it's enabled by default). To zoom into a page, push the scroll wheel away from you; zooming out is done by dragging the mouse (or stylus) wheel toward you, as shown here. If you don't care for this feature, you can restore mouse wheel action to scrolling by choosing Options (CTRL+J) | Workspace | Display, and then choosing Scroll from the Default Action For Mouse Wheel drop-down list.

NOTE   *If your zooms feel jerky when you're using the scroll wheel, this is not a CorelDRAW problem, but rather that of the physical wheel (the way it was designed). But you may be able to fine-tune the scroll action using the manufacturer's mouse driver options. The best place to check for mouse options is in Windows Start Menu | Control Panel | Whatever icon you see for your mouse (if any). If there's no icon for your mouse (or other input device) in the Control Panel, check Start | All Programs.*

Customizing View Shortcuts

Many of the Zoom and Hand tool commands in CorelDRAW have preassigned shortcut keys that can be changed. To access these shortcut key commands for viewing, follow these steps:

1. Open the Options dialog (CTRL+J) or choose Tools | Options.

2. On the left side of the dialog, under Workspace, click to expand Customization, and then click Commands to view the Commands page.

3. Choose View from the drop-down menu at the top-left corner of the right side of the dialog, and notice that a list of view items appears below it. In this list, click to select the tool or command to change, as shown next.

4. Click the Shortcut Keys tab at the top of the rightmost section of the dialog to display the shortcut key options. Click to make an insertion point in the New Shortcut Key box, and then press the key combination (or single key) that you want to assign as the new shortcut. If, as shown in this example, you want Zoom To Selection to be CTRL+SHIFT+Z instead of the default SHIFT+F2, you press CTRL and SHIFT and Z at the same time (you *don't* type "Shift" or "Ctrl"). If a conflict appears in the Currently Assigned To field, you can rethink your custom keyboard combo, or dismiss (overwrite) the default key assignment by just clicking Assign. Click the Assign button when you've got the keyboard key combo of your dreams entered.

5. To delete a shortcut that has already been assigned, click the shortcut in the Current Shortcut Keys box, and then click the Delete button.

6. Click OK to close the dialog and apply the shortcut key changes.

TIP   *You can quickly Zoom To All Objects on or off the document page by double-clicking the Zoom Tool button in the toolbox.*

Using the Pan Tool

The Pan tool—also commonly called the Hand tool—is a convenient alternative to using document scroll bars; it's your avatar for your physical hand while in CorelDRAW. The Hand tool's keyboard shortcut is H (for "hand"), and it works exactly as you'd anticipate. To use it, click-drag in the drawing window, and your view will travel in the same direction. The principal advantage to using the Hand tool over the document window scroll bar "thumbs" (that screen element in the center of a scroll bar you use to click-drag) is one of economy; you don't have to put in several "mouse miles" to change your view, and the Hand tool is great for adjusting your document view by a fraction of an inch, with precision.

The Hand tool's cursor looks like a hand (Corel engineers gave a lot of consideration to the cursor), and with a click-drag, you can scroll your view in any direction (often called *panning*) as you would with a camera. As you do this, the scroll bars and document rulers move in unison to reflect the new position.

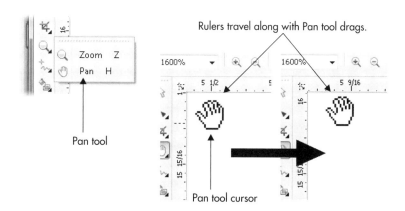

Rulers travel along with Pan tool drags.

Pan tool

Pan tool cursor

TIP   *Double-click the Pan Tool button in the toolbox to instantly center your page view.*

Controlling Zoom and Pan Tool Behavior

The Options dialog is where you can customize certain actions when using the Zoom and Hand tools. Right-clicks, by default, trigger Zoom Out for both the Zoom and Hand tools. However, you might want to reassign right-clicking for the Hand and Zoom tools to be more consistent with the right-click behavior—in other words, to display a pop-up context menu like the other toolbox tools do.

If this is your preference, you can change your right-clicks by opening the Options dialog (CTRL+J) and clicking to expand the tree directories under Toolbox | Zoom, Hand Tool, as shown here. In this dialog, you can set the behavior of the right-clicks, using either tool to open the pop-up menu instead.

Several shortcuts are available while using the Pan tool, some of which are for zooming, not panning. A right-click using the Pan tool results in a Zoom Out command, and a double-click causes a Zoom In command. You can also use the keyboard to pan the view of your document while any tool is selected by using these shortcuts:

- **Pan left** Press and hold ALT+LEFT ARROW.
- **Pan right** Press and hold ALT+RIGHT ARROW.

- **Pan up**   Press and hold ALT+UP ARROW.

- **Pan down**   Press and hold ALT+DOWN ARROW.

Special View Modes

Other types of views are found in CorelDRAW. In addition to viewing quality and resolution, you might have the need to change the page order in a multi-page document for a tidier presentation. Hey, you could certainly do with a preview setting that eliminates the workspace and puts the focus on your artwork!

The following sections explore these features, how to work with them, and how to provide views of your work you might not even have considered. You're going to *love* this stuff.

Page Sorter View

CorelDRAW Page Sorter view (covered in detail in Chapter 6) becomes available as a special view mode when your document has at least one page; two or more pages will be more useful, because it's silly to try to sort one page (and impossible if you have less than one page). To go into Page Sorter View mode, choose View | Page Sorter View. While viewing a document in the Page Sorter, you can browse several pages at one time and manage their properties as a collection instead of thumbing through single pages. While you're using this view, your pages and all their contents are displayed in miniature, but no other view in CorelDRAW can show you a complete document page flow and offer you the chance to reorder pages and their properties in one fell swoop. The Pick tool is the only available tool in this view, and the property bar displays several options unique to this document view. You can reorder pages by dragging them to different locations in the current order, or right-click specific pages to rename, insert, and delete them (see Figure 4-5).

Full-Screen Preview

To fill the entire screen with a view of your current document page at the current zoom level, use View | Full-Screen Preview, or press the F9 shortcut key. This view hides all of the CorelDRAW interface—including your cursor—and shows only the current view rendered in Enhanced view mode (the Full-Screen Preview default view). To return your view to Normal, press any key or click either mouse button.

> **NOTE**   *Depending on any desktop utilities you might have installed, there might be a conflict between the F9 shortcut to get to Full-Screen Preview and something such as a desktop calendar or local weather applet. You can use a number of remedies: you can define a different keyboard shortcut, use the View menu or the pop-up menu instead of a keyboard shortcut, or remove the desktop utility that probably doesn't tell you the correct weather in Kazakhstan anyway.*

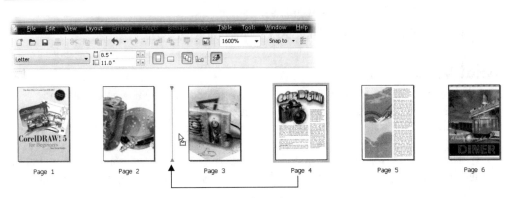

Page 4 is being scooted in front of Page 3.

FIGURE 4-5   Page reordering in a multi-page document is as easy as drag and drop.

While you're using Full-Screen Preview, the view mode and page border view appearance is set according to preferences in the Options dialog. To access these options, choose Tools | Options (CTRL+J) and click Display under the Workspace category on the left side of the dialog to access the Display options. Full-Screen Preview options, located in the lower part of the dialog, let you choose either draft or enhanced (the default) view as the view mode, and either show or hide the page border.

Previewing Selected Only

The Preview Selected Only command, available from the View menu, lets you preview only what's selected on the page before entering this mode. This option works using the Full-Screen Preview preferences and takes a toggle state either On or Off when selected. There are two caveats to using this command: if no objects are selected, the Full-Screen Preview offers a nice, energy-wasting white blank screen; you'll also get similar all-white views if the selected object is not in view before entering this mode. The result you get with Preview Selected Only depends entirely on what's framed in the document window at what viewing resolution you have defined before using the command.

Using the View Navigator

The View Navigator is a pop-up viewer that is indispensable for navigating your entire document page when you've zoomed in to 10,000 percent and need to quickly move to a different design area without zooming out to get your bearings. The View Navigator pop-up window is at the point where the vertical and horizontal scroll bars meet at the lower-right corner of the document window. To open the View Navigator pop-up, click-hold the button, the magnifying glass icon.

Click-holding the icon displays a pop-up thumbnail that represents the outermost region of the page and the application's desktop. The preview frame—the tiny rectangle with the crosshairs through it—within the View Navigator window indicates the viewing limitations according to your current Zoom settings. Click-drag within the View Navigator pop-up window to pan around your drawing in the document window; it's panning by proxy. As you drag, releasing the mouse button ends the navigation.

In Figure 4-6 you can see the View Navigator put to the test. Let's say you need to view or edit one of the gumballs in the machine. At 100 percent viewing resolution this would be a true hassle; luckily, by zooming in, it's easy to see the gumballs to such a detailed extent that you could wipe the foolish grin off the center one with the Shape tool, simply by homing in on this roguish piece of candy by panning the window using the View Navigator.

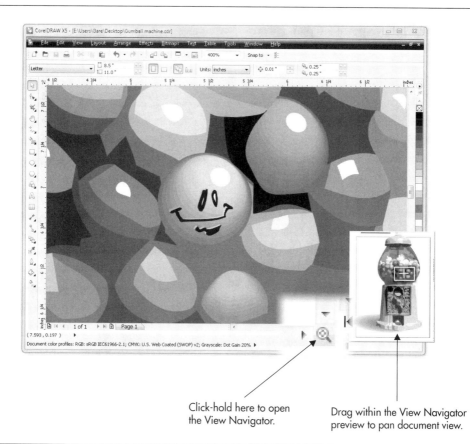

Click-hold here to open
the View Navigator.

Drag within the View Navigator
preview to pan document view.

FIGURE 4-6   The View Navigator steers you in the right direction for precise editing in very tight views.

Using the View Manager Docker

Imagine a bookmark feature in CorelDRAW that takes you to a location and viewing resolution on one or more pages just by clicking the link. This is what the View Manager does: you can define zoom levels and page locations, you can browse to any number of pages in the same document, and your document is not only better organized for future edits, but View Manager is a darned good presentation tool as well!

To open the View Manager, choose Window | Dockers | View Manager or press CTRL+F2. Figure 4-7 shows a practical use for the View Manager: here you can see an architectural drawing. All the different parts of the room have been "viewed," and different pans and zooms have been defined for the sunroom, the dining room, and so on. Now the illustrator or client can click around the structure to get a comprehensive virtual tour of the proposed design. The View Manager is also useful for tagging and returning to an exact point in a drawing where you might need to take a break! If you have a multi-page document, View Manager can accommodate your need to pinpoint any view on any page.

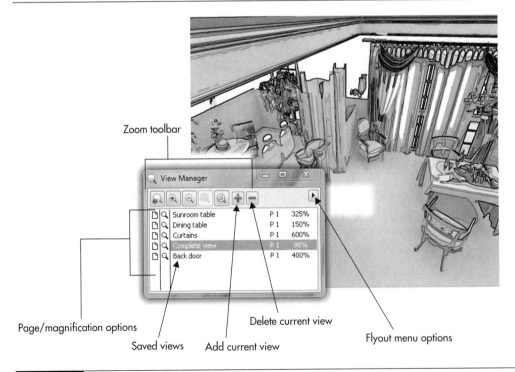

FIGURE 4-7 When you're working with complex drawings, the View Manager provides a quick way of saving and recalling views.

Exploring View Manager Commands

When a view is saved, its page number, position, and view magnification are recorded and become a new view in the View Manager docker window. The view *mode* isn't saved—such as Simple Wireframe, Draft, Normal, Enhanced, and so on—but this is trivial because you learned earlier in this chapter how to manually define view quality with any document at any time.

This sort of feature calls for a hands-on review, tutorial style. There are no "right" or "wrong" steps—this is just an exploration by-the-numbers!

Making and Taking a Structured View of a Document

1. Open an existing document containing a drawing, either completed or in progress, and the more complex the better, and then open the View Manager docker window (CTRL+F2).

2. Using page navigation commands and the Zoom tool, the Zoom command buttons on the Zoom property bar, and/or the View Navigator feature, go to a specific part of your drawing in the document window.

3. To create and save your current view, click the Add Current View button in the docker. Notice that a new item appears in the View Manager docker. By default, the new view is automatically named View-*nn-nnnn%*; the first numbers after "View" represent a sequence in which you save views, while the last digits before the percent symbol tell you the magnification level of the saved view. At the right on the docker is the page number for the saved view and the zoom percentage again. The zoom percentage is an important label at the right of each saved zoom and cannot be edited. However, you'll definitely want to replace the first zoom percentage with an evocative name for the zoom—this first zoom percentage field is just a default name for the saved zoom.

4. To name the view, right-click the name, choose Rename from the pop-up menu, and then type a name to enter the new view name. Your view is now saved. If you want, save more new views using the same procedure; change the view display in your document window each time, and then click the Add Current View button each time to save each view.

5. To go to a view, click either the page number or the view magnification title of the saved view on the docker's list. Your view is then changed to the exact point at which it was saved.

6. To delete a specific view in the View Manager docker, click to select the view, and then click the Delete Current View button. The view is immediately deleted.

In addition to the interactive methods you can use to save, name, recall, and delete saved views, the same operations can be accomplished by choosing commands on the flyout menu located on the View Manager's docker window.

Using Page and Zoom Options

To the left of each saved view in the View Manager, two options will appear. These options give you control over how your saved views are recalled and restored. For each view saved, you can toggle display of the Page Only and the Magnification Only to On or Off. Single-clicks toggle these options on and off; grayed-out options indicate an inactive state.

When the page symbol is deactivated, recalling the corresponding saved view causes only the magnification to be recalled; when the zoom symbol is deactivated, only the page display is recalled. While both are deactivated, the saved view does absolutely nothing.

Working with Views of a Document's Depth: Layers

CorelDRAW's layer feature provides invaluable ways not only to organize but also to view complex drawings. You can create several layers and move shapes between layers. You can also name layers, control their order and appearance, change object ordering within layers, group objects, and quickly see object information. One immediate advantage to adopting layers in your composition work is that you can hide layers. Suppose you have a lot of objects that need labels, and you need to print the objects with and without labels. The solution is to put all the labels on a layer. Hide the layer, print just the objects, and then unhide the layer and make a second print: easy!

Exploring the Object Manager

The Object Manager docker is your resource for viewing layer content and using layers options. With the Object Manager you can perform a whole range of actions: navigate document pages, create and name layers, select and move objects between layers, and set layers as editable, printable, and visible. To open the Object Manager docker, choose Tools | Object Manager; this is a good opportunity to give the Object Manager a shortcut key command, as described earlier: CTRL+ALT+O is available.

The Object Manager shows a listing of the layers, each accompanied by options and a flyout menu. A master page also appears and includes default layers for controlling guides, the desktop, and grid objects. Figure 4-8 shows a drawing and what the Object Manager reports for this composition. There is only one page, the drawing was created on two layers on Page 1, and highlighted on the Object Manager list is a group of ten objects, none of which has an outline color or width.

Navigating Pages, Objects, and Layers

The best way to use the Object Manager docker to navigate through your document, select layers, and to control layer options is by experimenting; the following steps are a guide.

4

Edit Across Layers

FIGURE 4-8 View, name, and alter info with the Object Manager.

You'll learn exactly how these operations are performed. Look at the next illustration, which shows a default layer structure for a new document.

Navigating and Mastering Layers

The next steps have no right or wrong execution; rather, they're simply exploration steps to get you comfortable with working with layers. This is why an illustration has already been created for you. You just work the steps and see how any of several techniques can be applied to your own work, future and present.

1. Open Alarming.cdr in CorelDRAW.

2. Open the Object Manager docker: choose Tools | Object Manager. Look at the status of the layers. The background—the pattern fill of the clocks—is locked so it cannot be moved at present. Also, there's a layer on top with a default name, and it's hidden, which means it's locked. Investigate a little now; unhide the top layer to see what's inside.

Layer is hidden.

Background is locked.

3. Okay, the author is trying to be funny here. The layer contains a third hand, yet within the context of an alarm clock, it's really a second hand. It's possible now to select the group of objects on Layer 3 by clicking them with the Pick tool, and if you click a second time, you can rotate the hand by dragging the rotation handles, and turn time itself back to Chapter 1. Click twice (slowly, don't double-click) on the name of Layer 3 on the Object Manager, and then type a name in the field that's more descriptive than "Layer 3" for future reference. Try **extra hand**, because why not?

4. Double-click the Extra Hand layer title to open its contents. The hand is several grouped objects, and they can be moved to the Clock layer. First, rename the group: click Group Of 36 Objects twice, and then type **third hand** in the field. Notice that control nodes are visible when a group or a single object is selected, and if you chose to assign Zoom To Selected to a keyboard shortcut earlier in this chapter, selecting items from the Object Manager is an easy way to select and then zoom into an object you want to work on.

5. Double-click the Clock layer title to open it, and then drag the Third Hand group down below the layer title, but above the Group Of 233 Objects entry. Layers have a hierarchy, and if you put the group below the Group Of 233 Objects, the third hand would be hidden from view by the 233 other objects.

Drag group down to clock layer.

6. Double-click the Extra Hand layer title. This action produces precisely nothing, which indicates that there is nothing nested within the layer. So it's okay to delete it—with the layer title highlighted, click the trash icon. Poof.

CAUTION *There is no confirmation box with the Delete trash icon; it's very similar to pressing the keyboard DELETE key. Be careful how you use it; to undo an inadvertent deletion, click the workspace to put the document (and not the Object Manager) "in focus," and then press CTRL+Z (Edit | Undo).*

7. Similarly, the background is expendable in this composition. Click the Wall Clock Paper layer title to select it. The layer is locked and you can confirm this by trying to move the clock pattern with the Pick tool. Click the Lock or Unlock pencil icon with the red slash over it to make the layer editable, and then click the Delete button.

TIP *Every object on the Object Manager's list can be renamed, down to single objects. Consider giving a very important object a custom name in your own work. Then, at any time, you can locate the object by conducting a search (see Chapter 14) with the Edit | Find feature, or just by scrolling through the list of objects.*

8. Create a new layer by clicking the New Layer button. Name it and then drag its title to the bottom of the layer stack on this page.

9. Lock the Clock layer.

10. Click the new layer highlighted on the Object Manager list, choose the Rectangle tool from the toolbox, create a rectangle as a background for the clock, and then apply a fill. Figure 4-9 shows a linear gradient fill (covered in Chapter 15) and a blend with transparency added to the new background layer—see Chapter 21 for the scoop on blends and contours.

Using Object Manager Editing and View States

Objects can be on different layers, and you can edit across layers in CorelDRAW. Create a new file that has objects on, let's say, three layers, to better learn through example about the editing and view states of CorelDRAW layers. Open the Object Manager docker. You'll see three view state buttons at the top of the docker where information about viewing and editing behavior is set. Clicking each button toggles its state on or off. Each button has the following effects:

 TIP *You can use Combine, Group, or Convert To Curves commands on objects in the Object Manager docker by selecting the objects, right-clicking them, and choosing a command from the pop-up menu.*

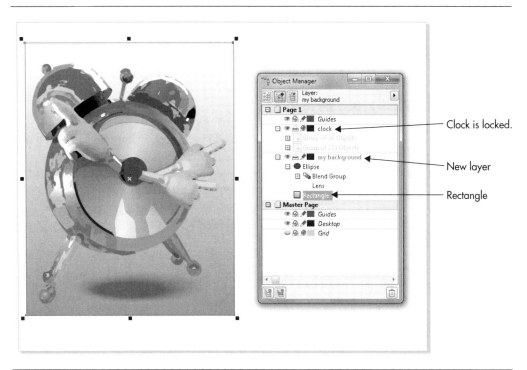

Clock is locked.

New layer

Rectangle

FIGURE 4-9   Working with layers takes full advantage of CorelDRAW's search capabilities and makes it easy to modify only certain elements in a complex drawing.

- **Show Object Properties**   Click the Show Object Properties button to set whether you want to view a detailed name for a layer's contents (color, type of object, and so on), or just the name, default, or your own custom name.

- **Edit Across Layers**   Click the Edit Across Layers button to set whether objects can be selected, moved, and copied between layers. While cross-layer editing is disabled, only objects on your current page layer and/or on the desktop can be selected or edited. While cross-layer editing is enabled, you can select, move, or edit any object on an unlocked layer.

> TIP   *Use the Object Manager to PowerClip, change object order, copy object properties, and group objects by using a right-click-drag action to drag one object onto another. After you do so, the pop-up menu lists the available commands. Grouping and PowerClip commands apply only when right-click-dragging objects within the same layer. PowerClip is discussed in detail in Chapter 11.*

- **Layer Manager View** The Layer Manager View button toggles your view to show only your document's layers. When working with complex drawings that have many pages, layers, and objects, using this view can make managing layer properties a lot easier. In this state, all page and object information is omitted.

Controlling Layer Properties

Using the Layer Properties dialog, you can control specific properties for each layer. To access these options, right-click a specific layer in the Object Manager docker, and choose Properties from the pop-up menu. You can access properties directly from the pop-up menu, or display a modeless dialog for defining the properties of a specific layer. There is a minor difference between using the dialog and the pop-up menu: the pop-up (right-click) menu has the Rename command, grouped with Delete, Cut, Copy, and Paste.

Options in this dialog control the following layer properties:

- **Visible** This option enables you to toggle the view state of a layer between visible or hidden. You can also control the visibility of objects on a layer by clicking the eye symbol to the left of the layer name.

- **Printable** This option toggles on or off the printing state of objects on the layer. You can also set whether layer objects are printable by clicking the Printer symbol beside the layer in the Object Manager docker to toggle the printing state of objects on the layer.

NOTE *Nonprinting layers will also not export. If you need objects selected on a nonprinting layer to be included when exporting, you'll need to turn on the layer's Printable option.*

- **Editable** Use this option to lock or unlock all objects on a layer. While a layer is locked, its objects can't be edited (or even selected), which is a little different from the Lock (object) command. You can also set whether layer objects are editable by clicking the pencil symbol beside the layer in the Object Manager docker to toggle the editing state of objects on the layer.

- **Master Layer** This option is only available after you've dragged a layer on the Object Manager onto the Master Page icon. Changing a layer to a master layer causes it to become part of the master page structure. Any objects on a master page appear on all pages. For details on working with master pages and master layers, see the next section.

- **Layer Color**   This selector sets the color swatch as it appears in the docker listing directly to the left of a layer name, for easy recognition. Layer Color also determines object colors when viewed using Normal or Enhanced views while the Override Full Color View option is selected. You can also set the color coding for a layer by double-clicking the color indicator next to a layer name to open a typical color selector menu and then clicking any color from the drop-down color picker.

- **Override Full Color View**   Use this option to control how the objects on the layer appear when viewed using either Normal or Enhanced view. While selected, it has the effect of displaying all objects in wireframe style, using the layer color specified.

Working with Master Page Layers

Whenever a new document is created, a master page is automatically created. The master page isn't a physical page in your document, but instead a place where document objects can be placed so that they appear on every page of your document. Objects on a master page layer are visible and printable on every page in your document, making this an extremely powerful feature. For example, a text header or footer, or a company logo, on a master page layer becomes a quick and easy way to label all the pages in a pamphlet or brochure.

Moving any object onto a layer on the master page makes it a master page object and causes it to appear on each page. Let's try out this feature.

 ## Working with Master Page Items

1. Open the Object Manager docker by choosing Tools | Object Manager.

2. Click the New Master Layer button at the lower-left corner of the docker and press ENTER. A new layer is automatically added to the master page with the default name "Layer 2."

3. With this new master layer as your current layer, create the object(s) you wish to appear on every page in their final position and appearance. By creating the object while the master layer is selected, you cause the object automatically to become a master layer object. You can also move objects from other pages onto the master layer by click-dragging them in the docker list from their position under a layer name to the master layer name.

4. Click to select the new master page object(s) on your document page. Notice that you can still select, move, and edit it. To toggle the lock or unlock state of your master layer objects, click the Edit button (the pencil symbol) beside the master page in the docker. Locking prevents any accidental editing of the master page objects.

5. Add pages to your document by clicking the + button at the lower left of the workspace. As you browse through the pages, you'll see the same object on all pages.

Several default layers already exist on your document's master page for controlling special items that appear in your document, such as Guides, Grid, and Desktop. These layers have the following purposes:

- **Guides layer** This is a global layer for guides you create; if you click the Master Guides entry on the Object Manager to select it, and then drag a guide onto the page, all pages in the document will display this guide. If you need a guide on only one page, you choose that Guides entry on the page you're working on, drag a guide from the Rulers, and that guide belongs to the page and is not a master item. Guides are covered in detail in Chapter 7.

> **TIP** *You can move a local guide, a guide you created on a page, to the Master Guides entry on the Object Manager to make it global—it will then appear on every page of your document.*

- **Grid layer** This controls the appearance of grid lines. You can control the grid color and visibility, but you can't set the Grid layer to be printable, nor can you change its editable objects or add objects to that layer. Options in the Grid Layer Properties dialog enable you to control the grid display color and to gain quick access to the Grid page of the Options dialog by clicking the Setup button in the dialog. To open the Grid Layer Properties dialog, right-click the Grid layer under the master page in the Object Manager docker, and choose Properties from the pop-up menu.

> **TIP** *Grid layer visibility can be toggled on or off by clicking its eye icon on the Object Manager.*

- **Desktop layer** This is a global desktop, the place outside of your drawing page. If you want to keep objects handy but don't want to print them on your page, drag the object to this entry on the Object Manager. If you put an object on the desktop from a layer, you can't hide it or keep it from printing, but if it's explicitly placed on the master desktop, you can hide it, keep it from being edited, and keep it from printing.

Hopefully, this chapter has shown you the way—both as an allegory and literally—to better get a fix on what it is you've drawn, what you *want* to draw, and what appears to need an edit or two. Thanks to zoom features that let you home in on a fly's eye or zoom out to a scaled drawing of Chicago, you now have a handle on the magnifying glass and other tools for panning, navigating, and recalling areas of interest in your work.

Chapter 5 is a departure from "The Basics" and a dive into just a little pure fun with CorelDRAW. If you've read Chapters 1–4 in sequence, believe it or not, you're ready to start creating amazing stuff. And even if you haven't, the steps are guided, the theme is designing a commercial logo, and your own results are going to astound you. Turn the page and help an author keep his promise!

CHAPTER 5

The X5 Test Drive

In very few guides to software applications will you read, as early as Chapter 5, "Okay, are you all ready to get going?" The *CorelDRAW X5 Official Guide* is one of them: this chapter takes you through the steps to create a *finished* design and print it!

This chapter builds upon what you know from previous chapters and also serves as a bridge between *understanding* CorelDRAW's features and putting them to practical *use*. If you're a new user of a graphics program, it's only natural for you to poke around tools and palettes to get a feel for what you've purchased: this chapter is a supervised "poking around session." You get hands-on experience with some of the advanced features used to create some basic commercial designs and learn how to integrate the features to put together a T-shirt logo for a fictitious company—after which you'll probably have the knowledge to apply these techniques to your own company logo.

But overall, this chapter is all about the *fun* you'll have designing with CorelDRAW. Everyone owns at least one manual whose documentation is dry from cover to cover. However, *this* book gets your feet wet without going over your head.

Begin a Design with a Concept

One of the most basic rules for creating a good design is to begin with a concept. This might sound strange, and you might be scoffing, "Of *course* I have a concept! I want to design a logo!" Designing a logo isn't a concept; it's a *need*. To address this need, you'll want to visualize the logo. In this chapter's example, you have a fictitious machine parts company, Dyson Gears, and they want all five of their employees to proudly wear the company's logo on T-shirts. The company has a name, but not a logo; therefore, it's thinking-cap time before moving on to CorelDRAW's tools.

One of the simplest and most effective approaches to logo design is through the use of an iconic representation. For example, if you ran an ice cream stand, a very simple and effective logo would be a drawing of an ice cream cone. Don't let the simplicity of this approach put you off: Apple, Inc., has done very well through the years with a logo of you-know-what! What sets apart a logo from every other logo that's a drawing of the vendor's product is the artistic treatment of the design. You can visualize an ice cream cone—it's basically a ball with a triangle beneath it. In CorelDRAW you can draw a circle and a triangle and then apply Artistic Media strokes to the paths to make the drawing look like a child's crayon rendering or a Victorian oil painting. You can copy and paste a dozen copies of the ice cream cone and then use the Arrange | Align and Distribute commands to pepper a page with all 12 flavors the ice cream stand sells. You can extrude the simple shapes and make a 3D ice cream cone; you can apply fountain fills to the objects…see how the treatment of a simple geometric shape offers you dozens of logos to choose from?

Along these lines of thinking, a logo for Dyson Gears would be visually outstanding if you took the initials "D" and "G", whose facing sides are rounded, and put gear teeth on them to reinforce the idea that Dyson Gears *is* gears, a literary conceit that works in commerce every day. That's the concept; read on to learn how to draw gears using a bold font as the base, create a visually stunning *treatment* for the gear design, add some compatible and striking text, and *realize* a concept.

Setting Up the Page for the Logo

Although CorelDRAW can open a new document by default when you launch the program, you need to set up guidelines on a default page so the T-shirt logo design will print edge to edge on a sheet of inkjet transfer paper. If you measure an average T-shirt, you'll see that about 7 inches is a good width for a logo. You can pick up T-shirt transfer paper at an office supply store (or even at the supermarket) that measures full-page letter size: 8½×11 inches. So you're in luck twice: CorelDRAW's default document size is the same as most T-shirt transfer paper, and the maximum width of the logo will fit the horizontal measure.

The following steps show you how to set up nonprinting guidelines on a default page: T-shirt transfer paper needs about ½ an inch in the clear on all sides so you can peel the transfer from the T-shirt (which still gives you 7½ inches for the maximum design width).

 ## Setting Up Guidelines

1. Launch CorelDRAW and then from the Welcome screen choose New Blank document. In the Create A New Document dialog, choose CorelDRAW Default from the Preset Destination drop-down list if it's not already chosen for you, choose Letter (portrait orientation) for the Size, name the file **Dyson Gears.cdr**, and then click OK.

2. You'll want to zoom into the ½-inch tick mark on the rulers for precise placement of the guides. Most of us have a scroll wheel on our mouse, and by default, CorelDRAW uses the wheel as a zoom feature. Put your cursor at the top left of the page you see in the drawing window, and then push the wheel away from you to zoom into this area. If your mouse doesn't have a scroll wheel, choose the Zoom tool from the toolbox (or press Z), and then diagonally click-drag an imaginary rectangle around the corner of the page (the gesture is often called *marquee-dragging* or *marquee-selecting*).

3. You can use any tool to drag guidelines from the rulers. Place your cursor first over the horizontal ruler at the top of the drawing window. Click-hold, and then drag from the ruler onto the page, to the vertical ½-inch tick. If you didn't get it quite right, you need to switch to the Pick tool (press the SPACEBAR), and then click-drag the guideline to the ½-inch tick mark.

4. Similarly, drag a guideline to the bottom ½-inch margin you'll need. Then drag vertical guidelines out of the vertical ruler (at the left of the drawing window) to create ½-inch vertical margins inside the page. Your screen should look like Figure 5-1 now.

5. Click the Save button on the standard toolbar. Save Dyson Gears.cdr to a location on your hard drive you can find later. Don't close the document; you're not having enough fun yet.

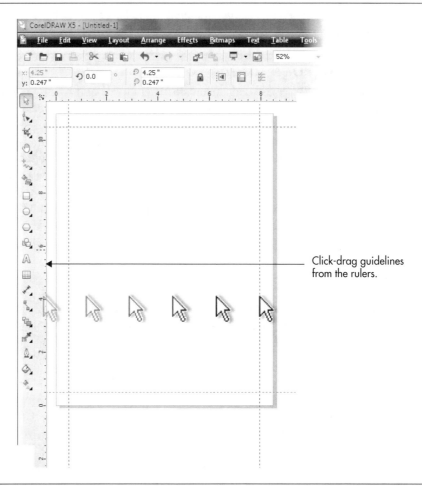

Click-drag guidelines from the rulers.

FIGURE 5-1 Set up your page so there is a ½-inch margin on all sides for printing to inkjet transfer paper.

Using the Polygon Tool to Design a Gear Shape

The Polygon tool might not seem like it has features to automatically create a gear shape and this is partially true. The Polygon tool produces symmetrical shapes that can be dynamically edited; they can be dramatically modified and still keep a special base property. Gears are symmetrical. The trick to creating a complex-looking gear to weld to the initials "D" and "G" is to slightly modify a polygon so it becomes a multi-spoke star shape first. Then you add a control node to the object and drag the node to reposition it. This is one of those things it's easier to see while you do, but in the following steps, you'll modify a polygon you create so that the spokes end in a blunt, straight edge instead of a point. This gets you 90 percent of the way to creating an elegant gear shape; the other 10 percent is demonstrated in the following sections.

Creating and Modifying a Polygon

1. Choose the Polygon tool from the toolbox (it's just below the Ellipse tool).

2. On the property bar, set the number of sides to 16. This will produce a polygon with 16 control points and control points in-between.

3. Hold CTRL (this constrains the shape to equal width and height), and then click-drag on the page until the width and height fields on the property bar (the second-from-left fields) tell you the shape you're creating is about 3 inches. At this point, release CTRL and your mouse button. Your polygon should look like the illustration here.

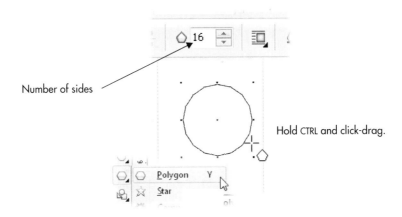

Number of sides

Hold CTRL and click-drag.

4. Choose the Shape tool; hold CTRL, click one of the control points along the path of the polygon, and then drag until the result is a star shape, shown here. The reason for holding CTRL as you drag is that it keeps the control point from drifting to the left or right as you move it. Otherwise this would produce a radial saw blade shape and not a star whose path segments mirror each other.

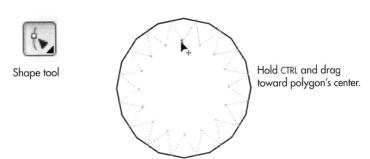

Shape tool

Hold CTRL and drag toward polygon's center.

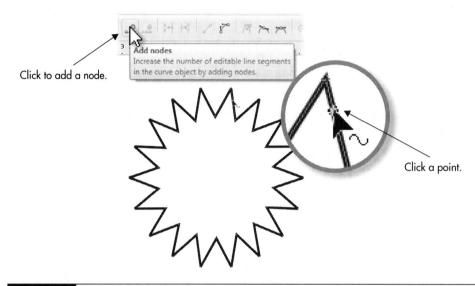

Click to add a node.

Click a point.

FIGURE 5-2 When you add a node to a polygon object, additional nodes are created symmetrically around the shape.

5. With the Shape tool still active, click a point on the path, as shown in Figure 5-2. Then click the Add Node(s) button on the property bar. You've created a change in the property of the path, although it doesn't look like a change yet. The polygon can still be dynamically reshaped. Look closely at the polygon path—you added a control node, but there are actually 16 added control nodes, because you made a change to a dynamic object.

6. Take your time on this step: with the Shape tool, drag the top control node a little to the left and then a little down. Stop when you have the shape shown here. The polygon looks very much like a 16-tooth gear now, doesn't it?

Click-drag to the left and then down.

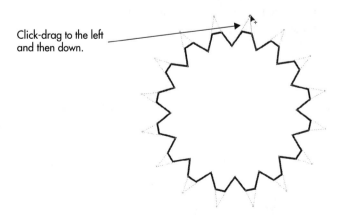

Welding an Edge to a Typed Character

CorelDRAW has a number of operations you can access from the property bar (and from the Shaping docker) when more than one object is selected; you'll achieve more dramatic objects that are the result of overlapping objects. These operations can weld two shapes into a single one and can trim the bottom object using the top object. These two operations— Weld and Trim—are used in the following sections to add only part of the gear you created to the rounded side of a capital "D."

 ## Shaping the Polygon

1. You can substitute any available font you like in the following steps, but if you own Futura XBlk BT—the filename is tt0148m_.ttf and it's in the Fonts folder on the CorelDRAW installation DVD—install it if you haven't done so already. It's a very good workaday typeface with scores of design uses, because it's very plain and extremely bold, ideal for adding a few gear notches without ruining its legibility.

2. Drag and drop a copy of the gear for future use; with the Pick tool, drag the gear off the page, but before releasing the mouse button, tap the right button to leave a duplicate of the gear.

3. Zoom into the original gear shape, choose the Text tool, and then click an insertion point directly over the gear, hold SHIFT, and type **D**.

4. Choose the Pick tool, and then with the character still selected, choose Futura XBlk BT from the Font list drop-down on the property bar. You can also highlight "24 pt" to the right of the font name and then type **300** in the Font size box. There are approximately 72 points to an inch in typesetting, so a ballpark estimate of the character's size makes it approximately the size of the gear. Click over the No Fill color well on the Color Palette to remove the fill of the character, and then right-click over the black color well to give the character a black outline. Now you can see both objects to reposition the "D".

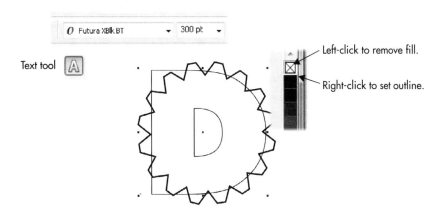

5. With the Pick tool, move the "D" so that its right side aligns to the gear. If necessary, hold SHIFT and then drag a selection handle away from or toward the center of the "D" to proportionately enlarge or shrink the "D" so that its right curve lies just a fraction outside of the gear.

6. Choose the Pen tool from the pen group on the toolbox; drag on the icon of the current tool to access any other tool in the nested group. Click points around the left side of the gear to make an object, shown next, that surrounds the left side of the gear, encompassing the hole in the character "D". You're going to remove these areas using this object and the Trim operation.

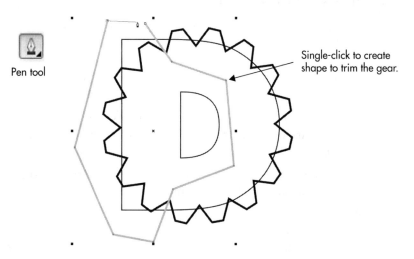

Pen tool

Single-click to create shape to trim the gear.

7. With the Pick tool, select the shape first, and then select the gear, holding SHIFT and clicking one object at a time. On the property bar, click the Trim icon.

8. By default, the shape that trims the bottom shape remains in the document, but it's now unnecessary. Select it and then press CTRL+X to delete it.

9. Select both objects by marquee-dragging with the Pick tool, and then click the Weld icon on the property bar.

You've done great. But the "G" needs to be added to the design with the same gear effect. Add a "G" to the page, and use the spare gear you duplicated in the previous Step 2. Alternatively, if you feel you've had enough of a workout (you haven't!), a Dyson Gears partially completed.cdr is available in the Chapter 05.zip file where you downloaded the tutorial files for this book.

A Brief Excursion into Gradient Fills

A linear gradient fill for the characters might make them look a little more metallic and will add to the complexity of the logo with a minimum of effort. For this example, let's do a little hands-on with the Interactive Fill tool and use the default Linear fountain fill style. The features you use in this test drive are cross-referenced at the end of this chapter; you'll learn how to expertly use the Interactive Fill tool later in this guide.

 ## Adding Visual Complexity Using Fountain Fills

1. Choose the Interactive Fill tool from the toolbox.

2. Click the "D" gear shape to select it, and then click-drag up and to the right (drag toward about 2 o'clock on the gear shape) and release the mouse button. By default, the "To" color of the Linear fountain fill is the place where you released the mouse. You work "From" your click-drag start point "To" your destination within the object.

3. Let's say you're not thrilled with the From and To colors in the fountain fill. To change a color, while the Interactive Fill tool is still selected and you can still see the control handles for the fill above the gear drawing, click the tiny From color marker—it's marked with the color you chose in the previous tutorial. Now the color is highlighted and available for editing. Click a light gray color well on the Color Palette. Then click the To color marker and click a medium to dark gray color well on the Color Palette.

> **TIP** *If you're careful, you can drag a color well color and drop it on the selected From and To color markers above the object to recolor them.*

4. Now let's say that the color transition between From and To in the fountain fill isn't dramatic enough, but you do like the two colors. Adjust the midpoint of the fill by dragging on the midpoint control, shown in Figure 5-3. You drag it toward the From color marker to emphasize the To color in the fill, and vice versa.

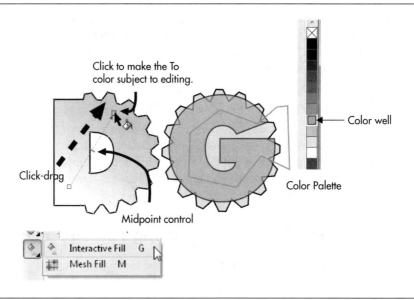

FIGURE 5-3 Use the Interactive Fill tool to embellish your illustration.

5. The "D" gear is looking terrific now, and it's going to look *more* terrific by the end of the chapter. To quickly add the same sort of fill to the "G" gear, choose the Attributes Eyedropper tool from the toolbox. Click over the D gear to sample its properties, and then click over the G gear to apply the sampled properties, as shown next—occasionally, you luck out in Life, and some things are simple… Press CTRL+S to save your work up to this point. In fact, just make it a practice to save your work every 10 minutes or so; it's only two keystrokes.

	Color Eyedropper
	Attributes Eyedropper

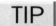 **TIP** *With the exception of the Text tool, pressing the SPACEBAR toggles your current tool to the Pick tool; a second press of the SPACEBAR toggles you back to the last tool you were using.*

Going 3D

Although CorelDRAW is a drawing program and not a modeling application such as Autodesk 3D Studio, you can indeed get dimensional effects with the Extrude tool to make a simple drawing such as this logo pop off the page…or off a T-shirt. The following sections take you through a basic and then an advanced editing technique that will make your audience wonder how on earth you accomplished this logo by reading one chapter in a book!

Using the Interactive Extrude Tool

The Interactive Extrude tool is a basic tool for defining edges that appear to extend into the third dimension of space, adding depth to the height and width of the object to which you apply this tool. However, once you've added depth to a selected object, it might not be apparent to you or your audience that this is a 3D shape because of the way it's "posed" on the drawing page. By default, the Interactive Extrude tool creates edges that appear mostly behind the extruded shape, because of an optical principle known as a vanishing point.

A *vanishing point* (tell your friends you know that da Vinci discovered vanishing points) is the point in 3D space where, if you drew lines marking the angles of an object with depth, the lines would converge. You see vanishing points all the time: say you're standing on train tracks (when a train isn't coming), and you look straight down the tracks. Where the rails converge is the vanishing point.

Similarly, to get the most out of the Extrude feature in CorelDRAW, you want to view an extruded shape off-axis, not straight-on, because looking at objects directly face-front removes the *perspective* from the object, flattening its appearance. CorelDRAW has additional features after you've made a shape into an extruded shape, one of which is a rotation feature—yes, you *can* rotate a 3D object on your drawing page—to show off all three possible facing sides of the extruded shape. An object viewed in ¾ view shows off the most visual detail (this is why portrait photographers try to get customers to point their head off-camera), and the following tutorial takes you through object extruding, rotating, and how to interactively adjust the depth of the object you extrude.

> TIP: *Extruded sides of an object by default inherit the fill from the parent object. Therefore, because the gear in this example has a fountain fill, so do the objects that make up the sides of the gear. Fountain fills aren't as visible when they're on the 3D face of a shape that has lighting, which you'll add in this tutorial. However, you can modify the fill of the control object (the shape you started with), the extrude:* CTRL-*click to select it from the group of shapes that dynamically make up the extruded object, and then modify the fill.*

Making a Logo into a 3D Logo

1. With the D gear selected on the drawing page, click-hold the Effects group button (just above the familiar-shaped Eyedropper tool) on the toolbox to reveal the flyout that has the Extrude tool. Select the Extrude tool from the flyout.

2. Click-drag *just a little,* straight down on the object, as shown in Figure 5-4. *Just a little* does the trick—you're establishing an extruded object and setting a *vanishing point* for the object at the same time. Stop dragging when one of the sides of the extrude object is visible. *Resist* the temptation that accompanies the natural thought, "the more I click-drag, the more extruded the gear will be." Nope—the more you drag, the farther the vanishing point is defined relative to the object, and it's very easy to set the vanishing point clear off the page, and possibly extend it to the Theophilus crater on the moon.

   Double-click the extrude group of objects while the vanishing point and other onscreen indicators are visible. You're now in a mode where you can rotate the extrude objects onscreen in three dimensions. If you deselected the shape, double-click an extrude area, and then single-click (this can be done with the Extrude or the Pick tool). Point the D gear a little upwards by click-dragging up and just a little to

Extrude tool

Click-drag just a little.

FIGURE 5-4   The Extrude tool is used to set a third dimension for your object. Other features help you set an angle of rotation and the depth of the object.

the left on the face of the object, as Figure 5-5 shows. The goal here is to create a visually dynamic logo that the audience is intimidated by, so the audience is looking up at this goliath of a company (yeah, yeah, it's trite, but it works). If necessary, drag one of the markers along the green ring encircling the D gear to rotate the object parallel to the screen; think of the ticks on a clock face, and you're rotating the D gear from 9 to 8 o'clock, for example.

3. Click-drag the marker shown in the following illustration toward the gear to decrease its depth. Dragging it away from the gear makes it deeper, and although this is illuminating advice, you will probably never need to make an extruded shape fatter. Also note that the vanishing-point line, the light blue dotted line, extends way off the page. This is of absolutely no consequence in your design work. The vanishing point does not print, and if your gear illustration looks fine right now, it is fine, regardless of onscreen guides.

Drag toward object to decrease depth.

Drag on face to rotate up, down, left, and right.

Drag to rotate parallel to screen

Vanishing point

Depth control

FIGURE 5-5 Use the Extrude Rotation feature onscreen to make the gear truly three-dimensional in appearance.

TIP *At any time in the future, you can change the rotation of the extruded shape, as well as the depth—it's a dynamically editable object. To quickly display the property bar options and the depth control marker on the object, and switch to the Interactive Extrude tool, you can double-click the object with the Pick tool.*

Adding Lighting and a Bevel

Let's polish the D gear part of the logo now; the G gear can take on the same look as the D once it's completed by copying its properties to the G. The Extrusion Lighting feature is available only when an object is extruded and is located on the property bar—it's the light bulb button. Lighting can be performed using one or up to three individual lights, and each light can occupy one of 16 possible positions around the object.

As an embellishment, you'll add a very small bevel edge to the front face of the D gear, just to add a little highlight to the edge where the extrude and the object meet. Realistically, industrial gears don't often have beveled edges, but they also aren't shaped in alphanumeric characters! This is Art and not a blueprint.

Here's how to add lighting and the bevel edge to the D gear.

 ## Finessing the Look of the Gear

1. With the D gear selected, right-click the No Fill color well on the Color Palette to remove the outlines. The extruded gear will take on a washed-out look, but you're not done yet.

2. Click the Extrusion Lighting button on the property bar.

3. Click the marker labeled "1" to add lighting to the extruded object.

4. Drag the "1" light to the front right position on the lighting cage surrounding the proxy sphere shape.

5. Click the Extrusion Bevels button, the cube with the "X" through its front.

6. Check the Use Bevel check box.

7. Put the cursor in the bevel height field and then type **0.07"**. Objects that feature concave edges, as this gear shape does, do not take a bevel of a much larger size…and still look recognizable.

8. Put the cursor in the bevel angle field, and then type **30**.

9. Click anywhere in the document to apply the new bevel angle.

Because the light is facing the right side of the gear, the lighting on the gear's teeth looks superb and quite intricate in design. The face, conversely, looks a little dim because it's facing away from Light 1. This is not a big design flaw; the face looks appropriate when contrasted against its side, but if you want to lighten it:

1. Click the extrude group to select the group. Then CTRL-click the front face to select it separately from the other objects.

2. Choose the Interactive Fill tool; the markers appear for the color stops of the Linear fountain fill.

3. Click a color marker and then choose a different color well from the Color Palette by clicking.

4. Alternatively, if you think a solid color would be better for the gear, deselect the gear and then drag a color well on top of the face of the extruded object. The extruded sides will take on this color. Press CTRL+Z to undo if you prefer your original to your changes.

> **NOTE** *The rotation properties of extruded objects follow the convention of 3D modeling programs. The X axis (top to bottom rotation) runs left to right through the object, the Y axis (rotation from left to right) runs top to bottom through the object, and the Z axis runs around the object parallel to the page in angles of rotation like those of an analog clock. Degrees of rotation are counterclockwise—negative values spin the object in a clockwise direction.*

Duplicating the Extrude Properties

When an extrude object is selected, a button is available on the property bar for duplicating the properties of the extruded object to a plain, unextruded one: Copy Extrusion Properties. This feature can change the angle and lighting of an existing extruded object, but that's not what you need to do right now. You want to get the G gear extruded at the same depth, with the same lighting and bevel, but you then want to change its rotation so it's facing away from the D in a mirror-like fashion.

Not a big deal! Follow these steps.

Creating Another Gear with the Copy Extrusion Properties Feature

1. Double-click the D gear's extruded side using the Pick tool to bring up the features on the property bar.

2. Move your cursor over to the G gear, and then click it to select it.

3. Click the Copy Extrusion Properties icon (shown next) on the property bar; because the G object has an outline, the outline remains on all edges of all the objects. Not what you had in mind for the finished art: right-click the No Fill color well on the Color Palette to remove the outline.

4. To *precisely* mirror the angle of the extruded G gear calls for a different feature than the onscreen interactive rotation: click the Extrude Rotation button on the property bar, the second from the left after the VP Locked To… button.

5. Click the Rotation Values button at the lower right of the "3" (shown next) to go to a number-field view of the current object's rotation.

6. To mirror the G gear from left to right is a Y axis rotation. Whatever value you see in the Y field, replace it by typing in an equal negative value. In this example, the Y aspect of the G gear (copied from the D gear) is –22, so typing in 22 rotates the G an equal and opposite amount compared to the D gear.

Extrude Rotation

Rotation values

Rotates from left to right

7. Click the Extrusion Light button, and then drag Light 1 from its upper-right position to the upper left. Artistically, it's usually bad form to mix lighting sources in a single illustration; however, this is a logo, with no real visual clue as to where the light is shining because the scene is incomplete. You can get away with this in the world of logos.

Adding Text to the Logo

You might call this assignment finished; you now have two stunning 3D oddly shaped gears in the document. But this assignment is for a logo, not for an icon that really would serve an advertising purpose only if it were painted on a shingle above a store in a hamlet in the 1600s. You need *text* to accompany the graphic: a fancy artistic text title above the graphic will serve the purpose of a logo quite well, and in smaller text Dyson Gears' web address will lessen the need of the viewing audience to ask the person wearing the T-shirt for contact info.

In the following sections, you'll use another effect, the envelope feature, which can mold a headline into any shape you can imagine, integrating into the overall design and catching an equal amount of audience attention.

Creating an Envelope Shape

CorelDRAW's Envelope feature is dynamic, just like Extrude and the Polygon tool, so you can shape and reshape an object until you're happy with the result. For this assignment, a good visual reinforcement of the mirrored gears might be to take "Dyson Gears" and reshape the name to look like a squared-off lozenge, larger in the middle than at either end. To perform this Envelope maneuver, you'll begin with a default Envelope shape and then customize it so that its sides are straight and not curved.

Making a Headline / Enveloping the Headline

1. Choose the Text tool from the toolbox.

2. Click an insertion point on the page, just above the gears.

3. Type in all caps (hold SHIFT): **DYSON GEARS**. Artistic text is editable as text, but as far as the envelope effect goes, text is a malleable object, just like any object you'd draw. It's also by default 24 points in height and Arial, which is not an exciting font. Select the text with the Pick tool, and then choose Futura XBlk BT from the Font list; it should be toward the top of the list as all recently used typefaces are ordered.

4. While holding SHIFT, drag a corner handle away from the text center until the text width is a little narrower than the gears. Alternatively, you can type 60 in the Font Size box to make the text 60 points in height, a little less than 1 inch; this trick is useful, however, only if you're familiar with how point size corresponds to inches. See Figure 5-6.

5. One entry above the Extrude tool in the Interactive Tools group on the toolbox is the Envelope tool; choose it and then select the text with your cursor. You'll see a faint dashed blue outline around the text now.

Drag and hold SHIFT to scale from center.

FIGURE 5-6   Use the same font as you used for the gear letters to avoid typeface style clashes.

6. By default, the envelope is in Putty mode, which presents both an advantage and a disadvantage. The advantage is that in Putty mode, you can delete envelope nodes; the disadvantage is that all the segments that join the nodes are curves, and you want straight envelope segments for this text. No problem: with the cursor, marquee-select the 3 and the 9 o'clock nodes. Then either click to remove them by clicking the Delete Nodes button on the property bar, or press – (minus) on the keyboard keypad.

7. Marquee-select all the remaining nodes, and then click the Convert To Line icon on the property bar. Then click inside the envelope to deselect the nodes. See Figure 5-7.

8. Click the top center envelope node, and then hold CTRL (to constrain movement to the first direction in which you drag) and drag upwards to make a peak in the center of the text.

9. Click the bottom center envelope node, hold CTRL, and then drag down until the bottom of the text overlaps the gears just a little, as shown in Figure 5-8.

TIP *You can also nudge envelope nodes by selecting one or more of them, and then pressing the keyboard arrow keys. This technique can provide precise editing of the envelope shape.*

Select and then remove middle side Envelope nodes.

FIGURE 5-7   Make an envelope with custom properties from the default envelope.

FIGURE 5-8   Create a dynamic headline for the T-shirt design by suggesting that the perspective of the text is coming at the audience from the center.

Applying the Conical Fountain Fill

Fountain fills, when used appropriately, can give a feeling of motion to static objects, and occasionally can soften the look of large objects without stealing from their visual importance. The DYSON GEARS is a tad overpowering as is, so a Conical fountain fill type will serve two purposes: to play down its massive presence just a little, and to make the text look a little metallic. Also, the headline should go behind the gears design; it will still be legible, and the slight overlap helps visually integrate the two groups of shapes.

Follow these steps to finish the headline work.

Applying a Custom Fountain Fill

1. Select the enveloped text with the Pick tool, and then press SHIFT+PAGE DOWN to send it to the back of the illustration. Vector objects have a page order; the last-created object is drawn on the top of the stack.

2. Choose the Interactive Fill tool from the toolbox.

3. Choose Conical from the Fill Type drop-down list on the property bar. The text changes color and the color wells for the Conical fill type appear above the text.

4. Drag the white color handle to 6 o'clock relative to the text to set the To position for the fill, and then with the color handle selected, click the 10% black color well on the Color Palette. Cool, eh? See Figure 5-9.

FIGURE 5-9 Add some flair to the text while also reducing its visual importance with a fountain fill.

Adding and Aligning Text

Congratulations! The hard work is behind you now—and it wasn't really all that hard now, was it? Next stop is adding the URL for Dyson Gears, performing a little alignment work, and then on to setting up the design for printing.

Adding a Visually Compatible Subhead

1. VAG Rounded is a beautiful, fairly serious typeface, and an ideal complement to the no-nonsense design of this logo. It's on the CorelDRAW Fonts installation CD, and its filename is tt0756m_.ttf. Install it now if you want to use it in the following steps.

2. With the Text tool, click an insertion point to the left and below the gears. Type **www.dysongears.com**.

3. Choose the Pick tool, and then with the text selected, choose VAG Rounded BT from the Font list, insert your cursor into the Point Size field, and then type **36**. Half an inch is a good size for the design when printed to a T-shirt.

FIGURE 5-10   Use Align And Distribute to perfectly center multiple design elements.

4. Marquee-select the envelope headline text and the gears. Press CTRL+G to group these two groups of objects.

5. Press CTRL+A to select all.

6. Choose Arrange | Align and Distribute | Align and Distribute to make it easiest to see and execute the controls for aligning objects.

7. Click the Center check box, as shown in Figure 5-10, and then click Apply. You can close the Align And Distribute box now. If you needed to do some heavy-duty, multiple aligning work in a design, you'd keep this box open and convenient for future use.

Align, Group, Scale, Flip, and Print

You're already familiar with most of the techniques covered in the upcoming tutorial that shows how to do one or two minor things to the finished logo to make it printworthy. Yes, you're coming in to home base and concluding the X5 Test Drive, but let's make this assignment a top-to-bottom, complete excursion. Follow these steps to brush up the logo design a little, and to set it up for output to an inkjet printer.

Getting Your Logo Design into the Real World

1. Select all (CTRL+A) and then press CTRL+G to group all the selected shapes.

2. Let's get your money's worth out of the print by making the logo that 7 inches maximum that was agreed upon at the beginning of the chapter (okay, you might not have actually agreed, but play along here). With the group selected, type **7** in the horizontal width field on the property bar, make sure the Lock Ratio (little lock) icon is depressed, and then press ENTER. Then press P to center the design relative to the page.

3. T-shirt transfers need to be printed as the reverse of the imprint; that is, the text needs to be mirrored so that when the inkjet page is ironed onto the shirt, it reverses back again to legibility. Click the Mirror Horizontally button on the property bar, which is easy enough to undo later if your logo is needed for a promotion other than T-shirts. See the illustration next.

4. Put a piece of *regular paper* in the inkjet printer, and print a copy of the design. Press CTRL+P, choose the correct printer, and then click Print. This is a "proof of concept" print; T-shirt transfers cost about a dollar each, while plain paper costs significantly less, cheaper still if you print on the backside of a page that has already been printed with something expendable. If everything seems to be satisfactory with the test print, do it for real with the T-shirt transfer paper.

With the exception of that all-night pizzeria around the corner, all good things must come to an end. You've passed the test drive. You're home safe and didn't dent a fender, and the best part is, you get to pocket the keys. You're going to need them when you take this high-performance Model X5 out on your own and take the bends and curves in the chapters to come!

The Test Drive Cross-Reference

You haven't really broken in all the features and tools covered in this chapter, so here are the signposts to learn more about the editing and transforming you performed in this chapter:

5

- Aligning and Distributing Objects: Chapter 9

- Extruding Objects: Chapter 19

- Guidelines and Rulers: Chapter 7

- The Envelope Tool: Chapter 20

- Working with Text: Chapters 12 and 13

- Filling Objects: Chapter 15

See Chapter 3 for the basics on the Color Palette, and for saving and opening documents. But you probably already know that stuff.

PART II

Getting Started with CorelDRAW X5

CHAPTER 6

Working with Single- and Multi-Page Documents

Y ou have an idea for promoting your product or service; you have your graphics, and you have some body copy and a snappy headline in mind. The next logical step is defining the space within which you express your promotional idea. Do you need a flyer? Or perhaps a four-page booklet? This chapter covers one of the most important aspects of any project: setting up pages in CorelDRAW. You'll learn about layout styles, page dimensions for your screen and for printing, and page reordering. In the process, you'll gain a good working knowledge of what you need to do—and what you can have CorelDRAW do—to create a page that suits your ideas.

Setting Up Your Document Page

Every new file you create, every file your coworker shares with you, and every CorelDRAW template you use has its own set of *page properties* that have two attributes: physical properties and display preferences. The *physical properties* refer to the size, length, and color of each page. *Display preferences* control how page values are viewed. Let's begin with the most common options and then move onto the more specialized features.

Controlling Page Size and Orientation

If you've unchecked the "Always show the Welcome screen at launch" check box, the default size whenever a new document is created is the CorelDRAW default, which might depend on the language version of CorelDRAW you use. For the U.S. author, this is U.S. Letter, 8 ½" by 11", but this can be changed in a number of ways. The quickest method is via the property bar while the Pick tool—and no objects—are selected. You must have a document in CorelDRAW's workspace, or you can't access the property bar. The property bar features options for setting your page to standard-sized pages, custom sizes, and orientation, as seen in Figure 6-1. In case you have a multi-page document, the property bar also has ways to change all pages at once, or to change only the currently visible page.

The Paper Type/Size and orientation options control the format for your document. When you have a specific format for a design you need to print, the following sections cover the options available to you in CorelDRAW X5.

Paper Type/Size

To choose a standard page size for your region, clicking a Paper Type/Size option in the property bar is the quickest method; from the drop-down box, you have Letter, Legal, Tabloid, and so on. If you have a limited need for different paper sizes, click the Edit This List button at the bottom of the drop-down list, and you can delete seldom-used sizes by clicking the Delete trashcan button in the Options box. Once you've made a selection, the dimensions are automatically entered as values into the Page Width and Height boxes in the property bar.

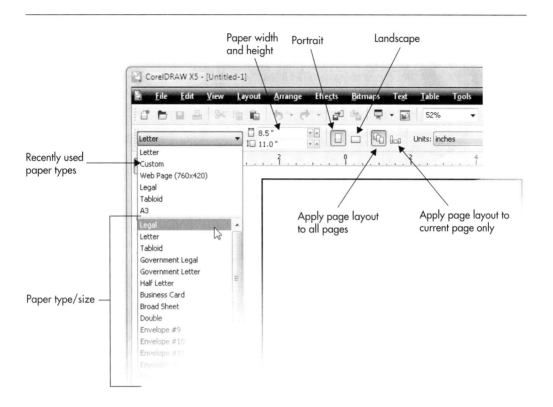

FIGURE 6-1   You change page size and orientation by using the property bar.

- **Page Width and Height**   For a custom page size, type specific values directly into the Page Width and Height boxes, and then press ENTER. Both page width and height values can be between 0.00333 and 1,800 inches. This is equivalent to 1 to 172,800 pixels if you do more web design work than printed page layout.

- **Landscape/Portrait orientation**   Clicking either Portrait or Landscape in the property bar while using the Pick tool (and having no objects selected) sets the page orientation. If the page width you enter is smaller than the page height entered, the orientation is automatically set to Portrait, and vice versa for Landscape. Changing from Portrait to Landscape (or vice versa) automatically switches the values in the Page Width and Height fields.

- **All Pages/Current Page**   In CorelDRAW X5, you can create a document up to 999 pages long, with different pages set to any size or orientation. The All Pages and Current Page buttons operate in "either/or" fashion like the orientation buttons, enabling you to set the page size either for all pages in your document at once (the default) or for only the current page. To set only the current page to be different from the others in your document, click the Current Page button (whose icon is different-sized pages), and set your new page size and orientation as needed. Other pages in the document aren't resized when you choose this option.

> **NOTE**   *If you've unintentionally removed a page size you need later, re-create the page size, go to the Page Size list on the property bar, and click Custom and Edit This List. In the Options | Page Size box that appears, click the Save (diskette icon) button, type a name for the page, and click OK.*

Page Viewing Options

With CorelDRAW at its default settings, when you choose File | New and click OK, you'll see a rectangle in the workspace. This rectangle represents your document page in height and width. However, what you *won't* see is how your page will be printed to a personal printer or to a commercial press. Whenever you print, you have areas called the *printable area* and the *bleed area*. You can add nonprinting guidelines to provide a page preview to see those areas, so objects and text at the edges of your work aren't partially printed. You want these features visible when designing for print because the grippers on printers often prevent edge-to-edge prints. To have CorelDRAW add bleed area and printable area (*safety*) guides to your page, press CTRL+J, and then choose Document | Guidelines | Presets; check the Printable Area and Bleed Area check boxes, as shown next. The bleed area extends to the edge of the page, and this is correct for personal printers; see the following Note.

> **NOTE**   Bleed *is the part of the printed image that extends beyond the edge of the page. When printing to a personal printer, there is no bleed, because bleed is only relevant when a page on a commercial press is trimmed to final book size. For example, if a commercial press uses 12″ x 14″ paper and the final trim size is 8 ½″ x 11″, you could set up a bleed area of 10″ x 13″ to make a design extend to the edge of the page the audience reads. You'll see in the next tutorial how to create a No. 10 envelope that features a bleed design.*

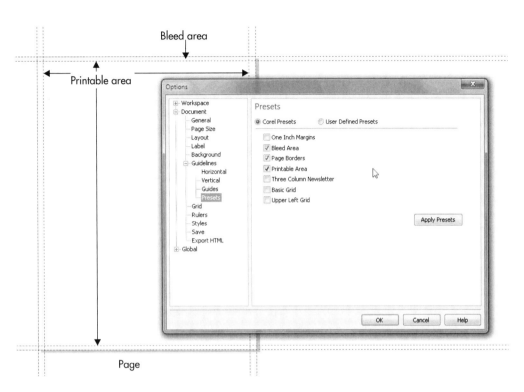

Bleed area

Printable area

Page

NOTE   *If you are printing to a borderless photo printer, your printable area will be the same size as your page border.*

The properties of Printable Area and Bleed Area depend on the printer options you choose in the Print Setup dialog, opened by choosing File | Print Setup:

Click to choose printer's page size and other features.

TIP *Setting a bleed amount is done using Tools | Options | Document | Page Size, using the Bleed option num box. The bleed amount can be defined anywhere from 0 (the exact edge of your page) to 900 inches.*

Creating Your Own Bleed Designs Using Your Home Printer

Suppose you have a need for an elegant No. 10 envelope whose design bleeds at the left side. With the knowledge you now have about bleeds and the printable page size, you can create a bleed envelope using your home laser or inkjet printer.

1. Choose File | New, choose Letter as the Size, and click the Landscape orientation button. Click OK to create the new document.

2. Choose File | Print Setup to access the printer's setup features. Click the Preferences button, and then click the paper/quality tab at the top (note: this location may differ depending on the printer make and model). Scroll the Paper sizes list to find Envelope #10. Click on the finishing tab (again, the location may differ) to set page orientation in the printer driver to Landscape to match the page orientation in the CorelDRAW document. Click OK and return to the empty page in CorelDRAW.

3. Select Tools | Options and navigate to the Guidelines | Presets section. Check the Printable Area box to put guidelines on the page that will show the shape of the envelope selected previously.

4. Place your design in your page border, but overlapping the printable page area in the position in which you want the design to bleed to the left, as shown in Figure 6-2.

5. Add an address and then choose File | Print (CTRL+P).

Controlling Page Background Color

To specify a page background color for your document, choose Layout | Page Background (CTRL+J) to open the Options dialog to the Background page.

- **Solid**   Choose this option and a color from the selector to specify any uniform color as the page background. Click Other in the color selector to use a color picker in different color models (RGB, CMYK, and so on), a mixer, or a specific color palette. Once a color has been chosen, the page background is set to that color, but the bleed area and the workspace are not.

- **Bitmap**   Choose this option to use a bitmap as the page background. Click the Browse button to open the CorelDRAW Import dialog, and locate and choose a bitmap. Background bitmaps are tiled as many times as needed to fill the page. You can also scale the number of repeating tiles by clicking the Custom Size radio button and entering values. The best bitmaps to use for patterns are ones that have been designed to tile seamlessly. In Figure 6-3, you can see an application of a Background Bitmap that is muted in tone (and therefore is suitable for white headline text) and that

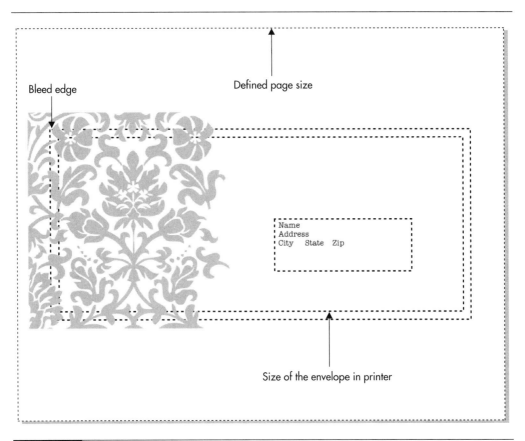

Bleed edge

Defined page size

Name
Address
City   State   Zip

Size of the envelope in printer

FIGURE 6-2 Creating the bleed design on the envelope

was designed to seamlessly repeat. The Bitmap option is terrific for creating several different signs or stationery that contain different text but must be tied together in a theme. You might, for example, create different text on layers such as "Swimsuit Sale," "Vacation Sale," and "Inflatable Theme Toy Sale," and then print different signs by hiding all but one layer for printing. You can't accidentally move the Background, and this technique is quick to set up when you have 12 different messages that need a common background.

- **Source** The Source options let you establish an external link to the bitmap file or store a copy of it internally with your CorelDRAW X5 document file. Choose Linked to maintain an external link or Embedded to store the bitmap with your document. While Linked is selected, the file path to the bitmap is displayed, and the bitmap itself must be available to CorelDRAW during printing. This option is very useful when you need to conserve on saved CorelDRAW file sizes; additionally, you

FIGURE 6-3 Use a bitmap as a Background for your design and text.

can modify the background bitmap in PHOTO-PAINT or Painter, and then reload the edited bitmap in the future.

● **Bitmap Size** This field contains "either/or" radio buttons. If you choose Default Size, the background appears on the page because the bitmap's original dimensions allow it to tile as many times as needed to fill the page. However, if you want a smaller bitmap as the background (more tiles), click the Custom Size button. The Maintain Aspect Ratio option is checked by default; you probably don't want the bitmap background to look smooshed or stretched—with Maintain Aspect Ratio turned on, all you need to do is enter one value in either the H or V field, and CorelDRAW automatically fills in the remaining field. Note that bitmaps are resolution dependent, unlike vector drawings. Thus, you can usually scale down a bitmap, but don't try to enlarge it, because the bitmap will go through something called resampling, and blurriness is often the result. Scale down = yes; scale up = no.

- **Print And Export Background**   Use this option to control whether the page background you've added to your document page is included when exporting your drawing files or when you print the document. It's available when either Solid or Bitmap is selected for the page background; by default, it's active.

Using Layouts and Labels

The property bar is used to set up the basic page and paper sizes and orientation. But designers often need to lay out designs for items such as labels, booklets, tent cards, and greeting cards that are printed on standard size paper, but that are definitely *not* laid out like a single-page flyer. So you don't have to sit at your workstation all day folding paper to try to figure out exactly where the fold lines are and where the text needs to be upside down. CorelDRAW X5 provides specialized layouts that are just a few clicks away. These timesavers are not on the property bar—you need to open the Options dialog to choose the one you want from the Layout drop-down box.

Choosing Specialized Layouts

On the Layout page of the Options dialog, you can choose from seven specialized layouts for your document including Full Page, Book, Booklet, Tent Card, Side-Fold Card, Top-Fold Card, and Tri-Fold Brochure.

Choosing one of these layout styles instantly divides the current document page size into horizontal and vertical pages, based on the preview supplied in the dialog.

- **Full Page** This layout style is the default for all new documents, and it formats your document in single pages, like those shown here.

- **Book** The Book layout format, shown right, divides your document page size into two equal vertical portions, and each portion is considered a separate page. When printed, each page is output as a separate page.

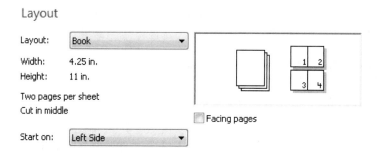

- **Booklet** In a similar arrangement to the Book layout, the Booklet layout format divides your document page size into two equal vertical portions. Each portion is considered a separate page. However, when printed, pages are paired according to typical imposition formatting, where pages are matched according to their final position in the booklet layout. In a four-page booklet, this means page 1 is matched with page 4, and page 2 is matched with page 3, as shown at right.

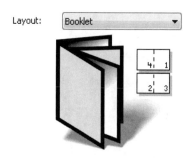

● **Tent Card**   The Tent Card layout format, shown at right, divides your document page size into two equal horizontal portions, each of which is considered a separate page. Because tent card output is folded in the center, each of your document pages is printed in sequence and positioned to appear upright after folding.

● **Side-Fold Card**   The Side-Fold layout format divides your document page size into four equal parts, vertically and horizontally. When printed, each document page is printed in sequence, and positioned and rotated to fit the final folded layout. Folding the printed page vertically, then horizontally, results in the correct sequence and orientation.

● **Top-Fold Card**   Like the Side-Fold layout, the Top-Fold layout format also divides your document page size into four equal parts, vertically and horizontally. When printed, each document page is printed in sequence, and positioned and rotated to fit the final folded layout.

● **Tri-Fold Brochure** Set your page orientation to Landscape using File | Print Setup, and you then have the ideal layout for travel brochures and restaurant tabletop stand-up menus. If your printer supports it, you can print both sides for a total of six panels, with live space measuring about 3 ½" wide and 8" high on the end panels.

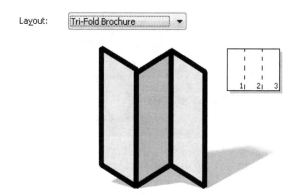

After you choose a layout style and return to your document, each subdivision of the layout can be viewed individually. You can also view pages in pairs by choosing the Facing Pages option in the Layout page of the Options dialog for several layout styles. When Facing Pages is selected in the dialog, you also have the opportunity to start your document on either the Left Side or Right Side for some layout styles by making a selection from the Start On menu.

Using Preformatted Labels

CorelDRAW has a comprehensive collection of label formats for preformatted paper stock from vendors such as Avery, Ace, and Leitz. Once you've clicked the Labels radio button, the Page Size page turns into the Label page, offering access to the label collection. After you've selected a specific label format, the preview window shows its general layout and indicates the number of rows and columns available, as shown in Figure 6-4.

After you choose a label format and return to your document, each of your document pages will represent an individual label. You'll need to add the exact number of pages to accommodate all of your labels. If you don't see the exact manufacturer for your specific

6

FIGURE 6-4   CorelDRAW has just the preformatted label template you need.

label type, you can create your own from scratch, or base it on an existing label format (see Figure 6-5). Choose an existing label from the Label Types menu; click Customize Label; set the number of Rows and Columns; and set the Label Size, Margins, and Gutters according to your own label sheet. Once the format is created, you may save your label by clicking the plus (+) button next to the Label Style drop-down list. You can delete a selected label format from the list by clicking the minus (−) button.

FIGURE 6-5 If you don't find the label you need, modify an existing label using the options.

Naming Pages

Whenever a new document is created, CorelDRAW automatically creates the names, such as "Page 1," "Page 2," and so on. These page names are only for your reference as you navigate your multi-page document. However, you can customize your page names by using several different methods.

When creating web page documents—where each document page is a *separate* web page—adding a unique name to the page creates a title for the exported page. When your document is printed, page names can also be printed in the margins, can indicate the contents of the page, and can provide other page-specific information.

 To quickly display the previous or next page in your document, you can press PAGE UP (previous page) or PAGE DOWN (following page).

Using the Rename Page Command

Use the Rename Page command to assign a unique name to pages. Either choose Layout |
Rename Page, or (more quickly) right-click the page tab at the lower left of your document
window, and then choose Rename Page from the pop-up menu to access the command. The
Rename Page dialog, shown here, can rename a page with a name of up to 32 characters,
including spaces.

6

Save Details with Your File

Document Properties is a CorelDRAW feature that provides details about a document you
save without having to type in the margins. To access Document Properties—to both enter
and view information—right-click on a blank part of the page. In addition to letting you type
yourself little reminders, Document Properties is also a very convenient method to tag
designs you export to JPEG and other bitmap file formats. As you can see in Figure 6-6, the
same information you type in Document Properties is available to Windows users when they
right-click your image in a file folder and choose Details.

> **NOTE**   *Users who don't own CorelDRAW cannot access Document Properties info you've
> embedded in a native CDR file by right-clicking. The solution to this problem is to
> make them buy CorelDRAW.*

Navigating a Multi-Page Document

To go to different pages in a document, click a page icon at the lower left of the document
window. If the page isn't in view, you can scroll to locate it, or (for lengthy documents) open
the Go To Page dialog, shown next, by clicking between the Next Page and Previous Page

FIGURE 6-6 Save your CorelDRAW files and exported bitmaps with Document Properties metadata.

buttons at the lower left of your document window. This dialog enables you to move quickly to a specific page in your document.

Click here to open the Go To Page dialog.

Using the Object Manager

The Object Manager docker offers the advantage of mass-editing page names from within a single docker. To open the Object Manager, choose Tools | Object Manager. Once the docker is open, click to ensure that the docker is set to Show Object Properties by deselecting the Layer Manager View button state, shown here:

In this view, all page and object names are displayed. To rename any page (or any object), click once directly on the page title to select the page you want to name or rename, click a second time to highlight the page name text, then type a name, and finally press ENTER. Page names appear in the page tabs at the lower left of your document window, accompanied by a numeral indicating the page's order in your document:

To see more (or less) of the pages of your document in the page tab area of your document window, click-drag on the vertical divider between the page tabs and the horizontal scroll bar.

Click-drag to expand/reduce page tab area.

Page Commands

There are several ways to add and delete pages from a document; three ways are using menu commands, using shortcuts while holding modifier keys, and using certain page views. However, quick is best, and in this section, you see the most convenient way as well as methods that are easiest to remember. You can decide for yourself which best suits the way you work.

Inserting Pages and Setting Options

From the main menu, choose Layout | Insert Page to open the Insert Page dialog, shown here, which features a host of options for specifying your new page properties and where you would like to add the new page in relation to your existing pages.

Enter the Number Of Pages needed in the Insert Page dialog, and choose to Place them either Before or After your current page, or between specific pages in your document by using the Existing Page box. You are not limited to the orientation or size of your current page when you add pages, unlike the constraints of traditional printed books and magazines!

 To quickly add a new page to the beginning or end of your document, go to the first or last page and click the plus (+) symbol on the left or right of the page buttons at the lower left of your document window. To add a page before or after your current page, right-click a page tab to the right of the + button on the right, and choose either Insert Page Before or Insert Page After from the pop-up menu.

Deleting Pages

Deleting document pages can be done by choosing Layout | Delete Pages from the main menu; you can delete one or more of the existing pages in your document. By default, the dialog opens to display the current page as the page in the Delete Page box, shown next, but you may select any page before or after your current page if you choose. To delete an entire sequence of pages, click the Through To Page option, which enables you to delete all pages in a range between the page specified in the Delete Page box through to any page following your current page. Pay careful attention to the word "Inclusive" after the last page number: if you type, for example, *10* when you want to delete pages 1–9, well, oops—there goes your day unless you press CTRL+Z immediately!

 To delete the current page, right-click the page name on the page tab, and then choose Delete Page from the pop-up menu. There is no confirmation when you delete a page, so make sure you've had your second cup in the morning before doing this.

Moving and Duplicating Pages

You're going to create such fantastic content in CorelDRAW that you might never want to delete it; instead you might want to move and/or copy pages. To move a page, use a click-drag action on the page tab to drag it to a new position. To copy a page—*and all its contents*—thus creating a new page order, hold CTRL while click-dragging the page tab, dragging the page to a new position. CorelDRAW does not duplicate the name of a user-named page; you'd wind up with an organizational nightmare if it did, so it's a good practice to name a duplicate page after you've created the copy.

Click-drag tabs to change page order.

Hold CTRL and click-drag to copy page and contents to a specific location.

Using the Page Sorter

Page Sorter is a view that provides you with a broad look at your document and all its pages. In this view, you can add, delete, move, or copy pages in a single view. You can also change the Paper/Type Size and the page orientation of all the pages or just selected pages. A CorelDRAW document can contain pages of different sizes, which can be very handy when you are designing matching business cards and letterhead or other similarly related materials. To open your document and all its pages in Page Sorter view, choose View | Page Sorter View. The Page Sorter displays all pages in your document.

TIP	*Using Page Sorter, you can quickly export either your entire document or only selected pages. Click to select the page(s) you want to export, and choose File	Export, or click the Export button in the standard toolbar to open the Export dialog. To export only specific pages, choose the option to Export This Page Only, which by default is not selected. Exporting is not to be confused with saving; exporting pages is usually done to get your work into bitmap format, Adobe Illustrator file format, or CMX (Corel Media Exchange) for sharing with users who have a compatible application.*

In Page Sorter view, a single click selects a page. Holding SHIFT while clicking pages enables you to select or deselect multiple contiguous pages. Holding CTRL while clicking enables you to select or deselect noncontiguous pages. The following actions enable you to apply page commands interactively to single- or multiple-page selections, as seen in Figure 6-7.

- **Move Page(s)**   To move a page and change its order in your document, click-drag the page to a new location. During dragging, a vertical I-beam appears, indicating the insertion point for the page or the first page of the selected sequence of pages.

- **Add Page(s)**   To add pages to your document, right-click any page and choose Insert Page Before or Insert Page After from the pop-up menu to insert a page relative to the selected page.

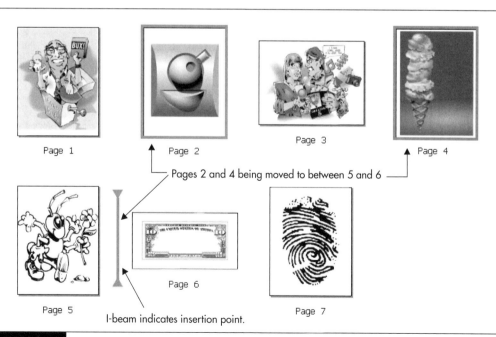

Page 1   Page 2   Page 3   Page 4

Pages 2 and 4 being moved to between 5 and 6

Page 5   Page 6   Page 7

I-beam indicates insertion point.

FIGURE 6-7   Page Sorter enables you to manage your document pages interactively while viewing all page properties.

- **Copy Page(s)**   To copy pages—and their contents—hold CTRL while click-dragging the page to a specific location. During dragging, a vertical I-beam appears, indicating the insertion point for the page copy or the first page of the selected sequence of pages.

- **Name or Rename Page**   To add a new name or change an existing page name, click the page name below the page to select it; click a second time to highlight the page title and enter a new name; then press ENTER. You can also rename a page by right-clicking a specific page and choosing Rename Page from the pop-up menu to highlight the page name for editing.

- **Change Page Size/Orientation of All Pages**   In Page Sorter view, the property bar displays typical page property options for applying standard or custom page sizes and for changing the orientation between Landscape and Portrait.

  If you want to change the orientation of *all* of the pages in the document, click the All Pages button on the property bar, and *then* click either the Portrait or the Landscape button to change all pages to that orientation.

- **Change Page Size/Orientation of Selected Pages**   If you want to change only the orientation of some of the pages, click the Current Page button. Then select the pages you want to change, and click the Portrait or Landscape button to change the page(s) to the desired orientation, as shown.

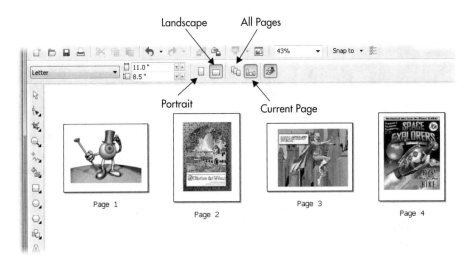

Changing the orientation in the Page Sorter not only changes the view, but also changes how the pages themselves are oriented in the document. As you can see, the second and last pages have drawings that look better in Portrait view; you CTRL-click pages 2 and 4 in this example, click Current Page, and both the Page Sorter view and the pages themselves are re-oriented. If you want to rethink this dynamic change, repeatedly pressing CTRL+Z (Edit | Undo) restores your document.

Exiting Page Sorter view is easily done; click the Page Sorter View button, or click any tool on the toolbox. Any changes applied while in the Page Sorter are applied to your document.

| TIP | *To exit the Page Sorter and immediately go to a particular page in your document, double-click the page.* |

Page definition, sorting pages, margins, bleeds, and enough other options have been discussed to fill a book! Now that you know how to set up a page, how large do you want that drawing you just created on the page? And how do you precisely move the drawing if you want it perfectly centered on the page? Fortunately, the answers are in the next chapter, which covers measuring and drawing helpers.

6

CHAPTER 7

Measuring and Drawing
Helpers

More than likely, a project you are beginning is composed to a specific page size. Within the design you've envisioned, you have graphics that need to be aligned, spaced, and proportioned to exact dimensions. Moreover, you might need to label what you've designed, adding callouts and even the dimensions of parts of a sketch so manufacturing can order the right size of packaging. Today is your lucky day: CorelDRAW not only has more ways of measuring objects than you can shake a stick at, but it also makes it easy for users of all skill levels to turn out professional, tightly composed pieces. In this chapter, you'll learn how to measure, scale measurements, align objects, work with guidelines, create your own guidelines, add measurements and callouts, and get objects to snap to other objects with pinpoint precision. Leave "a smidgeon," "a pinch," and "just a touch to the left" behind as you enter the world of CorelDRAW accuracy and layout perfection.

Using the Ruler

Although property bars and toolbars offer information about the size and position of an object (to three decimal places), something about using rulers bounding a page has tangible and easy to understand qualities. Additionally, CorelDRAW rulers are a resource for pulling nonprinting guidelines. Later in this chapter the Dimension and Connector tools, guides, and guidelines are covered. Now let's look at how rulers are configured and manipulated, and how they invaluably assist in your design work.

Accessing Rulers and Ruler Properties

Straight out of the box, CorelDRAW displays rulers on the top and left side of the page window. However, if someone experimented with your installed copy and turned rulers off, it's easy to restore their visibility. You can choose View | Rulers from the main menu, but a quicker way is via the pop-up menu. With any tool chosen except the Zoom tool, right-click over a blank area of the page (or outside of the page), and then choose View | Rulers from the pop-up menu.

Pop-up menu

Rulers in CorelDRAW look like physical rulers with major spacing (inches, for example) and minor spacing (the ticks between whole number amounts, such as 3/8 and 1/4). CorelDRAW detects when a mouse scroll wheel is active, and if you zoom the page in and out, you'll see an additional ruler nicety—the ruler ticks between major spacing have labels for fractional amounts when your zoom level is large enough to display them.

CorelDRAW rulers (see Figure 7-1) can be broken down into three components: the vertical ruler, the horizontal ruler, and the ruler origin. If you ever need the location of your cursor onscreen, you'll see a dotted line on the rulers, and the numerical value is right at hand on the status bar. CorelDRAW uses the standard convention of displaying horizontal position values as *X* values on the property bar, and vertical values as *Y.* For example, you create a rectangle using the Rectangle tool, and you're not sure you put the rectangle in the center of an 8½×11" page. A quick glance at the property bar will tell you that if the rectangle's X position is 4.25" and the Y position is 5.5", its center is at the center of the page.

The *origin* is the intersection of the vertical and horizontal rulers at the top left of the workspace. The origin is the page position reference where all measurements begin, but it does *not* represent the zero point for measuring the page. By default, the *lower-left corner* of your page represents the ruler origin 0 position. Try this: Create a shape near the center of the page. Then with the Pick tool move the shape up and to the right, while watching the X, Y position values on the property bar; the values increase. Conversely, if you move the shape down and to the left, the values decrease—eventually, if you move the shape off the page (down and left), you'll see negative X, Y values on the property bar, as the shape travels beyond the origin.

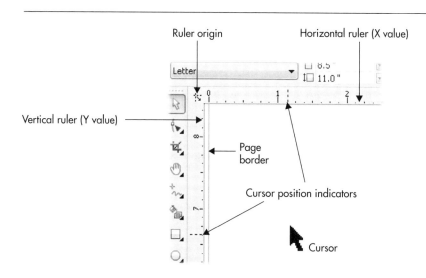

FIGURE 7-1   Elements of CorelDRAW's rulers

As with a physical ruler, you can move rulers in CorelDRAW to assist you in your design needs. Additionally, you can leave the rulers where they are and just move the origin of the rulers. This is something that cannot be done with a physical ruler; working with these features is covered in the sections to follow.

Setting the Ruler Origin

Say you're uncomfortable with measuring from the bottom left and prefer a more conventional set of rulers that start at the upper-left corner of a page. Click-hold your cursor on the origin, and then drag to a point at the upper-left corner of the page. Doing this thwarts the ability to use the property bar for easy-to-read X, Y positions for objects, because by convention—in drawing applications, CAD applications, and most advanced design programs—Y, the vertical measurement of space, always travels up in a positive direction. However, moving the origin not only can make the rulers suit your intuitions, but it's also a handy technique for measuring relative distance between objects, measured against each other and not as an absolute measurement against the page.

Two Inches to the Right, Please

1. Create two shapes; any shapes will do.

2. Move the shapes using the Pick tool so that they're horizontally aligned, and let's try 5 inches from each other.

3. You need the centers of the objects to be 2 inches apart. You click-drag the origin so that it's horizontally centered on the first object. The zero horizontal point is now at the center of the first object.

4. You move the second object so that its center is at the 2-inch major mark on the horizontal ruler.

5. With this shape still selected, take a look at the X, Y fields on the property bar. If the X value is not exactly 2.000, type **2.000** in the X field, and then press ENTER. See Figure 7-2.

It's easy to undo what you've done: to restore the origin of the rulers to the default setting, double-click the origin.

A more dramatic change you can make to the rulers is to actually *reposition* them in the workspace, not simply change where the units appear. To undock the rulers (they come as a set; you cannot undock only one ruler), hold SHIFT and then drag the ruler origin to where you want the rulers to begin. You'll see a dashed-line preview onscreen for the intended new location of the rulers; release the mouse button, and the rulers move to this position. To restore the rulers (to dock them), you hold SHIFT and then double-click the ruler origin. See Figure 7-3.

3

5

FIGURE 7-2   Specify a different origin for the rulers to measure relative distances between the centers of objects.

SHIFT+click-drag the ruler origin to undock and move.

Hold SHIFT and double-click to redock.

FIGURE 7-3   Rulers can be repositioned on the page.

Once the rulers are undocked, you're free to move them as needed, by holding SHIFT while dragging the origin. Regardless of where you place the rulers in the workspace, the zero for the increments on the rulers remains constant. To see this, move the view of the page by using the scroll bars at the right and bottom of the screen, or use the Hand tool (H); the increments on the undocked rulers move as you move your view. If you need to move the origin while the rulers are undocked, drag the origin.

Setting Unit Measure

In CorelDRAW, you have the same unit measurements as in the real world: millimeters, yards, and so on. *Units of measure* is the name of the setting in CorelDRAW, and they affect the look of the rulers as they increase and decrease in frequency with your view magnification setting. The actual units of measure are specified according to the drawing units currently defined on the property bar. To set the drawing unit measure, choose the Pick tool (click an empty area on your page to make sure nothing is selected), and then use the Units drop-down list on the property bar to specify anything from picas to kilometers.

Drawing units control the units displayed on rulers and also for other areas of CorelDRAW X5 where dimensions are displayed: page size, shape size, and nudge and duplicate offset commands.

Setting Ruler Options

Options for measuring in CorelDRAW can be found in Tools | Options | Document | Rulers; but the faster route is to double-click a page ruler, or to right-click a ruler and then choose Ruler Setup from the pop-up menu. In the Rulers area of the Options box, you'll find options in addition to the increments displayed on rulers. See Figure 7-4.

Nudging

At the top of the Rulers page are Nudge options, worth covering first here, although indirectly related to the page rulers themselves. When we nudge things in the real world, our intention

FIGURE 7-4   The Rulers area of Options is where you can set units, the independent display of units on rulers, nudge distance, and more.

is to move an object by a small, but fairly arbitrary distance—and we estimate the measurement. In CorelDRAW, however, nudging objects is precise, not at all arbitrary, and on the Rulers page you can set the distance for normal, Super, and Micro nudging. Nudging can be performed on a shape, several shapes at the same time, and even on a node or several nodes on a path when they are selected using the Shape tool.

Once you've specified values for nudging in the Rulers area:

- You set the normal nudge distance of an object by choosing the object(s) with the Pick tool or by choosing the node(s) using the Shape tool, and then pressing the keyboard arrow keys to nudge up, down, or across; one keyboard stroke equals one nudge distance.

- Super-nudging is performed the same way as normal nudging, except you hold the SHIFT key while pressing any arrow key.

- Micro-nudging is performed the same way as regular nudging, except you hold the CTRL key while pressing any arrow key.

The upper limit for nudge distance is 600 inches, which is fair enough, because, for example, nudging a shape 600 inches to move it is more easily accomplished by simply entering the intended position in the property bar's X and Y fields (then you press ENTER to apply the move).

 Nudge distance can be set on-the-fly within the workspace, and Super and Micro Nudge scale apply to the new nudge distance. With nothing selected, set a new value in the Nudge Distance box.

 There's an easy way to remember some modifier keys. In many applications, CTRL means "constrain," "to limit"—while SHIFT often means "to add to" or "to extend." So super-nudging can be thought of as an extension to normal nudge distances (you hold SHIFT while pressing arrow keys), and micro-nudging is a constrained version of normal nudging (you hold CTRL).

Specifying Units, Origin, and Tick Divisions for Your Rulers

In the fields below Nudge options, you'll find all the controls for what appears, and where, on the rulers displayed on your drawing page. Here's how each option controls ruler appearance:

- **Units** Units are measurement values. Choose a Horizontal unit measure to specify unit measures for all drawing units in your document. To specify different units of measure for vertical ruler and drawing units, click to deselect the Same Units For Horizontal And Vertical Rulers option, shown in Figure 7-4.

- **Origin** Although you can manually set the origin as described in the previous section, you can also perform precise origin definition using this field. The origin point can be set anywhere from –50 to 50 yards, in precise increments as small as 0.001 inch.

- **Tick Divisions** *Tick divisions* are the evenly spaced numeric labels seen bracketing the smaller increments displayed by your ruler—for example, if you are using inches as the unit, the tick divisions are 1, 2, 3, and so on. Tick divisions are automatically set according to the unit of measure selected. For example, standard measure displays a default of eight divisions per tick, and metric measure displays ten divisions. Desktop publishing and printing units such as didots, picas, points, and ciceros display using

2 tick divisions

8 tick divisions

Decimal labels for divisions instead of fractions

FIGURE 7-5   Choose tick divisions and whether fractions or decimals display on rulers.

six divisions per tick. The option to Show Fractions is also available and set by default while a unit measure is selected. The top of Figure 7-5 shows two divisions per tick; below it is the standard eight subdivisions; and at bottom, with the Show Fractions check box unchecked in the Rulers area of Options, decimals are now shown for ticks.

TIP   *To set the Spacing and Frequency of your ruler, see "Setting Grid Properties" later in this chapter.*

Editing Drawing Scales

Scale drawing is used when the dimensions involved in drawing actual sizes are either too large or too small to be practical. For example, a world atlas at 1-to-1 (1:1) scale would be hard to carry around, and almost as hard to print. You can set up a drawing scale by first setting the units; click the Units drop-down on the property bar. Then click the Edit Scale button in the Rulers page of the Options dialog (CTRL+J is the shortcut). In the Drawing Scale dialog, you can quickly apply a scale ratio, or set your own custom scale. By setting

1 foot to equal a mile (5,280 feet), it's then simple to draw accurate maps and directions around town.

The Typical Scales drop-down list includes a selection of the most commonly used drawing ratios ranging from 100:1 to 1:100, with the most common standard measure scales included. When selecting ratios, the first number represents the object *Page Distance*; the second number represents the *real-world* distance, labeled "World Distance." Usually small objects such as circuitry and clock parts are illustrated using ratios where the Page Distance is larger than the World Distance. Conversely, the best setup for a technical drawing of a skyscraper is to set Page Distance much smaller than World Distance.

The moment you change either the Page Distance or the World Distance, the Typical Scales selection in the drop-down list turns to *Custom*. Page Distance is the measured distance on your document page, while World Distance refers to the distance represented by your ruler and drawing units in your document. Settings can be made independently of each other and to different units of measure to a range between 1,000,000 and 0.00001 inches in increments of 0.1 inch.

Calibrating Ruler Display

You buy a Lamborghini Gallardo (about $200,000); you pull into a gas station, and you want to put Regular in the tank? No. Similarly, you can't expect precision when you use CorelDRAW on an uncalibrated monitor. CorelDRAW provides a very simple way to ensure what you see on your monitor screen matches real-world measurements. Occasionally, your display might not show perfectly square pixels, and as a result, your 5-inch line in a very important drawing might measure 4.88" when you print it. To calibrate the rulers in CorelDRAW to match your screen, to match real-world output, you'll need a plastic foot-long ruler (clear is better than solid, about $1 at a stationery store), about 30 seconds, and the following steps:

1. In a new document create a 5"-wide square. With the Rectangle tool, hold CTRL (constrains proportions to 1:1), and then drag while watching the size fields on the property bar. If you're close but not precisely 5", type **5.0** into either field with the Lock Proportions icon clicked (see following illustration), and then press ENTER.

2. Using the Zoom tool property bar options, set your view magnification to 100 percent.

3. Using your physical $1 ruler, measure the object you created on your screen. If both CorelDRAW's rulers and your physical ruler agree it's a 5" square, your ruler display is accurate. If the measurements *don't* match, CorelDRAW's toolbox Options dialog has the fix.

4. Open the Options dialog (CTRL+J).

5. Click to expand the tree directory under Workspace | Toolbox, and then click Zoom | Hand Tools. This displays the Zoom, Hand options on the right of the dialog. First, click to select the Zoom Relative To 1:1 option.

6. Click Calibrate Rulers to display the ruler calibration reference rulers and Resolution options, shown in Figure 7-6. Notice the vertical and horizontal ruler bars that intersect at the center of your screen. This represents your current ruler drawing units.

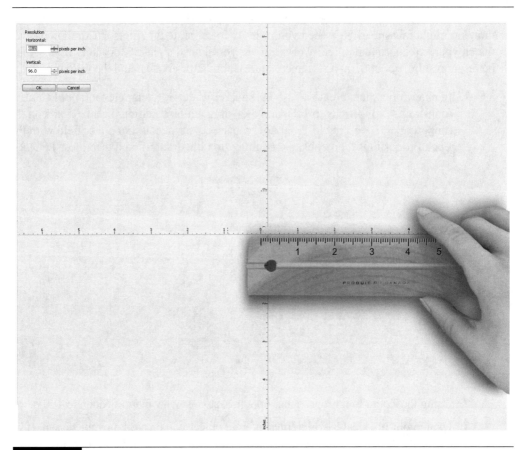

FIGURE 7-6   Clicking Calibrate Rulers displays reference rulers and Resolution options.

7. Using your ruler, measure both the vertical and horizontal rulers on your screen to see that they match. If they don't match, increase or decrease the Horizontal and/or Vertical options using the spin boxes until the onscreen rulers match your $1 ruler. See Figure 7-6.

8. Click OK to close the calibration dialog, and then click OK again to close the Options dialog. Your rulers are now calibrated.

Introducing the Indispensable CorelDRAW Grids

A page grid is a customizable, by default nonprinting, overlay that extends beyond the printable page onto the pasteboard area at all viewing resolutions and viewing qualities. It's not only an excellent visual reference for scaling and aligning objects vertically and horizontally, but it also can be used in combination with CorelDRAW's Snap To Grid option. To make the grid visible, right-click with the Pick tool over an empty area of the page, and then choose View | Grid from the pop-up menu. To modify the Grid, right-click over either ruler or the ruler origin, and then choose Grid Setup.

Show grid

7

Grid Setup (right-click)

Setting Grid Properties

You're going to have a variety of designing needs, which will certainly call for different appearances of grids, which is why they're customizable. Changing grid-line frequency and spacing is often needed. You can use options in the Grid page of the Options dialog to tailor your grid just the way you need it to appear. To open this page, as shown next, choose View |

Setup | Grid And Ruler Setup from the command menus, or right-click your ruler and choose Grid Setup.

TIP	*Use the Object Manager to set all grid properties, including visible, printable, and/or editable states. Grids are controlled by the Grid layer properties, which is a layer on the master page. To open the Object Manager, choose Window	Dockers	Object Manager (see Chapter 9).*

The Grid page's *Grid Lines Per Inch* and *Inches Apart* options for units might look similar, but there's an important distinction. The *Grid Lines Per Inch* ("frequency") option gives you control over the grid appearance according to the number of lines that appear within a given distance. The *Inches Apart* (called "spacing" in CorelDRAW version X4) option controls the physical space between the grid lines based on distance. Both are set according to the current drawing units choice, and you choose frequency *or* spacing; choosing both would be impossible. You can also set the horizontal and vertical spacing independently of one another, which is very useful when you have an object such as a tall fluted glass that you want to put etching on. You'd use more horizontal than vertical grid lines, and your design would turn out flawlessly.

| TIP | *When illustrating or drawing based on a specific unit of measure—such as inches—formatting your grid to match the ruler unit of measure is a smart thing to do. For example, if rulers are set to display inches using a Tick Division of 8 per inch, setting the grid to a Grid Lines Per Inch value of 8 vertical and 8 horizontal lines per inch causes grid lines to appear every eighth of an inch while using a Drawing Scale ratio of 1:1 (actual size).* |

Display Grid as Lines or Dots

Also on the Grid page of the Options dialog, you control how your grid appears—either as lines or as dots. By default, new documents are set to the Show Grid As Lines option. However, a design, for example, of a checkerboard might make the grid fairly invisible and as a consequence useless; you'd opt for the display of Show Grid As Dots. Conversely, you're going to lose a solar system or two if dots are chosen for grids when you're drawing an astronomy chart (use lines)!

Using Snap-To Commands

The Snapping feature helps you move a shape to an exact location when it's close to grid lines, guidelines, and other objects. Think of snapping as magnetism: you hold a paper clip, for example, close enough to a magnet, and eventually it snaps to the magnet. In CorelDRAW you use the Pick tool and Shape tool to get snapping. The *Snap To* drop-down menu on the property bar is your ticket to defining what snaps to what on your drawing page.

Snapping is one quick route to precise manual aligning and distribution of table callouts, symmetrical patterns, and just about any design that requires some regularity to placed shapes. And if you don't need it, it's easy to turn off.

- **Snap To Grid** To have your drawing shapes snap and align to the document grid, click the drop-down on the property bar, or press the shortcut CTRL+Y to toggle the feature on and off. When objects snap to a grid, they snap to the grid lines, and you'll feel an even stronger attraction when you move an object close to grid *intersection* points.

- **Snap To Guidelines**   Guidelines are covered later in this chapter. To cause your objects to snap to any type of guideline, choose this option from the drop-down list.

- **Snap To Objects**   To have objects snap to and align with other objects, choose Snap To Objects from the drop-down list; it's faster to remember the shortcut ALT+Z. When objects are set to snap to each other, they can use snap points on either the source (the magnet) or target (the object that's attracted) object. Snap points are set using options and modes in the Snap To Objects page of the Options dialog (see the later section, "Setting Snap Behavior").

- **Snap To Page**   When you want to draw an object that's aligned perfectly to any edge of the drawing page, use this Snap To option. Snap To Page is also great for snapping an existing object's edge or corner to the edge of the page.

- **Dynamic Guides**   This feature in CorelDRAW X5 is akin to *object* snapping. Press ALT+SHIFT+D, or use the drop-down menu to toggle the dynamic guides on or off. This feature is covered in detail in the next section.

 Snapping To It

1. You have a web page to design, with six 1-inch squares (three across, two down), with a ½-inch space between them. Don't get out a pocket calculator, and don't resort to colorful language—at their defaults, Snap To Grid and Snap To Objects make this task go like a charm. Enable Snap To Grid and Snap To Objects from the Snap To drop-down list and make sure Grids are turned on.

2. With the Rectangle tool, begin close to a grid intersection, and then drag down and to the right until the property bar tells you either the height or width of the rectangle is very close to 1". Release the mouse button when your cursor is over a grid intersection.

3. Choose the Pick tool.

4. Drag the rectangle over to the right until you see one vertical grid separating it from the original square, but don't release the mouse button yet. One space is on each side of this line, and together they represent half an inch.

5. Right-click while the left mouse button is still depressed, and then release both buttons to drop a copy. What you've done is duplicate the original square to a new position. This is an important, quick technique for duplicating shapes.

6. Repeat steps 4 and 5 to build the array of evenly spaced squares, as shown in Figure 7-7. Notice that when an object's edge is on, or even close to, the grid when Snap To is turned on, you'll see a tiny blue label indicating the snap-to point. You're not limited to shape edges as the origin of a snapping point; setting behavior for snapping origins is covered later in this chapter.

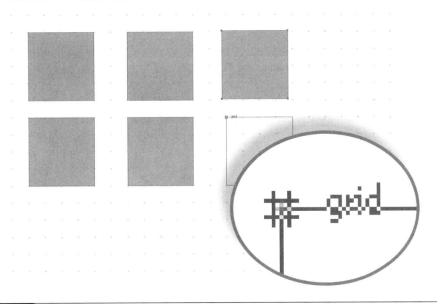

FIGURE 7-7   Duplicating and aligning objects makes accurate composition of a design a breeze.

 Snapping behavior isn't limited to the grid. In fact, you don't even have to have the grid turned on to snap objects to one another; press ALT+Z *and then all your objects are sticky.*

Setting Snap Behavior

On the Snap To Objects page of the Options dialog, you can control snapping behavior in precise detail when moving *and* drawing lines or objects. You choose Tools | Options (CTRL+J), click to expand the tree directory under Workspace, and then click Snap To Objects.

The Snapping Radius feature requires that you have a shape and a different object (or guideline or grid intersection) to which it snaps. Proximity to the "magnetic" snapping object is important—you can't have an object snap to a different object that is miles away. However, in the Snap To Objects page, you have control over the *strength* of the magnetism, by setting the Snapping Radius pixel distance.

To customize snapping behavior to suit the type of drawing you're building, you enable or disable the following features on the Options page:

- **Snap To Objects On**   Clicking this check box toggles the Snap To Objects feature on or off. You can also do this from the Snap To drop-down list on the property bar.

- **Snapping Radius**   Use this to set snapping sensitivity, based on screen proximity to snap points. Experiment with what works best for you in a specific design situation;

you can always return to this area and change the value. For example, choose 10 (the default), or 2 (weak magnetism), or 25 (akin to having chewing gum on the bottom of your shoe).

- **Show Snap Location Marks**   This option is on by default. Snap points are highlighted when your cursor is held over the precise points of a selected object or a target object while moving objects or drawing. When it is activated, you can also choose the Screen Tip option, which identifies the snapping point, highlighted with a text label. With Screen Tip turned on, the blue icons preceding the text labels represent some of the modes you've chosen. The types of snapping are covered next.

 When you reposition a shape by dragging it with the Pick tool, before you release the mouse button to finalize the move, the shape remains in the original position, but a blue, outline version of the shape appears at the intended new location. Use this feature as a visual guide for repositioning objects; this preview of a move offers positioning precision because you can "see through" to objects beneath the chosen object before you release the mouse button.

Choosing Object Snapping Modes

The Modes list includes nine object snap points you can define. You can toggle them on or off using the check boxes. Symbols beside the mode names identify the current snapping points on different object types. Use the Select All and Deselect All buttons to quickly activate or deactivate all the options in the list.

At times you might want snapping to occur at certain object points but not others—you can turn specific snap points on or off. Choose options from the Modes list to have objects snap to precise points on other objects in the following ways:

- **Node**   Use this mode to snap where nodes exist on objects or lines. A node is a break point along the path of a shape, and it's indicated by a very small (but noticeable) black outlined square.

- **Intersection**   Choose this mode to activate snapping where the outline paths of two objects cross, including the original position of an object you're moving.

- **Midpoint**   This mode snaps to a point equidistant between any two nodes on an object or path.

- **Quadrant**   This mode should only be used with ellipses and circles. It causes snapping to one of the four nodes that were created using the Ellipse tool (F7).

Below these modes are Tangent and Perpendicular; they work only in combination with dynamic guides, covered in the following section:

- **Tangent**   This mode shows a guide at a *tangent* (a straight line that touches a curve at a point) to a quadrant snap point. This mode applies only to ellipse objects.

- **Perpendicular**   Choose this mode to show a dynamic guide at right angles and to snap to the midpoint between object and segment nodes.

Finally, the following modes apply snapping regardless of whether other, additional snapping points are checked in this Options page:

- **Edge**   Choose this mode to have the outline path of an object act as a dynamic guide for snapping to.

- **Center**   This mode displays the center point (origin) of closed-path objects.

- **Text Baseline**   When snapping, all text objects take on the characteristics of a normal object such as a rectangle and have snapping points for edges, centers, corners, and so on. Additionally, the *text baseline* (the hypothetical line each character appears to rest on) is included in the snapping action.

7

Working with Guidelines, Dynamic Guides, and Guide Layers

Like the nonprinting blue pencil marks traditional designers used, CorelDRAW's page guides, dynamic guides, and objects you put on a guides layer don't print, but here the similarity ends. Regardless of whether you use one or all of the guide features in your work, you'll have the precision only a computer application can offer, plus the same speed and ease with guides as any object you'd draw on a page.

The following sections are the operator's manual for guides: how to use them and how to customize them.

Using Guidelines

Guidelines placed on your document page extend between the top, bottom, left, and right edges of the document window. Guidelines appear as vertical and horizontal dashed lines, but guidelines can also be *rotated*. In CorelDRAW, *guidelines* are considered unique objects—they have their own properties, but are manipulated in many ways like objects you draw.

To view and hide the display of guidelines in your document window, right-click an empty area of the page and then choose View | Guidelines. By default, a new document doesn't have any guidelines—you need to create them, which is shown next. To have objects *snap* to the guidelines you create, choose from the Snap To drop-down list on the property bar, where you found Snap To Grid earlier in this chapter.

Manipulating Guidelines

The following steps walk you through the tasks you'll need most often when working with guides:

- Make sure the rulers are visible; they're where a lot of the guides live. With the Pick tool chosen, and no objects selected, right-click and then choose to View | Rulers.

Then, using any toolbox tool you like, click-drag beginning on a ruler, and release the mouse button anywhere in the workspace. Although dropping a guide on the page is most useful, you can certainly create a guide on the pasteboard area to measure and align objects not currently placed on the page.

- To move a place guide, you need the Pick tool selected. Then hover the cursor over the guide you'd like to move; when the cursor turns into a double-headed arrow, all you need to do is drag the guide.

- If you want to eliminate a guide, hover over it with the Pick tool until you see the double-headed arrow cursor (to indicate you've selected it), click the guide to confirm the guide is "in focus" in the interface, and then press DELETE or CTRL+X. When a guide is selected, you'll see an onscreen confirmation before you delete it—the guide turns red.

- If you need a guide that travels uphill or downhill, you create a guide first. Next, click it to select it, and then click a second time, and you'll see a center and rotation handles. One of the neat things about rotating a guideline is that you can move its center point before dragging on the rotation handles to, for example, rotate a guide around the corner of a shape you have on the page. You move a slanted guideline exactly as you do with a perfectly horizontal or vertical guide—you click-drag it to reposition it. See Figure 7-8, where the design needs cartoonish shafts of light

FIGURE 7-8　Make your guides perform at the angle you need for a design piece.

emanating from a center point that is *not* the default center of a guide that's put into slant mode. No problem; you change the center of rotation, then drag a rotation handle clockwise or counterclockwise.

> **TIP**   *You can move and rotate several guidelines at once by pressing SHIFT to select or deselect them, and then click-dragging to move them. To rotate one or more guidelines while selected, click one of the guidelines a second time to display rotation handles, and drag one of the rotation handles.*

Controlling Guideline Properties

If you need several guidelines exactly spaced, manage all guidelines via the Options dialog (CTRL+J). Separate dialog pages are here for controlling the vertical, horizontal, and slanted guidelines. To see these dialogs, right-click either of the rulers and then choose Guidelines Setup. Additionally, while a guideline is selected in a document, you can open this dialog by clicking the Guidelines Options button on the property bar.

The Options dialog lists each of the guideline types individually on the left side of the dialog. Click one to select it in the tree directory under Guidelines; here's what the Vertical page looks like when some guides have been defined at 1-inch intervals:

By default, guidelines are a medium blue when added to the workspace, and their highlight color when they're selected is red. However, on the main page for Guidelines in Options, you can change the color of a guide as well as the color for preset guides. This is quite handy, for example, if you're designing a series of medium blue rectangles—naturally, you'd want to choose a contrasting color for the guides!

Adding, Deleting, and Moving Guidelines

You can adjust guides using the features in Guidelines in Options. Each dialog contains a listing of the existing guidelines on your document page. Here are the ways to perform the common tasks:

1. To create a new guideline, enter a value in the top-left num box according to the position where you want the new guideline to be created. Then click the Add button. A new guideline is created where you want it.

2. If you're in a Guidelines window and you can't see where to move or add a guideline, go to either the Horizontal or Vertical guidelines dialogs, and you can work there.

3. To move an existing guideline, click it in the list, enter a new value in the top-left num box, and then click Move. The selected guideline has moved, and on the list you can see it's been thoughtful and left a forwarding address.

4. To delete a specific guideline, select it in the list, and then click the Delete button. The selected guideline is gone from the page, and as you see the page from your current view, your document is immediately updated.

5. To remove all guidelines in the list, click the Clear button. All guidelines are deleted.

Locking and Unlocking Guidelines

All guidelines are editable by default; you can move or delete them using the Pick tool. But occasionally a guide that can move accidentally is as welcome as a friend who is holding your ladder moving accidentally. You can lock it using property bar options:

Lock button

1. To lock an *individual* guideline, click the guideline to select it using the Pick tool.

2. Using property bar options, click the Lock button. The selected guideline is locked, and the guide-specific property bar options become unavailable. You can also choose Lock Object from the pop-up menu when you've selected a guide using the Pick tool.

3. To unlock a locked guideline, right-click the guideline and choose Unlock Object from the pop-up menu. Your guideline is now unlocked, and the guide-specific property bar options become available again.

Working with Dynamic Guides

Dynamic guides are guides that you first set up with axes of rotation (0°, 15°, and so on), and then when you want a guide at a specific angle for aligning or drawing, it appears onscreen. It can snap the object you're positioning, and dynamic guides offer onscreen information about the result of a moving or drawing action. When using dynamic guides, drawing or moving your cursor over active object snap points will cause guides to temporarily appear to aid in placement of objects and nodes. You can move your cursor along these "sticky" guides, and view snap points, angle values, and distance measurements relative to object snap points (as shown in Figure 7-9). You can also have your cursor snap

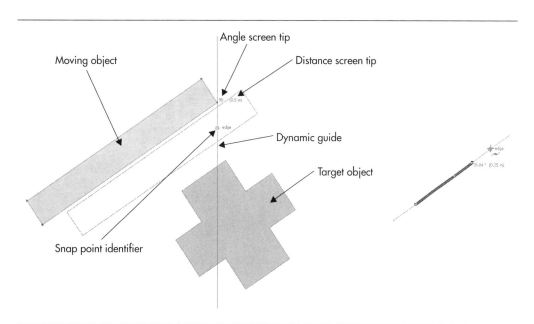

FIGURE 7-9   From the "sticky" guides, you can view snap points, angle values, and more.

to specific points along the guide path, based on a customizable tick value. To activate this feature, choose View | Dynamic Guides (ALT+SHIFT+D).

Dynamic guide behavior works in combination with your selected Snap To Objects modes (see "Setting Snap Behavior" earlier in the chapter), but has a unique set of options that control their behavior. To access these options (see the following illustration), choose Tools | Options (CTRL+J), and click Dynamic Guides under Workspace in the tree directory.

Here's how choosing each option will affect the behavior of your dynamic guides:

● **Dynamic Guides On**   Click this check box to turn dynamic guides on or off.

● **Angle Screen Tip**   Choose this to display angle values relative to snap points on your object.

● **Distance Screen Tip**   Choose this to display the distance between your cursor position on a guide and the current snap point. Unit measure is based on your currently selected drawing units.

- **Snap To Ticks**   This option offers to snap your cursor position to points along the guide according to the value you enter.

- **Guides**   This area opens up a whole world of possibilities for angles at which dynamic guides appear relative to the active snap point. Clicking a check box activates each of the default angles, which are preset at from 0° to 150° (in 15° and 30° increments), for a total angle of 180°, which effectively covers all possible angles, because Dynamic Guides appear bi-directional. The angle of each guide is displayed in the Guides Preview window on the right of the dialog. Enter a degree value in the num box above the list, and click the Add button to add a new guide. To remove a dynamic guide, click a guide either in the list or in the preview window, and then click Delete. When a new guide is added, it appears in the list; conversely, when you delete a guide, it's permanently removed from the list.

- **Extend Along Segment**   Choose this to display a guide at the same angle as straight line segments. This option is useful for Bézier and freehand drawing because this makes it easy for you to add new portions to straight lines at a constant angle (as shown in Figure 7-10).

Figure 7-11 shows a logo nearing completion by setting up dynamic guides at 45° increments. Using the Pen tool, the dynamic guides (set to snapping) show exactly when the tool has reached a 45° angle as well as a 90° angle. Try this feature for yourself; this illustration was accomplished using 25 clicks—precision has seldom been achieved so easily.

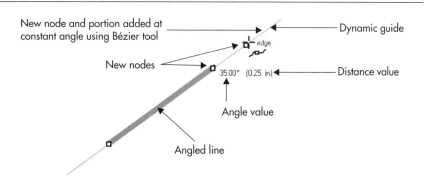

New node and portion added at constant angle using Bézier tool — Dynamic guide
edge
New nodes — Distance value
35.00° (0.25 in)
Angle value
Angled line

The Extend Along Segment option is useful for both Bézier and freehand drawing.

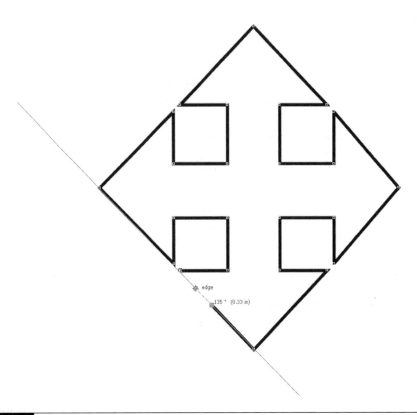

FIGURE 7-11   Use dynamic guides to assist in alignment and drawing when rulers don't suit the assignment.

Controlling the Guides Layer

Guides belong to a special layer, named Guides on the Object Manager, reserved just for these assistants. To view the layers in your document, open the Object Manager by choosing either Tools | Object Manager or Window | Dockers | Object Manager, and then click the Layer Manager View button at the top of the docker. The Guides layer is a Master Page layer; you'll find it with other layers controlling your Desktop and Grid. By default, all guidelines on the Guides layer are set as Visible, Non-Printable, and Editable. If you want, you can change any of these by clicking the symbols to the left of the Guides layer in the Object Manager docker, as shown here:

Edit Across Layers

Layer Manager View

Show Object Properties

Click to expand Master Page layer.

Visible option

Non-Printable option

Editable option

To set all options for a layer at once—including the display color of objects on the Guides layer in the Object Manager docker—right-click the layer name, for example, the Guides layer, and then choose Properties from the pop-up menu. Doing this opens the Guides Properties dialog to reveal further options.

Make an Object a Guideline

Where a straight or slanted guideline doesn't get you where you want to go, you can make almost any drawing shape into a guideline; going the other way around, you can also turn a guide into a drawing object. To do this, you use the Object Manager docker to move objects between layers. Moving any object to the Guides layer makes for all intents and purposes a guideline, with all the same properties as a typical guideline, except you might call it a guide-curve or a guide-spiral! After an object becomes a guideline, objects and anything you draw in its proximity snap to it, as long as the Snap To Guidelines option is active. Think of the artwork you can clean up and refine when you're tracing over the original with a drawing tool that snaps to the original.

Moving any guideline to a different layer automatically makes it a printable object. To move an object to the Guides layer, use these steps:

1. Create or select at least one drawing shape that you want to use as a guideline.

2. Open the Object Manager docker by choosing Tools | Object Manager.

3. Expand the tree directories in the Object Manager docker to locate both the Guides layer on the Master Page and the shape you want to make into a guideline, so both are in view.

4. In the Object Manager docker, click-and-drag your shape icon (not the shape on the page) from its current page and layer to any position under the Guides layer on the Master Page. As you drag, notice a horizontal I-beam cursor appears, shown next, indicating the shape's current position as it is dragged. When your cursor is over a layer—ideally, the layer you want to move the shape to—you'll see the default cursor replaced with a horizontal arrow "holding" a symbol of graphics content. The following illustration also shows a "before and after" of a star shape when it's moved to the Master Page Guides layer. Unlike guidelines you drag from rulers, the look of a user-defined guide doesn't have the dashed lines; it's a solid line with no fill.

Cursor between objects in docker indicates
current position during the drag action.

Generally, after moving a shape to the Guides layer, it's a good practice to lock the layer, as described earlier. A guide that moves when you don't intend it to is as useful as a crepe paper umbrella in a storm.

Using Guideline Presets

CorelDRAW's Guidelines feature comes with a group of presets that generate scripts to instantly add guidelines to your document. To use these scripts, press CTRL+J (Options); click to expand the tree directory under Document | Guidelines; and then click Presets, shown here. Click Apply Presets (you can add as many as you like in one fell swoop), and you have instant preset guides on the page. Basic Grid is a very useful preset because unlike with the Grid feature, you can move, and thus customize, any of the guidelines.

Many of the presets are page margins, many are timesavers, but you can also create your *own* preset. To define guidelines that automatically populate the page, choose the User Defined Presets option in the Presets page of the Options dialog. This displays a collection of options for you to create your own custom Margins, Columns, or Grid guidelines. To activate any or all of these preset guideline effects, choose the corresponding options and customize the associated preset values.

 To open the Options dialog quickly to the Presets page while you currently have an unlocked guideline selected, click the Preset Guidelines button on the property bar.

Altering Preset Guides and Saving Guides in a Template

Although preset guidelines behave like guidelines you drag from the rulers, if you want to alter the preset arrangement by dragging one with the Pick tool, the action triggers an *attention box*. This attention box is equivalent in seriousness to the tag you get on new pillows—it's for your own safety and is simply telling you that you're modifying a preset, your own or a Corel preset for guidelines. You can check the "Don't show warning again" box at the bottom-left of the Warning dialog box to avoid it in the future. Basically, you cannot destroy or modify a Corel guideline preset by moving one of the guides on the page—the option is always there from session to session. And there's really nothing to mess up by altering a user preset guideline on the page after you've created one. There is no saved list of user presets; if you've created a user preset of grids, margins, or columns and want to save the modified or the original arrangement, you choose File | Save As Template. In the future, you can load a fresh, new document based on the template, and your guides are all in place.

Using the Dimension Tools

If you need to annotate a drawing or an imported bitmap image with dimensions or labels calling out, for example, different parts of a machine, the dimension tools are expressly for this purpose. The lines you create with the four dimension tools will tag the bracketed area with units of measurement of your choice, and they dynamically update when you scale them. The 3-point callout tool is for adding text to a wide selection of arrowhead lines; you can choose a line style for the connector as well as width, a type of arrowhead, and any style of typeface that you have installed on your system. The text labels for callouts are also upright regardless of if you rotate the line, and a callout control line can be edited at any time with the Shape tool (F10).

Working with Callouts

When using the 3-point callout tool, you produce two elements: a line composed of two segments (the callout, as it's displayed on the status bar), and the control text. Callouts are not bound to an object; they can be moved anywhere on the page. But the text and the line are linked and cannot be moved independently of one another. You have a number of options on the property bar when the tool is active and also when a callout is selected (after one has been drawn):

- **Outline width** By default, you always begin a callout with a 0.5-point line width in black. It is not recommended to adjust the width before drawing a line; doing so triggers an attention box that asks whether you want the default line width—for any object you draw, not just callouts—to be changed. Instead, create your callout, and *then* adjust the width while the callout is selected. Because the callout belongs to the general class of line objects in CorelDRAW, you can change the color of the callout line by right-clicking a color well on the Color Palette while the line is selected.

- **Start arrowhead** This drop-down list will seem familiar if you've ever applied an arrowhead to a line by using the property bar. The same basic styles are available as on the Start arrowhead collection. You can even use an arrow *tail* for a callout.

- **Line style** Like any other line you draw with the Pen or other drawing tool, the callout can be solid, dashed, a series of dots—choose a style by clicking the pop-up box, and then click a style thumbnail.

- **Callout symbol**   You set the style for the callout text from this pop-up list of presets. The symbol doesn't affect the font; it's a style—a rectangle bounding the text, a straight line butted above or below the text—symbols add an element of polish to your presentation.

- **Offset**   Sets the distance between the tail of the callout line and the beginning of the text.

- **Character Formatting (CTRL+T)**   After creating a callout, you can select the text and use the property bar to change the font, font size, and so on, but Character Formatting also provides you with more controls and options. Clicking this button displays Character Formatting as a docker entry, persistent onscreen until you close the box.

To use the 3-point callout tool:

1. Click-drag to create a point where you want the callout to end (the node will eventually have the arrowhead), move the cursor to where you want the "elbow" of the callout line, and then click.

2. Move your cursor to where you want the control text, and then click.

3. Begin typing what you want the callout to read.

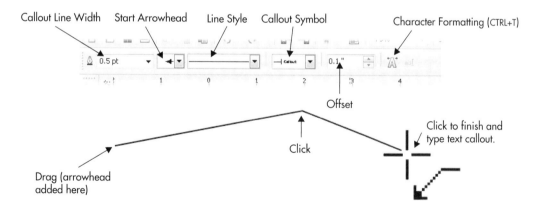

The following steps walk you through an imaginary assignment: you have an illustration of a custom bowling shirt, and you need to call out one or two selling points about the shirt. The shirt in League Shirts.cdr could use a callout for the name of the league that the vendor silk-screens on the shirt's back. Also, the vendor offers to embroider the name of the player above the front pocket in case the bowler forgets his or her name. These steps are simply a demonstration, and your finished assignment is neither "right" nor "wrong," but rather an exploration of the 3-point callout tool's features and ease of use.

Calling Out a Bowling Shirt

1. Open League Shirt.cdr. The layer with the illustration is locked so nothing can accidentally be moved.

2. Choose the 3-point callout tool from the Dimension Tools group on the toolbox.

3. Click-drag from "The Kingpins" logo on the back view of the shirt, and then release the mouse button inside the green bubble graphic. Doing this sets the first of two segments for the callout line.

4. Click below the shirt, and then type **Your Team logo**.

5. Choose the Pick tool. You cannot press ENTER to toggle to it, because technically, the Artistic text tool is being used by your cursor.

6. Select the callout line; notice that the options for the callout are now available on the property bar.

7. Choose 4 pt. from the Line Width pop-up list, and then choose a dashed line from the Styles pop-up.

8. Choose the third from the top symbol style for the callout. Depending on how the last node is positioned on the page for the callout, your text might have the bar for the symbol to the left or above it. Either is fine in this experiment, and you'll see shortly how to change the symbol's orientation.

9. Right-click over any color well you like with the callout line selected to change its color.

10. Choose the Shape tool (F10). Click anywhere on the line to select it.

11. Try moving one node of the line, and then another. Notice that the text is always oriented upright and adjusts to reflect changes you make to the connected callout line.

12. Click on the "elbow" node; let's say you want a 2-point callout and not this 3-point guy. Either press the minus key on your numeric keypad, or click the Delete Nodes button on the property bar. Voila! You can add a node by clicking the segment and then pressing the + keypad key, and even add a few more nodes. The overall property of the callout isn't destroyed by editing it. The text is still bound to the callout line.

13. Click a line segment, and then click the Convert To Curve button on the property bar. Then drag the segment with the Shape tool to create an arc.

14. With the Pick tool, select the text; the status bar should read "Control Text on…" Choose a typeface from the installed list of Fonts on the property bar. Try using a different size for the text you typed, and view how the symbol for the callout text adjusts to accommodate the new typeface size.

15. Finish up this assignment by adding a second callout to the front of the shirt, where the name "Spinny" appears. See Figure 7-12 for one of several graphical treatments you can now build with the 3-point callout tool.

FIGURE 7-12   Use the 3-point callout tool for fast, professional-looking labels for graphic designs.

Using Dimension Tools

Four Dimension line tool types are available, each of which creates a different type of line with a specific purpose. When the Dimension tool is selected, the property bar displays options to specify the style, precision, and unit values of your displayed dimensions, and to control the display and appearance of the labeling text, covered next. Figure 7-13 has the names of the areas you can access when using Dimension tools.

- **Dimension Style** This option is used to set decimal, fractional, or standard measuring conventions, the default of which is decimal.

- **Dimension Precision** This option is used to set a level of precision. While using Decimal as the measuring style, precision may be specified up to ten decimal places. While using Fractional, precision may be specified using fractions up to 1/1024 of a selected unit measure.

- **Dimension Units** Use this option to specify the measurement unit with which to display your text labels. You can choose any of the unit measures supported by CorelDRAW X5.

- **Show/Hide Units** This is a toggle button. If you don't want units appended to a dimension, leave the button turned off before you create a dimension line.

- **Prefix/Suffix For Dimension** With this feature, you can enter your own text so that it appears before and after the text label for your dimension line. For example, styles of merchandise, such as "Plastic" or a "Children only" sized garment, are uses for this option. Prefix and Suffix text may be any character you want and may be applied before or after the dimension line has been drawn.

FIGURE 7-13   The four Dimension tools each share a common set of options.

- **Show Leading Zero** When a value of less than one is a resulting dimension, a tenth of an inch, for example, you can add a zero before the decimal, or choose to leave it off by toggling this button off (the non-depressed state). If you have a series of columns of dimension lines, adding the leading zero will help keep the values aligned to the left or right.

- **Dynamic Dimensioning** This option lets you specify whether your measurement values are updated automatically as the size of the dimension line is changed. By default, this option is turned on for all new dimension lines. If you plan on resizing or changing the drawing scale of your drawing after creating the dimension lines, disabling this option freezes the values being displayed so that they remain fixed, whether your dimension lines are resized or not.

 If, for some reason, resizing a drawing applied with dimension lines causes the measured values to change, you can right-click the dimension line and choose Break Dimension Apart from the pop-up menu as a workaround.

7

- **Text Position** To specify a position for the text labels applied to your dimension line, choose one of the options from the Text Position drop-down list. Choose from top-centered, middle-centered, or bottom-centered for Auto, Vertical, Horizontal, or Callout dimension lines.

Checking Out Dimension Lines

The following steps walk you through the use for, and the technique used to build, dimension lines. Let's pretend in the "Urn While you Learn.cdr" file that the drawing of the antique urn is to size: it's 6 ¾" tall in the real world. Your assignment is a response from the antique dealer that she wants to know the overall height of the urn, the height of the neck, and the angle of the bottom decal on the bowl of the urn, as measured from tip of the bowl where it meets the neck. Moreover, she wants the drawing marked with fractional values and thinks metric amounts are for nerds and scientists. People go a little overboard when it comes to cataloguing antiques, but your success is ensured because you have these steps to guide you.

 Using Dimension Lines

1. Open the Urn While You Learn.cdr file, and then select the Horizontal or Vertical dimension tool from the toolbox.

2. On the property bar, set the Style to Fractional.

3. Click-drag from the top of the urn to its bottom, where you release the mouse button. With this tool, direction is set to vertical or horizontal by the direction in which you first drag.

4. Move the cursor to the left without holding either mouse button. Doing this defines a position for the control text, so make sure your cursor position is not over the urn drawing.

5. Click. You're done and the number value is called out now.

6. Choose the Parallel dimension tool; the neck of the bottle is slightly slanted, so this is the appropriate measuring tool.

7. Click-drag from the top of the neck (below the lip) to the part that joins the neck with the bowl; release the mouse button at this point.

8. Move the cursor to the right, away from the drawing, and then single-click to add the dimension line and number value.

9. Choose the Angular dimension tool.

10. Click-drag from the junction of the neck and bowl, and release the mouse button when your cursor is to the left of the bottom decal on the bowl.

11. Move your cursor to the right so it touches the right side of the decal.

12. Click. You're not finished yet. You now have the opportunity to set the position of the arc. Move your cursor toward or away from the vertex of the two angular lines, and then click.

13. The measurement probably will not read, being black against the dark urn. No problem: with the Pick tool, select the number value, and then click the white color well on the Color Palette. Figure 7-14 shows the completed assignment.

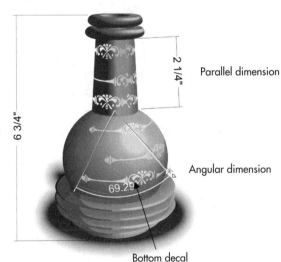

FIGURE 7-14   Use dimension lines to quickly and accurately annotate drawings and images.

Segment Dimensions

Whether you need to discover a value for technical comparison's sake, or want to make sure a part of a personal illustration is of an exact length, the Segment dimension tool is your ticket. This tool measures the distance between nodes on a path, whether the nodes are on a straight line or a curve.

To use this tool, you first select a line in your composition with the Pick tool. Choose the Segment dimension tool, and then marquee-select the two nodes you want to discover the distance between. Move the cursor away from the selection to create handles that bound the selected nodes and then click. As you can see here, the illustrator was curious about the length of the tips of this cartoon character's hair. We don't ask *why* he wanted to know, but we *do* know that they are 0.65".

Marquee-select nodes

Move and then click to finalize.

7

An Exercise in Dimensioning to Scale

All of the preceding info and examples are fine in theory; now, you're going to put the theory into practice in the next tutorial. You're handed a CorelDRAW document with a photo in it. Your boss—or any other person who is intimidating—wants the parts of the toy water pistol called out, but here's the catch: the image of the water pistol is *not* 1:1. So how does one measure all the parts of a 7 ½" long toy that is 6.78" on the CorelDRAW page?

As follows!

Drawing Scale, Windows Calculator, and Dimension Lines

1. Open The Neptune Soaker.cdr.

2. For laughs, choose the Horizontal or Vertical dimension line tool, and drag it from the beginning of the body of the water pistol to the right, and then release the mouse button at the end of the water plug, the yellow piece of plastic to the left of the red cap. Write this value down.

3. The boss says the body is 7 ½". In this example, the body length should be 5.76". You launch Windows Calculator (or use the physical home version in your workshop): 7.5/5.76 = 1.302 percent. This is the value by which this document's Drawing Scale must be adjusted, as you recall from the example earlier in this chapter.

4. Right-click over a ruler, choose Ruler Setup, and then in the Ruler Options box, click Edit Scale.

5. Page Distance should be 1 inch. Type **1.302** in the World Distance field, and then click OK to apply this new scale. See Figure 7-15.

6. Use the Horizontal or Vertical, the Parallel, and the Angular dimension tools to measure anything asked of you in this or your own drawing.

FIGURE 7-15 Adjust the World Distance scale to make measuring areas in photos and drawings accurate to scale.

As Figure 7-16 shows, when Fraction styles are used in combination with reassigning line and fill colors for text, you have a highly detailed, picture-perfect presentation for the manufacturing department and even print ads.

You've seen in this chapter that in addition to everyday paths and closed objects, there are also lines for labeling and organizing objects. You've also learned how to steer the power of CorelDRAW's rulers to suit your own design needs. You can now use those old-fashioned wooden rulers you have around the house for what they're *meant* for: to stir house paint.

Come explore the basic shapes you can create (and then measure!) in Chapter 8, as you get a feel for the speed and ease of CorelDRAW's preset shapes—there are a *lot* of them— and take the next step in creating visually complex illustrations.

FIGURE 7-16   Provide accurate object dimensions for a client—regardless of the print size of a document—with the dimension tools.

CHAPTER 8

Creating Basic Shapes, Applying Transformations

This is the "You have to begin *somewhere!*" chapter: drawing vector paths with CorelDRAW is all about creating objects that you then customize and refine through fancy fills and elegant outlines. Therefore, it's important to know the techniques for creating simple—and not so simple—geometric shapes, and to know how to edit your drawings to create exactly the shape you want to fill and stroke.

 Download and extract all the files from the Chapter08.zip archive to follow the tutorials in this chapter.

CorelDRAW X5's Smart Drawing Tool

Even if you use a graphics tablet and stylus, you're still drawing freehand, and using a mouse introduces even less precision when it comes to vector drawing. Fortunately, the Smart Drawing tool takes the guesswork out of drawing polygonal and rounded objects—in a nutshell, you sketch an approximation of what you intend, tune the options for the Smart Drawing tool a little, and in a jiffy you have a precise object of the proportions you need. Pictured here on the toolbox, the Smart Drawing tool instantly translates rough drawings into shapes you'd usually consider drawing with the Rectangle tool or Ellipse tool—or with other tools that require more effort and skill.

When the Smart Drawing tool is chosen, the property bar displays Shape Recognition Level and smoothing options (shown next) for setting the sensitivity CorelDRAW uses in translating your roughs into precise shapes.

Recognition and smoothing options

You control how precisely your sketch shape is translated into shapes by setting these options:

- **Shape Recognition Level**   This option sets how precisely your sketched shape is matched to a recognizable shape and can be set to one of five levels ranging from Lowest (sketched shapes are not easily recognized) to Highest (sketched shapes are easily recognized), with Medium being the default; None turns the feature off.

- **Smart Smoothing Level**   After you've completed a sketch by releasing the mouse button, a level of node smoothing is applied to make object recognition more, or less, precise. This option gives you total control over the smoothing action, much in the same fashion as using the Reduce Nodes spin box on the property bar when a path is selected with the Shape tool. Choose from five options ranging from Lowest (less smoothing applied) to Highest (more smoothing applied), with Medium as the default; None turns the feature off.

> **TIP**   *You can control the delay time interval between the moment you release the mouse button and stop drawing and the moment DRAW X5 determines a recognizable shape. By increasing the delay time, you can sketch several separate lines or shapes one after the other, and DRAW then recognizes them as a single compound path. To get to this option, double-click the Smart Drawing tool icon on the toolbox to open Options. The Drawing Assistance Delay slider can be set between 0 and 2.0 seconds. The higher you set the delay time, the more time you'll have to keep drawing before CorelDRAW steps in to assist you.*

Try the following steps to immediately get a leg up on drawing flawless objects.

CAD: CorelDRAW-Assisted Drawing

1. Choose the Smart Drawing tool and use a click-drag action to sketch the shape of a square or rectangle. Try to keep the sides of the shape vertical and horizontal as you draw; if the square shape looks like a melted ice cube, don't worry! When you release the mouse button, CorelDRAW X5 automatically translates your sketch into a rectangle shape.

2. Choose the Pick tool next, and check your status bar display. The shape you sketched is specified as a Rectangle, and the property bar shows options associated with shapes created with the Rectangle tool.

3. Choose the Smart Drawing tool(s) again, and sketch the shape of an oval or circle. Try to keep the shape parallel to the page orientation, but CorelDRAW can also intelligently refine a sketch of an oval that's rotated. On releasing the mouse button, CorelDRAW X5 translates your sketched shape into an ellipse shape.

4. Choose the Pick tool and check your status bar. The shape you sketched is specified as an Ellipse, and the property bar shows options associated with shapes created with the Ellipse tool, such as the Ellipse, Arc, and Pie properties.

 You can alter your sketched shapes on-the-fly using the Smart Drawing tool to backtrack and erase the path you're drawing. Hold SHIFT as the modifier key to reverse and erase. Release SHIFT to resume sketching normally.

The shapes you draw can also have special editing properties; use Figure 8-1 as a visual reference when you use the tool.

● Rectangles and ovals produced by using the Smart Drawing tool become CorelDRAW objects, identical in editing properties to the objects you draw with the Rectangle and Ellipse tools.

● Trapezoids and parallelograms produced with the Smart Drawing tool become Perfect Shapes, explained in a moment.

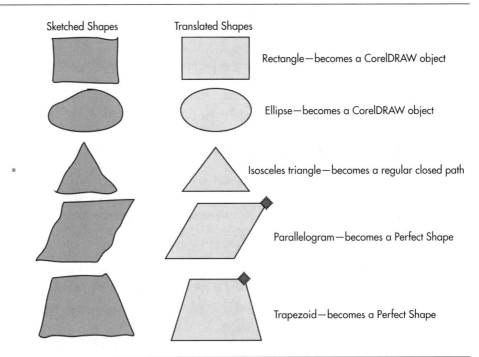

FIGURE 8-1 Perfect Shapes retain their properties even when you extensively edit their appearance.

- Other shapes you draw—triangles, arrows, stair steps, and so on—become regular curved objects, but the Smart Drawing tool intelligently smoothes out curves and straightens nearly straight line segments.

- *Perfect Shapes* are a special category of CorelDRAW objects and they have special properties. They feature "glyph" nodes (by default, a red-filled diamond)—which are different from regular nodes along a path—and the nodes can be manipulated to modify the shape without destroying any of its unique geometric properties.

Now that you've created at least one Perfect Shape and know how to make others, try these next steps to create variations on the basic appearance of a Perfect Shape.

Reshaping a Perfect Shape

1. Using the Smart Drawing tool, sketch the shape of a trapezoid (refer to Figure 8-1; two sides are parallel, the other two sides converge). When you release the mouse button, CorelDRAW translates your sketch into a Perfect Shape.

8

2. Choose the Pick tool and then look at the status bar. The shape is identified as a Perfect Shape, a special category of shape. Use the Shape tool next to click-drag the glyph node. You'll see that the parallel sides remain parallel, and the converging sides slope away and toward each other. By duplicating this Perfect Shape, you can edit with the Shape tool and create an array of trapezoids, all different in appearance but all editable indefinitely, and all retain the geometric structure of a Perfect Shape.

TIP | *To learn more about creating Perfect Shapes and manipulating glyph nodes, see "Using Perfect Shape Tools," later in this chapter.*

The Smart Drawing tool helps you quickly draw and translate a variety of sketched shapes into different, geometrically flawless shapes more efficiently than using multiple tools. Each of the translated shapes has its own special properties, which you'll learn in detail in the sections that follow.

Using the Rectangle Tool and Property Bar

The Rectangle tool is simple enough to use, but it doesn't just create a four-sided, right-angle polygon—it creates a rectangle that has *special properties* in CorelDRAW, and these special properties extend to rectangles drawn with the Smart Drawing tool. You'll find the Rectangle tool in the toolbox, or you can quickly select it by pressing F6.

Rectangle shapes offer you the option to apply corner "roundness" based on a percentage value. Roundness can be set either manually by dragging a corner with the Shape tool, or by using the property bar Corner Radius option available while a rectangle is selected. By default, you round all four corners equally and together. However, if you unlock the Edit Corners Together toggle button, you can manually enter different values for each of the four corners, discussed in the following section.

Corner Radius (roundness) values

 TIP *You can also choose the Rectangle tool while any shape-creation tool is selected (the Ellipse tool, for example) by right-clicking a blank space on the document page and choosing Create Object | Rectangle from the pop-up menu.*

Drawing a Rectangle

To create a rectangle, choose the Rectangle tool from the toolbox, and click-diagonal drag in any direction to define its corner positions, as shown here. The act of click-dragging begins by defining the first two corners. As you drag, the corner positions can be redefined, depending on where your cursor is on the page; and then, before you release the mouse button, you've defined the position for the remaining two rectangle corners.

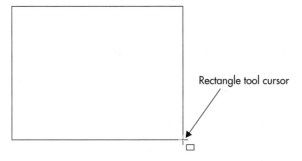

Rectangle tool cursor

While the Rectangle tool is selected, notice that the cursor is a crosshair with a small rectangle shape at its lower right. As you click-drag using the cursor, you'll also notice that the status bar and property bar show coordinates, width, and height properties of your new object shape.

Setting Rectangle Corner Properties

Round Corner is one of three different effects you can apply and dynamically edit when you're into rectangles. Round Corner, as well as the Scalloped Corner and Chamfered Corner styles, can be applied to a rectangle from a value of 0 to about one half the overall length of one of its sides. If we think about this, a 2" rectangle *can't* have more than a 1" rounded corner on each side! The Corner Radius amount can be changed anytime while the shape remains a native rectangle; that is, it has not been converted to curves. By typing 0 into any of the size boxes while the rectangle is selected, you remove the corner style. Round, Scalloped, and Chamfered Corner can be set uniformly for all corners (the default) or independently when the Edit Corners Together lock option is in the unlocked state.

 TIP   *Double-clicking the Rectangle tool button in the toolbox instantly creates a rectangular border around your current document page.*

8

Constraining Shapes While Drawing

Just like most Windows applications, CorelDRAW takes advantage of keyboard modifier keys you can use to modify shapes as you draw them. Holding modifier keys as you click-drag various tool cursors makes drawing your new object shape easier, you get more options at your cursor tip, and you work faster. These shortcuts are worth committing to memory:

- Hold CTRL while drawing new objects to constrain their shape to equal width and height.

- Hold SHIFT while drawing new objects to draw their shape from the center outward. This is particularly useful, for example, when you need a rectangle whose center is positioned at a specific point on the page.

- Hold CTRL+SHIFT while drawing new objects to constrain their shape from the center origin, *and* to equal width and height simultaneously.

It helps to mentally associate CTRL with "constrain" and SHIFT with "additional or added feature."

While a rectangle is selected, use any of the following operations to change corner properties according to your needs:

- Click the type of corner style you want on the property bar, and then either type in the size for the corner values, or drag the elevator buttons up or down to adjust the size of the corners.

- Set your rectangle's corners manually using the Shape tool by first unlocking the Edit Corners Together toggle button, and then CTRL-dragging any corner control point away from its corner (toward a side that makes up the rectangle). Enabling the Edit Corners Together option causes all corners to be rounded or scalloped in an equal amount by dragging on any of the control points.

- Use the Object Properties docker (press ALT+ENTER), click the Rectangle tab, and then edit any property you so choose.

Figure 8-2 shows rectangles with different types of corners; this is an ideal feature for building interesting signs, borders, and frames for documents.

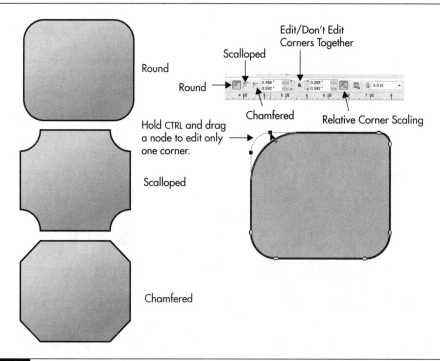

FIGURE 8-2   Rectangles can have almost any type of corner you can imagine.

Creating 3-Point Rectangles

If you want to create a rectangle and have it rotated all in one fell swoop, you have the
3-Point Rectangle tool. You'll find it grouped with the Rectangle tool in the toolbox.

3-Point Rectangle tool

Using this tool, you can draw new rectangles at precise angles, as shown in Figure 8-3.
The rectangle you create is a native rectangle shape, meaning you may round its corners and
manipulate it as any other shape.

To create a Rectangle using the 3-Point Rectangle tool, use these steps:

1. Select the 3-Point Rectangle tool, click to define the corner end point of one side of
   your rectangle, and then drag to define its width/height. As you drag the cursor, the
   angle of the line changes freely, enabling you to set the precise angle of the new
   rectangle. Release the mouse button to define the opposite side of the rectangle.

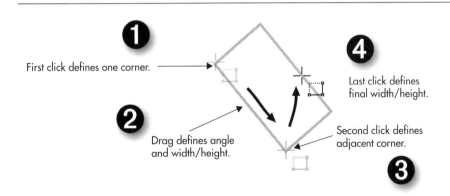

FIGURE 8-3   Draw new rectangles at precise angles with the 3-Point Rectangle tool.

2. As you move your cursor now, an angled rectangle preview shape is built on either side of the two points you defined. Your next click will define the final dimensions of your rectangle.

Using the Ellipse Tool and Property Bar

Ellipses are a staple of commercial design work, and essentially an ellipse is a circular shape that is not perfect. The Ellipse tool can be used to draw both perfect circles and ellipses, but in CorelDRAW an ellipse shape has additional, special properties, just like a rectangle can be a round-cornered rectangle. Ellipse shapes can be edited to create dramatically new shapes while retaining their elliptical properties. In contrast, an oval shape drawn with, for example, the Bézier tool always remains an oval.

Ellipses are easy enough to draw with the Ellipse tool and can be set in several different states: as oval or circular closed-paths, as pie wedges, and as arcs. Pie wedges are the portions of an ellipse—like a single slice of a pie, or conversely a whole pie with a slice removed. Arc shapes are the open-path equivalent of pies.

To create an ellipse, choose the Ellipse tool, shown at left, from the toolbox or press F7, followed by a click-drag in any direction.

While the Ellipse tool is selected, the property bar shows ellipse-specific options, shown next, that enable you to control the state of your new ellipse shape before or after it has been created. Choose Ellipse, Pie, or Arc. A complement is reserved for Pie and Arc shapes: for example, if you specify a 15° pie wedge, clicking the Change Direction icon changes the shape to a 345° wedge. Additionally, if you want a Pie or Arc to travel in a different path direction, double-click the Ellipse tool icon on the toolbox, which takes you to Options, where you can choose clockwise or counterclockwise path directions.

> | TIP | *You can also choose the Ellipse tool while any tool is selected by right-clicking in an empty space on your document page and choosing Create Object | Ellipse from the pop-up menu.*

Drawing an Ellipse

Let's walk before running; before creating pie and arc shapes, begin with creating circles and ovals. Start with these brief steps.

Round One with the Ellipse Tool

1. Choose the Ellipse tool (F7) and use a click-diagonal drag action in any direction. As you drag, an outline preview of the shape appears, as shown here. An ellipse shape has two overlapping control nodes (so onscreen it looks like only one node); if you drag down and left or right, the nodes will be located at 6 o'clock. Conversely, if you drag up and left or right, the control nodes will be located at 12 o'clock.

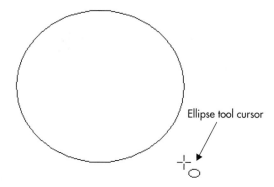

Ellipse tool cursor

2. Release the mouse button to complete your ellipse shape creation.

Controlling Ellipse States

All ellipses have two control points (*nodes*—a start and an end) that overlap each other and are visible when the ellipse is selected. When these control points are separated, they create either a pie or an arc state, and each control point determines either the *starting* or *ending* angle of the pie or arc.

You can separate these control points either by using property bar options or by dragging the points using the Shape tool. Dragging *inside* the ellipse's shape creates the Ellipse Pie state. Dragging *outside* the shape creates the Ellipse Arc state, as shown in Figure 8-4.

Dragging inside creates the pie shape.   Dragging outside creates the arc shape.

FIGURE 8-4   Dragging the points using the Pick or Shape tool creates different states.

Even though pies and arcs appear as if sections or path parts are missing, the portions are still there. They're just hidden from view.

To draw a new pie or arc without drawing an oval-shaped ellipse first, click either the Pie or Arc button in the property bar before you start drawing. You can also switch any selected ellipse between these states by using these buttons. By default, all pies and arcs are applied with a default Starting Angle of 0° and a default Ending Angle of 270°. Starting and Ending Angles are based on degrees of rotation from –360° to 360°; this is counterclockwise in orientation.

 To set the default properties for all new ellipse shapes, double-click the Ellipse tool on the toolbox; doing this brings up the Ellipse tool in the Options box. Choose an ellipse type, and then each new ellipse shape you create will be created according to the options you select, including the state of the new ellipse—Ellipse, Pie, or Arc—and the starting and ending angles for each.

Creating 3-Point Ellipses

The 3-Point Ellipse tool is the key for creating ellipses while setting a rotation angle (perfect circles show no possible rotation angle; we're talking ovals here). You'll find it grouped with the Ellipse tool in the toolbox, as shown at left.

This tool enables you to create ellipses at precise angles without the need to create and then rotate an existing one, as shown in Figure 8-5. The shape you create is still an ellipse with all associated properties, such as optional pie and arc states.

To create an ellipse using the 3-Point Ellipse tool, use these steps:

1. Choose the 3-Point Ellipse tool, click to define the midpoint of one side of your ellipse, and drag your cursor to define its radius. As you drag the cursor, the angle of the line changes freely. Release the mouse button to define the opposite side of the ellipse.

2. At this point, an angled ellipse preview shape is built on either side of the two points you defined. Your next click will define the final dimension of your ellipse.

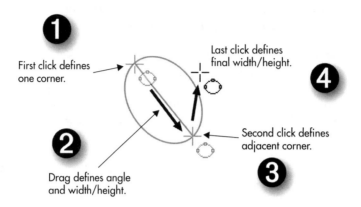

FIGURE 8-5 You can create ellipses at precise angles using the 3-Point Ellipse tool.

Using Polygons and the Property Bar

The Polygon tool (the shortcut is Y) is unique to the category of vector drawing software; competing applications offer a polygon tool, but CorelDRAW's Polygon tool produces shapes that can be edited—making dynamic changes, just like with CorelDRAW rectangles and ellipses. The shapes you create with the Polygon tool can have as few as 3 or as many as 500 points and sides; by default, all polygon sides are straight paths. You'll find the Polygon tool, together with the Spiral, Graph Paper, and other group tools.

While the Polygon tool is selected, the property bar offers the number of sides for the polygon you'll draw; CorelDRAW remembers your last used number of sides from session to session.

Drawing and Editing Polygons

Most of the trick to creating symmetrical, complex shapes with the Polygon tool lies in the *editing* of them. Read Chapter 11 before getting too involved with the Polygon tool, because you really need to know how to use the Shape tool in combination with the property bar to make the most of a polygon shape.

To create a default polygon, use the same click-diagonal drag technique as you use with the Rectangle and Ellipse tools. This produces a symmetrical shape made up of straight paths. Because you'll often want a shape more elegant than something that looks like a snack chip, it helps to begin a polygon shape by holding SHIFT and CTRL while dragging: doing this produces a perfectly symmetrical (not distorted) polygon, beginning at your initial click point and traveling outward. Therefore, you have the shape positioned exactly where you want it and can begin redefining the shape.

Here you can see the Polygon tool cursor and a symmetrical default polygon. Because the Polygon tool can be used to make star-shaped polygons, control points govern the points, and nodes in-between them control the coves between points. When you edit a polygon, the position of these points can be reversed. These control points have no control handles because they connect straight path segments. However, in the following tutorial you'll get a jump start on Chapter 11's coverage of paths and the Shape tool, and in very few steps create a dynamite polygon shape through editing.

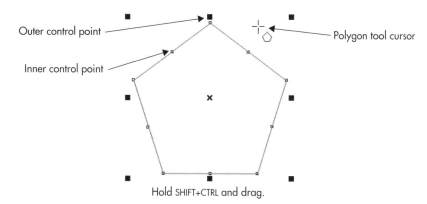

Outer control point

Inner control point

Polygon tool cursor

Hold SHIFT+CTRL and drag.

Here is a brief tour of how to create and then edit a polygon to design any symmetric object you can imagine, and a few unimaginable ones.

Reshaping a Polygon

1. Choose the Polygon tool from the toolbox, and before you do anything else, set the number of sides to 12 on the property bar.

2. Hold CTRL to constrain the shape to a symmetrical one, and then click-diagonal drag on the page. Release the mouse button after you have a polygon that's about 3" wide.

3. To better see what you're doing, left-click over the Color Palette with the polygon selected to fill it. By default, polygons are created with a small stroke width and no fill.

4. Choose the Shape tool from the toolbox. Click any of the control points on the polygon to select it, but don't drag yet. Hold CTRL and then drag outward, to constrain the movement of the cursor so that the polygon doesn't take on a lopsided appearance (although you can create interesting polygons by dragging in any way without holding CTRL). You should have a star shape now, as shown next.

5. Notice that on the property bar you now have a lot of icons that control how line segments pass through nodes and whether the segments are straight or curved. Click any line segment that makes up the polygon; your cursor should have a wiggly line at lower right, as shown next, meaning that you've clicked a line. Then click the Convert To Curve icon on the property bar, converting not only the line, but also all the lines in the polygon that are symmetrical to the chosen line, to a curve.

6. Drag the line you converted to a curve. Doing this, as you can see here, creates an interesting and complex symmetrical shape, and you can now see the control lines for the curves segment and can manipulate the control handles to further embellish your creation.

Figure 8-6 shows but a few creative examples of polygon editing: from gears to those vinyl flowers you put over shower stall cracks; you have immense design power at your disposal with the Polygon tool.

FIGURE 8-6   Shapes you can create using a Polygon object and the Shape tool.

After editing a polygon, you can change the number of sides. For example, you've created a 12-petal flower polygon, and your client wants only 8 petals. You select the edited shape with the Pick tool and then decrease the number of sides using the spin box on the property bar.

Stars and Complex Stars

You have variations on polygons at the ready in CorelDRAW, in the same group as the Polygon tool. The Star tool can be used to create pointy polygons with anywhere from 3 to 500 points. The Complex Star tool creates a number of combined polygons to make a star shape; you can create interesting symmetrical shapes by filling a Complex Star—the result contains both filled and vacant polygon areas as the component paths intersect one another.

Working with the Star Tool

The Star tool produces objects by using the click-diagonal drag mouse technique; CTRL constrains the shape to symmetry, SHIFT lets you drag from the center outward, and CTRL+SHIFT dragging creates symmetrical stars beginning at the initial click point and traveling outward.

On the property bar, when the Star tool is chosen, you have options for the number of points for the star and the "pointiness" (sharpness) of the resulting object—how severe the indents are between points. At a setting of 1, the star object becomes pointy not at all—you'll see that it looks quite like a Polygon tool object. So, if you can make a star using the Polygon tool, why would you ever choose the Star tool? The answer is because the geometric structure of a star shape is always perfectly symmetrical if you use the Star tool. Although you can use the Shape tool to manually tune the sharpness of a Star tool object's points, the angle between points is always consistent. In the next illustration, you can see a Star tool object compared with a Polygon tool object that has been clumsily edited. You can't perform this goof with the Star tool; its interior angles are always mirrored and symmetrical.

Star

Failed attempt at a polygon as a star

Using the Complex Star Tool

Think of the kaleidoscope images you enjoyed as a child (or still do!) when you choose the Complex Star tool, because with only an edit or two using the Shape tool, you can create mesmerizing symmetrical shapes, unlike with any other tool in CorelDRAW.

To use the tool, you know the drill if you've read this far! Click-diagonal drag to create a shape; by default, the complex star has 9 points of a sharpness value of 2 on a 1- to 3-point sharpness scale (available on the property bar, shown next).

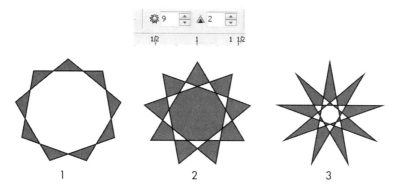

CTRL, SHIFT, and CTRL+SHIFT act as the same modifiers as they do with other shapes. One unique characteristic of complex stars is that they have two control points: one for the inner, negative space, and one for the points. When you edit using the Shape tool, holding CTRL constrains your edits on the control points to symmetry, but if you want a spiral treatment of a complex star, don't hold CTRL, and then drag any way you like on both the inner and outer control points. You'll probably want to assign a fill to a complex star as your first edit because unfilled complex stars aren't as visually interesting. The following illustration shows what you can create by moving the inner control point to outside the outer. Imagine the snowflake patterns you can build; and like snowflakes, no two complex stars are alike!

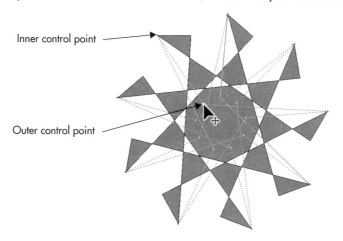

Inner control point

Outer control point

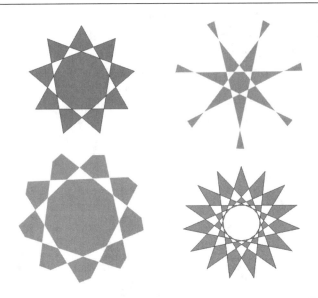

FIGURE 8-7   Complex stars are fast to create, fun to look at, and can serve many design purposes.

Figure 8-7 shows other examples of simply playing with the Shape tool on a complex star object. Also try assigning a wide white outline property to a complex star as a property to create still more variations.

Using the Spiral Tool

With the Spiral tool (press A as the keyboard shortcut), you can create circular-shaped paths that would be tedious if not impossible to create manually. Spiral objects are composed of a single open path that curves in a clockwise or counterclockwise direction. They can also be designed to expand in even segment distances or in *increasing* distances as the spiral path segments travel away from its center (called a *logarithmic* function). You find the tool in the toolbox, grouped with the Polygon and Graph Paper tools.

Spiral tool

Spiral tool options share space in the property bar (shown next) with options for the Graph Paper tool and include Spiral Revolutions, Symmetrical, and Logarithmic Spiral modes, and a Spiral Expansion slider.

The objects you can create can have between 1 and 100 revolutions, each of which is equal to one complete rotation around its center point. The direction of the revolutions is set according to the click-diagonal drag action during creation of the initial shape, as shown in Figure 8-8.

8

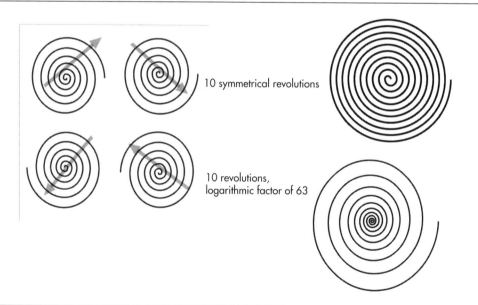

FIGURE 8-8   The direction of your spiral revolutions is determined by your initial click-drag direction.

Spiral objects are not dynamic; no special editing or redefining is possible once the spiral has been created. This means you must set their properties before they are created. Other than your using the Pick or Shape tool to edit its size or shape, spiral objects are a "done deal."

By default, all new spiral objects are set to Symmetrical. If you choose Logarithmic, the Spiral Expansion slider becomes available. Here's how the modes and options affect the spiral objects you can create:

- **Symmetrical vs. Logarithmic** A symmetrical spiral object appears with its spiral revolutions evenly spaced from the center origin to the outer dimensions of the object. To increase or decrease the rate at which the curves in your spiral become smaller or larger as they reach the object's center, you may want to use the Logarithmic method. The term *logarithmic* refers to the acceleration (or deceleration) of the spiral revolutions. To choose this option, click the Logarithmic Spiral button in the property bar before drawing your shape.

- **Logarithmic Expansion option** While the Logarithmic Spiral mode is selected, the Logarithmic Expansion slider becomes available—as well as a value field you can type into—and you can set this rate based on a percentage of the object's dimensions. Logarithmic Expansion may be set from 1 to 100 percent. A Logarithmic Expansion setting of 1 results in a symmetrical spiral setting, while a setting of 100 causes dramatic expansion. If you need a shape that is reminiscent of a nautilus, increase the Logarithmic Expansion to 50 or so.

Using the Graph Paper Tool

The Graph Paper tool (the shortcut is D) is used to create a grid containing hundreds (even thousands) of rectangles—an emulation of graph paper. Graph paper is invaluable in chart-making as well as for artistic uses. You find the Graph Paper tool, shown at left, grouped with the Polygon and Spiral tools. This tool's options on the property bar let you set the number of rows and columns for your new graph paper object. As with the Spiral tool, you must set options *before* drawing your graph paper object; a Graph Paper object cannot be edited dynamically.

The rectangles in a Graph Paper group are, in fact, native rectangles*; you can ungroup the rectangles (CTRL+U) and then make scalloped and rounded rectangles on each and every one of the graph paper component objects.*

Let's explore one of the many creative ways to create and use the group of rectangles the Graph Paper tool builds for you. This next assignment uses the Add Perspective effect to make a dimensional chessboard beneath a drawing of chess pieces and uses one or two tricky editing techniques, but you're guided step by step all the way. Watch how you can dramatically improve the look of a composition just by using the Graph Paper tool and some minor editing.

 ## Power-Drawing a Grid with Graph Paper

1. Open Chess set.cdr. A drawing has been created for you, and your assignment is to put a chessboard behind the drawing.

2. Choose the Graph Paper tool from the toolbox, or press D to select it.

3. Using property bar options, set the number of rows and columns to 8 for your new graph paper object.

4. Using a click-diagonal drag action, hold CTRL and drag to create the new object. Release the mouse button when the graph paper fills the height of the page.

5. Look at the status bar; it tells you that a group of 64 objects is selected. All the graph paper objects can take on a new fill and outline color in one fell swoop: click a medium gray color well on the Color Palette, and then right-click white to make the outlines white.

6. Because the objects are grouped, you have no outline pen width option on the property bar, and the white grouting outlines in this chessboard are a little too thin. No problem: with the Pick tool, right-click over the grouped objects, and choose Properties to display the Object Properties docker. (ALT+ENTER is the shortcut.) Set the outline Width to 2 points now, as shown in Figure 8-9.

7. Choose Effects | Add Perspective. You'll see a red dashed outline with four control points surround the group, but before actually *editing* the Perspective bounding outline—thus distorting its contents—let's perform a transformation.

FIGURE 8-9 Change the outline properties of a group of objects using the Object Properties docker.

8. Choose the Pick tool from the toolbox. Click the selected graph paper object to reveal the rotate and skew handles. While holding CTRL to constrain rotation, rotate the grouped rectangles by 45 degrees. By default, CorelDRAW constrains rotation to 15-degree increments; therefore, having two points of resistance as you CTRL-drag does the trick.

9. Choose the Shape tool (F10); the group's shapes again feature the Perspective control points.

10. Choose the top control point and then drag it down until you have a chessboard in perspective. You will know when you've dragged enough—the chess pieces drawing will visually fit right into place.

Hold CTRL and rotate 45 degrees.

Use Shape tool to drag top node down.

11. Optionally: with the grouped chessboard in its final perspective aspect (get happy with it because this step removes its editing properties), press CTRL+U (Arrange | Ungroup). Fill every other rectangle with a lighter color; doing this enhances the look of the chessboard, the overall illustration, and also lets the cast shadows from the chess pieces become more apparent.

Holding CTRL while you drag constrains the shape of the graph paper object, but not the cells in the graph. Therefore, you could, for example, create a 5-row, 2-column graph whose overall proportions are square, but the cells within the graph paper object would be distorted to rectangles.

Using Perfect Shape Tools

CorelDRAW X5 gives you the power to create objects called *Perfect Shapes*. This group of tools (see the following illustration) helps you to draw shapes, many of which would be a challenge to draw manually, and some of which can be dynamically edited.

Perfect Shapes often feature one or more control points called *glyph nodes*. These nodes enable you to edit specific parts of a specially formatted object dynamically, according to the shape's design. For example, the shape representing a dog-eared page features a single glyph node that enables you to set the diameter of the inner ellipse, leaving the outer diameter unchanged, or a glyph on a beveled rectangle shape enables you to set the bevel depth, as shown in Figure 8-10.

Once a specific Perfect Shape tool is selected, a collection of shapes becomes available on the property bar. Choose a specific type of shape from the property bar Perfect Shapes flyout selector, shown here, *before* drawing.

Click Perfect Shapes button to open the flyout selector.

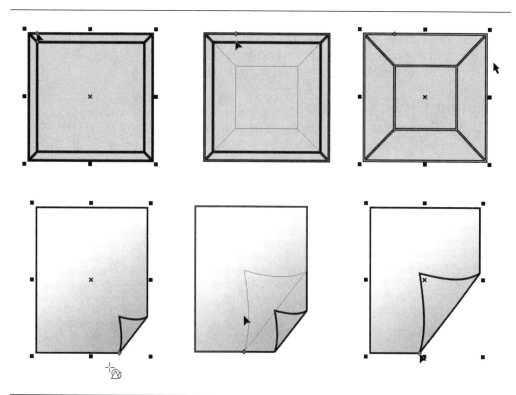

FIGURE 8-10   Glyph nodes can be used to control specific parts of these specially formatted objects.

Walk through these simple steps to quickly arrive at perfection in your CorelDRAW design work.

Creating Perfect Objects

1. Choose a Perfect Shape tool by clicking the toolbox flyout and selecting a category.

2. In the property bar, click the Perfect Shapes selector and choose a symbol. Use a click-drag action to define a size and position. For all symbol types except Callout, the direction of your click-drag won't matter because the symbols are created using a fixed orientation. For Callout shapes, the direction of your click-drag determines the object's orientation.

3. Once your shape has been created, you may notice it includes one or more glyph nodes that control certain symbol properties. In cases where more than one glyph node exists, the nodes are color coded. To position a glyph node, use a click-drag action directly on the node itself.

4. Once your object has been created and any glyph node editing is complete, your other basic shape properties (such as outline and fill) can be changed in the usual way. For example, you can change the width or height of your new shape by using the selection handles.

Editing Glyph Nodes

Glyph nodes are edited in ways similar to the control points on a polygon. As they are moved, the glyph nodes often have the effect of resizing, changing proportion, or dynamically moving a certain part of an individual symbol. Complex symbols can include up to three color-coded glyph nodes.

To explore glyph node editing, take a moment to try this:

1. Choose the Banner Shapes tool.

2. Choose the second style from the left on the property bar.

3. Using a click-diagonal drag action, create a new shape on your page. Notice the shape includes two glyph nodes—one yellow, one red.

4. Click-drag the yellow glyph node up or down to reposition it several times. Notice its movement is horizontally constrained; as it is moved, the vertical width of each portion of the banner changes.

5. Click-drag the red glyph node left or right to reposition it several times. Notice its movement is vertically constrained; as it is moved, the horizontal width of each portion of the banner changes to match your movement, as shown in Figure 8-11.

Glyph nodes can be edited using both the Perfect Shapes tool you used to create the shape and the Shape tool (F10). You can also edit glyph nodes by using the Object Properties docker for a selected Perfect Shape, as shown in Figure 8-12. This docker offers precise control over glyph node position; right-click your shape and choose Properties from the pop-up menu or press ALT+ENTER. Depending on the Perfect Shape you've selected, the Object

Converting Shapes to Curves

Any of the shapes discussed in this chapter can be converted to curves by using the Arrange | Convert To Curves command (CTRL+Q). Using this command removes any dynamic-editing properties. For example, an ellipse shape may be converted to a pie or arc (and vice versa); but after it is converted to curves, you'll no longer have the option of turning the object into a pie wedge. The same applies to rectangles, polygons, and so on. With the exception of the Undo command, once an object is converted to curves, you have no way to return the object to its dynamically editable state.

Glyph nodes

Yellow glyph
node moved up

Red glyph node
moved right

New object shape

Original Shape

Edited Shape

FIGURE 8-11   When movement is vertically constrained, the width of each portion of the
banner changes.

8

Color-coded glyph
node position sliders

Vertical adjustment

Horizontal adjustment

Auto Apply

FIGURE 8-12   Use the Object Properties docker to edit glyph nodes.

Properties docker might display one, two, or more controls. Also, Auto Apply can be locked or unlocked by clicking on the lock button next to Apply. This is a useful feature if you want to adjust several different node positions without CorelDRAW immediately updating a shape several times.

Using the Convert Outline To Object Command

A lot of the shapes covered in this chapter, the spiral in particular, are objects that have outline properties but no fill. So what do you do, for example, if you want a gradient-filled spiral? The Convert Outline To Object command converts any shape's outline properties to a closed path. To apply the command to a selected object, choose Arrange | Convert Outline To Object, or use the shortcut: CTRL+SHIFT+Q. Once the outline is converted, the resulting closed path looks exactly like the shape of the original, except it can be filled because it's not an outline but instead is a closed path object whose shape is based on an outline.

When an object is converted to an outline, CorelDRAW X5 performs a quick calculation of the Outline Pen width applied to the object and creates a new object based on this value. When applying this command to objects that include a fill of any type, a new compound-path object is created based on the outline width. If the object includes a fill of any type, the fill is created as a new and separate object applied with an outline width and color of None. When you're converting open paths, only the path itself is created as a single outline object of the path according to the Outline Pen width applied. Figure 8-13 shows a spiral shape with a thick black Outline Pen width that is converted to outline using the command.

Things are certainly shaping up now, aren't they? You've learned how to create basic shapes and smart shapes, and how to edit them to create scores of original and visually interesting items: think of how your next brochure will look with prices framed in elegant banners, fancy stars, and rounded-corner rectangles. This isn't the half of it; in Chapter 9 you learn to move, rotate, scale, and put your new objects anywhere you like on the page. Arranging and organizing objects is your next destination, and you'll find it to be a moving experience.

Original with 16-point outline applied   New fountain-filled object based on the outline

FIGURE 8-13   When an object is converted to an outline, CorelDRAW X5 performs calculations that create a new object.

CHAPTER 9

Moving, Scaling, Rotating: Basic Transformations

O ften when you create or import an object, it's not exactly where you want it on the page. Or it might be an inch away from where you want it, *and* a little too large. The object might also be rotated a few degrees off from where you want it to be—you get the picture. This chapter covers the common—and not so common—techniques to use in CorelDRAW for transforming objects, from the manual approach to pinpoint-precise numerical entry. You'll soon have the skills and know the steps for composing elements on a page the way you want them, and then you can stop cursing at the cursor.

Basic Object Selection

You choose the Pick tool from the toolbox and then click an object to move, scale, or create other transformations. The easiest way to select more than one object is to hold SHIFT; you then add to your existing selection by clicking other objects. With one or more items selected, you'll notice that information about the selected shapes is displayed on the status bar. The other workspace area to watch is the property bar, which shows the position, size of the selection, and offers options such as the number of degrees to rotate the selected object(s). Also, if you press ALT+ENTER with something selected, the Object Properties docker provides you with not only details about what you've caught, but also the opportunity to quickly *change* many of the object's properties.

Property bar

Status bar

Pick Tool Selections

Pick tool

The Pick tool can be used for several things, the most important of which are to choose an object or several objects, and to create a *change* in the selected object(s) by moving it and adjusting its selection handles.

Clicking an object once selects it. While an object is selected, *selection handles* appear—the eight black markers surrounding the object, as shown in Figure 9-1. Additionally, depending on the type and properties of an object, you'll see *nodes* at various areas around the object, which indicate the control points path (when a vector object is selected) or the edge of an object (when a bitmap is selected). A small *X* marker appears at the centermost point of the object, indicating its center origin. This origin can be moved, is quite useful for defining a center of rotation for an object, and will be discussed later in this chapter.

| NOTE | *Nodes are edited using the Shape tool, covered in Chapter 11. The Pick tool has no effect on nodes.* |

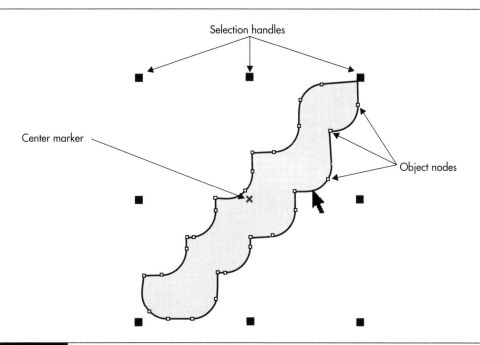

FIGURE 9-1   Select any object with a single click using the Pick tool.

Occasionally you or a coworker will create a shape with an outline stroke that's very narrow and has no fill, and you have trouble selecting the darned thing with the Pick tool. If zooming in doesn't make selecting it any easier, activate the Treat All Objects As Filled option. Open the Options dialog (CTRL+J) and choose Workspace | Toolbox | Pick Tool from the tree at left. Check the Treat All Objects As Filled check box, and then click OK to close the dialog, as shown in Figure 9-2.

Object Selection Techniques

You can use a number of tricks while navigating through a selection of objects or for selecting more than one object at a time using the Pick tool. Many of these object-selection

Check this option to treat all selected objects as though they have a fill.

FIGURE 9-2 Select unfilled objects by clicking anywhere on them using this option.

techniques can also be used in combination with each other as you adopt your own selection technique. Here's how you can make a selection of more than one object in one fell swoop:

- **SHIFT-clicking to select**   Holding SHIFT while clicking an unselected object adds it to your current selection. This also works in the reverse: holding SHIFT while clicking a selected object deselects the object.

- **Marquee-selecting objects**   To select all objects in a specific area, click-drag diagonally with the Pick tool to surround the objects; a dashed blue outline representing the rectangular area of selection appears until you release the mouse button. While you're marquee-selecting, all object shapes completely within the area you define become selected, as shown in Figure 9-3. The complete object's shape must be surrounded for it to become selected. Holding SHIFT while using the marquee-selection technique causes unselected objects to be selected, and it also causes selected objects to become unselected.

- **Holding ALT while marquee-selecting**   If you come to CorelDRAW from Adobe Illustrator, you can use the convention of selecting objects by merely touching a shape in a marquee-selection technique. Holding ALT as the modifier while click-dragging to marquee a specific area causes all objects within—and even those whose *edge* you touch—to become selected. Holding SHIFT+ALT while marquee-selecting causes the reverse to occur, deselecting any objects that are already selected.

FIGURE 9-3   A click-drag with the Pick tool in any direction marquee-selects the objects that are completely surrounded.

The Pick Tool's Shape Tool State

If you're getting an idea that the Pick tool has a host of hidden features, you're right. One of these is its alternate state—the temporary Shape tool state. The Pick tool can temporarily act like the Shape tool while a single object is selected and when held over object nodes. But this isn't its normal behavior, and you need to first enable this feature in Options.

Pick tool as Shape tool   Normal Shape tool states

Normal Pick tool state

Typically, the Pick tool is used for selecting and transforming objects, while the Shape tool is used for editing curves and selecting object nodes. The temporary Shape tool state lets you move object nodes without changing tools.

To access this, choose Tools | Options, and click to select Workspace | Display in the tree directory; then check Enable Node Tracking. This convenience gives you control to modify selected characters in a line of artistic text, to edit open and closed paths, and to modify an ellipse, star, polygon as star, graph paper objects, and even bitmaps. The next illustration shows this temporary state in action; you'll see in your work that when the Pick tool is outside of a shape, it looks like an arrow cursor. However, after an object is selected and the tool is positioned inside a shape, the tool presumes you want to perform an operation such as moving the selected shape, and it becomes a four-headed arrow:

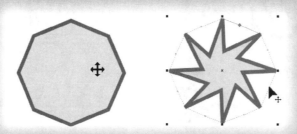

Pick tool moving selected object

Pick tool as Shape tool, moving object with object node selected

- **Pressing TAB to select next object**   Suppose you have a bunch of objects in a document, but some of them overlap, and you're getting nowhere by attempting to click the one you need. Pressing TAB alone while the Pick tool is active selects a shape and causes the next single object arranged directly behind your current selection to become selected (whether or not it overlaps the current object). Holding SHIFT while pressing TAB causes the single object arranged directly in front of your current selection to become selected. This tabbing action works because each new object created is automatically ordered in front of the last created object—no matter how the object was created (for example, using various duplicate, repeat, transformation, or object effect-creation methods). Tabbing cycles through single-object selection on a page, whether you have a current object selected or none at all. The key is to begin tabbing after you've chosen the Pick tool.

- **ALT-click to select objects covered by other objects**   To select an object that is ordered in back of and hidden by other objects, hold ALT while the Pick tool is selected, and then click where the object is located. Each time you ALT-click with the Pick tool, objects that are ordered further back in the stack are selected, enabling you to "dig" to select hidden objects.

TIP *Although you can select nodes with the Pick tool when Enable Node Tracking is active, you can't perform editing operations other than moving a node. To create curves from straight path segments and work with node control handles, you need to use the genuine Shape tool.*

Selecting Objects by Type

So far, you've learned to select any objects on or off your page. But you may also select objects by their type (such as text objects, guidelines, or path nodes) using commands from the Select All menu, shown in Figure 9-4. Each time you use a command, a new selection is made (and any current selection of objects becomes *un*selected).

Here's how each of the commands is used:

- **Select All Objects**   Choosing Edit | Select All | Objects causes all objects in your current document window to become selected. Quicker to use is the CTRL+A shortcut, which accomplishes the same result and is easy to remember because it's used by many professional software programs.

TIP *Double-clicking the Pick Tool button in the toolbox instantly selects all visible objects in your current document window view.*

CAUTION *You can't select what's locked or hidden. Check the status of layers with the Object Manager if there's an object that is apparently nailed to the page!*

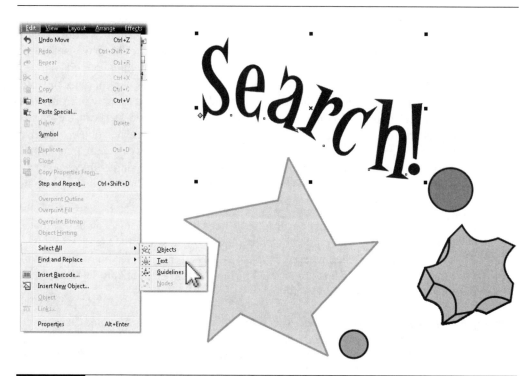

FIGURE 9-4   Select items in your document by using the Select All command.

- **Select All Text**   Choosing Edit | Select All | Text instantly selects all text objects both on and off the current document page. Both artistic and paragraph text objects become selected after using this command (unless they have been grouped with other objects, in which case they are ignored). Text objects applied with effects (such as contour or extrude effects) also become selected using this command.

- **Select All Guidelines**   Guidelines are actually a class of document page objects, different from objects you draw, but objects nonetheless. To select all guidelines on your document page, choose Edit | Select All | Guidelines. Selected guidelines are indicated by a color change (red, by default). To select guidelines, they must be visible and cannot be locked; use the Tools | Object Manager to edit the properties of guidelines before you try to select them. If guidelines you've placed aren't currently visible on your page, choose View | Guidelines.

TIP   *Guidelines can be created using a click-drag action from your ruler onto your document page. Choose View | Rulers to display CorelDRAW's ruler feature.*

- **Select All Nodes**   You must have both the Shape tool and an object selected (closed or open paths qualify) to use this Select All command. Choose Edit | Select All | Nodes to select all of the object's path nodes. For a quicker method in the same situation, use the CTRL+A shortcut. Special CorelDRAW objects such as rectangles, ellipses, and polygons can't be selected this way because their shapes are defined dynamically by "control" points instead of nodes.

 Shapes are often made up of two or more paths that are combined. To select all the nodes on a combined path, first select the object, and then double-click the Shape tool on the toolbox.

Moving Objects

When moving objects, it's important to lift using your legs and position yourself carefully to avoid back injury. However, moving objects in CorelDRAW is a lot less stressful, and you basically have two options: to move objects directly by using the Pick tool and dragging, or to use the keyboard arrow keys to precision-nudge objects in four directions.

 For information on moving and transforming objects, see the section "Applying Precise Transformations" later in this chapter.

Using the Pick Tool

Holding the Pick tool over certain areas of a selected object will cause the tool's positioning cursor to become active, as shown in Figure 9-5. This means a click-drag action on the area will move your selected object(s) in any direction. As you drag your object, you'll see a preview outline, indicating its new position. When the mouse button is released, the move is complete.

 If you're having difficulty selecting and/or moving an object because it's too small, you can increase your view magnification using the Zoom tool, or use the keyboard nudge keys, covered next.

Using Nudge Keys

As an alternative to using the Pick tool, you can also move selected objects by a distance you specify by nudging. You use your keyboard arrow keys; to nudge a selected object, press the UP, DOWN, LEFT, or RIGHT arrow key. Your object will be moved by the nudge value specified in the Rulers page of the Options dialog. You can customize the Nudge

Positioning state of Shape tool cursor   Preview outline

FIGURE 9-5 Moving objects with the Pick tool offers a preview before you actually move them.

distance by opening the Options dialog (CTRL+J), clicking to expand the tree directory under Document, and clicking to display the Rulers options page, as shown here:

You have eight possible directions in which to nudge your artwork. In addition to using an arrow key, you can also press two neighboring arrow keys to perform a diagonal nudge.

Using nudge keys, you can perform moves according to this value, or by larger or smaller values. These respectively are referred to as *super* and *micro nudges*. Like "normal" nudges, these values are set in the Rulers options page. Here are the techniques for using super and micro nudges:

- **Super nudge**   This action moves a selected object in larger increments than a normal nudge. To use super nudge, hold SHIFT while pressing the UP, DOWN, LEFT, or RIGHT arrow key on your keyboard. By default, this causes your selected object to move by 0.02 inch.

- **Micro nudge**   The pint-sized version of a typical nudge is the micro nudge, which moves your object in smaller increments. To use micro nudge, hold CTRL while pressing the UP, DOWN, LEFT, or RIGHT arrow key on your keyboard. By default, micro nudges cause the selected object to move by 0.005 inch.

Transforming Objects

A *transformation* is any type of object shape or position change, short of actually editing the object's properties. This includes changing its position, size, skew, and/or rotating or reflecting it. Dragging an object directly in a document is more intuitive than precision transformations—but both approaches to transformation have their own special advantages. In this section, you'll learn how to apply transformations using both techniques.

Transforming Objects Using the Cursor

For the intuitive method, the Pick tool is what you need to transform objects by the simple act of click-dragging. Depending on the type of transformation you need to apply, you can click-drag any of the four, black, square selection handles that surround the selected object or group of objects to change an object's size *proportionally,* by width only and by height only. Dragging any middle selection handle or side handle scales the object disproportionately—"smoosh" and "stretch" are the more common terms for disproportional scaling; see Figure 9-6.

During transformations, CorelDRAW keeps track of the object's transformed size, position, width, height, scale, and rotation angle. CorelDRAW remembers your object's original shape from the time it was created, regardless of how many transformations have been applied to it. You can remove all transformations and restore the object to its original state in a single command: choose Arrange | Clear Transformations to return your object to its original shape immediately.

9

Original   Proportional scaling   Disproportional scaling

FIGURE 9-6   Dragging these handles changes the size of an object proportionally or otherwise.

While transforming objects, you can constrain certain shape properties by holding modifier keys. Here are the effects of holding modifier keys for constraining a transformed object's shape:

- **To change object size (scale)**   Click-drag any corner handle to change an object's size *proportionally,* meaning the relative width and height remain in proportion to the original object shape. Hold ALT while dragging any corner selection handle to change an object's shape *disproportionally,* meaning width and height change, regardless of original proportions.

- **To change width or height only**   Click-drag any side, top, or bottom selection handle to change the size of the object in the drag direction. Hold SHIFT while doing this to change the width or height from the center of the object, or hold CTRL while dragging to change the width or height in 200-percent increments.

   When transforming an object using the Pick tool, click the right mouse button during the transformation, and then release both mouse buttons to "drop a copy." The active object you're dragging becomes a copy, applying the transformation to a duplicate, not the original. When combined with the CTRL key, this technique is a quick and easy way to mirror a duplicate and make symmetrical compositions.

You can also rotate or skew an object using Pick tool states that become available after you click a selected object a second time—you click an object once that is *already* selected to display rotation and skew controls around the object. This action causes an object (or group of objects) to look like Figure 9-7.

You control the point around which objects are rotated or skewed, by moving the center origin marker (anchor point) of an object or group of objects. Your cursor will change to display either the rotation or a skew cursor when held over a corner or side handle. A good

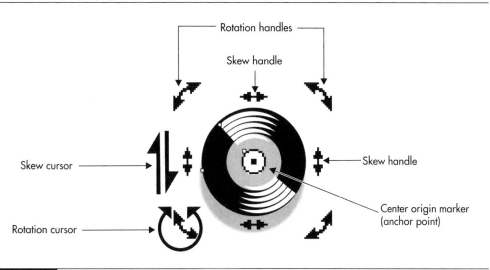

Rotation handles

Skew handle

Skew cursor

Skew handle

Center origin marker
(anchor point)

Rotation cursor

FIGURE 9-7 Clicking a selected object will cause these rotation/skew handles to appear.

creative example of offsetting the original center of an object is shown in the following illustration. The spade shape is a simple extrusion, and by putting its origin at the crosshairs in this illustration, holding CTRL to constrain rotation to CorelDRAW's default of 15 degrees while rotating, and then right-clicking to transform a duplicate, a wonderfully intricate pattern can be made in less than a minute.

 TIP *To flip a selected object quickly, either vertically or horizontally, use the Mirror Vertical and Mirror Horizontal buttons in the property bar while using the Pick tool.*

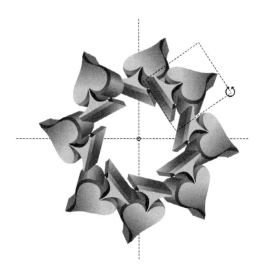

Using the Free Transform Tool

The *Free Transform* tool is the middle ground between controlling transformations entirely with mouse gestures, and the hands-off controls of the Transformation docker. When you use the Free Transform tool, the property bar offers four modes of transformation: Free Rotation, Free Angle Reflection, Free Scale, and Free Skew. Here, Free Angle Reflection is used to mirror the drawing's original location and left-to-right orientation.

Free Transform tool

To transform a selected object in one of these four modes, click to select the mode, and then use a click-drag action on your object. A live preview of the new object's shape appears. While using Rotation or Angle Reflection modes, a reference line appears as you drag to indicate the object's angle transformation from its original state.

Using Free Transform and then applying a little transparency can yield compositions that contain believable reflections. Free Transform works with bitmaps as well as native CorelDRAW vector objects.

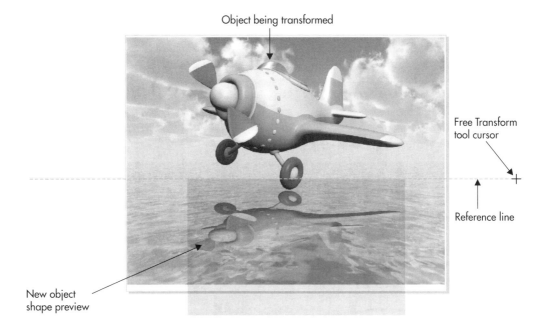

Object being transformed

Free Transform
tool cursor

Reference line

New object
shape preview

9

Copying Effects with the Attributes Eyedropper Tool

You can copy transformations between objects using the Attributes eyedropper tool.
To do this, choose the tool, have both the objects in view, and use these steps:

1. With the tool selected, click the Transformations button on the property bar,
   and then check the individual properties you want to sample. Click OK to
   close the flyout and save your choices.

2. Click the item whose transformation properties you want to sample and apply
   to a different object. Groups of objects do not qualify; however, the PowerClip
   items in the illustration you see next—the silverware drawings—do indeed
   qualify because a PowerClip is seen as a single object.

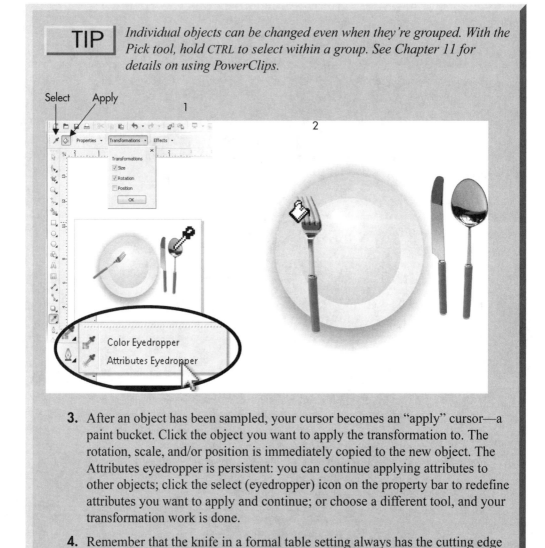

> **TIP** *Individual objects can be changed even when they're grouped. With the Pick tool, hold CTRL to select within a group. See Chapter 11 for details on using PowerClips.*

3. After an object has been sampled, your cursor becomes an "apply" cursor—a paint bucket. Click the object you want to apply the transformation to. The rotation, scale, and/or position is immediately copied to the new object. The Attributes eyedropper is persistent: you can continue applying attributes to other objects; click the select (eyedropper) icon on the property bar to redefine attributes you want to apply and continue; or choose a different tool, and your transformation work is done.

4. Remember that the knife in a formal table setting always has the cutting edge facing left; fortunately, this is a simple transformation.

Applying Precise Transformations

The Transformation docker is terrific for applying multiple transformations with a single command. The docker has five Transformation buttons: Position (Move), Rotate, Scale And Mirror, Size, and Skew, as shown in Figure 9-8. To open the Transformation docker, choose

Rotate   Scale and Mirror   Size

Position

Skew

FIGURE 9-8   The Transformation docker offers precision over position, rotation, size, and skew changes.

Window | Dockers | Transformations, or choose Arrange | Transformations, choose a command, and then click the button that applies to your task.

For all transformations, the procedure is the same: click the button for the type of transformation, enter the values you need, and then click the Apply button in the docker to transform the selected object(s). In this section, you'll learn what each area does for you and the options offered for each.

Using the Transformation Docker

Options in the Transformation docker vary by transformation type. In the illustrations shown in the next few pages, examples show only the specific transformation being discussed.

Positioning (Moving) Objects

Options for the Position page will move your object selection a specified distance, either *vertically* (*V*), *horizontally* (*H*), or to a specific point on your document page, as shown in Figure 9-9.

While the Relative Position option is selected, entering new values and clicking the Apply button causes your objects to move by a specified distance. If the Relative Position

Original position   New position

Object moved 2 inches

FIGURE 9-9   This object was precisely moved by applying a Position transformation.

option is *not* selected, new values you set for absolute, nonrelative position move an object to the absolute location shown on your current ruler position.

Rotating Objects

With Rotate, you can make multiple copies, and enter exact angles of rotation based on degrees and in default increments of 5 using the spin boxes. Figure 9-10 shows two very different results when using relative and absolute positioning and making two copies of the teakettle.

Entering negative values rotates an object clockwise, while positive values cause counterclockwise rotation. Selecting the Relative Center option allows either *V*ertical or *H*orizontal to rotate objects, according to the object's center marker position, and the position of that is specified as either *V* or *H*. You can specify a new center origin position for your object's rotation by changing the existing value in the *H* and *V* boxes. When Relative Center is *not* selected, your object is rotated according to the page center.

Scale and Mirror Objects

The Scale and Mirror transformation has features for entering precise changes in object size. You can also cause the object to be flipped either *V* or *H,* and/or simultaneously, by clicking one of the two mirror buttons, as shown in Figure 9-11.

When the Proportional option is unchecked, your object's new horizontal and vertical scale values are unlinked, meaning you can apply scaling commands to either the width or height, independent of each other. While the Proportional option *is* checked, width and height scaling operations are locked to each other. This means that scaling the width or height by a given percentage value causes the adjacent value to be calculated automatically to preserve your selected object's original proportions.

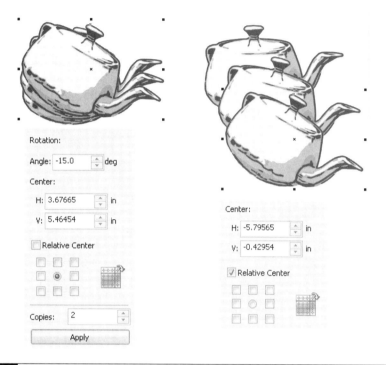

FIGURE 9-10 The Rotation transformation features an offset option when you choose Relative positioning for duplicates of the original object.

FIGURE 9-11 Both Scale and Mirror changes were applied to the drawing.

Sizing Objects

This transformation type gives you the option to change either the *V* and/or *H* measure of an object selection based on the values entered. For example, entering 2 inches in the *H* box and clicking the Apply button causes the selected object to be scaled to a width of 2 inches. When the Proportional option is unchecked, the width and height values can be changed independently. While the Proportional option is selected, width and height values are linked and calculated automatically to alter the size of the object proportionally.

Precision Skewing

The term *skew* means to change the position of two sides of a shape in a parallel fashion while leaving the other two sides alone; *slanting* is a more common term for "skew." The Skew transformation also gives you the chance to apply both vertical and horizontal skew independently or simultaneously by entering degree measures, in turn, transforming the object either *V* or *H*. As with rotation commands, negative degree values cause clockwise skews, while positive values cause counterclockwise skews. Choosing the Use Anchor Point option enables you to specify left, center, right, top, bottom, sides, or corner points as the point around which your objects are skewed, as shown in Figure 9-12. The skewed copy more or less looks like a cast shadow of the original symbol, doesn't it?

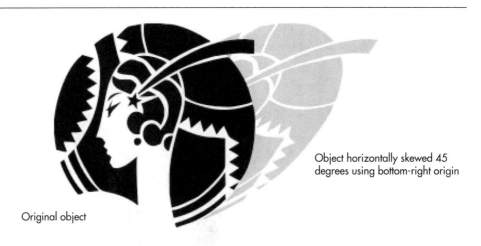

Object horizontally skewed 45 degrees using bottom-right origin

Original object

FIGURE 9-12   A precision Skew changes both the angle and the size of this object in a single command.

Controlling the Order of Things

How your objects are ordered is another consideration when organizing drawing objects in a composition. The order of objects determines whether an object appears in front of—or behind—another object. Your page and the pasteboard (the area surrounding your document page) are always the *backmost* point, while your screen is always the frontmost point. All objects are layered between these two points.

When overlapping objects are ordered, they appear in front of or behind each other, according to their order. As you create each new object, it is put in front of all existing objects *on the current document layer.* Changing the object order lets you rearrange overlapping objects without changing their position on the page. To do this, CorelDRAW has a series of order commands that let you shuffle the order of objects in various ways. You'll find them in the Arrange | Order submenu, but you can also apply them using shortcut keys; a list follows.

> **NOTE** *The* hierarchy *of object ordering on a layer is very different from* object layers. *Although layers each have their own collections of objects that can be ordered in a sequence, the layers* themselves *can* also *be ordered. This means that if you're trying to control the ordering of two or more objects, check the status bar to make sure they're on the same layer. If you skipped over Chapter 4, that chapter explains layers and provides some fun working examples of layers and the Object Manager.*

Here's how each of the object order commands works:

- **To Front Of Page (CTRL+HOME)**   This command puts objects on top of all objects on the uppermost layer. If your composition has only one layer, these two page commands simply do what To Front and To Back Of Layer do. You will receive an attention box concerning moving objects to different layers—you can permanently dismiss this box by checking the Don't Show Warning Again check box.

- **To Back Of Page (CTRL+END)**   The converse of To Front Of Page, this command puts the selected objects on the back of the object order on the bottom layer of the page.

- **To Front Of Layer**   This command shuffles your selected object(s) to the very front of the current layer. Press SHIFT+PAGE UP or choose Arrange | Order | To Front to apply it. The To Front command is also available as a property bar button when an object is selected.

- **To Back Of Layer**   This command shuffles your selected object(s) to the very back of the current layer. Press SHIFT+PAGE DOWN or choose Arrange | Order | To Back to apply it. The To Back command is also available as a property bar button while an object is selected.

- **Forward One**   This command shuffles your selected object(s) forward by one in the object order of the current layer. Press CTRL+PAGE UP or choose Arrange | Order | Forward One to apply it.

- **Back One**   This command shuffles your selected object(s) backward by one in the object order of the current layer. Press CTRL+PAGE DOWN or choose Arrange | Order | Back One to apply it.

- **In Front Of**   This command is interactive and puts your selected object directly in front of any object you specify in the current layer order. A targeting cursor will appear, and you use it to choose which object to shuffle your selection in front of. Choose Arrange | Order | In Front Of to apply it.

- **Behind**   This command also causes a targeting cursor to appear, enabling you to specify which object you want your object selection to be shuffled behind in the object order on the current layer. Choose Arrange | Order | Behind to apply it.

- **Reverse Order**   This command effectively shuffles the order of your selected object so that it's in the reverse of its current order on the layer. Front objects become back objects and vice versa, as shown in Figure 9-13. For example, if your objects were numbered 1, 2, 3, and 4 from front to back, applying this command would cause them to become reordered to 4, 3, 2, and 1. Choose Arrange | Order | Reverse Order to apply it.

Original order

Order after using Reverse Order command

FIGURE 9-13   You can quickly change the order of objects within a layer by using Reverse Order.

TIP   *When changing object order using the Reverse Order command, grouped objects are considered a single object, so their relative order in the group will be preserved. To reorder objects within a group, you'll need to Ungroup (CTRL+U) the objects before applying the command.*

Hopefully this chapter has shown you not only how to transform objects, but also your skill level with CorelDRAW. You now know how to move, scale, rotate, and perform other operations on page objects and their duplicates. You also know how to both manually transform and use the dockers and other features for precise moving and alignment of the elements you need for a terrific design. Chapter 10 takes you into *creating* these shapes that you now know how to move. Put Chapters 9 and 10 *together,* and your family's going to start missing you, because you'll be having too much fun designing to sit down for regular dinners!

PART III

Working with Object Tools

CHAPTER 10

Drawing and Editing Objects

If you thought learning to create basic and smart objects in Chapter 8 was fun and a learning experience, hold on: basic shapes will get your work only so far—CorelDRAW's path-building and editing tools move your cursor toward exactly what you have in mind. The Curve tools group on the toolbox has specific tools for drawing paths of any shape you can imagine, and some you *can't*! In the following sections, you'll work through the process of *editing* lines and their nodes, so there's no reason to draw something that's *close* to what you need. This chapter is the DRAW part of CorelDRAW.

NOTE   *Download and extract all the files from the Chapter10.zip archive to follow the tutorials in this chapter.*

Introducing CorelDRAW X5's Curve Tools

The most basic shape you can draw in CorelDRAW (and in any vector drawing program) is a *line*: a line is a path that passes through at least two points, called *nodes* in CorelDRAW. A line is actually a mathematical equation, and as such doesn't necessarily need an outline color or a width. It doesn't even have to be a straight line, but it does have a *direction*—the direction in which you draw the line. Actually, this is where the fun begins, because you can assign a line scores of different properties: arrowheads, a dotted look for coupons, colors, and varying widths galore. Joining the beginning and end points of a line (a *path*) closes the path, and if the beginning doesn't meet the end point, the shape is called an *open path*.

CorelDRAW X5's Curve tools group is made up of eight virtual pens, shown in Figure 10-1, located between the Zoom/Hand and the Smart tools groups on the toolbox.

The tools are task oriented; although they all produce paths, your choice of tool(s) for a task depends upon what you want to draw. For example, do you need to produce an object whose curves are flawless like those of a physical French curve? This task calls for the new B-Spline tool, although other drawing tools can approximate the same set of curves with

How to Fill an Open Path

Depending on how your CorelDRAW X5 options are currently selected, open-path objects—in which the beginning and end points are not joined—might not be available to apply a fill color to the inside area of the path, mostly because it has no inside. This might seem an inconvenience if you're accustomed to using other applications such as Adobe Illustrator that, by default, normally enable open paths to be filled. In CorelDRAW X5, you can fill an open path, but this option is not turned on by default.

Options are not set to fill open-ended paths, shown next, automatically, but you can change this if you so choose.

Unfilled   Filled

To change CorelDRAW drawing behavior to specify that all open paths be filled—without the need to close the path first—follow these steps:

1. Open the Options dialog by choosing Tools | Options (CTRL+J).

2. Click to expand the tree directory under Document, and click General to display the associated options on the right side of the dialog.

3. Click to select the Fill Open Curves option, and click OK to close the dialog.

After you choose this option, the open paths you draw can have an interior area.

10

a different approach and a little more work. Additionally, the Artistic media tool is prone to producing open paths, not closed ones, and although you *can* close and fill an artistic media path, if drawing an object you can fill is your goal, you'd choose a tool other than Artistic media. You can also "mix and match"; you can begin an object with one tool, and finish it with a different tool—your choice, or choices, depend on the object you want to create. Some of these tools work similarly, so it's best to become acquainted with what the cursors look like, as shown in Figure 10-1.

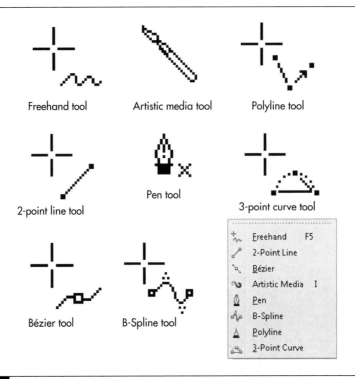

Freehand tool   Artistic media tool   Polyline tool

2-point line tool   Pen tool   3-point curve tool

Bézier tool   B-Spline tool

FIGURE 10-1 For visual reference while you work, each of the different drawing tools has a unique cursor.

Using the Artistic Media Tool

The Artistic media tool treats a path as though it's a skeleton to which you can apply any number of CorelDRAW preset "skins." There are five different types of artistic media "brushes," some with preset variations (the Preset, Brush, and Sprayer artistic media types) and some without presets (Calligraphic and Pressure artistic media types). It helps to think of a "paintbrush" metaphor; by dragging strokes, you'll wind up with anything from complex filigree strokes to elegant calligraphic handwriting. The underlying path to artistic media strokes can be changed at any time, which changes the corresponding look of the media—and you can see the dynamic changes for accurate visual feedback as you work. You can draw while an artistic media effect is enabled, and you can also apply these painterly strokes to existing lines. The Artistic media tool is located in the toolbox with other line-drawing tools.

Brush Sprayer Calligraphic Pressure

Options for current
artistic media type

Preset

Path guiding
shape of stroke

Preset   Brush   Brush   Calligraphic   Pressure

Sprayer

FIGURE 10-2 The property bar offers five different line-drawing modes, each of which has its own options.

10

With the Artistic media tool selected, the property bar offers five different line-drawing modes to choose from, shown in Figure 10-2, each of which has its own options. You have additional options on the property bar, directly to the right of your choice of artistic media, and the options change, depending on the media type you choose.

Applying Presets to Lines

Artistic media is an evolutionary result of CorelDRAW's Powerlines feature. Veteran users will be the most comfortable with the improvements over Powerlines—now called *Presets*— and everyone will be delighted with the new diversity of media types. The Artistic media tool surrounds your drawn lines with specific preset vector objects, which are dynamically linked to the underlying path; you choose from the Preset stroke list in the property bar after choosing a media type. The smoothness and width of the applied effect is set according to the Freehand Smoothing and Width options in the property bar, as shown here:

Freehand Smoothing   Artistic Media Tool Width   Preset stroke list

 TIP *If you've used previous versions of CorelDRAW, you'll notice that the smoothness with which you draw artistic media strokes has been refined quite a bit; you might not need to adjust your strokes for smoothness at all.*

Set the shape using one of the styles in the Preset stroke list. Smoothing is based on percent values between 0 (no smoothing) and 100 (maximum smoothing). Width can be set on a unit measure ranging from 0.03 to 10 inches. As you draw, a path is created in freehand style and immediately applied to your line.

Ready to take the Artistic media tool out for a spin? The following steps walk you through the completion of an illustration—adding cartoon "reaction lines," the sort of emanations a character has when they're struck with a revelation—just to get a feel for how the artistic media's Preset brush works and feels.

 ## Painting with a Drawing Program

1. Open Cartoon Reaction.cdr in CorelDRAW.

2. Choose Tools | Object Manager to make sure Object Manager is checked. In the Object Manager docker, click "add lines here" to select it as the current editing layer if it's not already highlighted. The underlying layer containing the cartoon is locked so it cannot accidentally be moved.

3. Choose the Artistic media tool, then click the Preset icon, the far left button on the property bar.

4. Click the Preset stroke list and choose a style. For this example, choose a style that has a rounded head and that tapers at the end to a point.

5. Think of how you'd draw a cartoon sun; drag strokes so the "sun" is the cartoon fellow's head. The target width for the strokes is about 0.35". If your current stroke width is something different, more's the opportunity to become familiar with artistic media features—while the stroke is highlighted, increase or decrease the width on the property bar.

6. The head of the Preset stroke begins where you begin your click-drag. If you drew a stroke backwards, this is easily fixed. Press F10 to choose the Shape tool, click to select the stroke (you'll see the red underlying path when the stroke is properly selected), and then right-click and choose Reverse Subpaths from the context menu.

7. Click the Artistic media tool of the toolbox, and you're ready to continue stroking. The Artistic media tool is persistent—it "remembers" your last-used stroke settings, styles, and all that good stuff.

8. The preset strokes you create are a special instance of an object surrounding a path. You can, therefore, recolor the default black fill. With a stroke selected, try clicking a color well on the Color Palette. The cartoon fellow's excitement is now in color, as shown in Figure 10-3.

10

Click a color well while the stroke is still selected.

NIGEL IS QUITE CHUFFED OVER THE FIDELITY OF HIS NEW DIGITAL MP3 DOOR CHIMES...

FIGURE 10-3   While a Preset stroke is selected, you can change its width, smoothness, and color.

9. Let's say you want to get adventurous and change the preset for one of the strokes. If the stroke is selected, you choose a different Preset stroke from the drop-down list…and every subsequent stroke you make will have its style. If you've deselected a stroke and want to change it, choose it with the Pick tool, and then use the drop-down list. It's important that you *click the edge of a stroke on the page* and *not its center.* The center of the drawn stroke is the parent—the *control curve* to which the stroke is applied—and it has no properties like the artistic stroke does. Alternatively, you can click (don't click-drag, though) a stroke on the page to select it, and then change the Preset stroke. Class dismissed, go answer that doorbell.

TIP   *If you're experimenting and turned the Freehand smoothing down to 0 while painting with the Artistic media tool, the result might be a stroke that has more nodes than you'd like, to create a smooth arc or straight line. At any time, you can choose the Shape tool, click the stroke to reveal its nodes, and then marquee-select all the nodes. Then use the Reduce Nodes spin box on the property bar to remove superfluous nodes along the path that is driving the artistic media stroke.*

Drawing with Brushes

In Brush mode, you can simulate the look of traditional, natural media, that looks very similar to the brushes in Corel Painter, with a notable exception. Because beneath an artistic media stroke lies a skeleton path, the strokes you make can be edited ad infinitum. In contrast, bitmap paint programs such as Corel Painter and Adobe Photoshop feature brushstrokes that can't be edited after making them—it's a done deal after you paint a stroke. As with the Presets category, artistic media brushes extend the full length of every path you create. Here's what the property bar looks like, and what your options are, when you choose the artistic media brush:

The Brushstroke list box offers a variety of different styles, only six of which are shown in Figure 10-2. Freehand Smoothing and Stroke Width options are used to change the appearance of the graphical object—the "skin"—applied to the underlying path.

 CAUTION *As with all trash-can-shaped Delete icons and buttons, don't click the Delete brush button unless you truly understand the consequences of deleting something (and your decision-making ability can be verified by friends).*

You can draw using a brush style, or alternatively, apply one to an existing line. To draw using a brushstroke, choose the Artistic media tool, and use property bar options to choose a brush style. Begin drawing by click-dragging on your page in a stroking motion. To apply a new brushstroke to an existing line, select the line using the Artistic media tool, choose the Brush mode, and use property bar options to choose a width and brushstroke style. You can load saved brushes by clicking the Browse button in the property bar, and save your own objects as brushstrokes and add them to the existing Brushstroke list. This is fun and useful stuff, as the following steps walk you through how to create, save, and use a custom brush.

TIP *By default, saved brushes can be found in C:\Users\(Your user account name)\ AppData\Roaming\Corel\CorelDRAW Graphics Suite X5\Draw\CustomMediaStrokes.*

Creating and Saving Your Own Brushstroke

1. Open Toothpaste ad.cdr. The layer with the image is locked, and the current editing layer should be above it—check Object Manager to ensure this before you begin.

2. Take a look at the light purple grouped object at the lower left of the page. This is a simple example of using the blend effect and then adding a few objects for highlights. Create something similar to this for these steps. See Chapters 8 and 21 if you don't already know how to build such a drawing; you can use the grouped objects to get right to these steps.

3. Select the shape(s) and then choose the Artistic media tool. Click the Brush button on the property bar.

4. Click the Save icon; save the stroke to whichever folder CorelDRAW offers (to make it easy to find later), give the stroke a name, and then click Save, as shown in Figure 10-4. Brush objects are saved using Corel's standard presentation file format (CMX).The next time you choose the Artistic media tool's Brush, a thumbnail preview of your custom brush is at the top of the drop-down list.

5. After you click Save in the Save As dialog, your new brush is immediately available for use. Try slowly click-dragging the brush above the toothpaste to write "New"; try stroking a daub of toothpaste on the toothbrush. The only thing you should watch out for is creating sudden changes in direction with your stroke, especially when the brush contains several small objects, as this toothpaste custom brush does. The brush has a difficult time negotiating sudden direction changes in the underlying path, and you might find unappealing corners in the resulting brushstroke.

6. Tutorial's done. Don't forget to brush twice a day.

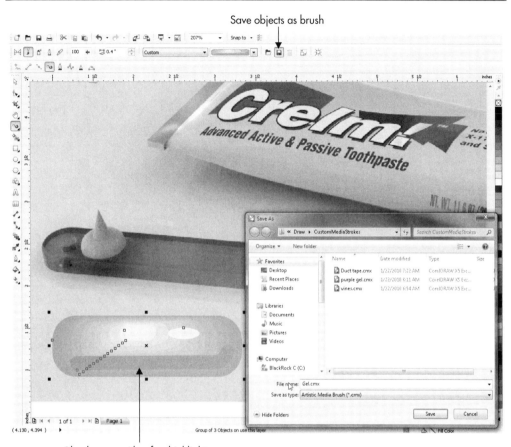

Blend group with a few highlights

FIGURE 10-4   The easiest part of building a custom brush is saving it.

Applying the Sprayer

The Artistic media tool's Sprayer mode is used to pepper the drawing page with a sequence of drawings, either by using your own that you save as a brush, or by choosing a preset from CorelDRAW's Sprayer collections. The Sprayer is quite like the Image Hose in Corel Painter, except changes to the underlying path and the objects used in a spray can be dynamically made at any time. The Sprayer objects repeat uniformly or randomly across the full length of a path. The Size/Scale, Spray Order, Dabs, Spacing, Rotation, and Offset values can be set using the property bar, shown in Figure 10-5.

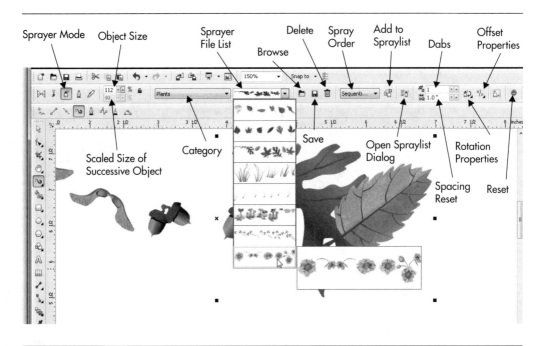

FIGURE 10-5 The Sprayer mode of the Artistic media tool offers a huge number of design variations.

Here's what the Sprayer property bar options give you control over:

- **Object Spray Size/Scale** These two options control the initial object size of the sprayer style (the objects that make up a specific spray type) based on a scaled percentage of the original spray object selected. When the Size/Scale options are locked, you can set the scaling of successive objects to be increased or reduced in scale relative to the size of the first object in the sprayer style.

- **Spray Order** This option lets you set the ordering of the sprayer objects: Randomly, Sequentially, or By Direction. If the sprayer style features only one object to vary, changing this option has no effect. Try the mushrooms preset; the Spray preset contains several different objects of different sizes, and you can get different looks by choosing Randomly and By Direction.

- **Dabs and Spacing** These two values set the *number of objects* to be placed along a drawn or existing path and *the distance between* the centers of each object. *Dabs* are the individual objects in the sprayer style; *Spacing* controls how many objects appear within a given distance. Think of Spacing as "population."

- **Rotation**   This option is used to set the angle for the first object of the sprayer style. The *Increment* option is used to compound rotation values for each subsequent object. Rotation angles and increment values can be based on the degree measure relative to the page or the path to which the objects are applied. For example, if you need a circular pattern whose objects are oriented toward the center of the circle, the rotation option is the ticket.

- **Offset**   This option sets the distance between the path you click-drag and the sprayer objects. *Offset* can be set to be active (the default) at settings between roughly 0.01 and 13 inches. The direction of the offset can also be set to Alternating (the default), Left, Random, or Right. To deactivate the Offset options, uncheck the Use Offset option in the selector, which sets the Offset measure to 0.

- **Reset**   Clicking this button returns all sprayer style settings in the property bar to their original default settings.

As with other Artistic media tool modes, you can draw while applying this effect, or apply an artistic media stroke to an existing line.

With a sprayer style applied and the line selected, you can use property bar options to edit the effect. Doing this edits the style *only as it is applied to your line* and *not* in the original style in the Sprayer file list. Figure 10-6 shows a sampling of the available sprayer styles applied using default settings.

10

FIGURE 10-6   These are a few of the sprayer styles available in CorelDRAW X5.

TIP *To create your own Sprayer brush, first open the Artistic media docker (Window | Docker | Artistic Media). Create several shapes—they can be groups of objects, and they can contain any fill you like—and then arrange them horizontally on the page. Select them, and then click the Save button at the bottom of the docker. Saving and choosing sprayers to use is almost identical to the way you save and use brushes.*

Calligraphy Pens and Applying Media

The Calligraphy tool mode produces results similar to adjusting the nib shape with any regular Pen tool; however, the width and angle can be conveniently changed dynamically when you use the Calligraphy tool. Additionally, your artistic approach with this tool is different than with drawing paths—you click-drag to produce an entire stroke instead of click-dragging to set a node and a path segment.

You have three options on the property bar when Calligraphic is selected: the Freehand smoothing (the degree of accuracy when you click-drag); the Stroke width, which sets the maximum width (because calligraphic stroke are alternately thick and thin); and the Calligraphic angle (increasing values in this field rotates the stroke evaluated from the vertical in a counterclockwise direction).

Freehand Smoothing   Stroke Width   Calligraphic Angle

If you use a mouse as an input device instead of a digitizing stylus, using the Calligraphy tool to draw elegant curves and handsome signatures becomes problematic. A mouse simply cannot express the degree of accuracy a tablet and stylus do. This doesn't have to be an obstacle to creating calligraphic designs, however. Follow this tutorial to learn how to apply a Calligraphic property—and any artistic media except Pressure—to an *existing* path.

Defining and Applying Calligraphic Brushstrokes

1. Open the Calligraphy.cdr file. There is a thin centerline on the top, unlocked layer. The bottom layer is just for reference. Mistral was used as the typeface and is a good example of calligraphic swoops, curves, and turns. Keep reading this chapter to learn how to guide a pen tool to create a similar centerline trace over a typeface.

2. With the Pick tool chosen, select the lowercase *a* after the initial *C*.

3. Choose the Artistic media tool, and then click the Calligraphic tool on the property bar. Do not deselect anything.

4. Here's the trick: click either the up or down elevator button to the right of the Width field (or type **.2** or **.1** in the field instead of using the elevator buttons). What you've done is get the Calligraphic pen to "recognize" that you want to change a value of the selected path's calligraphic width. The change isn't important, it's the recognition that applies the calligraphic property to the selected stroke.

5. Continue to adjust the Width (.2" works well at the path's scale here), and then play with the Angle—anywhere from 35° to 55° will look good in this example.

6. Because you began with an existing stroke, the calligraphic treatment has an outline and no fill. Click the black color well on the Color Palette, and then right-click the No Fill color well to remove the outline.

7. Perform steps 2–6 with the initial *C,* and then with the brush, dot the *i.*

Create a value change by clicking the elevator buttons.

Pressure Mode

The last of the artistic media modes was created for users of digital tablets; if you own a stylus and tablet, you can set up the drivers for the stylus to apply pressure, and CorelDRAW will read stylus pressure to vary the width of the stroke as you drag across the page. You have Freehand smoothing and Width controls on the property bar.

If you're using a mouse, you can:

● Hold the DOWN ARROW key to make the line smaller as you drag.

● Only after using the DOWN ARROW key, press the UP ARROW key to widen the stroke as you click-drag. The maximum width is the value in the num box, and you cannot exceed this width, so plan ahead.

Honestly, don't expect world-class art using the mouse and arrow keys; you might run into a design situation where you need to vary the width of a stroke, but there are other ways to edit an existing stroke that produce more refined results.

How to Draw in CorelDRAW

Using artistic media is fun and useful, but it's now time to learn how to build paths instead of brushstrokes. In the same group of Curve tools, you'll find CorelDRAW's path and node creation pens. They're used for both accuracy and artistic expression, and they have varying degrees of ease of use that correspond directly to their power.

Drawing with Freehand and Polyline Tools

The *Freehand* and *Polyline* tools share a common function, giving you the freedom to draw as if you were sketching by freehand on a physical sketchpad, but the tools work in slightly different ways. Sketched lines can create a single open or closed vector path. Both tools are in the toolbox, grouped with other line-creation tools. For mouse users and stylus users alike, click-dragging initially produces a start node for a path segment and then a path segment that follows; a node is placed when you release the mouse (or stylus) button, setting the end of the path segment. To use these tools:

1. Begin by selecting either the Freehand or Polyline tool. Your next step depends on which tool you choose.

2. If you chose the Freehand tool, you can create a continuous line by click-dragging a path shape. As soon as the mouse button is released, the line is complete, shown next. To draw a straight line between two points, click once to define the start point and a second time somewhere else to define the end point. As soon as you release the mouse button, the curve is complete.

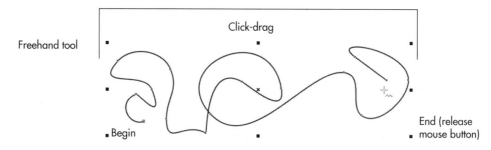

3. If you chose the Polyline tool, the technique is slightly different. Use a click-drag action to create a continuous freehand-style line, but after you release the mouse button, your cursor can continue extending the curve with path segments. You click-drag to freehand-style extend the path, or single-click to add a straight line path segment. A double-click action at your final point defines it as the end point.

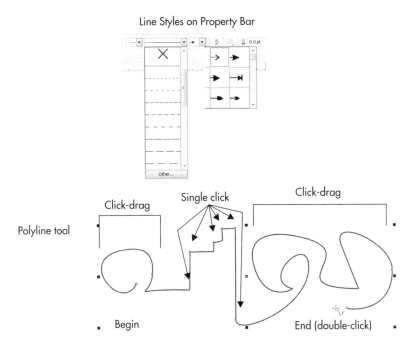

4. Both tools produce "bare bones" paths—no fancy strokes, no elegant calligraphic varying widths. This means you can use the property bar options to make your path begin with an arrowhead, make the line a dashed line, and change the stroke width.

Using either of these line tools, you have control over the smoothness of path shapes drawn using click-drag actions by adjusting the Freehand Smoothing option in the property bar *before* drawing your path. You can control smoothness after *drawing* a path by selecting nodes with the Shape tool and then using the Reduce Nodes spin box. Reduce Nodes has a range between 0 and 100 percent; lower values apply less smoothing, and higher values apply more smoothing, as shown in Figure 10-7.

Original Freehand path (no smoothing)

Path after applying Reduce Nodes

FIGURE 10-7   Freehand Smoothing and Reduce Nodes can change a crude drawn line into smooth curves.

Drawing Arcs with the 3-Point Curve Tool

The *3-point curve tool* was created for artists to build perfectly smooth arcing line segments, with complete control over the direction and steepness of the curve between two points. Making a smooth arc is accomplished in three steps, and you can then *extend* the curve by beginning a new 3-point curve at the first curve's end point, to then close the two curves as a single object.

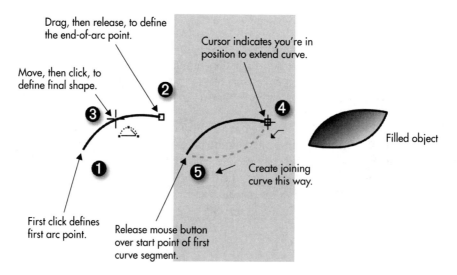

You'll quickly discover that part of the power of the 3-point curve tool is its use in building a series of connected arcs: you can design French curves and ornamental borders by

FIGURE 10-8   You can create smooth, connecting arcs quickly by using the 3-point curve tool.

designing a 3-point curve, positioning your cursor over the end point until you see the cursor signifying an extension of the last-drawn curve, and then building another 3-point curve. This is how the head, eyes, and pupils of the cartoon tabby cat in Figure 10-8 were drawn. Open Ginger tabby.cdr and take the 3-point curve tool out for a spin; Ginger tabby finished.cdr is the completed illustration you see here. The goatee was drawn using the artistic media Brush mode.

Using the Bézier and Pen Tools

The *Bézier tool* and the *Pen tool* are variations on the same theme of drawing connected curves and straight segments (unlike the 3-point curve tool) through the action of first clicking to set a path point, and then either dragging to define a curve behind the click point, or by clicking (no dragging) to define a straight path segment behind the click point. You'll find these tools grouped together with other line-drawing tools.

One of the less obvious differences between the two tools is that the Pen tool offers a "look ahead" point when you draw with it: before you click or click-drag a point, the proposed path between the point before you click and the previous (already defined) point on the path is shown in light blue. When you're just beginning with CorelDRAW, the choice between these tools might seem to be:

- The Pen tool provides intuitive results when you want a path that has both straight segments and curves.

- The Bézier tool excels at creating curved segments that are joined smoothly, and when straight segments are not your design goal.

The Science of Béziers

Bézier curves (pronounced *bezz-ee-aye*) were named after French engineer Pierre Bézier, who published papers on their use after seeing the need for mathematically describing very smooth curves that are easy to manipulate, to design automobile bodies. A Bézier curve is a parametric curve, which means it approximates a curve through 2D space, using a convex control hull that can be described by two points on a curve, and two points off the curve (called *control handles* in CorelDRAW) for intuitively reshaping the curve. The Bézier tool by its nature creates smooth connections between path segments, through the action of click-dragging to set a path point while at the same time defining the slope of the curve segment that is created behind the newly created point. When control points are on a curve, they are called *nodes* in CorelDRAW. You can also create straight path segments between curves by using the Bézier tool; it's a matter of technique. Click-dragging creates smooth curves that have smooth connections between segments, and the act of clicking without dragging sets a path point that is not smooth—if you click again in a different location, a straight path segment is the result.

Because the Bézier tool can produce both curved and straight path segments, there is almost no distinction between the terms *line* and *curve* in the discussions in this chapter. The shapes of Bézier lines are controlled in part by node properties and by the position of curve handles. Two paths can have nodes in the same relative page position, but they have completely different shapes (as shown in Figure 10-9).

Same Node Positions

FIGURE 10-9 These two paths each have the same relative node positions, but node properties make them appear completely different from each other.

Nodes and Control Points

Depending on the type of math used to describe a vector path, *nodes* (points) connect a beginning and end point, and the nodes have *control handles,* at the end of which are *control points,* the screen element you use to manipulate curves. The number of control handles and points depends on the segment connected by each node. For example, an arc (a curve) connected to a straight line segment has one control handle visible, and it controls the slope of the curve segment. When two curve segments are connected, you'll see two control handles if you click the connecting node with the Shape tool, and this node can have different connection properties (cusp, smooth—described later in this chapter). A straight path segment can be described as two nodes connecting the segment, and the control handles for the nodes coincide in position with the node itself. For all intents and purposes, the control handles can't be seen; they become visible when the segment is changed to a curved segment. The control handles appear on the segment, and you can move them away from the launch point of the curve and then freely manipulate the slope of the curve by dragging the control points.

Nodes can be defined as Cusp, Smooth, or Symmetrical, as shown in Figure 10-10. *Cusp* nodes can be used to create a discontinuity in direction between two line segments; in English, the two segments connect in a non-smooth fashion. Think of the moon being on the cusp; it's crescent shaped and this is the sort of shape you can create using cusp node connections. *Smooth* nodes cause the path slope and direction to align on either side of a node; their relationship is in 180-degree opposition, which has the effect of creating a smooth transition at the node point itself. Control handles surrounding a smooth node may be unequal distances from the node. *Symmetrical* nodes are not only smooth, but the control

10

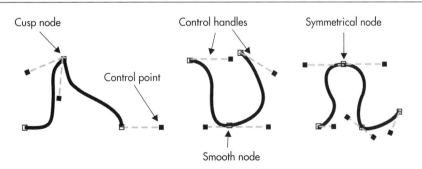

FIGURE 10-10   These paths use different node connection properties.

handles are also of equal distance from the node. You'll immediately appreciate the effect of a symmetrical node; when you drag one control point away from a node, the opposing control handle moves an equal distance from the node in exactly the opposite direction. The artistic effect is that the two joined path segments take on an almost circular appearance, which is very useful for technical illustration work.

Drawing with the Bézier and Pen Tools

Both of these tools are used to create compound paths (segments connected by a common node) by combining a series of clicks or click-drags, but each is used in slightly different ways for different results. Using either of these tools, single-clicks define new node positions joined by straight segments. Curve segments are created by clicking to define the node position, and then *dragging* to define the curve shape. Click-dragging in succession creates a continuous curved path shaped by multiple nodes and off-the-curve control handles. While using the Bézier tool, each click-drag defines and completes the curve segment. A little differently, while using the Pen tool, the cursor remains active, and a preview of the next curve segment appears, so you can define both the curve shape and the next node point. Double-clicking ends the series of path segments.

 When drawing with the Bézier tool, holding CTRL as you click to create new nodes constrains their position to align vertically, horizontally, or within constrained angles relative to the last created node position. Holding CTRL while dragging curve handles constrains their angles to 15-degree increments relative to the last node created.

Let's try out a new drawing method.

 ## Drawing Curves and Straight Line Segments

1. Choose either the Bézier tool or the Pen tool, and use a single click to define the first node position of your path. Click again to define a second point somewhere else on your page. The two nodes are now joined by a straight line.

2. Using the click-drag mouse technique, click to define your next node position, but continue dragging in any direction. As you drag, the second and third nodes are joined by a curved line.

3. If you chose the Bézier tool, you'll notice that two control handles appear joined by a dotted line. The point you are dragging is the control point that steers the control handle. The farther you drag the control point from the node, the larger the arc of the curve becomes. Release the mouse button and notice that the control handles remain in view, and your path is complete unless you'd like to move a node or refine the position of its control points some more.

4. If you chose the Pen tool, you'll notice that a preview of your next curve appears as you move your cursor, which remains active until the next node is defined. To specify a node as the last in the path, double-click to define the current node as the last point.

5. Using either tool, click your cursor directly on the first node you defined. This action closes the path and automatically joins the first and last nodes.

Editing Bézier Paths

All lines are controlled by properties of the nodes they include, which are edited using the Shape tool (F10). You'll find this tool, shown next, grouped with the Smudge Brush, Roughen Brush, and Free Transform tools.

Using the *Shape tool,* you can change node positions and curve shapes by click-dragging the nodes, their control points, and by directly click-dragging on a path segment. While using the Shape tool, icons appear on the property bar when one or more nodes are selected; you can select several nodes to change by marquee-dragging them or by SHIFT-clicking a few. These icons are used to set node attributes to Cusp, Smooth, and Symmetrical; to join node and break nodes to create individual path segments; and to create straight lines from curves (and vice versa) when you've selected a segment or a node connecting segments. The bevy of additional functions on the property bar provides exceptional control and flexibility in your design work. In short, get to know the functions for the Shape tool! The options are called out in Figure 10-11.

Each of these buttons changes the selected nodes, lines, and curves in specific ways. The following is a description of what the icons do and what they're called:

- **Shape Tool Selection Mode**   New to CorelDRAW X5, this mode can be used to marquee-select nodes the way users always have, by click-dragging a rectangular shape around the nodes you want to select, or by using Freehand style, which produces a lasso-like marquee you can use to be exacting about which nodes in a group you want to edit.

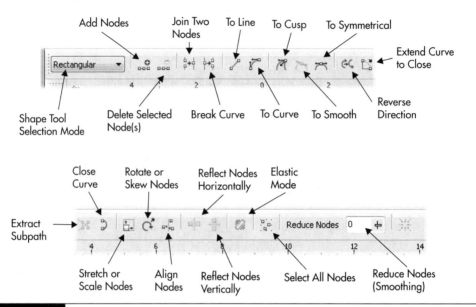

FIGURE 10-11   The property bar offers comprehensive control over path and node properties.

- **Add/Delete Nodes**   These buttons give you the power to add new nodes to a curve or to delete selected nodes after you've drawn a path, using the Shape tool and clicking at specific points on a path. To add a node, click any point on a line to highlight the new position, and then click the Add Node button. You can also add a new node to a line by clicking one or more nodes, and then clicking the Add Node button to add a node midway between the selected node and the next node on the path. Pressing the plus (+) key on your numeric keypad achieves the same thing, and you might find this a quicker method. To delete a node, click to select it with the Shape tool, and click the Delete Node button. You can also marquee-select (drag diagonally with the Shape tool to create a rectangle surrounding the nodes) and then delete all the selected nodes in one fell swoop. Pressing the minus (–) key on your numeric keypad or your DELETE key also deletes selected nodes.

- **Join Two Nodes/Break Curve**   When two unconnected nodes on an open path are selected, for example, when the start point is close to the end point, clicking the Join Two Nodes button connects them to create an unbroken path. On single paths, only the unjoined beginning and ending nodes may be joined. On compound paths (paths that aren't necessarily close to one another, but that have been joined using the Arrange | Combine command), the beginning and ending nodes selected on two existing—but separate—paths can also be joined. While a single node is selected or while a specific point on a segment is clicked, clicking the Break Curve button results in two nodes becoming unjoined, in turn breaking a closed path into an open path.

TIP   *Unjoined paths are not the same as separate objects. Two paths, for example, can be located nowhere near each other on a page and yet still be part of a single path. If you want to break a path into its component subpaths, you first select the nodes using a marquee-selection technique with the Shape tool, click the Break Curve button, and then choose Arrange | Break Curve Apart. Pressing CTRL+K is the shortcut, and it's one of a handful of essential CorelDRAW shortcuts you'll want to commit to memory.*

- **Convert Line to Curve/Convert Curve to Line**   These two buttons are used to toggle the state of a selected straight line to a curve state, and vice versa. A single click with the Shape tool selects a line or curve indicated by a round black marker on the line. When curves are converted to lines, the path they follow takes on a shortcut (as in "the shortest distance between two points"); when converting a straight line to a curve, the path remains the shape, but control handles appear directly on the "line," and the quickest way to make the control points visible is to drag on the line to force it into a curve shape. When a curve is selected, you can also adjust the shape of the curve using a click-drag action at any point on the curve and dragging to reposition the path followed by the curve.

- **Extend Curve to Close**   For this command to be available, you must have both the beginning and ending nodes of an open path selected (marquee-select the points, or SHIFT-click to select them both). Under these conditions, clicking the Extend Curve To Close button joins the two nodes by adding a straight line between them and closes the path.

- **Close Curve**   While an open path is selected, clicking this button joins the beginning and end nodes to form a closed path by adding a new straight line between the two nodes; it's a similar command to Extend Curve To Close, but depending on the closeness of the start to the end path nodes, you might not even see a visible straight line connection. You can also join the end points of a selected curve by using the Close Curve option in the Object Properties docker opened by pressing ALT+ENTER; then click the Curve tab to find the Close Curve check box.

- **Reverse Direction**   While a curve path on a line is selected, clicking this button has the effect of changing the direction of the path. By doing this, the start point of the path becomes the end point (and vice versa). The results of using this command button are most noticeable when the start or end of the line or path has been applied with an arrowhead, meaning the arrowhead is applied to the opposite end of the line or path. You may also notice subtle changes in the appearance of line styles applied to a path after using this command button.

10

In addition to making arrowheads point in the right direction, Reverse Direction is also a handy way to enforce PostScript conventions when you print to a PostScript printer. Adobe Systems' PostScript language is a page description language that has very fixed and definite rules about the direction of paths in a compound shape, such as the letter o. If your compound path o appears to be filled and not hollow, it's not "speaking" PostScript language. You click the subpath of the compound path, reverse the path direction using this button, and the o will then print properly.

- **Extract Subpath** This option becomes available only when a compound path is selected by clicking one of its nodes with the Shape tool. After you click the Extract Subpath button, the selected path is separated from the compound path, converting it to a separate path. Using this command on a compound path composed of only two different paths is essentially the same as using the Break Apart command. It's more useful when you need to extract a specific path from a compound path made up of three or more paths.

- **Stretch or Scale Nodes** This is a very powerful CorelDRAW feature not available in competing applications. When at least two nodes on a path are selected, clicking the Stretch Or Scale Nodes button allows the transformation between nodes using their relative distance from each other vertically, horizontally, or from center. Eight selection handles become available, just as with object selection using the Pick tool, and you can use a click-drag action from any corner or side selection handle toward or away from the center of the node selection. Holding SHIFT constrains the stretch or scale operation from the center of the selection.

- **Rotate or Skew Nodes** Similar to Stretch Or Scale Nodes, when at least two nodes on a path are selected, clicking the Rotate Or Skew Nodes button lets you rotate or skew the selected nodes; this is a great feature for refining a shape just a little, and also for creating more dramatic appearance changes (see the following illustration). Eight selection handles appear, and you can click-drag from any corner selection handle to rotate the nodes in a circular direction either clockwise or counterclockwise. Dragging from any side handle enables you to skew the node selection either vertically or horizontally.

- **Align Nodes**   When two or more nodes are selected, clicking this button opens the Align Nodes dialog, where you choose among the Align Vertical or Align Horizontal options that automatically align your node selection accordingly. In addition to these options, while only the beginning and ending nodes of an open path are selected, you can also choose to align control points. This has the effect of moving the two end points of the line to overlap each other precisely. This is a wonderful command for quickly sketching a zigzag (perhaps for an illustration of a saw blade), and then in one step, aligning the nodes to create a precise illustration.

- **Reflect Nodes Horizontally/Vertically**   These two buttons become available when two or more nodes are selected. You use these options to move nodes by using nudge keys (the UP ARROW, DOWN ARROW, LEFT ARROW, and RIGHT ARROW keys on your keyboard) or using click-drag actions in opposite directions.

> **TIP**   *To quickly access the same eligible Shape tool node and curve commands available using buttons in the property bar, right-click the nodes or segments of a path, and choose commands from the pop-up menu.*

- **Elastic Mode**   With this command, you move selected nodes according to their relative distance from each other; the effect is like experimenting with a rubber band. For example, while a collection of nodes is selected, dragging one of the nodes causes the others to be dragged a shorter distance in relation to the node that is being dragged. While Elastic mode is off, all the selected nodes are moved equal distances. Try this option to add a more organic and natural feeling to a drawing you might feel looks a little too studied and stiff; it adds expression to a path.

- **Reduce Nodes**   When you use this command, CorelDRAW evaluates the overall shape based on the nodes you've selected, deletes nodes that deviate from a predictable course along the path, and then repositions the remaining nodes—the effect is to smooth the curve. For past CorelDRAW users, this was called the Curve Smoothness slider. To use this feature, select the nodes controlling the segments you want to smooth, and drag the Reduce Nodes slider control position toward 100. As you drag the slider, the shape of the curves becomes smoothed, and you'll notice that superfluous nodes disappear from the curve. This option is useful for smoothing lines drawn using the Freehand tool with either the mouse or a digitizing tablet stylus.

- **Select All Nodes**   This button selects all the nodes in a path (or compound path) using one click. It's a great feature for users who aren't expert with the marquee-selection dragging technique yet. You may also select all the nodes in a path with the Shape tool by holding CTRL+SHIFT and clicking any node on the path.

10

TIP | *To quickly switch from Rectangular to Freehand node-selecting mode, hold ALT. Any nodes located within the area you lasso are selected.*

Are you ready to test-drive the Shape tool? Follow along here.

 Editing Paths with the Shape Tool

1. Choose the Ellipse tool (F7) and create an ellipse of any size. Convert the ellipse shape to curves (CTRL+Q) to create a closed path with four nodes joined by four curved lines.

2. Choose the Shape tool (F10). Notice that the property bar now features all the line and node command buttons. Click the Select All Nodes button to select all nodes on the path.

3. With the nodes still selected, click the Add Node button (or press the + key on your numeric keypad). Notice that four new nodes are added midpoint between the four original nodes.

4. Click any of the segments once, and click the Convert Curve To Line button. The curve is now a straight line, and the curve handles have disappeared.

5. Click a node on one of the other existing curves, drag either of the curve handles in any direction, and notice how they change the shape of the path.

6. Using a click-drag action, click near the middle of the curve segment and drag in any direction. As you drag, the curve handle positions at both ends move, and the shape of the curve is changed accordingly.

7. Click any node on the path to select it, and first click the Cusp Node button, and then click the Smooth Node button. Drag the curve handle of this node in any direction. Notice that the curve handle may be dragged only in a single direction. Click the Cusp Node button, and then perform the same action. Notice that the lines on either side of the node can be curved in any direction independently of each other.

8. With this node still selected, click the Break Curve button to split the path at this point. Although it may not be obvious, two nodes now exist where the original node used to be. Drag either of these nodes in any direction to separate their positions. The nodes are now control points because they break the path to form beginning and end points.

9. Select one of these nodes, hold SHIFT while clicking the other, and click the Extend Curve To Close button. Notice the curve is now closed again, while the two nodes have been joined by a straight line.

10. Undo your last action (CTRL+Z) to unjoin the nodes and, while they remain selected, click the Align Nodes button to open the Align Nodes dialog. If they aren't already selected, click to select all three options (Align Horizontal, Vertical, and Control Points) in the dialog, and click OK to align the points. Notice that they are positioned to overlap precisely. Click to select both nodes, and click the Join Two Nodes button in the property bar. Your path is now closed, and the nodes are joined.

11. Hold SHIFT and click to select two or more nodes on your path. With your nodes selected, click the Stretch Or Scale Nodes button, and notice that eight selection handles appear around your node selection. Hold the SHIFT key (to constrain from center), and drag one of the corner handles toward or away from the center of the selection. All node positions are scaled relative to each other's position, and the lines joining the unselected nodes also change shape.

12. With the nodes still selected, click the Rotate Or Skew Nodes button in the property bar. Notice that eight rotate and skew handles appear around your selection. Drag any of the corner rotation handles either clockwise or counterclockwise to rotate the nodes. Notice that they are rotated relative to their current position, and the lines joining the unselected nodes also change shape.

The preceding tutorial is only a sampling of what can be accomplished when editing nodes using the Shape tool. You'll want to invest some quality time practicing your editing skills using all the available node-shaping command buttons, because the payoff is better artwork, artwork that's closer to what you have in your head, and in the long run, you'll save time creating wonderful pieces.

 TIP *To set the drawing behavior of the Freehand and/or Bézier tools, double-click either of their tool buttons in the toolbox to open the Options dialog to the Freehand/ Bézier tool page. Options are discussed in the next section.*

Controlling Freehand and Bézier Tool Behavior

The settings to control how Freehand and Bézier tools create the curves and lines you draw are set using a series of options in the Freehand/Bézier Tool pane of the Options dialog, shown next. To access these options, choose Tools | Options (CTRL+J), expand the tree subdirectory under Toolbox, and click Freehand/Bézier tool. The quick way to get to this box is to double-click the Freehand or Bézier tool buttons after choosing them from the Curve tools group.

Here's how the options work:

- **Freehand Smoothing** The Freehand Smoothing option enables you to set the default value of the Freehand Smoothing option in the property bar while drawing with the Freehand tool. Smoothing may be set based on percent within a range between 0 (minimum smoothing) and 100 (maximum smoothing). This option is largely redundant with the Freehand Smoothing option available in the property bar when a curve and the Shape tool are selected.

- **Corner Threshold** This option is for setting the default value for corner nodes when drawing with the Freehand or Bézier tool. Lower values cause nodes to be more likely set to cusp nodes, and higher values cause them to more likely be smooth nodes. The range may be set between 1 and 10; the default is 5.

- **Straight Line Threshold** This option pertains to how the shapes of lines or curves are created when drawing with the Freehand tool. Lower values cause nodes to be more likely set to straight lines, while higher values cause them more frequently to be curved. The range may be set between 1 and 10; the default is 5.

- **Auto-Join** This option sets the behavior of the Freehand or Bézier tool while drawing closed-path objects. This value represents the distance in pixels your cursor must be when clicking *near* the first node of a newly created path to close the path automatically. Auto-Join can be set anywhere within a range between 1 and 10 pixels; the default is 5 and is probably the best overall choice for large screen resolutions commonly run today.

Working with Compound Paths

Compound paths have at least two separate paths (either open or closed) composing a single shape. To examine an example of a compound path, use these steps:

1. Choose the Text tool (F8), click once to define a text insertion point, and then type an uppercase *Q* character. You can assign the character any typeface you like; the more ornamental the character, the more obvious the compound path soon will be. This character shape shown in Figure 10-12 has two paths that are combined: one represents the "positive" space, and one represents the "negative" space shape.

2. While the text object is selected, convert it to curves (CTRL+Q). The status bar now indicates the object is a Curve on Layer 1.

3. Change your view to Wireframe; choose View | Wireframe.

4. Press CTRL+K (Arrange | Break Curve Apart). With the Pick tool, click an empty area of the page, and then click one of the objects and drag it to move it; clearly the two paths are now separate. As shown in Figure 10-13, you have just converted a compound path featuring two subpaths into two individual objects. Go back to View and restore your view quality to Enhanced.

Combining Objects

10

When separate objects are combined, they behave as a single object. When two or more closed paths are combined, they form positive and negative spaces within the object. Applying a fill to this type of object causes the positive shapes to be filled, and the negative shapes remain clear, as shown in Figure 10-14. You can use the Combine command by choosing Arrange | Combine, or by using the CTRL+L shortcut. You can also click the Combine button in the property bar, or choose Combine from the pop-up menu.

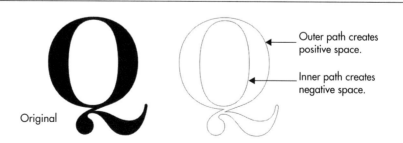

Original

Outer path creates positive space.

Inner path creates negative space.

FIGURE 10-12 In vector artwork, "holes" in objects are achieved through compound paths, paths that are combined to create a single object.

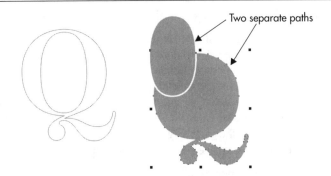

Two separate paths

FIGURE 10-13 Break a compound path apart to work with the component objects.

Combining objects that normally feature unique properties—such as rectangles, ellipses, polygons, and perfect shapes—permanently converts them to curves.

NOTE *If you intend to output to PostScript, it might not be a good idea to combine paths that overlap each other. Again, it's one of the limitations of the PostScript page description language—in human terms, a PostScript printer or image-setting device gets "confused" when a single closed path intersects itself; the device doesn't know which areas to fill and which to leave empty. If you have a design need for a shape that looks like it self-intersects, ensure proper PostScript output by using the Shaping docker or the buttons on the property bar when multiple objects are selected using the Pick tool to create the illusion of a self-intersecting object.*

Original objects   Combined objects

FIGURE 10-14 You can make two or more separate objects into a single compound path with the Combine command.

Breaking Paths Apart

You can separate the individual paths in a compound path using the Break Curve command (CTRL+K). This command is available when a compound path composed of at least two subpaths is selected. (Using the Extract Subpath command button in the property bar also does this, but only for the *selected* path.)

Converting Objects to Curves

Converting special types of objects to curves—such as shapes auto-created with the Rectangle and Ellipse tools—frees them to be manipulated with the Shape tool as if they were ordinary paths. Choose Arrange | Convert To Curves, press CTRL+Q, click the Convert To Curves button in the property bar, or right-click the object and choose Convert To Curves from the pop-up menu.

Converting an object to curves removes any special editing properties; text loses its ability to be edited as text, and rounded rectangles can no longer be edited to refine the curvature of the rounded corners. Converting to curves applies to polygon, ellipse, artistic text objects, and certain effects objects such as envelopes and perspective effects.

In this chapter, you've seen different tools for creating paths, but the results are more or less the same; objects have path segments and nodes, and paths can be open or closed. You've also learned how to edit paths using the Shape tool. You'd be well served to bookmark this chapter; there's an awful lot of power in CorelDRAW's drawing and editing tools, and this chapter can be a good reference in the future. After all, the program isn't called CorelFILL or CorelRECTANGLE—drawing is what good vector design is all about.

10

CHAPTER 11

Editing Objects

L et's say you've drawn an object and you're fairly pleased with it, *except* for that little corner that you couldn't draw *just* right. Editing objects is the theme of this chapter, where you'll learn various techniques to massage that almost-perfect shape into *exactly* the shape you've envisioned. Because every object you draw on a page can be broken down into rectangles, ovals, path segments, and so on, this chapter covers the tools and features for doing exactly this: breaking down shapes, combining them, subtracting a little of this, adding a little of that. Often, arriving at a design of your dreams can be most quickly accomplished by creating an approximation of the shapes you need. Then, with a pull and a tug here and there, erasing a tiny area, perhaps you'll get quicker results than if you had built the object from scratch. You'll see in this chapter that editing objects not only provides you with the best results, but also lets you add visual complexity and embellishments that would be hard to achieve using other methods.

 NOTE *Download and extract all the files from the Chapter11.zip archive to follow the tutorials in this chapter.*

Reshaping Things

You have a choice of two places to begin when you want to edit an object: you can use operations (commands you make with the click of a property bar button), or you can use the hands-on approach; both are covered in this chapter. Both approaches will serve you well, and your choice largely depends on what you need to edit, and then what type of operation is required.

Shaping and Reshaping Object Shapes

Drawing shapes from scratch is often a tedious and time-consuming process, but CorelDRAW has great shaping commands to speed the process. Shape commands such as Trim, Weld, Intersect, and Create Boundary make creating complex shapes quick and painless. You'll also find three other shape commands at your disposal: Simplify, Front Minus Back, and Back Minus Front. In this next section, you'll learn exactly how you can use these commands to shape and reshape your objects. Before getting into the specifics of each type, though, let's take a look at where you can find them in CorelDRAW X5.

Shaping Commands and the Property Bar

CorelDRAW X5's property bar provides shaping command buttons that enable you to shape selected objects instantly. These property bar options become available only while at least two objects are selected—and they make shaping commands available whether or not the objects are positioned to overlap. Property bar shaping buttons are shown here:

Welds all selected shapes

Trims selected shapes

Intersects selected shapes

Simplifies selected objects

Front Minus Back

Back Minus Front

Create Boundary: makes new object that surrounds selected shapes

| TIP | *When you use property bar shaping buttons, shapes are subtracted, added, and so on, but the original objects—except when you use Create Boundary—go away. To keep your original objects, use the Shaping docker, which offers options to specify that the* source *object (the one performing the operation—the "scissors") and/or* target *object (the object receiving the operation—the "paper") should remain after shaping.* |

| TIP | *When using the Shaping docker and the Weld and Intersect operations, you have an additional helper: the Intersect With or the Weld To button (shown next) at the bottom. When only one object is selected, naturally it's hard for CorelDRAW to perform these operations. The idea behind this option is that if you have several objects nestled together (making a target object hard to select), you click the Weld To or the Intersect With button, your cursor changes to a unique shape, and you then click the desired target object to complete the operation.* |

11

Boolean Shaping

The mathematical term for what is called "shaping" is *Boolean operation.* It was named after the 19th century mathematician George Boole, who invented a logic system in algebra for describing certain functions in plain English terms, such as "show me A and B together," where A and B are geometric shapes. Other shaping operations when translated to these logical statements include "and," "not," "or," and so on. The statement "show me A but not B" can describe the function of the CorelDRAW Back Minus Front shaping operation, as another example. This is the basis for the operation CorelDRAW performs when you use one shape as a target and a different one for the source in a shape operation.

Now that you know where to find the buttons to launch these commands quickly, it's time to examine what you can do with them. The following section explains the results of applying each command to at least two selected objects:

- **Weld** The *Weld* command creates a new shape based on the outline shape of two (or more) objects whether they overlap or not, as shown here. You can specify via the Shaping docker whether the *original* shapes remain on the page.

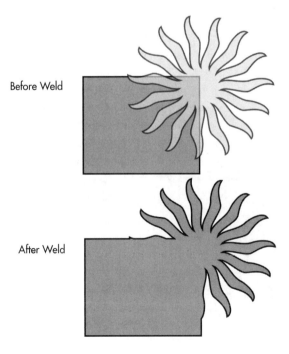

Before Weld

After Weld

This illustration shows a polygonal, sun-like shape with partial transparency applied to better show the order of objects on the page: the rectangle is behind the sun shape. Not only did the Weld operation create a single object from the two, but it also gave the result object the *color* of the *bottom* object. The important thing to know when welding objects is:

● If you marquee-select two objects for the Weld operation, the bottom object's color is the resulting object color.

● If you select two or more objects one at a time with the Pick tool (by SHIFT-clicking), the last object you choose—*regardless* of whether it is on top or bottom in the stack of objects on a layer—contains the fill color that will be the result color in the welded object.

● **Trim** The *Trim* command removes any overlapping areas of the object in front from the object(s) in back *when marquee-selection is used,* as shown next—the rectangle in front is partially transparent to make the effect more obvious. The original objects are automatically deleted, and no color change takes place (the back object does not inherit the front object's color, transparency, or any other trait). If you select the objects one by one (click, then SHIFT-click), the second object is trimmed.

Sun is in back   After Trim   Rectangle is moved

● **Intersect** The *Intersect* operation creates a new object based on the overlapping areas of two or more objects. The original objects remain on the page, and the result is not obvious because the new object is in the same position as the overlapping parts of the original objects. In the following figure, the sun shape was on the bottom, and the resulting shape takes on the color of the bottom object, because

11

marquee-selection was used. Intersect is a great operation for creating difficult crops of complex objects. The new sun shape would make a nice logo for a tanning salon!

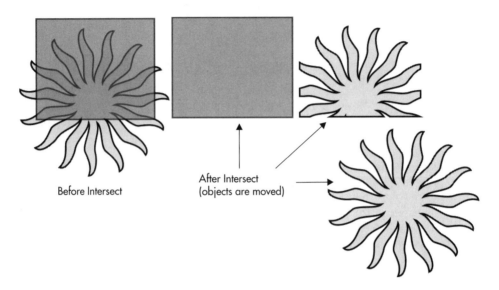

Before Intersect

After Intersect
(objects are moved)

- **Simplify** The *Simplify* command removes all hidden areas of objects that "underlap" foreground objects, as the example shows here. This command is great for uncomplicating an intricate drawing, and it can also make a design that otherwise might not print to PostScript correctly, print just fine. As you can see at middle, there is no apparent change to this simple design after the Simplify command is applied, but at right, you can see that when the objects are moved, overlapping areas of the sun in back have been erased, similar but not identical to the Trim and the Back Minus Front operations. Different order and arrangements of objects will result in slightly different results.

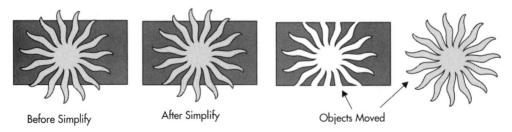

Before Simplify

After Simplify

Objects Moved

- **Front Minus Back** When two or more shapes are selected, applying the Front Minus Back command removes the hidden area of the object in back from the shape in front. When more than two shapes are selected, it removes all portions where the shapes in back are overlapped by the object in front, leaving only the object in front remaining, as shown here:

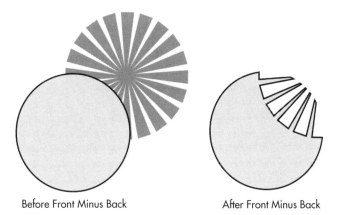

Before Front Minus Back   After Front Minus Back

Front Minus Back is a trim operation, "A but not B" in Boolean terminology, and the advantage to using this operation to trim objects is that it removes the guesswork of, "Gosh, what's the order of the objects in this design?" Front Minus Back is an unambiguous, straightforward trim operation.

● **Back Minus Front**   This shaping command works in reverse of Front Minus Back. While at least two shapes are selected, applying the Back Minus Front command removes the portions of the shape layered in front from the shape in back. When more than two shapes are selected, it will remove all portions where the shapes in front overlap the shape in back, leaving only the shape in back remaining, as shown here:

11

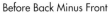

Before Back Minus Front   After Back Minus Front

● **Create Boundary**   This is similar to the Weld operation, except it leaves the target objects on the page. Also, if there are empty spaces between objects, Create Boundary ignores them when making the combined single object. Here is an example of several objects selected and the resulting shape. By default, the new object has no fill and is ordered on top of the target objects. Just click a foreground color on the color strip, and the new object will become immediately apparent.

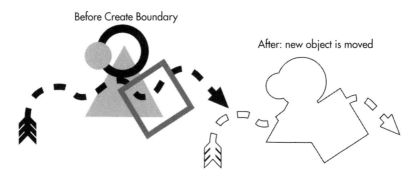

Before Create Boundary

After: new object is moved

> **NOTE** *You can use shaping operations on bitmaps. See Chapter 24 on how to create invaluable cropping effects on your photos using shaping operations and other techniques.*

Using the Shaping Docker

Under the Arrange menu, you'll find all the shaping commands. Also, the Shaping command is on this menu, which opens the Shaping docker in the workspace. As with all dockers, you can detach (undock) this palette so it floats near your work (demanding fewer "mouse miles"), and this docker offers more options than when you use the shaping operations from the property bar. Because of their operation, Simplify, Front Minus Back, and Back Minus Front only have an Apply button, and Create Boundary has Place Behind Selected and Leave Original check boxes.

The first three shaping commands in the selector are applied in slightly different ways from the others. To Weld, Trim, or Intersect, you must have at least one object selected and another unselected (but still in view) for the commands to be available. Once Weld, Trim, or Intersect is selected, the docker will display available options, shown here. Clicking the docker command button begins the action.

Shaping command selector

Preview window

Object options

Command button

The preview window on the docker doesn't actually change; it's an illustration that shows the result of using each operation. The Object options check boxes are what you use to set what object, if any, remains after an operation. Leave Original is equivalent to "make a copy so I don't lose my originals," and the options are as follows:

- **Source Object(s)** When this option is selected, the object you selected before the shaping operation remains after the command has been applied.

- **Target Object(s)** With this option selected, the object you Trim, Weld to, or Intersect with remains after the command has been applied.

Let's give this docker a spin. First, create two shapes; the Rectangle tool is fine to make shapes you won't need later, so they're expendable in this example:

1. If you haven't already done so, create the objects on which you want to base your new shape, and position them in such a way that the shape created by their overlapping portions represents your new shape.

2. Select one of these overlapping objects, and open the Shaping docker by choosing Window | Dockers | Shaping.

3. Choose Weld, Trim, or Intersect from the selector at the top of the docker.

4. Choose which original object(s) you want to remain after the command has been applied by clicking Source Object(s) and/or Target Object(s), and then click the command button at the bottom of the docker to apply the command. Notice your cursor has changed to one of three targeting cursors, depending on your shaping operation.

5. Click the object you want your selected object to Trim, Weld to, or Intersect with. Your new shape is immediately created based on the overlapping area of your existing objects.

 The outline and fill properties of newly shaped objects are determined by the properties of the target object.

Choosing Simplify, Front Minus Back, or Back Minus Front requires that at least two objects are selected. If only one object is selected, you'll get an attention box politely telling you so and asking if you'd like to try again. With any of these commands, the shaping is applied when you click the Apply button in the Shaping docker.

Working Examples of Object Shaping

If you've seen some stunning CorelDRAW creations and said to yourself, "Wow, that must've taken that artist ages to do all that work," nope, it probably didn't: the artist put *object shaping* to work. The following shows just three of thousands of creative possibilities for shaping operations; these are just a few examples to kindle your efforts.

Here is an example problem and a solution using the Trim operation. The chicken came first, then the need to make the chicken drawing look as though it's peeking through the broken eggshell. The chicken drawing is composed of several grouped sub-objects; the Trim operation trims all objects in a group. Walk through the next set of steps to see how the Trim operation solves a lot of the manual effort of editing dozens of objects to visually integrate the chicken drawing into the scene. All the shapes needed to perform the Trim operation have been added for you; just focus on how to use the Trim operation.

Trimming a Chicken

1. Open Chicken.cdr. The goal is to place the toy chicken drawing so that it looks as though it's peeking out of the half-shell at right.

2. With the Pick tool, drag the chicken group's objects, and position them so the lower half of the chicken is over the eggshell.

3. Choose Arrange | Shaping | Shaping to display the Shaping docker.

4. Select the dashed outline shape. If you were designing this composition from scratch, the Pen tool would be ideal for drawing such a shape. The blue dashed outline is only to call attention to the object in this example—the shape can be any outline color or style.

5. Choose Trim from the drop-down list. Put a check in the Target Object(s) check box so a copy of the whole chicken remains in the drawing. Why spoil a perfectly good drawing?

6. Because only one object is selected, you now *click* Trim on the Shaping docker, and the docker queries you on what you want trimmed.

7. With the special cursor, click over the chicken.

8. With the Pick tool, move the lower (whole) chicken out of the way to see the results. Try a click-drag over the wing.

With the outline selected, click Trim, and then click the chick.

Target object retained and moved

Figure 11-1 shows a combination Weld and then a Trim, although Back Minus Front would work as the second step, too. The problem in this composition is that a specific font is needed in stencil style, but the artist doesn't have such a typeface. So Arial is first used, and then:

1. Draw several rectangles over areas that need to be removed from the text to create the stencil effect.

2. Create duplicates of one narrow rectangle by using the drop-a-copy technique: drag a rectangle to a new location, and then tap both mouse buttons before releasing both buttons. Doing this keeps consistency between areas to be removed from the text.

3. After all the rectangles are in position, marquee-select the rectangles, and then use the Weld command to make a single object out of the rectangles.

4. Remove the single shape from the text by using it as the Source object in the Trim operation. The text is trimmed.

5. Finally, use Effects | Add Perspective to make the text appear as though it's on the 3D crate. The text probably could use some rotation, but you get the idea.

Black rectangles are welded.

Welded rectangles trim text.

Effects | Add
Perspective plus
transparency

FIGURE 11-1   Weld and then Trim are used to make a stencil treatment out of the text.

Figure 11-2 uses Back Minus Front, Weld, and an Arrow shape (covered in Chapter 16) to create a complex-looking design for a corporate logo. First, a circle is drawn using the Ellipse tool in combination with holding CTRL (to constrain ovals to perfect circles). Then, to put a smaller circle centered inside the first, you hold SHIFT, drag the original circle's corner-bounding box handle toward the center, then right-click before releasing the left mouse button to create a scaled duplicate. Back Minus Front is chosen on the Shaping docker with both objects selected; click Apply and you have a perfect doughnut object. The Arrow shapes come in all four directions on the property bar; four arrows are dragged to create with this tool, they're arranged, and then all four arrows are selected. The Weld operation is chosen on the Shaping docker. Then with the large arrow cursor, the doughnut is clicked to indicate it's the target object. This could be the end of the story, but in only a few clicks, the resulting shape can be extruded and rotated. See Chapter 19 for the complete details on object extrusion—3D is yours to experiment with within CorelDRAW.

Back (larger circle)
Minus Front

Weld arrow
shapes to
doughnut object.

Extrude with bevel edge.

FIGURE 11-2   Complex illustrations don't need to take a lot of time. Get to know the Shape
tools, and what you envision is only a few clicks away.

Fillet/Scallop/Chamfer

The Fillet/Scallop/Chamfer docker can be displayed by choosing it from Window | Dockers,
and with it, you have your choice of truncating sharp corners of an object you draw. This
docker will not alter a curved path segment: a shape that consists of straight paths is the best
to use with this feature; objects with a combination of curved and straight segments will
only be affected along the convergence of two straight path segments.

When Fillet/Scallop/Chamfer evaluates sharp direction changes along a path, it "rounds
off" the point of a convex area toward the inside of the path and increases concave areas.
This is a terrific feature for quickly building elegant objects such as furniture pieces,
machine parts, and nice ornaments for desktop publishing documents. When you enter a
positive value in the Radius field (or use the elevator buttons on the docker), you see a faint
outline preview in your document, and then you click Apply when you're happy with the
preview. Fillet/Scallop/Chamfer is a destructive operation, unlike the shaping operations, so
if you want to keep your original object, duplicate it before using this docker.

- **Fillet**   Rounds the corners of an object

- **Scallop**   Trims a semicircle from the corner of an object

- **Chamfer**   Lops a straight angle off a corner at an angle perpendicular to the
  interior angle of the corner

11

Figure 11-3 shows the effects of the Fillet/Scallop/Chamfer docker on the same zigzag object created with a single-click and the Pen tool. Because the Radius of this trimming effect is measured in page units, it's usually a good idea to keep rulers visible in your document, and to refer to them to achieve the exact degree of corner truncation you need.

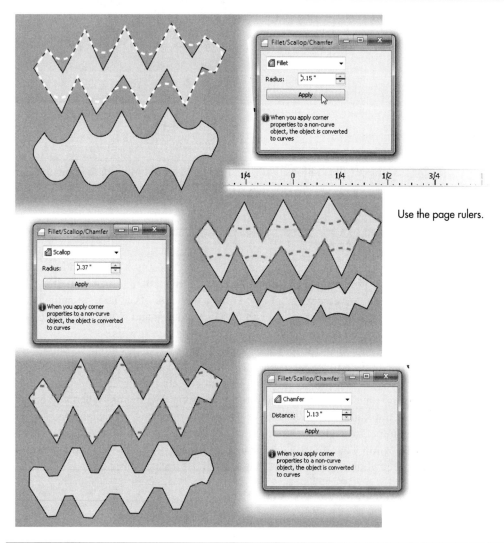

Use the page rulers.

FIGURE 11-3   Use the Fillet/Scallop/Chamfer docker to take the corners off an object with intricacy and classic style.

PowerClips

CorelDRAW PowerClips change the appearance of a shape by hiding certain areas of its exterior with a different shape. This, unlike other reshaping operations, is completely nondestructive, and the clipping object can release the inner clipped object(s) at any time. Consider the usefulness of PowerClips: You can hide most of an object from view and put other objects behind the PowerClip. You can play a dozen possible scenarios for the composition you have on a page, and never commit to any of them, unlike with trimming an object.

To give you an idea of the creative power of PowerClips, follow these steps with a document whose objects have already been created for you. The assignment is to put a design on the bottom of a flower vase, stencil-style, so parts of the vase's original color still show through in different regions. It's not hard work when you're familiar with PowerClips.

PowerClipping a Design onto an Object

1. Open Flower and Vase.cdr. To the left you'll see a grouped pattern with transparency. Below it is the same pattern with an envelope applied to make the pattern look bulged, as it would when viewed on the surface of a round shape such as the vase drawing here. At right, over the vase, is a thin yellow outline shape that is a fairly accurate trace over the vase. This will be your PowerClip shape for the pattern—it will hide all shapes outside of it. If you'd like to use the Envelope tool to experiment with the non-enveloped grouped pattern, Chapter 20 provides the complete documentation on this feature.

11

Pattern with transparency

Pattern with transparency and an envelope

Clipping object

2. Select the bottom pattern with the Pick tool, and then drag it over so it's on top of the yellow outline object, making certain that all parts of the pattern overlap the outline. You don't want gaps in the pattern as it's displayed on the vase.

3. Choose Effects | PowerClip | Place Inside Container.

4. A huge arrow becomes your cursor. Click the cursor over the yellow outline, and the pattern scoots inside the container object.

5. The container object is now selected. Right-click over the No Fill color well on the Color Palette to remove the outline, or alternatively, choose None for the Outline Width from the drop-down list on the property bar. See Figure 11-4.

Although the preceding example shows how to mask the exterior of a group of shapes, a PowerClip container can also have an outline width, color, and a fill. In any case, the nondestructive property of PowerClips will serve you in a number of design situations.

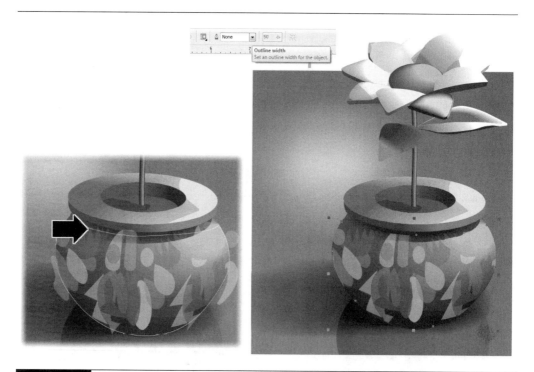

FIGURE 11-4   Let empty areas in patterns and other complex drawings show through a PowerClip object.

Occasionally, an object "inside" the PowerClip container might not be aligned perfectly relative to your overall composition. You also might like to do a little editing to the contained object(s). This is not directly done on the page. Here are the editing options for a PowerClipped object:

- To reveal the object for editing or repositioning relative to the PowerClip object, right-click over the object, and then choose Edit Contents from the pop-up menu. A blue outline indicates the size and position of the PowerClip container. When you're done editing, right-click and then choose Finish Editing This Level.

- To undo the PowerClip effect, you can press CTRL+Z right after making the command, or right-click over the PowerClip object, and then choose Extract Contents. Your PowerClipped object(s) and the container are restored to their original condition, but not always to their original position on the page.

- To quickly reposition the contents of a PowerClip container, right-click and then choose Lock Contents To PowerClip. This is a toggle on and off state: when it's unlocked, you can reposition the container by dragging with the Pick tool. You can also scale and rotate the container without affecting the contents. When it's locked, the contents travel with the container objects wherever you drag.

The Knife Tool

The Knife tool functions like a knife you'd use in the real world—except you can run with it and it requires no sharpening— and feels quite natural to use. You begin by hovering over an object area where you want to begin the cut, your cursor changes its appearance to signify it is ready, and then you click-drag to the end of the cut, the other side of the object. The result is two separate closed objects. As with many of CorelDRAW's tools, SHIFT and CTRL can be used as modifier keys as you work with the knife, and in the case of the Knife tool, these modifier keys add precision to your cuts. You'll find the Knife tool in the toolbox grouped together with the Crop, Eraser, and Virtual Segment Delete tools.

Knife tool

Types of Cuts with the Knife Tool

There are three ways to cut a shape with the Knife tool, and each one requires a different keyboard/mouse technique.

- **Straight cuts**   Suppose you want to slice an object into two separate shapes as you'd do with a workshop saw. To produce straight lines on sides of both objects, you aim the cursor on the near side of the object, hover until you see it change from an angled cursor to an upright one, click, release the mouse button, and then click the far side of the object, as shown in Figure 11-5.

- **Freeform cuts**   This technique can be used, for example, to quickly create an illustration of a sheet of paper roughly torn in half. You hover the cursor until it turns upright, click-hold the near side of the object, and then drag until you reach the far side of the shape, as shown in Figure 11-6.

- **Bézier cuts**   If you need to guide the Knife tool to make smooth jigsaw-like cuts, you hold SHIFT, and then click-drag points, beginning at the near side and completing the cut at the far side, as shown in Figure 11-7. Notice that not only do the cut result objects inherit the original shape's fill, but this applies to all types of fills, including gradients. The shapes in this figure each have a gradient start and end point inherited from the original shape, and if you choose the Interactive gradient tool, you can adjust each object's gradient directly and come up with a visually interesting jigsaw puzzle composition or other complex drawing.

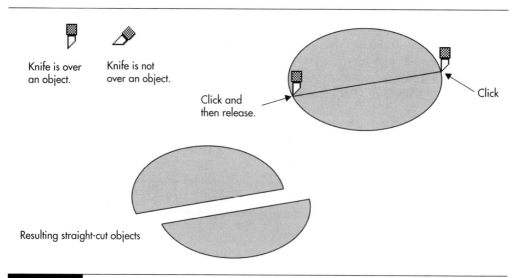

FIGURE 11-5   Click, release, then click to create a Knife tool straight cut.

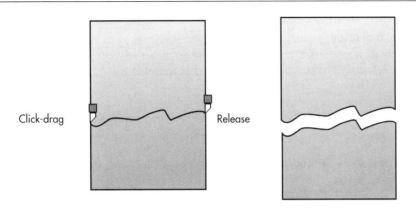

Click-drag   Release

FIGURE 11-6   Click-drag to create a freeform cut.

Naturally, if you have a specific cut in mind, you'll get the best results using the shaping operations, and you cannot edit a Bézier cut's path as you make the cut, but the Knife tool does provide fast and easy results.

 If you hold both SHIFT and CTRL while click-dragging to make a Bézier cut, doing so constrains the direction of the path to 15-degree increments for more predictable results in making the edge of the cut.

11

Hold SHIFT and drag.

Cut objects inherit the original object fill and outline.

FIGURE 11-7   Bézier cuts guide the Knife tool with the precision of using a digitizing tablet and stylus.

Setting Knife Tool Behavior

Using the Knife tool results in just what you'd expect—several objects out of a single one. However, you do have options, the two property bar options shown here. Each of these options toggles on and off to suit a specific cutting requirement.

Leave As One Object —————▶ ◀————— Auto-Close On Cut

- **Auto-Close On Cut mode**   This option, on by default, sets the Knife tool to create closed-path objects following any style of Knife tool cutting. If you turn this option off, the Knife tool divides an object into two open paths and removes any fill. This can be a useful mode for breaking a closed shape into open paths. To use this option, don't drag with the Knife tool, but instead click a near point and a far point.

- **Leave As One Object mode**   This option is active by default; if you disable it, the Knife tool cuts an object, but the result is a combined path—in other words, you don't get two separate objects. This option is useful on occasions (for creating characters in typefaces, for example), but it probably would not be an everyday mode of operation for your work.

 Both the Eraser and Knife tools can be used on imported bitmaps; you can perform a little photo retouching with these tools exactly as you would with vector objects. The only restriction is that a bitmap (BMP, TIFF, JPEG, and so on) has to actually be imported to the document; if it is externally linked, the tools can't be used on this reference to bitmap images.

Using the Eraser Tool

The Eraser tool, shown next, completely removes areas of selected objects you click-drag over—just like a real art eraser, but without the stubble landing in your lap. The Eraser tool comes in two different shapes, and you can define the size by using the property bar. You'll find it in the toolbox grouped with the Knife, Virtual Segment Delete, and Crop tools.

Working with Eraser Operations

With this tool, you can remove portions of shapes in four ways:

- **Double-clicking** When you double-click a selected shape, you remove an area that is the shape of the cursor. Therefore, if you double-click a lot with the circular cursor chosen, you can quickly design a slice of Swiss cheese.

- **Single-click two points** If you single-click, move your cursor, and then click a second time, the Eraser tool erases a straight line through the selected object.

- **Click-drag** This is the most common method of erasing, and the results are totally predictable. If you click-drag, you erase the area you've dragged over on a selected object.

> **NOTE** *Grouped objects do not qualify for use with the Eraser tool. However, if you CTRL-click an object in a group to temporarily isolate it, you can indeed erase part of the object.*

- **Hovering and pressing TAB** This technique creates several connected straight-line segments, and after you get the hang of it, it will feel like you're painting with an eraser, and you'll be able to quickly produce phenomenally expressive and complex drawings.

Walk through the following tutorial to see the power of this hover-TAB erasing technique and to make it your own.

Power Erasing

1. Open Don't Litter.cdr, an incomplete international symbol that tells the audience, "Put refuse in the appropriate place; don't be a pig." The orange areas are guides for you; they're locked on the Guides layer.

2. Select the main object. Choose the Eraser tool and then set the nib style to rectangular by clicking the default nib style (the circle) on the property bar. For this example, set the nib size to about **.18"**.

3. Single-click at the top left of the wastebasket guide. Move your cursor over to the bottom left of the wastebasket guide, but don't click. Notice as you move the Eraser tool that a path preview follows the cursor.

4. Press TAB, but *don't click* your mouse button. Notice that a new erasure appears between the first single-click point and the point where you pressed TAB.

5. To define a third point, move your cursor to a new point (without clicking the mouse button) and then press TAB again. A third point is defined, and the path between the second and third points is erased. To stop using the Eraser tool, click at the end to halt CorelDRAW from connecting the points you click with a line between them.

6. When you're done with the wastebasket, set the nib style to round, and then add limbs to the thoughtful international guy. Use the TAB technique, for example, to extend a forearm from the guy's shoulder, and once this segment has been erased, double-click where you think his hand would be to extend the erasure. Single-click to end an erasure. Figure 11-8 shows the work in progress.

  Each time the Eraser tool cursor is clicked to erase portions of your object, CorelDRAW considers the action as a unique and separate erase session. This means that Eraser tool actions can be reversed using the Undo command (CTRL+Z) in steps, depending on which erase technique was used. While using the single-click technique, an Undo command is needed to reverse each erase point. During a continuous erase using the click-drag action, a single Undo command reverses each continuous erasing session.

Setting Eraser Tool Properties

The width and shape of the Eraser tool are set using property bar options, as shown next. The complexity of the removed shape, the number of path segments, and the connecting nodes created during an erase session can also be controlled. These properties significantly affect the shape of erased object areas.

Single-click

Pressing TAB defines points; single-clicking defines end.

FIGURE 11-8 Press TAB to define intermediate points between your first and last erase-path points to create connected, straight-line erasures.

TIP   *As with most of the toolbox tools, you can get to the options for the Eraser tool in Options by double-clicking the button on the toolbox.*

Eraser Width

Width can be set between 0.001 and 100.0 inches either by entering values in the property bar combo box or by pressing the UP and DOWN ARROW keys on your keyboard to increase or decrease the size. Naturally, you might never need a 100-inch eraser; it makes more sense to use the shaping operations—but you do have this latitude.

TIP   *Use the keyboard to change the cursor size while you erase. Press the UP ARROW and/or DOWN ARROW key while click-dragging, and the result can be a tapered brush, as shown here. After you release the mouse button, the Eraser tool resets to its original size, so you don't have to worry about starting out a new erase stroke with a yard-wide tip!*

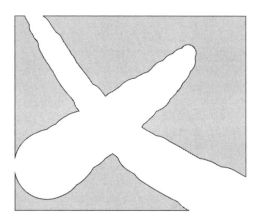

Reduce Nodes Mode

Erasing continuous paths removes portions of objects to create new sides that are made up of normal vector path segments and nodes. How closely the new edges follow your erase path is determined by the number and properties of the nodes that are produced. The more nodes, the more complex and accurate the erased shape will be. While selected, the Reduce Nodes option affects the complexity of the resulting erased shape when erasing in continuous freehand-style paths.

Adding nodes to an already-complicated object, however, can create an overly complex object, something that can slow you down—the excess nodes don't contribute to the artwork and may result in inconvenient screen redraws of effects you might apply. The Reduce Nodes option lets you reduce the complexity of erased area shapes at the price of what's usually trivial inaccuracy. To activate the Reduce Nodes option, click the button to the depressed position (the default), or deactivate it by clicking it to the undepressed state.

The Eraser tool's Reduce Nodes settings are set according to the Freehand smoothing default setting used by the Freehand and Bézier tools, which can be set between 0 and 100 percent (the default is 50). To set this option, double-click the Eraser tool button on the toolbox. By default, it's enabled.

Using the Virtual Segment Delete Tool

The Virtual Segment Delete tool is used to delete specific portions of objects, specifically, overlapping areas. Additionally, this tool removes portions of an object's path where they intersect paths of *other* overlapping objects.

To use this tool to delete path segments where an object intersects itself, use these quick steps:

1. With the Freehand tool, draw a path that loops around and crosses itself.

2. Hold your cursor over the segment to delete—you don't need to have the objects selected to use this tool. You'll notice the cursor becomes upright when an eligible segment is hovered over (shown at top here).

3. Click the cursor directly on the segment you want to delete. The segment you targeted is immediately deleted.

After deleting portions of a path with this tool, what remains is either an open curve with just one path, or a compound curve with two or more subpaths. For example, if the object you're deleting segments from is a closed path, deleting one segment will result in an open curve. Deleting a segment from a rectangle, ellipse, or polygon object will convert the resulting shape to curves and remove the dynamic object properties. To delete segments that are hidden behind an overlapping object, temporarily set its Fill to None.

> **TIP** *If the object you are deleting segments from is a compound path (an object composed of more than one open or closed path), the Virtual Segment Delete tool will work best if the object is first broken into individual curves using the Break Apart (CTRL+K) command.*

Cropping an Illustration

The Crop tool, located in the group with the Knife and the Eraser tools, brings a bitmap effect to vector drawing. If you have experience with Corel PHOTO-PAINT or another photo-editing program, you already are familiar with a crop tool: you select an area within a photo, perform a command such as clicking inside the crop area, and the area outside the crop is deleted and the image is resized.

The Crop tool in CorelDRAW behaves exactly like an image editor's crop tool. Objects do not have to be grouped; you just drag a rectangle around the area of your design you want cropped, double-click inside the proposed crop area, and all object areas outside the crop box are deleted. In Figure 11-9 at left you can see two objects: the goal is to leave only the comedy mask and to get rid of the tragedy mask. In the middle the Crop tool is dragged around the desired area, which then is double-clicked. At right you can see two separate objects: the cropped gray background and the cropped mask. This is a powerful and potentially very destructive tool, but fortunately you can work with the proposed crop box before cropping. You can drag a *corner* crop box handle before cropping to proportionately resize the crop; dragging a *middle* handle disproportionately resizes the crop area.

11

Original   Crop   Cropped Objects

FIGURE 11-9 The Crop tool removes all areas of every object that lies outside the crop box.

Additionally, once you've made a proposed crop, clicking, then clicking again inside the box puts the box in rotation mode, and you can actually crop a diamond shape. If you want to cancel a crop operation, press ESC and the crop box goes away.

Using the Smudge Brush

The Smudge brush tool is yet another paint tool in a drawing program: not only is this tool a lot of fun to use, but you can also dramatically alter shapes in a natural, painterly fashion whose results would take hours using any other method. You move areas of a vector object by dragging from a starting point inside the object, dragging outward, or by starting outside and dragging inside the object. The result is a smear, but with all the crispness of a vector design. You'll find the Smudge brush, shown next, in the toolbox, grouped with the Roughen brush, the Shape, and Free Transform tools.

Applying Smudge to Shapes

Using the Smudge brush, you can alter the outline shapes of open or closed paths by click-dragging across the outline path, in either an outward direction (to add a bulge) or an inward direction (to create a pucker). As you drag, the path is altered according to your drag action and to the shape settings of the Smudge brush cursor. Figure 11-10 shows a creative example of using the Smudge brush: the cartoon head has long, spiky hair now; the editing took less than 5 seconds, and the resulting path can be edited for refining by using the Shape tool and other CorelDRAW features.

 TIP *If you're trying to smudge shapes that have been applied with an effect (Envelope, Blend, Contour, Distortion, Extrude, or Drop Shadow), you'll first need to break apart the effect. If the shape is part of a group, you'll need to ungroup it first (CTRL+U). Smudging cannot be applied to bitmaps.*

Choosing Smudge Brush Property Bar Options

In case you haven't noticed, the Smudge brush works quite differently from other tools. You can control how the Smudge brush effect is applied by varying tool properties such as the

FIGURE 11-10   The Smudge brush treats vector objects as though they're made of liquid.

tilt, angle, and size of the nib; or by adjusting how quickly the effect diminishes; or by using optional pressure stylus settings.

   While the Smudge brush is selected, the property bar offers these options for controlling the shape and condition of your Smudge brush cursor:

Changing each of these options has the following effect:

- **Nib Size**   Nib Size can be set between 0.02 and 2.0"; the default is 0.1".

- **Pen Pressure**   If you have a digitizing tablet and stylus that supports pressure, choose this option to have the Smudge brush react to pressure you apply while increasing the width of the nib.

11

- **Dryout** This option sets a rate for the effect of gradually reducing the width of a smudge according to the speed of your click-drag action and can be set between −10 and 10. Higher values cause your smudge to be reduced in width more quickly (as shown next), while a setting of 0 deactivates the Dryout effect. Interestingly, negative Dryout values make your stroke begin small and eventually widen as you click-drag.

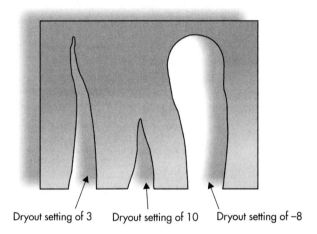

Dryout setting of 3   Dryout setting of 10   Dryout setting of −8

- **Tilt** The Tilt value controls the elliptical shape of the Smudge tool nib. Tilt is measured in degrees set between 15° (a flat-shaped nib) and 90° (a circular-shaped nib), as shown next. Tilt and Bearing values (discussed next) work in combination with each other to control the smudge nib shape.

Tilt = 15°,   Tilt = 45°,   Tilt = 90°,
Bearing = 0°   Bearing = 0°   Bearing = 0°

● **Bearing** Bearing lets you set the angle of the cursor in circular degrees (0 to 359°). The effects of changing Bearing are most noticeable at lower Tilt values—such as 15°, as shown here. It's the rotational angle of a non-circular tip.

Tilt = 15°,   Tilt = 15°,   Tilt = 15°,
Bearing = 30°   Bearing = 45°   Bearing = 90°

Using the Free Transform Tool

The Free Transform tool, located in the same group as the Smudge brush, the Shape tool, and the Roughen brush, is your one-stop shop for performing rotations, skews, and other object transformations using an onscreen guide.

Rotate   Reflect   Scale   Skew

Property bar options

Free Transform tool

Unlike with the Pick tool for object transformations, the Free Transform tool has a handle by which you steer and have precise control over the object you manipulate. To use the tool, you choose it from the toolbox, choose a transformation type on the property bar, and then with the object selected, you click-drag on a control point (or any object node) to set the center of the transformation; dragging reveals a handle that also serves as a visual indicator of the amount of transformation you're creating. This preview of the transformation is in effect until you release the mouse button. As you can see in this illustration, it's obvious the rectangle is being rotated, where the center of rotation is, and the extent of the rotation before the transformation is actually made.

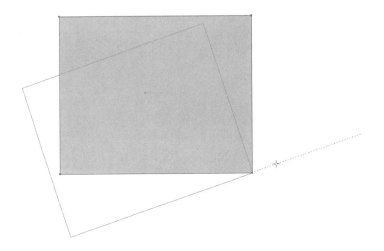

The Roughen Brush

To add a touch of character and imperfection to ultra-precise objects, you have the new Roughen brush in the group with the Smudge brush, shown here:

The Roughen brush alters the course of an outline path on an object, and depending on the setting you use on the property bar, you can achieve effects that range from lightning bolts, to really gnarly lines, to zigzag patterns, just by dragging on the edge of a shape. The options you have when using the Roughen brush can be seen here on the property bar; they're similar to those of the Smudge brush:

- **Brush Diameter**   This sets the size of the Roughen brush. It's usually a good idea to scale the nib in proportion to the selected object you want to roughen. By default the scale of the nib is measured in inches.

- **Pressure Sensitivity**   If you use a digitizing tablet and stylus that responds to pressure, this option can be used to vary the nib width as you drag over object areas. The option is dimmed on the property bar if CorelDRAW doesn't detect a digitizing tablet hooked up to your system.

- **Frequency**   You'll see that the Roughen brush creates irregularity on an object edge that is similar to the peaks and valleys of a mountain range—it varies the object outline in an "in and out" fashion. At low Frequency values, the roughened object outline will feature large, varying areas. At high Frequency settings, you'll attain a zigzag effect. The range of Frequency is from 1 to 10 (10 produces zigzags).

- **Dryout**   Like the Smudge brush, the Roughen brush can "dry out" at the end of a stroke you drag with the cursor. The range of dryout effect is from –10 (the stroke tapers in the opposite direction in which you click-drag) to 10 (the stroke tapers and fades). At 0, the stroke remains consistent. The greater the Dryout setting, negative or positive, the more natural a roughened appearance you can achieve.

- **Tilt**   This option measures your stroke with the Roughen brush perpendicular to the edge on which you stroke. Therefore, if you have an edge that travels straight up and down, at a 90° setting you'll achieve very little effect. In your experiments with this tool, try 45°, an overall good setting for all angles of edges on most objects. When you roughen an edge that already has roughening applied, you overwrite the previous distortion of that edge. Figure 11-11 shows two examples of the Roughen brush; at left a small nib is used at a low Frequency, and at right a large nib is used at high Frequency.

11

> | TIP | *Shapes that have special properties, such as rectangles and ellipses created with the Rectangle and Ellipse tools, need to be simplified using the Arrange | Convert To Curves command (CTRL+Q) before they can be roughened. If you try to use the Roughen brush on such a shape, you'll get an attention box telling you that the object needs simplifying, but then CorelDRAW will automatically do the operation for you. So if you want to avoid the attention box, press CTRL+Q while a shape is selected, so you can get right down to editing.*

This chapter has taken you through several processes by which you can create minor and big-time alterations to just about anything you draw; additionally, many of the operations apply to bitmaps you bring into the workspace. Use the command that best suits the task you have in mind, and use your judgment as to which operation will get you to your goal fastest. Personal computers are productivity enhancers: there's no need to labor over something when CorelDRAW and your PC can do it for you in less time.

Use the Roughen brush to achieve object complexity in a fraction of the time needed using other tools.

Now that you have one, or two, or a dozen shapes on your drawing page, it would be nice to mix them up with some honest-to-gosh text: a headline here, a little body copy there. Shapes and words live together, practically no one publishes an image-only website, and Chapter 12, Part IV of this guide gets you into the language of typography and the features in CorelDRAW that make your keyboard a professional communications tool.

PART IV

Working with Text

CHAPTER 12

Getting Artistic with Text

CorelDRAW is all about communication and expressing yourself; this chapter and the others in this part show you how to use text in a CorelDRAW creation to support and enhance your ideas as expressed on a page. This chapter gets you started with the Text tool and other CorelDRAW type features and shows you how to present your thoughts and ideas invitingly and clearly. Text and graphics go hand in hand in presentations; whether it's a poster, a newsletter, a banner, or a logo, you have the tools at your disposal. This chapter shows you how to access and work with them.

Download and extract all the files from the Chapter12.zip archive to follow the tutorials in this chapter.

CorelDRAW's Text Tool

All text you want to enter on a page in CorelDRAW is created with the Text tool, the tool with an *A* as its icon in CorelDRAW's toolbox. To begin designing, click its button in the toolbox, press F8, or double-click an existing text object. The Text tool cursor is a small crosshair with an *A* below and to the right, which becomes an I-beam (a text-editing cursor) when it's over a text object.

A shortcut to reselect the Pick tool while the Text tool is selected is CTRL+SPACEBAR— for all other tools, you can press either SPACEBAR or CTRL+SPACEBAR.

When you use the Text tool, you can produce two different types of text objects in a document: artistic text and paragraph text. Figure 12-1 shows a simple layout that uses artistic text in combination with the Text | Fit Text To Path command—the path is hidden in this illustration. The smaller body text uses paragraph text; the top paragraph wraps around the top of the image by use of a CorelDRAW envelope (see Chapter 20). Artistic text and paragraph text have different properties, but are added to a document by using the same Text tool. Artistic text, by the way it's produced in a document, is easy to reshape and distort— you'll find it simple to do artistic things with it, such as creating a company logo. Conversely, paragraph text is optimized for longer amounts of text, and it's a great text attribute for quickly modifying columns of, for example, instructions, recipes, short stories, and so on. In short, *paragraph* text is best used for several paragraphs of text in a composition, while *artistic* text should be reserved for headlines and just a few lines of text you might want to curve along a path, extrude, or do something else unique and fancy with.

Although artistic text and paragraph text have some similarities, you're best off using one or the other depending on the type of text element you want in your design.

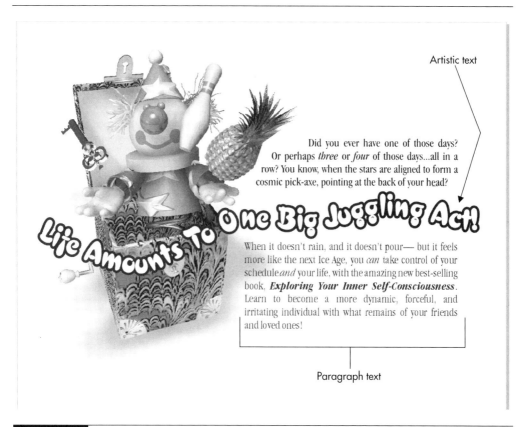

Artistic text

Did you ever have one of those days? Or perhaps *three* or *four* of those days...all in a row? You know, when the stars are aligned to form a cosmic pick-axe, pointing at the back of your head?

When it doesn't rain, and it doesn't pour— but it feels more like the next Ice Age, you *can* take control of your schedule *and* your life, with the amazing new best-selling book, ***Exploring Your Inner Self-Consciousness***. Learn to become a more dynamic, forceful, and irritating individual with what remains of your friends and loved ones!

Paragraph text

FIGURE 12-1   Artistic text and paragraph text have different attributes, and each is suited for different text treatments in a design.

12

NOTE   *Text copied from the Clipboard can be pasted when the Pick tool is your current tool. Usually, unformatted text—text from a TXT file you copied from Textpad, for example—will import as paragraph text.*

- Text imported *without* a Text tool insertion point entered on the page comes in as paragraph text.

- Text pasted *with* an insertion point made on the page imports as artistic text.

NOTE   *Text copied from word processors will import as a document object; double-clicking the object offers in-place editing exactly as you'd edit a WordPerfect or Microsoft Word document. It's usually best to choose Edit | Paste Special when pasting Clipboard text, to ensure that correct formatting and the original fonts are used, and to use the Text tool's I-beam cursor to insert pasted text.*

Entering and Editing Artistic Text

Artistic text will serve you best for illustration headlines, callouts, and on any occasion when you want to create text that has a special effect such as extrusion, an envelope, text on a path, and so on. To add a line of artistic text to a document, use the Text tool to click an insertion point, and then type your phrase; alternatively, after clicking an insertion point, press CTRL+V to paste any text you have loaded on Windows' Clipboard. Creating several lines of artistic text simply involves typing and then pressing ENTER to put a hard return at the end of the line; you then continue typing. By default, all artistic text is set in Arial 24 point; later in this chapter you'll see how to change the default.

Artistic text is also easy to convert to curves so you can modify a character in a word: for example, Microsoft's logo has a tick missing in the second "o". To duplicate this effect (but not Microsoft's logo!), you'd begin with artistic text for the company name, press CTRL+Q (Arrange | Convert To Curves), and then edit using the Shape tool. Artistic text, as editable text, can be fine-tuned using the features on the property bar when the text is selected using either the Pick tool or the Text tool. The options are shown in Figure 12-2.

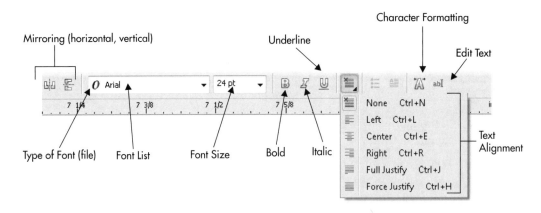

FIGURE 12-2   Use the property bar to get artistic text to look exactly the way you want.

- **Mirroring (horizontal and vertical)** In addition to creating special effects, the mirroring buttons are also useful when, for example, you want to print a T-shirt transfer with your company name. The name needs to be reversed (mirrored horizontally) to print on the transfer paper, so the un-reversed print on the T-shirt reads correctly (or at least without the need for a mirror).

- **Type of Font (file)** To the left of the font name displayed in the Font list drop-down box is an icon signifying what file format the font uses: OpenType, Type 1, or TrueType. This is a nicety when you're sorting your fonts in Bitstream Font Navigator or Windows' Fonts utility in Control Panel.

- **Font Name** This is the name of the typeface you select. By default, you're using Arial 24 point. You change fonts in a new document by selecting text you've typed with the Pick tool and then choosing a different font from the Font list drop-down. If a font has family members, a right triangle can be seen to the right of the font name when the drop-down list is extended, and you can choose it by clicking the (flyout) triangle. You can also perform a speed-search by clicking the current name in the Font list box and then typing the first few letters of the font you want. The drop-down list immediately scrolls to the neighborhood of installed fonts, making your selection a fast and effortless one. Note also that on the Font list drop-down, at the top (above the divider bar), are the fonts you've chosen recently—from previous documents and even from previous CorelDRAW sessions.

- **Font Size** Text has traditionally been measured in points; with current digital typeface technology, the traditional 72.27 points has been rounded off to 72 points to the inch. Artistic text used as a headline can ideally be anywhere from 24 points for a flyer headline to 72 points for an impactful newspaper headline to 300 points and up (there's no hypothetical limit to how large artistic text can be)—which is over 4 inches in height—for headlines that fairly shout at the reader.

- **Bold and Italic** These buttons on the property bar are shortcuts to defining a whole line of text or only selected characters as bold and italic members of the typeface shown in the Font list box. If a specific font has no family members, CorelDRAW doesn't "fake" a bold or italic look, and the buttons are dimmed. If you need an italic treatment of a font that has no italic family member, a quick fix is to use the Transformation docker and then to set Skew to about $-12°$ to apply to the artistic text.

- **Underline** An underline is an effect available for every font you have installed—you click the button when text is selected and CorelDRAW renders an underline. You can modify the style of the underline to your choosing by pressing CTRL+T, and then on the Character formatting docker choose from the Character Effects | Underline drop-down. If you don't see the preset you want, choose Edit from the list, and then build the underline width and style you need. Underlines are great for professional documents, particularly legal ones, but an underline *isn't* the most clever way to emphasize a phrase in an advertisement. Use a bold font instead

12

or a colored outline or a gradient fill to attract attention artistically. Although underlines are effects, they're very real, and if you convert an underlined phrase to curves (CTRL+Q), the underline becomes an object.

- **Text Alignment** This drop-down lets you set how lines of text are aligned relative to one another. Although justification will serve you best when using long columns of paragraph text, artistic text takes on a more polished look, too, when you apply, for example, Center justification to two or three lines. By default, there is no justification for newly entered artistic text, but for all intents and purposes, this is left-justified text. Full Justify creates a splendid, professional look for columns of paragraph text, but tends to generate an awkward look for artistic text, because a line containing only one word with only a few characters has to take on very wide character spacing. Similarly, Right justification is not an everyday choice for audiences who read Western languages (from left to right). Right justification is a "slow read"; hyphenations and line breaks between words usually look awkward, and this type of justification should be reserved for a page layout where the right edge of the text needs to align perfectly to the vertical of a graphic and the left side of the column can be flowing and freeform. *Force* Justify creates lines of text whose left and right edges are perfectly vertical, like with *Full* Justify, but with an important difference. Force Justify gives equal emphasis to the spacing between characters; although it can sometimes create unsightly gaps (called *rivers*) in paragraph text, it's usually a good alignment choice for correcting justified lines of text where there are too few words on a line, and when hyphenation is not used. Force Justify can also be used as an artistic treatment of paragraph text, as shown in this illustration.

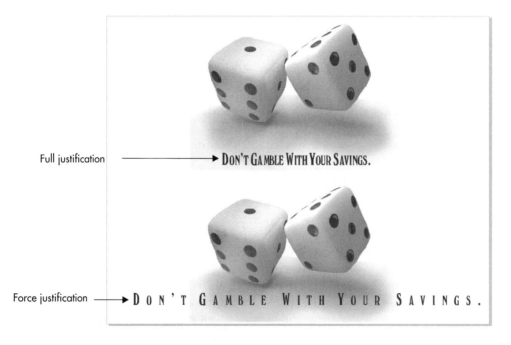

Full justification ⟶ DON'T GAMBLE WITH YOUR SAVINGS.

Force justification ⟶ D O N ' T   G A M B L E   W I T H   Y O U R   S A V I N G S .

- **Character Formatting**   This button will serve the most creative purposes when you have one or only a few characters selected using the Text tool. You can underline a single character, change its font type, family member, point size, and even rotate the selected character(s), all through Character Effects and Character Shift on the Character formatting docker. See the following section, "Character Formatting" for more information.

- **Edit Text**   This button displays a text-editing box, which also appears when you click a piece of text to which is applied an effect such as an envelope or an extrude. CorelDRAW is designed with text-editing flexibility in mind, so to transform text using just about any feature—and to allow the text to still be editable—you work in a proxy box so you don't have to start over when you make a typographic error. Here's a visual example: You've chosen a lovely font to express a lovely sentiment for a card and have extruded the font. In the morning, you find you've misspelled "Happy". No big deal. You click an insertion point in the text where the fix is needed by using the Text tool; the Edit Text dialog appears, you enter the additional characters, and finally click OK. Occasionally, you might need to modify an envelope containing text if you're adding a lot of characters, but the Edit Text dialog is your friend in a jam, and as you'll see, you can even change the font of selected characters, the family members, and the point size.

Character Formatting

You'll often want to change the look of only one or two characters in an artistic text phrase in your document. Character formatting can be accomplished using:

- The Shape tool in combination with the property bar.

- The Text tool in combination with the Character formatting docker.

As you can see in Figure 12-3, you have some options using the Shape tool to select characters, but you have a more complete set of options when you highlight a character with the Text

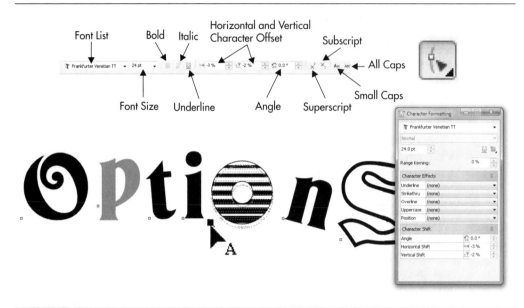

Format and reformat text characters using the Character Formatting box and the property bar.

tool and then click the Character Formatting button on the property bar. For quick and simple reformatting, it's the Shape tool, and for extensive reworking of your artistic text, use the Text tool. You have additional options for lines running under, over, and through selected characters, and if, for example, you've used the Character formatting docker to put a Double Thin Underline beneath your text, you can remove this underline later using the property bar while character nodes have been selected using the Shape tool. Character nodes appear black when selected (as shown in Figure 12-3), and your cursor is a clear indication you're editing text with the Shape tool and not an object path node.

Artistic Text and the Shape Tool

The Shape tool can be used to make various changes to the text, including repositioning individual characters within the artistic text object, changing the horizontal and vertical spacing of all the text at once, and selecting nonconsecutive characters, so you change their properties without changing the rest of the text in the object.

Selecting and Moving Characters with the Shape Tool

To select any characters in an artistic text object, select the text object with the Shape tool (F10)—the cursor changes to the Shape tool pointer with an *A* next to it. With the text object selected in this way, a small, empty box or "control handle" appears at the lower-left corner of each character, as shown in Figure 12-4.

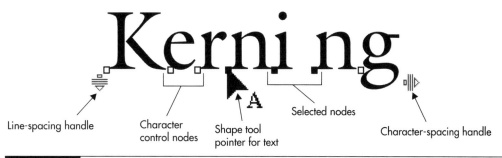

Line-spacing handle   Character control nodes   Shape tool pointer for text   Selected nodes   Character-spacing handle

FIGURE 12-4   Set character and line spacing, and reposition individual characters with the Shape tool.

To select any character, click its control handle using the Shape tool. To select nonconsecutive characters, hold SHIFT (not CTRL as you'd anticipate) while clicking. You can also marquee-drag around the nodes you want to select with the Shape tool. With the control handles selected, you can modify the text formatting, fill, outline, and position of those characters.

To move one or more characters selected with the Shape tool, click-drag one of the selected control handles—all the selected characters will move together. Unless you're striving for a humorous effect, however, it's usually a good idea to keep the characters you move horizontally aligned: hold CTRL while dragging—vertical moves do not accept the CTRL key for constraining movement.

Moving characters with the Shape tool changes the horizontal- and vertical-shift values of them, and the new values can be seen in the Character Formatting box (CTRL+T). Moving characters with the Shape tool is useful for manually adjusting the position of characters visually to improve the *kerning,* the inter-character spacing. Although repositioning character nodes can create fun, freeform headlines, it's also useful if you own a "bum font," a digital typeface whose poor coding results in certain characters neighboring other characters too tightly or too loosely. Then again, almost every typeface has poor kerning for the word "HAWAII"; at the top of the next illustration is the way the characters align as typed. There is usually too little space between the *II*s, and the *A* and *W* should tuck into each other, but do not. At bottom, after 30 seconds with the Shape tool, the word not only has a better relationship between negative and positive areas, but the word is also shorter (which is good when design space is cramped).

The Shape tool can be nudged after selecting character nodes and nodes along object paths. Therefore, you can create better headline kerning by first adjusting the Nudge Distance in Tools | Options | Document | Rulers and then using the keyboard arrows to create a professionally typeset headline.

Adjusting Spacing with the Shape Tool

When an artistic text object is selected with the Shape tool, two additional handles appear at the lower-left and lower-right corners of the object, as shown in Figure 12-5. These two handles modify the line spacing and character spacing for the entire block in one go.

To increase or decrease the word and character spacing, drag the handle at the lower-right corner of the selected text object right or left with the Shape tool. To increase or decrease the line spacing (also the before-paragraph spacing), drag the handle at the lower-left corner of the selected text object down or up with the Shape tool.

All spacing values modified with the Shape tool can be viewed and edited in the Text | Paragraph Formatting Docker.

Combining and Breaking Apart Artistic Text

You can combine several artistic text objects into a single artistic text object: select all the artistic text objects with the Pick tool, and then choose Arrange | Combine or press CTRL+L. Each text object starts a new paragraph in the new text object. Ordinarily, the Combine command converts CorelDRAW objects to simplified ones, but text objects retain their editability as text.

A line of text here,
and a line of text there,
and eventually you have
a paragraph.

A line of text here,
and a line of text there,
and eventually you have
a paragraph.

FIGURE 12-5   *Leading* (inter-line spacing), *kerning* (inter-character spacing), and inter-word spacing can be tuned using the text handles.

The text objects are combined *in the order in which they are selected*—if you select several objects in one go by dragging a marquee around them, they will be selected from front to back. Text objects that do not contain spaces are combined onto a single line. If any of the selected objects is not a text object, all the text objects will be converted to curves and combined with the nontext object.

> **TIP** | *If the text doesn't combine in the order you want or expect, you can reverse the stacking order of the original text objects by first pressing CTRL+Z (Edit | Undo) and then choosing Arrange | Order | Reverse Order.*

Artistic text can also be broken apart from several lines of stacked text to individual lines, all unique objects. To break apart artistic text, choose Arrange | Break Artistic Text, or press CTRL+K. With multi-line text objects, the break apart command results in one text object for each line or paragraph from the original object.

Also, using the break apart command on single-line text objects results in one text object for each word. As you'd expect, breaking apart single-word text objects results in a new text object for each character.

Converting Artistic Text to Curves

Many effects can be applied directly to artistic text, but you might want to apply effects that cannot be applied as a "live" effect to editable text. To achieve the desired effect, the artistic text objects first need to be converted to curves: choose Arrange | Convert To Curves, or press CTRL+Q. Text that has been converted to curves is *no longer editable with the Text tool* and must be edited with the Shape tool instead, just like any other curve object. As mentioned earlier, converting text to plain objects with paths and control nodes is a good way to begin creating logos. The following illustration shows a treatment of artistic text converted to curves. With a push of a node here and a pull there, the result is a workable party store sign. See Chapter 11 for the details on how to use the Smudge brush to produce this effect.

12

Entering and Editing Paragraph Text

Paragraph text is very much like the frames of text that professionals work with in desktop publishing (DTP) applications such as CorelVentura and Adobe InDesign; however, in CorelDRAW you'll soon see options and features that DTP applications don't provide. The largest difference between artistic text and paragraph text is that paragraph text is held in a container—a frame—so *you don't directly edit,* for example, the width of characters in a paragraph text frame simply by yanking on a bounding box handle with the Pick tool. In Figure 12-6 at top are duplicate paragraph frames; they're easy to spot and differentiate from artistic text because even when not selected, they have a dashed outline around them signifying the paragraph text frame. The duplicate at top right has been scaled so it's wider

The Pick tool modifies the container for paragraph text.

The Pick tool directly modifies artistic text.

FIGURE 12-6 When you edit paragraph text with the Pick tool, you're only changing the shape of the frame, not the text itself.

than at left: note that the lines of text flow differently, but the characters remain unchanged, as does the spacing between characters and words. At bottom the same historic American address has been entered as artistic text, and then at right the bounding box was dragged to the right using the Pick tool. The words per line don't rearrange, but what does happen is that the characters themselves are stretched, which is often unwanted. That's the biggest difference between paragraph and artistic text: if text doesn't have a frame, then you're scaling the text.

Working with paragraph text can be a challenge, a little more complex than riding a bike but a lot less complex than rocket science. However, once you get the hang of it (and the following sections are your guide), you'll find paragraph text indispensable for business designs, and those Tri-Fold and Top Fold page presets you learned about in Chapter 6 will spring to life and a new purpose. Your brochures will look as slick as can be.

To create a paragraph text object, select the Text tool in the toolbox, and then click-drag diagonally to create a rectangle into which you'll enter the text. In the next illustration, the arrow at left shows the click-diagonal drag technique (commonly called a *marquee drag*), and at right you see the result. The text inside the paragraph frame is simple a visual prompt, and it disappears after you've added text. A paragraph text frame has resizing, kerning, and leading handles (artistic text features these as well), discussed later in this chapter. You have three ways to fill a paragraph text frame with text:

- **Type in the frame** Manually, it's probably best to leave spell checking on as you go.

- **Paste from the Clipboard** You'll see a dialog before you can paste if you press CTRL+V or choose Edit | Paste (and Edit | Paste Special). Here you can choose to keep or discard the formatting of the text on the Clipboard. If your cursor is inserted in a paragraph text block when you choose Paste Special, the result is a new block of artistic text, regardless of your cursor's insertion point. If you want to paste into existing paragraph text, pressing CTRL+V—the simple Paste command—does the trick.

- **Import a text file** Depending on the text file type, you might be prompted to install a compatibility pack, especially for older MS Word documents. With a broadband connection, the process takes about 3 minutes, you don't have to quit CorelDRAW, and you can paste after the compatibility program is installed. In contrast, a plain TXT file with no font or paragraph attributes will import perfectly after you choose a style of import from the Importing/Pasting Text dialog.

12

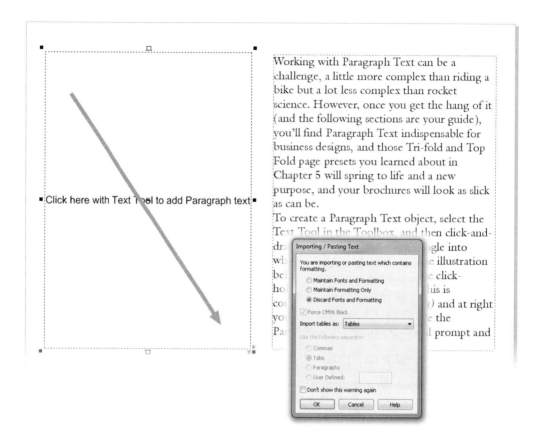

Especially if you're pasting text from the Clipboard, the frame you drag for paragraph text might not accommodate the amount of text. As a result, the text is hidden; the frame is a dashed red outline instead of black. To reveal the text, drag down the "window-shade handle," the small square tab (bottom center) on the text frame; when there's hidden text, the handle has a down arrow in its center.

One of the most useful things you can do with paragraph text frames is to link them; instead of spoiling a design by increasing the size of the frame, you can create a second, third, or any number of additional frames, and flow the excess text into the new frames as you create the frames. The advantage to this is that you can move the linked frames around in your design, and the content (the printed message of the paragraph text) remains in perfect order. For example, if you need to break a paragraph into two frames in the middle of "Now is the time for all good people to come," you do this, and in the future if you need to resize the first paragraph text frame, the excess of words "pours" into the second frame, regardless of its position on the page. This is too neat to simply describe with words, so let's try creating linked text frames in the following steps.

Creating Linked Paragraph Text Frames

1. In a word processor or plain text editor, copy some existing text to the Clipboard; it doesn't matter what the text is. Highlight a few paragraphs and then press CTRL+C.

2. In CorelDRAW, choose the Text tool and then click-diagonal drag to define a paragraph text frame. Try to make the frame smaller than the text on the Clipboard (eyeball it).

3. Insert your cursor in the frame, and then press CTRL+V to paste the Clipboard text. If you copied from a word processor, CorelDRAW will flash you the Import/Pasting Text dialog, where you have the option of retaining the formatting (if any) created in the word processor—font choice, point size, justification, and tabs are all attributes of text formatting. Go with it; click the Maintain Fonts And Formatting button and then click OK.

4. Click the bottom-center text handle (the box with the black arrow), and your cursor is now loaded with all the text that was hidden from view because your frame is smaller than the text you pasted into it. Your cursor takes on a new look, shown in the following illustration.

Ipsum lorem de facto incognito. Et tu gorilla e pluribus unum. Olympian triouts souvlaki ignitus. Homo sapiens nolo contendre. Telli phonus sodium glutimate. Marquis attendee est plural ad nauseum. Unix incognito. Et tu gorilla e pluribus unum. Olympian triouts souvlaki ignitus. Homo sapiens nolo contendre. Telli phonus sodium glutimate. Marquis attendee est plural ad nauseum. Unix interruptus ipsum lorem. Gyros sic tempus fugit. interruptus ipsum lorem. Gyros sic tempus fugit. Congolium et plutonium et baklava. Caveat emptor.Quid pro quo a omnibus. Glorious apprehende sic hic infinitum. Los Angeles carborundum unitus Mercedes. Circus clownus e minutae. Glorious hiatus sic hic infinitum. This sentence goes on and on and on. Ipsum lorem de facto Ipsum lorem de facto incognito. I

Click to load cursor with paragraph text overflow.

5. Click-diagonal drag to create a new, linked text frame. The excess text from the first frame automatically flows into the new frame, shown here. A light blue line with an arrow indicates the relationship between the text in the first and the second frame (don't worry, this screen element does not print). Try repositioning the two frames now using the Pick tool. Then try resizing the first frame. You'll see, dynamically, the second frame take the overflow from the first frame.

Web-Compatible Paragraph Text

If you are designing web pages in CorelDRAW, you should make all paragraph text web compatible. *Web-compatible* paragraph text will be exported as real text in the final HTML web page. Web-compatible paragraph text has a limited subset of normal paragraph text properties: font, size, bold, italic, underline, alignment, and solid color, but no tabs, bullets, or other advanced features you might find in a DTP program. All other properties are removed from the text. All text that is not web compatible (symbol fonts, certain extended characters, and so on) is exported as bitmaps when the page is published to HTML. Bitmaps do not scale on dynamic HTML pages; they take more time to download than live text and do not render to screen as crisply as actual text.

 To export text as web-compatible text and not as a bitmap, choose File | Export HTML. Don't *choose Export For Web. See Chapter 28 for the details on exporting text and graphics for website design.*

To make paragraph text web compatible, right-click the paragraph text object with the Pick tool, and choose Make Text Web Compatible from the pop-up menu.

Editing Text: The Comprehensive Tour

A few of the basics of text entry and editing have been discussed to get you up and running. However, as your needs arise for more complex character formatting and fancy text layout, you'll want to become more familiar with the nitty-gritty of everyday typography and publishing. The good news is that CorelDRAW's text-handling features are very similar to your favorite word processor or desktop publishing program. Just select the Text tool (F8) and begin the exploration.

Navigating with the Insertion Point Cursor

You can use the text cursor to select text a character at a time, by whole words, or even by whole paragraphs, just by dragging to highlight. You can also use the UP, DOWN, LEFT, and RIGHT ARROW keys on your keyboard to quickly navigate the cursor insertion point around large amounts of text.

Selecting Text

To place the text cursor (the I-beam) in the text where you want to start typing, click with the left mouse button. Any text you type will be inserted at that point and will have the same style as the character *to the left* of the insertion point.

To select text with the Text tool cursor, click-drag with the primary mouse button from the point at which you want the selection to start, and release the mouse button where you want the selection to end. Alternatively, click once to place the cursor in the text where you want the selection to start, and then, while holding down the SHIFT key, click where you want the selection to end—all the text between the two clicks is selected. Double-clicking a word selects that word. Triple-clicking selects the entire paragraph in which you triple-clicked.

You can move the cursor with the cursor keys (the keyboard arrow keys) as well as with the mouse.

- To move left or right a word at a time, hold CTRL while moving the cursor with the LEFT or RIGHT ARROW key.

- To move up or down a paragraph at a time, hold CTRL and press the UP or DOWN ARROW key, respectively.

- To expand or contract the selection, hold SHIFT while moving the endpoint with the arrow keys.

- To move to the beginning or end of the current frame, hold CTRL and press the HOME or END key, respectively. Alternatively, use the PAGE UP or PAGE DOWN key to move up or down a frame.

Moving Text

You can move a selection of text with the mouse by dragging-and-dropping; select the word or phrase you want to move, and then with the primary mouse button click-and-drag the text to its new location in the current text object—or in any other text object. A vertical bar indicates the insertion point at the new location; the cursor becomes the international "no" sign (a circle with a slash through it) if it is not possible to drop the text at the current location.

Dragging with the *right* mouse button causes a pop-up menu to appear when you drop the text, with options for what to do with the text. The options are Copy Here and Move Here, and Add To Rollover doesn't do anything unless you have a web-page rollover defined. You can use this special editing gesture to copy and move words within paragraph and artistic text, but you can also put the copied or moved text outside of the body of artistic and paragraph text. In this event, the text is no longer in line with the text from which you copy or move, so only use this command (particularly Move) for a very good reason.

Converting Between Artistic Text and Paragraph Text

To convert a block of artistic text to paragraph text, right-click the artistic text object with the Pick tool; then choose Convert To Paragraph Text from the pop-up menu. The menu command is Text | Convert To Paragraph Text, and the keyboard shortcut is CTRL+F8. All the text formatting is maintained as closely as possible each time you convert between the two text types, although some formatting, such as paragraph text columns and effects, cannot be applied to artistic text and is lost.

Going the other way, from paragraph text to artistic text, is similarly simple. However, all the text in a paragraph text frame must be visible: it cannot be hidden and you cannot convert a linked paragraph text frame. With the Pick tool, right-click over the paragraph text, and then choose Convert To Artistic Text (CTRL+F8 works, too).

Paragraph text objects that are web compatible cannot *be converted to artistic text. You need to first (with the Pick tool) right-click over web-compatible text, and then uncheck the Make Text Web Compatible check box.*

The Text Bar and Special Paragraph Formatting

Let's dig deeper into paragraph text options and discover new ways to embellish your printed message; create or open a document now that contains a paragraph text frame. Because of the large screen resolutions we enjoy today, we can view pages at almost a 1:1 resolution as they would print, but this also means we might need to scroll and mouse around a document more than is healthy for the wrists. The solution in CorelDRAW is a simple one: if you're working extensively with text, you float the Text toolbar close to the area of the document in which you're fine-tuning. Right-click over any area of the property bar, and then choose Text from the pop-up menu. You can drag the Text toolbar to hover over any area you like.

The Text toolbar can be used to edit single characters in artistic text and paragraph text, but its real strength is in the offering of options for making paragraph text look polished and sophisticated. When the Pick tool or the Text tool is active, all the features shown in Figure 12-7

12

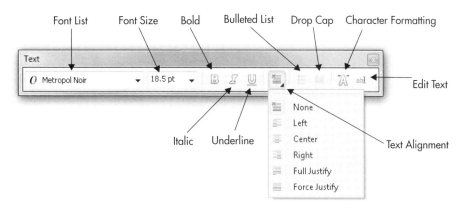

| **FIGURE 12-7** | The Text toolbar is a convenient gateway to the text formatting you need on a daily basis. |

are active and at your disposal. Additional modifications to the available options are described a little later in this chapter.

TIP   *The Text toolbar and the Text options on the property bar when the Pick or the Text tool have selected text are essentially identical. The Text toolbar is simply a more portable device for working closely with text.*

Drop Caps and Bulleted Lists Formatting

A *drop cap* is a dropped capital character at the beginning of a paragraph, much larger than the rest of the text, extending three, four, or more lines down in the paragraph…and it adds a touch of class to a document, particularly if you're illustrating a fairy tale.

Bulleted lists are a common necessity for page layouts: restaurant menus, assembly instructions, just about anything that's a list that doesn't need to be a numbered list! In the following sections, you'll see not only how to create a bulleted list, but also how to choose any character you like for the bullet and even create a hanging indent for the bulleted list for an ultra-professional presentation.

Creating a Drop Cap

You have a lot of options, hence a lot of design opportunities, for drop caps in a CorelDRAW document: you can decide on the drop cap's height relative to the lines of paragraph text of its neighbors, whether it's nestled into the body of the text or stands to the left (called a hanging indent), and even choose the font used for the drop cap.

First, the Drop Cap button on the Text toolbar and property bar is available when the Pick tool is used to select paragraph text, and when the Text tool is used to highlight a paragraph within a paragraph text frame. This is a show/hide *toggle* button: it turns the default attributes for a drop cap on and off within the selected text. Therefore, you can create a drop cap for paragraph text in one click, but if you want to add your own input, you need to additionally work with the Drop Cap options box, as demonstrated in the following steps.

Adding a Drop Cap to Your Paragraph Text

1. Create some paragraph text, as described earlier in this chapter.

2. Use the Text tool to highlight a paragraph that you want to lead off with a drop cap. You can create drop caps by simply selecting a paragraph text frame with the Pick tool, but doing so will put a drop cap at the beginning of every paragraph (after every hard return), which might be overdoing the effect.

3. On the Text toolbar or the property bar, click the Drop Cap button; you'll get the default drop cap effect, as seen in the illustration below.

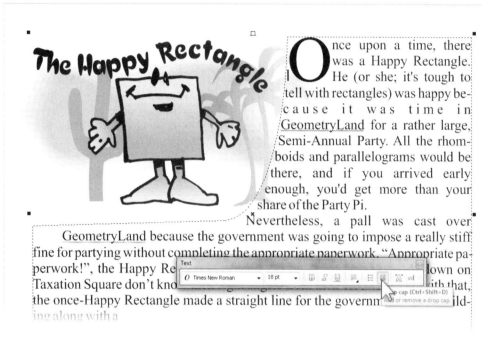

4. The easiest way to make the drop cap into an ornamental drop cap is to toggle the Drop Cap on the property bar to hide it; then highlight the first letter, and change the font for this one character. Then, with the I-beam cursor in front of the letter, click the Drop Cap button once more.

12

TIP | *Barock Caps (a regional spelling of "Baroque," not the U.S. president) is a wonderfully intricate storybook-style typeface. It's available for free at http:// moorstation.org/typoasis/designers/steffmann/index.htm.*

5. Choose Text | Drop Cap to display the *options* for the drop cap. The most common customizing would be to change how many lines the cap is dropped; by default, it's three, but four or even five can look interesting, depending on the font you use. If you feel there isn't enough air between the paragraph text and the drop cap, use the Space After Drop Cap spin box to increase the space to the right of the drop cap. You also have the option to Use Hanging Indent Style For Drop Cap, which casts the drop cap to the left of the paragraph text while the paragraph text then takes on a flush-left indent. The following illustration shows the completed effect; a hanging indent was not used because the design uses paragraph text inside a path (discussed later in this chapter) to wrap the text around the cartoon, and an indent would spoil the overall composition.

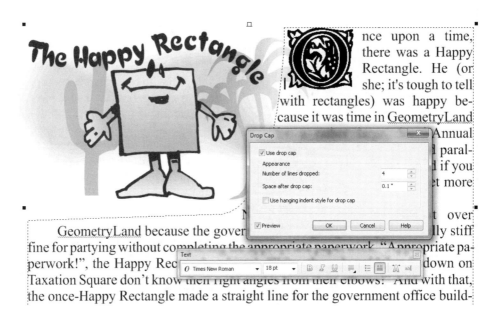

Making Bulleted Paragraph Text

Like the toggling Drop Cap button, the show/hide Bulleted List button can be your one-click stop for creating bulleted lists; however, you'll surely want a custom bulleted list that looks as artistic as your document layout. On the Text menu you'll find the Bullets command; it's straightforward and you'll quickly achieve great results. Find or create a list of something, and follow along to see how to work the options for bullets.

Creating a Bullet Motif

1. There's no real harm in simply using the Pick tool to select the paragraph text you want to make a fancy bulleted list: every line break in the list begins a new bulleted item, so select the text and then click the show/hide Bulleted List button on the property bar or on the Text toolbar. See the following illustration.

2. Choose Text | Bullets.

3. Choose a typeface that contains a character that works well with the theme of the bulleted list composition. The illustration is an "All-Star Recipe," so a bullet shaped like a star is appropriate. Microsoft's Wingdings font is installed with every copy of Windows, and it features some nice symbols: choose Wingdings from the Font drop-down list in this example, and then click the Symbol drop-down arrow, and locate a good star shape.

4. Click the Use Hanging Indent Style For Bulleted Lists check box to get a polished look for the list.

5. Increase the point size by dragging upward in the center of the spin box control for Size.

6. Most likely, the baseline of the enlarged symbol won't look right compared with the text in the list (it'll be too high). Drag downward on the Baseline Shift spin box control until the bullets look aligned.

12

7. Optionally, if your symbol is crowding into the list text, increase the Bullet To Text spacing. Similarly, the paragraph text frame might be too tight to the left of the bullet; in this case, you increase the Text Frame To Bullet amount. See the following illustration for the completed design.

Working with Columns

Although you can manually create flowing columns of paragraph text, it's often less time-consuming to use the automated Columns feature in CorelDRAW. Text columns divide paragraph text frames into several vertical columns separated by *gutters* (margins). Multiple columns can be created only in the Text | Columns dialog. This section describes how to manipulate columns with the mouse. You must have paragraph text selected with the Text tool to work with columns: the tabs do not show on the rulers using other tools.

Select the frame in which you want to place columns, choose Text | Columns, and then set the Number Of Columns on the Column Settings dialog. It is always a good idea to keep the number of columns balanced, so each column is neither too wide nor too narrow. A good rule of thumb for legibility is: each line of text should be no wider than 6 inches or 16 words, but it should be wide enough to have at least 4 words per line.

To change the width of the columns and margins, drag the column guides, column-boundary markers, gutter handles, and horizontal-resize handles, as shown in Figure 12-8. When dragging the column guides or boundary markers, if the Equal Column Width option is selected in the Column Settings dialog, all the gutters will be resized together; the gutter handles are available only when this option is not selected.

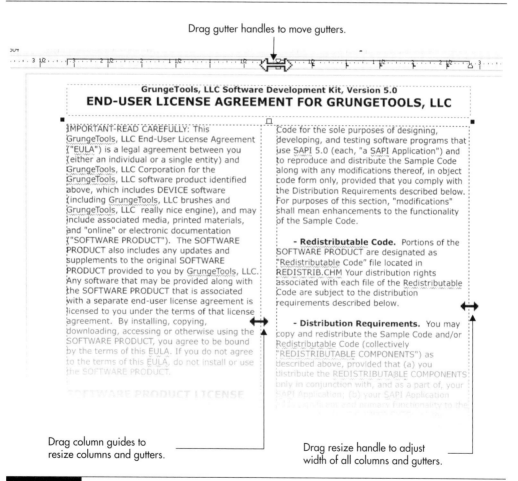

FIGURE 12-8   Column widths can be edited directly by dragging with the mouse.

Columns can be applied only to whole paragraph text frames and cannot be applied to individual paragraphs or artistic text.

Column Settings

Once you've created a paragraph text object with columns, you can refine and make precise columns and gutter widths through the Column Settings dialog (Text | Columns), shown in Figure 12-9.

To add extra columns, first set the Number Of Columns, and then set the Widths of the columns. The Gutter value is the distance between the selected column and the next one. If Equal Column Width is selected, changing the width of any column or gutter changes the

FIGURE 12-9   Use the Column Settings dialog to apply columns to paragraph text.

width of all columns or gutters to the same value. If Maintain Current Frame Width is selected, changing the width of any column or gutter will not change the overall width of the frame, so the other columns and gutters will be resized to accommodate the change. A preview of the column settings is shown in the preview frame on the right side of the dialog.

Text in columns (even if only one column is used) can be justified via the Text toolbar and the Paragraph Formatting box.

 You can have more control over columns by laying them out as multiple text frames, each one containing a single column.

Formatting Paragraph Text

Stepping inside the frame and column formatting of paragraph text, CorelDRAW has extensive options for specifying how lines of text look compared with one another, how tightly characters and words are spaced, and how you want individual paragraphs to separate from each other. The following sections cover the use of the Paragraph Formatting box.

Paragraph Alignment

The Alignment settings on the Paragraph Formatting box affect the spacing for the entire selected paragraph; you can choose the entire paragraph text object using the Pick tool, or choose only pages by highlighting them with the Text tool. Horizontal and Vertical Alignment at the top of this box pertain to the orientation of the language set of the font used; American and European users will want to use Horizontal Alignment.

Spacing

12

Below Alignment on the Paragraph Formatting box are controls for inter-line spacing (leading), for how much space should go before or after a paragraph, for inter-character and inter-word spacing, and finally for indent preferences. Note that proper typographical form dictates that separate paragraphs are usually indicated by either a first-line indent or a line space between paragraphs, but not both.

Paragraph and Line Spacing

Depending on your layout, you might choose to separate paragraphs by using the Before Paragraph or the After Paragraph spin boxes, but not both. The spacing between paragraphs is measured by default as the "% Of Char. Height" (percent of the character height), the total height of a character in a digital font, which is not always easy to discern; typically it's about 30 percent taller than a capital letter in the font. If this proves to be too time-consuming to calculate, you can always choose Points or "% Of Pt. Size" (percentage of point size) from the drop-down list. In the following illustration, 200% of the character height is chosen to separate paragraphs. This is an option you want to experiment with, depending on the typeface you're using. Anywhere from 125% to 200% can work from an artistic standpoint.

Line spacing is used to let some "air" into paragraph text and is especially useful when you have a font whose ascenders or descenders are unusually tall. You can also use very wide Line spacing to create an artistic effect when starting, for example, a magazine article. It's been fashionable in layout for several years now to put about 300% Line spacing in the opening paragraph: it lightens the page when using a bold font and also allows the reader to see more of any decorative background.

Language, Character, and Word Spacing

If you're typesetting, for example, an article using an Asian font, Language spacing will be useful to space non-left-to-right sentences; if not, you have very little use for this option. You can set how much extra space is added to the default inter-character space for the paragraph as a whole by using the Character spacing. The values are a percentage of a normal space character for the current font. You can also modify the inter-word spacing—this has the effect of adjusting the width of the space character. The following illustration shows some adjusted text at right (highlighted), and you can compare the effect to the default paragraph text at left.

Remember the control handles on the bounding boxes of paragraph text. They offer less precision when setting character and line spacing than the Paragraph Formatting box, but they're quick to use and provide a good coarse view of how your layout is shaping up.

Indentation and Margins of Paragraph Text

You can set the sizes of the indents of the left and right margins, as well as the size of the first-line indentation, just as you do in a word processor. These can be set precisely from the Paragraph Formatting box, or you can set them with a little less precision using the triangular markers on the ruler, which are shown here:

Left indent marker   First-line indent marker   Right indent marker

Handle for moving both left-hand indent markers together.

Formatting Tabs

Tab stops for paragraph text can be edited either directly in the ruler or in the Text | Tab Settings dialog, as shown in Figure 12-10. CorelDRAW supports left, right, center, and decimal tabs, just like most word processors do.

Adding, Moving, and Deleting Tabs from the Dialog

Tabs can be added to the current paragraph in the Text | Tab Settings box by first entering a value in the Tab Location spin box, and then by clicking Add. To set the type of the new tab, choose from the drop-down list associated with the tab. Similarly, you can adjust an existing tab by clicking its position (thus opening the value for editing) and then typing in a new value. To delete a tab, select it in the list, and then click the Remove button.

When you create a new paragraph, unless you have modified the default paragraph style, tab stops are positioned every half-inch. To remove all the tabs, click the Remove All button.

Formatting Tab Leaders from the Dialog

You can choose whether text positioned to any tab has a leader between the tab settings from the Leader Settings box reached by clicking the Leader Options button in Tab Settings. *Leading characters* are often used in tabulated lists such as tables of contents and menus to join the section titles or menu items on the left with their respective page numbers or prices on the right.

Leaders are usually displayed as a series of dots, but they can be changed to any of the characters shown in the Character drop-down list (unfortunately, you can't make a leader using a font other than the one used in the paragraph text). To change the leader character,

12

Edit tab stops by using the Text | Tabs settings.

select a Character from the drop-down list. The distance between the leader characters is set with the Spacing setting: this value is the number of space characters to insert between each leader character. A preview of the leaders appears in the Preview box.

Using the Ruler to Set Tabs

To edit tab stops on the ruler, the ruler must be visible (choose View | Rulers), you use the Text tool in selecting the paragraph text, and you click to set or edit the tab stops. To view tab characters in the body of your paragraph text, press CTRL+SHIFT+C (Text | Show Non-Printing Characters).

 Before creating new tabs, you should delete all the tabs that are already in place— select Remove All from the Tab Settings dialog.

To create new tabs with the ruler, use the Text tool to select the paragraphs to which you want to add tabs, and then click on the horizontal ruler where you want to add the new tab stop. The type of the tab can be set by right-clicking over the tab. There is also a selector button where the ruler origin usually is when working with paragraph text. Clicking the selector button cycles between the four tab states: left–right–center–decimal. See Figure 12-11.

To move a tab, drag it to its new position on the ruler. To delete a tab, drag it off the ruler and into the workspace. To change the type of a tab, delete it and create a new one of the correct type, right-click it in the ruler, and select a new type from the pop-up menu, or change its type in the Tab Settings dialog. Tabs cannot be added to artistic text.

Here's a practical example of the value in knowing how to set up tabs: create a folding menu design, and then create paragraph text with menu items and their corresponding prices on the same lines (make up anything you like; have fun here!). Here's how to create a dot leader so the guests can see the prices at far right easily, based on the menu items at far left.

12

FIGURE 12-11   Tab stops can be edited directly on the horizontal ruler when editing.

Picking Up the Tab

1. With the Text tool cursor inserted in the body of the text, choose Text | Tabs.

2. Create a tab at the end of the line, just short of the end of the paragraph frame; give it the Right tab property.

3. Unfortunately, you can't have a decimal leader and a regular text leader on the same line of text, but this, for the most part, is okay. With most typefaces the decimal in the price column will line up fairly evenly with a leader tab in place on lines. Click Leader Options.

4. Choose a period as the character, or if you want something fancier, you might try a single right-pointing angle quote ("›"; ALT+155) if your font supports this character.

5. Set the Spacing for the leader character. Notice that your document updates live, so you can preview how your dot leader looks before clicking OK.

6. Click OK and the menu will certainly look more appetizing after applying your newfound typographer's skills.

Wrapping Text Around Other Shapes

You can apply text wrapping to shapes in CorelDRAW so that any paragraph text placed close to the shape will flow *around* the object instead of over or under it, as shown in the examples in Figure 12-12.

Several types of wrapping are available.

- **Contour wrapping**   The text is wrapped a line at a time *around* the outline of the object.

- **Square wrapping**   The text is wrapped around an imaginary rectangle that bounds the object with the wrap (its *bounding box*).

FIGURE 12-12   There are six contour and square text-wrapping options available and one non-wrapping option (None).

In either case, the text can be made to flow down the left or right of the object, or straddle it (flow down both sides). Square wrapping also supports Above/Below, where no text flows to the sides of the object.

To apply Contour Straddle, right-click the shape and select Wrap Paragraph Text from the pop-up menu. To set a different wrapping type, select it from the General tab of the Object properties docker (press ALT+ENTER). Then set the margin distance, which is the gap between the outline or bounding box of the shape and the paragraph text wrapped around it.

NOTE *Grouped objects will accept Contour Straddle, but not all complex objects will. For example, if you want to straddle text around a blend group, group the blend objects first, or the Wrap Paragraph Text option will be dimmed.*

Puz · zle[puhz–uhl]

noun, verb, -zled, -zling.

—noun

1. A toy, problem, or other contrivance designed to amuse by presenting difficulties to be solved by ingenuity or patient effort. 2. Something puzzling; a puzzling question, matter, or person. 3. A puzzled or perplexed c o n d i t i o n ;   bewil derment. 4. A c r o s s w o r d   puzzle: Did you do the puzzle   i n   t h e n e w s p a p e r   today? 5. A jigsaw puzzle.   —verb (used with object) 6.   To   p u t (someone) at a   loss; mystify; confuse; baffle: Her attitude puzzles me. 7.   To frustrate or confound, as the   understanding; p e r p l e x : T h e   problem puzzled him for weeks. 8. To   exercise (oneself, one's brain, etc.) over some problem or matter. 9. Archaic. to make intricate or complicated. —verb (used without object) 10. To be perplexed or confused. 11. To ponder or

12

It's important to understand that text legibility can be at peril when you wrap text around a highly freeform shape; it's just not good layout, for example, to create a zigzag-shaped wrap, causing the reader's head to whiplash every other line. Use wrapping text as a creative element, but use your artistic eye to avoid unnecessarily hard-to-read paragraph text.

TIP *Wrapping affects only paragraph text. Text wrapping is not applied to the wrapped text itself, only to the shapes that are wrapped by the text.*

Fitting Text to Curve

Wrapping text around an object has its alter ego: putting text inside a shape, so it looks as though the text itself forms a shape. And there's a third variation called Fit Text To Curve—

you can have artistic text follow an arc, a freeform line, an open or closed shape, and you have options for the style in which the text follows your line.

Pouring Text into a Shape

The simplest way to form text so it appears to have a geometry other than rectangular, is to first create a shape, copy some text to the Clipboard if you don't have a message in mind, and then carefully position your Text tool just inside the line of the shape (perhaps 1/8 of a screen inch inside) until the cursor turns into an I-beam with a tiny text box at its lower right, and then click to start typing, or click and then press CTRL+V to paste your Clipboard text. Text inside a shape is paragraph text, and it obeys all the paragraph text formatting conventions covered in this chapter. Here's an example of a creative use for shaped paragraph text: the following mock article is about buttons, so the shape of the paragraph text might look appropriate if it was shaped like…a button.

Creating a Round Text Frame

1. Open Sew what.cdr in CorelDRAW. The text has been provided for you in the margin.

2. With the Ellipse tool (F7) hold CTRL to constrain the ellipse to a circle, and then drag a shape in the document about 6" in width. Check the property bar if necessary to get an approximation of the 6" circle.

3. Copy the text at left to the Clipboard. It's easiest to do this with the Pick tool; the Text tool can also be used. Highlight the text and then press CTRL+C to copy or CTRL+X to cut.

4. With the Text tool, hover the cursor just inside the circle until it turns into an I-beam cursor with a tiny "AB" to the bottom right, and then click. Do not click if the cursor features an "A" with a wavy line—this is the indication that you can put text along a curve, the wrong feature for this example. With the insertion point for text inside the circle, you could start typing, but for these steps, press CTRL+V to paste text from the Clipboard.

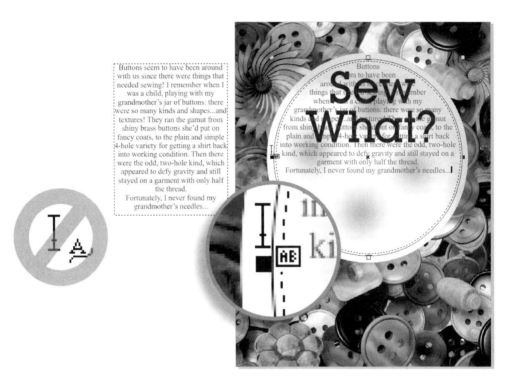

5. Choose Text | Paragraph Formatting. If you'd created a half-circle into which you poured the text, it would not obscure the headline in this example. However, the text doesn't fill the circle container, so you can align the text to the *bottom* of the circle: choose Bottom from the Alignment | Vertical drop-down list on the Paragraph formatting docker.

6. With the text selected, choose an appropriate typeface from your list of installed fonts, accessed from the property bar. Then choose a font size of your liking. Times New Roman—a Windows system font—works quite well for this short text passage at 18 points.

7. If the text proves to be too large in point height, resize the container using the Pick tool—hold SHIFT to contain the scaling, and magically the text reflows dynamically until you release the object. You don't always need to scale text; sometimes scaling the text's container is a more inspired way to finish a design.

8. Make the circle containing the text invisible: select the circle with the Pick tool (check the status line to make sure the circle and not the text is selected), and then right-click the no outline well on the color palette, the top one with the "X" in it. Figure 12-13 shows the assignment nearing completion.

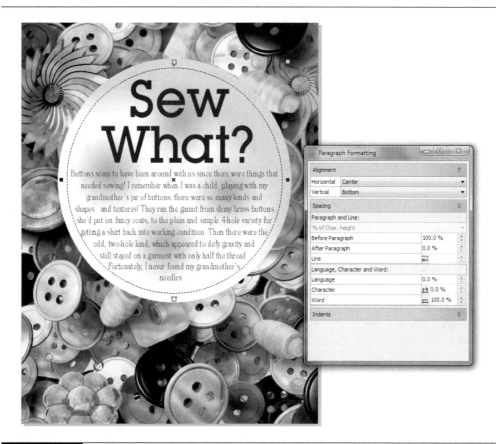

One very popular treatment for text "bound" to an object is the arc of text. This is accomplished by first creating the arc shape (a circle usually works well) and then instead of clicking inside the shape, hovering your cursor above the shape until your Text tool cursor becomes an I-beam with a tiny swooping curve beneath it.

Follow these steps to flow text in a semicircle.

Text Along a Curve

1. Open Loving Cup.cdr. The graphic of the trophy could use some text surrounding the top.

2. Create a circle using the Ellipse tool.

3. With the Shape tool, drag the Ellipse node away from the center of the circle to create an open arc. Adjust each node until you have an arc centered above the loving cup. See Chapter 8 if you're unfamiliar with editing CorelDRAW objects.

4. With the Text tool, position the cursor just along the outline of the circle, and then click an insertion point and begin to type. You'll see that the text follows the curve. What you type is up to you, but "Congratulations" is a solid starter for graphics that involve a trophy!

5. If the text isn't aligned to your liking, use the Offset spin box on the property bar to correct it.

6. If you'd like the text to be a little off the curve, use the Distance From Path spin box.

7. If you'd like a truly wild and interesting style, a treatment of the text such as a 3D ribbon look, check out the drop-down list at left on the property bar. Click any of the styles to apply them. Figure 12-14 shows an example of an award; the circle still has an outline, but it takes one right-click to correct that.

FIGURE 12-14   Use Fit Text To Curve to make your message a flowing one.

Embedding Objects into Text

Graphic objects and bitmaps can be embedded into blocks of artistic and paragraph text—in the layout profession, this is called an *inline graphic*. This is great for adding special symbols to text such as logotypes, bullet points, or horizontal separators, or for embedding instructional graphics such as mouse cursor images.

You embed an object into text in two ways:

- **With the Clipboard** Copy or cut the object to the Clipboard (CTRL+C or CTRL+X), click the Text tool in the text where you want the object to be placed, and paste the object (CTRL+V).

- **Drag-and-Drop** Select the object with the mouse, and then drag it with the *right* mouse button to the position in the text where you want it to appear—a vertical bar between characters in the text indicates where the object will be placed. Release the mouse button and select Copy Into Text or Move Into Text from the pop-up menu.

Embedded objects are treated as "special characters"—they can be selected only with the Text tool or the Shape tool. To resize an object after it has been embedded, select it and set its point size on the property bar as if it were a typographic character.

To delete an embedded object, select it with the Text tool and press DELETE.

Changing and Proofing Formatted Text

Once you have your text formatted the way you want, it's still editable text; if you've entered it by hand, you should probably proof it before sending it off for printing. There's no equity in 12,000 four-color posters that proudly exclaim, "Enter The Millyun Dollar Speling Contest!", right? Proofing for spelling and grammar is easy: you select the text with either the Pick or the Text tool, and then press CTRL+F12 (or right-click and then choose Spell Check from the pop-up menu). You'll see that you have not only a spelling, but also a grammar checker and a thesaurus right there at your cursor tip.

Spell checking is only one area of CorelDRAW that you can use to put the finishing touches on your text message; the following sections take you through other features and a little text preflight for your work.

Changing Text Case

Occasionally you'll receive text from a client who doesn't know where the CAPS LOCK key is on the keyboard, or you have a really, really old plain-text file created using a DOS application. In any event, using all caps in a text message, unless it's a very brief headline, can be a real eyesore.

To change the case of text you have typed, insert the Text tool cursor in text, and then right-click the text: choose an option from the Change Case submenu. Changing the case of characters replaces the original characters with new characters of the correct case.

Hyphenation

It's bad form to have two or more consecutive lines of text with a hyphen at the end, and this sometimes happens when you use a specific column width or frame shaping.

- To remove hyphenation from a paragraph, choose the text with either the Pick tool or the Text tool, then choose Text, and then uncheck Use Hyphenation.

- To manually hyphenate a line after hyphenation is turned off, you can put your cursor between the characters you want to break and then press CTRL+-. Alternatively, click the insertion point with the Text tool, and then choose Text | Insert Formatting Code | Optional Hyphen.

Converting Paragraph Text to Curves

It is possible to convert paragraph text to curves. By converting text to curves, the resulting shapes can be extensively modified, reshaped, and restyled. This is also a method for preventing others from making any text modifications to the document. It is also an acceptable way to prepare text-heavy illustrations for sharing when you're confident that a coworker doesn't own a font you used in the document.

To convert a paragraph text object to curves, select it and choose Arrange | Convert To Curves. Or, right-click the text object with the Pick tool, and choose Convert To Curves from the pop-up menu or press CTRL+Q. Because paragraph text as curves can have thousands of nodes, don't perform this sort of thing thoughtlessly, and be prepared to wait a while during the conversion of large paragraphs. CorelDRAW converts paragraph text to curves quite intelligently; it breaks the text into groups, groups almost never consisting of a single shape that has more than 1,000 nodes. PostScript printing language has a complexity threshold of 1,000–1,200 nodes along a single path. If you ever arrive at a single curve shape that has more than this amount, you're best off breaking the shape (Arrange | Break Curve Apart; CTRL+K) and then joining shapes that should be joined (Arrange | Combine; CTRL+L). Too many nodes, and a PostScript job will fail, and a commercial printer is not likely to thank you for your business.

Text and Styles

After you've created a specific look for text, it would be a shame not to be able to save it as a style so it can be reused later. You can create styles for artistic and paragraph text in CorelDRAW. *Styles* store the text attributes from one object and can be used to apply those attributes to other

12

objects at a later time in the same document (styles are by default local properties). If you edit the properties of a style, all the text formatted with that style is updated immediately.

To save a style, with the Pick tool, choose the text, right-click, and then choose Styles | Save Style Properties, and you'll get a box that looks like the following illustration. This box is valid for objects as well; object styles can also be applied for fill and outline settings.

Creating and Editing Styles

In the Save Style As dialog, only select those formatting options that you want as part of the style. If, for example, you select the Text option but clear the Fill and Outline options, then applying this new style to some text will only modify the type-related properties and will keep the existing fill and outline.

Give the style a new, unique name. Click OK, and the style is created and ready for use on the Graphic and text styles docker, which is opened by pressing CTRL+F5 or by choosing Window | Dockers | Graphic And Text Styles. You drag the title of your saved style and drop it onto a text object you want formatted. Alternatively, right-click the text object and choose Styles | Apply in the pop-up menu; then choose the style you want from the list.

Editing Text Styles

To edit a style, right-click its title on the Graphic and text styles docker, and then choose Properties. This opens the Options dialog at the Styles page under Document, with the style selected in the list, from where you can enable and disable features of the style. You can also edit the settings of the style by clicking the Font, Fill, or Outline Edit button in the Options dialog.

To delete a style from the docker, right-click it and choose Delete. You cannot delete default styles.

| TIP | *To revert some text to its assigned style, either reapply the style, or right-click and choose Styles | Revert To Style from the pop-up menu.* |

You have in front of you a very handy and thorough documentation of how to make a text message stand out in the marketplace—how to attract attention in a polished, professional manner. From drop caps to justification, leading to indents, these aren't just a typographer's tools, but the tools of everyone who needs to communicate visually. After a while, what you used to consider an extraordinary effort to accomplish with text will feel quite natural and even ordinary. Now that you know how to drive CorelDRAW's text engine, let's learn the rules of the road in Chapter 13. Fonts are like any artistic element: there are wise and poor uses for typefaces, and you'll want your message to read as well as it looks.

12

CHAPTER 13

Typography Rules and Conventions

The art of typography isn't easily separated from the art of illustration—text and graphics have coexisted on the printed page since there was a printed page. This chapter is a departure of sorts from regular documentation of CorelDRAW because before you drive the CorelDRAW text engine, you need to know the rules of the road. For example, the physical appearance of text should complement an illustration. Think of a font choice as the attire in which your message appears and CorelDRAW as the boutique where you shop for accessories to dress up your message.

Like successful design work, typography has rules, such as hyphenation, punctuation, justification, line spacing; in addition to the rules, typography is subordinate to the design it appears with. Nothing spoils a good display sign like 15 exclamations marks misused to stress a point. Give this chapter a thorough read-through before moving on to the chapters on working with text later in this part of the book. This chapter has great examples of typographic dos and don'ts, and the tips you'll learn will enhance the worth of your printed message—and at the very least this chapter has good examples of punctuation.

Font Families and Font Styles

When beginning a project, it's usually best to cruise the Installed Fonts drop-down list in CorelDRAW, see what you think is an appropriate typeface choice, find fonts that work harmoniously if you need more than one typeface in the design, and then, if you're drawing a blank, check out the typefaces you own but have *not* installed. It's generally a bad idea to pick the first font on the installed fonts list; Arial is a good workaday font, but it's most appropriate for text on aspirin bottles and caution signs because of its legibility at small point sizes and its authoritative, clean but spartan look.

The following sections describe the anatomy of a font, what *stroke width* means, *serifs* and font characteristics, and basically explain why a typeface looks the way it does and therefore becomes appropriate for a design idea. Also, the better you understand the characteristics of characters, the better you'll be able to communicate a specific need to a typographer or a press operator, and to conduct a quicker search on your drive and the Web for the typeface you need.

Styles and Types of Typefaces

There are two basic categories of typefaces a designer uses daily:

- **Roman**   The characters (called *glyphs* by typographers) consist of thick and thin stems (called *strokes*) providing good contrast between characters to make long paragraphs at small point size easy to read.

- **Gothic**   The characters are made up of strokes of even or almost-even widths. This makes a Gothic font an excellent choice for headlines with impact and for official signs.

Within the categories of typefaces, there are two more branches: *serifs* and *sans* (from the Latin "without") *serifs*. Serifs are an embellishment at the end of a stroke in a character; their original purpose was both as a flourish when scribes would hand-copy manuscripts and, as typesetting was invented, serifs made the wooden and metal slugs easier to remove from the surface the slug was pressed into.

Typographers ages ago decided that a Gothic font could benefit from serifs and, conversely, a Roman typeface could become more functional as a headline-style font by removing the serifs. Designers now enjoy the use of both Roman and Gothic type cast in serif and sans serif treatments, examples of which are shown in Figure 13-1.

 In typographer's language, a font *is usually part of a* family *of typefaces. Optima, for example, has normal, italic, bold, and bold-italic as part of the font family; additionally, other weights of Optima, part of the Optima* family, *are available from several vendors you can find online.* Typeface, *in contrast, is generally used to describe either a single member of a family (Optima Bold is a typeface) or a typeface that has no family members, such as Rockabilly.*

Eurostyle
Futura
Futura
Helvetica
Handel
MACHINE
Kabel

Gothic Sans

Galliard
Rundfunk
Albertus
Bookman
Bodoni

Roman Sans

Stymie
Serif Gothic

Gothic Serif

Optima
Serpentine Sans

Roman Serif

FIGURE 13-1   Examples of Gothic and Roman typefaces in serif and sans serif styles

Other Types of Typefaces

The design world would be a fairly boring place today if there weren't other types of fonts designed by professionals. Variations on the traditional Roman and Gothic typefaces abound in the desktop publishing world and many defy classification. On the CorelDRAW installation disk(s), you'll also find about a thousand typefaces, many of which would fit in the category of "designer" fonts: from classic to classy, from appropriate for packaging to logo treatments. In the world of digital typefaces, an element of playfulness has snuck in, and we have "grunge" fonts that look as though the office photocopier's having a bad hair day, elegant script typefaces that are ideal for wedding invitations, Blackletter typefaces that span usage from fairytales to metal band logos, fonts that look like handwriting, and Pi (picture) fonts. In Figure 13-2 you can see a small collection of different types of fonts gathered from the CorelDRAW disk and third-party vendors such as Émigré, The Font Bureau, and Stu's Font Diner.

Distant Cousins in Typeface Families

Often, font families are written for normal, bold, bold-italic, and italic variations on a typeface. However, as the need arose for specific printing purposes, typographers extended font families to include expanded versions—compressed, condensed, engraved, stenciled, and professional sets that include characters not regularly written to standard typeface sets. For example, Helvetica, Futura, and Goudy come in more than 17 "flavors" from different typeface foundries. Typeface manufacturers have retained the name "foundry" from the days

FIGURE 13-2 Examples of fresh and uncommon styles of typefaces

What Is a Digital Typeface?

Fonts you use in CorelDRAW and most every other Windows application are actually applications, specifically *runtime applications* that require a "player" to display, print, and otherwise use the characters contained in the typeface. Fortunately, after you add a typeface to the Fonts folder in the Windows Control Panel, you don't have to worry about the player; it's in the operating system, and most applications recognize a recently added typeface immediately.

A digital typeface has outlines that describe the shape of the individual characters. This is why you'll see a lot of picture fonts available on the Web for free: characters can be anything in a font, and it requires less skill to draw a tiny picture than to design a professional font such as Times New Roman for desktop publishing. Because the shapes are vector in nature, fonts can be small in file size, they scale smoothly to any size you might need, and CorelDRAW can simplify characters you type in a document so they become regular vector shapes that can be manipulated in any way you like. Common file extensions for digital typefaces are .OTF (OpenType font) and .TTF (TrueType font), and older fonts come in two parts: PostScript Type 1 fonts have the .PFB file extension for the *binary* data part, which contains the outlines of the characters, and an accompanying .PFM file holds header and *metrics* information (information character width, space surrounding characters, and so on). Windows and CorelDRAW can handle all three types of digital fonts.

Later in this chapter you'll learn how to use CorelDRAW's Symbol Manager to catalogue characters you use often in a specific font that are frequently hard to locate.

when typefaces were cast from metal using a forge, much like a metal foundry that manufactures machine parts. When shopping and using Bitstream Font Navigator (included with CorelDRAW, discussed later in this chapter), it's important to know a few of the fancier variations on typeface families. On the next page are examples of a small caps typeface: it's appropriate for formal announcements and doesn't assault the reader as ALL CAPS does! Look for *SC* in a font name; typographers often use it to denote this special font. Also, some Roman serif typefaces have *swash* members: Bookman, Goudy, Garamond, and other popular fonts for body text can be purchased with characters that have strokes that sweep under and above neighboring characters for an elegant look. OldStyle versions of fonts contain numbers that alternate in position to make long sequences of digits easier to read, and frequently their filename is appended with *OS*.

Finally, a well-designed, professional typeface of any family member will contain extended characters. An *extended character* is one you can't directly access from the keyboard; instead you must first hold ALT and then type four digits on the numeric keypad area of your keyboard. For example, if you want to put a pause in a sentence, one way to punctuate is with ellipses (three periods when we used typewriters). However, the proper punctuation in today's typesetting is the ellipse character, which is accessed from standard-encoded typefaces by pressing and holding ALT, then typing **0133**.

Some typefaces don't come with extended characters, some come with a few, and the more professional typefaces have ligature characters in the extended range of the font. Ligatures were first invented by scribes several centuries ago to get more words per line on parchment and to even out the look of certain words, usually Latin. For example, (in today's English) the word "find" looks awkward in certain typefaces because of the proximity of the *f*'s extension to the right, hitting the dot in the *i*. Because today's digital typefaces can contain thousands of characters including entire foreign-language character sets, a specific typeface might have a ligature for *fi* with the dot missing from the *i,* but this ligature is nearly impossible to look up to use. Fortunately, you can add an *fi* ligature, an *fl,* or any other extended character through the Insert Character docker (CTRL+F11), demonstrated later in this chapter. If you're into typesetting, it's a good idea to remember this keyboard shortcut.

 Ligatures occasionally come as part of an Expert set of a specific typeface, making it easier to locate the ligature you need. These sets are often called "Extras" in their filename.

The Anatomy of a Font

When looking for a font that seems appropriate for a specific design, the shape of the individual characters might or might not work out the way you intend; you want the spacing between lines of text (called *leading*) to be extremely tight, but the ascender on certain characters is too high and juts into the preceding line of text. What's an ascender? The vertical strokes in characters have names typographers use and you should, too, when describing an ideal font or when seeking one:

- **Character height**   Used to describe the overall height, which includes not only the character but also the space above the character, this is usually coded in by the person designing the typeface. Character height determines how much interline spacing you'll need to make more than one line of text.

- **Cap height**   This is the height of a capital letter in a typeface, which is usually not the same as character height, nor is it necessarily the height of all characters (which is called the *ascender*).

FIGURE 13-3 The heights of the strokes in a typeface

- **Ascender** This is the height of the tallest character in a font; usually it's the *f,* the *h,* or a swash if the font contains this embellishment.

- **Descender** This is the lowest part of a character; usually a *g* or a *y,* except when a font has swashes.

- **X-height** This is the measurement of a lowercase character, traditionally measured by the letter *x* in the font.

- **Baseline** An imaginary line where all the characters should rest.

Figure 13-3 shows all the measurements just described.

TIP *A few typographic elements have characters not found in a digital typeface, but instead are built by CorelDRAW and other applications. For example, an underscored character, used a lot in legal documents, in CorelDRAW is built from any typeface: you select the character(s) to be underscored, click the Underline button on the property bar, and you're done. Similarly, if you need a Superscript or Subscript character (see the next illustration), CorelDRAW builds one from any font. However, a Superscript is a special treatment of a character, and you need to first choose the character's glyph node with the Shape tool (not with the Pick or the Text tool). Then the Super and Subscript buttons appear on the property bar and you're home free.*

13

Super 1ˢᵀ and Subscript H₂0

Finding the Font You Need

In this age of online transactions, you might find it hard to simply walk into a store and ask a knowledgeable person for a specific font. This is not a problem; fonts are small enough in file size to be downloaded in seconds, you can find the font you need in scores of places, and

CorelDRAW X5 has a feature that makes it a snap to identify a font you want to own. The following sections take you through the browsing process at MyFonts.com and get you up and running with Bitstream Font Navigator for previewing fonts. Let's face it, "tt1040m_.ttf" doesn't tell you that the typeface is actually Bitstream Amazone or that it's a really cool script typeface!

Working with Font Navigator

Because the engine for displaying and printing fonts from Windows 95 up until Windows 7 was written to accommodate a hypothetically unlimited number of installed fonts, today's designer enjoys an incredibly wide selection for pamphlets, flyers, and other needs. However, just because you have over 1,000 fonts at hand on the CorelDRAW install disk, doesn't mean it's a wise idea to install *all* of them! Managing your typeface collection is similar to arranging your sock drawer: it's not a glamorous task, but you're glad you've done it when you have a 9 A.M. meeting, it's 8:30, and showing up with a blue sock and a black one is not a fashion statement.

Happily, Font Navigator comes with CorelDRAW; if you chose not to install it during setup, you might want to install it now—it's a must for previewing, organizing, and installing typefaces. Here are the simple instructions for using Font Navigator…

Launch Font Navigator exactly as you do any other application: click the Windows Start button, choose All Programs, and then choose CorelDRAW Graphics Suite X5 | Bitstream Font Navigator. Alternatively, you can double-click the Font Navigator icon in a folder window if the program doesn't show in the Programs menu. The default path to FontNav is C:\Program Files (x86)\Corel\CorelDRAW Graphics Suite X5\FontNav.

Font Navigator immediately recognizes the disc in your drive and offers up all the fonts on the disc for previewing and organizing. If you want to browse a different collection, choose a different drive or folder from the drop-down list. If you scroll up the drop-down list, you'll see that the Font Catalog above My Computer is an index of the fonts you decide to catalogue. It's not a location for fonts on your hard drive, but rather it's just an index. Therefore, when you browse a disk or folder location for fonts, you've moved from the Catalog to a hard drive or other location such as a USB thumb drive or optical disk. To browse a folder, you navigate the drive(s) from the drop-down list; to do some indexing, you go back up the folder tree on the drop-down list and choose Font Catalog.

The four-pane interface is easy to understand, and everything you want to do can be accomplished by click-dragging. At upper left is the Contents Of Font Catalog list of fonts. At upper right is the Installed Fonts list of fonts you currently have on your system. These fonts were most likely installed through Windows Control Panel | Fonts and an application that auto-installs the fonts it needs. At lower left is the Font Groups area, and by default there's nothing in it. At lower right is a preview panel, Font Sample, which can display samples of any typeface far faster than the Windows Fonts utility can. To view a font you haven't installed yet, click a name in the upper-left Font Catalog panel to highlight it, and instantly the preview shows at lower right in the Font Sample panel. It's the same deal with an installed font; click the name in the upper-right panel to preview the installed font. Typefaces don't always have names indicative of what they look like, and occasionally you might find an installed font you don't want installed. If you want to remove a font from your system, the easy way is to open Windows Control Panel | Fonts, right-click and then delete the font; be sure you have a backup copy available whenever you delete something.

Font groups are a handy and welcome feature. Any font that is installed can be put in a group and the group named anything you choose. At any time in the future, you can add or remove a group and the icons in that group folder. For example, let's say you had a job for a Halloween party and you needed to use bold, striking, and truly *ugly* typefaces for the project. If you put them in a group, you can now uninstall them in one fell swoop, keeping your installed fonts in tidy and useful order.

Performing operations in Font Navigator is as simple as its interface suggests:

- To add any typeface to the Catalog for indexing, choose it from the upper-left list, right-click it, and choose Add To Font Catalog. You'll then be asked through a dialog whether you want to install the font and whether you want to copy the font file to a new location, an easy and convenient way to keep all your font files in one central location. After a font has been catalogued, its icon features a tiny yellow star tag, as shown here.

 In the catalog

 Not catalogued

- To install a font from the upper-left pane, drag the font name into the Installed Fonts pane, or right-click the font name and then choose Install Font.

- To create a font group, right-click in the Font Groups pane, and then choose New Group (the menu command is File | New Font Group). A new folder icon appears with its default name highlighted, ready for you to type a name for the group. Organization here is key; you might like to create groups by the name of an assignment so you can install and uninstall them as the occasion calls for it. **Megatronics Presentation**, **Birthday Cards**, **Truck Signage** are examples of group names…you get the idea. Alternatively, you might want to create groups by types of fonts: **Headlines**, **Body Text**, **Unusual**, **Picture Fonts** will help you sort out the fonts you need quite quickly. To add fonts you choose to a new group, drag their names into a group from the catalog in the upper-left pane. To install and uninstall groups of fonts, right-click the folder icon to show these options.

The illustration below shows the Font Navigator interface; a font in the Catalog is being dragged into the Installed Fonts list, and immediately Windows is updated and the font's ready to use in CorelDRAW and other programs with no need to reboot or restart an application.

NOTE *You might have a problem viewing OpenType previews using FontNav in Windows 7 64x. If this creates a workflow problem, try the freeware NexusFont previewing and cataloguing utility at http://xiles.net/programs/, thanks to Junghoon Nog, who accepts donations for his work at his site!*

Looking Up a Font

You have a wealth of font choices on the CorelDRAW disc, and now you know how to preview them using Font Navigator. So what if you're looking for a font you've seen used in a layout or advertisement and you don't own it and you don't even know its name?

An invaluable resource for font finding and purchasing is MyFonts.com, probably the largest clearinghouse for type foundries ranging from large such as Linotype and Bitstream to cottage-industry independent font authors. A new feature in CorelDRAW is an URL on the Text menu called WhatTheFont?!—to use it, you need an active Internet connection and an understanding of how this command works.

WhatTheFont (part of MyFonts.com's site) is an automated utility that intelligently matches a bitmap of a sample of text to a best guess at what the name of the font is. Like any software, WhatTheFont (WTF) is "intelligent" up to a point, and your best chance of finding, for example, the font used on a wedding invitation, is to make sure that the bitmap you have

13

of the invitation has the characters neatly spread apart and that the bitmap is of a pixel resolution large enough for WhatTheFont to clearly "see" the outlines of the characters in the bitmap. Also have sufficient blank space surrounding the text so that WhatTheFont isn't confused with surrounding text and graphics. Consider using Corel PHOTO-PAINT to edit the bitmap before using the WhatTheFont?! command in CorelDRAW.

Here is a working example of how to use WhatTheFont to find out what a specific font used on an invitation is called so it can be purchased:

1. Start a new document (press Ctrl+N). In the Create A New Document dialog, set the page size to Letter, but also set the Rendering Resolution to **96** dpi—this is screen resolution and CorelDRAW's WhatTheFont?! command captures an image of the font you want to discover at screen resolution. Click OK to create the new page.

2. With the Pick tool chosen, specify Pixels from the Units drop-down list on the property bar.

3. There is an maximum area size that WhatTheFont?! can accept for capturing the text: 400,000 pixels combined maximum width times height, so first, press Z (Zoom tool) and then choose 100% viewing resolution on the property bar. Now your screen resolution matches your page resolution.

   With the Rectangle tool, drag a rectangle on the page that's 800 pixels wide and 500 pixels tall. This area measures the maximum size recommended by WTF of 400,000 pixels.

4. Press CTRL+I to import the bitmap containing the mystery text, locate it in the Import dialog, click Import after you select the file, and then click-drag the loaded cursor so the placed bitmap falls within the rectangle you put on the page. Resize the bitmap by dragging a corner handle with the Pick tool if necessary. If the imported bitmap doesn't have an 8×5 orientation, you can resize the rectangle, but you need to use Windows Calculator or another utility to recalculate the proportions. Calculating 400,000 divided by the width in pixels will give you the ideal height, and vice versa. Delete the rectangle when your imported bitmap text is scaled to accommodate WTF's recommendation.

5. Choose Text | WhatTheFont?!

6. Your cursor actually has tiny text that explains what to do now; you drag a box with your cursor to highlight the text you want to send to WhatTheFont. In Figure 13-4, you can see the bitmap at top, and what your screen looks like after you've click-dragged to define an area around the text. If you make a mistake, reset by clicking outside of the box you defined, and then click-drag the crosshair cursor again.

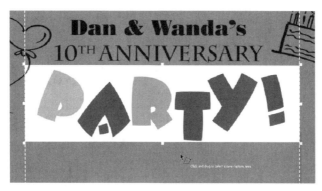

400,000 pixels maximum size

FIGURE 13-4   Click-drag around the text you want to send to WhatTheFont as a bitmap copy.

7. After you click inside the box, WhatTheFont on the Web guides you through any help it might need to identify the typeface, as shown in Figure 13-5. At left you can see that this automated routine occasionally asks you for help identifying characters; for example, 1's and exclamation marks are sometimes mistaken for each another.

8. Once you've scrolled to the bottom of the characters you captured, click Continue. As you can see, WhatTheFont offers a number of foundries for Beesknees, the font used in the invitation.

Font Foundries

Digital typeface files can be broken down into two parts: the information about the characters themselves—the vector outlines that are pure artistic design work—and the coding that allows the characters to run as a small application, so you can type using a font. Copyright issues concerning the ownership of a typeface can also be broken into two parts: what the font looks like and who owns the name. It might sound weird, but you will find several different names for what essentially looks like the same font, because the design of characters in a digital typeface isn't copyrighted, but the brand name is.

This strange legality can easily confuse a consumer: for the most part, the Bitstream typefaces on the CorelDRAW CD are trademarked by Bitstream; their names are clear and

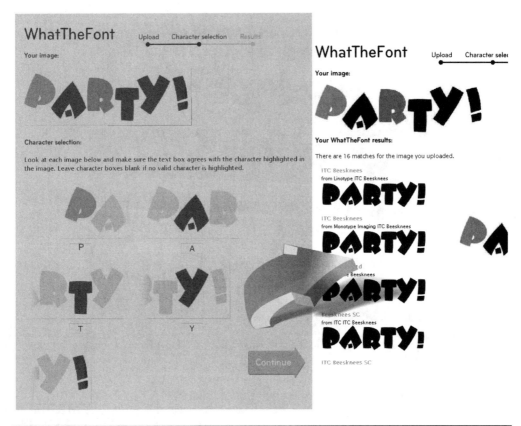

WhatTheFont identifies a typeface you have in a bitmap version of an invitation or other printed material.

forthright and easy to look up in any traditional typeface specimen book or on the Web. You'll also see the same font name distributed or owned by different foundries and vendors. In this case, such as with Clarendon, the original character designs were sold as physical artwork ages ago, and several digital foundries traced off the characters, usually embellishing them with their unique style. Almost all the time, if you didn't own Clarendon and wanted to buy it, the smart thing to do would be to shop around and buy the best-priced version of Clarendon.

However, a foundry such as Bitstream might have licensed both the design of the font and its name to a different vendor; in this case, Bitstream still offers the typeface, using its original character designs, but offers it using a nonstandard, unique font name. This is why WhatTheFont?! is an invaluable CorelDRAW menu command—you might own a typeface but not recognize the unique name! For example, Exotc 350 on the CorelDRAW install disc has a different industry standard name: Peignot. Use Font Navigator and WhatTheFont to explore what you own; your personal type case might be better stocked with workaday classic fonts than you imagine.

Finding Fonts on the Web

For a specific assignment, you might want to shop for a fresh, unusual typeface. The following URLs are reputable places where you can buy or download for free some interesting typefaces whose themes run from staples (basic fonts you can't live without) to retro to novelty to "goth":

- **Linotype Library**   www.linotype.com/

- **ITC**   www.itcfonts.com/fonts/

- **Bitstream**   www.bitstream.com/

- **URW**   www.urwpp.de/deutsch/home.html

- **Monotype**   www.monotypefonts.com/

Also, clearinghouses for fonts are the distributors and only occasionally the creators:

- **The Font Bureau**   www.fontbureau.com/

- **Adobe Systems**   www.adobe.com

- **MyFonts**   www.myfonts.com/, probably the largest distributor

Smaller type shops also offer quality, refreshing selections:

- **Acid Fonts (www.acidfonts.com)**   The collection is uneven; you may need to do some sifting to find quality typefaces you find useful, but you can't beat the price, and Acid Fonts is one of the largest repositories of free and shareware typefaces on the Web (about 4,700 free fonts).

- **Harold's Fonts (www.haroldsfonts.com/)**   Harold Lohner advertises that he vends "homemade fonts," but they're actually clean and professional in every regard. Harold offers over 100 free fonts including fonts designed to look like famous product logos.

- **Stu's Font Diner (www.fontdiner.com)**   Stu offers all retro fonts and has free downloads of some very nice pieces.

- **1,001 Fonts (www.1001fonts.com/)**   Another clearinghouse for free and shareware typefaces. Quality is uneven, but overall a very handsome collection.

- **Dieter Steffman's Font Repository (http://moorstation.org/typoasis/ designers/steffmann/index.htm)**   A collection of excellent freeware ornamental, unusual, and Blackletter-style fonts designed by a professional font craftsman.

13

The Last Word on Accessing Installed Fonts

Depending on the programs you've used before working with CorelDRAW, accessing the fonts you've installed might or might not feel familiar. The steps to follow are a brief guide to getting the most out of all the fonts you've installed for your design work. Although working with text is covered in detail in chapters to come, you might like a jump start so you can get right down to business with that job that was due five minutes ago!

The Text tool (F8), accessed from the toolbox (the icon with the *A*), operates in two different modes: Artistic Text and Paragraph Text. Artistic text is usually the best choice for brief headlines. Selecting, manipulating, and otherwise editing artistic text is accomplished differently than with paragraph text. Paragraph text is intended for typesetting long blocks of text (a short story, an instruction manual) and has different properties than artistic text, explained in Chapter 14.

To create artistic text, you choose the Text tool and then click an insertion point in your document. Then you type. By default, the font you use is Arial 24 point, No justification, which, by default, is justified to the left. You can change the default to anything you like: with the Text tool selected, you choose the font, point size, and justification on the property bar, and CorelDRAW displays a Text Attributes box. Here you can redefine artistic and paragraph text for all future default documents.

> **TIP** *A* point *is a typographic term, a measurement of the height of text. Traditionally, there are 72.27 points to the inch, but with the advent of digital fonts, this measurement has been modified to 72 points to the inch. Because typefaces are designed by hundreds of different professionals, the actual size of, for example, 24 point Arial is not necessarily the same size as 24 point Palatino. It's always a good idea to measure the height of text cast in different fonts using rulers in CorelDRAW to ensure consistency. Usually, paragraph text is set in anywhere from 9 to 14 points (except for aspirin labels, which seem to be set in 2 point type), while fonts used in headlines look best at 24 points to 72 points on a page that measures standard letter 8.5×11".*

Paragraph text is entered the same way as artistic text and in the same way as most other Windows applications, but you define paragraph text by marquee-dragging a frame into which paragraph text flows. Marquee-dragging is accomplished by click-holding the primary mouse button and then dragging diagonally; top left to bottom right is the most common technique. Then you release the mouse button, a frame appears, and you type in the frame (or paste from the Clipboard when you have copied text).

- To change the font and the point size of the font after you've entered text, you select either artistic or paragraph text with the Pick tool, and then choose a different font and point size from the property bar. The Text tool can also be used to select and change the font of the text.

● To change a single character in text you've typed, you highlight only that character and then use the drop-down lists on the property bar to make the change(s). The property bar lists installed fonts alphabetically, with their names shown in the font style itself as a convenient preview method. A font family is listed on the flyout for a font name on the list; you click the triangle and then choose a family member. Single-member fonts have no little triangle to the right of their name. The following illustration shows two lines of text being edited to change family members. Additionally, at the top of the fonts list are the most recently used fonts, a handy way to access the same font in a document you're continuing from two hours ago.

13

Finding and Saving Important Characters

Picture (Pi) fonts, also called Symbols, are terrific for embellishing design work, but locating a specific character within a Pi font isn't straightforward because your keyboard has letters and not very many symbols; no two font designers agree on a specific mapping for symbol sets, although occasionally there is a progression as you type across your keyboard. For example, some picture-font designers code an upper-left ornamental frame corner as "a", the upper-right frame corner as "s"—if the users are intuitive enough, they can type across the left end of the second row (a-s-d-f) on the keyboard to make a sequentially correct four-corner picture frame from such a symbol font.

Using the Insert Character Docker

CorelDRAW, via Text | Insert Symbol Character (CTRL+F11), removes the guesswork in locating a character or symbol in any font you have installed. When you choose this command, the Insert Character docker appears, and you have two ways to insert a character:

- **As text** If you need, for example, a fancy bullet that is inline in existing text in your document, you place the Text tool cursor at the location in the text where you want the character, click the character on the docker to select it, and then you click the Insert button (or double-click the thumbnail of the character). You might not always want to choose this method; the advantages are that the character is editable text and stays aligned to the text that comes before it and after it. However, the disadvantage is that as a designer, you might want to move this ornamental character around on the page—but as inline text, the inserted character is bound to the line of text you added it to.

- **As a collection of editable shapes** To add a character to your document as a shape you can immediately edit with the Shape tool, you first select the Pick tool instead of the Text tool. Then you drag the thumbnail of the symbol you want onto the page. It's easy to spot the difference between an inserted Symbol on a page and a Symbol added as a shape: shapes have a default black outline and no fill, so they're easy to single out in a document. The disadvantage to adding a Symbol as a shape is that you can't edit it with the Text tool, but overall, you have an endless supply of special characters at your cursor tip with the Insert Character docker, so mistakenly adding the type of symbol you don't want to a document is corrected in a flash.

Figure 13-6 shows the process of adding a Symbol to a document by dragging a thumbnail into the document; you locate the installed font from which you want a symbol by using the drop-down list at the top of the docker, set the size of the symbol at the bottom (a symbol can be resized at any time in the future by scaling it with the Pick tool), and then drag and drop. Notice in the enlarged inset graphic in this figure that the Insert Symbol docker provides you with the extended character key combination for the symbol you've clicked. This feature is a great help if you're coming to CorelDRAW from a word processor such as WordPerfect. You might already be familiar with certain extended character codes; for example, standard font coding for a cents sign (¢) is to hold ALT, then type **0162**. Therefore, for any font you've chosen on the Insert Symbol docker, if the font has a cents sign and you want to choose it quickly, you type **0162** in the Keystroke field, press ENTER, and the docker immediately highlights the symbol—it's easy to locate and equally easy to then add to the document. Conversely, when you click a symbol, the Keystroke field tells you what the keystroke is; you can then access a cents sign, a copyright symbol, or any other

FIGURE 13-6   The Insert Character docker is your ticket to quickly looking up and adding special extended characters to your designs.

extended character you like in any application outside of CorelDRAW. You just hold ALT and then type the four-digit keycode in, for example, WordPerfect or Microsoft Word, and you're home free.

Using the Symbol Manager

Now that you've located the perfect symbol for a design by using the Insert Character docker, it would be nice to save the symbol so you can reuse it in the future instead of hunting for it again! This is where the Symbol Manager (CTRL+F3) under Window | Dockers is an invaluable resource. The Symbol Manager provides you with information about symbols contained and saved only to a document you have open and also provides User Symbols, an area on the Symbol Manager where you can duplicate a catalogued symbol into any document at any time.

Let's say you've found a great symbol for a layout, you've placed it in your document, and you decide you want to reuse it tomorrow. Here are the steps for cataloguing the symbol

13

and for accessing an *instance* (a duplicate that takes up less saved file space in a document) of it tomorrow:

1. With an object selected, choose Edit | Symbol | New Symbol.

2. In the Create New Symbol box, type a name you'll remember later in the Name field and then click OK. As you create more and more new files using CorelDRAW, you'll definitely want to stay tidy in your cataloguing work. Cross-referencing is a good practice; in Figure 13-7, the Name of the symbol refers to the typeface it was copied from. Later, it's easy to look up the name of the symbol and use it in a program outside of CorelDRAW.

FIGURE 13-7 Define a symbol and then save it to a Symbol Library.

3. Open the Symbol Manager and then click on the Symbol1 title. A thumbnail of the symbol you just saved appears.

4. A tiny Export icon becomes active; click it, it's the Export Library command. This is not much of a library, but you need to start somewhere!

5. In the Export Library box, it's best to save the new library to where CorelDRAW recommends (to better allow the program to locate it in the future; Symbols is a good location). Name the library and then click Save. You're done.

6. In any new document, open the Symbol Manager, click the User Symbols + icon to open the collection, and then click the name of the library you saved in step 5. Now all you need to do is drag the thumbnail into a document, and you have an instance of the symbol you saved.

In Windows 7, if you install CorelDRAW X5 Graphics Suite to the default hard disk location, your saved Symbol Library should be in your boot drive directory (usually C:\)AppData\Roaming\Corel\CorelDRAW Graphics Suite X5\Symbols. This is good to know when you want to load your collection by clicking Add Library on the Symbol Manager docker, to add symbols to a Local document.

 With the Pick tool, right-click over any object you create, and you can then choose Symbol | New Symbol and Symbol | Symbol Manager from the context menu.

Symbols saved to a library are always *instances* and as such, duplicates you add to a document cannot be edited using the Shape tool or other shape-editing features. You can apply transformations such as scaling and rotating, but you cannot edit the nodes of a shape instance. However, you can edit the original shape as saved in the Library, and all future instances you use reflect your edits. To edit a symbol in your library, right-click the shape thumbnail in the Symbol Manager and then choose Edit. After you've edited the shape, right-click the shape in the document window, and then click the Finish Editing Object button to the left of the document horizontal scroll bar. Every instance in every document is updated to reflect your edits.

13

TIP *It's easy to tell the difference between an instanced symbol and one that can be edited in any document. Choose the shape using the Pick tool. If the bounding box dots are blue, it's a shape instance. If the bounding box handles are black, it's a regular shape and you can perform any CorelDRAW operation on the shape.*

Font Etiquette: Using Fonts with Style and Appropriateness

It's easy for anyone to mistype a word or use fractured grammar in an email message. However, an ad posted on the Web and a sign hanging in a store window for thousands to see is *not* a use of "relaxed" typography between friends—and it's hard to retract. A badly designed sign from a typographic point of view hurts the product, the company, and your reputation as a professional. The following sections discuss common mistakes we try to avoid from the planning stage of a printed message; you'll work with CorelDRAW's type features in future chapters, but now it's time to learn to walk before you learn to fly with new talents and skills.

Font Appropriateness and Very Basic Layout Rules

When an audience looks at a printed message, they don't simply absorb what the message says, but they additionally look at the *presentation*: the choice of capitalization, emphasis through bold and italic family members, how lines of text are stacked (justification), point size, font color, and how well the printed message harmonizes with any accompanying graphic. With most digital typefaces, the artist casts a tone on the typed message. Headline, sans serif Gothic fonts, for example, are rather hard-edged and cold yet impactful, while Roman serif fonts tend to lull the audience with rounded strokes, swooping serifs, and swashes. Roman typefaces generally send a warm but clean and professional signal to the viewer, while Gothic fonts wake up the reader, perhaps even warning them—hence their appropriateness as a headline typeface.

Figure 13-8 has two obvious sight gags demonstrating inappropriate uses of specific fonts. At left, the use of all uppercase, Gothic stencil contrasts extremely distastefully with both the message and the graphic behind it. At right, the choice of fonts on the page the officer is showing to someone about to be detained clashes with the message to the extent that the officer will probably have a hard time getting the cuffs on the person rolling on the pavement laughing.

A quick fix to these two bad examples would be to swap the fonts around, so the stencil font is used in the Miranda rights, and the slightly silly typeface is used for "I Love You." But better still, a quick trip to Font Navigator and the CorelDRAW Fonts CD will show you that Staccato 222BT (its industry name is Mistral) is warm, loose, and splendid for a valentine, and the font that commonly goes by the name *Machine* (distributed by ITC among other vendors) is serious, functional, and perfect for the arresting officer. You have the choices of fonts at hand; all you need to do is apply your artistic sensibilities to the selection.

When you have more than one line of text in a headline, legibility is a concern, and this, too, is accomplished by an appropriate choice of fonts. You want a "quick read" from the audience, especially on billboards and vehicle signage that appears and disappears as the sign or the reader moves.

Let's take a simple example headline, pull it apart, examine it, and make it work hard for your money. "The best deals in town" is a common slogan. In Figure 13-9 you can see this headline cast in text three different ways, with icons beneath them to indicate their merit as a sales message.

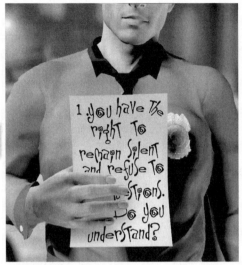

FIGURE 13-8   Don't undercut your message with the wrong font.

FIGURE 13-9   From clownish to professional, your message stands or falls based on fonts and layout.

First, the sign above the clown suffers from the following abuses of typographic conventions and rules:

- The use of Times New Roman, a Roman serif font, is stale (it's a Windows default typeface used since 1991 on the PC) and artistically defeats the message. It's large yet the characters aren't bold enough to present an impactful message.

- The use of all capital characters looks particularly inappropriate; Roman typefaces have upper- and lowercase characters, and the message looks like the designer had the CAPS LOCK key enabled. Also, it's plain bad form to "shout" a message unless a typeface has no lowercase letters and the designer is firm about the choice of fonts.

- The use of several exclamation marks suggests that if the business owner shouts loudly enough, someone will buy the product. One exclamation mark is sufficient for stressing a message; often a headline is adequately emphasized with no exclamation at all. It is redundant to cast a headline in all caps followed by several exclamation marks.

- The use of quotes is for quotations, *not* for emphasizing a phrase. When a designer puts quotation marks around "BEST" in this example, it creates in the reader's mind the suggestion that the retailer is speaking *euphemistically.* For example, when someone writes, "Get that 'antique' out of my parking lot in 15 minutes," they aren't actually referring to your 10-year-old car as a valuable antique, but rather as a piece of junk to which they're referring euphemistically or sarcastically. The word "BEST" in quotes will surely be interpreted by anyone with writing skills as, "They really aren't the best deals; they mean something else."

- The alignment of the headline is wrong. Although left justification is acceptable for Western language countries, the second line is much shorter than the third line. As a result, the reader has a hard time focusing to quickly read the message.

The center example in Figure 13-9 is a vast improvement and gets a checkmark because it's acceptable as a headline. Here's what is going right for this treatment of the slogan:

- The use of sans serif Gothic fonts makes the headline easier to read quickly.

- The emphasis created by using a bold, italic font to stress "BEST" makes it the first word a casual passerby will read. What this design does is create a hierarchy of importance within the message. It directs the reader to the most important, then to the second most important area of the slogan.

- The slogan uses center justification and the lines are stacked to align well; no line is too long or short, and both legibility and neatness have been added.

The middle example is short of ideal for two reasons:

- Because "BEST" is italicized, it might be design overkill to also make it all capitals and bolder.

- The exclamation mark at the end is not really necessary. The message's importance is already well supported by the use of the fonts. Generally, if you've graphically punctuated a slogan, you don't need to add an exclamation mark to overdo the importance of the slogan.

The example at right, which earns four stars, works the best for the slogan. Here's why:

- The lines of text have been stretched to fit, by using the Pick tool and scaling horizontally, disproportionately. You can do this with CorelDRAW artistic text. The result is a very neatly stacked presentation of words.

- The word "BEST" stands out through the use of a different color. In design, you don't necessarily have to use black to emphasize something, not when text surrounding a particular word is set in black. Contrast can be achieved through emphasis, or by "negative emphasis"; when objects surrounding the most important one are gray, you make the most important object black. And conversely, a gray object gets noticed when surrounded by black objects. Additionally, uppercase for "THE" and "BEST" works in this example because the other words are upper- and lowercase. In art, you first learn the rules, and then when you understand them well enough, you can *break* the rules with style.

- The hierarchy of importance of the words is proper and reads well. "BEST" is read first, then the surrounding text, and then "in town"—because a thin typeface is used, a script type font, it becomes subordinate in visual importance.

It's not hard to think up a more compelling and fresh sales slogan than "The Best deals in town." Once you have that ideal slogan, consider the good and bad points in the previous example, approach your sales message with taste and sensitivity, lean but don't push, and you cannot go wrong.

You've seen in this chapter how to define a font, how to find a font, how to find and save an individual character, and how to put the whole of your acquired knowledge into motion with some good working rules for the ambitious sign-maker. There's a lot more in store in the following chapters on working with text. It's not just about signs: you'll see how to work with the Text tool to its fullest potential, creating extraordinary logos and headline treatments, and then work your way up to outstanding page layouts and special design needs such as reverse printing, flawless character alignment, special effects, and more.

You've *read* enough text in this chapter; let's move on and actually *work* with text!

13

CHAPTER 14

Getting Your
Words Perfect

Y ou want your text to look as good as your drawings, and the good news is that the same powerful grammar and spelling tools offered in Corel WordPerfect Office suite are right inside CorelDRAW. Proofing tools including a spell-checking system, thesaurus, and grammar checker—in 25 different languages—are at your fingertips. This means you don't have to duck out to your word processor just to proof text that you've entered on-the-fly in a CorelDRAW document.

CorelDRAW also has the same QuickCorrect feature that's in WordPerfect for correcting common typos and spelling mistakes *as you type*. With QuickCorrect, you can also automatically replace something you've typed with something else—which is extremely helpful for words that you commonly mistype and for common extended characters such as © or ™.

Both CorelDRAW and WordPerfect use the same writing tools, dictionaries, word lists, and configurations. If you add a word to your user word list in WordPerfect, it is there for you in CorelDRAW. Therefore, when you know how to use the writing tools in WordPerfect, you already know how to use them in CorelDRAW and vice versa. If you're a Microsoft Word user, CorelDRAW's proofing tools are as easy to learn as WordPerfect's—the dialogs and labels are a little different in appearance, but you'll soon get the idea. This chapter takes you through the steps and options you have to step up to the title of Literary Wizard in addition to CorelDRAW Design Guru.

Using CorelDRAW's Writing Tools

Frequently, small to medium businesses communicate with customers around the world; with text proofing in 25 different languages available right out of the box, CorelDRAW makes it easy for you to get your sales language proofed perfectly regardless of whether you minored in French at school. When you install CorelDRAW, choose the languages you are most likely to use (you can go back at any time and install more), and you are ready to check the spelling and grammar of anything that comes your way.

By default, CorelDRAW assigns a language code and checks all text using the proofing tools that correspond to the language your operating system uses. For example, if you use a U.S. English copy of Windows, CorelDRAW automatically installs English–U.S. proofing tools and assigns all text to U.S. English (ENU).

Assigning Language Codes

If your document contains text in a language other than the default language, you need to select the foreign language text and assign the proper language code to the text so CorelDRAW will use the appropriate proofing tools. The language currently assigned to selected text is noted by a three-letter code in parentheses next to the font description in the status bar, as shown, for example, by "(ENU)" here.

To change the language assignment of any character, word, or paragraph of artistic or paragraph text in a document, select the text and then choose Text | Writing Tools | Language. When the Text Language dialog opens, you can choose any one of the 122 different language and language variants that appear in the list. Click OK to make the selection.

Why Language Codes Are Important

You want your text to be spelled correctly, including accent and other orthographic marks (text indicators of how a word is pronounced), regardless of what language you use. When text is tagged with the proper language codes and you've installed the corresponding proofing tools, it's as easy to check foreign language text as it is to check your native language text.

For example, suppose you're working on a package design that contains text in English, French, and Spanish on a system that uses U.S. English. To proof in multiple languages, you select each piece of French text and assign it a French language tag, select each piece of Spanish text and assign that text a Spanish language tag, and so on. CorelDRAW has already assigned the English language tag, so you don't have to do that. Now when checking the document for spelling and grammar, CorelDRAW will use English, French, and Spanish proofing tools (if you installed them) to check the text for foreign language spelling errors.

14

Corel's proofing engine is also capable of proofing text to meet the spelling and punctuation standards of different regional and national variations for a number of major languages. This ensures, for example, that text that has been tagged as French Canadian will be checked using the French (Canadian) proofing set and rules that reflect correct French Canadian spelling, grammar, and word choice. If the French text in the document is intended for French speakers in Belgium, France, Luxembourg, Monaco, or Switzerland, instead of Canada, you would tag the text to match French (Belgium), French (France), French (Luxembourg), French (Monaco), or French (Switzerland) so that the appropriate proofing tools would be called into use by CorelDRAW.

Using the Proofing Tools

To use CorelDRAW's spell checker, thesaurus, or grammar check on text in your document, select the text with the Pick tool or the Text tool, and then choose the appropriate writing tool from the Text | Writing Tools menu. Alternatively, you can right-click a text object with the Text tool and then choose a proofing tool from the pop-up menu. You can also right-click with the Pick tool and choose Spell Check, or press CTRL+F12. This opens the Writing Tools dialog to the Spell Checker tab, as shown here:

NOTE   *If you have the WordPerfect Office suite installed on your computer, you will also have a Dictionary tab to the right of the Thesaurus tab in the Writing Tools dialog.*

Common Buttons

The Spell Checker and Grammatik tools share common buttons in the Writing Tools dialog. These buttons perform the functions described here:

- **Start**   The Start button starts the Spell Checker or Grammatik. This button is visible only if Auto Start is off—it is on by default. To enable or disable the Auto Start option, click the Options button in the Writing Tools dialog, and make a selection from the drop-down menu.

- **Replace**   As the check is performed, when a misspelled word or grammatical error is found, the Start button changes to Replace, and the misspelled word or grammatical error is highlighted. Select the suggested correction from the list, and click Replace to apply it. You can also edit the replacement word in the Spell Checker's Replace With box, or type in a new word before replacing it. After the replacement has been made, the checker rechecks the replacement and continues checking.

- **Undo**   The Undo button reverts the last correction to its previous state.

- **Resume**   After you correct a mistake, if you move the insertion point—for example, to a different part of the text—the Start button changes to the Resume button. Simply click it to recheck any selected text and to continue checking from the insertion point.

- **Skip Once and Skip All**   If the word or sentence that a checker has queried is actually correct—for example, a brand name such as Pringles or Humvee—you can click one of the Skip buttons to have the checker ignore it. Skip Once causes the check to continue, but future instances of the same problem will stop the checker. Skip All tells the checker to ignore *all* instances of this spelling or grammatical error.

- **Add**   Add allows you to add a word to the current user word list. Many unusual names and technical terms are not included in the Spell Checker's dictionary, and these can be added to the user word list for the current language. In the future, these added words will not be queried. If a word appears in the Replace With box or in the Not Found box, clicking Add immediately adds the queried word to the default user word list. Otherwise, if no word appears in either box, clicking the Add button opens an input box, where you can type the word you want to enter into the user word list.

- **Auto Replace**   If you choose an alternative spelling for a queried word, the Auto Replace button becomes active. Clicking this button will add the misspelled word and its replacement to the default user word list, *and* if QuickCorrect is enabled, then the next time you type the same mistake, the correct word will be automatically substituted.

14

- **Options** The Options button displays a drop-down menu that contains various settings for the current Writing tool.

- **Check** By using the options from the Check drop-down list, you can set the range of text for performing a spell check or a Grammatik check. The available options depend on whether text is selected with the Text tool or the Pick tool.

 When Auto Start is enabled, so spelling and grammar checks are performed as soon as the dialog is opened, you cannot choose the range before the check is performed. Disabling Auto Start means that CorelDRAW does not perform the check until you click the Start button, so you can change settings before the check begins.

Setting Spell Checker Options

You can click the Options button on the Spell Checker page of the Writing Tools dialog to access various settings that affect how the Spell Checker works. The Options drop-down menu is shown here:

Setting the Checker's Language

The Language option sets the current language for the Spell Checker. When you click Language, the Select Language dialog appears, as shown next, in which you can select the language for the checker to use. By checking Show Available Languages Only, you reduce the list to those languages for which dictionaries are installed.

Selecting a different language and checking Save As Default Writing Tools Language causes both the Spell Checker and Grammatik to use this language by default in all future checks.

TIP | *Although you can change the Language of the Spell Checker, it is much better to select the text and then to set the language of the text via Text | Writing Tools | Language, than to change the language from the Writing Tools dialog. When you change the language of the text, the checker language is automatically changed to match, but the reverse doesn't happen. Changing the Language option of the text saves the change to the file so that the proper proofing tools will be used without additional user intervention.*

You can also add new language codes by clicking the Add button to open the Add Language Code dialog, as shown:

14

NOTE | *Adding a new language code does not create or install a dictionary or user word list to go with it. CorelDRAW does not come with a utility to create or edit main dictionaries, but if you have WordPerfect, you can use the Spell Utility that comes with it to create main and user dictionaries to use with your custom language code.*

Using Word Lists

CorelDRAW's writing tools maintain word lists that contain all the valid words and phrases for spelling checks. If a word in your document is not in one of the active lists, it is flagged as being incorrectly spelled. CorelDRAW has two types of word lists:

- **Main word lists** These lists are provided by Corel and contain the most common words and spellings in each language. One main word list exists per language and this list is not editable.

- **User word lists** These lists contain words that are not in the Corel-supplied lists but rather are made up of words you have added during a spell check by clicking the Add button. It is up to you to ensure that the words you add to a user word list are spelled correctly! User word lists also contain the QuickCorrect entries for the text's language. Each language has at least one user word list.

  You can create your own user word lists with the WordPerfect Spell Utility, or you can use third-party created lists. Specialized user word lists such as those containing medical, legal, engineering, scientific, or other words and phrases that are common to an industry are very useful to create. The Spell Checker compares each word in your text to those in the main word lists and then to the user word lists that you have chosen for that word's language.

> **NOTE** *You should include the user word lists in your regular data backups. That way, if you have to reinstall CorelDRAW, you can also reinstall the latest versions of your user word lists. User word list filenames have the extension .UWL, and main word lists files use .MOR. When running Windows 7, the UWL files can be found in [USER]/AppData\Roaming\Corel\CorelDRAW Graphics Suite X5\WritingTools, and the MOR file(s) in C:\ProgramFiles (x86)\Corel\CorelDRAW Graphic Suite X5\ WritingTools.*

Using Main Word Lists

The main word lists are predefined by Corel and cannot be edited by CorelDRAW. Main word lists contain only words used by the Spell Checker—no QuickCorrect word pairs are included.

Which main word list is currently being used changes according to the Language setting. After pressing CTRL+F12 to display Writing Tools, click Options, and then choose Main Word Lists, select a different language, and CorelDRAW will use the main word list for the new language you chose. Changing which word list CorelDRAW is currently using does not change the language code of the selected text but rather temporarily proofs that text using the new main word list.

You can also *add* extra main word lists to a language by using the Add List button. For example, some U.S. English users might want their *U.S. Spell Checker* to include Spanish words. By adding the Spanish word list, the Spell Checker will first check words against the English lists. Then, if the words are not found in the English list, the checker compares against the Spanish list. Only if the check fails against both lists will the Spell Checker display an error. Using this method, you don't have to specifically set a language code for the Spanish text.

Setting Options in User Word Lists

To choose which user word list is used, and to edit entries in a user word list, open the User Word Lists dialog. From the Writing Tools dialog, click the Spell Checker tab, and then click the Options button; then choose User Word Lists from the drop-down menu. From the User Word Lists dialog, shown in Figure 14-1, you can add existing user word lists you might have, set the default list to which new entries are added, as well as add, delete, and edit entries in any existing user word list. Also, you can edit the AutoCorrect entries contained in the selected list and manually add new entries to the currently selected user word list.

14

FIGURE 14-1   Use the User Word Lists dialog to set options for new lists.

Setting Current Language

User word lists are language dependent, and at least one list is created for each language. You can choose which language's user word lists to edit with the Change button, located at the top right of the dialog. The Change button opens the Select Language dialog shown in the earlier section, "Setting the Checker's Language." This does not change the language of the text or of the writing tools—it changes which language's settings are shown in the dialog. Changing the current language offers you the chance to edit the user word list of *other* languages.

Adding User Word Lists

Clicking the Add List button in the User Word Lists dialog adds new lists to the current language; each language can have more than one list. This is useful, for example, for adding company- and industry-specific word lists to everyone's installation of CorelDRAW without having to enter the words individually on each computer.

To choose which user word list will be the one that is used to store new words added when you spell check, choose the list you want to use in the User Word Lists field, and then click the Set Default button to the right.

Browsing and Editing User Word List Contents

You can browse and edit the user word list contents. Just scroll up and down the list to view the contents, or enter a word or the first few characters of a word into the Word/Phrase box to scroll to a certain point in the alphabetical list.

| NOTE | *The list contains words that you have added. It also contains QuickCorrect entries that you have added with either the Spell Checker's Auto Replace button or in the QuickCorrect section of CorelDRAW's Tools | Options dialog.* |

Hacking a User Word List

If you don't have the Spell Utility, you can create a user word list by use of a little backdoor maneuvering. Close CorelDRAW. In Windows 7, go to the Users*current user*\AppData\Roaming\Corel\CorelDRAW Graphics Suite X5\Writing Tools folder on your hard disk. Locate the user word list that corresponds to the default language you use; for example, WT15US.UWL is the U.S. English user word list file. Press CTRL+C and then CTRL+V to copy and paste the copy into the same directory. Select the copied file and rename it to a descriptive name with a .UWL file extension, for example, "Aereospace.UWL." Next time you open CorelDRAW, you can use Aereospace.UWL—add it to your list, add to or delete entries from it—as you would any other user word list.

You can scroll through the list to view any particular word. Each entry has two parts: the word or phrase for which CorelDRAW checks (Word/Phrase), and the word or phrase with which CorelDRAW replaces the incorrect word (Replace With).

Adding a New Entry   If you want to add a new word or phrase to the user word list, enter the word or phrase that you want replaced into the Word/Phrase box. In the Replace With box, enter the text you want to use to replace the Word/Phrase, or leave the box empty if you want CorelDRAW to ignore the spelling of the word or phrase. Click the Add Entry button to add the new word to the list. For example, if you perennially type *Ive* instead of *I've*, enter **Ive** in the Word/Phrase box, enter **I've** in the Replace With box, and click Add Entry.

 To add a word that is spelled correctly but that is not in any list, type the word in the Word/Phrase box and then type it in the Replace With box. If you put the correctly spelled word in both boxes, Corel will not put the red squiggle under the word. If you leave the Replace With box empty, CorelDRAW adds "<skip>" to the Replace With column, which tells QuickCorrect and the Spell Checker to ignore this word.

Deleting Entries   If you have an entry in the user word list that is misspelled or simply not what you want, you can delete it. Select the item and click the Delete Entry button. You'll see a confirmation box asking whether you really want to delete the word—yes, you do—just confirm it and it's history.

Editing Entries   You can also correct or edit any entry. Click the entry in the list to select it, make your changes in the Replace With box, and then click the Replace Entry button.

Setting Entry Properties   The property set for each word in your user word list is important to consider and may need tweaking to get the results you want for the particular entry. With the word or phrase selected in the list, click on the Properties button to display the Entry Properties dialog. From here, the Entry Type can be set to Skip Word, which causes the proofing tools to ignore the word. Choose Auto-Replace Entry to have CorelDRAW substitute what you typed with what you've entered in the Replace field.

Other Spell Checking Options

Some other options available from the Options drop-down menu of the Writing Tools dialog are described here:

- **Auto Start**   The Spell Checker and Grammatik start the check automatically when the Writing Tools dialog is opened or when that checker's page is opened in the Writing Tools dialog.

- **Check Words With Numbers**   Checks or ignores words that include numbers.

- **Check Duplicate Words**   Flags words that appear twice in succession.

- **Check Irregular Capitalization**   Checks for words that have capital letters in places other than the first character.

- **Show Phonetic Suggestions**   Makes *phonetic* suggestions—replacement words that *sound* like the unrecognized word.

Main Spell Checking Options

The Workspace | Text | Spelling section of CorelDRAW's global Options dialog (CTRL+J) also includes various options that modify how the writing tools work.

- **Perform Automatic Spell Checking**   Check this if you want to check spelling as you type. When it is turned on, unrecognized words are underlined with a red zigzag line while you're editing text with the Text tool.

- **Visibility Of Errors**   Choose here to have all errors underlined in all text objects or just the text object being edited.

- **Display Spelling Suggestions**   Set the number of suggestions to display in the pop-up menu after you've right-clicked a misspelled word with the Text tool. The maximum and default number of suggestions is 10.

- **Add Corrections To QuickCorrect**   When this option is checked, CorelDRAW will add a correction pair to the user word list based on a correction made from the right-click pop-up menu.

- **Show Errors Which Have Been Ignored**   When you right-click a word, the pop-up menu includes an Ignore All command, which tells the Spell Checker to ignore this word. With this option set, CorelDRAW will still show ignored errors, but it will use a blue zigzag line to indicate that they have been ignored.

Using Grammatik

Spelling errors aren't the only proofing goof that can make your work look unprofessional. Poor grammar is a big, red flag that reflects on your education and communication skills. To make you look in print as smart as you are in person, CorelDRAW includes the Grammatik grammar checker, in many of the languages that spell checkers are available in. Grammatik is a flexible, powerful tool for checking your work. Grammar checking is a much harder task than spell checking; no program can serve as a proxy for an educated, native speaker's judgment. What Grammatik excels at is calling your attention to parts of your text that *might be* grammatically incorrect; it second-guesses you, and it's always good to have this resource at 1 A.M. when all your coworkers are sensibly asleep at home! Grammatik encourages you to stop and think about what you've written and offers helpful suggestions to fix the problem it *thinks* is a thorn in your rosy prose.

Grammatik has different sets of rules that it uses to judge the correctness of your grammar. When you use Grammatik, you should choose the rule set that corresponds to the level of formality and complexity of your writing. You can also edit any of Grammatik's rules to suit a specific situation.

Mastering every in and out of Grammatik combined with the intricate nature of grammar for a given language is beyond the scope of this book. However, the day-to-day operation of Grammatik is not difficult to manage, as you'll see in the next section, where the basics are covered.

Checking and Correcting Grammar

To check your grammar, select the text objects to check with the Pick tool, or select sentences with the Text tool; in the Writing Tools dialog open the Grammatik tab, shown in Figure 14-2, by choosing Text | Writing Tools | Grammatik. As with all of the other writing tools, you can also select text and then use the right-click pop-up menu to launch the tool you want to use. It's common to use a word that sounds like the word you want: in this figure "affects" is indeed a real word, correctly spelled, but it's a homonym—a word that *sounds* like the intended word—"effects."

Grammatik literally highlights potential grammar problems.

If Auto Start is enabled, Grammatik will immediately start checking the text; otherwise, you must click the Start button.

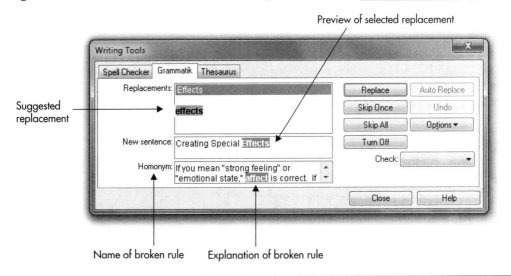

14

FIGURE 14-2   Grammatik catches errors in your writing that spell checking wouldn't alert you to.

If Grammatik finds something that breaks the rules of grammar using the current settings, it displays an explanation of the problem next to the name of the broken rule—the "Rule Class" that has been broken. Grammatik may make one or more suggestions of better grammar, and if you click an option, the new sentence is shown so that you can decide if that's what you meant to say. Click Replace to apply the change and continue checking.

Turning Grammatik's Rules On and Off

When Grammatik finds fault with your grammar, you might not always agree with its suggestion. If you don't want Grammatik to check a certain kind of grammatical error, you can tell it to ignore it. As soon as Grammatik pops up a grammar query, the Add button in the Writing Tools dialog changes to Turn Off. If you click Turn Off, the specific grammar rule that is currently being used will be deactivated for as long as the Writing Tools dialog is open. If you want to turn it back on again, choose Options | Turn On Rules, which brings up the Turn On Rules dialog. Choose those rules that you want to reactivate and click OK. The next time you perform a check, these rules are included.

After you have pared down the rules to the ones you want to keep, you can save this new "profile" for future use: Choose Options | Save Rules. The Save Rules dialog opens, and you can either click the Save button to update the current style or click Save As to create a new checking style.

Using the Thesaurus

When the word you're using doesn't convey exactly the right shade of meaning or if you've already used it three or four times, check out the available synonyms with the Thesaurus writing tool. Right-click with the Text tool on the word you want to replace with a better word, and then choose Thesaurus from the pop-up menu. Alternatively, choose Text | Writing Tools | Thesaurus. The Writing Tools dialog opens with the word in the word look-up box, as shown here:

Word look-up box

It's extremely costly to put in a new bathroom, and almost as costly to install new tiles. What makes home rennovation the most costly, however, is the high-price of *towels* to put in your new bathroom. Have you ever *seen* the price tags on even the less-costly ones? You're usually better off staying wet!

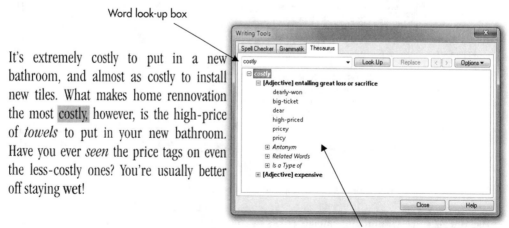

Suggestions area: similar words and phrases, opposite meanings

The word look-up box contains the word that you want to look up. The suggestions area of the dialog contains a folder-like tree view list of alternative words and meanings for the word you are looking up. Find one that matches the message you are trying to present, and click to expand the entry. If you find the word you want to use, select it and click the Replace button to insert the word into your text. You can also choose *the opposite meaning* of a word in case inverting a sentence is a style of writing you like—*antonyms* are available for the word you chose in the expandable tree in the suggestions area.

If you find a word that is close, but not exactly the right word for you, double-click the word to automatically open another suggestion area in the dialog that makes suggestions for words that are similar to the selected word. Up to three panes of suggestions are visible at once, but you can keep clicking suggestions and open more panes that you can navigate through using the left and right navigation buttons at the top of the dialog. To use a word in one of the alternate panes as your replacement word, select it and click the Replace button.

Setting Thesaurus Options

You can set various options for the Thesaurus by clicking the Options button in the Writing Tools dialog and clicking the Thesaurus tab to view the drop-down menu; the most useful ones are described here:

- **Auto Look Up**   This option speeds up your work by starting the process right away.

- **Auto Close**   When turned on, it closes the dialog as soon as the Replace button is clicked.

- **Spelling Assist**   When enabled, if the word that you selected to check in the Thesaurus is not recognized, a list of similar words from the Thesaurus is shown. Click the word that best matches the correct spelling of the word you typed, and then click Look Up. The suggestions area will contain alternatives.

- **Synonym**   This option displays synonyms of the look-up word in the list of suggested alternatives.

- **Antonym**   This option displays antonyms of the look-up—a lifesaver for those times when you can't think of an opposite for the word you want.

- **Language**   Choose this to change which language's Thesaurus is used for the current session. This does not change the language of the text in your document, but any replacements will be set to the new language. This only works with languages you have currently installed.

14

Using QuickCorrect

QuickCorrect is a dynamic part of CorelDRAW's writing tools. QuickCorrect works with you *as* you type, much like Auto Spell; it replaces words that you commonly mistype or misspell with the correctly spelled versions. It can also be used to replace an abbreviation with the full-word form to save you having to type a word or phrase each time.

How QuickCorrect Works

While you are typing, every time you "leave" a word by typing a space, period, tab, comma, or linefeed, QuickCorrect compares that word with its user word lists. If it finds the word—or possibly a phrase in one of its lists—it replaces that word or phrase with the replacement in the list. For example, people often mistype the word *the* when typing quickly; the English word lists already include an entry to change *teh* to *the*. Similarly, *don't* is the QuickCorrect replacement for *dont*, *misspell* for *mispell*, *you're the* for *your the*, and *weird* for *wierd*.

QuickCorrect also manages other automated text-correction features, such as capitalization of the first words of a sentence and the names of days, correcting consecutive capitals, and adding typographic or "smart" quotation marks.

 To remove an unwanted QuickCorrect change, choose Edit | Undo or press CTRL+Z. The QuickCorrect change is undone without undoing any other *typing. You then continue typing and the word that you typed is as it is.*

Setting QuickCorrect Options

To set QuickCorrect's options, open CorelDRAW's global Options dialog (CTRL+J), and navigate to the QuickCorrect section of the tree, as shown in Figure 14-3.

The available options are listed here:

- **Capitalize First Letter Of Sentences**   Does exactly that.

 If you use a lot of symbol fonts in your text, the sentence capitalization option is notorious for capitalizing those symbols when you don't want this. In these instances, you might want to disable this feature.

- **Correct Two Initial, Consecutive Capitals**   This option automatically corrects for holding the SHIFT key down too long when typing.

- **Capitalize Names Of Days**   This option capitalizes the first letter of days of the week.

- **Automatically Hyperlink**   When this option is enabled, typing *www* (followed by the rest of the URL) creates an Internet hyperlink. You might not want this if you're creating flyers, but if you are creating Acrobat PDF documents, it's a welcome option.

FIGURE 14-3 Use this dialog to choose your QuickCorrect settings.

This next Language section of the dialog is used to customize how a specific language deals with single-quote (apostrophe) and double-quote marks. Different languages use different glyphs to mark quotations. When you choose a language in the Language drop-down list, CorelDRAW automatically displays the traditional characters that language uses if they are available. To change which characters are used when working with a specific language, choose from the drop-downs. All of the settings are language specific, and you will need to set them for each language you use.

- **Change Straight Quotes To Typographic Quotes** QuickCorrect changes single- and double-quotation mark characters from the plain typed form to the appropriate left or right typographic quotation mark.

14

● **Use Straight Quotation Marks After Numbers -6'** Choose this if you work with measurements a lot. It looks awkward and unprofessional to denote six inches as the number 6 with a closed double-quote mark after it instead of a double-prime.

 If you need to use prime symbols for foot-and-inch measurements (such as 1' or 12"), copy the prime (or straight apostrophe) or double-prime (straight double-quote) symbol to the Clipboard from the Windows Character Map (Start | All Programs | Accessories | System Tools | Character Map) or other application. When the Importing/Pasting Text dialog opens, make sure that Discard Fonts And Formatting is checked. Click OK and the character will be inserted into your document without being intercepted by QuickCorrect.

● **Replace Text While Typing** When enabled, QuickCorrect replaces those words in the Replace list with the corresponding word in the With list. Entries to a language's QuickCorrect or directly into a user word list were shown earlier in this chapter, in the section "Adding a New Entry."

Finding and Replacing Text and Special Characters

All too often you may find yourself in the situation of having to find a specific piece of text so you can change the font or formatting or even the content of the text itself. CorelDRAW has terrific tools for searching for and replacing text—and text attributes—regardless of whether your layout is a paragraph or a multi-page document.

Finding Text

To find a word, phrases, and other marks such as dashes, hyphens, and special characters like tabs, paragraph breaks, and spaces, open the Find Text dialog by choosing Edit | Find And Replace | Find Text. In the Find box, enter the word or exact phrase you want to find.

You can include special characters such as an Em or En Space or Dash, a ¼ Em Space, a Non-Breaking Space, a Non-Breaking Hyphen, a Column/Frame Break, an Optional Hyphen, a Space, a Tab, or a Hard Return in your search. To enter the search tag for a special character into the Find box, click the right arrow next to the Find drop-down, and choose the character you want to include in your search.

If you know the exact character case of the word or phrase, enter it and check the Match Case check box—if the Match Case check box is cleared, all matching words will be found, regardless of the case of the characters (a case-insensitive search). The Find Text dialog is shown here:

Click the Find Next button to find the next instance of the searched text within the document. All the text objects in the document—paragraph, artistic, and fitted text—will be searched, starting with the current page and working to the end of the document. You will be asked whether you want to continue from the start of the document when you reach the end: Clicking Yes takes the search back to page 1, and it will continue through to the start position, so the whole document is checked once. If the search text is not found, CorelDRAW tells you.

Replacing Text

If you want to replace a word, phrase, or special character in the text with another word, phrase, or special character, use the Replace Text dialog, shown next, which is accessed by choosing Edit | Find And Replace | Replace Text.

14

You enter the word or phrase you want to find into the Find box, and enter the replacement word or phrase into the Replace With box using the same process as described for finding text in the previous section. Click the Find Next button to find the first instance of the search text. When the search text is found, click the Replace button to replace it with the replacement text, or click the Find Next button to skip over the found text and to find the next instance to replace.

If you are sure that you want to replace *all* instances of the Find text in the current document with the Replace With text, click the Replace All button.

NOTE *The ability to search and replace special characters in addition to text is incredibly useful when you are cleaning up imported text, changing five spaces into a tab, and removing column/frame breaks (soft returns). It is also a useful feature if you want to tweak your typography; for example, you can search for a hyphen between numbers and replace it with an en dash. You can also give your text some breathing room and search for all the em dashes in your text and put ¼ em spaces on either side of the em dash.*

Finding and Replacing Text Properties

You can also find and replace text properties using the general Find And Replace Wizard interface, invoked by choosing Edit | Find And Replace and then choosing one of the two wizards that can be used, either Find Objects or Replace Objects.

Finding Text Properties

Using the Find Objects Wizard, you can find text based on its type, such as Artistic, Paragraph, or Text On A Path (Fitted); on its contents; and on its styles. To find text in the current document, use these steps.

 ## A Simple Text Hunt Based on Object Properties

1. Open the Find Objects Wizard by choosing Edit | Find And Replace | Find Objects. Then choose Begin A New Search and click Next.

2. On the next page, from the Object Types tab, choose the type of text you want to find, or just check the Text box in the list, which will select all types of text. Then click Next.

3. On the next page, you must provide the settings for each text type individually. Click a type in the left box to choose it, and then click the Specify Properties For button. This will open the Specific [*Attribute*] dialog, where you choose the properties that the text must have in order for it to be found. The Specific Paragraph Text dialog is shown in Figure 14-4.

4. The properties shown selected in Figure 14-4 must all be present for the text to qualify: For example, if you type "village" and choose the font Comic Sans MS, and then choose Normal from the Weight field, the artistic text object containing the word "village" will be selected *only* if it is in the correct Font *and* Weight (the style of the typeface); CorelDRAW will select the text object but not any words within the object.

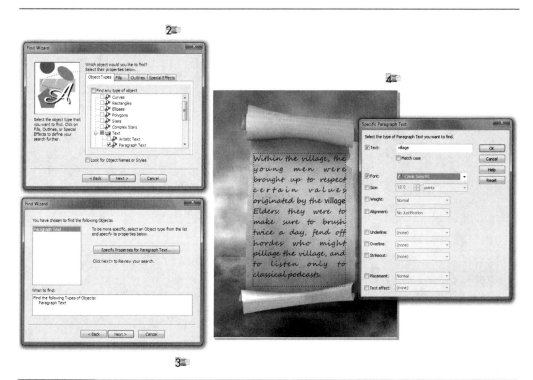

FIGURE 14-4   Use this dialog to give the properties of the text that needs to be located.

5. Click Finish and use the button bar, shown here, to jump between the found instances:

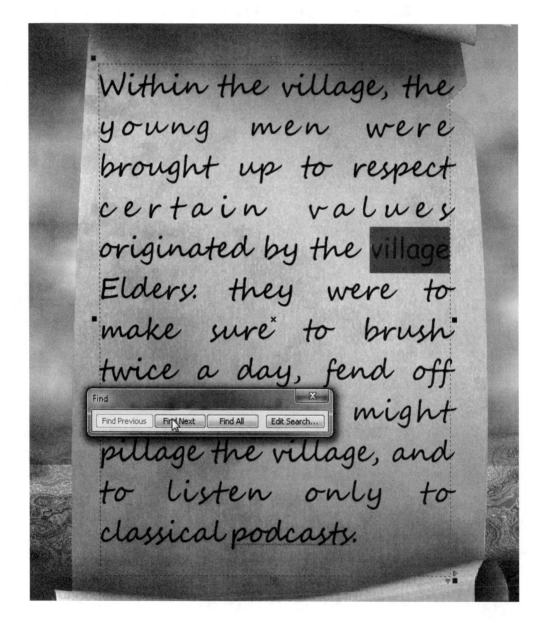

Within the village, the young men were brought up to respect certain values originated by the village Elders: they were to make sure to brush twice a day, fend off might pillage the village, and to listen only to classical podcasts.

Find

Find Previous | Find Next | Find All | Edit Search...

To find the occurrences of text objects containing text that uses a Text Style, check Look For Object Names Or Styles at the bottom of the first page of the Find Wizard. When this option is checked, clicking Next takes you to a page where you can choose the Style Name or a Style Type that you want to search for from a list.

Replacing Text Properties

The Replace Wizard replaces one set of matching text properties with another set. When you start the wizard, you can choose whether to restrict the search only to the text within the selected text objects or to search the whole document.

In the first page of the wizard, choose Replace Text Properties and click Next. You can now set the search and replace criteria for text properties, as shown in Figure 14-5.

You can set the Font, Weight, and Size of the text to find, and you can replace one or all of those settings with new ones. Click Finish and use the button bar to decide whether to find each match one at a time or just to replace them all in one go.

FIGURE 14-5   Set the Find and Replace With properties for your text.

Tables

With CorelDRAW's Table tool tucked into the toolbox, you no longer have to struggle to neatly and attractively present tabular data in your documents. Creating datasheets or directories, or displaying spreadsheet data no longer hinges on setting up elaborate networks of guidelines, or paragraph text blocks with a generous handful of tab and column settings thrown in. Drag out a table with the new Table tool, or import a table from your word processor or spreadsheet program, and you're all set to use CorelDRAW's tools to make the data look good.

Creating a Table

You can create a new table with either the Table tool in the toolbox or from the Create New Table command on the Table menu. If you use the Table tool to create the table, you can click-drag to position and size the table exactly where you want the table to be inserted. If you create the table using the menu command, the table will be inserted in the center of the document. In either case you can drag the table to a new position or resize it just as you would any other object, such as a rectangle that you create with toolbox tools.

Using the Proper Tool for the Job

Customization of a table takes place on several levels: the entire table, a single cell, a range of cells. The content you place inside a cell, such as text or graphics, is controlled with the same tools and settings that would affect it if it were not inside a cell. Which tool you have active, and what you've selected with that tool, if anything, determines what customization options are available to you at that moment from the property bar or the menus.

Table Options When the Pick Tool Is Active

With the Pick tool, click anywhere in or on the table to select the entire table. You can use the Pick tool to select, move, resize, stretch, skew, or rotate the entire table. When the Pick tool has been used to select the table, the following commands and options appear on the property bar, as shown in Figure 14-6. These options apply to the entire table.

The table's position on the page and the overall dimensions of the table use the same common entry fields on the left of the property bar that other objects such as rectangles or polygons use. Other important options are:

- **Rows And Columns**   Use the top control to enter the number of rows you want your table to have and the bottom one to enter the number of columns you require. You can change these entries at any time. For example, if a table currently has 2 rows and 2 columns, entering *6* in the row field and *4* in the column field causes the table to immediately reconfigure itself to contain the new number of rows and columns.

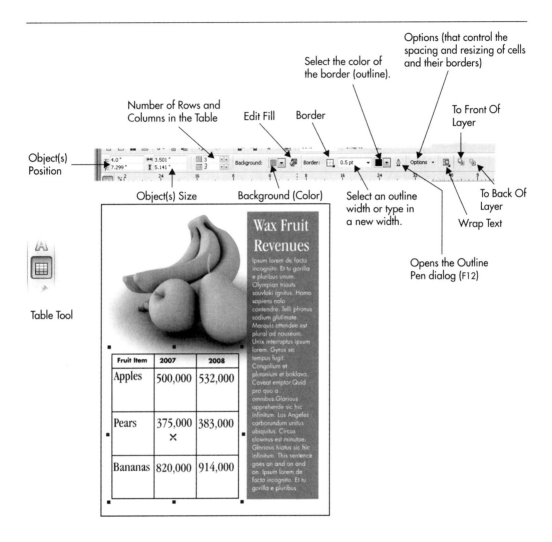

FIGURE 14-6   Use the property bar to customize the look of a table.

If you reduce the number of rows or columns, they are removed from the bottom up and from the right to the left. Any content you have in the columns and rows is lost, so do this with aforethought!

● **Background**   Choose a uniform color for all the cells from this drop-down list. You can also accomplish the same thing by choosing a color from the Color Palette.

- **Edit Fill**   If you've given the table a background fill, you can go directly to the Edit Fill dialog by clicking this icon. By default, tables are filled with a uniform fill. If you want your table to have any other fill type, such as fountain or pattern fill, you must first select the table, and then change the fill type from the Object Properties docker (ALT+ENTER).

- **Border**   "Border" refers to the outline of each cell and the table as a whole. You can show or hide the interior cell outlines and/or combinations of the top, bottom, left, and right sides of the table.

- **Outline Width and Outline Color**   These options control the width and color assigned to the borders you have set. For more advanced control, click the Outline Pen icon to open that dialog.

- **Options**   The options that can be set here are Automatically Resize Cells While Typing and Separated Cell Borders. The first is useful when the amount of content you need to enter in each cell is not uniform. Enabling this prevents your content from overflowing and moving out of view. The second option lets you space out your cells horizontally and vertically so that each cell is still contained in the table but is not in immediate proximity to the adjacent cell.

- **Wrap Text**   This important option determines how *paragraph text* flows around the table and how close the paragraph text box can get to the table—this option has nothing to do with the text content of the table. Tables are objects; text can be made to flow around them, over them, or under them. Artistic text is not affected by the Wrap Text setting.

- **To Front Of Layer and To Back Of Layer**   These icons become available if another object is layered on top of or below the table. Clicking these icons changes the position of the table in the stacking order.

Table Options When the Shape Tool Is Active

When you want to select a single cell or multiple cells in a table, use the Shape tool. To select a single cell, click in it with the Shape tool. To select adjacent cells, click-drag across the row(s) or column(s) that you want to select. To select non-adjacent cells, hold the CTRL key and click in the cells you want to select. Diagonal blue lines shade the cells you've selected. These lines are an onscreen visual indicator and not an actual fill.

Once cells are selected with the Shape tool, you can use the options available to you on the property bar, as seen in Figure 14-7, to customize the cells. The attributes you apply to cells override any you set for the table. The first control group on the left now will set the

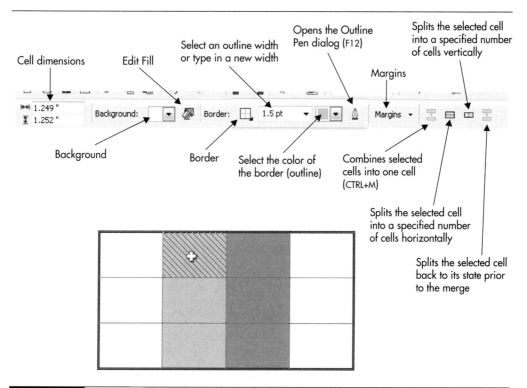

Cell dimensions

Edit Fill

Select an outline width or type in a new width

Opens the Outline Pen dialog (F12)

Splits the selected cell into a specified number of cells vertically

Margins

Background

Border

Select the color of the border (outline)

Combines selected cells into one cell (CTRL+M)

Splits the selected cell into a specified number of cells horizontally

Splits the selected cell back to its state prior to the merge

FIGURE 14-7   These options are available for table customization when the Shape tool is active.

dimensions of the selected cells as opposed to those of the entire table. The Background and Border options work the same as before, but making changes with them now only affects the selected cells. New to the property bar are the Margins drop-down, which sets the top, bottom, left, and right margins within the cell's bounds, and a group of controls to merge or split the selected cells into fewer or more cells.

You can also use the Shape tool to select an entire column or row. With the Shape tool click on the left border of the table next to the row you want to select. When the cursor turns into a small arrow, click again to select that row, or click-drag to select additional adjacent rows. To select columns, click on the top table border over the column you want to select, wait for the arrow to appear, and click again to select the column, or click-drag to select additional columns.

To select non-adjacent rows or columns, follow the preceding procedure, but hold the CTRL key and then click next to or over the rows and/or columns you want to select.

14

Editing a Table When the Table Tool Is Active

The Table tool is used to create the table by click-diagonal dragging in your document, but it is *also* used to edit the table once it is created. Right-clicking in a table row, column, or cell and choosing the appropriate option from the Select menu in the context menu is a quick way to select a single row, column, or cell. To select the entire table, choose Table from the Select command on the pop-up menu.

The Table tool can also be used in the same way the Shape tool is used to select multiple columns and rows, but it is easier to use the Shape tool and avoid the possibility of creating a table instead of a selection.

You can add or delete columns or rows from your table by clicking in a row or column and then choosing Delete | (Row or Column) from either the Table menu or the right-click context menu.

Working with Text and Graphics in a Table

Entering text into a table is easy; just use the Table tool to click in a cell, and enter text using any method for text entry. You can type text directly into the cell, import text from the File menu or from the Edit Text Box dialog (CTRL+SHIFT+T), or paste text into the cell from the Clipboard.

Text in tables is handled as paragraph text and can be proofed, edited, and formatted in the same ways. If you want to draw a paragraph text box within the table cell, you can do so by click-dragging the Text tool in the cell. Artistic text cannot be *created* in a table cell, but you can create it elsewhere on the page, copy it, and then paste it into a table cell.

You can paste any graphic into a cell, but which tool you use to select the cell that will hold the graphic makes a huge difference. If you use the Shape tool to select the target cell, the graphic will be pasted into the center of the cell as a graphic object. If you use the Table tool to select the cell and then paste the graphic into the cell, the graphic will be pasted in as an inline graphic whose size matches that of the default or current font size being used in that cell. This operation can take some time if the size reduction is great.

Once a graphic object has been placed in a cell, you select it by clicking it. You can then use the control handles to resize, rotate, and skew it. You can even extrude it if you like. If you want to move the graphic to another cell, select it with the Pick tool, and drag it into a different cell in the table. You can drag a graphic *out* of a table, but you cannot drag a graphic into a table.

Converting a Table to Text

A table can be converted into a single paragraph text box at any time by selecting the table and then choosing Table | Convert Table To Text from the menu. The Convert Table To Text dialog that appears offers you the option to separate the contents of each cell with a delimiter—a comma, a tab, a paragraph, or the character of your choice. If you choose to separate the cell contents with a comma, a tab, or one of your own choice, each row of cells will be saved to a paragraph with the individual cell contents separated in that paragraph by the delimiting character you choose. If you choose to separate cell contents by paragraph, you will get a paragraph for each cell.

 Converting a table to text sometimes produces results you don't like, so be prepared to undo the conversion. Saving a copy of your file before converting isn't a bad idea either.

Converting an Existing Text to a Table

Existing paragraph text can be converted into a table in a process that is basically the reverse of the process outlined in the previous section. Select the text you want to convert, and choose Table | Convert Text To Table from the menu. From the Convert Text To Table dialog, choose the delimiter you've used to break up the text into the chunks that you want to go into each cell. CorelDRAW analyzes the selected text and guesses what will work best as a delimiter. Because commas and tabs are frequently used within a section of text, they might cause the creation of many more cells than you were expecting. The bottom of the dialog shows you how many rows and columns it is going to create. If the number sounds wrong, cancel and go back to your text. Mark the end of each piece of text you want transferred into a cell with some other character—an asterisk (*) or a tilde (~), for example. Then choose User Defined and enter the character you choose as a delimiter into the field.

Importing a Table from Another Application

You don't have to create tables in CorelDRAW to use them in CorelDRAW. You or your client may have created a table in a document or spreadsheet that you want to include in a CorelDRAW document.

To import a table, choose File | Import from the menu. Use the Import dialog to navigate to the spreadsheet or word processing document. Select the document, and then click the Import button. When the Importing/Pasting Text dialog opens, choose how you want to handle importing formatted text. Your choices are Maintain Fonts And Formatting, Maintain Formatting Only, or Discard Fonts And Formatting. Then be sure to choose Tables from the Import Tables As drop-down list.

If you chose to maintain fonts and you don't currently have a font installed that was used in the table, you will have to work your way through the Font Substitution For Missing Fonts dialog. See Chapter 12 for information on font substitution.

Your cursor will be loaded with the table; you then click in your document to place the table. This is a live, editable, customizable table that you can use all of the CorelDRAW table tools on to make it exactly the way you want.

14

NOTE *If the existing table looks just the way you want it to look in CorelDRAW, by all means choose one of the first two "Maintain" options in the Importing/Pasting Text dialog just described. Although CorelDRAW is pretty good at interpreting what other applications did and mapping them accurately to CorelDRAW features and functions, the translation may not be perfect. Once the table has been imported, you may be able to make some simple fixes to make it look like it did in the other application. It may be a more effective use of your time to import your table without any formatting or fonts and to spend your time styling your table from scratch, instead of trying to fix the imported formatting.*

And this is the last word on typography in CorelDRAW! You now know how to spell check, grammar check, find and replace text, and how to create a text-driven table for your work. Our next stop is setting properties for filling objects and outline properties for paths. Let's get your objects—*including* text objects—looking as handsome and as visually captivating as you'd like them to be.

PART V

Attributes for Objects and Lines

CHAPTER 15

Filling Objects

A shape without a fill on your drawing page is like a brand-new coloring book. To make a coloring book—and your CorelDRAW artwork—more visually meaningful, you need to *fill* your shapes with colors and textures. CorelDRAW has more than a half-dozen different types of fill you can apply to your shapes, and these types have hundreds of variations. In computer graphics, you have over 16 million solid shades of color at your disposal; imagine what you can do with *blends* of colors, colors in different patterns, and colored *textures*! The worst part of filling CorelDRAW objects will be deciding on a style of fill. The *best* part, as you explore filling shapes in this chapter, is that it's very difficult to color outside of the lines.

NOTE	*Download and extract all the files from the Chapter15.zip archive to follow the tutorials in this chapter.*

Examining the Fill Types

Each type of CorelDRAW fill has its own special characteristics:

- *Uniform* fills apply flat, solid color.

- *Fountain* fills make a color transition from one color to another, in different directions—sometimes also called a *gradient fill.* You can also create a fountain fill composed of more than two different colors. CorelDRAW ships with a lot of preset fills that this chapter demonstrates how to pick and apply.

- *PostScript* fills are good for repeating patterns. Although PostScript is a *printing* technology, you don't need to print a CorelDRAW document to see a PostScript fill, and you can indeed export a PostScript filled object to bitmap format, and the fill will look fine. PostScript fills support transparency and are ideal for exporting to EPS file format to use in desktop publishing programs. And, naturally, a PostScript fill is valid for printing to a PostScript printer.

- *Pattern* and *texture* fills can fill shapes with bitmaps, including photographs, and a large supply of preset bitmaps is included with CorelDRAW.

- *Mesh* fills take multicolored fills and present you with the option of "smearing" colors within the fill, much like finger-painting.

Every fill type is applied in a slightly different way through the use of onscreen tools, docker windows, or the Interactive fill and Mesh fill tools (see Figure 15-1).

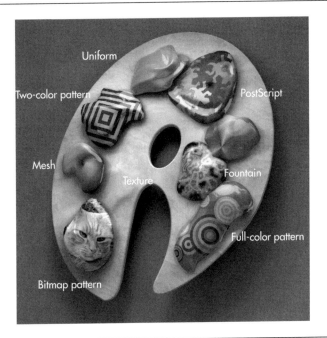

FIGURE 15-1 Fill your shapes in a composition with exactly the fill type that draws attention to your design work.

Using the Color Palette

With color selection, the Color Palette is an excellent starting point, and to apply a uniform (solid) fill to a selected object, you just select an object with the Pick tool and then left-click a color on the Color Palette. You can also drag a *well* (a color swatch) from the Color Palette, drop it onto a shape (which does not have to be selected), and the object is filled.

Perhaps one of the most interesting features in CorelDRAW is selecting not only a color from the Color Palette, but also a shade or a tone of that color—in color theory terms, these are called *analogous colors*. To pick a shade of a color on the Color Palette, you first select the object you want to fill, click-hold on a well color, and a small pop-up menu of shades and tones of that color appears. While holding the mouse button, drag to the exact shade you want, release the mouse button, and the object is filled. This pop-up menu features shades

15

that vary in *hue* from top to bottom, and in *brightness* as you drag your cursor from left to right. It's like having 49 possible colors at your cursor tip when you choose one color.

Selected shape

Color Palette

Click-hold to choose analogous color.

Uniform fills can also be assigned to all objects right from the get-go. With no objects selected in the drawing window, left-click a color you want to use for all objects, artistic text, and/or paragraph text from now on. CorelDRAW then displays a dialog, shown next, that asks what sort of object you want filled when it's created from now on. You can cancel out of this operation, but you can choose objects, text, or both.

 If you need to set the default fill for all documents you create in the future, go to Options | Document, where you can check Save Options As Defaults For New Documents, and then check Styles, which applies the fill you've chosen to Default Graphic (the properties for all new objects).

From Uniform to Non-Uniform Object Filling

The quick way of applying any of the fill types is by using the Interactive fill tool, shown here. You'll find it at the bottom of the toolbox; to quickly select it, press G. You'll see a hint here that the Interactive fill tool is also a selection tool—the cursor is an arrow cursor with a paint bucket. You don't need to have the object that you want to fill selected when you use this tool. You can click an unselected shape with the Interactive fill tool; it becomes selected, and then a second click-drag on the object by default applies the linear style fountain fill, making a transition from black to white. You can then change the colors used, or choose a different fill type from the property bar by clicking the Fill Selector drop-down list.

While you're using the Interactive fill tool, the property bar displays fill options that change depending on the type of fill you choose from the selector. If your selected object features no fill color at all, the selector displays the type as No Fill, and the property bar displays no options. The selector, shown next, is where you can choose from any of ten fill types: Uniform Fill, four fountain fill types (Linear, Radial, Conical, and Square), two Color Pattern fill types (Two Color and Full Color), Bitmap Pattern, Texture Fill, and PostScript Fill. In this section, you'll learn to control every fill type using property bar options and the control handles on the Interactive fill tool.

15

The technique you use to set angle and position (among other properties) of fills varies a little from fill type to fill type, so let's run through the basics for a moment.

Filling an Object, Setting Fill Properties

1. Select the object to fill, and then choose the Interactive fill tool (G) from the toolbox.

2. If your object *already* has a fill (excluding a shade of a color well on the Color Palette), the property bar automatically displays the fill type and the current properties of that specific fill.

3. Use the Fill Type selector to choose a fill type. As you do this, the object is filled with the selected style, and the property bar shows options for this style, which is applied with default color, direction, pattern type, and so on. Your object will also display control handles for the direct manipulation of the current fill type.

4. Use the property bar to define properties of your fill, which are instantly updated in the object in the drawing window.

The following section covers the property bar options specific to the fill type when the Interactive fill tool is selected.

Uniform Color Fill Options on the Property Bar

Uniform fills are like the paint chips at the hardware store; it's a solid color, no variations, and a uniform fill floods an object within the boundaries of its outline with the color you choose. The Color Palette is a fast, easy way to assign a uniform color; however, when you choose the Interactive fill tool, you have several different color models from which to choose. See Chapter 17 for details on color theory—if you're already familiar with the CMYK printing color model, the intuitive HSB color model, and others, you'll feel right at home using the property bar to mix up color values (and better still, entering values a client might have telephoned to you for that big advertising job).

The following illustration shows the color models you can use the Interactive fill tool to choose when Uniform Fill is selected from the property bar Fill Type selector. Most of us prefer to visually mix up a color. So while the property bar displays fill options, click the Edit Fill button at the far left; this displays a palette in which you drag a marker and move sliders to specify the color you need, and then click OK to define it.

Edit Fill · Palette · Uniform Fill Palette Color · Color Tint (Spot Colors Only)

Uniform Fill Selected · Uniform Fill Type Selector (Color Models) · Color Values · Copy Fill Properties

Saturation/Brightness Marker · Hue Slider

TIP   *HSB and RGB color models occupy the same color space, the extent to which a color can be expressed onscreen. Therefore, you can arrive at an identical color using either color mode. This means you can switch color models for a filled object, and between RGB and HSB there will be no real color change.*

15

Applying a Fountain Fill

Fountain fills can fill objects with a smooth transition between two (or more) colors, and they come in various styles. Many commercial pieces of artwork are created today that imitate the traditional airbrush (popular in the mid–20th century) by using fountain fills. You can apply a fountain fill in different ways, and the following tutorial shows you the quickest, most artistically satisfying way.

Creating Fountain-Filled Objects

1. Select an object and then choose the Interactive fill tool (G) from the toolbox.

2. Click-drag, beginning at one side of your object and dragging to the opposite side at any angle; try dragging from 10 o'clock to 4 o'clock, for example. A default linear fountain fill is created using the object's current fill color, making a color transition from the defined color to white, indicated by settings in the property bar. If your object has no fill, a default black-to-white fountain fill is created.

3. For a different fountain fill type, choose Radial, Conical, or Square from the Fill Type selector. As you do this, the shape of your fountain fill (and the available property bar options) changes.

4. Experiment with changing the appearance of the fill by dragging to move the color markers and midpoint slider control. Notice how the position changes affect your fill. The midpoint slider is used to influence the point at which the *From* color and the *To* color in the fountain fill are exactly a 50/50 mix of the colors. So if, for example, you want to create a shaded sphere, you begin with an ellipse object, fountain fill it with the radial fill type, and then move the midpoint closer to the white marker than to the black to make a small, subtle, sharp highlight on the object: bingo, you have yourself a dimensional sphere!

Using these steps, your click-drag action specifies several properties. The first click sets the From color position, and the drag direction defines the angle. The length of the drag defines the distance, and the mouse release defines the To color position. A series of interactive markers shows the position of each of these values. It's important to understanding how fountain fills are applied; other fountain fill operations are variations on this theme. The following sections examine each fountain fill type in detail (see Figure 15-2).

- **Linear** This is the default fountain fill style and is most useful for shading rectangular shapes to suggest lighting on a dimensional plane or 3D object. The color marker positions mainly control its appearance.

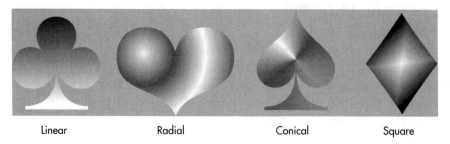

| Linear | Radial | Conical | Square |

FIGURE 15-2 A different fountain fill type can bring out the dimensional qualities of almost any shape.

- **Radial**   This type makes a color transition outward in a circular style, terrific for shading round objects and objects you'd like to soften in appearance. During use of radial fountain fills, the center offset controls where the fill begins.

- **Conical**   This might not be a fill type you use every day, but if you need to simulate the look of the playing side of a DVD or an aerial view of a grain silo, Conical produces a strongly shaded and unique transition between two or more colors. The From color of a conical fill is the beginning and the end of the conical fill, and the To color shades all the in-between blend steps. The center control handle can be used to increase the contrast of the effect by dragging it toward the From color marker along the dotted-line arc of the control handles; dragging the center toward the To marker creates less contrast and a milder effect.

- **Square**   This style produces a look like a four-pointed starburst. The center marker controls contrast; the To marker sets distance and direction for the fill.

Chapter 22 documents object transparency types. Here's advance notice if you haven't read this chapter yet: Fountain fill styles are also transparency styles—all four types of fountain fills can make a transition between opaque and transparent. You therefore can build an elegantly shaded object by, for example, applying a radial fountain fill to an object and then giving it a linear transparency property.

Controlling Fountain Fills Interactively

The interactive fountain fill markers (hovering on top of an object you've drawn), combined with the property bar, give you control over the look of your fill. Among these, you'll see color selectors, a Midpoint option, Angle and Edge Pad options, and a Fountain Step Lock/Unlock option, shown here:

Many of these fountain fill property bar options correspond to interactive markers surrounding your object, but the marker positions can be changed to produce different looks, according to the type of fountain fill. Although the property bar offers precision, dragging the markers is extremely intuitive and often is a preferred method to make a custom fill. In Figure 15-3 you can see the different interactive marker positions that appear around each fountain fill type.

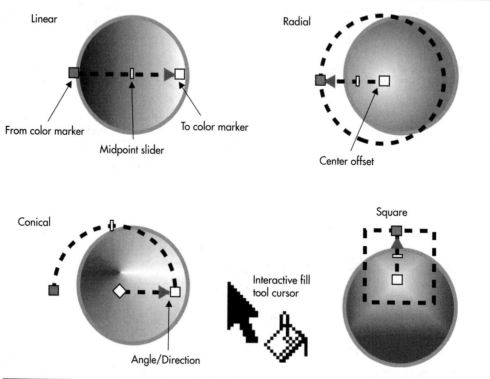

FIGURE 15-3 Interactive markers surround each fountain fill type while you're using the Interactive fill tool.

Moving any of the markers will change the fill appearance in different ways. The following explains the purpose of options you'll see in the property bar while dragging interactive markers and what the effect is on the fill:

- **Color Markers** Use these to set the position and colors in your fountain fill. Each fountain fill type has to have at least two colors. To change a color, click to select it and click a color well in your onscreen palette, or drag a color well directly onto a color marker. To move a marker, click-drag it in any direction, which changes the properties of the filled object, usually relocating the center of the fountain fill.

- **Midpoint** This slider control is available only while a two-color fountain fill is applied; if you use more than two colors for the fill, the midpoint marker goes away. The midpoint marker is used to set the point at which the From and To colors are equal in value. This value is measured in terms of percentage—by default, it's 50 percent.

- **Angle**   The Angle value applies to linear fountain fills and is set in degree values between 360 and –360 (a negative value). Positive angles rotate the fill counterclockwise, while negative values rotate the fill clockwise.

- **Edge Pad**   This option sets the amount of contrast between the To and From colors, expressed as a percentage. The default setting, 0, creates smooth, even blends at the slowest possible rate. Increasing this setting causes colors to change more abruptly, as shown next. Edge Pad can be set within a range of 0 to 49 percent, and this can also be adjusted in Object Properties (ALT+ENTER) and in the Fountain Fill dialog (F11). Moving the color markers of a linear fill away from or toward your object's outline increases or decreases this value; try dragging the To and From color markers to positions outside of the object, for example, to decrease the edge pad effect.

Edge pad 0   Edge pad 15   Edge pad 30

- **Center Offsets**   Radial, conical, or square fountain fills feature this marker; you change the center position of the fill relative to your object's center by dragging the marker. Dragging the center marker of a radial, conical, or square fill away from or toward your object's center also increases or decreases the edge pad value.

- **Steps**   This setting affects both the display and printing of fountain fills. A fountain fill is actually calculated by blending neighboring bands of color in succession, but you don't see this banding effect because so many shades of intermediate colors are used between the To and From color. The Fountain Steps option is fixed at the maximum setting of 256 by default, but can be increased to a maximum of 999. However, you might be *looking for* a banding effect, to create shirt stripes or other geometric patterns. To lower this setting, click to unlock the Lock button. Lowered step values cause the color gradation in your fill to become unsmooth, as shown

15

next. While 256 steps is set and locked, fountain fills will display and print using the maximum capabilities of your monitor and printer resolution.

256 steps

20 steps

12 steps

Using Custom Fountain Fills

A default fountain fill features two colors, but you can *add* colors to make any type of fountain fill into your own version. When you make multi-colored fountain fills, the appearance of your artwork can change dramatically. The position of added colors is shown by node positions on the dashed line guide joining the two default colors. After you've added color markers and clicked them to select them on the object, the property bar will display their position and color, as shown here:

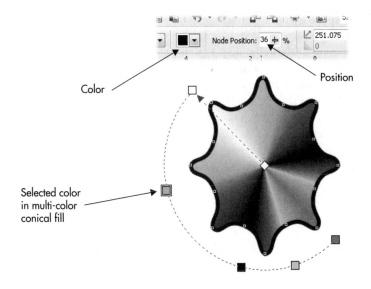

You can add, move, and delete fountain fill colors you've added to a default fountain fill type in several ways, but you *must* have both the object and the Interactive fill tool selected, or you'll wind up editing the object and not the fill. To explore doing this, follow the steps in this tutorial.

Editing a Fountain Fill In-Place

1. Select the object to be filled, choose the Interactive fill tool (G), and then apply a fountain fill by choosing Linear, Radial, Conical, or Square from the property bar Fill Type selector.

2. With a default fill applied, double-click a point on the guide between the two existing color markers where you want to add a color marker. Doing this adds a color that is based on an average of two existing marker colors, so your custom fountain fill probably looks the same as the default fill.

3. Decide on a new intermediate color (choose one in this example on the Color Palette), and drag a color from the color well (drag the swatch) onto your new marker. You have a three-color gradient now.

4. Try a different technique to add a color marker position and a color at the same time: drag a Color Palette well directly onto the same fountain fill guide, but at a different location.

5. To reposition an added color, click-drag it along the guide path. As you do this, the color's node position changes, as indicated by the Node Position value on the property bar.

6. To change any fountain fill color, click to select it, and choose a color from the property bar selector, or click a color well on the Color Palette.

7. To delete an added color, right-click or double-click it on the guide. To and From color nodes can't be deleted, but they can be recolored.

Additionally, color can be added when a color node position is selected, and you choose from the color selector to the right of the Fill Type selector on the property bar.

 You can drag a color marker "through" a neighboring marker to change the order of color nodes along any fountain fill object.

Setting Fountain Fill Dialog Options

The interactive way is great for controlling fountain fills, but if you want deeper and more precise controls, you can use the Fountain Fill dialog, shown in Figure 15-4.

15

The Fountain Fill dialog provides some options common to the property bar and others unique to this dialog.

You can open the Fountain Fill dialog while a fountain fill is applied to a selected object and while using the Interactive fill tool by clicking the Edit Fill button in the property bar. Or, with your object selected and while any tool is in use, press F11.

The Fountain Fill dialog options that aren't available while you're using the Interactive fill tool property bar are listed and explained here:

● **Color Wheel Rotation** This option is available only while a two-color blend is selected. You can choose to blend directly from one color to the other (the default), more or less "jumping" the hue cycle the traditional color wheel goes through, or choose Counterclockwise or Clockwise to blend between colors while cycling through a standard color wheel's colors, traveling around the outside edge of the wheel. This might seem like a trivial option, but CorelDRAW is one of the few design programs that can shortcut through the traditional model of visible colors. For example, in other applications, a fountain fill that goes from red to blue necessarily has to travel through green, somewhat muddying the fountain fill. Not so if you choose Direct Blend here.

- **Interactive preview**   You have some manual control over where you want the center and/or direction of a fill to take place within an object by dragging in the preview window. In Figure 15-4, you can see that the radial fountain fill will be positioned beginning in the upper-right of the filled object because this is where the center has been dragged in the small preview window.

- **PostScript Options**   When a two-color fountain fill is selected with both the From and To colors specified as *spot color inks,* the PostScript Options button becomes available. PostScript Options offer halftone screens of special fills to certain dot shapes. Possessing PostScript level 3 capabilities, CorelDRAW features an expanded collection of screen styles including CosineDot, Cross, various Diamond styles, various Double and InvertedDoubleDot styles, various Ellipse and InvertedEllipse and other styles, Euclidean, Grid, Rhomboid, Round, Square, and Star shapes. While any of these styles is selected, Frequency and Angle options are available in the PostScript Options dialog, enabling you to override default printing settings for your selected spot color inks. An easy visual indicator that you are using spot colors is the small circle tick inside the chosen color swatch in the Fountain Fill box.

Tick indicates spot color.

If you're unfamiliar with spot colors, it's the printing process used to add a color to packages, for example, that cannot be reproduced using standard press inks, such as that reflective silver logo on a box of cereal. See Chapter 27 for the lowdown on spot versus process colors and for a guide to commercial printing of your CorelDRAW work.

- **Presets** The Presets drop-down menu includes a variety of sample fountain fill types, colors, and positions. Use them as they are, or edit them to suit a specific need. To select any of these, choose a name from the drop-down list. While you're browsing the alphabetical list, a preview of the highlighted preset is displayed in the fountain fill preview window in the upper-right corner of the dialog. A preset can contain any of the properties associated with a two-color or custom fountain fill color.

- **Add/Delete Presets** The two small buttons to the right of the Presets drop-down list can save you hours of custom fountain fill creation time. First, the button labeled with the minus (–) symbol deletes your current selection from the list of preset fountain fills after presenting a confirmation dialog, just to ensure that you don't delete a factory preset by accident. The button labeled with a plus (+) symbol is for saving the current fountain fill as a preset.

To save your selected fountain fill settings, follow these steps.

Saving Your Own Fill as a Preset

1. With your custom fountain fill colors and options set in the Fountain Fill dialog, enter a name in the Presets box.

2. Click the + button. Your custom fountain fill is immediately saved alphabetically in the list of available presets.

3. Click OK to apply the saved preset and close the dialog.

4. To retrieve and apply your saved preset to fill a selected object, press F11 to open the Fountain Fill dialog, click Custom to view the Presets menu, choose your saved preset from the list, and click OK to close the dialog and apply the saved fountain fill.

Applying Pattern Fills

Pattern fills are rectangular-shaped tiles that repeat vertically and horizontally to fill a closed-path object completely. They come in three different varieties: Two Color, Full Color, and Bitmap, each with its own unique qualities, shown in Figure 15-5.

Two-color pattern Full-color pattern Bitmap pattern

FIGURE 15-5 Pattern fills come in three types.

While a pattern fill is applied, the property bar includes a host of options that can be used to apply dramatic changes to the fill's appearance, as shown here when the Two Color Pattern fill has been applied to an object, and the object is currently selected:

15

In addition to altering pattern properties, the property bar has features to control the appearance of your pattern in the following ways:

- **Fill Selector**   Use this drop-down box to choose from existing pattern fill libraries.

- **Front/Back Color Selectors**   When a two-color pattern is selected, these two selectors let you set colors other than black and white for a pattern.

- **Tile Size Buttons**   Use these buttons to set your pattern to Small, Medium, or Large preset width and height sizes.

- **Tile Width/Height**   The Width and Height sizes of your selected pattern can be set individually using these two options, each of which can be set between 0.1 and 15 inches.

- **Transform Fill With Object**   When this option is active, transformations applied to your object will also be applied to your fill pattern. This is a useful feature when you need to scale an object larger and don't want your pattern to "shrink"!

- **Mirror Fill Tiles**   Using this option forces a transformed pattern tile back into a seamless pattern.

Two-color patterns are limited to *exactly* two colors, with no additional edge colors to create anti-aliasing. This means that the edges of the design can be harsh and somewhat jaggy if you export your work to a screen resolution of 96 dpi. However, if you *export,* for example, a TIFF copy of your work, the jagged edges you see onscreen will *not* appear in the exported bitmap image.

Full-color patterns are composed of vector shapes, but the pattern itself already has color applied and cannot be altered. Additionally, these full-color fills cannot be extracted as vector shapes from the pattern. Therefore, when making your own pattern, save a copy of your pattern to CDR file format for editing in the future, and forget about the Break Apart and Convert To Curves commands in an attempt to reduce a full-color pattern to its vector component shapes. Bitmap patterns are carefully edited bitmaps; some of the presets are taken from photos, while others are paintings, and all of them are relatively small in dimensions. The difference between a full-color and a bitmap fill is that the vector-based pattern tiles for the full-color fills can be resized without losing design detail, focus, or introducing noise, but enlarging bitmap pattern tiles carries the same caveat as enlarging any bitmap—the more you enlarge it, the better your chances are that the component pixels will eventually become visible. You can scale bitmaps down, but not up—computers are "smart," but they can't create extra visual data from nonexistent data.

Controlling Pattern Fills Interactively

You can edit the look of an applied pattern fill by adjusting the interactive markers, and using the various property bar options common to all pattern styles.

The interactive handles surrounding a pattern fill help you to set the tile size, offset, skew, and rotation of the pattern. To experience this firsthand, open Platonic.cdr and work with the uncompleted group of objects on the left of the page. Use the right side duplicate of the Platonic geometry as a reference.

Customizing a Pattern Fill

1. Select an object in the group at left, and then choose the Interactive fill tool (G).

2. Choose Two Color Pattern from the Fill Type selector. By default, a two-color dot-style pattern fill featuring Black as the Front color and White as the Back color is applied to your object featuring fill markers.

3. Insert the cursor in the top Edit Tiling field, and then type **1.2**; then type **1.2** in the bottom Edit Tiling field. You've made the polka dot pattern a more pleasing size for one of the Platonic object faces. Clicking on the Small, Medium, and Large Tile buttons performs the same thing, but without precise size control. Dragging the Rotation/Size handle while holding CTRL to constrain the rotation angle also changes the size.

4. Drag the diamond-shaped center origin handle slightly in any direction. Notice that the center origin of the pattern changes.

5. Drag the white marker, governing the Back color, up and right to skew the pattern so it looks more like it's on the face of the object, viewed in perspective.

6. Click the white Back color marker, and then click the Back color icon on the property bar—choose a light gray. Now the face of the Platonic object looks a little more properly shaded.

7. Repeat steps 3–6, varying the Front and Back colors to complete filling in other objects.

8. To quickly complete the assignment, while the Interactive fill tool is chosen, click a solid fill object, and then click the Copy Properties button on the property bar. Then click over a corresponding object in the completed design at right.

Figure 15-6 shows the marker handles around a two-color pattern fill.

15

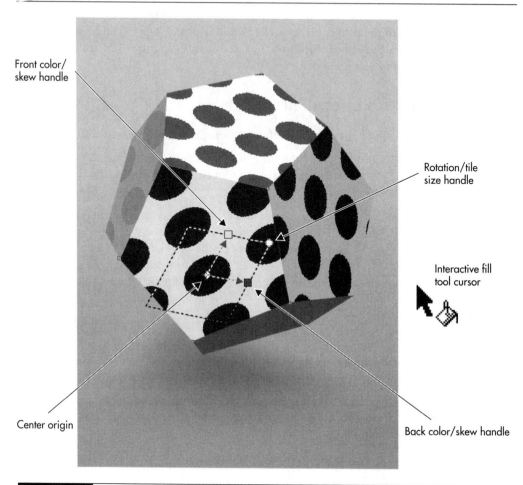

Front color/
skew handle

Rotation/tile
size handle

Interactive fill
tool cursor

Center origin

Back color/skew handle

FIGURE 15-6 The interactive markers surrounding a two-color pattern fill are there for you to control the pattern's colors, size, and skew.

Using Pattern Fill Dialog Options

The Pattern Fill dialog offers an alternative way to control pattern fills (see Figure 15-7). To open this dialog (which is nearly identical for two-color, full-color, and bitmap pattern fills), click the Edit Fill button in the property bar while a pattern fill type is in effect.

FIGURE 15-7   The Pattern Fill dialog provides an alternative method for setting pattern fill properties.

Here's what each of the options in the Pattern Fill dialog controls:

- **Origin**   The X and Y Origin options are used to offset the center of the pattern from 0 within a range between 30 and –30 inches. Positive X or Y values offset the origin right or upward, while negative values offset the origin downward or left. Using the interactive origin handle in the workspace performs the same thing.

- **Transform**   These options are Skew and Rotate, each of which is measured in degrees. Skew values range between 89 and –89 degrees, while Rotate values can be set between 360 and –360 degrees. These options work in combination with each other to apply vertical and/or horizontal distortion to the fill pattern. Rotation and Skew can be performed directly on an object onscreen; however, undoing a skew and rotation, and performing these distortions with precise values, is not easily done in the workspace.

15

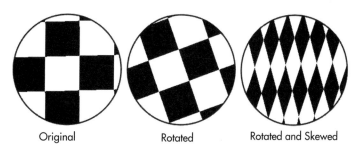

Original   Rotated   Rotated and Skewed

● **Row and Column Offsets** By default, pattern tiles join to appear seamless. However, you can *intentionally* ruin the pattern (or just create an "interesting" one) by offsetting the pattern seams through either of these two options. To apply an offset, choose either Row or Column as the offset option, and enter a value between 0 and 100 percent, as shown here:

Column offset 40 percent   Row offset 40 percent

Create Your Own Two-Color and Full-Color Patterns

Two-color patterns are harder to think up than they are to create, and the details are covered right after this section. Full-color (vector) patterns are created by sampling an area on the page. While the Interactive fill tool is active and the Fill Type selector in the property bar has Full Color Pattern selected, click the Create Pattern button. This opens a dialog for specifying the new pattern type and resolution. After you choose the type and resolution, crosshairs appear on your screen, and you then click-drag to define an area in your document to use for the new pattern.

The saved pattern is located in C:\Users*your user name*\AppData\Roaming\Corel\ CorelDRAW Graphics Suite X5\Custom Data\Patterns. To apply a custom pattern, you need to click the Edit tool on the property bar to display the Pattern Fill box, where you click Load.

Two-color patterns are created using a special editor box displayed by clicking the Edit Fill button on the property bar when the Interactive fill tool is active and the Fill Type selector is set to Two Color Pattern. Once the Pattern Fill box is displayed, click Create. As you can see in Figure 15-8, two-color patterns are created by choosing a bitmap size, a pen size, and then left-dragging and/or clicking to set the foreground pattern. Right-clicks and right-click-drags act like an eraser. Alternatively, you can click Load if you've created a

TUTORIALS
At A Glance

This color section shows what you can achieve (and probably improve on) by working through some of the dozens of tutorials in this guide.

Chapter 11 is your guide to permanent as well as nondestructive object editing. Learn how to use the Shaping docker to remove the parts of a drawing's group that you want to hide. Also see how to use the PowerClip effect in combination with envelopes and transparency to decorate dimensional surfaces such as in this vase illustration.

In Chapter 19, you'll learn how to add depth to objects by using the Extrude tool. Combining manual editing and adding objects, you'll be able to make your ideas leap off the page without a net.

The Lens docker is your ticket to creating views of your illustrations, to magnifying areas, and to creating color inversions and other visually arresting special effects. All the steps are in Chapter 22.

CONTAINS NO ACTUAL FRUIT JUICE. WHAT DID YOU EXPECT?

Get some perspective on things! Chapter 18 demonstrates how to use the Add Perspective command on the Effects menu to create scenes with depth. Using the command in combination with the Drop Shadow tool, you can build a digital diorama!

Then check out Chapter 20 for the many uses of the Envelope tool. Treat finished drawings as though they're soft, flexible, and fun objects in your compositions.

Sew What?

Buttons seem to have been with us since there were things we needed to sew them on and a thread! I remember when I was a child, playing with my grandmother's jars of buttons: there were so many kinds and shapes...and textures! They ran the gamut from shiny brass buttons she's put on fancy coats, to the plain and simple 4-hole variety for getting a shirt back into working condition. Then there were the odd, two hole kind, which appeared to defy gravity and still stayed on a garment with half the thread.
Fortunately, I never found my grandmother's needles collection.

Chapter 12 takes you on an exploration of CorelDRAW's Text tool; see how to use artistic and paragraph text in combination with true desktop publishing features to create logos, page layouts, and special effects. Shown here are two different examples: wrapping text within an object and aligning the text to the container shape.

VIOLIN

The violin is sometimes informally called a fiddle, regardless of the type of music played on it. The word violin comes from the Middle Latin word vitula, meaning stringed instrument; [1] this word is also believed to be the source of the Germanic "fiddle".[2]

The violin, while it has ancient origins, acquired most of its modern characteristics in 16th-century Italy, with some further modifications occurring in the 18th century.

Someone who plays the violin is called a violinist or a fiddler. The violinist produces sound by drawing a bow across one or more strings (which may be stopped by the fingers of the other hand to produce a full range of pitches), by plucking the strings (with either hand), or by a variety of other techniques

Chapter 26 features some pretty tricky special-effects image-editing techniques using PHOTO-PAINT. Learn how to replace the background in images to create invisible retouching; also see how to build animated GIF images for the Web.

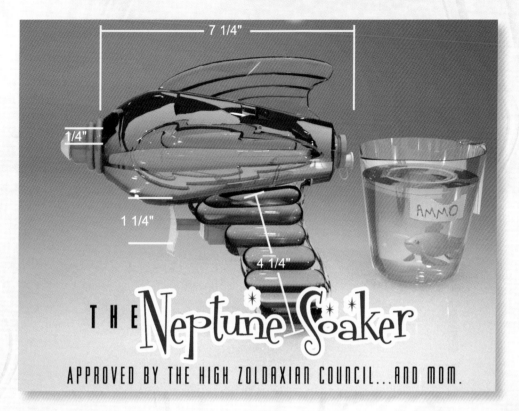

7 1/4"

1/4"

1 1/4"

4 1/4"

THE Neptune Soaker

APPROVED BY THE HIGH ZOLDAXIAN COUNCIL...AND MOM.

Chapter 7 provides all the details you need for letting CorelDRAW assist you with precise measurements—calibrating your screen, creating callouts for technical drawings, and putting your rulers exactly where you need them. And in Chapter 15, you'll have your fill: you'll use patterns, textures, and even your own designs to fill objects in no time.

Chapters 23 through 26 uncover the secrets to working between CorelDRAW vector objects and bitmap images. Learn how to filter photos to look like artwork, blend images together, and add shadows to glass objects that make your artwork look photorealistic!

personal
GARDENING

July 2011
$4.⁹⁵ US &
Canada

Flex
That
Green
Thumb!

INSIDE: Gardening Tips of the Stars 🍵 Gardening Hints from Ordinary People 🍵 How to transplant a tree 🍵 Secrets to building a better rock garden: start small 🍵 Much much more!

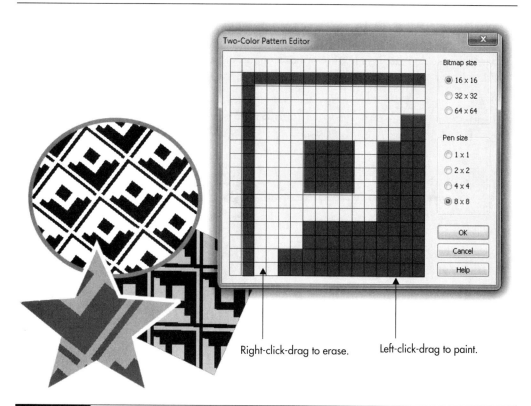

Right-click-drag to erase.   Left-click-drag to paint.

FIGURE 15-8   Create your own two-color pattern by clicking the Create button in the Pattern
Fill dialog; then edit an existing preset pattern.

bitmap image (a two-color one works best, so the Editor doesn't brute-force a tonal image to
black or white); the Editor accepts TIF, BMP, and other image file formats. Two-color
patterns you create are immediately applied to a selected object, unlike full color patterns,
which are saved to a PAT file on hard disk. If you want to later load a two-color pattern
you've designed, click Load in the Pattern Fill dialog.

 TIP   *You can also create patterns by using the Tools | Create | Pattern Fill menu
command.*

15

Applying Texture Fills

When the Interactive fill tool has been chosen and you then pick a texture fill, the property bar (shown next) displays texture options, including a Texture Library selector, a Texture Fill selector, and options for controlling the appearance of the texture.

The interactive handles surrounding a texture fill are the same as those for pattern fills; they're there for you to set the size, offset, skew, and rotation of the texture. If you have experience manipulating pattern fills by click-dragging the control handles above the object, you'll discover bitmap fills are exactly the same. However, because these are *bitmap-based* textures, you'll need to take note of some transformation limitations, covered shortly.

As you'll discover next, each texture is based on a range of variables specific to a style type. To view these core styles, you'll need to open the Texture Fill dialog by clicking the Edit Fill button.

You'll notice that the same options available in the property bar are in the dialog above—but also included when you click the Edit Fill button are the texture variables. There are settings for texture, color, frequency of properties of the textures, and so on. Don't hesitate to drag a spin box value and then to click Preview; although several of the values might seem to have strange labels for the values, they'll indeed modify the texture preset (changing the Texture # is a great place to begin experimenting). Also, it's very hard to give a label to some of the properties of fractal math; they're abstract attributes and fairly difficult to write in the first place! Start by choosing a type of texture from the Texture List, and then use different values in fields such as colors (another good starting place). Click Preview, and if you like what you see, save it as a Preset, click OK to apply the texture, and then use the control handles for the Interactive fill tool to adjust the fill as it appears in the selected shape.

15

What Is a Fractal?

Fractal geometry is based on mathematical equations, whose core is beyond the scope of this book. However, fractal geometry usually appears to have the following visual characteristics:

- **Self-similarity** Fractal designs branch with variations set by the mathematician writing the fractal math, but typically a fractal design repeats a basic structure within itself at smaller scales, branching from a main body in the design. This is why many fractals look like organic forms such as ferns, broccoli, and seashells—these designs in nature also obey fractal math.

- **A recursive structure with irregularities** As with self-similarity, fractals repeat, with variations, as they branch. If you're familiar with Euclidean geometry, fractal math is too unpredictable when plotted to 2D space to be described in Euclidian geometric functions.

- **Exist within a domain of 2D or 3D space** Fractal math is used in several 3D programs to generate organic sculptures. KPT Frax4D, in fact, is a plug-in for PHOTO-PAINT and other bitmap programs that can generate fractal designs in 3D space. Fractals were once described by a mathematician using this analogy: if a square represents the number *2* and a cube represents the number *3*, fractals live somewhere between these two integers.

Not all the texture fills use fractal math; some use procedures (a recipe of equations), but overall, they're just *fun* to add to a design. And because they're math based, they can be rendered to the size you need—this is part of what the Regenerate button on the property bar is for.

The textures are based on more than a hundred different styles ranging from bubbles and clouds through minerals, raindrops, ripples, rock, and vapor.

 Many of the fractal patterns in the Samples libraries do not seamlessly tile all on their own. Fractal math can be coded as non-terminating (which creates an infinite branching and can be quite processor-intensive) and terminating, which means the math ends at a certain point, and you'll see a tile edge in your design once in a while. To fix this: click the Mirror button on the property bar when the object is selected and when the Interactive fill tool is chosen. Alternatively, this option is available by clicking the Edit Fill button on the property bar, which displays the Texture Fill dialog, where there's a Tiling button. Clicking this takes you to the Tiling box, where you can check Mirror Fill and set other options. The texture fill will then appear in your object as a seamless one, regardless of how you scale, rotate, and skew the pattern.

Setting Texture Fill Options

Besides being able to set the appearance of your texture fill interactively and to customize the fill using the value fields in the Texture Fill dialog, you'll want to be able to set other options, too. For example, if your texture fill looks like it's been pushed through a screen window, it means the resolution is too low, as measured in pixels per inch (called dots per inch [dpi] in the dialog). To increase the texture size and its resolution, click the Texture Options button in the property bar to open the Texture Options dialog.

By default, texture fills are initially created at a resolution of 300 dpi and at a tile width of 2,049 pixels. Increasing both of these settings will reduce harsh areas and add definition to your texture, as shown here:

Original filled object

45 dpi   120 dpi   300 dpi

15

Calculating the Resolution of Texture Fills

If you're the ambitious, professional sort, you can use a very non-nerdy equation to determine your maximum tile width setting. Calculate the value based on twice the final line screen multiplied by the longest object dimension in inches. Line screens are what PostScript laser printers and commercial printer image-setting devices use for reproduction. You're good to go with 133 lines per inch (lpi; this value is half of 266 dpi, which is commonly used in high-quality art books); 1,200 dpi laser printers can use 85 lpi. Inkjet printers don't arrange dots in a logical order (they sort of splatter ink on the page), but a ballpark estimate (if inkjets were to render lines of dots) would be about 180 lpi for inkjet printers manufactured as late as 2007. Or you can overestimate, be on the safe side, and use 300 dpi, which vendors often suggest because it's an easy number to remember. Enter your calculated value in the Maximum Tile Width box, or choose the next highest preset value available.

Texture options affect the appearance of your texture fill in the following ways:

- **Bitmap Resolution** The Bitmap Resolution option sets the amount of detail in the bitmap image created. By default, the bitmap resolution setting is 300 dpi, but it can be reset to preset values ranging between 75 and 400 dpi, and to a maximum value of 9,999 dpi.

- **Texture Size Limit** This option should be set according to both the desired resolution of your texture and the size of your object. To avoid seeing seams between your texture's tiles (which will ruin the effect), set the tile larger than the object it fills *and* ensure that the tile seams are hidden from view; use the Mirror button on the property bar if necessary.

NOTE *Increasing the Bitmap Resolution and Maximum Tile Width settings of your texture fill can dramatically increase your saved CDR file size and the time it takes for high-resolution textures to display on your monitor. For screen display, you can usually get an accurate view of a texture at 1:1 viewing resolution (100%) with a texture resolution of 96 dpi (pixels per inch, dots per inch). Coincidentally, this is also an ideal texture resolution for web graphics, because visitors to your website are also viewing your texture at 1:1 on their monitors.*

Creating and Saving Texture Samples

Once you've gone to the effort of selecting or editing a texture fill to suit your needs, you may wish to save it for later retrieval. To save a texture, click the + button to the right of the Texture Library selector drop-down list. You'll then be prompted in the Save Texture As dialog for the name of your texture (type any name you like), and for the name of the library in which you want the texture saved. Click a library name found in the drop-down list, click OK, click OK in the Texture Fill dialog, and your custom texture is ready to be applied to the selected object.

Applying PostScript Fills

PostScript fills are vector based and use PostScript page-descriptor language to create a variety of patterns from black-and-white to full color. Each PostScript fill included with CorelDRAW has individual variables that control the appearance of the pattern, much the same way as you can customize texture fills. PostScript pattern styles come in a variety of patterns, as shown in Figure 15-9, and also come as non-repeating fills.

While using the Interactive fill tool with PostScript Fill selected in the property bar Fill Type selector, very few options that relate to the individual fills are available on the property bar. You need to click the Edit Fill button on the property bar to get access to line widths, how large the pattern elements should be, and to color options, depending on the specific preset.

The image you see onscreen is an accurate representation of the actual pattern that will be printed; again, PostScript is a printing technology, but Corel Corporation has made the technology viewable in CorelDRAW and printable without the need for a PostScript printer.

15

FIGURE 15-9   PostScript fills come in a variety of repeating and non-repeating patterns.

Note that PostScript fills will print exceptionally well to any PostScript device; that's what the fills are intended for, but you don't necessarily have to use PostScript. However, *you must be using Enhanced View to see it* (choose View | Enhanced).

To apply a PostScript fill, use these steps:

1. Create and then select the object to apply any PostScript texture fill, and then choose the Interactive fill tool (G).

2. Using property bar options, choose a PostScript fill texture from the selector by name.

3. To customize the fill, click the Edit Fill button in the property bar to open the PostScript Texture dialog, shown in Figure 15-10. To view your currently selected fill, check the Preview Fill option. Notice that each fill has its own set of Parameters that can be changed.

4. Make any changes to your fill, and click the Refresh button to view the results of your new settings.

5. Click OK to accept the fill, close the dialog, and apply the new fill to your object. Your object is now filled with a PostScript texture fill.

FIGURE 15-10 The PostScript Texture dialog lets you customize a PostScript fill.

PostScript fills can be very useful in schematic and roadmap illustrations, and if you use no background color when you customize many of the fills, the fills support transparency. So you can actually apply, for example, crosshatching, over a color-filled object to enhance the shading.

Applying Mesh Fills

Mesh fills can be used to create the effect of several blending-color fountain fills over a mesh of vertical and horizontal Bézier curves. Editing a mesh grid creates a sort of fill that doesn't really look like a fountain fill but instead looks very much like a *painting*. Mesh fills make it easy to create, as you'll see in the following figures, most of the visual complexity of a reflective sphere—*using only one object and one fill*. Add to the visual complexity the capability to set transparency levels to each patch of a mesh fill individually, and in no time you'll be creating scenes that look like paintings, using a fraction of the number of individual objects you'd imagine. You'll find the Mesh fill tool, shown at left, in the toolbox grouped with the Interactive fill tool; or press M for speedy selection.

While the Mesh fill tool is selected, the property bar features a number of options, shown next, for controlling this truly unique fill type. Use these options to set the vertical and horizontal size in the mesh grid, to change node and path properties, and to set the smoothness of curves.

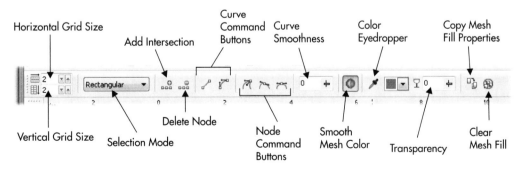

Applying a mesh grid to an object is a quick operation. Mesh fills are dynamic, so they can be edited and reedited at any time. Editing the shape and color of a mesh grid can be a little bit of a challenge your first time out, but to be able to smear and to almost paint on a fill will make the effort worthwhile to you and to your work. Node- and curve-editing actions to move fill areas are done exactly the same as for Bézier curves. For information on how to do this, see Chapter 11.

Mesh Fill Options

On the property bar, when the Mesh fill tool is used and an object is selected, you have control over the following attributes of your mesh-filled object:

- **Resolution of the Patches** By default, a new mesh fill is created on an object with two horizontal and two vertical sets of patches. These patches are linked at the edges by paths and at their vertices by nodes. You can use the numerical entry fields or the spin boxes with these fields to increase or decrease the number of columns and rows of patches. If you right-click a node or a path segment, you have the option to create a node or an intersection by choosing from the pop-up menu.

- **Add Intersection/Delete Node** When you've clicked a path segment and a marker appears, this is your opportunity to add an intersection, either by clicking the Add Intersection button, or by pressing + on the numerical keypad. When you add an intersection, you add a row or a column to the mesh fill, depending on whether you've added a point to a vertical or a horizontal mesh path segment. You must first select a node to then delete it, and doing so by clicking the Delete Node button or by pressing DELETE on your keyboard removes both the mesh node and its associated intersecting path segments—reducing the number of columns or rows of mesh patches. Deleting nodes can yield unanticipated results, so give some thought before you delete a node.

- **Curve and Node Command Buttons** By default, path segments that make up the mesh fill are curves, bound by nodes that have the smooth property at intersections and the cusp property along the edges of the object. To change a path segment to a line, you use the Convert To Line button; click Convert To Curve to create the opposite property. Nodes can be changed to cusp, smooth, and symmetrical properties by clicking the associated property bar button; the commands can also be found on the right-click pop-up menu when your cursor has selected a node.

- **Curve Smoothness** Suppose you've added far too many nodes to a path segment, and your mesh fill looks like a bad accident in one area. If you marquee-select the nodes that bind this path segment, the Curve Smoothness slider and numerical entry field act like the Node Reduction feature in CorelDRAW. You reduce the number of superfluous nodes (CorelDRAW decides on the meaning of "superfluous"—you have no control) by entering a value or using the slider.

● **Selection Mode** By default, you can select nodes in Rectangular mode, which means you marquee-drag a rectangular shape with your cursor to select nodes, and then change their properties such as color, position, and transparency. Your other selection choice is Freehand mode; your cursor behaves like a real-world lasso, and you are unconstrained by a selection shape for nodes. Additionally, you can SHIFT-click and select non-neighboring nodes to edit. When using Freehand mode, patches cannot be selected—selecting patches by clicking within them is only available in Rectangular selection mode.

● **Transparency** When selecting using Rectangular mode, transparency can be applied to a patch by clicking the patch once with the Mesh fill tool, and then using the numerical entry field or the slider to assign from 0 (no transparency) to 100 (completely transparent) to the patch. You can also set a transparency value to a mesh fill node by selecting it and then using the Transparency controls. Transparency on a mesh fill has no blending mode like the Transparency tool offers for entire objects—transparency is applied in Normal mode. However, once your mesh fill object is completed, you can use the Transparency tool on the toolbox to assign the object different types and modes of transparency as a single object.

● **Smooth Mesh Color** This is a toggle on/off button that can produce smoother color blends in your fill without changing the position or properties of the mesh nodes and curve path segments.

● **Color Eyedropper** When a patch or node is selected, you can choose a color anywhere on your Windows desktop by dragging the Color eyedropper over to any point. You can also sample from objects on your drawing page, but that might not be as much fun!

● **Color Palette** You have a mini color-palette flyout on the property bar with which you can select colors for selected nodes and patches. Click the flyout button to access the default color palette, or choose from other preinstalled CorelDRAW palettes. Clicking a color well on the (regular) Color Palette applies color, too.

● **Copy and Delete Mesh Fill Properties** These buttons are common to most all effects in CorelDRAW; use them to copy a mesh fill to a different object on the page, or to remove the mesh fill effect from an existing object.

When working with the mesh fill, you'll get far more predictable results if you apply colors to the nodes instead of dropping colors onto patches. Also bear in mind that regardless of how you create a shape, the mesh fill makes the object "soft"—the control

15

nodes that make the closed path of the object are also mesh fill nodes. So, unavoidably, if you want to move a node you've colored in at the edge of the object, you're also *moving the associated path segment.* This is fun and creative stuff, actually, and if you need the fill to be soft with the object's original shape intact, you can put your finished object inside a container by using the Effects | PowerClip feature.

> **NOTE** *You cannot mesh fill a combined shape; an object made by subtracting a circle from a rectangle so it looks like an awkward doughnut will not take a mesh fill, although the property bar will offer you mesh fill options.*

The following tutorial guides you through the creation of a mesh fill within a shape that's been created for you, with the finished example on the right of the page in Shiny Sphere.cdr. The goal is to create a mesh fill that gives a simple circle object the appearance of being a dimensional, highly reflective sphere, complete with a soft cast shadow beneath it.

Take a look at Figure 15-11 before you begin these steps; it's not only a comprehensive visual guide for the steps to follow, but also is a handy reference to accompany your independent mesh fill adventures.

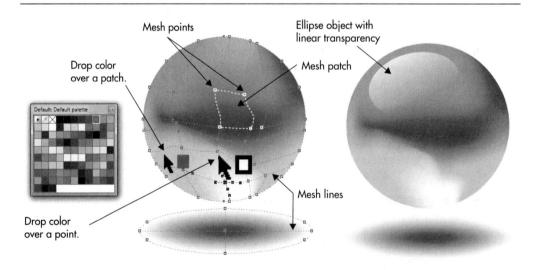

FIGURE 15-11   Mesh fills use control handles very similar in appearance and function to the paths you draw with the Pen tools and edit with the Shape tool.

Blending Colors Using the Mesh Fill

1. Open Shiny Sphere.cdr, select the top circle at left, and then choose the Mesh fill tool. A default mesh fill grid is applied to the object: 2 rows, 2 columns. Increase the resolution to 4 rows, 4 columns for starters.

2. In a lasso marquee–drag motion, select the horizontal nodes along the center of the sphere, and then click the black color well on the Color Palette.

3. Marquee-select all the nodes below the horizontal center nodes you selected in step 2, and then choose a rich brown from either the Color Palette or from the flyout palette on the property bar.

4. Select only the bottom center node, and then click a lighter brown.

5. Choose the Freehand selection mode from the property bar, then select the five top nodes that define the top edge of the circle, and then fill them with a purple-blue medium color. Select the first row, the five nodes below the top circular edge nodes, and fill them with a light blue.

6. Click the second node in this row, and fill it with a deep gold color to suggest a sunset on the horizon of the little desert painting you've created. Often, traditional airbrush illustrators have created photorealistic chrome spheres using the reflection of a desert as the primary visual content. You've done this; now it's time to distort the desert scene to suggest the dimensionality of a 3D sphere.

7. Select the gold node and drag it down a little.

8. Select, one by one, the nodes that are colored black, and create a slight wavy effect.

9. Select the light brown node at bottom center, and move its control handle up a little.

10. Finesse the color nodes to suit your personal artistic taste. Then select the bottom oval, apply a white fill, and apply the default 2 by 2 Mesh fill grid.

11. Click the center node with the Mesh fill tool, and then click black on the Color Palette. You now have a feathered, soft drop shadow that would take two of three additional steps to get right if you'd used the Drop Shadow tool on the toolbox. The Drop Shadow tool is often, but not always, the right tool for creating a shadow effect.

12. With the Pick tool, drag the oval highlight object currently over the completed example at right; tap the right mouse button before releasing both buttons to drop a copy on top of your shiny sphere at left.

15

> **NOTE** *After a mesh fill has been applied to an object, the object cannot be filled with any other fill type unless the mesh fill effect has first been cleared. To clear a mesh fill applied to a selected object, click the Clear Mesh button in the property bar.*

Sampling and Applying Fill Colors

After you've experimented and come up with a lot of interesting and valuable fills you've applied to objects, a natural question to ask is: I've got this once-in-a-lifetime, truly excellent color (or texture), and I want to use the fill on other objects. How do I do this?

Version X5 has integrated the color-sampling process and improved it so that a single tool now can be used to sample a color and apply that color to a different object. Additionally, when an object fill has more than one color—such as fountain fills—you have the Attributes eyedropper at hand to sample and duplicate any fill to a new object or group of objects.

To use the Color eyedropper tool:

1. Make sure your view of the page includes both the object that is filled with the color you want to copy, and the target object. Zoom out or pan your view if necessary.

2. Choose the Color eyedropper tool from its group on the toolbox.

3. Click over the object with the color you want to sample. The cursor changes to a paint bucket, as does the function of the tool.

4. Click over the object you want to apply the sampled color to. Notice that after you click, the cursor remains in the paint bucket state. If you want to apply the sampled color to additional objects, you do it now. However, if you want to pick a different color sample—starting the process all over again—click the eyedropper icon on the property bar. The tool is now reset to sample, not apply, color. Applying samples is not limited to fills: click the paint bucket cursor over the outline of an object, and you apply the color to the object's outline.

Additional options with the process of color sampling are on the property bar:

- **Select From Desktop** When you click this button, you can sample more than a CorelDRAW object color. You select any color on your screen. This means, for example, you can sample the color of the Zoom tool on the toolbox, any color on the Color Palette, and you can even click CorelDRAW's minimize/restore button above the menu bar, move the CorelDRAW window a little, and sample from your Windows desktop.

- **Selected Color** This is not only a good visual reference as you work, but while the Color eyedropper tool is in use, you also can drag this color well on top of any object—selected or unselected—and the current selected color is applied to that object, or to the outline of the object if your aim is precise.

- **Add To Palette** If you want to keep using your sampled color long after you're done with the Color eyedropper tool, click this button to add the sampled color to the Document palette, located in Window | Color Palettes | Document Palette.

- **Sample Size**   Before clicking to sample, you have the option to sample a single point—one pixel on your monitor's screen—or a 2×2 average area, or a 5×5 average color area. The use and importance of this feature is covered next.

Eyedropper tool

Paint Bucket tool   Choose color from any point on screen.   Point   2×2   5×5

Color Eyedropper
Attributes Eyedropper

The usefulness of sampling colors with a "big" eyedropper will become evident when you've imported a bitmap and want to approximate a color you see in the bitmap for a border or text in your composition. Figure 15-12 illustrates the use of a large, averaged color sample. The background of the ceramic moon is dreadful, and a harmonious color value sampled from the moon sculpture itself would be splendid. But the color at left was taken using a "point sample," 1×1 pixel. Bitmap images have pixels that vary from neighboring pixel to pixel, especially with JPEGs that by their nature have noise—similar to film grain, random distribution of color pixels that don't belong in image areas. So the 1×1 pixel Eyedropper tool sample is a dud, even after three tries. The 2×2 averaged sample (at center) did better, but at the right, when the same area in the circle is sampled using the 5×5 setting, a color has been sampled correctly for artistic purposes, and a nice average of a 25-pixel area yields a suitable color for the background on the moon.

Sampling Above and Beyond Uniform Fills

You will love to work with the more complex fills in CorelDRAW, and naturally, you'll want to apply one you've deliberately created or even stumbled upon to other objects. Multi-color fills fit into a category called Styles, and to copy them, you need to use the Color eyedropper's cousin tool, the Attributes eyedropper. To sample and apply fills such as fountains, texture fills, and all the others, choose the Attributes eyedropper from the toolbox, and then click

15

FIGURE 15-12 Increase your Color eyedropper sample size to get a general color instead of the exact underlying pixel color.

the Properties button and choose Fill. You can use the Attributes eyedropper to copy just about anything an object displays, but for making a rectangle's fill look like that fountain-filled circle next to it, for example, you only check Fill before clicking with the tool.

Alternatively, you can drag an object using the right mouse button, and drop it on top of an object to which you'd like to apply any style of fill. The pop-up menu appears when you release the right mouse button, and you then choose Copy Fill Here. The position of the source object does not move using this drag technique.

When a shape is selected, double-clicking the Fill box in the status bar opens a corresponding dialog where you can edit the current fill of the object and also add it to a Preset list for safekeeping for future needs. This saving option doesn't apply to PostScript fills, which cannot be fundamentally edited in CorelDRAW.

If you've had your fill, this is okay…so have your objects. You've learned in this chapter how to tap into CorelDRAW fills, and hopefully you've also seen how important fills can be to your drawings. Fills can actually contribute to the visual robustness of a composition more than the shape of objects. Take a cardboard box, for example. The shape of the box isn't that interesting and takes only a few seconds to draw. But the *texture* of a cardboard box is where the object gets its character and mood.

Outline properties and attributes are covered in the following chapter. You can do as much with customizing the thing that goes *around* an object as with the object itself.

15

CHAPTER 16

Outline Attributes

Chapter 15 covers only half the story about how you can flesh out a visual idea by using CorelDRAW. Although an object can usually live its life just fine without an outline, the attributes you can apply to a path can add a touch of refinement to an illustration. The right outline color can help visually separate different objects. Additionally, you can simulate calligraphic strokes without using artistic media when you know how to work with the Outline Pen dialog; you can even make a path a dashed line, complete with arrowheads for fancy presentations and elegant maps. In fact, an outline, especially an open outline, can live its life in your work just fine without defining a filled object! You don't have to draw the line at fills and effects in your CorelDRAW artwork. This chapter shows you the ins and outs of properties you apply to your paths, from beginning to end.

> **NOTE** *Download and extract all the files from the Chapter16.zip archive to follow the tutorials in this chapter.*

Applying Outline Pen Properties

By default, when you create an open or closed path, it's given a ½-point-wide outline in black, with no fancy extras. Part of the rationale for this default is that vector paths can't really be seen without some sort of width. In contrast, bitmap artwork by definition is made up of pixels, written to screen and written to file; so when a user draws an outline, it always has a width (it's always visible). Happily, vector drawing programs can display a wide range of path properties, and unlike with bitmap outlines, you can change your mind at any time and easily alter the property of an outline.

In a number of areas in CorelDRAW, you can apply a property such as color, stroke width, and other fun stuff to an open or closed path (and even to open paths that don't touch each other but that have been unified using the Arrange | Combine command). The following sections explore your options and point out the smartest and most convenient way to travel in the document window to quickly arrive at the perfect outline. When an open path or an object (which necessarily has to be described using a path) is selected on the page, the property bar offers a lot of options for outline properties. Some shortcuts for performing simple property adjustments are also covered on the long and winding path through this chapter.

Outline Pen Options and the Property Bar

Although it doesn't offer all options for path properties, the property bar is probably the most convenient route to outline properties. It actively displays a selected path's *current* properties, which you can change when a path is selected. The property bar, shown next while a path is selected, has width, style, and arrowhead options—you can make an open path with a head, tail, two heads—it's up to you. Other options give you control over wrapping text around an object, showing or hiding a bounding box around a path, and items not directly related to the look of the outline. Closed paths, naturally, can't have arrowheads, but your options for dashed lines and other attributes are available for rectangles, ellipses, all the polygon shapes, and for freeform closed curves you've drawn by hand.

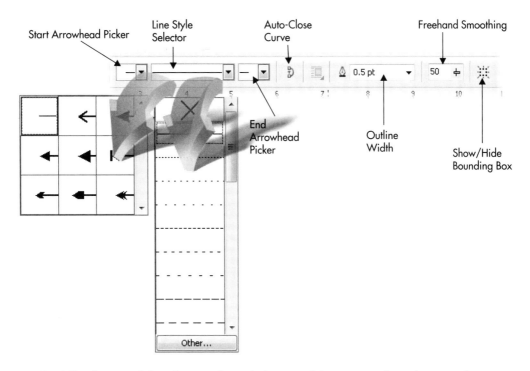

The following tutorial walks you through the use of the property bar when you draw a path.

 Going Long and Wide

1. Choose any drawing tool—the default Freehand tool is fine—just drag a squiggle and then press SPACEBAR to switch to the Pick tool; the path is selected now.

2. On the property bar, choose an outline thickness using the Outline Width selector, or enter a value and then press ENTER.

3. For arrowheads (on an open path), click the Start or End Arrowhead picker, and then choose an arrowhead style from the pop-up. The Start option applies an arrowhead to the first node of the path; the End option applies it to the last. Therefore, this might not be the direction in which you want the arrow to point. You just have to perform a little mental juggling.

4. To apply a dashed or dotted-line pattern to the path, click the Line Style selector, and then choose from one of the presets. Creating custom dashed patterns is covered later in this chapter.

16

5. Try increasing and decreasing the outline width, and see what happens to dashed line styles and arrowheads; they scale proportionately to the width of the outline.

As you apply outline properties from the property bar to your object or path, the effect is immediately visible, making this method both quick and convenient to use.

 TIP *To quickly set the color of an object's outline, right-click over any Color Palette color well when it's selected.*

Using the Outline Tool

The toolbox method is a different way to define the properties of a path. The Outline pen tool isn't really a tool; rather it's a flyout selector of options, shown next. If you're working on outlines a lot in a design, the Outline pen tool—like all the toolbox tools—can be floated as a palette. Just right-click first over the toolbox area and uncheck Lock Toolbars, and then drag the flyout (by the tread marks at the top of it) into the workspace. At the lower left in the illustration, you can see access points to the Outline Pen dialog, which offers options not available on the property bar; to the Outline Color dialog (which is a one-shot deal); and to the Color docker, which has some options similar to those in the Outline Color dialog, but here the docker is a persistent element, always available to use. Also, you have ten preset widths for outlines, and an *X,* which removes a path's outline width, making it invisible. If you want labels on the various commands instead of iconic representations, right-click over an empty area of the toolbar once it's floating, and then choose Customize | Outline Flyout Toolbar.

Right-click over vacant area to reveal options for toolbar.

Click-drag to float Outline tool as a toolbar.

Unlock to float any toolbar.

Opens Outline Pen dialog

Opens Outline Color dialog

Opens Color docker

Set display options for floating toolbar.

Exploring the Outline Pen Dialog

Use the Outline Pen dialog for total control over a single object's outline or over a selected group. It includes the same set of options available in the property bar, plus several more.

 The Color eyedropper tool can be used to sample and apply outline properties between objects.

The Outline Pen dialog includes options for specifying outline color, editing arrowhead and outline styles, and setting nib shape and transformation behavior; this is the only place in CorelDRAW where you'll find all these options together. To open the Outline Pen dialog, shown in Figure 16-1, the quickest way is to double-click the Outline well on the status bar, but you can also choose the dialog from the Outline flyout (pressing F12 gets you there, too).

FIGURE 16-1   The Outline Pen dialog has comprehensive options for outline properties.

Setting Outline Color

Using the Color selector in the Outline Pen dialog, you can choose a color for your selected path(s). Pen color affects only the color of the object's path; object *fills* are not changed. Outline color can be set only to CorelDRAW's uniform colors from the drop-down palette. To access every color collection and color model for outlines, click the Other button at the bottom of the palette. The Outline Color dialog provides access to all CorelDRAW's color palettes, including custom swatches and the Color Mixer.

Click to display the main color dialog.

If you want color control and don't need to fuss with dashed outlines, arrowheads, or other outline attributes, don't choose the Outline Pen dialog—click the Outline Color dialog button on the Outline Flyout in the toolbox. And if you're not particular about a specific shade of color, right-click a color well on the Color Palette to set an outline color.

Choosing Outline Styles

For a quick way to apply a dashed- or dotted-line pattern to the path of a selected object, the Line Style selector offers more than 28 preset variations.

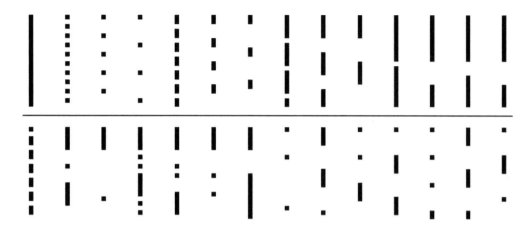

Applying an outline style causes a pattern to appear along the entire path, which is a must for anything you need to visually suggest to the reader that they go running for the scissors: coupons, tickets, you name it. Styles are repeating patterns of short, long, and a combination of dashes that apply to the entire path. Line styles can be applied to any open or closed path object, as well as to compound paths—paths that look like two or more individual paths, but are bound using the Arrange | Combine command. The quickest way to apply a dashed style is to use the Pick tool and the property bar Style selector when one or more paths are selected, as shown here.

Click here to remove outline properties.

Preset styles

Click here to open Edit Line Style dialog.

16

Once you have a nice custom outline set of properties defined and want to apply all the parameters to a different path, you can copy outline properties of one path to another by right-clicking and dragging one path over on top of the target path (this doesn't move your original path; it's a special editing technique). Release the mouse button when a crosshairs cursor appears over the target path. Then choose Copy Outline Here from the pop-up menu.

Creating and Editing Outline Styles

If you're looking for a special dashed-line style, one of your own invention, you can always *build* it. Choose Other from the Style selector in the property bar while a curve is selected, or within the Outline Pen dialog click the Edit Style button. Both actions open the Edit Line Style dialog, shown here:

Creating a custom line style of dots and dashes is a fairly intuitive process, very similar to drawing a line in a paint program; your cursor serves as both a pencil and an eraser. Click a black dot to erase it, click a white (space) dot to add to or begin a line. Once you save a style by clicking Add, it becomes available throughout CorelDRAW wherever outline styles are offered. Your only limitation—*read the legend at the bottom left of the editor*—is that you can't create a sequence consisting of more than five dashes or dots; two or more single dot marks count as a single dash. To create and save your own custom outline style, follow these steps.

 ## Drawing a Dotted Line Style

1. Create and/or select a path to serve as a host for your new line style, open the Outline Pen dialog (F12), and then click the Edit Style button, or click the Other button at the bottom of the Style selector on the property bar.

2. In the Edit Line Style dialog, you see a horizontal pattern generator featuring a slider control, a preview window, and a set of command buttons.

3. In the pattern generator, drag the slider left or right to change the style length. Click (or click-drag to make a long dash segment) on the small squares to the left of the slider to set the on/off states of the pattern. If you want to erase a segment, you click or click-drag on the black square(s) you've drawn. As you do this, the preview window shows the new pattern.

4. Click the Add button to add the new style to the list (or click Replace to overwrite the style currently selected in the Style selector) to return to the Outline Pen dialog. New styles are added to the bottom of the selector list.

5. Verify that your new line style is available by choosing it in the selector and clicking OK to apply your new outline style; it will be at the bottom of the drop-down list, and as with the preset styles, there is no name for custom styles—you search by the look of the saved thumbnail. The line style you created is now applied to the object.

If the pattern applied to a path doesn't exactly match its length—for example, the pattern is longer than the path it's applied to—you might see a "seam," especially when applying outline styles to closed paths (as shown next). You have two ways to cure the problem. One is to go back to the style editor, and then to increase or decrease the length of the pattern. This is a trial-and-error edit, but it doesn't change the path to which the style is applied. The other method (a desperate measure) is to lengthen the path by using the Shape tool, or to scale the path by using the Pick tool. In either of these edits, you change your design and not your custom preset—it's your call, but editing the style is usually the best way to avoid seams on a case-by-case basis.

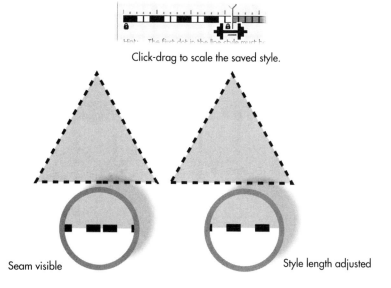

Click-drag to scale the saved style.

Seam visible

Style length adjusted

16

Setting Outline Arrowheads

Arrowheads are both heads *and* tails on an open path, and although you have a handsome collection of preset arrows, they can be almost anything you decide to draw. Most of the preset styles are arrowheads, but some are symbols that represent a tail. Figure 16-2 shows several of the styles, and many of the tails match the visual style of the arrowheads. When applied, arrowheads can be set to appear at the start and end points of open paths, at both ends, one end, or by default, at neither end.

Here's a trick to defining the size of an arrowhead or tail proportional to your line. Select the line, then press ALT+ENTER to display the Object Properties docker, and then click the Outline (the pen) tab.

- If you check the Scale With Image check box, whenever you use the Pick tool to scale a line with an arrowhead, the line's width will increase or decrease, but the arrowhead remains a constant size.

- If you leave Scale With Image unchecked as a property, the arrowhead scales with the width of the line when you scale the path using the Pick tool.

If you don't scale a path but instead change its outline width using the box on the property bar, no object scaling is really taking place. The path is the same length when you change its width, and this trick doesn't apply. This is your ticket to making an arrowhead exactly proportional to the path's outline.

FIGURE 16-2   CorelDRAW includes these arrow styles, and you can design your own. Heads, you win.

The quickest way to apply an arrowhead is by using the Start and/or End Arrowhead selectors in the property bar when an open path is selected, as shown here.

Arrow start (first node on path)

Arrowhead 7

Arrow end (last node on path)

<table>
<tr><td>NOTE</td><td>*Applying an arrowhead to a closed path has no visible effect unless the path is broken at some point.*</td></tr>
</table>

Creating Custom Arrowhead Styles

Realistically, CorelDRAW could not have the ideal arrowhead (and tail) for your (and every other user's) assignment as a preset, or the preset selector would need a head and a tail itself—from here to the moon! That's why you have the Tools | Create | Arrow command— don't choose the command yet; you'll need to draw the arrowhead first, as covered in the following tutorial. The best arrowhead should be simple in its construction and needs to be a single or compound path. Fill makes no difference in creating the arrowhead because a finished and applied custom arrow style gets its color from the outline color you use on the selected path in your drawing. The orientation of the arrowhead needs to be in landscape, too, before entering the Create command. In other words, the top of your custom arrowhead design needs to face right, not face the top of the page.

To create a new arrowhead and save it, follow these next steps. If you'd like a jump-start, open Shovel.cdr first. It contains the elements needed to make both a head and a tail.

Drawing, Saving, and Editing an Arrowhead Style

1. Give some thought and planning to what would make a good arrowhead and tail. Shovel.cdr has a drawing of the business and the user ends of a common garden shovel. This works for designs of gardens (an arrow pointing to "dig here"), treasure hunts, and certain civil engineering projects. Allowing about 3" for your symbols to be used as arrowheads seems to work well and gets you around the need to edit the size later. When you've drawn your arrowhead (a tail is optional for this tutorial), rotate it so its pointing side faces the right of the drawing page.

2. With the shape selected, choose Tools | Create | Arrow.

3. Type a name in the upper-left field for future reference. The Create Arrowhead box gives you the chance to set a size for the arrowhead; by default, it's the size you've drawn it on the page. Click OK and your arrowhead is saved to the arrowhead selector list at the bottom of the list. Possibly you're done now. Let's check, before calling it a day, to see how the arrowhead looks when applied to an open path.

4. With the 2-point line tool, click-drag a two-node path. Straight is good for checking out the arrowhead, but in the future a curved path can be more visually interesting if it's capped off with your work.

5. On the property bar with the path selected, choose the 10 pt outline width so you'll have a clear view of the arrowhead you defined (or the shovel head if you used the Shovel.cdr file).

6. On the property bar, choose the arrowhead from the last node drop-down selector, the one on the right on the property bar. Let's suppose you're not 100 percent happy with the look of the arrowhead; you'll now access additional options for modifying the saved arrowhead. With the path selected, double-click the Outline Color icon (either the pen icon or the color swatch) on the status bar to display the Outline Pen box. Click the Options button beneath the thumbnail of your arrowhead and then choose Edit.

7. Here's where you can correct a number of problems with your arrowhead; you cannot, however, edit the path of the arrowhead itself. If, for example, your arrowhead is pointing the wrong way, you Mirror | Horizontally, as shown in the following illustration. You also have the option to rotate the arrowhead, for corrective or creative reasons, as well as to move the head away from its parent line (the Offset options), and for proportionately or disproportionately smooshing or stretching the selected arrowhead. If you've made a mistake drawing the arrowhead, you cannot change it in the editor, but instead need to revise your drawing and then redefine the arrowhead.

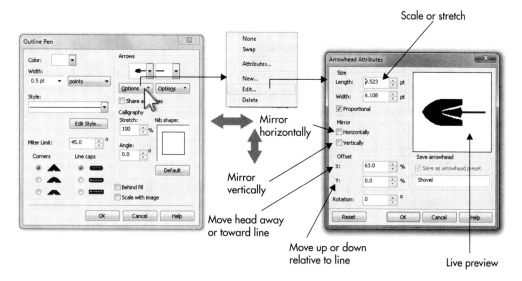

8. Click OK to overwrite your saved arrowhead, or rename it to add it to your collection. The Edit Arrowhead dialog can also be used to modify *existing* preset arrowheads, but only to the extent that you've just modified your custom arrowhead in step 7. End of tour!

Here you can see a few uses for a shovel. Don't hesitate to mix and match outline styles; in the middle illustration here, a dashed outline style happily coexists with a custom arrowhead.

At work   Under construction   Uri Geller was here…

16

Other Arrowhead Options

While an arrowhead style is applied, other convenient options are available from within the Outline Pen dialog. Just below each Arrowhead Style selector are two Options buttons. Click either the start or end buttons to open a drop-down menu that features the following commands:

- **None**   Choose this command to clear the arrow style you selected from your path. This can also be done from the document window using the property bar.

- **Swap**   This command switches the styles currently selected for the Start and End arrowheads. This cannot be done, at least not as easily, from the document window.

- **New**   Choose this command to open the Edit Arrowhead dialog and to create variation on a default style to add to the existing collection. New does *not* offer custom arrowhead creation; you need to use Tools | Create, as you learned earlier, to make a truly new arrowhead.

- **Delete**   While an existing style is applied, choosing this command permanently removes the selected style from the collection.

Setting Corner Shape

Frequently, you'll create a path whose segments join at a node in a cusp fashion; the connection is *not* smooth—for example, a crescent moon shape has a least two "sharp" cusp connections between path segments. When shapes have *discontinuous* connections—when a path abruptly changes direction as it passes through a node—you can set the appearance of the node connection through the Outline Pen dialog, the only area in CorelDRAW's interface that offers these options. Therefore, it's always a good idea to remember that double-clicking the Outline box on the status bar is your quickest route to defining how nodes look as they join two segments. Figure 16-3 shows the visual effect of Square (the default), Round, and Miter joints on a path that has cusp nodes. Notice that at extremely sharp node connection angles, the Square joint option produces an area of the outline that extends way beyond the path, an exaggerated effect you might not always want in a design. You can use Corner properties creatively to soften the appearance of a node connection (Round works well) and also to keep a severe cusp angle from exaggerating a connection. Miter corners can often keep a path more consistent in its width than the default corner can.

Setting Line Cap Shape

Line caps, the beginning and end of an open path, can look like their counterparts, the corners, covered in the previous section. One of the greatest visual differences you can create is that the true width of a path is extended using the Round and Extended choices—the outline width overshoots the true path's length, proportional to the width you choose for an outline. Figure 16-4 shows examples of your end cap options.

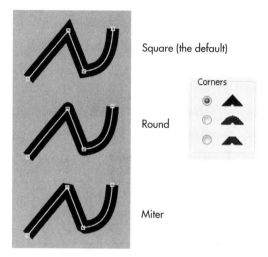

Square (the default)

Round

Miter

FIGURE 16-3   Corners can be set to one of these three styles.

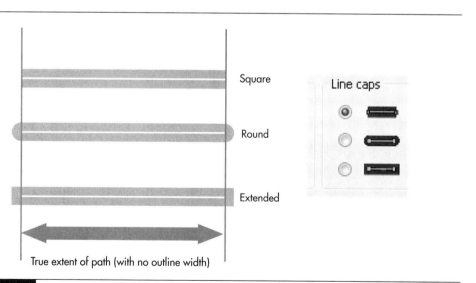

Square

Round

Extended

True extent of path (with no outline width)

FIGURE 16-4   End caps can be set to one of these three styles.

16

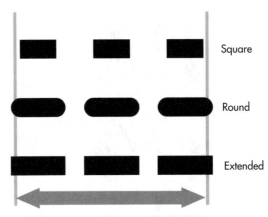

Square

Round

Extended

True extent of path (with no outline width)

FIGURE 16-5 Applied line caps will affect the appearance of dash patterns applied to your outline path.

Applying line cap options to the end points of an open path affects not only the first and last nodes' appearance on an open path, but it also affects dashed and dotted line styles, as shown in Figure 16-5.

> **TIP** *Line cap options control the shape of* all *end points in an open path simultaneously; therefore, a compound path receives your choice of end caps at all two, four, six end points, and so on, depending on the structure of such a compound path. Also, end caps are not "mix and match"; for example, if you choose Round, both end caps in a two-node path are rounded—there is no facility in CorelDRAW for a two-node path that begins Round and ends Square.*

Outline Pen Calligraphic Effects

The term *calligraphy* has come to be accepted today as a handwriting craft, the result of which is text and ornaments that have a varying width along strokes due to the popular use of a flat-edged pen nib held at an angle. The same effect can be achieved using the Calligraphy options in the Outline Pen dialog.

Calligraphic options are applied using a set of options and an interactive preview window used to define the shape of the nib that affects a path you've drawn. *Stretch* controls the width of the nib using values between 1 and 100 percent. *Angle* controls the nib rotation in 360 degrees (the minimum, –180°, produces the same "12 o'clock" stroke angle as the maximum, 360°). Click the Default button to reset these parameters to their original state. Stretch and Angle values work together to achieve the nib shape. Set them numerically by entering values, or better still, set them interactively, by placing your cursor in the preview window and then click-dragging to shape the nib. By default, all paths in CorelDRAW are created using a Stretch value of 100 percent and an Angle value of 0°. As you can see in Figure 16-6, varying the Stretch and Angle of a calligraphic nib changes the look of an outline, but the *shape* you begin with also has an impact on the final look of the design. For example, these three pairs of interwoven B-spline paths are identical, but the one at left perhaps is more visually interesting and elegant with its 45° angled nib. The point is that if you have an object that you think will look more refined and elegant with a calligraphic stroke, keep changing the angle until you're happy with the finished artwork.

> **TIP** *The Artistic media tool has a Calligraphic style that can be used as a brush; you just drag on the page, and it immediately produces angled paths. See Chapter 10 for details.*

FIGURE 16-6 Calligraphic effects can be used as ornamentations to a piece of work or to imitate handwritten phrases.

16

Scaling and Behind Fill Options

Two more options for controlling outline properties available in the Outline Pen dialog are very important for controlling how outlines display in particular design situations. The following sections explain how Scale With Image and Behind Fill work.

Scale With Image

Choose Scale With Image to increase or decrease the outline width applied to an open path or closed object when you scale the object at any time after the outline width has been applied.

For example, a 2-point outline width applied to a path will become 1 point if the object is scaled in size by 50 percent. In most illustration work, where drawings commonly change size before they are complete, choosing this option is a smart move. However, if you leave the scale constant (leave Scale With Image unchecked), you can duplicate, for example, 50 stars, arrange them on the page at different sizes, and the design looks good because the outline width is consistent from star to star. The illustration here shows copies of a pretzel shape reduced with and without the Scale With Image option selected. If this were a drawing of a *salted* pretzel, the one in the center—Scale With Image—would be less likely to cause high blood pressure and other heart risks if eaten by a drawing of a person.

Original object

Reduced using Scale With Image option

Reduced without the Scale With Image option selected

Behind Fill

Behind Fill sets outline properties to print and display in *back* of the object's fill. One of the many practical uses for using Behind Fill is in a sign or other simple illustration where you need rounded corners along the outline, but sharp and crisp edges along the fill, the important and recognizable part of many illustrations. Next you can see at left the ubiquitous recycle symbol with a 16-point rounded-corner outline. The arrows are lost in the design. However, at right, a 32-point outline is used with Behind Fill checked in the Outline Pen dialog. Therefore, the same outline width has been achieved (visually); however, because the outline is behind the fill, the points on the arrows are undistorted, even in weight, and will print crisply.

16-point outline in front of
fill; most edges are soft.

32-point outline behind fill;
edges are crisp and detailed.

Setting the Outline for All New Objects

Each time you create a new object, CorelDRAW automatically applies a set of default outline properties, as follows:

Width = 0.5 point
Color = CMYK black (from Corel's default custom palette)
Style = Solid line
Corners and Line Caps = Square
Calligraphy: Stretch = 100%, Angle = 0°
Behind Fill, Scale With Image = Off

To change any or all of these default properties, open the Outline Pen dialog (F12) while *no objects* are selected.

By choosing Graphic, Artistic Text, or Paragraph Text, you can control the defaults for new objects. Unless you have a specific reason for changing the default outline properties of text objects, it's wise to accept Graphic as the object types to apply, and then to click OK to proceed to the Outline Pen dialog to change the outline pen defaults.

16

Turning an Outline into an Object

A fancy calligraphic property for an outline, arrowhead, and even for dashed outlines can be freed from being non-editable *outline* properties when you convert an outline to an object. Consider this: an outline is constrained to solid fills, while an object that *looks* like an outline, that was originally *based* on an outline, can have any type of CorelDRAW fill. To make an outline into a shape, you choose Arrange | Convert Outline To Object—but this will disturb your workflow less if you perform this on a *copy* of the path you slaved over! In Figure 16-7 you can see the command on the Arrange menu (the shortcut is similar to

FIGURE 16-7　Convert a path to an object, and all outline properties become editable objects.

Convert To Curves; it's CTRL+SHIFT+Q). This path is fully loaded, using a calligraphic nib, a dashed line, an arrowhead, and a tail. It is about to become a shape that's freely editable with toolbox tools and that will accept all of CorelDRAW's effects such as contours and fountain and texture fills; even the Extrude tool can turn this shape into elegant, abstract, bizarre artwork.

In Figure 16-8 you can see at left that the path of Figure 16-7 is now a shape that will take, in this example, a linear style fountain fill—in contrast, you can't fill an open path. See also in this figure that the arrowhead path that's now a shape can be extruded. To come full circle, the new object based on the path can have an outline; in this figure at right a black outline behind the fill is used artistically to visually separate the linear fill areas.

This chapter has taken you from simply assigning one property to a path, to using several, more complex properties. As you gather more understanding of options in CorelDRAW, you add to your personal, creative wealth of design options. Dashed lines, arrowheads, and calligraphic strokes will come to your rescue during 11th-hour assignment crunches, just as will other features that have been covered in previous chapters. Chapter 17 takes a side-step from object creation to defining a color for that object you just created. You've probably read things on digital color *theory,* but the following chapter puts theory into *practice.*

And practice makes perfect.

FIGURE 16-8   If you need to edit certain areas of a fancy outline, you can do it more easily and more precisely by first turning the outline into an object.

CHAPTER 17

Digital Color Theory
Put to Practice

P ut away those crayons and fling that color wheel out on the front lawn. *Digital* color obeys *none* of the rules we were taught in school. Digital color models are what you use to fill objects that CorelDRAW displays on your monitor, and defining colors is an art that even professionals occasionally struggle with. The good news is that CorelDRAW makes it as simple as can be to apply exactly the color you have in mind to an object, through an extensive collection of industry-standard swatches, color models that are intuitive to use, and color mixers that make color definition more like play than work.

This chapter covers color theory and how it's put to practice in your CorelDRAW work. If you've ever faced picking out a tie to match your shirt at 8:30, in a dimly lit closet, you have an appreciation for the importance of choosing harmonious and intriguing color schemes. Similarly, your color work is out there for the public to evaluate; this chapter guides you through the digital process of choosing colors and making certain what you print is what you see onscreen.

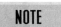 *Download and extract all the files from the Chapter17.zip archive to follow the tutorials in this chapter.*

Digital Color Terms and Definitions

Let's say you've created a rectangle on your page; by default, it has no fill and you have two quick fixes to fill it. You can left-click a color on the Color Palette, which offers a nice selection of preset colors, but let's say you want a specific color. Double-click the Fill icon on the status bar, shown in the following illustration, and you can work in the Uniform Fill dialog, a combination of interface palettes that has tabs for Models, Mixers, and Palettes.

Double-click to display
Uniform Fill dialog.

Where do you get colors in CorelDRAW? From palettes, mixers, and models. Palettes are predefined collections of color swatches. Mixers are covered later in this chapter. Let's begin with models, an area worth some serious documentation here.

First, the terms that set the stage for color exploration in this chapter are used in digital color descriptions and also to define real-world colors you apply to paper, plastic, and so on. They'll give you a handle on a variety of attributes that colors have. They're also somewhat interrelated; when you change a parameter in one, most of the time you change a parameter in a different class of color description.

- **Color model**   A *model* is a representation of something that's intangible or too ungainly in other respects to directly manipulate. For example, a child plays with a model airplane because this representation fits in his bedroom better than an actual airplane would, and passengers around the world feel safer. Color models are used in CorelDRAW to make it easy to deal with the relationships between colors; without a model of the intangible qualities of the spectrum of light, it would be a challenge to choose the colors you need. Additionally, a color model *scales* all the available colors you have when working on CorelDRAW and other programs, in the same way a model airplane can be rotated to see all its sides—which is hard to do with a full-sized airplane. Today, users have at least 16.7 million possible colors from which to choose in design work; a color model makes color selection much easier than choosing colors from a palette containing 16.7 million swatches.

- **Color space**   Think of a color model as a piece of architecture: it's a structure. If you were having a house built, your structure would need to take up space, usually on some land. A color space is that "land" for your color model "architecture." Different color models require different color spaces. Let's say you have a CorelDRAW file you want a commercial press to print. Print presses usually use the CMYK color model as the basis for reproducing the colors you've filled objects with in your document; CMYK color is covered later in this chapter. Unfortunately, digital color, the color you see on your monitor, has its structure in a fairly wide color space; RGB colors have a wider range of expression (more possible colors) than CMYK color space. What can happen (unless you read this chapter thoroughly) is that some colors you use in your CorelDRAW document look fine onscreen, but they don't print as you anticipate. The reason is that CMYK color space is smaller than the color space of your monitor, and some of your original design's colors are *clipped* when printed. They've been arbitrarily moved to a color that's *similar* to the color you used, or they just don't print, or you get a nice splotch of muddy brown on the printed page. You certainly want more control over how a CorelDRAW design prints, and that's why CorelDRAW offers a CMYK color picker and also a Gamut Alarm. *Gamut* is a term that means the expressible range of color; in other words, colors that fall into a specific color space. When you choose a color that falls out of the range of the color space, it's called an *out of gamut* color, and these colors won't print correctly because they're like a structure that is built on a part of the land you don't own.

17

> **NOTE** *The K in "CMYK" indeed stands for "Black," and it's fair to ask, "Why don't we call it CMYB" color?" The K is for "key"; the key plate in CMYK printing is the last plate that is printed. In this case, Cyan is pressed first, then Magenta, then Yellow, and finally the key, Black. In printing, a key plate is the plate that prints the detail in an image. As you can often see in a progressive proof of a print job, C, M, and Y inks don't provide much image detail. We use the term "key plate" in printing because black is not always used. For example, in two-color print jobs, the key plate is the darker of the two colors. In general, however, K means "Black" and you'll often see CMYK written as "CMY (black K)" to avoid ambiguity.*

- **File color capability** If the extent of your CorelDRAW work is to create CDR files, print them, and save them, you have no concerns about a file format that can hold all the colors you've picked and applied to objects. The CDR file format will retain the colors you've used. But if you intend to export a design to bitmap file format, you'll want to check out Chapter 23. Different bitmap file formats have different ceilings of color capability, which relates to color space in many ways. TIFF images as written by CorelDRAW, for example, can contain 16.7 million unique colors, and this file format can be written to the RGB color model, the CMYK color model, and even to some color *modes* such as Grayscale, which offers no color at all but instead only brightness values. On the other hand, GIF images continue to be written for the Web, and these images can hold only 256 unique colors, pretty meager when compared with 16.7 million colors, so you need to know how to design using only 256 colors, tops.

The sections that follow are a step-by-step documentation of topics. They range from the structure of digital color, to the space in which color resides, through how you manipulate color models in CorelDRAW to define colors you want, or to match color values a client might have read to you over the telephone.

Subtractive and Additive Color Models

The world of color models has two distinct categories: *subtractive* and *additive* color models. You, the designer, use both: when you print something, you use a device that uses the subtractive color model. When you design for the Web or an onscreen presentation, you use an additive color model. How these models are similar, where their differences lie, and how you access these models in CorelDRAW are the subjects of the following sections.

Subtractive Color Models

From the moment the first caveperson depicted an antelope on the family room wall, humans have been using a *subtractive color* model for painting. Subtractive color is what a lot of artists were brought up on, mixing physical pigments; and as we all know, when you mix a lot of different pigments together, you eventually get black. This is what the traditional subtractive color model is all about: you *remove* part of the visible spectrum as you overlay one color upon another. CMYK is a subtractive color model used in commercial printing, and in theory, if you put Cyan, Magenta, and Yellow pigments together at full intensity, you should get black—Cyan, Magenta, and Yellow are the primary colors in a subtractive color model. However, due to chemical impurities in physical pigments such as ink and paint, you get a deep brown and not true black. Hence, a black printing plate is used in addition to the C, M, and Y plates to reproduce a wide spectrum of colors available in CMYK color mode.

NOTE	*If you take your kids out to a family restaurant where they have crayons and menus that the kids color, notice that the crayon colors are not cyan, magenta, and yellow. More than likely, they're red, yellow, and blue, and if you're lucky, green also comes in the little box. You might rightfully wonder why commercial presses use CMYK and your kids are using red, yellow, and blue. The answer is that red, yellow, and blue have traditionally been the primary subtractive colors used by painters throughout history,* before *scientific color theory proved that cyan is more of a* pure *subtractive primary than blue, and that magenta describes a component of subtractive color better than red. Green was introduced as a primary subtractive because of the human mind's perceptual bias that green is a* perceptual *primary color, although it's not used at all in CMYK commercial printing.*

The RGB Additive Color Model

The *additive* color model describes color using *light,* not pigments, and a combination of the primary additive colors Red, Green, and Blue, when combined in equal amounts at full intensity, produces white, not black as subtractive CMYK color does. RGB is a common additive color model, and it is not at all intuitive for an artist to use. However, CorelDRAW has different views of the RGB color model that make it easy and intuitive to work with.

Because a color model only does one thing—*it shows a mathematical relationship between values that are intangible*—the visualization of the relationship between Red, Green, and Blue can use any model anyone cares to use, with the goal being to make color picking and color relationships as painless as possible to perform! Figure 17-1 shows the default view of the Uniform Fill dialog. This chapter walks you through how to customize your onscreen display and your color choices for both the RGB and CMYK color models.

Let's take these controls in Figure 17-1 slowly and one at a time. It's quite likely that a color attribute you're looking for right now can be defined in this dialog.

- **Color Model** This selector drop-down list includes CMYK, CMY (as explained earlier, black is more a part of the printing process than a part of the color model), RGB, HSB, HSL, Grayscale, YIQ, LAB, and Registration. These models are covered later in this section. If you're in a hurry: CMYK should be chosen for in-gamut colors for printing, and RGB is the color model for doing work that won't be printed, such as JPEG images destined for the Web.

17

FIGURE 17-1 The Uniform Fill dialog is one of several areas from which you can pick colors in CorelDRAW.

- **Color field and Hue slider** Here is something tricky, a little confusing, and totally wonderful on the Models tab. A model is a representation of a hard-to-grasp thing or idea. CMYK is an intangible item, and choosing colors using a CMYK model is hardly a fun pastime. Corel Corporation thought ahead on this stumbling block; when you choose CMYK mode, the *HSB* color-choosing field and slider are presented to you, even though you're not choosing HSB colors. To manipulate Brightness, you drag the little rectangle up or down in the color field. To manipulate Saturation, you drag left or right; and obviously you can navigate both Brightness and Saturation at the same time. The Hue slider to the right of the color field sets the predominant, recognizable attribute of the color you're picking. Designers usually set the Hue first, and then play with the amounts of Saturation and Brightness.

- **Current Color/New Color** The color well at the top shows you the current color of the selected object on the page. The bottom color well shows you any changes you've made, and the two together provide a convenient way to compare color changes.

- **Components** The field at left provides a numerical breakdown of the current color, as expressed in the components of the current color model. In Figure 17-1, the current color is a blue, and its HSB numerical values are H: 240 (degrees on a color wheel), S: 41 (percent), and B: 36 (percent). However, these values are not static; in fact when you click the icon to the right of any value (the icon that looks like a slider), a slider pops up, and you can adjust the color you want by dragging any component value up or down. This offers a more precise adjustment of the filled object's color; you can also insert your cursor into the number field (it's a live field), double-click to select the entire value, and then type in a new value. The fields to the right of the current color model fields are a secondary, static readout that gives you the selected color's equivalent using a different color model. You can see in Figure 17-1 that Hex is chosen, which only requires one component field. You set the secondary field by clicking the button title above the component fields.

- **Name**   The Color Palette, the strip docked to the right of the drawing window, contains colors that are tagged with names such as Desert Blue and Mint Green. To quickly search for a preset color on the Color Palette, you can choose from the drop-down list, or begin typing a name in the Name field—as you type more characters, the dialog narrows the search. If you have a custom palette loaded, you can't search for it using the Models tab of the Uniform Fill dialog; you conduct a search using the Palettes tab.

- **Add To Palette**   This button adds the current color you've created to the Color Palette's document palette. You can then retrieve this color directly from the Color Palette at any time without visiting the Uniform Fill dialog; choose Window | Color Palettes | Document Palette. This is one way to save a custom color; see "Using the Color Styles Docker" later in this chapter for a more feature-filled way to save a custom color.

- **Bring Color Into Gamut**   This button will not appear in the dialog unless you've chosen a color in an additive color model, and then switched to the CMYK color model. There's a chance that your chosen RGB color might be available in the CMYK color space (in which case you won't see the button), but intense RGB colors cannot be expressed in CMYK. If the button appears when you're switching color models, click it to let CorelDRAW bring it into gamut, using the rendering intent you set up under Tools | Color Management | Default Settings. Rendering intent is covered in Chapter 3, and yes, this *is* a lot to intellectually digest, so take it slowly here!

- **Options**   In this drop-down, you can swap the current color with the old color (if you've modified the current color). The Swap Colors option switches the order of the New and Old colors displayed at the top right of this box.

Options also offers a choice of color selection interfaces for your chosen color model. This deserves a little explanation: to represent the components of color models, the various color models necessarily need to be graphically represented in their unique structure. Some color models such as HSB are blessed with a structure that is intuitive for mere mortals to use; others are less intuitive. Figure 17-2 shows the RGB model using the four available models. The *HSB Hue Based* model is the easiest for artists to use; alternatively, the *HSB Brightness Based* picker might be popular with those who want to dabble in a large hue-based field instead of using the slider. The *HSB Wheel Based* picker will make Corel Painter users feel right at home, and the *RGB 3D Additive* model is offered to accommodate particle physicists and Martians. Try it, you'll hate it—although the model itself is mathematically sound, it just isn't user friendly, and a slider is necessary *in addition to* the 3D picking cube because this model is hard to visualize.

RGB as HSB Hue Based

RGB as HSB Brightness Based

RGB as HSB Wheel Based

RGB as 3D Additive

FIGURE 17-2   Many color pickers' views can be assigned to color models through Options in the Uniform Fill dialog.

| NOTE | *For reasons unknown, the color wheel in the Uniform color picker travels counterclockwise instead of in the traditional clockwise direction for hue. If you get a little confused that hues run from red to orange to yellow counterclockwise, note that hue is measured in degrees, and this wheel does indeed follow increased degrees for colors counterclockwise. For example, green is at 120 degrees on the color hue wheel in CorelDRAW, the same as it is in Photoshop, the same as it is in Microsoft products. The model might look novel, but the color value is the same and can be easily communicated accurately if you email someone the color values.* |

The HSB Additive Color Model

The HSB color model is to designers what the RGB color model is to software engineers; HSB serves the non-programming community for intuitively choosing colors, and HSB and RGB occupy the same color space, but use different components. HSB is the acronym for Hue, Saturation, and Brightness. It's occasionally called HSV (the *V* is for "Value"), and HSL (*L* is for "Lightness"), but it all boils down to a user-friendly model for working with digital color. HSB, in fact, was modeled by Dr. Alvy Smith, cofounder of Pixar Studios, former Microsoft Fellow, and an accomplished artist. The HSB color model has the same number of colors (the same color space, discussed later in this chapter) as the RGB color model. However, HSB organizes the relationship between components of colors differently, and in a friendlier fashion, than RGB does. The components of HSB color are as follows:

- **Hue**   The distinguishing characteristic of color. When we tell a friend, "Oh, that's a very nice blue tie" and "The TV set is a little orange, isn't it?" we're describing the hue component of the color. Hue is usually expressed in degrees on a hue wheel; technically, hue is determined by light wavelength.

- **Saturation**   The presence of color, the purity, the predominance of a hue. We often use the component of saturation when we talk about how *juicy* the colors are in a photograph. If there's a lot of noticeable blues in a photo or a drawing, the blue hue is said to be quite saturated in that color. Conversely, colors you often see on today's household appliances, such as "Oyster," "Putty," "Ivory," or "Bisque," are neutral; they have no strong dominance of hue, and therefore have little saturation. You can't make out the hue in such an appliance's color; you usually describe it as off-white or a warm gray. The pages in this chapter have no saturation, but offer a lot of brightness.

- **Brightness**   The amount of illumination a color has. Brightness, as described in digital color terms, is somewhat elusive, but an analogy from traditional painting with pigments (subtractive color) provides some clarity here. When you mix a pure color with white, you're increasing its brightness; in industries where color description is critical (fashion design, house paints) bright colors are a *tint* of a pure color, also called a pastel color. Then there are darker colors: a *shade* is the mixture of a color with black. Mixing with white increases lightness, while mixing with black reduces it. In both digital and traditional color, mixing black, white, or a perfectly neutral value in between black and white leaves hue unchanged.

17

X-Rite has emerged as the color industry's heavy-hitter after adding Pantone (the color-matching people) and Gretag Macbeth (proofing systems, monitor calibration hardware/software) to Munsell and other acquisitions in recent years. If you have any questions about printing, packaging, paints, plastics, or just color in general, Xrite.com is the place to visit. Their website contains not only catalog areas, but also many areas with seminar listings and free downloads of collateral material— all about color.

LAB Color

LAB is both a color space *and* a color model. CorelDRAW offers LAB as a color model; however, LAB—the color space—is device independent, and therefore it can be used to describe colors you see in the drawing window, on a physical plastic bottle of soda, and even on a basketball. Almost 100 years ago (this was before PCs) the Commission Internationale de l'Eclairage (the CIE, the International Commission on Illumination) was established as a worldwide organ for standardizing and exchanging color specifications. They are responsible for creating the LAB color model. It successfully replicates the spectrum of human vision, and this is why there is a disproportionately large area of green in LAB color space. This is because the human eye responds to this region of the visible spectrum more strongly than to other hues. LAB is modeled after one channel of *Luminance*, one color channel (named *A*) that runs from magenta to green, and another channel (named *B*) from blue to yellow. When you use LAB to describe a color, you're (theoretically) assured color consistency. LAB, the color space, is frequently used by software engineers as a conversion space. When you want, for example, to convert an RGB bitmap to CMYK, the LAB color space is larger than both, and as a consequence, colors are not driven out of gamut when the pixels in such a bitmap are reassigned new component values.

YIQ

The YIQ color model is similar in its components to LAB color; however, its purpose is for working with designs and text that are video-legal, as defined by the National Television Standards Committee (NTSC). YIQ's components are one channel of luminosity, and two of chromacity (color). Standard definition TV is brighter than PC monitors, the color range is smaller, and if you get an assignment to draw a logo for a commercial, you'd use this color model. HD television changes a lot of the broadcast rules concerning video-legal colors; check with your client before choosing YIQ as a color space for designing titles or anything for a TV assignment.

Grayscale

You'd use the Grayscale color model (which actually has no hue) if you're designing for one-color commercial printing and for laser print output. You might find that a color design you've drawn doesn't look right if printed to a laser printer: blue areas seem too faint, and reds look much too dark. By using Grayscale, you take the influence of hue out of the color equation, and what you see onscreen is what you get on paper.

Registration

You do not design with this color model; it's only one color. Registration is used for an object when you want that object to be printed on all commercial press plates, including spot color plates. As the name suggests, registration applied, for example, to hairline paths around the border of a design helps commercial press operators to see and keep all the printing plates in registration when they review progressive proofs of the plates. Also, if your design calls for spot-color inks, you can use an object with registration color to manually knock out (remove) areas on all other plates. For example, if you want a headline printed using a spot color on top of a photograph, a registration-colored object can be used to knock out the exact area on the C, M, Y, and K plates where printed areas of the underlying photograph would obscure the overprinted spot color.

The following sections bring relevance to all of these explanations of color; you want to put color to *use* in CorelDRAW, so it's only fitting to move into where the palettes and other features are *located*!

Using Color-Related Dockers

If you've been doing some independent exploring, you've certainly discovered the Uniform fill option on the toolbox, but you've also noticed that it doesn't dock; it is not a persistent part of the interface. The good news is that it's not *supposed* to be. Two dockers—covered next—are used to handle almost all commands that define and edit color. These are the Color docker and the Color Palette Manager docker. Let's examine these features.

Using the Color Docker

The Color docker, shown in Figure 17-3, is extremely convenient to work with and, essentially, it's the Uniform Fill dialog—smaller, dockable, and persistent in the workspace. When an object is selected, you can specify whether the color applies to the outline *or* fill color of the object, and any changes to colors are immediately applied. To open the Color docker, click-hold on the Fill tool on the toolbox to reveal the flyout group of tools—Color is at the bottom. It's also available when you choose Window | Dockers | Color. Unlike with Uniform Fill, you don't need to have an object selected to call it.

The Color docker is organized into three areas: color viewers and color sliders—as discussed earlier on the Uniform Fill dialog—and fixed palettes (actually, they were never broken…). You can display each area by clicking one of three buttons at the top of the docker. Each area is geared toward specifying a color using its unique parameters, and to then applying that color to the fill and/or outline of a selected object. Here's how each of the three areas is used for specifying color:

- **Color sliders**   You can mix the components of any color model you choose from the drop-down selector at top by dragging the sliders or entering percentages in the number fields. Notice that the sliders are in color and change dynamically, instantly

17

Color sliders   Color viewers

Fixed palettes

Flyout menu options

Apply lock

Click to apply fill.   Click to apply outline.

FIGURE 17-3   The Color docker is your one-stop shop for choosing by component values, by using a color model, and for choosing from custom predefined colors on the Palettes area.

updating to show you how much of a component affects the overall color, and the relationship between one component and the others.

- **Color viewers**   The color viewers (occasionally called *color pickers* in other programs) on the Color docker basically offer the same options as the color viewers on the Uniform Fill dialog; the Options button is simply located in a different place so the palette is more compact onscreen.

- **Fixed palettes**   Use this area to choose a color from a swatch collection from vendors such as Pantone, Trumatch, Focoltone, and others from the palette selector. Use the flyout options menu to display a color by name; if you have tooltips turned on (Tools | Options | Workspace | Display), the names of the swatches appear when you hover your cursor, as shown in this illustration. The slider at the bottom of this docker is dimmed if you've loaded Uniform Colors or any user or custom palette. This slider is for creating a mathematically precise color tint of an industry-standard solid color, such as any swatches in the Pantone Fashion + Home Cotton collection. Solid colors can take tints, thus producing pastels, because the printer or a vendor of paints can mix white into this real-world, solid color according to numerical values. Therefore, you can use this tint slider with solid predefined colors, but not with process colors; *process colors* are created in the physical world through separate passes of C, M, Y, and K pigments, and as a consequence it's impractical to tint the four components. However, CorelDRAW professionals make spot colors for designs by applying a tint to a solid. The technique works because a spot color always requires a separate printing plate.

Tint slider

17

TIP   *Solids colors can be turned into a tint when you print by assigning an object a percentage of the solid. For example, if you want a tint of PANTONE 357 green, fill an object with 50% of the solid swatch. When making the separations for your design, solids and percentages of color solids will print to the same plate. Effectively, the white of the paper becomes the "white paint" you mix with the solid to produce the tint.*

Solid Colors and Swatches

To quickly set up a tint of a solid CMYK or RGB color, you can click-hold on a swatch, release the mouse button after the flyout appears, and then choose from increments within the pop-up selector from solid at bottom right to white at top left. You click the tint on the flyout, and then click Fill or Outline to apply the tint. When you try this with a spot color, you'll see one horizontal strip with solid at the left, and 0% at the right. Also, if you choose a color from any of the spot color collections, you can use the Tint slider to create a percentage of the color, because spot colors are considered to be solids, while process colors use a combination of pigments.

Drag and drop swatch.

Click-hold to choose.

Swatches on the Color docker are "drag and drop"; alternatively, you can click the Fill, Outline, or both buttons in succession for "no miss" object coloring. You can click-drag a color onto an object, selected or unselected, to instantly fill it. If you have good skills with your mouse or other input device, you can set an outline color for an object by dragging and then dropping a color swatch on the edge of an object; even if the object has no outline attributes, the action of drag-dropping a color forces the object to take on a 0.5-point outline. If you miss the edge and the object itself while attempting to apply a color, CorelDRAW lets you know this by changing the cursor's appearance. If you release the mouse button over an empty area, this is the same action as redefining all object fill and/or outline properties, and you'll get an onscreen confirmation box about this action. You probably want to Cancel such an action—you might grow bored with having every new object you create filled with Pale Avocado.

Using the Color Palette Manager Docker

The Color Palette Manager docker, shown in Figure 17-4, gives you the option to manage multiple palettes and palette colors. To open the Color Palette Manager docker, choose Window | Dockers | Color Palette Manager. The docker is structured as a tree directory so you can view palettes by folder as you browse, and it includes handy palette command buttons.

To make your own palettes and to work with this docker, which you'll use frequently in your work, follow these example steps.

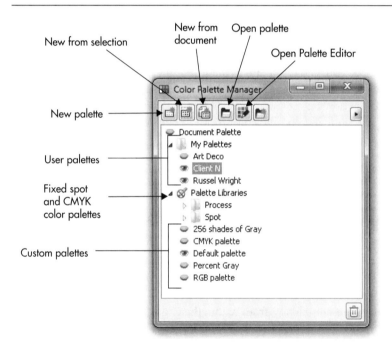

FIGURE 17-4 Choose from a wide selection of palettes with the Color Palette Manager docker.

17

Accessing Color Palettes

1. Open the Color Palette Manager docker by choosing Window | Dockers | Color Palette Manager. To open a palette—which docks to the left of the default color palette in the workspace—click the eye icon from its closed appearance to an open eye. To close an open palette, click the eye from open to closed. You can float an open palette by dragging the top of the color palette strip into the workspace.

2. Create several objects (seven rectangles are fine), and then fill them with different colors using the (default) Color Palette wells. Just select an object with the Pick tool, and then left-click a color well on the Color Palette.

3. Press CTRL+A to select all, and then click the Creates A New Palette From Selected Objects button on the top of the docker. CorelDRAW prompts you for a new palette name and a location in the Save Palette As dialog. Fill in the required information and then click Save. As a result, all seven colors (plus black, derived from the object outline) now appear on a color palette to the left of the default in the workspace. This is an invaluable method for saving colors you've spent a lot of time defining, and the palette can now be used on a new or existing document anytime. If two objects share an identical color, the color is not duplicated on your palette.

4. To open a saved palette, click the Opens A Palette folder icon on the top of the Color Palette Manager.

Using the Color Styles Docker

Color Styles is the route to follow in CorelDRAW to create, name, and apply colors and color *relationships* to objects.

 Because all styles are associated with individual documents, you must have at least one document open to use the color tools available in the Color Styles docker.

Color styles are managed completely from within the Color Styles docker, shown in Figure 17-5, which is opened by choosing Tools | Color Styles. The docker features command buttons for creating new styles, child colors, and shades.

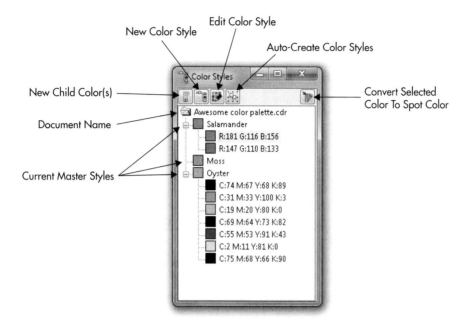

FIGURE 17-5 The Color Styles docker has commands for creating new styles and tints of master colors.

Follow these steps for an introduction to working with color styles.

Saving a Color as a Style

1. Open the Color Styles docker by choosing Tools | Color Styles.

2. Click the New Color Style button in the docker. The New Color Style dialog opens. Select a color and then click OK to create the style.

3. To name your new style, select and then click the default color component label field, enter a new name, and then click outside of the style text field to complete the naming. By default, each style you create is named by its color values. For example, a typical CMYK color would be labeled "C:18 M:45 Y:9 K:0."

4. To edit a selected style's color, click the Edit Color Style button to open the Select Color dialog. Click OK to complete the editing operation and close the dialog.

17

 To apply a master or child color from the Color Styles docker, drag the color directly onto an object in the drawing window. To add an object's current color as a style, drag the object into the docker window's field area below the document folder icon.

Creating Child Colors

Child colors have a dynamic relationship with a defined master color style. The child colors remain the same hue as the master color, but their brightness and/or saturation can be different. Any hue changes made to the master color are automatically updated in the child colors, which is the real power of setting up a drawing using master color—in less than 30 seconds you can recolor a drawing so it's significantly different from your original.

To explore the master/child color relationship controlled using the Color Styles docker, run through these tutorial steps.

Building a Parent-Child Relationship

1. Open the Color Styles docker by choosing Tools | Color Styles.

2. Click the New Color Style button to open the New Color Style dialog. Pick a color for your new style, and then click OK to create the style. Select and click the style name, and then enter a unique name of your own for the color.

3. With your style selected in the list, click the New Child Color(s) button in the docker to open the Create A New Child Color dialog, shown in Figure 17-6.

FIGURE 17-6   Control the number of child colors, the diversity of shades, brightness, and saturation through this dialog.

4. By default, the child color is based on the Hue component of the master. You can change the Saturation and Brightness of the child colors by dragging their sliders or by typing a value in their numeric fields.

5. Enter a name for the new style or accept its default name, and click OK to close the dialog. The new child color appears in the Color Styles docker.

6. Select the master once again, and click the Edit Color Style button in the docker to open the Select Color dialog. Change the style's color to any other color, and click OK to close the dialog. Notice the style's color is updated, and so is the hue of all the child colors. This same effect applies to any of the objects that feature either the master color style or its associated child color.

 As an alternative to using the docker buttons, you can right-click a color style in the docker, and then select commands from the pop-up menu.

A practical example of the usefulness of master and child colors is in a situation when you know in advance that a client will want to see several different color schemes for an illustration of a product, logo, or package label. You begin with a set of parent colors, create children for these "master" colors, design your design, and then when your client asks for a revision (or several), changing the parent colors automatically changes the child colors. This is a very powerful feature, and for this reason color styles are local to a document—you can edit a parent color in a file without worrying that you're messing up a color in a different file you also have open.

 You can create up to 20 shades of a master color in the Create A New Child Color dialog. If you need more, try creating a child of a child color. The result is that all the shades appear below the master color, so you could have, hypothetically, scores of child colors based on one master.

Creating Styles from Selections

The Auto-Create Color Styles command button in the Color Styles docker lets you create a collection of related color styles based on a selection in your document. Clicking the Auto-Create Color Styles command button opens the Automatically Create Color Styles dialog, shown next.

To create a collection of color styles and child color styles from a selection of existing colored objects in your document is quick and easy, as follows.

Sampling and Saving Colors from a Document

1. Press CTRL+A to select everything on the page, or select individual objects. Open the Color Styles docker by choosing Tools | Color Styles.

2. Click the Auto-Create Color Styles button to open the Automatically Create Color Styles dialog.

3. Choose the properties on which you want to base your new collection of styles by choosing the Use Fill Colors and/or Use Outline Colors check boxes.

4. Choose Automatically Link Similar Colors Together for flexibility in future revisions to your document, or choose Convert Child Palette Colors To CMYK if you think you'll have a future need to use only CMYK values for objects you'll add to the drawing.

5. The Many Parents Or Few Parents slider can be used to alleviate the world's overpopulation crisis. *Only kidding*—use this slider to limit the number of parent (master) colors generated, which is quite useful if you have hundreds of unique colors in the document.

6. To review the styles that will be automatically created and listed in the Color Styles docker before committing, click the Preview button. The color styles CorelDRAW is about to create are listed in the preview window.

7. To accept the previewed listing and close the dialog, click OK. Your styles are automatically created.

Moving from Color Models to Other Ways to Define Color

Although color models provide the designer with an intuitive device for picking colors, CorelDRAW offers alternative methods in the form of the color mixer and palettes—an extensive collection of swatches that simulate real-world ink, paint, and plastic colors on your monitor to match the colors manufacturers use from Pantone and other vendors. The following sections explore how to "mix it up" with the other tabs on the Uniform Fill dialog.

Using Color Mixers

Color mixers provide ways to create as many coordinated colors as you need automatically. Anytime you find yourself choosing a color in CorelDRAW's Color dialog, you have access to the color mixers. Mixers create colors using "color harmonies" and color blend tools. Select any object in your document, and press SHIFT+F11 to open the Uniform Fill dialog; then click the Mixers tab.

Mixing with Color Harmonies

Click the Options button at the bottom of the Mixers tab dialog shown in the next illustration, and choose Mixers | Color Harmonies. This is the default mixing type for Mixers. The term *color harmony* means that the color spectrum is organized using *equal emphasis*—equal space is devoted—on each color of the spectrum. Think of color harmonies as *organization* in the same way that color models show *structure*. To arrive at several colors that *work well together in a composition* is a manual task; no computer program can decide which colors work well together for *you*. The harmonies mixer features a color wheel and control handles you drag to choose which hue you want to make variations from, and which other hues, if any, should be used to create variations. Again, the color mixer creates variations you can choose from and can display other hues that have a math relationship to your chosen hue, and the related hues can be used to generate their own variations. However, the mixer is a mixer; it does not generate a "Oh, these colors all work together well in a drawing" color palette.

Use the Model drop-down selector to choose a color model on which to base a collection of color variations you can save. Choose one of the configurations from the Hues drop-down list, and then click-drag to rotate the color wheel markers to alter the collection of swatches displayed at bottom left. Choose from Primary, Complementary, Triangle (1 and 2), Rectangle, or Pentagon hues to create color markers that move as you change the primary hue marker around the color wheel; the related color markers range from a single point to five points. Use the Variation drop-down selector to choose among Cooler, Warmer, Lighter, Darker, and Less Saturated "children" of the target color you've defined on the color wheel. If you want a preference in your mix of a certain hue—and you've chosen Triangle, Rectangle, or Pentagon from the Hues drop-down—you can favor certain hues over others around the wheel.

17

First choose the hue—drag the black triangle to your choice, and then drag any of the white-circle color markers toward or away from their current location, distorting the polygon.

Reshape polygon to shift hues away or toward target hue.

Color Relationships

It is through color harmonies that you can better see the relationships between primary, secondary, and complementary colors. In the additive color model, the primary colors are red, green, and blue. Complementary colors are the color opposites of primaries and lie at 180 degrees in opposition on a color wheel of hues. For example, the digital complementary color of Red is Cyan; the opposite of Blue is Yellow; and these complements are largely responsible for the A and B color channels in the LAB model, discussed earlier in this chapter. Secondary (additive) colors are the result of mixtures of two primary colors: Red + Green yields Yellow, Green + Blue produces Cyan, and Red + Blue produces Magenta, which is the basis for the CMYK (subtractive) color model. It should be noted, however, that color harmonies, relationships that are described based on math, are not necessarily the sort of "harmony" you think of when designing a scheme, for example, for the living room. The "color explorer" utilities you can download online typically do exactly what CorelDRAW's mixer does. Usually showing only contrasting colors (color opposites, complementary colors), color mixers have no intelligence; they describe only relationships between hues, and therefore can choose, for example, college sports team colors, but you truly have to use your own mind's eye when designing an *eye-pleasing* palette of colors to use in your work.

In RGB, the complementary color of Red is Cyan. Quoting from Wiki:

In the RGB color model (and derived models such as HSV), primary colors and secondary colors are paired in this way:

- red and cyan
- green and magenta
- blue and yellow

However, in art and design, complementary colors are defined differently. Using Wiki again:

Because of the limited range of colors that was available throughout most of the history of art, many artists still use a traditional set of complementary pairs, including:

- white and black
- red and green
- blue and orange
- yellow and violet

(from http://en.wikipedia.org/wiki/Complementary_color)

Here is a set of steps you can use to gain experience with the features of the color mixer's Color Harmonies mode.

 ## Experimenting with Color Harmonies

1. You might not want to mess up the default Color Palette in your workspace, so before exploring mixers, create a new palette: click the menu options button on the default palette, as shown at left in the following illustration, and then choose Palette | New. When prompted for a new palette name, name it "Test" or anything you'll remember

later. A new blank palette appears to the left of the default Color Palette at the right edge of the drawing window.

2. With an object selected on the page, open the Uniform Fill dialog (SHIFT+F11), click the Mixers tab, and choose Options | Mixers | Color Harmonies. Choose a color model from the Model drop-down menu.

3. Choose a Hue type—in the illustration shown next, Triangle1 is selected. A four-pointed rectangle shape appears around the color wheel. Click-drag the black marker to change hue, and click-drag the white markers to reshape the rectangle. Triangles and other multi-point harmonies can be reshaped, too. By making the rectangle wide and short, you narrow the range of complementary colors to red (the selected color); yellows, greens, and violets are eliminated from the mixer swatches, in preference for cyans and blues.

4. Choose a Variation type to change the swatch collection below the color model, based on the color marker positions on the model. If you choose None from the Variation drop-down list, only one color per marker appears in the collection, and the Size slider is dimmed. In the case of the Rectangle harmony, four markers appear.

5. Choose a Variation other than None, and then choose a Size for your collection using the Size slider control. Choose up to 20 different variation colors per marker.

6. Work on this color collection using different harmonies and variations until you arrive at something you think you'll use in the future.

7. To save the collection now to the palette you created in step 1, click the first color well (the color swatch), and then SHIFT-click the last color well to select them all. Alternatively, if you have some colors you feel are useless, CTRL-click only the valuable color wells. Highlighted color wells take on a bevel-edge highlight.

8. With your colors selected, click the down arrow to the right of the Add To Palette button, and then choose your palette. You're not done yet: click the Add To Palette button, and your collection of colors is saved to your custom color palette.

9. At any time, you can add a color directly to the custom palette by dragging a filled object into the palette, whether it is docked or not. You can also rearrange the order of colors by dragging from one position on the palette, and then releasing the swatch when it's over its desired position.

Save selected color wells
(swatches) to new palette.

Drag a filled object over the
palette to add its color.

> TIP *To add an object's fill and its outline color at the same time to a custom palette, drag the object aboard the palette. A shape with a fountain fill can also add colors to a custom palette. For example, a four-color multi-step fountain fill will add its four primary color transition points to the custom palette if you drag the object onto the palette.*

Mixing with Color Blend

The Color Blend mixer (shown in the following illustration) is the other mode of the Mixers module, where you define colors almost literally by mixing them, very much like when you create a multi-stage fountain fill. You can choose four different colors and then generate a collection of up to 1,024 unique values, and then choose the ones you like to create your

17

own color palette. All these color options are easier to mentally sort by task: when you want a specific color, you use the Models module. When you want a palette of colors based around your tastes, you use the Mixers module.

To access the Color Blend feature from within the main Uniform Fill dialog while you're on the Mixers tab, choose Options | Mixers | Color Blend.

Here's how to work the Color Blend feature to create a small collection, and then to choose the colors you want to save as a palette.

Using the Color Blend Mixer

1. Create an object, select it, and then double-click the Fill Color button on the status bar to open the Uniform Fill dialog.

2. Click the Mixers tab and then choose Options | Mixers | Color Blend.

3. Choose four colors for your blend by clicking each of the four color selectors in view and choosing a color from the palette displayed. You do not need to blend from four colors: you can choose the same color from two or more of the flyout palettes to home in on a range of colors, making your decisions easier. Each time a selector is changed, the color field changes, as do the available colors from which to choose.

4. Choose a Size for your collection using the Size slider control.

5. Save some of the more useful colors to a palette; let's use the palette you saved in the previous tutorial. Remember that if you've got some eye-pleasing colors in the collection, you don't have to save a huge, all-inclusive collection; you can create shades of your favorite colors on-the-fly using the child colors feature covered earlier in this chapter. CTRL-click on the color wells in the collection to select only, let's say, your eight favorite colors. See the following illustration.

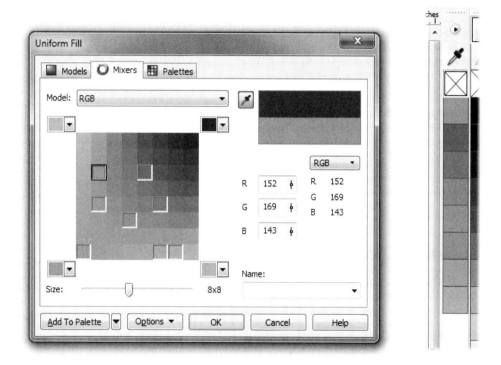

6. Choose a palette from the drop-down list, and then click the Add To Palette button. Your color blend collection is saved.

Using Fixed and Custom Palettes

A *fixed* palette is a collection of ink colors prepared by an ink manufacturer, such as a specific process or spot color. Because these color specialists have spent a good deal of time preparing combinations of inks and other pigments to match as closely as possible between your monitor's display and how the colors look on real-world packaging and other goods, you don't edit these colors as you can with models and mixers. However, if you choose a collection made up of one solid ink color (not a process color) such as Pantone Solid Uncoated, you can specify a Tint of this solid color (the Tint slider is below the color samples); the professional mixing the color for you simply adds white pigment. Fixed palettes are like small color catalogs. Manufacturers such as Pantone, Trumatch, and Focoltone have supplied color simulations for CorelDRAW users. You might use only one color collection, but you have a wide variety from which to choose, and these simulations are as faithful in the "What You See Is What Will Print" arena as technology can bring you today.

Using Fixed Palettes

Some of the palettes are for use in commercial print—they provide simulations for metallic inks, inks that will be printed to coated or uncoated stock (in English: glossy and matte finishes), and so on. Other palettes you'll find in this area of uniform fills are geared for the Web and not for print. The World Wide Web has color specifications, too. Using a specific color palette usually ensures that colors you use in a design fall within the capabilities of the reproduction or display technique used to show off your work.

To apply process color values (CMYK, usually, although Pantone Hexachrome fixed-palette inks use six values) to your work, the very first thing you do is talk with the commercial press operator. They might want to use substitution values (less expensive inks), or they might not even own the physical equipment to reproduce Hexachrome. You always work backwards when your final output is to be printed—you find out what can be reproduced on what budget, and then you choose your colors. Here's a short tutorial on how to specify a color from the Palettes list.

 Choosing Predefined Colors for Print

1. With an object selected on the page, in the Uniform Fill dialog (press SHIFT+F11), click the Palettes tab.

2. Choose a palette from the Palette drop-down menu. Colors appear in the main selector window, and you can pick swatches by clicking them; their names appear in the Name list at bottom right. You can more quickly thumb through colors by choosing Options | Show Color Names; the selector window changes from swatches to larger color samples with the name in the center of the color. The vertical selector to the right of the selector window lets you navigate through the available colors *very* quickly.

3. Click the color you need.

4. If you've chosen a process color collection, the Tint slider is unavailable. However, if you've picked a Metallic, Pastel, or other *solid* color collection, choose a percentage value for your color by using the Tint option. By default, tints of selected colors are set to 100 percent of the ink, but you can specify any value between 0 and 100 percent. However, choosing zero for a Tint just changes the chosen color to white; printing white on white paper probably won't earn you big bucks with your client!

5. Click OK to apply the palette color or a tinted value of the color.

Information about the Palettes You Can Use for Printing Assignments

Here's a quick rundown on each of the commercial palettes you can choose in the Palettes tab of the Uniform Fill dialog:

- **SVG Colors**   This collection was designed to address the need for standardized colors for Scalable Vector Graphics (SVG), an emerging technology that allows designers to post vector images as vector images (and not bitmaps) on web pages. These colors were agreed upon by the W3 Consortium.

 For a chart featuring user-friendly names for SVG colors, visit www.w3c.org/TR/ SVG11/types.html#ColorKeywords.

- **Pantone**   Pantone dominates the publishing industry with its color-matching system. CorelDRAW offers all of Pantone's color-matching simulations including coated, uncoated, and matte color versions for solids, as well as process and Hexachrome colors. CorelDRAW also features Pantone's metallic, GoeBridge, Color Bridge, pastel, solid-to-process EURO, and process-coated EURO palettes.

- **HKS (Hostmann, Kast, and Schmincke)**   This palette collection uses CMY components that occasionally (depending on the color) don't require a black plate. The HKS collections use a Euroscale color space, ISO 12647:2 2002, the FOGRA standard. If you're a Westerner, you probably won't use this color collection. HKS palettes include HKS Colors, HKS E, HKS Z, HKS N, and HKS K.

- **Focoltone**   This 750-color palette was designed from the ground up to be ICC compliant. If your commercial printer supports Focoltone (an abbreviation for "Four-color tone"), your client insists on color consistency between printed material and packaging, and you, the designer, need some flexibility in choosing colors and tints, you might want to try this collection.

- **Trumatch**   The Trumatch process-color palette is made up of more than 2,000 printable colors. Trumatch has specifically customized its color-matching system to suit the digital color industry by using the Computer Electronic Prepress System (CEPS). The palette has 40 tints and shades of each hue. Black is varied in 6-percent increments.

- **Web Safe**   The Web Safe Palette contains the 216 colors of the Web Safe color model. Colors are defined using the hexadecimal scheme; one of the six shades of each color (red, green, and blue) is combined together to create each color in the palette.

- **TOYO and DIC**   The TOYO and DIC color-matching systems are widely used throughout Asia—Japan, in particular. Each system contains its own numbering system and collection of different process colors. The TOYO collection of colors has been developed using its own process ink colors. The DIC (Dainippon Ink and Chemicals, Inc.) brand of process color inks is divided into three categories: DIC, DIC Traditional, and DIC Part II.

17

"Web Safe" Colors

Although the W3 Consortium publishes standards, you might feel a little confined choosing from only 216 colors that are Web Safe. *Web Safe,* by definition, means that these colors can be displayed accurately on a VGA monitor without color dithering, and that the colors display somewhat consistently whether you have color management on your computer turned on or off. Realistically, three people on earth still have a VGA monitor and a video card with less than 10MB of RAM. Additionally, designers tend to work with designers, and very few of us don't run a color management system—color management actually has been at the core of CorelDRAW and Windows since 1995.

There's something commendable about "playing to the cheap seats," but in actuality, very few designers bother with Web Safe colors. Every day, millions of people post JPEG images to the Web that look just fine, and these JPEGs decidedly have colors that fall outside of Web Safe standards.

Loading and Creating Custom Palettes

Through dialogs, the Color docker, or an open Color Palette, you can manage your color collections. The fastest way is to click the flyout arrow on a Color Palette and then to choose Palette | Open from the pop-up menu. This displays the Open Palette dialog, where you can browse what's available. The pop-up menu also includes Save, Save As, Close, and New palette commands.

The Palette Editor, shown in Figure 17-7, is the ideal place to rework custom palettes. In this dialog you can create, save, edit, and manage new and existing palettes using convenient command buttons. While editing palette colors, you can also access CorelDRAW's other color features.

Refining and redefining your palettes is easy, fun, and often necessary to keep palettes for client colors up-to-date. Try these steps to appreciate the ease of this powerful dialog.

 ## Editing Color Palettes

1. Open the Palette Editor; choose Tools | Palette Editor. Choose a palette by clicking the drop-down selector; open the directory tree for Custom Palettes or User's Palettes; click a palette name to choose it.

2. To edit an existing palette color, click a color and then click Edit Color. The Select Color dialog opens to offer color models, mixers, and palettes, exactly like the Uniform Fill dialog.

FIGURE 17-7   Manage custom palettes in the Palette Editor.

3. To begin a new palette, click the New Palette button in the Palette Editor dialog to open the New Palette dialog. Enter a name and then click Save. Your new palette is automatically opened, but there are no colors yet.

4. To add colors, click Add Color, which takes you to the Select Color dialog. Define your new color—with the Mixers module, you can choose a whole color range in one fell swoop—then click the Add To Palette button. New colors are immediately added to your new palette.

5. Once your colors have been added, click OK to return to the Palette Editor dialog. In the Name box, here's where you get to name a new color. When you use the edited color palette, the color name will appear on the status bar and in tooltips pop-ups instead of the component values.

6. To remove a selected color, click Delete Color and confirm your action in the prompt that appears. To reorganize your palette colors, click Sort Colors and then choose from Reverse, Name, Hue, Brightness, Saturation, RGB Value, or HSB Value. You can also click-drag a color well (color swatch) to reorder swatches as they appear on the Color Palette.

17

7. To name or rename an existing color, select the color in the palette, highlight its current name in the Name box, and then enter a new name. Existing names are automatically overwritten once a new color is selected.

8. Use the Reset Palette button to restore your palette to its original state before any changes were made, or click OK to accept your changes and close the dialog.

Now that you know how to create, save, and load color palettes, take a look at Russel Wright.xml. This palette was created by sampling photos of some of the art of historic ceramicist Russel Wright, whose work was exalted as modernist in the 1930s and 1940s. It's a nice, small, named palette for use when you need a truly retro look to a design.

There's one more way to make and save a user-defined palette: if you like the color of objects you have on the page, choose Window | Color Palettes | Create Palette From Selection (if you have objects selected in advance), or Create Palette From Document. This opens the Save Palette dialog, where you can name and save the colors you've used as a unique palette.

You can quickly copy color properties between two objects (including groups) by right-click-dragging an object on top of a different object. Release the mouse button once the source object is in position, and then choose Copy Fill Here or Copy Outline Here.

Color and Color Correction

Without defining a master color, creating relationships between parent and child colors, and without getting elaborate, you have another way to change colors in a CorelDRAW design. The Effects | Adjust menu has color and tone (brightness) corrections you can apply to an object—vector or bitmap—so you can modify all or parts of a design, and thus create variations on copies of your work. These changes are permanent; you should use the commands only on copies of your illustrations, or have the Window | Dockers | Undo docker handy in the workspace. These effects are mutually exclusive, and depending on the color solution you seek, you might need to apply one, and then a different one.

NOTE *Be sure every time you use the effects commands to click Reset. All command palettes remember your last used settings.*

- **Brightness/Contrast/Intensity** This command displays a palette where you can compress or expand the range of tones between the lightest and darkest (Contrast), add or subtract illumination from the selected object (Brightness), and use Intensity as an inverse operator to Brightness to make an object's colors more pronounced— decrease Brightness and then increase Intensity to see a working example of Intensity.

- **Color Balance**   Cyan is the additive color opposite of red, magenta's the opposite of green, and yellow is the color opposite of blue. Use this command palette to remove color casting in your selection in the three different tone areas. For example, the Compass.cdr file you'll experiment with shortly has a lot of deep reds toward the top of the grouped objects. Suppose you want to cool down only the deep reds, but not the medium reds. You put a check in the Shadows Range box, and then drag the Cyan-Red slider toward Cyan. Preserve Luminosity is an option when you want to shift the color in the selected object without changing its brightness. Color is linked to brightness, as you'll observe when using the HSV color model; when you change hue, you frequently also change brightness.

- **Gamma**   In video electronics, there is a "sag" (a non-linearity) when plotting signal to brightness; it's a physical drop-off that visually affects the midtones in images and designs you work with. The relationship between brightness and signal is called *gamma,* and the practical (nontechnical) purpose for gamma adjustment is to open up or block in midtones in a selected graphic or photo without impact on the lightest and darkest points in the brightnesses. Drag the Gamma slider to the right to increase the range of midtones, and drag it left to compress the midtone range.

- **Hue/Saturation/Lightness**   Use this command palette to shift certain hues to different ones, increase or decrease the richness of hues, and to increase or decrease the amount of white in the selection.

When you use any of the preceding commands, a pop-up menu offers the other Effects menu items. If you've selected a bitmap, you can use any and all of the commands, but if you have a vector object selected, most commands are unavailable, except two:

- **Invert**   This is a one-pop command with no options or command palette. It chromatically reverses color and tone areas. For example, deep red areas become light cyan.

- **Posterize**   This command has one slider marked "Levels." From a minimum of 2 to a maximum of 23, this effect moves all the colors in the selected object to a small, fixed range of colors. Although its use is perhaps best with photographs that you want to make look like rubber-stamp art or a silk-screened poster, objects with fountain fills and full-color pattern fills can take on an interesting look, too. Posterize and Invert are both under the Effects | Transform menu.

There is no "right" or "wrong" goal in the following steps: the intention here is simply to get you comfortable with adjusting colors in a composition by using the Effects menu. Open Compass.cdr now, and let's say a client wants a brighter, lighter version of this drawing, and you didn't create master colors, and the darned thing has over 80 objects you'd have to recolor…

17

Changing Colors with Effects

1. Duplicate the illustration first and then move it to one side so you can compare your results with the original.

2. Choose Windows | Docker | Undo, so you can undo any effect at any time.

3. With the copy selected, choose Effects | Adjust | Brightness/Contrast/Intensity.

4. Click Reset, as a matter of practice. Drag the Contrast slider to about 25, and then click Preview. Hmm, the colors are more pronounced, but not lighter, so half the request is addressed.

5. Drag the Intensity slider to about 35 and then click Preview. The graphic is improved, but the colors might need some saturation. Click OK to apply this effect.

6. Choose Effects | Adjust | Hue/Saturation/Lightness. Click Reset.

7. Click the Red channel button to correct only the predominantly red areas of the graphic.

8. Drag the Saturation slider to about 45 and then click Preview. Hmmm, better, but the red is now too light.

9. Drag the Lightness slider to –7 and then click Preview. Compare the graphic to its duplicate. For this example, let's consider the job well done—it's a much lighter, more lively graphic now, as you can sort of see in Figure 17-8. Click OK to apply the filter.

10. The phone rings, it's the client, and they decide they like the original. On the Undo docker, click Duplicate to send the original back in steps to before you applied any adjustments. Sure, you could delete the original and use the duplicate, but then you wouldn't have learned how to use the Undo docker to save time! Charge the client extra for the time they don't know you saved on revisions.

You've seen in this chapter that color is important; color sets a mood for an illustration, and the artistic use of color can actually remedy an illustration that lacks visual interest or complexity. And you now know how to define and save not only a color you need, but also an entire palette. This concludes the section on colors and fills. From here we travel to the land of very special effects—take what you've learned, take what you've drawn, and bend it, distort it, and in general, make it a unique piece by learning how to sculpt vector shapes.

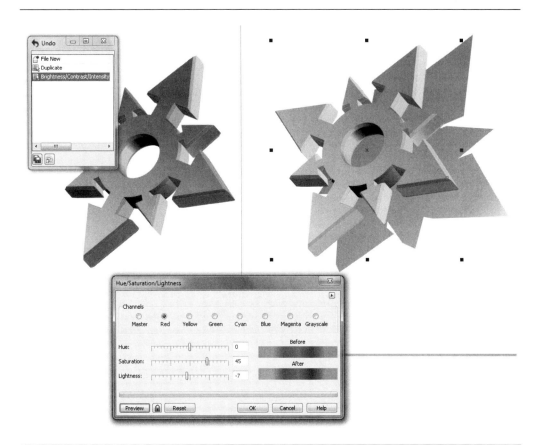

FIGURE 17-8 Change the colors of grouped objects selectively with the Effects | Adjust commands.

PART VI

Creating the Illusion of 3D Objects

CHAPTER 18

Working with Perspective

The property of visual perspective was first documented by Leonardo da Vinci and used in his technical drawings to give an accurate sense of depth to his 2D (two-dimensional) pieces. Perspective in drawings can be calculated today by CorelDRAW and other applications, and this chapter takes you through a definition of perspective, how to use CorelDRAW's perspective effect, and how to feature the artistic quality of perspective in your work to produce lifelike illustrations. If you want your audience to be drawn *into* your work and not simply to stare at it, consider adding some perspective...so your *audience* will see it, too!

> **NOTE** *Download and extract all the files from the Chapter18.zip archive to follow the tutorials in this chapter.*

The Optical Principle of Perspective

We've all witnessed the effect of perspective; for example, you make sure a train isn't coming, and then you stand on the tracks and look into the horizon. Apparently, the train tracks converge as they vanish at the horizon. Naturally, the tracks don't actually converge, or it would be difficult to put a train on them. This is an optical illusion that demonstrates the very real optics of the human eye. Any object that has parallel sides (a milk carton, most tables) when viewed at an angle other than face-forward will look as though its parallel sides converge at a point somewhere in the distance. This point, whether you can see it on train tracks or imagine it by mentally extending the parallel lines, is called the *vanishing point,* and CorelDRAW's perspective effect offers an onscreen marker for moving a shape's vanishing point when Effects | Add Perspective has been applied to an object or group of objects.

Depending on the angle at which you view an object—let's use a cube as an example—you can see one, two, or three sides of the cube. When you draw a cube face-front in CorelDRAW, you've drawn a square; there is no perspective, and it's not a visually interesting representation. If you can see two faces of the cube, you're viewing from a perspective point; the object is said to have *one-point perspective.* Naturally, you can't see more than three sides of a cube at one time, but when you do see all three front-facing sides, this is called *two-point perspective.* It's very visually interesting to pose an object (or draw one) using two-point perspective, and CorelDRAW helps you set up an object for two-point as well as one-point perspective.

What Is Normal?

Before getting into the wildly distorted perspectives you have available in CorelDRAW, it's probably a good idea to cover what the human eye normally sees with respect to perspective. In your design work, you might occasionally want to portray an object in "normal" perspective—learn how to do this, and you can increase and exaggerate perspective quite easily.

It's simple to calibrate and measure a camera lens when compared with measuring what the human eye sees, because the human eye is in constant motion, and there's a brain behind the eyes that interprets and occasionally *mis*interprets the optical signals it receives.

However, three things come into play that determine the appearance (including the apparent perspective) when using your eye or your eye through a lens:

- **Distance of lens from subject**   In CorelDRAW you might be surprised when you copy a perspective setting to a new object—depending on the perspective, the object might grow or shrink in dimensions. Not to fret; this is covered later in this chapter—perspective *changes* the apparent distance of objects. Because you're drawing on a flat plane in a CorelDRAW document, the program scales objects according to their perspective to simulate depth in a composition.

- **Field of view**   CorelDRAW's perspective effect has no field of view setting, but in the real world, this property affects how distorted an object looks and is related to focal length. Humans have anywhere from 140° to 180° field of view, but much of this is peripheral vision, not truly in focus, and the consensus is that we usually use about 40° normal field of view.

- **Focal length**   Focal length is the distance between a lens and the imaging surface and is proportional to field of view: as one changes, so does the other. This property is the most responsible for the distorted or undistorted appearance of objects. It's generally agreed that humans have a focal length of 50–55mm. As this relates to CorelDRAW, to simulate short focal lengths (such as a fish-eye lens on a camera), the vanishing points for the perspective effect are quite close to the object. As focal length increases, a telescopic effect is achieved, and the perspective of an object is lessened. For example, if you wanted to simulate a 500mm telescopic camera lens in CorelDRAW, the vanishing point for the perspective on the object would be clear off the page, probably in the parking lot somewhere.

This illustration of a child's toy block was rendered to a fairly accurate representation of what a normal human eye would see from a two-point perspective. The focal length is 50mm, and the field of view is about 40°. The lines you see along the parallels of the block indicate the direction of the vanishing points: a normal lens on the child's block puts the vanishing points off this page.

Parallels converge

Parallels converge

Focal length: 50mm
Field of view: 40°

18

Getting a Perspective on Perspective

Now that you understand what a "normal" lens does to perspective, let's take a look at a few abnormal (but artistic and creative) perspectives, beginning with no perspective and working our way up. In Figure 18-1 you can see at left an *isometric* view (also called an "orthographic" view) of the kid's block. Regardless of the term, it's unrealistic because the parallels of the cube do not converge. Isometric views of objects are quickly accomplished in CorelDRAW by putting an object into rotate/skew mode (clicking once and then a second time), and then skewing the object by click-dragging a middle control handle. Isometric views are completely the province of computer graphics and geometry. They don't exist in the real world with human eyes, but they are useful in illustration to put equal emphasis on all visible sides of an object. For example, if you want your client to read the side panel of a proposed cereal box design but want the box posed to show more than one side, you'd use an isometric view (occasionally called "isometric perspective"). At right you can see the same kid's block using a wide-angle perspective. In CorelDRAW such an illustration is accomplished by putting the vanishing points outside of the drawing page. It's exaggerated mostly because the human eye does not have a field of view as large as 76°, that is, the view is not entirely in focus.

Planes do not converge
on a vanishing point.

Planes eventually converge
in the distance.

Isometric view
(no perspective)

Focal length: 28mm
Field of view: 76°

FIGURE 18-1   Examples of isometric views and a fairly wide-angle view of the same object.

Two-point perspective

Vanishing point

Focal length: 14mm

Field of view: 104°

FIGURE 18-2   Vanishing points that are close to objects suggest an extremely distorted perspective.

Figure 18-2 goes way over the top; the vanishing points are quite close to the object, and the result is very dramatic, unrealistic, and unsuitable for presenting a product design. As you read through this chapter, you'll learn that on some occasions you want a vanishing point on the drawing page, and on other occasions you want perspective of the "normal" human-eye type.

Experiments in Perspective

It's a lot more fun and rewarding to experiment with the perspective effect than it is to read about it. The operations are fairly simple and straightforward, and you'll probably get ideas for future illustrations just by playing with it! Single objects and object groups can be put in perspective. You can change the angle of a perspective shape (or group) by click-dragging any of the four control corners or by click-dragging the vanishing point(s), which changes two of the four control corners at once. Let's begin with a simple perspective, performed on an object that will immediately, visually give you a reference for what's going on: a 12×12-cell graph paper object. The perspective effect displays subdivisions in red dotted lines on top of the object you're manipulating, which provides good visual feedback. With a graph paper object, you'll see exactly how the grid corresponds to the visual changes in the graph paper cells.

18

Creating One-Point Perspective

1. Press D, the keyboard shortcut for the Graph paper tool. On the property bar, set the number of columns to 12 and the number of rows to 12.

2. Hold CTRL while you click-drag to constrain the graph paper object to a square. Make the object fairly large, about 7" is good. Because the perspective effect can appreciably shrink one or more sides of an object, it's a good design practice to create objects that are a little exaggerated in size.

3. Choose Effects | Add Perspective, as shown here. It might not be obvious, depending on the color of the selected object, that it now has control handles around it. Notice that your current tool has changed to the Shape tool. The Shape tool is used during perspective creation. Additionally, if you intend to edit a perspective effect while you're working on a different area of a design, all you need to do is choose the Shape tool, and then click an object that's in perspective.

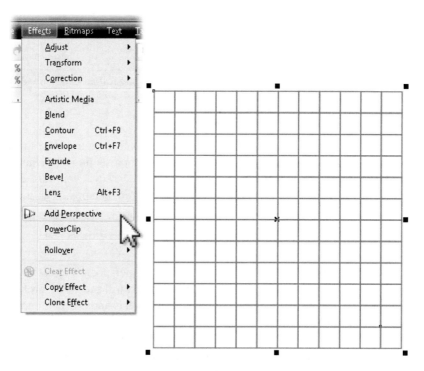

4. Click the top-right handle of the perspective effect box surrounding the graph paper object. Hold CTRL to constrain the movement of your cursor to the first direction in which you drag, and then drag down to about the second or third cell in the right column, as shown next. You've created a perspective effect on the object, as you can

see the cells align more or less with the effect's red-dotted overlay reference, and a vanishing point appears directly to the right.

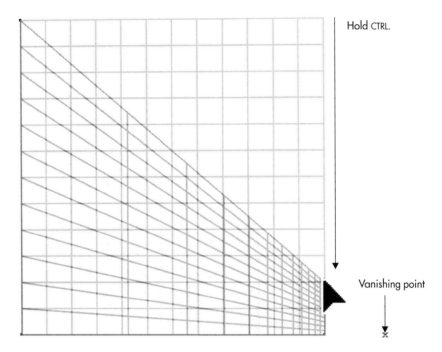

5. Click-drag the vanishing point up and then down as long as this is an experiment and not playing for points. Notice what happens: you've defined one-point perspective—this is the right side of a hypothetical cube, and one-point perspectives have only one vanishing point. So the left side of the object is anchored; it doesn't change with the perspective change.

6. Click-drag the vanishing point left and right. The left side is still anchored, and what you're doing is making the hypothetical box's right side deeper and shallower, extending to and from an imaginary horizon on the page.

7. Save this document; you'll work with it in a moment, so don't close it. This is only the beginning of the experiment with suggesting depth in a 2D document!

There has to be a practical use for what you've just learned; adding one-point perspective to a graph paper object by itself is about as exciting as watching grass grow. Next you can see the result of grouping some text with the graph paper object before applying the perspective effect. It's a simple drawing and it certainly could use some embellishment, but the point here is that one-point perspective can establish a *ground plane*

18

for a dimensional composition. A ground has been suggested in this illustration by the effect, the "scene" has depth, and the illustrator obviously can't read signs.

Working with Two-Point Perspective

Any 2D drawing can be made by the perspective effect to look as though it extends into space, as you proved in the previous tutorial. However, it's time to up the stakes and create a *second* vanishing point. This will make this graph paper object look as though it occupies space, suggesting visually that the grid recedes away from the page, and that its depth is traveling in a direction. This is going to be fun; by the end of the following steps, you'll have created a great high-tech, sci-fi background you can use in several design situations.

 ### Creating a 3D Ground Plane

1. With the graph-paper document you saved in the previous tutorial open, choose the Shape tool and then click the object to reveal its perspective effect control handles and the vanishing point you defined.

2. Click-drag the top-right control handle up and toward the center of the object, until you see a second vanishing point marker at about 12 o'clock on the page. You might want to zoom out to better see the second vanishing point, because it will initially be defined quite far away from the object. Use your mouse scroll wheel to zoom whenever you have a drawing or editing tool chosen; scrolling toward you zooms the window view out, and scrolling away from you zooms it in. Here you can see how the graph paper object should look now. Notice also that because this two-point perspective is so extreme, the graph-paper outlines are actually curved to accommodate the severely distorted perspective. This is not an optical illusion (the lines are indeed curved now), but it does mimic the human eye's perception of parallel lines viewed at exceptionally wide angles.

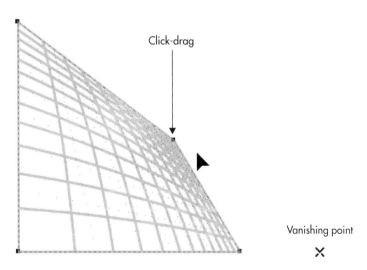

3. Choose the Pick tool, and with the graph paper object selected, click it to put it into Skew/Rotate transformation mode. Rotate the object about 45° counterclockwise— stop click-dragging when the property bar reports that you've rotated the object by about this amount. It would be difficult to change the orientation of the object by only changing the vanishing points' positions.

18

4. Choose the Rectangle tool and then click-drag a rectangle to cover the graph paper object.

5. Choose the Interactive fill tool, and then click-drag from top to bottom on the object so the top is black, fading to white at the rectangle's bottom.

6. Choose the rectangle with the Pick tool, and then press SHIFT+PAGE DOWN to put the rectangle on the back of the drawing page, behind the graph paper object.

7. Choose the graph paper object, and then right-click the white color well on the Color Palette. Then double-click the Outline Color swatch on the status bar to open the Outline Pen dialog.

8. Type **4** in the Width field, and then click OK to apply this width. You're done and your composition will look like the illustration here.

| NOTE | *The Outline properties of an object possessing the perspective effect do not diminish in width along with the shape of the object. If you need outlines to follow a perspective, you need to first convert the outlines to objects: press CTRL+U, for example, to ungroup a graph paper object, and then choose Arrange | Convert Outline To Object (CTRL+SHIFT+Q) before applying the perspective effect.* |

Copying Perspective and Creating a 3D Scene

Like many of the features in CorelDRAW, a perspective can be copied from an object and applied to a different object, by use of the options on the property bar. Being able to instantly copy and match perspective between objects in a composition can turn the entire drawing into a 3D event, as the following tutorial guides you through.

The characters in the Commuters.cdr file will make a nice part of a composition as you angle them using the perspective effect in the steps to follow, but you can use an illustration of your own if you prefer. The idea is that these fellows are so self-absorbed that they're going to miss the train pulling in behind them unless they look to the right a little. So you'll apply a perspective to one guy, and then copy the instance of the perspective effect to the rest of the gang, and then you'll embellish the composition a little to give the drawing true depth.

Perspective Scenes via Copying

1. Select the left guy on the page, and then choose Effects | Add Perspective.

2. Click the top-right control handle on the object, and then drag down a little. Then click-drag the bottom-right control handle, and drag up and to the right until the commuter is facing right in perspective, as shown in Figure 18-3. You might not see the vanishing points on the page because this perspective is not dramatic or severely distorted.

FIGURE 18-3   Create just enough perspective to give the shape some dimension.

18

3. You can keep using the current tool, the Shape tool; click the guy with his hat in his hand. Then choose Effects | Copy Effect | Perspective From. Click over the guy at left who has perspective as shown here, and the second object adopts the perspective of the first.

4. Repeat step 3 for the guy holding the writing pad.

5. Create a graph paper object that fills most of the page, and then give it a medium-gray fill and a white outline. Put it to the back of the illustration layer by pressing SHIFT+PAGE DOWN.

6. Put the graph paper in perspective to make a ground plane. Next, drag the top-left control handle to the right, and then drag the top-right control handle to the left until you see a vanishing point just above the graph paper object. Now drag the top and right-top control nodes down until the perspective looks like that shown in the figure. This object will not and should not be in the same perspective as the characters, but instead its perspective should be very distorted, suggesting a horizon at about the chest level of the characters.

7. Create a second graph paper object, fill it with medium gray, and give its outline a white property exactly like you did with the first object in step 5. Put it to the back of the drawing (SHIFT+PAGE DOWN).

8. If you haven't already read Chapter 22 on shadows, here are the simple steps to "grounding" the characters on the graph paper below them: click one of the fellows, and then choose the Drop Shadow tool from the Effects group of tools on the toolbox.

9. Choose Perspective Top Left from the Presets drop-down on the property bar. With your cursor, click-drag to adjust the black control marker for the shadow until it looks correct.

10. Repeat step 9 with the two other commuters: select a guy, and then choose Effects | Copy Effect | Drop Shadow From, and click the first shadow (not the object casting the shadow) you defined. You can also add a shadow to the train and the cloud group of objects. Additionally, try moving the commuters up or down from their original position to increase the sense of depth in the scene. Your scene should look like Figure 18-4 now.

The preceding tutorial might have been a bit of a workout, but look at what you've accomplished. Often, the effect you seek is accomplished through the use of a *combination* of CorelDRAW features. Unfortunately, there is no "create a complete piece of artwork" tool in CorelDRAW!

 Any object that has the perspective effect can be quickly put into editing mode when the Pick tool is the current tool, by double-clicking the object.

| FIGURE 18-4 | With the perspective effect and the use of a few drop shadows, you can build a virtual diorama. |

18

Mirroring Perspective Control Handles

Occasionally in your design work, you might need to add perspective or adjust the existing perspective of an object so that the perspective is symmetrical. This is accomplished by holding CTRL+SHIFT while you click-drag a perspective control handle. Here's a creative example of the use of a symmetrical perspective: in a new document, import Bowling.png, and then follow these steps.

 ## Building a Bowling Alley

1. With the Rectangle tool, create a tall rectangle, about 1" wide and 5" high. Fill it with a light brown color.

2. Drag and drop three copies, each to the right of the preceding one; first, hold CTRL to constrain your moves, then drag right, tap the right mouse button while holding the left, and then release both buttons to drop the copy.

3. Group the four rectangles; after selecting them, press CTRL+G, and then press SHIFT+PAGE DOWN to put them behind the imported PNG picture.

4. Choose Effects | Add Perspective.

5. While holding CTRL+SHIFT, click the bottom-right control node and then drag right. Strike! In Figure 18-5 you can see that this technique is a convenient way to set up symmetrical perspective. Optionally, you might want to use CTRL+SHIFT and then drag the top control nodes a little closer together to get the artistic effect, but you know the techniques now.

Pre-Visualizing Designs in Perspective

Often you'll design something such as a pattern and want to see what it will look like as a garment, gift wrap, or some other physical piece of art before you pay to have the design printed; this is called *pre-visualization* (preVis), and you can do this in CorelDRAW with the perspective effect. In the following example, you'll create a simple gift-wrap pattern; then, using perspective, you'll virtually wrap a package. The package is provided for you as an image on layers in a CorelDRAW document.

The following set of steps begins with importing A present.cpt, a layered PHOTO-PAINT image. You'll move the image's upper layer—the bow—to a new layer and then create an additional CorelDRAW layer to work below the bow but above the package to create a very effective illusion of gift wrap on the package.

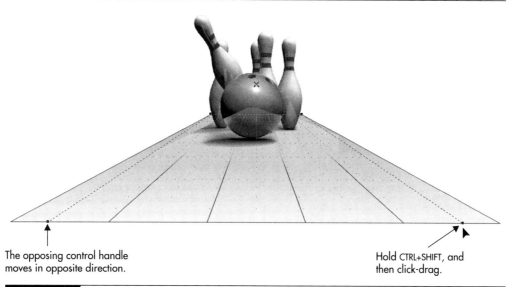

The opposing control handle
moves in opposite direction.

Hold CTRL+SHIFT, and
then click-drag.

FIGURE 18-5   Create symmetrical perspective by holding CTRL+SHIFT while you drag a
control handle.

Let's use CorelDRAW's Artistic media tool to create the gift wrap for the present in the
following steps. After completing the tutorial, you can use a design of your own with this
file in the future.

Pre-Visualizing a Design on a Product

1. After creating a new document (choose Landscape orientation), press CTRL+I to
   import A present.cpt. Just click at the upper left of the page to place it to size.

2. Open the Object Manager from the Tools menu. Expand the A present.cpt entry to
   reveal the two image layers. To retain your sanity dealing with these "Layer" default
   names, click the "Layer 1" bitmap name to select it, click it a second time to open
   the name for editing, and then type **Bow**, because it's the red bow on top of the
   present.

3. Click the New Layer button at the bottom left of the docker. Doing this creates a
   new default named "Layer 2."

18

4. Click-drag the "Bow" entry on the Object Manager, and place it on the Layer 2 title to move the bow image to the new layer.

5. Create a new layer, by default named "Layer 3." Click-drag it to below Layer 2. This is where you'll be designing the gift wrap.

6. Choose the Artistic media tool from the Pen tool group on the toolbox. Then choose the Sprayer button on the property bar. You can use any preset you like; one of the festive Food presets is shown in the following figures.

7. Create a rectangular area by scribbling up and down, like making several *W*s.

8. Choose Arrange | Break Artistic Media Apart (CTRL+K works, too). With the Pick tool, delete the parent black path that's now visible. See Figure 18-6.

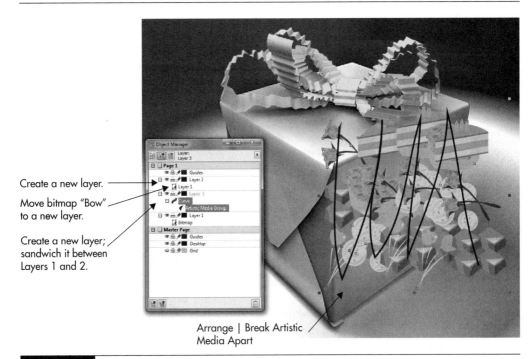

Create a new layer.

Move bitmap "Bow" to a new layer.

Create a new layer; sandwich it between Layers 1 and 2.

Arrange | Break Artistic Media Apart

FIGURE 18-6 Create a pattern with the Artistic media Sprayer tool.

9. Choose Effects | Add Perspective. With the Shape tool, drag, one at a time, the control handles for the effect to match the four corners of the face of the present, as shown here.

10. Duplicate the pattern (press CTRL+D), and then use the Shape tool to edit this duplicate (which also has the perspective effect applied) so it matches the four corners of the top side of the present. Because the bow is on the top layer, you're actually adding the top pattern in perspective below the bow so it looks optically correct.

11. Repeat step 10 to create the left panel of the pattern on the present.

12. The pattern shouldn't look totally opaque, but instead should take on a little of the shading on the blank present. The quickest way to apply transparency to the scores of objects that make up your artistic media stroke is to first turn it into a bitmap. First, let's check out the resolution of the present image so the conversion of the gift wrap pattern isn't unnecessarily larger than the present or bow images. Click either the Bitmap or the Bow entry on the Object Manager list, and then look at the status bar. The correct answer is 96 dpi.

18

13. Select one of the patterned sides, and then choose Bitmaps | Convert To Bitmap. In the Convert To Bitmap dialog Resolution box, choose 96. Check the Transparent Background check box and then click OK.

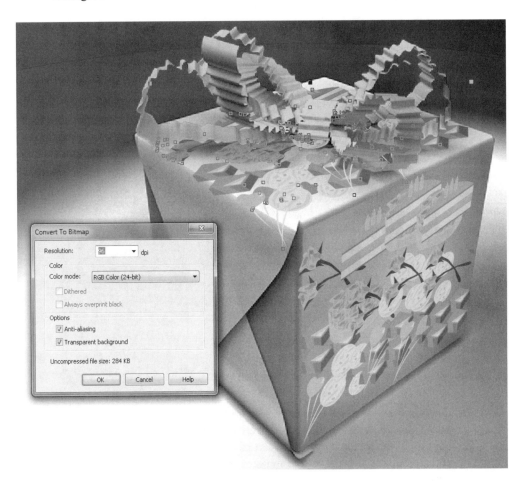

14. With the new bitmap selected, choose the Transparency tool on the toolbox. On the property bar, choose Uniform Transparency type, Multiply style, and then play with the amount of transparency your eye tells you looks best and that blends the pattern into the present. Repeat steps 13 and 14 with the other two sides of the gift, be sure to include a card, and then send it to someone who deserves a gift.

This finished pre-visualization provides you and your client with a view of the goods you've designed as they will appear from the customer's point of view, and perhaps this is the best "perspective" effect of all, as shown next.

You've seen in this chapter how to take a drawing, several objects, and even a complete design, and put a 3D spin on it. Perspective effects can help a client visualize what a design should look like when projected into real space, and at the least the perspective effect is a fun and quick method for embellishing a drawing that needs a "certain something" to lift it off the page. Chapter 19 takes you into a more complete visualization of 3D within a 2D drawing, as you explore the extrude effect in CorelDRAW. Bring along what you now know about vanishing points, and bring along an object or two that you want to add another dimension to—*literally*!

CHAPTER 19

Extruding Objects

Although CorelDRAW is a 2D vector drawing application, the extrude feature adds objects to create an illusion of a third dimension, one of depth. Depending on the intricacy of the parent object—and how you pose the object and light it—extruded objects can open up a whole new world of design opportunities and extend your style of illustration to present your audience with scenes they can step right into! This chapter takes you through the rich feature set of the Extrude tool, offers some creative possibilities for its use, and gets your head around the initial challenges of navigating 3D space in CorelDRAW.

 Download and extract all the files from the Chapter19.zip archive to follow the tutorials in this chapter.

How Extrude Works

CorelDRAW's extrude effect examines the geometry of an object, which can be a single or a compound path (two or more combined paths). Then, with your input, it creates extensions to all path segments, which are dynamic objects that are created to suggest that they recede into the distance to a vanishing point. (See Chapter 18 on perspective vanishing points.) Figure 19-1 is a rendered illustration of the 3D scene.cdr file, one of the several files you downloaded. By the end of this chapter, you'll know how to un-extrude the compositions, how these extrudes are designed, and how to create similar work. One thing to remember: even the most complex object you extrude probably won't convey a complete artistic idea— you need to use other CorelDRAW tools to complete a scene you're happy with. For example, the train composition uses *several* extruded objects, the toaster uses a Contour effect to create the shadow beneath the objects, and the tabletop was first created by extruding shapes, but then all the shadows you see were manually drawn on top of areas that look stark without a supporting shadow object here and there. The Extrude tool can get you 75 percent of the way you want to go with design, but you need to be imaginative to place the extruded object in context, within a scene, to build a complete graphical idea. That's what the *rest* of this book is for!

When an extrude effect is applied to an object, the original becomes a *control object,* and the extrude effect objects become a dynamically linked group. Any editing you then perform on the properties of the control object, such as fills and edits to the outline of the control object, are immediately updated in the linked extrude group. The extrude group itself can also be modified in ways that increase the intricacy and photorealism of the effect; you can change the depth, color, lighting, and rotation of the extrude effect.

Be aware that both lighting and the control object's geometry have an impact on how many extrude group objects are created. Although you don't usually need to concern yourself with how many objects are dynamically created to make an extrude, the sheer number of objects can slow down redraws of your page when you have, for example, hundreds of objects in the extrude group. When CorelDRAW creates an extrude group, it calculates lighting (when you *use* lighting, covered later in this chapter) and creates extrude

FIGURE 19-1   Imagine what an object looks like when projected into a third dimension, and then manually add what's missing from your complete idea.

group objects based on curved path segments in the control object. Here you can see a star-shaped control object with lighting; the object has a Radial fountain fill, and it's an interesting design in Enhanced view. At right, the page is viewed in Wireframe, and 48 objects are grouped in the extrude effect.

Extrude on straight path shape,
with lighting, Enhanced view

Wireframe view, 48
extrude group objects

19

Here, a much more complex control object is used for an extrude. It not only is a compound path, but also its path segments are curved. In Wireframe view it's evident that the extrude group is composed of more objects than the star-shaped extrude. No lighting is used in the extrude effect, which in turn limits the number of extrude group objects CorelDRAW has to create, and it is a fairly interesting design.

Extruded object with flat fill

Wireframe view, 118 extrude group objects

If lighting is now applied, you can see that the number of extrude control objects created to represent the curved paths with added lighting is an order of magnitude more. This *isn't* a warning to fellow Corellians to limit the intricacy of extrude objects you design, but rather a point of information. If you own a video card with lots of RAM yet suddenly find you're getting slow screen redraws, consider going to a less refined view such as Normal or Draft via the View menu. Also consider reading "Simplifying an Extrude" later in this chapter. CorelDRAW uses fountain fills for extrude objects on two occasions:

- When the control curve (the parent object) has a fountain fill and your Color setting for the extrude shapes is set to Object Fill.

- When you use the Color Shading setting for extrude objects.

Either of these conditions not only can create a lot of extrude shapes, but each shape also has a more complex fill than Uniform color. As you learn to create elegant extrude objects, consider these two circumstances if you're not printing the objects as seen on your monitor (you might not have enough printer memory), or if your screen redraws are slower than you expect (you're commanding too many operations).

Extrude on curved path shape, with lighting, Enhanced view

Wireframe view, 890 extrude group objects

Choosing and Applying an Extrude Effect

The extrude effect can be applied interactively using the Extrude tool, located in the toolbox with other effects tools, or you can choose from the Presets list to instantly create a 3D object.

While you're using this tool, the property bar provides all the extrude options for setting the properties of the effect. Browse the property bar options, as shown in Figure 19-2. Options are grouped into areas for saving your applied extrusions as Presets, controlling the shape, depth, vanishing point position, rotation, lighting, color, and bevel effects.

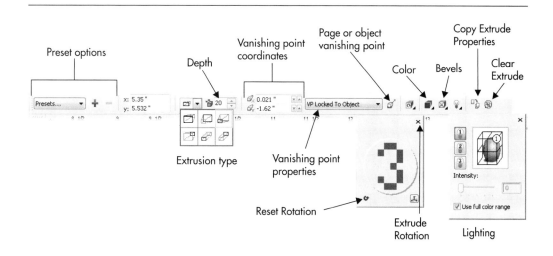

FIGURE 19-2   The property bar holds all the options for defining and saving the look of an extrude.

19

NOTE	*This happens to almost all CorelDRAW users: you've made only one copy of an object you've extruded, and now that you've extruded and rotated it, you want to save a copy of the object in its original form—not extruded, and not distorted or rotated. Do* not *copy and paste the Control Curve; doing this does not return it to its original orientation on the page. Instead, make a copy of the entire extrude group, double-click the group using the Pick tool to display Extrude options on the property bar, click the Extrude Rotation button, click the Reset Rotation icon at bottom left, and then click the Clear Extrude button on the property bar. Your original shape now contains the same number of nodes, the same curve segments, and the same color.*

Navigating the Interactive Markers

When you decide to manually extrude a shape, interactive markers appear around the resulting object after you perform the first step in an extrude: you click-drag the face of the object you want to be the control object. The interactive markers offer you control over the position, depth, and vanishing point position for the 3D object. You'll be creating a 3D object by hand in the following tutorial, so it's good to familiarize yourself now with the elements that surround a 3D extruded shape, as shown in Figure 19-3.

Vanishing point marker

Extrude outline preview

Extrude group

Depth slider

Extrude Tool cursor

Center marker   Original object

FIGURE 19-3   These control handles are used after an object is initially extruded, to change the appearance of the extrude.

Alternatively, you can apply a Preset extrude effect to receive a 3D version of a shape in lightning time; however, you might want hands-on control over the creation of an extrude effect. Follow this tutorial to get a handle on what some of the property bar options do to an extrude effect; in no time, you'll be able to "sculpt" whatever you envision as a scene that has objects with depth.

Getting Deep with the Extrude Tool

1. Create an object to be the control object for the extrude. A rectangle will produce results that make the relationship between the face of the object and the sides very clear, but not very artistic unless you're into cubism. Try a star shape for more dramatic extrude results. Give the shape a fill (a fountain fill will produce a stunning effect), and give the outline a contrasting color such as white so you can visually track where the extrude objects are created.

2. Choose the Extrude tool, and your cursor changes to the Extrude Tool cursor, hard to mistake for the Pick or a pen tool. When held over your object, the cursor indicates a start extrude position by using a tiny shape with a direction line below the symbol of an extruded cube.

3. Drag from the center of your object outward in any direction, but don't release the mouse button. The control object now has interactive markers and a wireframe preview of the front and back boundaries of the extrude, the front of the object is bound by a red outline, and the back of the 3D shape is bound by a blue outline. The preview indicates the length and direction of the extrude effect and the X symbol you're dragging is the *vanishing point.* As discussed in Chapter 18, a vanishing point is a geometric indicator of where parallel lines on a surface would converge at the horizon if the surface actually were to extend into the horizon.

4. Drag the vanishing point X symbol around the page; not only does the preview outline change, but more importantly, the view on the 3D object also changes. When the vanishing point is above the control object, you're looking down on the object; similarly, you move your view to expose the side of an object in direct correlation to the position of the vanishing point.

5. As you use the Extrude tool, you define both the direction of the 3D object and the depth. Try dragging the Depth slider toward and then away from the control object. Notice how you first make the extrude a shallow one, and then a deeper one, all the while the sides extend in the direction of the vanishing point. At any time from when you create the object by releasing the cursor, you can also set the object depth by using the depth spin box on the property bar.

6. Click outside of the object, and the extrude operation is complete. However, because extrude is a *dynamic* effect, you can change the appearance of the extrude at any time in the future by double-clicking either the extrude group or the control object with the Pick tool to once again display the interactive handles.

19

Using the Extrude Tool and Property Bar

Like other effects, extrusions can be set using the property bar. Using the Extrude tool, you'll see several cursor states depending on where the cursor is, which indicate what operation can be performed at any given point on the extrude group. Let's take a look at the different cursors and what they indicate in the following sections.

Interactive Extrude Tool States

The Extrude Tool cursor, shown here, changes appearance based on what it's over in your document. When the cursor is held over an object that can be extruded, the cursor features a start symbol. If an object cannot be extruded, the cursor features the international "No" (⊘) symbol. Most shapes you draw with the pen tools except artistic media can be extruded. If you have your heart set on extruding artistic media strokes, the strokes need to be first broken from the control path (CTRL+K) and then grouped; bitmaps cannot be extruded at all (but the 3D effects on the Bitmaps menu can be used to make perspective and emboss effects). You can only extrude one object at a time: you'll get the "No Can Do" cursor if you select more than one object and then try to use the tool. Grouped objects can be successfully extruded; however, you can no longer ungroup them—you need to clear the extrude before you can select and edit only one of the group.

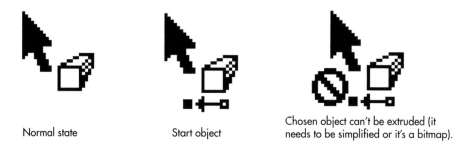

| Normal state | Start object | Chosen object can't be extruded (it needs to be simplified or it's a bitmap). |

TIP *Objects you want to extrude don't have to be filled. You can create interesting wireframes similar to those you'd see in a technical drawing by extruding objects that have an outline width but no fill.*

Setting Extrusion Shape

The Extrusion Type selector, shown next, offers six different shape types with which you can control both the direction of the extrude and whether you need wide-angle, small perspective, or totally isometric (no perspective) 3D objects. Depending on the type you choose, your extrusion can extend toward the back or front relative to the control object. Choosing a front style causes the vanishing point to project from the front of your object; choosing a back style does the opposite. Because you're working with geometric solids, when you choose a back style, the direction of the extrude will looked mirrored, although in wireframe view it's clear that the object inverted itself, its back side projecting forward instead of into the distance. Icons in the selector indicate each shape type, with the darkened outline indicating your original object. Here are examples of the six different perspectives, which were created in order from the selector; see how the selector icons fairly represent each style.

Small Back   Small Front   Big Back

Big Front   Front Parallel

Back Parallel

- **Small Back**   This option (the default setting) causes the extrusion and vanishing point to be layered behind your original object. Small Back is perhaps the most commonly applied extrusion type.

- **Small Front**   This causes the extrusion and vanishing point to be layered in front of your original object.

- **Big Back**   This option causes the extrusion to be layered behind your original object, while the vanishing point is in front.

- **Big Front**   This causes the extrusion to be layered in front of your original object, while the vanishing point is in back.

19

- **Front Parallel**   This causes the extrusion to be layered in front of your object so that the extruded surfaces appear parallel to the original surfaces. When this option is selected, the vanishing point sets the depth of the extrusion, while the actual depth option is unavailable. It's interesting to note that if you light a Back Parallel and a Front Parallel extrude with the same light setup, the two extrude groups appear to be lit differently.

- **Back Parallel**   This option causes the extrusion to be layered behind your original object so that the extruded surfaces appear parallel to the original surfaces. When this option is selected, the vanishing point sets the depth of the extrusion, while the actual depth option is unavailable. No true vanishing point is used in this style.

Setting Extrude Depth

Extrude Depth is based on the distance between the control object and the vanishing point. You will get different appearances using the same Depth value but different styles, and Extrude Depth can be set as high as 99. Figure 19-4 shows a shallow and a deep extrude, using two different Depth values but the same extrude style. You can control object depth manually by dragging the interactive depth slider on top of the object, or enter values in the num box on the property bar (press ENTER after typing a value; the spin box controls update the object without the need to press ENTER).

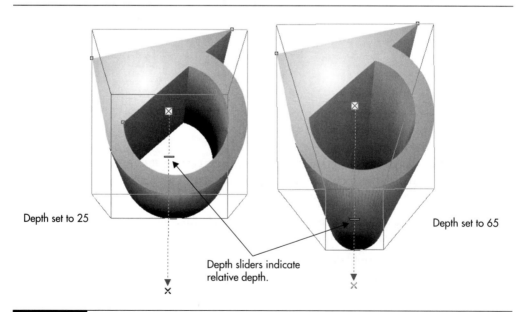

Depth set to 25

Depth set to 65

Depth sliders indicate relative depth.

FIGURE 19-4   Go for the subtle—or the dramatic—by changing the Depth setting on the extrude effect control object.

Setting Vanishing Point Properties

The direction of the vanishing point determines only the point toward which objects diminish; it does not control whether the extruded portion extends from the front or back of the object.

Vanishing points can be set on four of the six extrusion styles: Small Back, Big Back, Small Front, and Big Front. The sides of the extruded portions created in the Front Parallel or Back Parallel types never converge; these are isometric views, and therefore there is no horizon, so no vanishing point.

Using the property bar options shown here, you can lock an extrusion's vanishing point, copy vanishing points from an existing extrusion, and share vanishing points between extruded objects.

Here are the options for vanishing points—how they can be set and shared between different extruded objects:

- **Locking to the object**   Choosing the VP Locked To Object option (the default setting) fixes the vanishing point to a position relative to the object, regardless of where the original extruded object is positioned.

- **Locking to the page**   VP Locked To Page offers the option to tack the vanishing point to your page, forcing the extrusion to diminish toward a fixed page position, no matter where the original object is moved. Try this out to see for yourself the worth of this setting: lock the vanishing point of an extruded object to the page, and then move the object; you'll see that the sides of the extrude dynamically update to always show the correct perspective of the object.

- **Copying VP from**   Copying a vanishing point by using the Copy VP From command lets you set up several extruded objects on a page; in a few clicks the objects all appear to be facing the same direction, at a common point of view from the audience's perspective. Immediately after you choose Copy VP From, your cursor changes to a vanishing point targeting cursor (a really, really large arrow), which you use to target any other extruded object on your document page, with the

19

goal of copying its vanishing point position. For this command to be successful, you must have at least one other extrude effect applied to an object and in view. After the vanishing point has been copied, the property bar indicates the object's vanishing point as VP Locked To Page.

- **Sharing vanishing points** Choosing Shared Vanishing Point enables you to have multiple objects share the *same* vanishing point, but you must have applied at least an initial extrude effect to your objects before using this command. Immediately after you choose this option, your cursor changes to a vanishing point targeting cursor, which signifies that you now target any other extruded object for the purpose of creating a common vanishing point position for multiple objects. This creates a similar effect to copying vanishing points, but the overall effect is that every object on the page is in the same scene. The objects are positioned in different areas, but it's one big, visually integrated scene. Shared Vanishing Point can be repeated for as many objects as you like. When multiple objects share a vanishing point, they can be repositioned anywhere on your document page, and the perspective on the 3D object updates to maintain the relationship of a common vanishing point. Figure 19-5 shows the results of setting up a shared vanishing point arrangement with four objects. The figure has been retouched (you can't view more than one vanishing point at a time) to show the converging point for all the objects' sides, their depth aspect.

- **Setting a relative position for vanishing points** The Page or Object vanishing point option in the property bar is used to toggle the measurement state of object vanishing points between page and object. While the option is inactive (meaning the button is not depressed), the vanishing point position boxes enable you to specify the vanishing point relative to your page origin—a value determined either by the lower-left corner by default or by the zero markers on your ruler origin. While the option is active (the button is depressed), the center of your currently selected object is used as the measurement value, which changes according to the object's page position. You will see this most noticeably if you have a depth on an object of more than 40 and drag the object around the page with the Pick tool. The extrude group actually changes to reflect different vanishing point views.

Setting 3D Rotation

Until now, the extrudes you've created and read about have been based on the control object facing you; this is a good beginning point in your 3D experience, but it's not always the most visually interesting of poses for your 3D objects. You can rotate extruded objects; the extrude group follows and aligns perfectly with the control object, and you have two ways to perform 3D extrude rotations: via the property bar and with the interactive control handles. Create an extrude group of objects, and then let's begin with the precise, noninteractive method of rotation you access through the property bar when the Extrude tool is chosen and an object is selected.

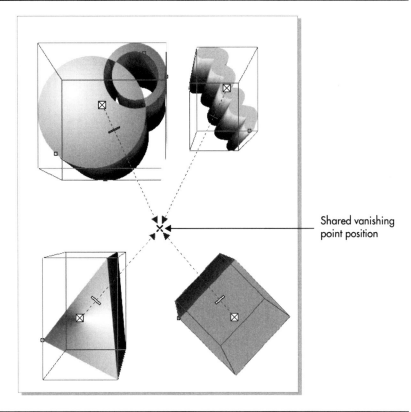

FIGURE 19-5   These four objects share the same vanishing point, applied using the Shared Vanishing Point command.

The Rotation pop-up menu offers a proxy box that you use by click-dragging on the *3,* as shown next. As you drag, a very faint yellow line appears on the *3,* indicating the current rotation of the object and the proposed new rotation once you release the mouse button. You might not always get the exact look you need using this technique because of the position of the object's vanishing point—your experience can be similar to levering an object seesaw-fashion when the pivot point (the fulcrum) is 15 miles away! To avoid imprecision, you can click the toggle button labeled in the next illustration to move to a number field display of the X, Y, and Z rotational values (see the following sidebar). The value fields have spin box controls that increase and decrease the values by 5; you probably want to enter values manually, because a single degree of rotation can be quite significant, considering only 201 of them are in this pop-up box. If at any time you've gotten too deep in this 3D rotation

19

stuff, clicking the "undo" curved arrow icon on the lower left of the selector, shown here, resets all rotation values to zero.

Extrude Rotation button

Drag

Resets rotation to zero

Toggle display in selector

Rotational Directions in 3D Space

The creative rewards of knowing how to extrude and rotate objects in CorelDRAW require that you learn how to navigate in 3D space as you would in any true modeling program such as Cinema 4D, Poser, or 3D Studio. Directions in space are measured much the same as on a CorelDRAW page: positive X values (measuring width) move to the right, positive Y values (height) travel bottom to top, and the values of depth (Z) travel from back to front. Rotation direction travels positive in a counterclockwise direction, and this might take some familiarization to better use your time. Fortunately, you have an excellent mnemonic device at hand, literally, *your right hand.*

Modeling usually uses the right-hand coordinate system: stand in front of a mirror if you don't want your hand to cramp, face your palm upward, and then extend your forefinger to your right. This is the X measurement of 3D space, and X rotation travels counterclockwise around your forefinger. Now point your middle finger straight up to indicate the positive motion along the Y axis. The rotation of an object along Y is also counterclockwise. Point your thumb at yourself. Z motion travels toward you, and rotation along Z is counterclockwise, following the curl of your fingers.

Therefore, when you want to rotate a CorelDRAW extruded object so its top is leaning toward you, this is the X axis, your forefinger. You enter positive values in the

X field in the pop-up box. If you want the left side of the extruded object to face you, this is your middle finger, and you enter positive Y values in the pop-up box, as shown in this illustration.

Overall, the best teacher is experience, particularly with manipulating your view of a 3D object in CorelDRAW. Set aside some quality time, and you might even be pleasantly surprised by some of your errors!

Using the Rotation Tools

You don't have to use the rotation pop-up box on the property bar to rotate an extruded object: you can define a degree of rotation along the X, Y, and Z axes of any object by click-dragging the object directly. To do some manual rotation, the object needs to be extruded and first put into Editing mode—you can double-click on the extrude group of objects with the Pick tool to put the object into Editing mode, and then a second click exposes the control handles shown here. Before you leap in, read on for an explanation of what the interactive controls do and what you do with them to achieve the desired result.

X and Y axis rotation cursor

Rotation reference markers

Circular (Z axis) rotation cursor

Extrude vanishing point marker

X axis rotation cursor

Y axis rotation cursor

NOTE *While either Back Parallel or Front Parallel is selected, extrude rotation controls are unavailable; parallel extrusions have no vanishing point, so there's nothing to pivot with. Also, when the vanishing point is locked to the page, extrude rotation cannot be performed.*

TIP *When an object is rotated, the vanishing point controls on the property bar cannot be used, mostly because mathematically, the vanishing point is nowhere near your drawing page! If you need to adjust the vanishing point of an object, you must work backwards; on the Extrude Rotation pop-up panel on the property bar, click the Reset Rotation icon. Then the vanishing point options and controls become active (and your object is no longer rotated).*

Rotating an Extrude Effect

Because a rotated extrude graphically describes an object more completely than a face-front view, the following tutorial will come in handy when you've extruded an object that has some built-in visual interest. Extrude something interesting now, and let's take the manual, interactive rotation feature out for a spin.

Putting a New Spin on an Extruded Object

1. With the Pick tool, double-click the extrude group or the control object, to expose the editing handles. Alternatively, you can use the Interactive extrude tool to select the object, and it's immediately put into Editing mode.

2. Single-click the *extruded* portion a second time. The interactive rotation markers appear, and circular guides surround the effect. The inside and outside areas of this circular area determine the tool's cursor state.

3. Move the cursor outside of the green dashed circle, and notice that it changes to the rotation cursor. This cursor is used to rotate the face of the object, the Z axis, counterclockwise and clockwise. Dragging right and down creates a clockwise rotation, and left and up rotates the face of the object counterclockwise.

4. Move the cursor inside the green dashed circle area, and it changes to the X/Y axis rotation cursor. Using this cursor is a lot like using an onscreen trackball; you just drag in any direction to simultaneously rotate the X and Y axes of the extrude object. It's fun, you can see the vanishing point move to reflect the new aspect of the object, and it's also not as precise as it could be when you only want to, for example, rotate the object along the top-to-bottom (Y) axis.

5. Release the mouse button for a moment and then hold CTRL. Then click-drag upward (downward is okay, too); you're now constraining rotation to the X axis of the object.

6. Release the mouse button again and then hold CTRL. Now click-drag left or right; you're constraining rotation to the Y axis of the object and not touching the X axis rotation.

7. When the amusement has worn thin or your task is accomplished, click a blank space on the document page way outside of the interactive rotational cursor area to deselect the effect. The cursor returns to the normal extrude cursor state. You've just completed manually rotating an extrude object.

NOTE *After an extrude effect has been rotated, you can still adjust the extrude depth of the effect, but not the vanishing points.*

Adding Lights

Adding lighting to an extruded object can spell the difference between an effect and a piece of artwork that truly attracts a viewer with its realistic appearance; many of the figures in

19

this chapter use the Lighting option. To access the lighting controls, click the Extrude Lighting button on the property bar while an extrude effect is selected, as shown here:

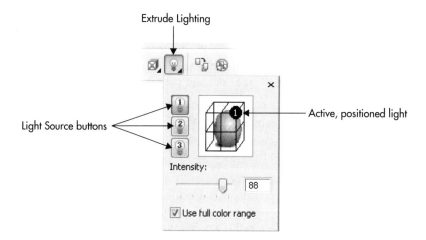

Working with the Options in the Lighting Control Window

Three independent light sources can be activated, positioned, and adjusted for intensity and for whether all of the control object's colors are used in the extrude group (the Use Full Color Range option). These lights are unidirectional; they can be positioned, but not aimed as you would a real flashlight or spotlight. Light intensity is set on a light-by-light basis between 0 and 100 percent by using the slider control when each is selected. One of the nice things about setting up light intensity and position is that response is immediate—there is no Apply button, and your object's light changes as you make changes in the control window.

When you first open the Extrude Lighting control window, all lights are inactive. To activate a light, click one of the three Light Source buttons—the numbering is for your reference; it's just a label. There is nothing special about light 3 versus light 1, for example, in any of its properties. Once a light button is clicked, a circle with the light's number inside appears in the front, upper-right position on a 3D grid surrounding a sphere, which represents the extrude object (see Figure 19-6). The lights themselves aren't visible on the drawing page, but the lighting effect you define displays highlights and shaded areas on your extrude object, particularly evident when the sides of the control object are curved. The light sources can be posed by adding them to the grid and then dragging them—there are 16 possible positions for lights; some of the positions can create very interesting "edge lighting" on your object.

Every time you activate a new light, it appears on the grid in the default position of front, top, right. This means that if you click to activate two or three Light Source buttons in succession without first moving them, you'll stack them on top of each other and wind up with one extremely intense light source on the object. When this happens, drag the individual lights to reposition them at different points.

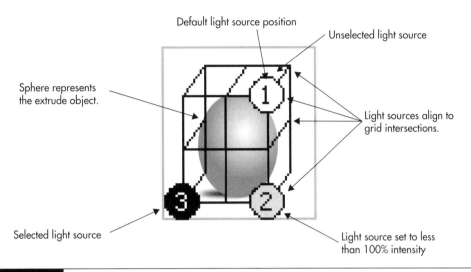

Default light source position

Unselected light source

Sphere represents
the extrude object.

Light sources align to
grid intersections.

Selected light source

Light source set to less
than 100% intensity

FIGURE 19-6   The 3D grid represents light positions relative to the selected extrude object.

A *selected* light is shown as a black circle in the preview; unselected lights are shown as white circles. Lights set to brightness levels less than 100 percent appear in shades of gray. As these light sources are dragged around the 3D grid, they automatically snap to line-intersection points on the grid. You cannot position lights at the back-mid-center or back-center-bottom position, but this is not really a creative limitation, because lights in these positions would not significantly contribute to the shading of the extrude shape.

 NOTE   *There is no option to set the color of lights; all lights cast white. If you want a spotlight effect, read Chapter 22 on lens effects for techniques on shading objects with color.*

Adding and Editing Extrude Lights

The following tutorial obliges you to put on your stagehand cap as you work the lights in a scene, adding them to the extrude object's properties and learning how to position them and turn the wattage up and down.

 ## Working with Extrude Light Options

1. Create a color-filled object and apply an extrude effect to it.

2. Using the Interactive extrude tool, click the Extrude Lighting selector in the property bar to open the Light Source option.

19

3. Click the Light Source 1 button, and a light source symbol appears in the upper-right-front corner of the grid, shown as a black circle numbered *1*. The Intensity slider becomes active; Light Source 1 is now active, and the colors of your extrude effect are altered (brightened and possibly a little washed-out) to reflect the new light's contribution to the extrude effect.

4. Drag the symbol representing Light Source 1 to a different position on the 3D grid; notice how the coloring of the effect changes in response to the new lighting position.

5. With Light Source 1 still selected, drag the Intensity slider to the left approximately to the 50% position, and notice how the color of the object becomes darker and more saturated.

6. Click the Light Source 2 button to activate it. Notice that it appears in the same default position as the first light source, and the symbol representing Light Source 1 is gray, indicating that it is not selected and it is not at 100% Intensity. When an unselected light is at 100% Intensity, the symbol is white. Drag Light Source 2 to a different grid position—in classic scene lighting, a secondary light of, say, 50% of the main light's intensity, is usually positioned directly opposite the main light to make objects look rounder, deeper, and overall more flattering with more visible detail than using only one light source.

7. Click the activation buttons for Light Sources 1 and 2 to toggle them off, and the color of the extrude object returns to its original state. To finish editing lights, click anywhere outside the Extrude Lighting selector.

Occasionally in your design work, you might like the perspective you've created for the face of an extrude object, but might not need the extruded side, the extrude group of objects. You can remove an extrude effect from an object and keep its perspective and position on the page by clicking on the extruded portion of the effect and choosing Effects | Clear Extrude. You can also use the Interactive extrude tool by clicking the Clear Extrude button in the property bar.

Controlling Light Properties

Two additional options available when you're using lighting have the following effects on your extrusion:

- **Lighting intensity** As mentioned in the previous tutorial, the Intensity slider determines the brightness of each light. While a light is selected, the range can be set between 0 and 100%; higher values cause brighter lighting.

- **Full color range**   Below the Intensity slider you'll find the Use Full Color Range option, which directs your display to use the full *gamut* of colors when coloring the surfaces of your original object and its extruded portion. Gamut is the expressible range of colors available to CorelDRAW, which depends on the color mode (see Chapter 17) of the original object and the extrusion. When working in CMYK process or RGB color, you might find the shading on an object to have too much contrast; the lighting might look too harsh and might create washed-out surfaces. The remedy then is to uncheck Use Full Color Range; the gamut of colors is then limited, and the dynamic range of available colors becomes narrower. You just might wind up seeing areas that are hidden in deeply shaded zones when Use Full Color Range is not checked.

Setting Extrude Color

In addition to shading an extrude group using lighting, you can further embellish and draw out photorealistic qualities by using color options for the extrude. You might need to perform some technical illustration with extrude objects, and you might need cross-hatching in addition to lighting, for example. This is when you turn to the Extrusion Color option on the property bar; you have three different ways to shade an extrude group: object fill color, solid color, or color shading (much like a fountain fill transition from one color to a different color).

In the Color control window, shown next, you can see the various modes you can use when you click the property bar Extrusion Color button.

Object Fill   Solid Color   Color Shading

19

You can achieve effects that range from flat, technical illustrations to highly polished metallic surfaces—which actually can work on their own without the need for lighting the object—and it all depends on the choices you make on the Color control window:

● **Using an object's fill** The Use Object Fill option is the most straightforward to use, but it does not automatically create any sort of shading—if you choose to use the default object fill and the object is filled with a uniform color, it's usually a good idea to give the control object an outline width whose color contrasts against the object fill color. When Use Object Fill is selected, the Drape Fills option also becomes available (and is selected automatically). Drape Fills is discussed shortly; here is an example of a fountain-filled control object, with and without Drape Fills.

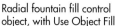

Radial fountain fill control
object, with Use Object Fill

Radial fountain fill control object,
with Use Object Fill, Drape Fills

● **Choosing your own solid fill** Choose Use Solid Color to set any uniform color to the extrude portion of your effect, regardless of the fill type currently applied to your object. The secondary color option becomes available only when Use Color Shading is selected.

 TIP *If an object has no outline width/color applied, it might be difficult to see the edges between the original and extruded portions. Applying an outline to your original object might help define the edges of overall composition.*

● **Using color shading** Choose Use Color Shading to add depth by using your object's color as the From color and using black (by default) as the To color. If the object to which you've applied your extrude effect is already filled with a fountain fill, Use Color Shading is selected automatically. Visual separation between the extrude group objects and the suggestion of depth is easy to create using color shading.

Extrude color applied with
Use Solid Color option

Extrude color applied with
Use Color Shading option

- **Draping your object's fill over the extrude effect** *Draping,* as used in CorelDRAW's extrude effect, means, "treat each extrude group object's fill as a unique item." Say, for example, you have a patterned piece of cloth and you drape it over a coffee table: you will see discontinuity in the pattern as each angle of the folds of cloth travels in different directions in 3D space. Similarly, draping creates discontinuity in a pattern and fountain fill you apply to both the control object and the extrude group of objects, as shown in Figure 19-7. At left, with Drape Fills enabled, the polka dot shape (with some lighting applied) truly looks dimensional, even though the two-color bitmap fill doesn't change perspective (bitmap fills do not take on the rotation angle of extrude objects; they're always face forward). At right, with Drape Fills turned off, the pattern proceeds across the object and the extrude group of objects in a continuous pattern, as though it's *projected* on the surface of the shape instead of *being* the surface of the shape.

CAUTION *Drape fills can be artistically ineffective when your control object has a lot of nodes and curve segments. If an extrude yields a lot of facets, consider using a shading other than Drape Fills.*

- **Using bevel color** This option becomes available only if you've applied the Bevel effect to an extruded shape. Bevel options are located on the Bevels selector in the property bar (covered in the next section). This is an important option to enable when your object and its child extrude group have a fountain or bitmap pattern fill. Enabling Drape Fills does to the bevel edges what Drape Fills does to the extrude group—it breaks up the pattern continuity, which in turn makes the overall object more realistic in appearance.

19

With Drape Fills
Pattern is discontinuous (looks realistic).

Without Drape Fills
Pattern is continuous (looks hokey).

FIGURE 19-7 The Drape Fills options can make or break the realism you're trying to illustrate.

 To detach an extrude effect, right-click the extrude group and choose Break Extrude Group Apart. This breaks the link between your original and its effect portion, making it a separate group that can be further broken down using the Ungroup command (CTRL+U). The result is that the control object adopts the perspective of the extrude effect; you can independently edit all objects for color and outline properties, and do some editing to manually increase the realism of your composition—some examples are shown at the end of this chapter. This is a destructive *edit, be forewarned, and the only way to reverse the process is via the Undo docker or by pressing CTRL+Z.*

Speak of the Bevel!

Bevels in the real world are the flattened edges where two planes meet on furniture to give it an ornamental look, to make the furniture safer for kids romping around the living room, and to make furniture more expensive. Similarly, the Bevel option in CorelDRAW's extrude effect creates new objects, in perspective, that join the face and sides of an extrude object.

Bevel effects are built to put a cap on the front end of the control object. Therefore, if an extrude is defined using a style that projects from front to back, the bevel is created as a group of objects facing you. However, if you choose the Small Front style, the bevel will go to the back face of the object, and without rotating the object the bevel will be hidden from view. Bevel shape is based on the angle and depth defined using the Extrusion Bevels button, shown here:

- **Using bevels**   The Use Bevel option causes the bevel effect to become active and makes available the remaining options in the control window. Bevel effects can be used only after an extrude effect has been applied.

- **Showing bevels only**   You might want not the extruded side but only the bevel effect of an object to be visible; this is a quick and easy way to make a fancy, engraved headline from artistic text. Choose the Show Bevel Only check box, and the extrude for the selected object is hidden, but can be restored at any future time by unchecking this box. You can rotate an object that has a Bevel effect, but the extrude parts are hidden.

- **Setting bevel shapes**   The Bevel Depth and Bevel Angle options can be defined by entering values in the corresponding fields on the Bevel pop-up on the property bar; you can also click-drag in the proxy window to interactively define the angle and depth. Bevel Depth can be set between 0.001 inch and 1,980 inches. Bevel Angle may be set to a maximum of 89°. Shallow angles of less than 30° often provide the best visual results. At significant depths, you might get self-intersections in the bevel because control objects that have sharp curves along the path segments are difficult for the bevel effect to reconcile mathematically. If you see a "bad" self-intersecting area, try reducing the Bevel Depth and/or changing the angle. Figure 19-8 shows the results of applying a bevel effect with and without an extrude effect involved.

19

Original extrude

Extrude effect with
bevel applied

Show Bevel Only
option selected

FIGURE 19-8   The shape of a bevel is determined by Bevel Depth and Bevel Angle.

Simplifying an Extrude

If you've created an extrude group you really like but clearly you can see that it's
made up of scores of shapes and you're experiencing a problem working with the file
due to the sheer number of objects, you can perform some *editing*.

At the heart of any extrude group, as with any dimensional piece of artwork, lies
color at any given point, and a geometry that supports colors. You'd be surprised at
how few objects that use fountain fills or even uniform fills can be used to substitute
for the scores of shaded objects that make up a bevel and the extrude side of an
extrude group. Open Simplified.cdr (Figure 19-9); the extrude group at left is made up
of 105 individual objects. At right, the extruded circle missing a notch is represented
almost identically by using 7 objects. Actually, the gradient on the object at right is
smoother because its shading is represented by a fountain fill and not by dozens of
individually colored shapes.

To edit an extrude group such as this one, you first make a duplicate. Then you
press CTRL+K to break apart the duplicate so it's no longer a dynamic extrude effect
but is now a collection of objects. With your choice of pen tools, you trace over the
perimeter of a group of objects used in the extrude, and then assign it a fountain fill
using multiple steps (covered in Chapter 15). It helps to move groups of extrude
objects to a new layer, because when you ungroup them to keep only certain shapes,
you'll wind up with a *lot* of unwanted objects. However, editing an extrude group
down to its essentials and replacing objects is not time-consuming if you're
experienced in drawing new shapes, and this practice also puts a little more of your
artistic ingenuity into the process of creating great designs.

105 objects   7 objects

FIGURE 19-9   Simplify an extrude group to make it look more the way you want it, and to make it easier to print and export.

Using Vector Extrude Presets

You might spend an hour or two creating the exact extrude effect you've envisioned, and naturally it would be nice to save the parameters you've defined to later apply them to other objects. When the Extrude tool is active, you have an area on the property bar for applying factory-designed presets as well as for saving and ditching presets, as shown in Figure 19-10.

Extrude presets are used the same way as all other CorelDRAW presets. You can save and reapply them to any object that qualifies for the effect (in other words, no artistic media, bitmaps, or objects that have an incompatible effect already in place). If you've never used extrude presets or any other preset options before, do not pass "Go," collect your wits, and move on to the following tutorial.

19

Click to add selected extrude effect as a preset.

Click to delete selected extrude preset in list.

Extrude Presets list

Preview of selected preset

Sample extrude added to Presets list

Target with applied preset

FIGURE 19-10 Use these options to save your extrude properties as presets.

 ## Working with Extrude Preset Options

1. If you've already designed an extrude group, make sure the object you're going to save as an extrude preset looks good, because when you save it, CorelDRAW builds a full-color preview thumbnail.

2. If you're just starting and want to try out a factory preset, select an object and then choose the Extrude tool.

3. Using the property bar, choose an extrude effect from the extrude Presets list. The properties of the extrude effect are immediately applied, and its properties are shown on the property bar.

4. To save an existing extrude as a preset, select the extrude group (not the control object), and then click the Add Preset (+) button. The Save As dialog opens. Enter a name for your new preset in the File Name box, then click Save, and your extrude preset is added to the Presets list.

5. To delete an extrude preset, while no object is selected, choose the preset from the Presets list and then click the Delete Preset button (–) in the property bar. The saved preset is immediately deleted, and there is no Undo command for this operation.

Using the Extrude Docker

If you're a longtime CorelDRAW user, you may have grown accustomed to applying extrude effects using a docker; new users will probably find the interactive editing methods and the options on the property bar to be more convenient to access, but the extrude docker is available via Window | Dockers | Extrude. The Extrude docker is organized into five areas: Camera (referring to shape), Rotation, Light, Color, and Bevels, as shown here.

Copying and Cloning Extrude Effects

As with other effects in CorelDRAW, you can copy or clone from existing extrusions. Neither operation requires the Extrude tool; both are accomplished by using menu commands.

When copying an extrude effect, at least one extrude effect must be in view, and at least one object must be selected. To copy an extrude effect, choose Effects | Copy Effect | Extrude From. The cursor becomes a targeting cursor (the large right-facing arrow guy). Use this cursor to indicate to CorelDRAW the extrude portion of an existing extrude effect to copy all applied extrude properties. If you're using the Extrude tool, you can also copy the effect by clicking the Copy Extrude Properties button on the property bar and then clicking to target an existing extrusion.

Cloning an extrude effect produces a slightly different result. When an effect is applied through cloning, the master clone effect object controls the new effect. Any changes made to the master are immediately applied to the clone. To clone an extrude effect, you must have created at least one other extrude effect and have this object in view. You must also have at least one object selected onscreen.

To clone an extrude effect, choose Effects | Clone Effect | Extrude From. Your cursor becomes a targeting cursor. You then click the existing extrude effect you want to clone by clicking directly on the extrude group portion of the effect. The clone effect is not the same as Edit | Clone. Effects | Clone Effect | Extrude From creates a clone object based on the shape of your choice, while Edit | Clone creates a daughter object without the need for an existing object to select from.

Although these options are organized differently from the property bar, all the options are there. Using the docker method for extruding objects lets you choose extrude settings before applying them.

Controlling Extrude Complexity Using Facet Size

When you apply the Use Color Shading option, the smooth curves and shading that are the visual result require complex calculations and produce a large number of extrude group objects to maintain curve smoothness. The smoother the curve and shading, the better the display and print quality.

When CorelDRAW creates an extrusion, the smoothness of curves and the number of objects used to create shaded extrusion fills are controlled by a value called a *facet*. Facet size can be increased or decreased to control curve smoothing and object count. This is what facet size is and does, so right now would be a good time to reveal where this option is *located,* right?

Click the Options button on the standard toolbar. Under Workspace | Edit, the option itself is named Minimum Extrude Facet Size and has a range between 0.001 inch and 36 inches—the default is 0.05 inch.

Controls complexity of curves, with Use Color Shading applied

Saves value with document

In Options, you can also choose Save Facet Size With Document to avoid the need to change the facet size each time your document is reopened. Higher facet values cause extrude curves to display and print less smoothly; lower values increase the smoothness of extruded curves, but significantly increase display and printing times. Figure 19-11 shows a minimum facet size of 1" and a shape that has a lot of curved segments and lighting that needs to be rendered using a correspondingly high number of extrude facets.

In Figure 19-12 the Minimum Extrude Facet Size has been reduced to a fraction of an inch; the little cocopelli guy looks extruded, the curved edges look smooth, and the wireframe view shows why.

Extruding shapes is something many artists who compete with you for jobs might not be able to offer, especially if they don't own CorelDRAW! However, it's probably not a career-enhancer to use the extrude effect (or any other effect) as a substitute for your own talent as a designer. Use extrude with good judgment. Use it when you're in a design rut and need that certain something to perk up a piece, and don't let yourself get branded as the Extrude King or Queen (it even *sounds* rude!).

As a bonus for completing this chapter, you can download "Extrude examples.cdr," a page of novel uses in a design assignment for the extrude effect. The text has been converted

19

Minimum facet size set to
1 inch; facets are apparent.

Wireframe view

FIGURE 19-11 This extrude's minimum facet size is too high; the extrude edges, as they change color to reflect the lighting, are very obvious.

Minimum extrude facet size set to
0.001 inch; facets are nearly invisible.

Wireframe view

FIGURE 19-12 Extrude facet smoothness is proportional to the number of facets needed to create the smooth impression.

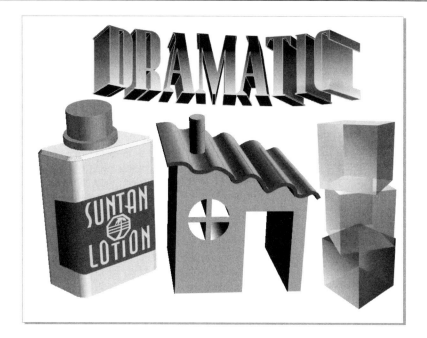

FIGURE 19-13   Four examples of strange and inspired use of the Interactive extrude tool

to curves, and the effects are live in this document, so you can use the Copy Extrude From command to sample and apply any of these effects to objects you've drawn.

In Figure 19-13 you can see the file, and an explanation of what was done and why will give you some ideas of your own based on the principles behind the novel use of the effect.

- The artistic text spelling out "DRAMATIC" is not a "straight" extrude, but instead it was created by extruding the first character and then rotating it. Then the extrude effect was copied to every other character via the Copy Extrude From button on the property bar list. Finally, the Rotation pop-up was used in Numerical Value mode to rotate the characters progressively by about 10° difference to create an arc of text instead of a somewhat flat and planar treatment of this flashy headline.

- The suntan lotion bottle takes advantage of the fact that an extrude doesn't have to face forward; the *side* of the rounded rectangle is exposed to view to represent the bottle, a circle was extruded to make the cap, and similarly, you see the extrude group edge more than you do the control object circle. When you extrude something, you're dealing with a 3D object, and it's up to you, the artist, to decide which side of the 3D shape is the most visually interesting. The label on the bottle was created by using the perspective effect, covered in Chapter 18.

19

- The little tin-roof hut is another example of using the extruded sides instead of the face of the extrude to convey an artistic idea. The roof is a squiggle created with the Bézier pen tool, and then the outline was converted to a shape (CTRL+SHIFT+Q) to extrude (you can't really extrude open paths). The shed itself is a compound shape, and the chimney is an extruded circle, rotated along its X axis so it's almost at a 90° angle to the roof.

- The glass cubes were made from extruded rectangles, but they were then simplified (CTRL+K), and the three faces hidden by the original extrude were drawn in by hand (using Snap To Objects for precision). The extrude effect does not create back-facing facets. Then transparency was applied in Linear style, at different amounts to allow the back faces to show in certain areas and remain hidden in others.

The real lesson here is that the extrude effect can sometimes be a jumping-in point for an idea, and not necessarily the finished product. When you break the extrude group from the control object, you're free then to manually edit all the objects to arrive at *exactly* the design you had in mind.

Chapter 20 continues *The Official Guide* "Effects Extravaganza," with envelopes and distortions the highlights. Learn to get an object or group of objects from close to what you want to draw, to *exactly* what it is you have in your head. Just rotate this page 180° counterclockwise along your local X axis.

PART VII

Creating Special Effects

CHAPTER 20

Envelope and Distortion Effects

Y ou've probably seen this effect in stores a dozen times: the words "Fresh Fish" shaped in the silhouette of a fish. In CorelDRAW this is called an *envelope effect*. With it, you can shape words and other objects (and groups of objects) to conform to a different shape. And to add to your creative effects in CorelDRAW, there's also the Distort tool, a kissing cousin of the envelope effect, which provides much more dramatic reshaping options, and which makes quick work, for example, of reshaping a simple flower petal shape to look more natural and intricate.

Remember when you were a child and played with that putty that came in a plastic egg? This is the theme of this chapter; in it, you'll learn how to treat apparently solid and stiff objects as though they had the flexibility of putty. In the process, you'll gather several practical and creative uses for the envelope and distort features…and discover that work can be fun!

What Does an Envelope Do?

In CorelDRAW you can start with a fresh envelope around an object, use presets, copy a shape to use as an envelope of a different shape, and edit the envelope until the object suits your need. Envelopes are nondestructive; your original artwork can be restored at any time. The property bar has a "remove envelope" button when an enveloped object is selected with the Envelope tool. Once an envelope has been defined, you edit the envelope exactly as you would a path—you can drag on segments and nodes, and change the node control points to your heart's content.

Figure 20-1 demonstrates both the ease and usefulness of the envelope effect. In the top illustration, the artistic text object is enveloped, and the envelope is based on an existing shape seen at right. The bottom illustration shows the envelope control segments and nodes in the process of being edited. It's true: the CorelDRAW envelope effect is just like playing with silly you-know-what!

Envelope shape copied
from the object

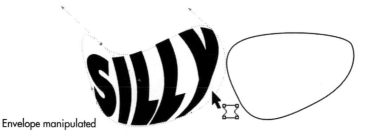

Envelope manipulated

FIGURE 20-1 Use the Envelope tool to create different object looks.

Creating Envelope Effects

When applying envelopes, you can choose from three different methods:

- Shape your envelope from scratch by defining a default envelope and then manually reshaping it.
- Copy an envelope shape based on an object on the drawing page.
- Apply a preset.

Let's begin working with the first technique.

Using the Envelope Tool and Property Bar

Using the Envelope tool along with the property bar options is the most intuitive way to apply envelopes. You'll find it in the toolbox grouped with other interactive tools, as shown here:

Envelope tool

With both the Envelope tool and an object selected, the property bar displays the options shown here:

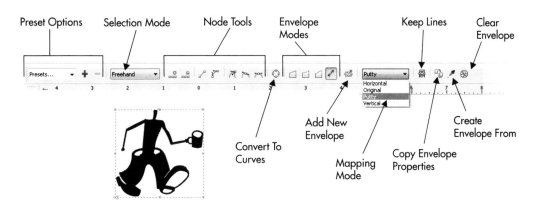

You'll get the best results from the envelope effect if you follow a sequence of moves in CorelDRAW. Let's work through some basic maneuvers using the following steps.

The Envelope, Please

1. Create or open an object (or group of objects) that you feel would make a good target for the envelope effect, and then choose the Envelope tool from the toolbox. Notice that the property bar shows envelope options. The more intricate the object, the more noticeable the effect will be. In general, don't choose a rectangular shape to which you want to apply a rectangular envelope; the effect would be more or less redundant.

2. Click the mode button resembling a square with one corner higher than the other— the Straight Line mode button—and notice the markers surrounding your object.

3. Drag one of the nodes on your object in any direction. Notice that the direction of movement is constrained, and the shape of your object changes to match the envelope as you release the mouse button.

4. Click the next mode button, resembling a square with one curved side—the Single Arc mode button. Drag any node in any direction, and notice that the object changes, but this time you have some curvature going on with the edges of the envelope and the object(s) inside. The Double Arc mode provides more distortion, most noticeably when you drag a center envelope node instead of one of the four corner bounding nodes.

5. Notice that you can drag an envelope node to reshape the object, but the direction handles on either side of the node are fixed and won't budge. Click the Unconstrained Mode button, the rightmost envelope mode on the property bar. Now try dragging nodes and then their direction handles. The following illustration shows the object group in its original state, and then at right it's been worked over a little in Unconstrained mode…it looks reminiscent of how your packages occasionally arrive on Mondays, doesn't it? In all seriousness, however, this is a prime example of the plasticity with which you can reshape objects through the envelope feature. Nothing is hard and fixed in a CorelDRAW drawing and no changes are permanent.

Original

Unconstrained Envelope Mode

You've applied a basic envelope effect to your object, but the inherent shape of the object remains intact. Clicking the Clear Envelope button in the property bar removes the envelope, returning everything to normal.

CAUTION *There is a limit, particularly with grouped objects in an envelope, to how much you can reshape before the paths that make up an object begin to self-intersect. This is usually an unwanted effect, so the remedies are to take it easy on the extent of the envelope, to ungroup the group and apply similar envelope effects to individual objects, or to use the distort effect, shown later in this chapter.*

Using the Envelope Docker

The Envelope docker provides an alternative to using the interactive method. This docker enables you to select options before they are actually applied. To open the Envelope docker, shown in Figure 20-2, choose Effects | Envelope, or press CTRL+F7.

TIP *The main difference between using the Envelope tool and the Envelope docker is that the docker is more visual—you have a good view of presets, but the set of editing tools on the docker is not comprehensive. The docker might be for a less experienced Corellian to use, while using the property bar with the Envelope tool and the Shape tool after an envelope has been created is the sport of designers who want hands-on, low-level control over the effect.*

20

Preset selector

Mode buttons

Mapping options

Create From

FIGURE 20-2 The Envelope docker lets you select options before they are applied.

To apply the effect using the Envelope docker, follow these steps.

Creating Envelopes via the Docker

1. Create or import an object, select it, and then open the Envelope docker (CTRL+F7).

2. Click the Add Preset button; notice how the preset selector window fills with thumbnails of the presets. Choose one (try the heart shape) by clicking the thumbnail; you can see a dashed outline preview surrounding your object on the page. You *could* click Apply to apply the preset, but don't do that right now.

3. In any direction, drag a node on the envelope bounding box surrounding your object. Depending on the preset shape, you can also drag a direction handle—straight line presets don't have node direction handles, but curved objects such as the heart do. Notice that the Apply button is now dimmed; when you edit a preset bounding box, CorelDRAW assumes you've accepted the preset shape, so there's no fussing with the Apply button.

4. The Reset button does not reset the preset object; instead, it calls the last-used preset. If you want to clear the envelope now, notice that the property bar features the Clear Envelope button and other options as long as the docker is onscreen.

Envelope Tool Cursor States

By following either of the previous tutorials, you'll have noticed your cursor changes its look, as shown next. These *cursor states* are visual signals that you're about to edit the envelope in different ways, depending on what part of the envelope your cursor is over.

While you're shaping your envelope, the cursor becomes active. But when your cursor is held over envelope nodes or segments (the dotted lines surrounding your envelope object), the Shape tool takes over, letting you change the position and properties of the nodes and segments by click-dragging (see Figure 20-3).

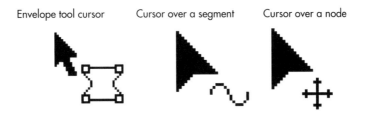

You don't necessarily have to reach for the Envelope tool to edit an enveloped object. You can use the Shape tool, and as you can see in the previous illustration, the Envelope tool's cursor looks exactly like the Shape tool's default cursor when it's over an envelope segment or node. When you're repositioning or changing the property of envelope nodes,

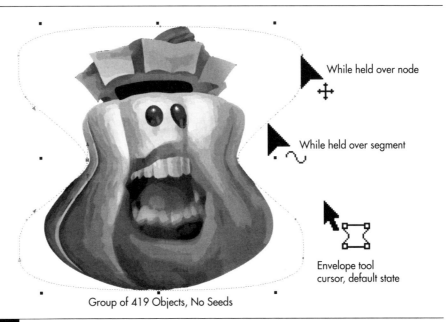

FIGURE 20-3   The Envelope tool has these three cursor states.

your cursor looks like the Shape tool's reposition cursor—indicating the node can be moved, and that you can use the property bar's envelope node tools to convert, for example, a smooth envelope node to a cusp node. When held over an envelope segment, your cursor will change into the Shape tool with a tiny curved-line symbol, indicating the segment can be edited. Using either cursor immediately alters your envelope, but editing envelope curves can be done only while the Unconstrained Envelope mode is selected.

 For speedy envelope editing, use the Pick tool to double-click any object that has an envelope. The enveloped object is immediately available for editing, and surprise, the Pick tool is now the Envelope tool. A single click with the Shape tool also opens an enveloped object for editing.

Choosing an Envelope Mode

The envelope mode you choose has no initial effect on the envelope you apply to an object; however, as you begin to move envelope nodes, the mode of the envelope offers features or limitations, depending on what it is you want to accomplish. Depending on the mode, corner and segment nodes take on different properties, which result in different capabilities to edit the envelope, as seen here:

 At any time while editing an envelope, you can change its mode just by clicking a button on the property bar. This capability gives you control over the overall shape you're trying to create. Any previous mode limitation is inherited with existing nodes, but nodes you've not changed inherit the new node property. For example, suppose your envelope is in Double Arc mode, and you drag a node to make a swooping arc, and then you click the Straight Line mode button on the property bar. The arc remains an arc, but all the other nodes can now only be edited as connectors to straight lines.

These modes have the following effects during shaping operations:

- **Straight Line**   This mode (the default) causes envelope segments to be straight lines; in effect, you're manipulating an eight-point polygon when the envelope is in Straight Line mode. Dragging an envelope node creates a different polygon object, and this mode will serve you well for imitating the shape of a traffic sign, a simple house shape, and other outlines you create with straight line segments. In this case, all node positioning is constrained to vertical and horizontal position changes.

- **Single Arc**   This mode sets the resulting envelope segments to curves, sets side nodes to smooth nodes, and sets corner nodes to cusp nodes; you can't change the angle of the cusp for corner nodes directly, but you do change it when you reposition a side envelope node. When you're using this mode, dragging corner nodes creates a curved side on the envelope, while side nodes align with the path of the resulting curve. Node movement is constrained to vertical and horizontal movement, while side nodes can be moved independently of corner nodes.

- **Double Arc**   This mode creates the effect of sine-wave-shaped sides. Behind the scenes, corner points become cusp nodes, while side nodes become smooth nodes. However, the curve handles of side nodes remain stationary in relation to the nodes, causing the segments to take on a double-arc shape. The same vertical and horizontal constraint restrictions as with the previous modes apply. Side nodes may be moved independently of corner nodes, but they apply a similar curve effect, as with the Single Arc mode.

- **Unconstrained**   The Unconstrained mode gives you complete control over nodes, segments, and control handles for envelope elements; it's probably the mode of choice for ambitious enveloping artists. You can position either side or corner nodes as if they were ordinary vector path object nodes. In this mode, the Envelope tool gives you unlimited flexibility (you can *severely* reshape objects), and nodes can be dragged in any direction to shape the envelope in any way. Unconstrained mode also provides the options to add or delete nodes, change any line segment state to straight or curved, or to change the properties of nodes to Cusp, Smooth, or Symmetrical using property bar buttons for these tasks.

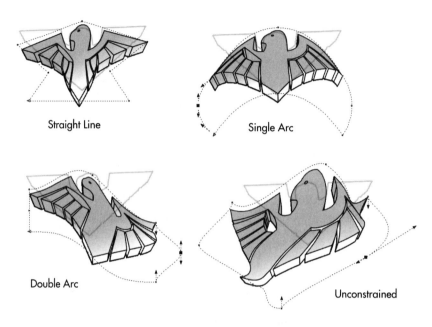

Straight Line

Single Arc

Double Arc

Unconstrained

Saving and Applying Envelope Presets

The property bar Preset list (shown in Figure 20-4) contains saved presets and options for applying, adding, and deleting preset envelope objects.

You can add a shape you've created as a new envelope object, and delete presets from the list using the Add Preset (+) and Delete Preset (–) buttons. It's best to create an envelope

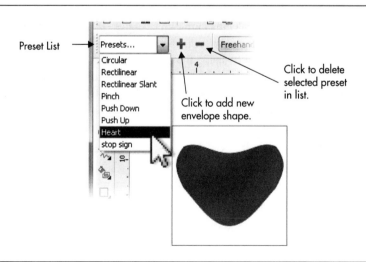

FIGURE 20-4 Use the property bar Preset list to access saved presets.

object from one, single path (no sub-paths). An object with a hole in it, for example, will produce an envelope that's unusable except for abstract artwork. For hands-on, truly warped experience, follow these steps.

Creating and Using an Envelope Preset

1. Create a simple closed path you think would make an interesting envelope; an egg shape would work well, for example.

2. Choose the Envelope tool and notice that the property bar now features envelope options.

3. To add the shape of your object to the Preset list, click the Add Preset (+) button on the property bar. The Save As dialog opens with the Save As Type drop-down menu automatically listing preset files. Enter a name for your new preset. CorelDRAW will automatically append the name with the .PST file extension; then click Save to add it to the list.

4. To apply your new preset, create an object (it shouldn't look like your new preset envelope) or a group of objects, and then choose your new preset from the list selector. The new envelope is applied.

5. To delete an envelope shape from the Preset list, make sure no objects are selected (it helps to switch to the Pick tool and then back to the Envelope tool), and then choose a saved preset from the list selector.

6. With the preset selected, click the Delete Preset (–) button. Confirm your delete action in the prompt dialog that appears and your preset is deleted.

Choosing Envelope Mapping Options

You have envelope mapping options both for the Envelope docker and while using the Envelope tool and property bar options, which offer control over how the shape of an envelope changes your object's shape (see Figure 20-5). As you can see, Original and Putty mapping provide almost identical results for this particular group of objects and the envelope shape used here, but Horizontal and Vertical Mapping afford the design opportunity to ignore the other envelope axis (Horizontal Mapping ignores the vertical aspect of the envelope, and vice versa). This is useful when you want limited distortion of an envelope but don't have the time (or need!) to create a unique envelope for several different design purposes.

20

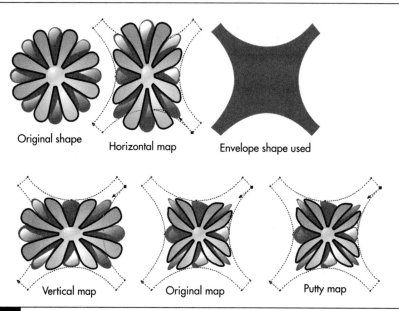

Original shape   Horizontal map   Envelope shape used

Vertical map   Original map   Putty map

FIGURE 20-5   This object group uses the same envelope but different mapping options.

Mapping options give preference to the shape of your original object's node positions and path shapes. Four types are available: Putty (the default), Horizontal, Vertical, and Original, as shown here:

The four envelope mapping options, plus a special option for text and another to preserve lines, are worthy of explanation here:

- **Putty**   This option (the default) distorts the shape of your object to match the envelope as closely as possible; the envelope's nodes are given priority over the nodes in your object being enveloped. The Putty option maps the envelope shape to your object and results in a smoothly mapped effect.

- **Horizontal**   This option maps the lines and node positions in your original object to match the horizontal shape of the envelope, without significantly altering the vertical shape of the original object.

- **Vertical** This option maps the lines and node positions in your original object to the *vertical* shape of the envelope, with the horizontal shape mostly ignored.

- **Original** This mapping type is similar to Putty. The main difference is that Original maps *only the outer shape* of your original object to the envelope shape. Corner nodes are mapped to the corner nodes of your original object's shape, while node positions and line shapes toward the inside of your object are mapped using an averaging value. The result can be less distortion. If Putty mode is too severe, try Original.

- **Keep Lines** Using this option changes only the node positions in your object to match the envelope shape being applied, leaving any existing straight lines unaffected. If your object is already composed only of curved lines, choosing Keep Lines has no effect, as shown at right in Figure 20-6, which looks like Keep Lines has been turned off. While Keep Lines is not selected (the default), all node positions and lines in your original object are reshaped to match the envelope object—even if this means changing straight lines to curved lines.

- **Text** This option becomes available as the only mapping option when a paragraph text object frame is selected. Text mode applies an envelope to the *frame* properties of a paragraph text object; the actual text and line of text are not distorted. This feature presents a wonderful opportunity to walk through a tutorial.

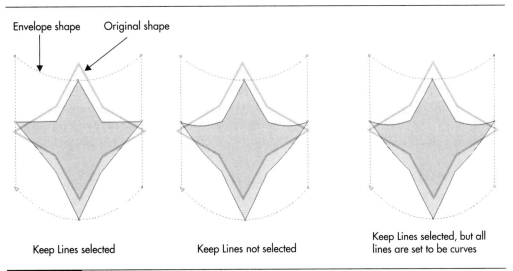

Envelope shape   Original shape

Keep Lines selected   Keep Lines not selected   Keep Lines selected, but all lines are set to be curves

FIGURE 20-6 The Keep Lines option changes node positions but not any straight lines in the target object to match the envelope shape.

20

In the next set of steps, you'll use the Violin.cdr file, which contains a silhouette drawing of a violin and a block of paragraph text attributed to Wikipedia. Your task is to fit the text inside the profile of the violin drawing. It's a class act, and this technique can be used for scores of designs. Especially music scores.

Creating a Text Envelope

1. In the Violin.cdr document, choose the violin object with the Envelope tool.

2. On the property bar, click the + sign to the right of the Preset list. In the Save As box, save the custom envelope with an obvious name such as Violin.pst. Click Save to save and exit the box.

3. Select the block of paragraph text with the Envelope tool. Click the Preset list and then choose Violin from the list.

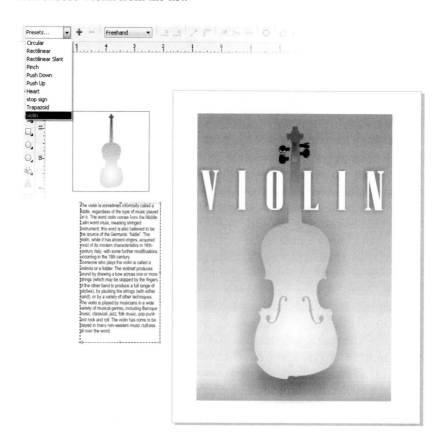

4. The edge of the newly enveloped text is going to look a little busy with the text offset margin and the envelope path around it; no big deal—choose the Pick tool (the envelope outline disappears), and move the text to fit over the violin drawing.

5. The "fit" is not perfect because the envelope effect is distorting the dimensions of the paragraph text block (but not the text itself) to match the proportions of the violin. Click-drag the object selection handles, and adjust the text so it fits neatly within the violin drawing.

6. With the Text tool, insert your cursor at the beginning of the paragraph, and then press ENTER to kick the text down so none of it is in the neck of the violin, which looks awkward, reads terribly, and makes it hard to play the instrument. See Figure 20-7 as a reference for where your composition should be now.

7. Optionally, choose a more elegant typeface than Arial. Select the text with the Pick tool, and then on the property bar choose a font you have installed. Figure 20-8 shows Bernard Fashion used. End of exercise, pretty fancy graphic use of the Envelope tool!

FIGURE 20-7 Perform a little manual editing to make the envelope text fit within the violin drawing.

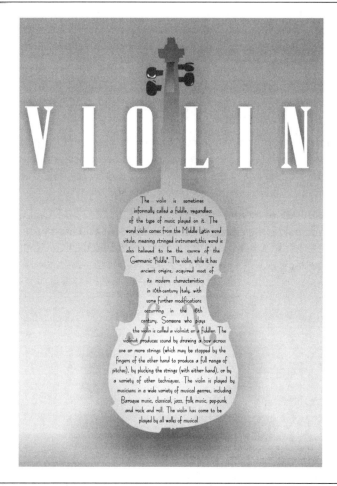

FIGURE 20-8   Create an elegant symbiosis of text as a graphic combined with a simple CorelDRAW drawing.

Constraining Single Arc Envelopes

Modifier keys offer valuable ways to constrain the shaping of an envelope while using *Single Arc* mode. By holding key modifiers, you can quickly shape two sides concentrically or simultaneously. Hold SHIFT and drag any side or corner node to have the corresponding node on the opposite side move in the *opposite* direction. Hold CTRL to move the corresponding node on the opposite side of the shape in the *same* direction and by an equal distance, as shown in Figure 20-9.

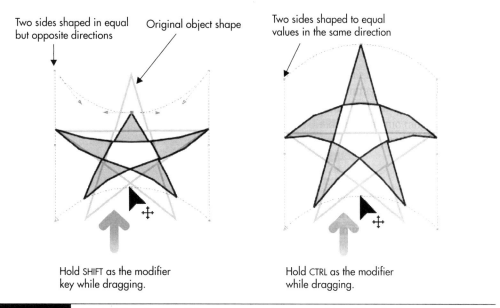

Two sides shaped in equal but opposite directions

Original object shape

Two sides shaped to equal values in the same direction

Hold SHIFT as the modifier key while dragging.

Hold CTRL as the modifier while dragging.

FIGURE 20-9   By holding key modifiers, you can shape two sides either in the same direction (concentrically) or in opposite directions.

Using Envelope Shapes Between Objects

You can copy single-path objects—and even other envelopes—that already exist in your drawing, and use them as envelopes. The commands for these operations are available from the Effects menu and by using the shortcut buttons in the property bar when the Envelope tool is selected.

Create Envelope From

Copy Envelope Properties

Clear Envelope

Copying Properties from Other Envelopes

If you've taken the time to create an envelope effect but you'll only use it a few times so it's not worth creating a preset, you can copy its properties to another object using the Copy Envelope Properties command. To copy an envelope's properties, try the following steps.

20

Envelopes Based on Existing Envelopes

1. Select the object you wish to apply the envelope shape to, and choose the Envelope tool.
2. Click the Copy Envelope Properties button in the property bar. Your cursor will change to a targeting cursor.
3. Click to target the object with the applied envelope effect you wish to copy. The envelope effect is immediately copied and applied to the new object, as shown here:

Original object

Envelope shape targeted   New object with envelope applied

TIP   *If the envelope effect you need to copy from is on a different page of your document, try dragging a copy of the object onto the desktop (the pasteboard outside the document page). You can copy envelope shapes from the desktop.*

Creating Envelopes from Objects

Creating envelope shapes from existing objects is another common operation that enables you to create and apply new envelope shapes based on the targeted object's shape. The steps are shown left to right here:

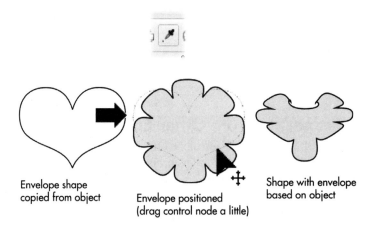

Envelope shape
copied from object

Envelope positioned
(drag control node a little)

Shape with envelope
based on object

Unlike using the Copy Envelope Properties feature, copying a shape to apply to a different object as an envelope requires a little additional step. First, you target the object to be enveloped using the Envelope tool. Click the Create Envelope From button on the property bar, click the source object, and then a preview of the envelope shape appears around the target object. It doesn't actually transform until you drag one of the control nodes just a little, or click an envelope path segment; then the target object transforms.

Clearing an Envelope Shape

Removing an envelope effect from an object is a quick operation. If you applied envelope effects in succession, all shaping can be removed at once. To remove an envelope effect, select the object bound to the envelope effect, and choose the Envelope tool. Click the Clear Envelope button.

 The Clear Envelope command is also available by choosing Effects | Clear Envelope.

 ## Copying Envelopes with the Attributes Eyedropper Tool

You can copy applied effects (including envelopes) from one single object (not grouped objects) to another by using the Attributes eyedropper tool. To do this, have both the objects in view. Got 'em? Follow these steps:

1. Choose the Attributes eyedropper tool from the toolbox.

2. On the property bar, click the Effects button, select the Envelope check box in the list, and then click OK.

3. Click the object currently applied with the envelope effect you want to copy using the Attributes eyedropper tool cursor to sample its properties.

4. Click the object you want to apply the effect to.

 TIP   *You can apply several instances of an envelope, an envelope enveloping an envelope, and so on, if you need a truly gnarly effect. After you've sampled the envelope, click the cursor over the target object three or four times until your laughter subsides.*

Mastering Distortion Effects

Distortion effects apply complex math to the curve paths that make up your object. But artists don't need to know what's under the hood in order to take advantage of these wonderfully intricate equations and to produce outstanding and very naturalistic artwork.

The Distort tool and options are also *dynamic,* which means they create distortion without ruining your original. Distortion properties can be edited at any time. Your custom distortions can be saved as presets, and they can be cleared from your object, just like with envelopes.

Distortion effects also change your object without affecting its other properties such as outline width and fill. Using distortion, the curve values and node properties are dramatically changed, and the more complex your object is to begin with, the more dramatic the distortion effect will be. Adobe Illustrator users will feel right at home; although distortions are similar to Punk & Bloat, they go beyond this effect in variety and complexity, and when you're using CorelDRAW distortions, you can restore your objects at any time. Distortion effects are great for a number of illustration challenges, including simulating organic-type effects, as shown in Figure 20-10. Believe it or not, the simple star shape at top left was used to generate the primitive cave scrawling. You can create flower shapes, zippers, swirly galaxies in space—not even the sky's the limit.

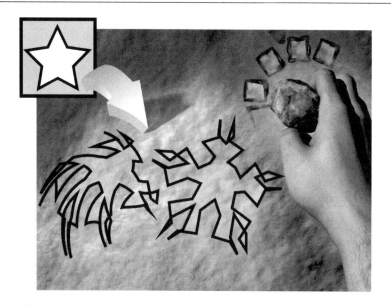

FIGURE 20-10   These primitive drawings were created by applying the Distort tool effects.

20

Using the Distort Tool and the Property Bar

Apply your distortions using the Distort tool, shown next, which is found in the toolbox grouped with other effects tools and is used together with these property bar options.

Property bar options for distortion

Distort tool and cursor

You'll notice three distortion modes: Push And Pull, Zipper, and Twister. With each mode, a different set of parameters is available. Amplitude and Frequency values can be varied in combination with certain other options (covered next) controlled interactively or by setting values on the property bar. Let's first look at the property bar when one of the modes, Zipper distortion, is chosen. All three modes offer slightly different options; by reviewing Zipper mode, you'll get a handle on many of the options.

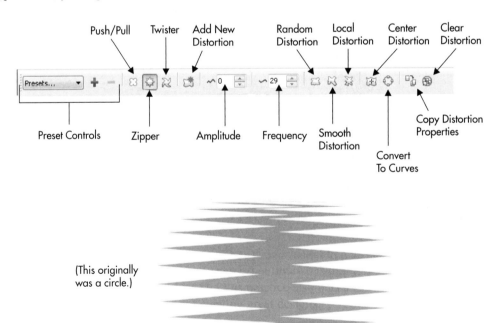

(This originally was a circle.)

Choosing Distortion Modes

If you've tried using this effect, even just a little, you probably have a newfound appreciation for "steering" this effect—it's akin to slipping into a Ferrari right after your dad took the training wheels off your bike. However, chin up, examples and explanations for this powerhouse of an effect follow, and as you read on (and get hands-on), the Distort tool will grow on you, and the intimidation factor will dwindle.

During a distortion session, interactive markers provide much of the control over this effect. Interactive markers vary by the mode selected. The distort modes are covered in the sections to follow in digestible, easy-to-assimilate, fun-size servings.

Push and Pull Distortion

Push and pull distortions can inflate or deflate the slope of your object's curves by amplitude. The *amplitude* value affects the extent of the effect, sloping the curves of paths from an object's original path from shallow at low settings to severe at high settings.

Amplitude can be set from 200 to –200 percent. Negative values cause the effect to distort the path *away* from the center origin of the object, which creates the "push" condition of the distortion. Negative values (which you can also define interactively with the Distort tool—it's fun and creatively therapeutic) can be used to illustrate flower petals, a cartoon splash into a pond, a thought balloon—all beginning with a rectangle object. Positive amplitude values cause the effect to be distorted *toward* the object's center origin, the "pull" condition. Again, if you use a rectangle as the target object, you can almost instantly produce anything from a diner sign from the 1950s, to a sleek, aerodynamic auto or airplane, to a nice 3D visualization of a TV tube viewed in perspective. The amplitude of 0 has no distortion. Figure 20-11 shows the effects of both negative and positive Push and Pull amplitude settings.

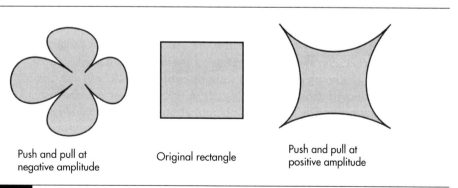

Push and pull at negative amplitude   Original rectangle   Push and pull at positive amplitude

FIGURE 20-11   Amplitude can be set from 200 to –200 percent. But a little goes a long way!

Zipper Distortion

Zipper mode distorts the paths in your object to resemble a zigzag or stitching pattern. Here, amplitude can be set between 0 and 100 percent and can be used together with a frequency value and options for Random, Smooth, or Local distortion, as shown here:

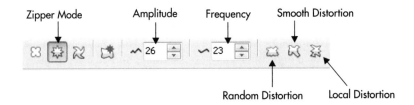

Interactive markers are made up of an outer marker controlling the amplitude and a slider controlling frequency, which enable you to set the number of zigzags within a given distance. Both can be set within a range of 0 to 100 percent. You can see the dramatic effects of various amplitude and frequency values while applying a zipper distortion in the next illustration. When beginning to work with the distortion effects, you might prefer to use only the property bar to define an effect, but as you grow more comfortable with distortion, you'll surely want hands-on control by dragging the control handles directly with your cursor.

After the effect has been created, you can slant the zipper line by dragging the Start handle left or right, as shown here:

Move Start handle left or right.

TIP *You can invert the direction of the zigzags on a line or closed shape by repositioning the control handles for the effect. For example, begin by placing the Start and End handles so they bisect the line that is affected. Then arrange the handles so both the Start and End handles are above the line; notice where the peaks and valleys are on the line. Now move the Start and End handles so they're below the affected line. You'll see that where there were peaks there are now valleys, and vice versa.*

In addition to amplitude and frequency, three additional options are available for setting the shape and size of the zigzags. Each can be toggled on or off, so you can mix and match to create the following effects:

- **Random** Choosing the Random option causes the zigzag Zipper distortion on your object's path to vary randomly between the current Amplitude values and zero. This creates the appearance of nonrepeating frequency and varied wave size, creating an uncontrolled distortion appearance. In this illustration you can see two examples of Random set at 25 and then at 74. Notice where the interactive frequency marker is on the controls just above each object. You can slide this marker instead of entering values on the property bar.

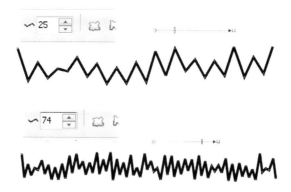

- **Smooth** While the Smooth option is selected, the cusps of the zigzag Zipper distortion become rounded, instead of the default sharp corners normally seen. This is a great option if you need to simulate sound-wave frequencies and equipment monitors in hospitals. The next illustration shows *constant* (Random is toggled off) Amplitude and variations in Frequency when the Smooth option is active.

Frequency = 48

Frequency = 21

- **Local**   Using the Local distortion option has the effect of varying the Amplitude value of your distortion effect around the center origin. At the center of the distortion effect, Amplitude is at its maximum value. Amplitude then tapers to 0 as the distortion emanates from the center origin of the effect. The results of applying the Local distortion option while the Frequency is varied are shown here:

TIP   *To clear a distortion effect, click Clear Distortion Effect in the property bar or choose Effects | Clear Distortion. If you've applied successive distortions, each distortion is cleared individually in order, from the last distortion applied to the first, so you can step out of the effect incrementally.*

To bring all this Zipper talk down to a practical level, the following illustration shows two creative, commercial uses. At left, the Zipper distortion is used as a coupon border. The only finessing needed was to apply a dashed Outline pen style. At right, the diagram of a sewing pattern is gussied up a little by making the cut marks look as though real pinking shears were used.

Twister Distortion

Twister distorts the outline paths and nodes of objects by rotating the outer areas around the center (which is largely undistorted), either clockwise or counterclockwise, to achieve an effect much like a child's pinwheel toy. Twister options on the property bar include rotation direction, rotation amount, and degree of additional rotation.

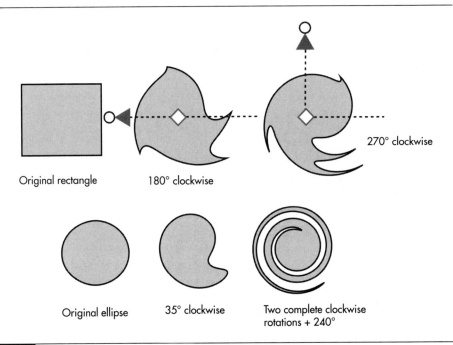

Original rectangle   180° clockwise   270° clockwise

Original ellipse   35° clockwise   Two complete clockwise rotations + 240°

FIGURE 20-12   Using simple objects and the Twister mode of the distort effect, you can create wild, organic shapes.

Controlling a Twister distortion is simple; rotation can be clockwise or counterclockwise, but increasing the rotation really dramatizes the effect of this mode. Whole rotations can be set to a maximum of 9; additional rotations can be added up to 359°—nearly another full rotation. Figure 20-12 shows some of the widely differing effects that can result—it all depends on the number of rotations and the object used as the target for the effect.

Objects applied with a distortion effect can't be edited using the Shape tool unless the effect is cleared. However, you can convert *a distorted shape to curves (CTRL+Q), and then edit to get the object you need.*

Getting Hands-On with the Distortion Tool Markers

The best way to shape a distortion is interactively, by dragging directly on the Distortion tool markers with your cursor. Depending on which distortion mode you're using, these interactive markers serve different purposes.

Which interactive markers are available depends on which mode (Push And Pull, Zipper, Twister) you've chosen, but basically you have a Start handle shaped like a diamond, which sets the center of the distort effect. The Start handle is connected to the End handle, which is used to define the direction of the effect and also the *amplitude* (with the Push And Pull and

Zipper modes). Generally, interactive markers involve a center marker and at least one other, each joined by a directional guide. When Zipper distortion is being applied, a small extra slider appears between these two markers and controls the amount of *frequency* applied. In the case of Twister distortions, the outer marker serves as a handle for determining the degree angle and amount of rotation you apply to an object.

NOTE	*To realign the center marker (the Start handle) with the center of the distortion, click the Center Distortion button in the property bar while the Distortion tool and the distorted objects are selected. It's the button with the + symbol, to the left of the Convert To Curves button.*

Changing Push and Pull Interactively

Push and pull distortions are controlled using two markers: a diamond shape indicates the center of the distortion, and a square marker controls amplitude. The center marker can be moved around the object, but the amplitude marker movement is constrained to left or right movement. Dragging the amplitude marker left of center changes the negative amplitude values, causing the push effect. Dragging it right of the center marker changes the positive values, causing the pull effect. Figure 20-13 shows the effects of different marker positions.

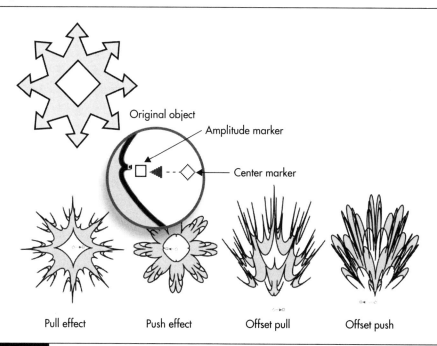

| Pull effect | Push effect | Offset pull | Offset push |

FIGURE 20-13   Push and pull distortions are controlled by a diamond shape and a square marker onscreen.

Working with the Zipper Control Handles

Using Zipper distortion, the movable diamond marker represents the center origin, and the square marker to the right controls the amplitude value. Use the small rectangular slider on the dashed blue centerline to set frequency by moving it left or right. Dragging it right increases the frequency, adding more zigzag shapes to your object's path, while dragging it left does the opposite. You also have the opportunity with Zipper mode, unlike the fixed positions of the markers in Push And Pull mode, to move the amplitude handle to slant the zigs and zags in a direction.

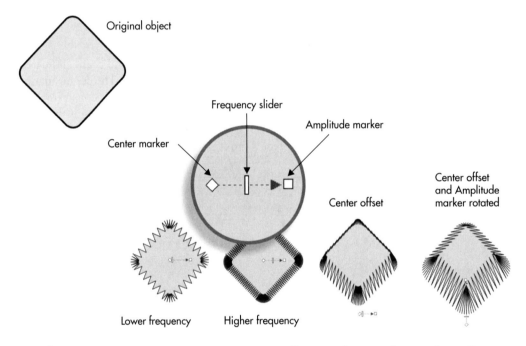

Original object

Frequency slider

Amplitude marker

Center marker

Center offset

Center offset and Amplitude marker rotated

Lower frequency

Higher frequency

> TIP *Exactly as with envelopes, the distortion effects can be copied using the toolbox Attributes eyedropper tool.*

Changing Twister Interactively

Controlling Twister distortions by dragging with your cursor over the markers is the most productive (and fun) way to apply this distortion mode; one click-drag lets you set two properties at once, both of which have a dramatic effect on the distortion. The markers during a Twister distortion are a diamond-shaped center marker and a round-shaped rotation handle. Dragging the rotation handle around the center marker causes distortion based on the angle of the guide between the center and rotation markers and the number of times the rotation marker is dragged completely around the center marker. You'll also see a dashed blue line connecting the markers, which provides a quick visual reference of the beginning

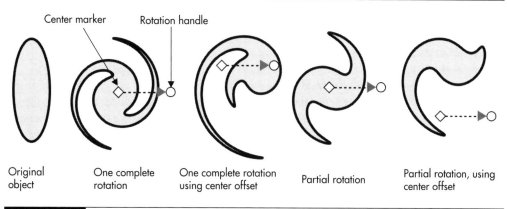

Original object | One complete rotation | One complete rotation using center offset | Partial rotation | Partial rotation, using center offset

FIGURE 20-14 It's best to use the control handles to create Twister distortions.

angle of the Twister distortion and the current angle of distortion you define. Figure 20-14 shows examples of Twister distortions and positions of the markers.

 To copy a distortion to a new object, select an object, click the Copy Distortion Properties button in the property bar, and use the cursor to target an existing distortion.

Using Distortion Presets

The property bar Preset list for distortion effects gives you the power to apply, save, and delete saved distortions, as shown here:

Exploring Distortion Presets

When the Distort tool is the current tool selected, choosing a preset from the list immediately applies a new distortion effect to a selected object. If you've created a really awesome distortion effect and you want to save the effect while the distorted shape in your document is selected, you can add it as a new distortion preset by clicking the Add Preset button. The Delete Preset button *permanently* removes a selected distortion preset from the list; therefore, think twice about ever clicking this button. To delete a preset, nothing must be selected on the page; then the minus button becomes active. Only user presets can be deleted, not CorelDRAW shipped-with presets.

Between distortion and envelope effects covered in this chapter, you should be well on your way to massaging an object or object group from something close to what you like to *exactly* what you like and need. Remember, these are dynamic effects, so you don't permanently change that shape you've worked for hours on. And if you need to exchange data with a client or coworker who doesn't own CorelDRAW:

- Take pity on them.

- Convert *a copy* of your effects work to curves (CTRL+Q), and then export the distorted or enveloped object to any number of file formats CorelDRAW supports. Effects are proprietary to CorelDRAW, but vector information can be used in other vector design programs and modeling programs or exported as typefaces—you name it.

Blends and contours are the topic of the next chapter, each with their own use, and you can actually take what you know now about distortions and apply a contour to a distorted object. Will it look weird? Yep, and *interesting*. Just think of it as adding to weirdness, and building on your knowledge!

CHAPTER 21

Blends and Contours

Although they're different effects, blends and contours share the common trait of creating many shapes based on control shapes; the additional shapes are dynamically linked to the control object, and the "in-between" objects will vary in size, color, and outline shape depending on how you set up the effect. Blends and contours are a boon to the designer who wants to add shading to flat color fills in a way that fountain fills do not. Additionally, blend objects can be used to illustrate the transition between two objects of similar or completely dissimilar shape. This chapter takes you through the use of blends and contours so you can add these effects to your bag of illustration tricks and create outstanding, intriguing work.

Blend and Contour Effects: Similarities with Distinctions

The blend effects create a series of objects *between* objects in a number of steps you define—an object can be a closed path, a group of objects, and even a line (an open path). The properties of each step are influenced by the objects used in the blend. The contour effect also creates additional objects in steps; however, only one object is used to produce a contour. When you imagine a contour effect, think of an object surrounded by the same shape radiating outward (or inward) in a concentric pattern, like the waves produced when you drop a pebble in a still pond. Depending on the assignment, you'll choose the contour or blend to achieve the exact look you need. The following sections explain the properties of the effects you can manipulate, and then you can decide which effect to reach for when you need a complex graphic or a smooth, shaded fill in an illustration area.

Blending as Illustration Shading

If you've ever tried to add depth to a drawing and found that you're not up to speed with the Mesh fill tool and that a fountain fill doesn't do the trick, the solution is to blend a large shape through transition objects to a smaller object inside the large one. By making, for example, the outer shape darker than the inner one, you can position a highlight wherever you need it on the face of a drawing of a hardware tool or a fork or a drinking glass . . . you get the picture. Similarly, a contour can be used to create a highlight; however, the contour object should be symmetrical, such as an ellipse, to achieve the highlight effect. You'll often see blend effects used in illustration work for creating photorealistic illustrations, but regardless of whether the visual content of a drawing is real-life accurate or a whimsical cartoon, with blends you add depth and suggest lighting and the type of material on an object. The left side of Figure 21-1 shows a decent drawing of a frankfurter in perspective, but you and other viewers detect that there's something missing from the illustration. At right, you can see a Wireframe view of the same drawing, except several blends and contours have been added on a new layer in CorelDRAW. You'll see how to do this stuff later in this chapter.

In Figure 21-2 you can see the finished illustration in Enhanced view in CorelDRAW's drawing window. About eight pairs of objects were used, different sizes and different colors, and what you see here is smooth shading and highlights that suggest lighting and a little

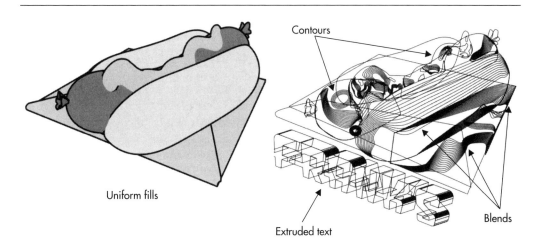

Contours

Uniform fills

Extruded text

Blends

FIGURE 21-1 A drawing, especially a perspective drawing of an object, can appear flat until you add shading with blends and contours.

FIGURE 21-2 The main difference between this illustration and that in Figure 21-1 is *depiction* in Figure 21-1 and *illustration* here. Illustrations are complete visual ideas, from outline shape to interior fills.

Photorealism Is Achieved Through Complex Fills

Many world-class designers—particularly in the field of 3D animations—have made the observation that the shape—the silhouette—of an object is usually not as visually interesting as *the texture* on the surface of that object. This is one of the reasons for using CorelDRAW blends and contours to make drawings not only more visually interesting, but also more photorealistic in appearance. For example, just about anyone can draw rectangles that represent a box viewed in perspective; in fact, this task takes about 1 minute using the Extrude tool. However, your audience probably won't immediately see the drawing as a box until it has shading; the side facing a hypothetical light source would be lighter than the side(s) facing away from the light. Additionally, some text or a simple drawing placed in the correct perspective on one face of the box drawing would also help convey an image of a box. Graphics inside of graphics add visual complexity to illustrations. They are the "fills" for objects, and the more complex you make an illustration, the more closely the drawing suggests a real object: the world is a visually complex place.

The more attention you pay to fills for objects, the more quickly and successfully you'll communicate a visual idea to an audience. With the speed of today's communications, you need to make your point—a selling point or just a point about fine art—fast and thoroughly before someone loses interest and moves on to a different web page!

shininess on the frankfurter, thus creating a visual impression of strength, size, and other qualities that help the audience read very quickly, "Oh, that's a *frankfurter*! It looks really large and bright! It probably has a lot of calories and nitrites, and the bun doesn't look like whole wheat…" Seriously, the more complexity you build into an object's fill, the more you tell your visual story, and the more readily the audience will pick up on that story and fill in *more* details. And before you know it, you've *sustained your audience's attention.*

Blends can also be used to create a lot of similar objects very quickly; the trick is to blend between similar objects that are quite a distance apart on the page. Figure 21-3 shows an example of two groups of objects blended to create a bar graph; the reference lines were blended from two identical lines. This is a graph with an even, upward progression. However, when you need to create similar blend objects that *don't* follow an even progression, you use the Break Apart (CTRL+K) command to break the relationship between the blend control objects, then ungroup the blend group, and finally, you edit the individual blend objects to create a more random transition from object to object.

FIGURE 21-3   Objects in this chart were created using blends.

The Blend Tool and Property Bar

The tool to use for the blend effect is the Blend tool; it's in the toolbox, grouped with other effects tools, shown here.

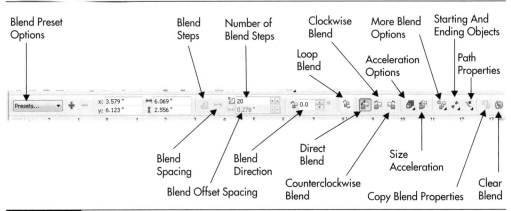

FIGURE 21-4 When the Blend tool is used, the property bar has options to customize your blend effects.

When the Blend tool is chosen, the property bar offers options (shown in Figure 21-4) for customizing the effect. By default, 20 intermediate steps are created between two blend control objects.

Creating a Simple Blend Effect

You might want to work with similar objects to create blends that look like repeats—rubberstamped copies of the original objects—but there's another creative use for the Blend tool. You can morph totally dissimilar objects, and the resulting blend will probably contain a lot of interesting and useful transitional shapes. Work through the following tutorial to experiment with a basic blend effect between a star and an ellipse object.

A Basic Blend Between Very Different Shapes

1. Choose the Star tool; it's in the group on the toolbox with the Polygon tool. Click-drag a star that's about 1" in size at the top left of the drawing page. Fill it with yellow on the Color Palette, and give it a 4-point blue outline. First, choose 4 pts. from the Outline width drop-down box on the property bar, and then right-click any blue color well on the Color Palette.

2. Choose the Ellipse tool (F7) and then click-drag an ellipse at the top right of the page. Fill it with blue and give it a yellow outline, but keep the outline width at the default of 0.5 pt.

3. Choose the Blend tool from the toolbox. Your cursor changes and the property bar's options are all dimmed because a blend doesn't exist yet on the page.

4. Click inside the star and then drag until your cursor is inside the ellipse. Once you release the mouse button, a series of new objects appears, and the property bar comes to life with almost all options available.

5. Twenty steps is too many for this example: type **2** in the Blend Steps field on the property bar, and then press ENTER. As you can see in the following illustration, the blend shapes make an interesting progression; the outline color makes the transition from blue to yellow; the fill color transitions from yellow to blue; and the intermediate shapes are some interesting stars in stages of distortion as they become the ellipse. These intermediate star-like objects are actually a little difficult to make using the standard drawing tools!

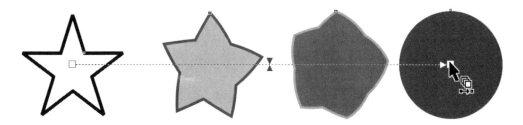

TIP   *To remove a blend effect, click the blend portion of the effect to select it, and choose Effects | Clear Blend; or, while using the Blend tool, click to select the blend effect portion, and click the Clear Blend button in the property bar.*

Looking at the Components of a Blend

The blend effect you built in the previous tutorial creates a fun composition, but to build on your *knowledge*—to be able to create more complex blends—it's a good idea to now examine what really went on, and what properties the objects on your page now have. A two-object blend includes several key components: the original objects become *control objects*; any changes made to either the star or the ellipse will change the blend itself. The effect portion—called a *blend group*—and the control objects maintain a relationship as long as the blend exists.

Each of the interactive markers around a blend effect corresponds to an option in the property bar. Figure 21-5 shows the various parts of a two-object blend.

Editing a blend is a little more of a challenge than making dinner reservations, but significantly less challenging than brain surgery. With the Pick tool, click the blend group to begin editing it using the property bar options. Single-clicking selects both the blend and its control objects. To select either control object, click only the control object itself. You'll see that the status bar tells you that a "Control *Whatever*" (Object, Curve, Rectangle) is selected, confirming that the correct object is selected for editing. To display the interactive control handles for the blend, double-click the blend, the intermediate objects.

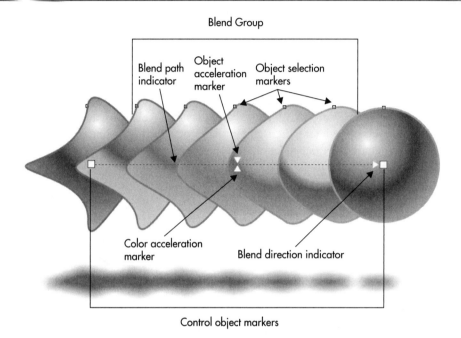

Blend Group

Blend path indicator

Object acceleration marker

Object selection markers

Color acceleration marker

Blend direction indicator

Control object markers

FIGURE 21-5 This blend between two objects shows the interactive markers controlling the effect.

The Blend tool has several different cursor states, as shown in Figure 21-6. Cursor states tell you when you're over a control marker and can extend a blend to include another object (more on this shortly), when you're over an object or acceleration marker (you can then move the marker and change the effect), and when you're over an area where the tool can't do anything, such as a blank space on the page.

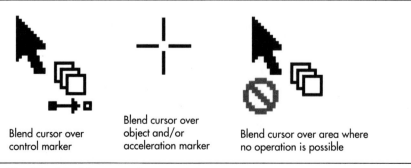

Blend cursor over control marker

Blend cursor over object and/or acceleration marker

Blend cursor over area where no operation is possible

FIGURE 21-6 The Blend tool has several cursor states.

Editing Blend Effects

You can create a custom blend effect by directly manipulating markers and objects with your cursor, setting specific values for options using the property bar, and occasionally by using a combination of the two interface elements. The following sections take you through the features you'll use most often; then it's on to useful but less frequently used options. Think of this as a journey from mildly amusing, to wonderful, and then on to totally bizarre effects as you progress through these sections.

Setting Blend Options

Options controlling a blend effect can have an impact on each intermediate step of the blend itself. You can change the steps' value, rotation, color, and the acceleration of the blend objects, as well as save the effect you've custom-designed as a preset.

Controlling Blend Steps

The number of steps in the blend group can be set within a range of 1 to 999, as shown in Figure 21-7. To set a number of steps, enter a value in the property bar Blend Steps num box and then press ENTER. Notice that as you set higher step numbers, depending on the closeness of the blend control objects, they might overlap. This is an interesting effect, but if you need intermediate blend objects that don't touch one another, you can resize both blend control objects, or move them farther apart from one another.

Specifying Blend Spacing

To set spacing values between blend steps, use the Blend Spacing option, which becomes available *only* if a blend has been applied to a path, as shown in Figure 21-8. This limitation is because the distance between the blend control objects must be fixed by the length of the

5-step blend effect

20-step blend effect

FIGURE 21-7   You can create dozens—and even hundreds—of objects and object groups by using a blend effect.

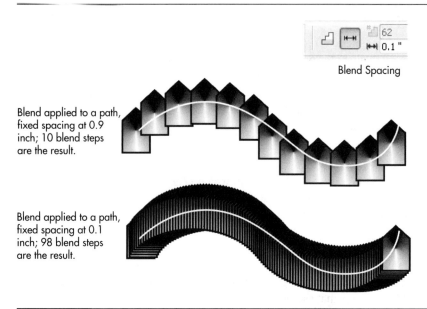

Blend Spacing

Blend applied to a path, fixed spacing at 0.9 inch; 10 blend steps are the result.

Blend applied to a path, fixed spacing at 0.1 inch; 98 blend steps are the result.

FIGURE 21-8 Fixed spacing between blend objects applied to a path can be controlled using the Blend Spacing feature on the property bar.

path. Use the Blend Spacing option in the property bar; enter the value to a specific unit measure. CorelDRAW automatically calculates the number of objects required to fit the path's length. Blend Spacing works within a range of 0.010 inch to 10.00 inches, in increments of 0.010 inch. To learn how to blend objects along a path, see "Assigning a Blend Path," later in this chapter.

Rotating a Blend

You can rotate the objects in a blend group by fixed degree values using the Blend Direction option, shown in Figure 21-9. Enter an angle value (based on degrees of rotation). Positive values rotate the objects counterclockwise; negative values rotate them clockwise. With a rotation value specified, the last object in the blend group is rotated the full angle, with the intermediate steps rotated in even increments starting at 0° rotation—the rotation value of the Start blend control object. This is a handy feature for suggesting action or even an animation.

When Blend Direction is set to anything other than 0° on the property bar, the Loop Blend option is available. Choosing the Loop Blend option has the effect of applying both rotation and path offset effects to the blend group. Looping a blend works in combination with the Blend Direction value, offsetting the objects from their original direction and rotating them simultaneously, as shown in Figure 21-10. If you then modify a blend control object, as done in the illustration on the bottom, you can achieve a different loop effect, sort of like one of those children's toys that never really got the hang of walking down stairs.

Blend Direction

Last object in a blend group rotated 45°

FIGURE 21-9 Rotate the objects in a blend group using the Blend Direction option.

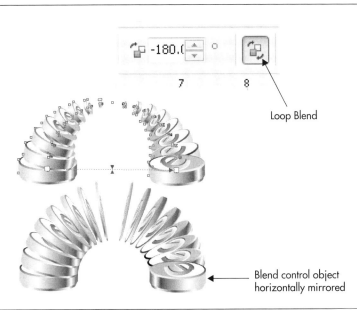

Loop Blend

Blend control object
horizontally mirrored

FIGURE 21-10 The Loop Blend option applies rotation and path offset effects to the
blend group.

Changing Color Rotation

By default, the object colors in your blend group are blended *directly* from one color to the next to create a smooth color transition. However, you can change this using either Blend Clockwise or Blend Counterclockwise on the property bar. Ideally, if you want, for example, a rainbow effect, one control object should be red and the other filled with blue so the Blend Clockwise and Blend Counterclockwise can cycle through the visible spectrum.

Acceleration Options

Acceleration increases or decreases the rate at which your blend group objects change shape; think of it as "preferring" one control object over the other—the technical term is *bias*. When a default blend effect is applied, both of these settings are at the midpoint of the blend; the blend group objects change in color and size evenly between the two control objects. You change object and color acceleration rates simultaneously (the default) when the two options are linked, or make acceleration changes independently of one another by clicking the link button to toggle it to the off state, shown here.

Object acceleration marker

Link

Color acceleration marker

Moving either slider in this popout box to the left of the center position reduces (or slows) the acceleration from the Start object toward the End object of the blend effect. Moving either of the sliders to the right increases the acceleration of your blend group objects from the Start object toward the End object of the blend effect. Interactive acceleration markers can also be used to adjust these values. While the two rates are unlinked, changing the Object acceleration affects only the progression of shapes in the blend group. Figure 21-11 shows the effects of increasing and decreasing the Object acceleration.

Object acceleration decreased, slider moved left of center

Object acceleration increased, slider moved right of center

FIGURE 21-11 By modifying Object acceleration, you can increase/decrease how many intermediate objects appear in the blend.

With Object acceleration sliders unlinked, changing the Color acceleration affects only the change in progression of the fill and outline colors between the two objects, leaving the blend group's shapes unchanged. Moving the sliders, or the interactive markers, left or right changes the acceleration. Changing the Color acceleration also affects the width properties applied to outline paths of objects. Figure 21-12 shows the results of changing the Color acceleration unlinked from Object acceleration.

Using Blend Presets

It's taken up to now to learn how to change blend steps, rotation, color, and acceleration rates of blend effects; naturally, you want to be able to save an elegantly customized blend so you can apply it to other objects. Saving your hard work as presets is accomplished through the Blend preset list when a blend is selected; you can also tap into some nice *existing* presets on the list, shown here:

NOTE *Blend paths, multipoint blends, and multi-object blends (covered later in this chapter) have to be created manually and cannot be saved as presets.*

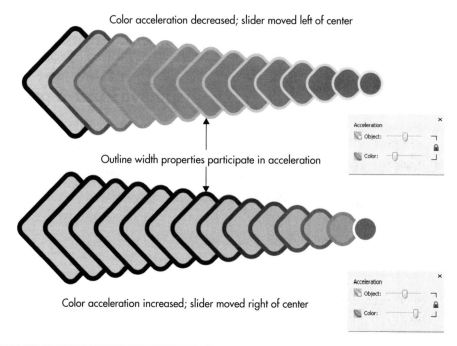

Color acceleration decreased; slider moved left of center

Outline width properties participate in acceleration

Color acceleration increased; slider moved right of center

FIGURE 21-12   The Object and Color acceleration options in this blend have been unlinked. The rate at which the blend group objects are shaped remains constant.

Blend presets are used the same as other CorelDRAW preset controls and can be saved and applied to two or more different objects.

Creating Extraordinary, Complex Blend Effects

More advanced blending can solve illustration challenges when a standard, direct blend can't. The following sections show you how to create *multipoint blends,* how to *map* blend control object *nodes,* and how to apply blends to paths. Yes, this is the "good part" of this chapter!

Creating Multipoint Blends

You can set the intermediate objects *in* the blend group as *child objects* of the blend, which causes them to behave as blend *control* objects. The properties of these child blend objects can be edited in the same way as control objects, which in turn affects the appearance of the blend effect applied between the *original* parent control objects and/or other child blend objects.

The action is referred to as *splitting.* When split, the blend objects between the child objects and the control objects become *child blend groups.* By creating and moving child blend objects, you can have a blend follow an indirect path between its parent control objects. This affects the appearance of the child blend groups between the child and control objects. As byzantine as this sounds, the effects can be absolutely spectacular; they more than pay for your mental gymnastics, and this is as difficult as it gets for complex blends.

Child objects controlling a split blend can also be returned to their original state as blend group objects, which eliminates the split. This is called *fusing* and is done using the Fuse End command. Figure 21-13 shows in detail the before-and-after effects of a split blend; familiarize yourself with what the visual effects are of splitting and fusing a blend effect.

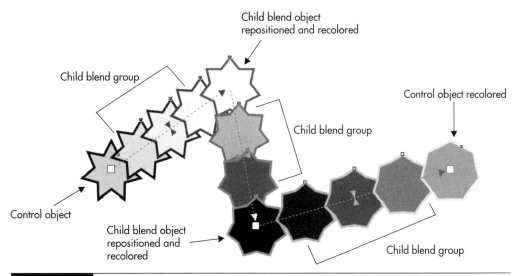

FIGURE 21-13   A blend between two polygons with different colors is fine. But when two of the blend group objects are split, and the child objects are repositioned and then assigned new fills, you're talking something visually complex and fascinating!

In splitting, two blend objects within a blend group are specified here as child blend objects and then moved, resulting in a multipoint blend. Each time the blend is split, a new set of interactive markers appears between the control and child blend objects on the path of the child blend group.

Splitting and Fusing a Blend

You can split an existing blend effect by using the Blend tool and property bar options. Fusing a split blend is done the same way as using the Fuse End command. Let's take a dip in the deep end of the pool in the following tutorial and put all these explanations to hands-on use.

Splits and Blends: The Fun Never Ends

1. Create two objects and then use the Blend tool to make a blend of about 12 steps.

2. Choose the blend group object whose position in the blend is the point at which you want to make a split, and then double-click this object. Your blend effect is now split.

3. While the blend control markers are visible, click-drag the object's marker to move it around on the page. The effect should remind you of editing a path with the Shape tool—this child blend object is a "node," and you alter the path of the blend by moving this object.

4. You can also change the shape of the blend path by click-dragging the child blend object with the Pick tool; try this now.

5. Drag a color well (a swatch) from the Color Palette, and then drop it onto the child blend object. Notice that there are two color transitions happening now in the total blend; one from the Start blend control object to the child, and a different one from the child to the End blend control object. Think of the drawings of fuzzy caterpillars that are easy to create using child blend objects.

6. Make the blend a contiguous one now by removing the child blend object's "childhood": choose the Blend tool, click the blend to reveal the child blend object's marker, and then double-click the marker. This is called *fusing* and it can also be performed using the More Blend Options button on the property bar. You'll see that the blend reshapes itself to make a Direct Blend transition across the page and that the color transition you created in step 5 is removed.

You can also use property bar options to split a blend, which is handy when you have a lot of blend steps, and a precise point in the blend is difficult to select. To do this, click the More Blend Options button on the property bar and click the Split button, as shown next. The entries in More Options are actually little buttons—you need to click *the icon to the left of* the word "Split"—not the word itself. The cursor changes to a targeting cursor, and then you can click the object on the blend group where you want the split to be.

 TIP   *Because a blend with child blend objects is more or less a blend within a blend, the markers between control objects and child objects also include acceleration marks for objects (their positions) and colors. You can make use of the acceleration markers with child objects to create phenomenally complex arrangements from blends, such as autumn leaves scattered on a sidewalk and a box of marbles someone carelessly dumped on the floor.*

Mapping Control Object Nodes

When a blend is applied, the blend group is built of a series of intermediate objects between the control objects. When you use two completely different shapes as control objects, the chances are that they won't have the same number of nodes connecting path segments; additionally, the position on the page of the first node you draw is usually arbitrary, depending on your style of drawing. By default, CorelDRAW blends two different objects using *node mapping*: the blend effect makes an assumption that the blend should start with the first node on the Start object and should end at the first node on the End object, and that all objects in the blend itself make the transition based on the same node position on the page as the Start and End control objects.

Occasionally you might get a blend that looks like a parade of crumpled sheets of paper, or something similarly nasty—it's interesting, but not what you had in mind!

Fortunately, you can match the nodes of your control objects in a few clicks. To map the nodes in a blend, click the More Blend Options button, and click the Map Nodes button. The cursor becomes a targeting cursor, your signal to click the nodes you want matched. Node mapping is a two-step operation: click a node on the Start blend control object (the operation temporarily increases the size of the nodes so it's easy to tell what the targeting cursor wants you to do), and then click the corresponding node on the End blend control object (see Figure 21-14).

FIGURE 21-14   The blend is confused; you need to remove the kinks by node mapping the control objects to make a smoother blend transition.

NOTE   *Node mapping is unavailable if a blend effect has been split into a multipoint blend.*

Assigning a Blend Path

Making a blend travel along a path can produce anything from kaleidoscopic patterns, to numbers on a clock, to a handsomely illustrated directions map. Blend paths can be set to evenly space a number of objects along a path; with a little skill, you can even adjust the acceleration of the objects along the path, thus adding a bit of a random quality to this effect. Blend objects on a path can also be rotated, offset from the path, and set to fill the full path or only part of the path.

There's a "down and dirty" way to create a blend effect while simultaneously directing the blend along a path: with two objects on the page, choose the Blend tool, and then while holding ALT, click-drag a path from one object to the other. The only real disadvantage to using this technique is that the path you define probably won't show the steadiness of a path drawn, for example, with the Bézier tool, and the blend along the path might look a little shaky. The following tutorial takes you through the more studied and precise approach to binding a blend to a path, using the Path Properties pop-up, shown next:

Path Properties button

 ## Blending Objects along a Path

1. With a blend effect already created and an open or closed path in view on the page, choose the Blend tool, and then click the blend group portion of your effect to select it, not the control objects on either end of the blend.

2. Click the Path Properties button and then choose New Path. Notice your cursor changes to a targeting cursor.

3. Click the open or closed path with this special cursor; the blend now follows the path you clicked. Notice also that the blend has changed position to align with the path exactly where it's positioned. Figure 21-15 shows a blend effect applied to a path.

Choosing New Path while a blend effect is already applied to a path lets you assign a new and different object as the blend path. To remove a blend effect from a path, use the Detach From Path command. If the blend includes so many steps that the path is hidden—or if the path itself is not visible because it has no outline color applied—use the Show Path command to select and highlight it for editing. Show Path is also a good command for editing a path you created using the ALT+click-drag technique described earlier. Remember: as long as the path is visible (in any view mode), you can change its course by using the Shape tool to edit the path's nodes.

 TIP *If you don't want a path to be visible in the final effect, set its Fill and Outline colors to None. This way you can edit the path later.*

Path targeting cursor

Blend path object

FIGURE 21-15 These two objects were set to follow an open path by using the New Path command.

Rotating Blend Objects

Objects set to follow a path do so using their original, unaltered orientation by default. For example, a blend involving vertical lines when blended to a path results in the centers of objects aligning with the path, but their orientation will remain vertical. If you need your blend group objects to *align* with the orientation of the path itself, choose the Rotate All Objects option in the More Blend Options pop-up menu in the property bar, shown here, which is available when a blend on a path is selected.

Click to align object
rotation to path.

Doing this applies rotation values to each of the objects in the blend group to align with the direction of the path. In Figure 21-16, 3D stars were created using the Star tool in combination with the Extrude tool; the extrude effect was simplified (Arrange | Break Extrude Group Apart), and then the objects were grouped and duplicated to make a Start and an End control object for the blend effect. Clearly, the bottom illustration, where Rotate All Objects was used along an arc path, is more visually interesting.

Blend Along Full Path

If the path you've applied your blend effect to is the right size and length to cover your blend completely, you may automatically set the blend group and control objects to cover the entire path. To do this, choose the Blend Along Full Path option from the More Blend Options pop-up. Using this option, you can move the center origins of the control objects in the blend to the first and last nodes of the path. Figure 21-17 shows the effect when a blend is applied to an open path.

Once a blend group is bound to a path, you can manually space the blend objects by click-dragging the Start control object with the Pick tool. This is a good feature for visualizing how you want spacing to occur in a blend.

Controlling Blend Object Path Alignment

When a blend follows a path, the point at which all objects align with the path is determined by their center origin. The *center origin* is where all objects are rotated during any default

Rotate All Objects
option unchecked

Rotate All Objects
option checked

FIGURE 21-16   The Rotate All Objects option can create a scaling progression between blend
group objects.

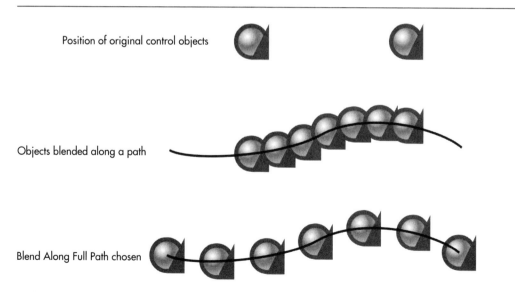

Position of original control objects

Objects blended along a path

Blend Along Full Path chosen

FIGURE 21-17   You have the option either to blend along the full length of a path or to retain
the same original distance between control objects.

rotation. Controlling how a blend aligns to a path is one of those hidden features you won't find in any dialog or property bar. Instead, the center origin is moved manually using the Pick tool, with object rotation and skew handles in view. By moving the center origin, you can control how the objects align to the path.

By default, the blend aligns all objects on the path using the object's default center. If you reposition the center origin of a control object, the blend effect aligns with the path to create a different overall composition. To move an object's center origin, select the object with the Pick tool, click it a second time so the object is in rotate/skew transformation mode, and drag the center origin marker in any direction. Once the center origin is moved, the blend is updated automatically. Figure 21-18 shows an illustration of a zipper; the artist wanted the zipper to begin exactly where it begins at the top illustration, but felt it should swoop downward as it travels from left to right. The simple and quick solution is to move the End control object's center upward, offsetting its relationship to the path, and the blend group follows this change gradually and smoothly.

Working with Multi-Object Blends

Blending between *more* than two objects can produce an effect quite unlike splitting a blend, and it's just as easy to do. You click-drag between different objects on your document page. Each time you do this, a new blend group is created. The dynamic link is maintained between all objects in a multi-object blend, which means you can change control objects,

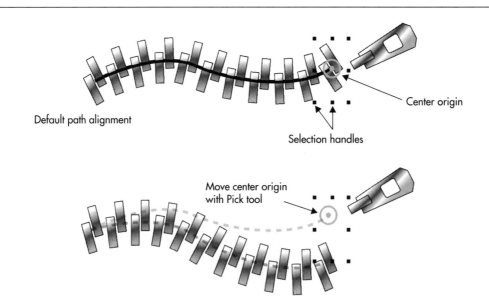

FIGURE 21-18   The center origin of these control objects was moved to change how the blend aligns with the path.

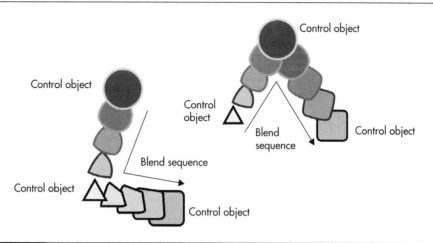

FIGURE 21-19   These three objects are blended in different sequence.

and the blends are instantly updated. Figure 21-19 shows two blend effects applied to three different objects with the multi-object blend defined in different directions.

Each blend of a multi-object blend is considered a separate effect; each has its own control objects with defined Start and End blend objects. You can change the Start and End blend objects using the Start And End Properties pop-out menu commands, shown next, available on the property bar. The Start and End blend objects are the key to making blends that change shape all over the place in very intriguing patterns.

With a blend selected, you first need to locate the Start or End blend objects—choose either the Show Start or Show End command. Choosing New Start changes the cursor to a targeting cursor, so you can then unlink the blend effect from one object and target a different one. Doing this creates a new effect each time a different object is targeted. Choosing New End works similarly.

When working with multi-object blends, clicking any blend group in the effect selects all control objects and all blend groups. To select individual blend groups, hold CTRL while clicking. Blend effect properties across multiple objects can be edited only individually and only while selected.

After a blend has been made, you might need to dismantle it and break the link between the control objects. This is easily done, but keep in mind that it can't be reversed without using the Undo command (CTRL+Z). To dismantle a blend, choose the Pick tool, right-click the blend group portion, and choose Break Blend Group Apart from the pop-up menu. The control objects then become separate objects, leaving the blend intermediate objects grouped. To further dismantle the arrangement, select only the blend group by using the Pick tool, and then choose Arrange | Ungroup (CTRL+U).

Copying and Cloning Blends

You can also copy or clone from existing blends. Neither command requires that you have the Blend tool selected as you do this, and both operations are done through command menus.

To copy a blend, at least one blend must be in view, and at least two objects must be selected. To proceed, choose Effects | Copy Effect | Blend From. Your cursor then changes to a targeting cursor—click the blend portion of an existing blend to copy all its properties. The selected objects then adopt the blend effect you targeted. This command can also be performed using the Blend tool by clicking the Copy Blend Properties button on the property bar.

Cloning a blend effect produces a slightly different result than copying the effect. When an effect is applied by cloning, the master clone effect object controls the new effect. Any changes made to the master are applied to the clone. However, any changes made to the clone override the properties of the master; any properties you've *left alone* with the clone still link to the master clone effect. To clone a blend effect, you must have created at least one other blend effect and have this in view. A Clone blend group affords limited editing: you can choose from one of the presets on the property bar, or choose Clear Blend.

 If you select a blend group and then choose Edit | Clone, you might find that you have more control over changes you make in the master blend affecting the clone object. This is not the same effect as cloning a blend; however, you can change master objects colors as well as make other edits and see the change in the clone.

To clone a blend, choose Effects | Clone Effect | Blend From. Your cursor becomes a targeting cursor used to target the existing blend to clone. Be sure to click directly on the blend group portion of the effect.

Using the Blend Docker

The Blend docker provides an alternative way to apply blends. Like all dockers in CorelDRAW, it's a handy and persistent interface element, and all the functions you can access on the property bar are located on this detachable palette.

FIGURE 21-20   The Blend docker provides an alternative way of applying blends.

Choose Effects | Blend or choose Window | Dockers | Blend to put the docker in the drawing window. Blend options in the docker are organized into four docker pages: Steps, Acceleration, Color, and Miscellaneous Options blends, shown in Figure 21-20. Unlike with the options on the property bar, the Blend docker lets you choose all your blend options before applying them; no changes are made to the selected objects in your drawing until you click the Apply button. As with the property bar, the control options available in the Blend docker change depending on the type of blend, for example, whether the blend is on a path.

Tapping into Contour Effects

Contour effects are slightly less complex than the blend effects but nonetheless powerful. Contour effects instantly create perfect outlines of shapes or paths by the dozens or even hundreds. The result is similar to viewing a topographical or *contour* map, hence the name.

During a contour effect, dynamically linked shapes are concentrically created outside or inside an object's path. CorelDRAW effectively calculates the shape of each contour step and applies progressive outline and fill colors based on the original object's properties and selected contour options.

While a contour effect is linked to an object, the object itself becomes a control object, and the new shapes created become the "contour group." Changes made to the properties of the original immediately affect the linked group. While the contour group is selected, its properties can be edited at any time—without your having to begin the effect from scratch.

Exploring CorelDRAW's Contour Effects

First, let's see what contour effects enable you to do. One of the more popular uses is to simulate depth.

Figure 21-21 shows two illustrations of climate zones in the Urals region of Russia. At left, uniform fills (solid colors) occupy the objects; at right, the same objects have contour effects. In the contour version, the control objects still use uniform color, but the contour uses different colors for the outermost and innermost objects. This is one of the uses of the contour effect. As with blends, intermediate objects are generated from the beginning object; however, you don't have to draw the end—the inner object—it's part of the contour effect function. Because the contour effect uses a large number of steps, you can see a smooth color transition in most of the objects. Also note that some of the objects have a small number of intermediate objects, producing banding, which can be useful in your design work. Just use a low number of steps when drawing a map of the Steppes.

Figure 21-22 shows two versions of the contour effect applied to text. At top, a two-step contour runs inside the word "Opera," creating an engraved look. At bottom, 25 contour steps are used outside the word to create a glowing effect; a duplicate of "Opera" with Linear transparency was put on top of the design as an embellishment. You do not have to convert text to curves to apply a contour effect.

Original filled with solid colors

Finished artwork with contour effects

FIGURE 21-21 Contour effects create a smooth color transition.

2-step contour effect inside text

25-step contour effect outside text with transparent overlay

FIGURE 21-22   Achieve two different looks for the text by using different options for the contour effect.

Using the Contour Tool and Property Bar

To apply contour effects, you'll need to use the Contour tool, shown here, in combination with the property bar. You'll find the tool in the toolbox, with other interactive tools: Blend, Distort, Drop Shadow, Envelope, Extrude, and Transparency.

While you're using the Contour tool, the property bar displays options for customizing the effect. These options include contour presets, contour direction, steps and offset spacing,

FIGURE 21-23 Use the property bar to make the fullest use of the Contour tool.

color rotation, outline and fill color, and buttons for copying and clearing the effect, as shown in Figure 21-23.

Let's dig right into the use of the Contour tool's features.

Applying a Contour Effect

1. Create an object (a polygon or star shape is a great seed shape for contours); apply a fill and (optionally) outline properties. If you'd like to go wild with this contour tutorial, try filling the object with a fountain fill—contours produce interesting results with fountain fills.

2. Choose the Contour tool. Notice that your cursor changes, and the property bar now displays contour options.

3. Click the object and drag (click-drag) in the direction you want the contour to be applied. Dragging from the center outward creates Outside contours; dragging in the opposite direction creates Inside contours. The angle of the drag action has no effect on the contours themselves—only inward and outward count. Notice that as you drag, a silhouette of the final size of the contour effect appears in inverted screen colors.

4. Release the mouse button, and your effect is finished and ready for customizing.

These steps created a contour in its default state. Adjusting the effect to suit your needs takes a little more work with the property bar options. The contours outside or inside the object can also be controlled using the interactive markers surrounding the effect. The next section explains the use of these markers, their purpose, and how to manipulate them.

 To remove a contour effect, click the contour portion of the effect using either the Contour tool or Pick tool and choose Effects | Clear Contour, or click the Clear Contour button in the property bar.

Editing Contours Interactively

The easiest way to edit a contour effect is by doing it hands-on, using the Contour tool to change the interactive markers in combination with adjusting property bar options. Use them to adjust the direction, spacing, and offset values of the effect.

The black diamond-shaped marker indicates which object is the control object of the effect. The white rectangle marker indicates the final object in the contour group, and its position sets the distance between the control object and the last object in the effect. A slider between these two enables you to adjust the spacing between the contour steps interactively, which, in turn, sets the number of steps by dividing the difference. Figure 21-24 identifies the interactive markers and their purpose.

> **NOTE** *Different types of objects are eligible for contour effects in CorelDRAW. You can apply contours to closed paths, compound paths (such as a doughnut shape), and grouped objects. These object types don't have to have a fill, but obviously they'd need an outline width, or you'd be applying a contour to an invisible object. Applying a contour effect to a group applies the effect to the entire group. Depending on how a group is arranged, if objects overlap, the contour will "trace" the silhouette of the objects as though the two shapes were combined using the Weld operation. An object applied with the contour effect is not eligible for other effects unless it's first grouped with its linked contour effect object.*

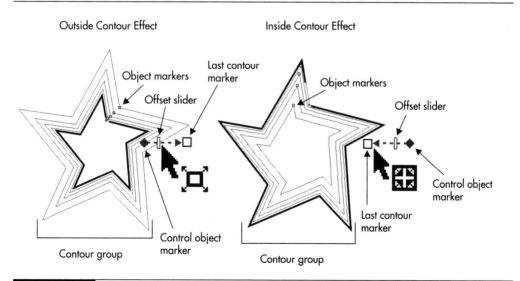

FIGURE 21-24   These two objects have contours applied in opposite directions.

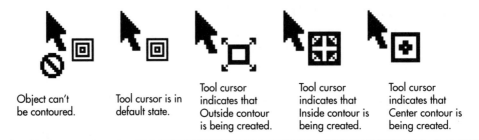

Object can't be contoured.

Tool cursor is in default state.

Tool cursor indicates that Outside contour is being created.

Tool cursor indicates that Inside contour is being created.

Tool cursor indicates that Center contour is being created.

FIGURE 21-25   The Contour tool cursor lets you know what's going on.

You'll also notice that the Contour tool cursor changes its appearance as you drag outside, inside, or to the centermost point of your selected object, as shown in Figure 21-25. While held over an object, the cursor will also indicate whether the object is eligible for the contour effect.

 To quickly edit a contour, double-click the effect portion of an existing contour with the Pick tool.

Choosing Contour Direction

In addition to click-dragging a contour to set its direction, you can also use property bar options, shown here. Choosing To Center, Inside Contour, or Outside Contour causes the contours to be applied in the direction relative to the object's outline path. When Inside Contour or Outside Contour is selected, you can set the number of steps and the offset spacing between the steps by entering values in the Contour Steps and Contour Offset boxes in the property bar, and pressing ENTER.

Inside Contour

To Center

Outside Contour

 To separate an applied contour and break the dynamic link to the original object, right-click directly on the effect (objects), and then choose Break Contour Group Apart from the pop-up menu.

The effect's contour direction, spacing, and offset values affect one another. In the sections to follow, remember that when you change one parameter's values, a different parameter will probably auto-change.

Contour Inside

With the exception of the 47 clowns that can get out of a Volkswagen, there's a real-world and mathematical limit to how many steps you can create a shape within a shape. For contours, if the offset spacing value you enter in the Contour Offset box (on the property bar) exceeds the number of steps the distance allows, the Contour Steps value is automatically reduced to fit. Figure 21-26 shows some results of applying Inside contours to different objects; as you can see, compound paths produce quite elegant contour steps. Remember: open paths are not eligible for Inside contour effects; it can't be done mathematically, and it can't be done in CorelDRAW.

Contour Outside

Choosing Outside Contour creates contours *around* your object, and yes, you can use an open path, as shown in Figure 21-27, with outside contouring. It creates an interesting effect you can use for designing everything from neon signs to expensive paperclips. The Contour Steps value can be set as high as 999, and the Contour Offset values travel within a range of 0.001 to 300 inches.

Contour To Center

The To Center direction creates the contour inside the selected object, but it does so using as many steps as mathematically possible. The number of steps depends on the Contour Offset value (editing the number of steps is not available)—in any case, your object is filled with a contour. This is a terrific option for illustrating game mazes—with a little editing after

FIGURE 21-26   These objects have identical Inside contours.

FIGURE 21-27   The same objects as shown in Figure 21-26 look a little different when Outside Contour is chosen as the contour style.

making a contour of a bicycle or a flower in a pot, you could fill a book with games like you see on children's menus in restaurants. Here, the Contour Offset value is the only parameter that can be changed; the number of steps is calculated automatically. Figure 21-28 shows contours applied using the To Center option; as with the Inside Contour option, open paths cannot take a To Center contour.

Setting Contour Colors

Controlling the progression of color between your original object and the colors of the contour effect is important to create great illustrations; CorelDRAW is a wonderful drawing program, but *you* are the artist! You can set color in several different ways, specify a

FIGURE 21-28   The To Center option creates contours to the center of an object while the number of steps is calculated by CorelDRAW.

nonlinear color rotation, control pen and fill colors, and even set fountain fill colors for individual contour steps.

Color Rotation Options

A default contour creates fill and outline colors in a steady progression between the base object and the final contour (the End object if contours were blends). However, you can rotate these colors to create rainbow contours and other special effects. To do this, choose either Clockwise or Counterclockwise Contour Colors, as shown here, which has the effect of applying fill and outline colors based on color positions located around a color wheel— red, orange, yellow…you get the idea!

Linear Contour Colors

Counterclockwise Contour Colors

Clockwise Contour Colors

Outline Color

The Outline Color option, handsomely screen-captured here, sets the outline color of the last contour in the effect, meaning the colors change steadily from your original to the last contour object. If your object doesn't have an outline color applied, this option still displays black as the default color, but no color will be applied to your contours. To set the outline color, click the Outline Color selector and choose a color.

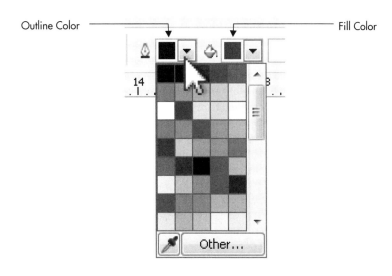

Outline Color

Fill Color

Fill Color

If you want to wow your audience, definitely play with Fill Color to create significant changes along the steps of a contour. If an object doesn't have a fill, although you can set a contour color, the contour will not have a fill. This creates an interesting effect if you have outline width and colors applied to the base object, but with no fill and no outline set for the base object to which you want to apply a contour, it's an exercise in artistic futility. To set the fill color, click the Fill Color selector and choose a color.

NOTE *Although base objects cannot have a transparency effect in place when you use the Contour tool, you can do some interesting things if you first create a contour, break it apart (CTRL+K), and then apply the transparency effect to the group of objects that used to be a dynamically editable contour. Try using Uniform transparency at about 90% in Xor mode on a group of 10 to 20 objects. Without a lot of preplanning, you can easily generate a color palette simply by experimenting.*

Creating Special Effects with Contours

Because contour intermediate steps travel concentrically from the control object to the end of the effect, you can accomplish certain things that would take hours or perhaps not be possible using other tools and effects. For example, a blend effect is simply the wrong tool choice when you want interior shading in an object, because when you scale an irregularly shaped object (such as the letter Q), it scales disproportionately. As a result, when you blend, say, a Q to a smaller Q you've centered inside the larger Q, the intermediate blend objects scale different areas disproportionately. Therefore, a key to creating smoothly shaded objects is to use a contour effect with many steps and a small Contour Offset value. Here's an example recipe: with the Artistic text tool, type the letter **Q** (uppercase), choose a bold font such as Futura, use black as the Fill Color, and make it about 200 points in height. With the Contour tool, choose Inside Contour on the property bar, set the Contour Offset to about 0.001", create about 150 steps, and choose white as the fill color. The result is a very smoothly shaded piece of artwork that will print beautifully with no banding, because 150 intermediate steps from black to white within relatively small objects is just about the upper limit for laser printers and most inkjet printers.

TIP *Grayscale images—those composed only of shades of black—are usually written to an image file format such as BMP and TIFF as 8-bit-per-pixel images. Eight bits of brightness values yield 256 possible shades from black to white, and this number is a good one to remember when you want to create smooth transitions with the blend and contour effects. In theory, you should see no banding in contour steps if you use 254 steps between a white and a black object of small size on your page. The greater the distance between blend and contour effect objects, the greater the chance you'll need to increase the number of steps, but 254 is a good bench value to begin your work with if a smooth transition is your goal.*

However, a smooth contour transition might not always be your artistic goal; by using no fill but only an outline width on objects, a small number of steps, and a relatively high Contour Offset value, you can indeed design topographic maps, magnetic fields, and other illustrations in the technical vein. In Figure 21-29 you can see an object with the top edge suggesting a landscape—created by using the Roughen brush. The contour objects are white lines, they have a high Contour Offset value so they're clearly visible, and then the Effects | Add Perspective command was used to suggest contour effects that have depth in the illustration. The text also has a contour effect; a Linear transparency was then added from top to bottom.

Fountain Fill Color

Contour effects also support the use of certain fountain fills in linear, radial, conical, and square modes. If you've applied a fountain fill to your original object, the color fill properties of the contour group are also applied with the same fill type. If you've contoured an object that has a fountain fill, use the property bar to set the last color in the Contour fountain fill; if the fountain fill uses multiple colors, the Contour fountain fill ignores the transition colors. If an object doesn't include a fountain fill, the color selector on the property bar is unavailable.

FIGURE 21-29   Make smoothly shaded contour effects or make the effect obvious; the technique you choose depends on the illustration assignment.

Copying and Cloning Contour Effects

You can also copy and clone contour effects to other objects, just as with blends as discussed earlier. To perform either operation, the effect you want to copy or clone must be in view on your screen at the same time as the object to which you want to copy or clone the effect. To copy an existing contour effect to your selected object while using the Contour tool, first click a target object to which you want to copy the effect. Then click the Copy Contour button on the property bar, and use the targeting cursor to click an existing contour effect. You can also use the Attributes eyedropper tool when you've checked the Blend entry in the Effects drop-down list on the property bar. While using the Pick tool, select the target object first, and then choose Effects | Copy Effect | Contour From, and use the same targeting operation. To clone a contour effect to a selected object, use the Pick tool and choose Effects | Clone Effect | Contour From, and target the existing effect.

Controlling Contour Acceleration

Just like blends, Contour Acceleration options have the effect of either increasing or decreasing the rate at which the contour group objects change shape (and color) as they progress between the control object and the final object. You can choose Object and Color Acceleration options on the property bar when a contour effect object is selected in the drawing window. When a default contour is applied, both these settings are at a default midpoint—the contour objects change in color and size evenly. Change both acceleration rates simultaneously (the default) while the two options are linked, or change them individually by clicking the unlink acceleration (lock icon) button, shown here.

Click to unlink Object and Color Acceleration sliders.

To access acceleration options, click the Object And Color Acceleration button in the property bar, and adjust the slider controls and/or choose the unlink acceleration button. Moving sliders to the left of the center position reduces (or slows) the acceleration rate between the control object and the final contour in the effect. Moving sliders right increases the acceleration. While the two acceleration options are unlinked, changing the object acceleration affects only the progression of shapes in the contour group. Figure 21-30 shows the effects of increasing and decreasing acceleration.

When the Object Acceleration slider is unlinked, changing the Color Acceleration affects only the change in progression of the fill and outline colors between the control

Object Acceleration decreased,
slider moved left of center.

Object Acceleration increased,
slider moved right of center.

FIGURE 21-30   Acceleration rates can dramatically change the look of an object that has a contour effect.

object and the final contour in the effect, leaving the object shape acceleration unchanged. Moving the sliders (or interactive markers) left or right increases or decreases acceleration between the control object and the final contour. Figure 21-31 shows the results of changing the Color Acceleration rates while unlinked from the Object Acceleration values.

12 contour effect steps;
default Color Acceleration

The same 12 contour steps;
Color Acceleration increased,
slider moved right of center

The same 12 steps; Color
Acceleration decreased,
slider moved left of center

FIGURE 21-31   Acceleration rates are unlinked; you can increase and decrease the illustration's contrast by changing only the Color Acceleration.

Changing the Color Acceleration also affects the color properties applied to outline paths of objects.

Using Contour Presets

Up to this point, you've learned about the effects of changing contour direction, steps, offsets, color rotation, and pen and fill colors of applied contour effects. Next, it's only natural to save your efforts as presets to apply to other existing contours using the Presets options, as shown here:

Contour presets are used in the same manner as other preset effects. Contour presets can be saved and quickly reapplied to different objects.

Using the Contour Docker

Although the Contour tool is the most intuitive way of applying contours, you can still apply them using the old Contour docker as an alternative.

To open the Contour docker, shown next, choose Effects | Contour, or choose Window | Dockers | Contour (CTRL+F9). The Contour docker is organized into three areas accessed by clicking buttons for Steps, Color, and Acceleration. The docker's options are organized a little differently than on the property bar, but the same options are found here. One advantage to using the docker is that as with the Blend docker, you can choose all your options before applying them.

In this chapter you've seen where to find the options for controlling and customizing blends and contours, so you know where things are, but as with operating heavy machinery:

● You don't take prescription medicines an hour before beginning.

● You turn the key and the real fun begins!

Dig into blend and contour effects; add shading to simple objects to make workaday illustration work an inspiring endeavor and to reap the reward of the automation that's possible within CorelDRAW. You can knock off 20 signs an hour using these effects instead of only two or three. Don't forget, either, that you can break these effects into groups (CTRL+K), ungroup the objects (CTRL+U), and rearrange the objects to suit your specific assignment. Blends and contours are one of the best ways to generate scores of similarly shaped objects, so fill your page with tiny drawings to make patterns, charts, you name it.

Chapter 22 continues with a survey of CorelDRAW effects, turning now to applying photographic qualities to your drawings through transparency, shadows, glows, and lens effects. Bring along some drawings you want to spruce up, and also bring your thinking cap. Specifically, your *lens* cap.

You can groan now…

CHAPTER 22

Lens Effects, Transparency, Shadows, Glows, and Bevels

When you need something more than distortions, blends, and contours, but your design doesn't require a full-blown 3D extrude look, *elements* of photorealism can push a design in your intended direction. This chapter takes a look at automated—and a few manual—techniques you can use to add shadows, an engraved look, and reflections and highlights to a composition. You'll also learn to use the Lens docker, a device for color correcting both vector and bitmap artwork. Many looks you'd like to achieve that use transparency, or a distorted, colored look through a virtual camera lens are easily accomplished with lens effects. The only hard part is deciding what type of effect works best in your illustration!

> **NOTE** *Download and extract all the files from the Chapter22.zip archive to follow the tutorials in this chapter.*

What's Behind a Lens Effect

Looking at your drawing with a lens effect object resting above it is like looking through a window or a magnifying glass. What you see through the lens effect object is influenced by the *properties* of the glass. For example, tinted glass in the real world makes objects in the distance appear darker—this phenomenon can be easily simulated by using the Color limit lens applied to a 50% black object.

The remarkable thing about lens effects is that this feature doesn't care whether a lens effect object is over a vector drawing or a bitmap—you'll get the same results. One of the more popular uses of this feature is to partially overlap a shape possessing a lens effect over a drawing area, to see affected and original areas at once. In addition to putting a lens effect shape over a drawing area, you can freeze the lens object, capturing whatever's underneath the lens, and then move the lens object around, retaining the original view within the object.

Using the Lens Docker

Later in this chapter the Transparency tool is covered; this tool can create wonderful shading effects, and its function slightly overlaps some of the lens effects features. Let's start with the easier of the two effects, which is called in sections to follow simply the *lens*.

The only way to apply a lens in CorelDRAW is through the Lens docker, opened by choosing Effects | Lens (ALT+F3). Figure 22-1 shows the Lens docker, whose options change depending on the function you choose. The way to operate the Lens docker is to first place an object—which becomes the lens object—over a *different* object (or several objects, vector or imported bitmaps), pick a lens type from the drop-down menu, and then choose among different property options.

When an object is selected, the Lens docker preview window shows a thumbnail of what you're about to apply; if no objects are targeted for the effect, the preview window features a graphic of a circle over a rectangle. Options are covered in following sections, but for now, let's take the Lens docker out for a trial spin.

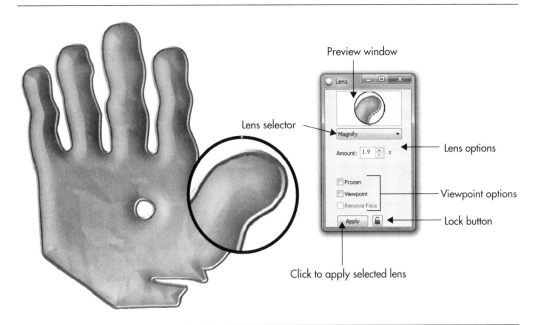

Preview window

Lens selector

Lens options

Viewpoint options

Lock button

Click to apply selected lens

 FIGURE 22-1   The Lens docker is where you customize effects to create a specific type of lens you need.

TIP   *Selecting the Lock button on the Lens docker causes lens effects to be applied immediately with no need to click the Apply button.*

 ## Working with a Lens Effect

1. Create a rectangle and then with the Interactive fill tool, click-drag to create a default linear fountain fill from black to white. This rectangle will serve for this demonstration; you'll most certainly get better effects using artwork of your own.

2. Create an ellipse and then with the Pick tool arrange the ellipse so it partially overlaps the rectangle, so you can better see the creative possibilities of applying a lens to the ellipse object.

3. With the ellipse selected, open the Lens docker (ALT+F3).

4. Choose Custom Color Map from the docker's selector drop-down list. Choose a deep blue from the From mini-palette, and then choose a bright green from the To mini-palette.

5. Click the Apply button. The lens effect has remapped deeper shades in the rectangle to blues and remapped lighter shades to greens. But areas of the rectangle not covered by the ellipse are still a black to white fountain fill.

6. With the Pick tool, move the ellipse around a little to see how the lens effect changes only those areas of the rectangle that the ellipse covers.

7. With the ellipse partially eclipsing the rectangle, select the Frozen box and then click Apply.

8. Move the ellipse around. As you can see, its contents colors remain constant, even when you move the ellipse totally away from the rectangle.

9. Call your friends over and show them this effect. This is *fascinating* stuff!

Exploring the Lens Effects

CorelDRAW has 11 lens types, and each has different properties you set using the docker controls. Each lens type and its options are covered in detail here so you can better judge your starting point when you want to dress up an illustration with a certain type of lens effect. The figures in this chapter are in black and white, but some of the really interesting effects that benefit most from showing them in color are highlighted in this book's color section.

Brighten Lens Effect

Colors in objects seen through a Brighten lens can appear brighter *or* darker, depending on the Rate you define in the number box. The Rate can be between 100 and –100; positive values brighten underlying colors, while negative values cause them to darken, as shown in Figure 22-2. This is a handy effect when, for example, part of an illustration you've worked on for days looks under- or overexposed when you print it. The solution is to design an object to use as the lens and place it directly on top, perfectly aligned with the area that prints poorly. The Brighten lens can also be used for creative effects, as shown in the figure, to make the hat look more stylish.

Color Add Lens Effect

The Color add lens fills the lens object with the color you choose by clicking the Color drop-down mini-palette and then combines all underlying colors in an additive fashion (see additive color models in Chapter 17). For example, if you created an object with a red to blue fountain fill, and then put a red Color add lens over it, the result would be that the red areas will look unaffected at all Rates, while the blue areas will move to cyan. This effect is good for adding a tint to isolated areas of an illustration and imported bitmaps. Any color can be added within a range of 0 to 100 percent in increments of 5 percent. Higher values add more color; 0 adds no color at all.

Color Limit Lens Effect

The Color limit lens produces an effect that looks like the opposite of the effect produced by Color add. Color limit tints underlying areas and decreases brightness in all underlying areas

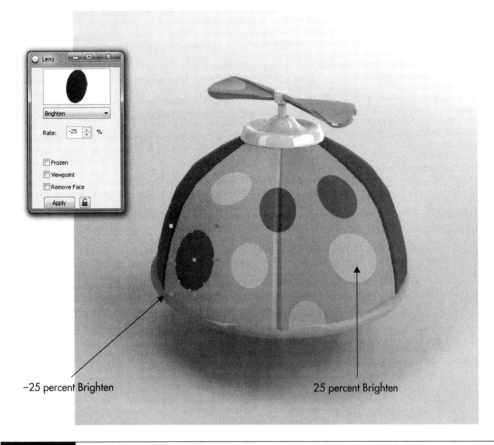

−25 percent Brighten   25 percent Brighten

FIGURE 22-2   Use the Brighten lens to correct the exposure in an area of a drawing or imported photograph.

except for the hues in colors you choose from the docker. This can be visually explained very easily.

Deepening a Selected Color Area

1. In a new document (specify RGB color mode to avoid any attention boxes), import Test tubes.jpg and place it on the page at full size by clicking the cursor at the page's upper-left corner.

2. With the Rectangle tool, drag a horizontal strip about an inch tall through the test tube image.

3. Choose Window | Dockers | Lens.

4. With the rectangle selected, choose Color Limit from the Lens selector list, and then click the Color mini-palette flyout.

5. Click the eyedropper at the bottom left of the palette, and then click a red area of the left test tube. If the Apply button is locked, you'll immediately notice that the areas covering the green and blue test tubes with the lens rectangle become a lot darker, but not the red tube. If the Apply button is unlocked, click Apply now to see the result.

6. Try increasing the Rate to 100, and then try sampling green and then blue using the Color eyedropper. You'll see that the colors sampled from the image retain most of their color after applying the Color limit lens, while the contents of the other two tubes gets a lot darker.

The Color limit lens can be quite useful, for example, in highlighting an object in a composition by de-emphasizing all other objects, as shown in Figure 22-3.

FIGURE 22-3   The color limit lens effect shown here limited all the colors except red in the image below the red lens rectangle.

Custom Color Map Lens Effects

A custom color map lens object looks at the original colors in the underlying objects—giving preference to brightness in its calculations—and then reproduces the design with the remapping colors you specify on the Lens docker. Usually, you want to choose a deep From color and a light To color; this tints and colorizes a drawing or bitmap in a traditional, stylized way. You can also remap your drawing colors in an untraditional way by using different hues with similar brightness values and also by using the Forward Rainbow and Reverse Rainbow options, all of which are ideal for re-creating Fillmore West rock posters from the 1960s.

Mapping options consist of three palette-mapping choices:

- **Direct Palette**   Choosing this option offers two colors (From and To) and maps the colors found in your objects evenly between the brightness values of colors found directly between these two around the color wheel.

- **Forward Rainbow**   This option has the same effect as Direct Palette, but in this case, each of the object colors is mapped to *all* colors between your two chosen colors in a clockwise rotation. For example, if you choose red as the From color and green as the To color, instead of a blend between these two colors throughout your illustration, distinct areas of red, magenta, blue, and green are mapped with equal emphasis to the underlying design. Orange and yellow are not included in the color map, because on a color wheel, these hues don't appear between the chosen red and green when you travel clockwise. If you want the entire spectrum of the rainbow, you'd choose red as the From color and an orange, *almost* red as the To color, so that the From and To colors cycle through the visible hue spectrum almost full-circle.

- **Reverse Rainbow**   The Reverse Rainbow option has the effect of mapping the colors in your object to the RGB brightness values of all colors between your two chosen colors in a counterclockwise direction. If you choose this option after setting up Forward Rainbow colors, you'll get a chromatic inverse of Forward Rainbow color mapping, a highly "solarized" look, much like what developed physical film looks like if you opened the back of the camera before rewinding the film.

 To quickly swap your selected From and To colors in the Lens docker while applying custom color map lens effects, click the small button located between the From and To color selectors, and then click Apply.

Fish Eye Lens Effect

A conventional camera "fish eye" lens is usually 18mm (compared with the standard 43.3mm) with a very wide angle of view—famous architectural photographs feature 90 degrees of vision and more. CorelDRAW's Fish eye lens performs the virtual equivalent; you can produce exceptionally distorted artwork, which can be interesting if not an everyday effect in commercial design. The Fish eye lens is controlled by setting the rate of distortion within a range of 1,000 to –1,000 percent. The effect is so dramatic at maximum settings that objects viewed through this lens can become unrecognizable. At lower rates, the effect is subtle while retaining a sense of drama and dynamics.

Although Burger.cdr—the file you'll work with in a moment— is a good illustration, let's say the fictitious client, Mr. Beefbarn, wants to "accentuate" his 1/16th of a pound all-beef special by plumping up the illustration for the advertisement instead of showing the actual weight of his product. You can occasionally use an envelope effect (see Chapter 20) to manually create a fish eye effect, but with groups of objects (the burger is made up of 138 objects, many of them simplified blends) you always run the risk of unpredictably bent objects within a group. Instead, what you can do in a few mouse clicks is create a shape that roughly fits over only the burger in the drawing, and then apply the Fish eye lens.

Changing Object Size with the Fish Eye Lens

1. Open Burger.cdr; with a Pen tool, draw an object that roughly matches the shape of the hamburger, just a little larger so the lens effect works the best. If you want to cut to the chase, creating an ellipse around the burger provides decent results.

2. On the Lens docker, with the object selected, choose Fish Eye. Set the Rate to 45%. If the Apply button is unlocked, click Apply to see the results. Try moving the lens object around a little if the illusion that the burger is almost twice its original size isn't perfect.

3. Suppose Mr. Beefbarn gets on a health food kick and wants you to design a leaner burger. Okay, just crank the Fish Eye lens to –90% and then click Apply. In one click and perhaps by moving the lens object, today's health-conscious culture will buy the MicroBurger over the BloatBurger without a second thought.

In Figure 22-4 you can see at left the result of an ellipse object with the Fish eye lens type, at a rate of 45%. The burger bulges toward the viewer, and Mr. Beefbarn is happy. At right a negative rate, –90%, is defined using the same lens object. Happy client, very little editing work.

Heat Map Lens Effect

The Heat map lens is similar to the color map effect, except the colors are predetermined (there are no specific color options). The effect simulates "black body" physics: a hypothetical object (in space) absorbs all light, and the presumption in this hypothesis is that the body is

Fish Eye rate at
45 percent

Fish Eye rate at
–90 percent

FIGURE 22-4   Two different Fish Eye lens effect settings are used to bloat and pucker the
underlying drawing area.

warm. With the Heat map lens, colors in underlying objects on the warm side of the color
wheel (red, orange, yellow) appear in shades of red or orange. Cool colors—green, blue, and
violet—appear in shades of white, yellow, purple, blue, and light blue. By default, colors in
the resulting composition tend to feature more warm than cool colors, but you can offset the
color mapping by using the Palette rotation spin box. This is an effect that you really need
to experiment with on your own, and to get a lot of clients who want simulated infrared
photographs!

When you use the Palette rotation spin box, values between 0 and 49 usually cause
colors to appear warmer, and values between 50 and 100 cause colors to appear cooler.

Invert Lens Effect

The Invert lens applies color inversion to the colors of underlying objects. In this case, colors
are directly mapped to colors found on the opposite side of a color wheel. Black areas change
to white, light grays turn to dark grays, reds turn to greens, yellows turn to blues, and so on.
To make a "day and night" composition as shown here:

1. Open the Sundial.cdr image.

2. Put the black half-circle over the left half of the logo.

3. Choose Invert from the selector list on the Lens docker.

Magnify Lens Effect

The Magnify lens produces a straightforward and predictable effect, but it can make underlying objects larger *or* smaller, depending on the settings you enter for the Amount value. The Amount can be set within a range of 0.1 to 100, where values between 1 and 100 cause increased magnification, and values less than 1 cause reduced magnification. Figure 22-5 shows one of scores of creative possibilities for putting a magnifying glass in a drawing. You can try this for yourself by opening Swamp Water.cdr. Bitmaps are resolution dependent, so there's a limit to how much you can magnify the image of the bottle. However, the text in this composition is pure native CorelDRAW vectors. Place the ellipse over the fine print in the image, and then magnify it 8 times or even higher if you like, and the text remains crisp, legible, and in this example, a little reminder about what you drink. Later in this section you'll learn about the Frozen, Viewpoint, and Remove Face options for the lens effect.

Tinted Grayscale Lens Effect

By default, the Tinted grayscale lens converts the colors of underlying objects to grayscale values, which is terrific if you're into black-and-white photography, but you can use any color you like, thus tinting photos and drawings, just by choosing a color from the color selector. It would be silly to show you a figure here of a grayscale lens effect; you'll see the results yourself in your own work. Remember that digital images use the additive color model, so the lighter the lens color, the fainter the resulting composition will be. This might be an effect you want, however; try light grays and light warm browns to make new photographs look like they were taken in the 1940s.

FIGURE 22-5   A Magnify lens effect rate of just 8 times enlargement is enough to make
5-point text in an illustration completely legible.

Transparency Lens Effect

The Transparency lens is a simplified version of the effects that can be achieved using the
Transparency tool on the toolbox. Blending modes are unavailable and the object itself—
not the underlying objects—becomes transparent to varying degrees, based on the rate
you set on the Lens docker. The perk to using a transparency lens effect over using the
Transparency tool is that you can freeze the effect and then move a partially transparent
copy of the underlying area anywhere you like on the page.

Wireframe Lens Effect

The Wireframe lens converts the color and outline properties of objects to specific colors;
this is a very useful effect for pointing out the technical details in an illustration. You can set

the outline and fill colors of objects beneath the lens to any uniform color you choose by using the color selectors. The fill and outline colors of your objects are replaced with the selected colors, while outline properties—such as applied widths and line styles—are ignored. Wireframe produced a fixed width outline, and if your illustration has no outline width on an object, no wireframe effect is produced.

Using Lens Options

Only one option has been discussed so far with the Lens docker, the *types* of effects. You'll gain more control of your effects in a moment, while the other options on the docker are explained in the following sections. Locking an effect, altering viewpoints, and controlling whether the page background is involved in an effect will open extra doors to this docker.

Using the Frozen Option

The Frozen option causes the view seen through any lens effect to remain constant—even if the lens object itself is moved. This gives you the option to apply and freeze the lens object view and use it for other purposes. Behind the scenes, some complex calculations are being performed. A Frozen lens object can actually be ungrouped to reveal a set of objects based on the lens you've applied. If the effect is applied above a bitmap, the result is often a complete copy of the image area, filtered, and can be exported as a bitmap.

After the Frozen option is chosen, the lens object can be ungrouped (CTRL+U). This action breaks the dynamic link between the lens object and the view of objects seen through it and converts the effect to a collection of ungrouped vector and/or bitmap objects. Each of the objects representing the complete effect becomes a separate object, including the lens object, the page background, and the objects within the lens view.

Walk through the following tutorial to see how the Wireframe lens is used in combination with freezing a lens object so that the lens object can be moved and edited independently of the spanner illustration. Open Spanner.cdr now.

 ## Making a Frozen Treat

1. Choose the Polygon tool (press Y) to make this a mechanical-looking composition. On the property bar, set the Points or Sides to 7, and then hold CTRL and drag to create a symmetrical polygon about 2" in width.

2. With the Pick tool, select the spanner group of objects and then right-click over black on the Color Palette. Wireframe doesn't work if the underlying objects have no outline, and ostensibly doing this action ruins the look of the illustration, but you're not done yet.

22

3. Put the polygon over any area of the spanner, and then on the Lens docker, choose the Wireframe type, set the Outline color to white, and then set the Fill color to blue, to create a blueprint-style lens effect. You can't change the Outline width, so the effect might look a little wimpy right now; just wait a few steps to dramatically enhance the Lens view.

4. Select the Frozen check box (see Figure 22-6). A lens can be frozen and unfrozen (thawed?) and then moved; however, if you alter the contents of the frozen object, it is no longer a lens object—it becomes a group of objects.

5. On the toolbox, click the Outline tool, and then choose 2 pt from the list.

Freeze lens

FIGURE 22-6   Freezing a lens object lets you move and edit it without affecting the underlying objects.

6. Move the polygon around if you like. Notice also that by applying a 2-point outline to the frozen lens object, background areas such as the grid the spanner is resting on become visible. Everything under the lens is now part of a group of vector objects—you can press CTRL+U now to ungroup the objects and individually recolor them if you like.

Changing a Lens Viewpoint

The Viewpoint option offers the chance to move a lens object but also to retain the view of the objects the lens was originally over. The Lens Viewpoint option lets you move a lens and keep the view inside the lens constant—like freezing a lens—but this option *keeps the effect dynamic.* When you check Viewpoint on the Lens docker, an Edit button appears. You then click-drag interactively to reposition the viewpoint of the lens effect either by using your cursor (indicated onscreen by an *X*) or by entering numeric values in the X and Y page position boxes.

Lens object with
Invert applied

Edit/End button

Numeric entry boxes for
viewpoint page position

New viewpoint
marker position

TIP *The view seen through a lens object is dependent on object order on a layer—all objects layered below the lens object appear in the lens. When the Viewpoint is repositioned, you may find that an object might not appear visible. Arranging objects in back of the lens object causes them to be affected; arranging them in front of the lens object prevents the lens effect from changing them.*

The default viewpoint position of a lens effect is always the center of your object, but you can move it anywhere you like. After moving it, click the Edit button and then the Apply button on the Lens docker to set the new position. The Viewpoint option does not use the auto-apply lock feature.

Using the Remove Face Option

Remove Face is available for only a few types of lens effects and lets you specify whether other objects and the page background participate in the effect. By default, whenever a lens effect is applied, the background—your page, which is usually white—is involved in the effect.

However, if the lens you are using alters colors—such as Custom color map—and you *don't* want your background to be changed within the view seen through the lens object, choosing the Remove Face option leaves the background unaltered.

Clearing Things Up with the Transparency Tool

Transparency is an effect CorelDRAW users have leveraged for many years to illustrate scenes that have a very photorealistic look. The Transparency tool is quite different in use and in the effect you achieve than the Transparency lens. You have directions for transparency such as linear and radial, and also various operators (styles of transparency) available from the property bar to set how a partially transparent object interacts with objects below it. Any "look" from stained glass to a bleached-out overexposure is possible to create using the different operators.

One thing is good to keep in mind when working with transparency in a design: this is the way you blend colors between objects. That's it; your work doesn't benefit from a totally transparent object—there has to be *some* influence from the object to which you apply transparency, and it's usually color. Therefore, an alternative way to think about transparency is to think about color blending.

One of the keys to accomplishing amazing artwork using the Transparency tool is *the fill* that a semitransparent object has; in addition to uniform fills, fountain and pattern fills can also take on transparency. You put fills and transparency together, and you're talking seriously sophisticated compositions! Another key lies in how you approach a drawing in which you plan to feature partially transparent objects. To illustrate a real-world object such as a piece of jewelry, transparency plays a part—the gem in the jewelry, for example—but there will certainly also be *nontransparent* objects in such a drawing, so don't overindulge in transparency when only certain parts of an illustration make the best use of this effect. In the next illustration, you can see what is today a fairly common button for a web page; it suggests glass. At left you can see a Wireframe view; not a lot of objects went into a fairly convincing drawing of a glass button. Combining use of the Transparency tool with your own designer's eye, you can illustrate gases, smoke, fog, mist, and steam; you can also add reflections and highlights to your work to add detail, interest…and a touch of glass.

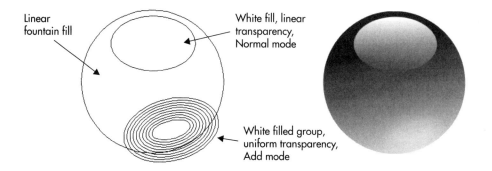

Using the Transparency Tool and Property Bar

The transparency effects discussed next are applied using the Transparency tool located in the toolbox grouped with other interactive tools, shown here:

| TIP | *When creating a transparency, you can set whether the fill and outline properties of objects are included in a transparency effect. Choose All, Fill, or Outline using property bar options.* |

While the Transparency tool is chosen, the property bar displays all options to control the transparency effect. These options, as shown in Figure 22-7, are used together with any interactive markers surrounding the target object.

Often, the most rewarding way to discover and gain control over a feature in CorelDRAW or any program is to dive straight in. The following tutorial might seem a little challenging because an explanation of the transparency options is provided on the fly, sort of like getting directions *while* you're driving, but you might want the power of transparencies at hand *right now*, as we all do with valuable stuff! Follow along here to create a fairly realistic composition of a child's marble; transparency will take care of the shading and the highlights. You can check out the Marble.cdr document to see and take apart the components at any time.

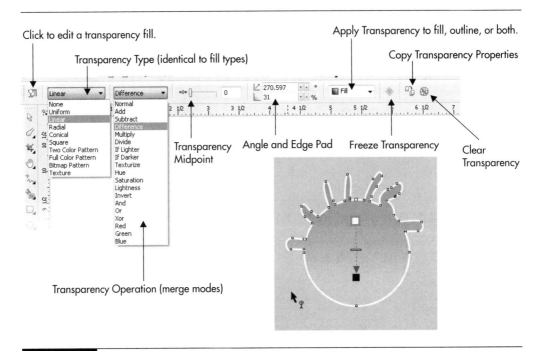

Click to edit a transparency fill.

Transparency Type (identical to fill types)

Apply Transparency to fill, outline, or both.

Copy Transparency Properties

Transparency Midpoint

Angle and Edge Pad

Freeze Transparency

Clear Transparency

Transparency Operation (merge modes)

FIGURE 22-7 Use the property bar to customize a transparency object.

Creating a Dimensional Drawing Through Transparency

1. Create a circle (choose the Ellipse tool and then hold CTRL while you drag). Give it a bitmap pattern fill by first choosing the Interactive fill tool; choose Texture Fill from the Fill Type selector on the property bar, choose Samples from the Texture Library drop-down, and then choose the third (pinkish) pattern from the drop-down on the property bar.

2. Press CTRL+C and then CTRL+V to put a duplicate of the circle directly above the original. Click the black color well on the Color Palette to give this duplicate a uniform black fill.

3. Choose the Transparency tool. Choose Radial as the Transparency type from the property bar, and then choose If Darker from the Transparency operator list on the property bar.

4. Click-drag the interactive marker, the black one that shows the start of the radial transparency, and move it just a little toward 10 o'clock. Then click-drag the end marker (the white one) toward 4 o'clock until the shading of this semitransparent

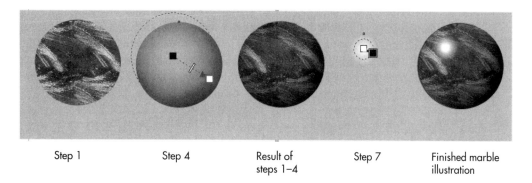

| Step 1 | Step 4 | Result of steps 1–4 | Step 7 | Finished marble illustration |

FIGURE 22-8   Use the Transparency tool to create shading for simple objects that you want to look dimensional.

object lends to the underlying bitmap-filled object the appearance of light coming into the scene from 10 o'clock. This is a classic *key lighting* effect used by photographers, so the composition should look a little photorealistic now. Refer to Figure 22-8, because you were promised directions while you're driving, and this figure is a roadmap!

5. Create a small white circle, about 1/10th the size of the circle. Fill it with white and then choose the Transparency tool.

6. Set the transparency type to Radial for the circle, and leave the Transparency Operator merge mode at the default of Normal.

7. By default, the Radial type of transparency produces the opposite effect than the one desired here: this object should serve as a highlight on the child's marble; on the Color Palette, drag the black color well onto the end marker of the interactive transparency, and then drag white to the start marker.

8. Drag the end marker to just inside the circle object; doing this ensures that the object is 100% transparent at its edges, creating a perfect highlight object. Put it at the upper left of the marble drawing, and consider this a frenetic tutorial well done!

Setting Transparency Properties

If you have experience with CorelDRAW's Interactive fill tool, you're 99 percent of the way to mastering the transparency fill types with the Transparency tool. Because transparency isn't the same as an object's fill, the following sections take you through some unique properties. You'll find wonderful design potentials you can leverage by choosing your transparency type according to what you need to design.

Uniform Transparency

Uniform transparency is the default for objects to which you assign transparency; the object will feature a flat and even transparency value. The way this semitransparent object blends with underlying objects is completely predictable. For example, if you assign a red rectangle and then a blue rectangle with 50% (the default transparency amount) and overlap them, yep, you'll see violet in the intersection.

The Uniform transparency type has no control markers over the object as other types do.

Fountain Fill Transparencies

Transparent objects that use any of the fountain fill direction types are an exceptionally powerful tool for illustration, as you'll see in a moment. What governs the degree of transparency at the start and end points are the control markers, not only their position relative to the object underneath, but also *the brightness value* of the markers. Fountain fill transparencies are driven by any of 256 shades, from black to white. Let's use the Linear transparency type; if you understand this type, all the others (Radial, Conical, and so on) will become obvious. When you click-drag using the Linear transparency on an object, the start marker is white, indicating full opacity, and the end marker is black, indicating no opacity at all.

Here's Trick No. 1 in creating an elegant fountain fill transparency: you can change the degree of opacity at the start and end points by using two methods, or a combination of the two:

- Reposition the start and end markers. If you position the markers way outside of the object, the transition between full and no opacity will be gradual, and the outermost parts of the transparent object will be neither completely opaque nor completely transparent.

- Change the brightness; the markers can have any of 256 shades of black. Let's say you have the start and end markers exactly where you want them; you like the angle of the fountain fill transparency. But you don't want the end (the black marker) to be 100 percent transparent. You click-drag a deep shade of black from the Color Palette and then drop it onto the black end marker. The end of the transparency then becomes mostly but not 100 percent transparent.

Trick No. 2 is to choose the transparency object's color to influence (usually to tint) the objects below the transparency object. Figure 22-9 shows an example: black paragraph text is on the bottom of the drawing page. On top of it is a rectangle. At left, the rectangle is filled with white, and a Linear fountain fill transparency is click-dragged from top to bottom. The text appears to be coming out of a fog. In the center, a 50% black fill is then applied to the rectangle, and a different visual effect is achieved—the paragraph text still looks like it's in

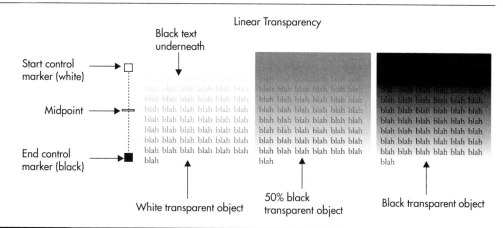

FIGURE 22-9 Use the marker positions, the marker brightness values, and the color of a transparency object to create interesting effects.

a haze, but more of it is legible toward the top. At right, black is the fill for the rectangle, and now the top of the text is as illegible as in the white rectangle example, but a different artistic sense of drama has been achieved. You now know two different methods for shading with transparency fills of the fountain type: change the control markers and change the color of the transparency object.

Property Bar Options for Transparency Effects

Some CorelDRAW users prefer the hands-on controls of interactive markers, while others choose the precision offered by the property bar's numeric entry fields and sliders; let's look at what is available on the property bar when the Transparency tool is chosen and a target object is selected. In Figure 22-7 you saw the Midpoint slider, and the Angle and Edge Pad fields called out; here's what they do.

 If no object is selected and you want to make any object partially transparent, the Transparency tool is a selection tool in addition to controlling the interactive markers. With the tool selected, click once to select the object to which you want to apply transparency, and then click-drag to add and set the control markers.

- **Midpoint slider**   This slider controls where the 50% point in a transparency is located. It does not indicate where an object is 50% transparency, but instead sets a relative 50% break point, because as mentioned earlier, you can set the start and end markers to any brightness value you like.

- **Angle**   When you click-drag, for example, a Linear transparency, you might not get the angle exactly the way you'd like it. Use this box to set an exact angle for the transition. Setting 90° runs a Linear fountain fill from transparent at top to opaque at bottom, and the angle measurement decreases as you travel clockwise.

- **Edge Pad**   Increase or decrease the "speed," the contrast of the fountain transparency. The highest value is 49, at which the transition is so abrupt you could shave yourself with the edge between the start and end opacity amounts.

> **TIP**   *By default, when you hold CTRL and drag a control marker for a fountain type transparency, you constrain the angle you're setting in 15-degree increments. You can also straighten a crooked fountain transparency you've manually defined by CTRL+click-dragging.*

Here is a practical example of a Linear transparency used in an illustration to imitate the "glass icon" reflective look. In this illustration, the folder design has been copied and then mirrored horizontally. Then the Linear transparency is applied to the duplicate group of objects, from almost 100% opaque where it meets the original, to 100% transparent at the bottom. Transparency is good not only for simulating glass but also for simulating reflective objects.

Additional Fountain Transparency Types

You also have Radial, Conical, and Square fountain transparency types at hand when you design something you need to look more dimensional. The Radial type transparency effect is fantastic for making spectacular highlights—brilliant but soft-edged highlights you commonly see when sunlight hits a highly polished metal or smooth plastic object. A Conical transparency is good to use when you need a pie wedge–shaped area, and this, too, is good for simulating highlights and reflections. The Square transparency type might not prove useful on a day-to-day basis, but it's very easy to create soft-edged highlights to use as windowpanes and other right-angle geometric areas you want to visually emphasize.

Before covering the bitmap type fills—listed below the fountain transparency types on the property bar drop-down list—let's take a detour in this documentation to explain *transparency operations*. Also called "merge modes" and "blend modes," operations have an additional effect on all objects that have a transparency effect. Operations can get you out of a design predicament when a transparent object doesn't seamlessly blend with objects below it.

Using Transparency Operations (Merge Modes)

The property bar has a list of *modes* for you to set how your transparency colors interact with the colors of underlying objects. These options further the visual complexity of semitransparent objects, and their use is for professional-level illustration work. For example, a red plastic drinking glass on a yellow tablecloth will show some orange through it due to the nature of colors that mix as light passes through the glass. However, the shadow cast by the nontransparent areas of the glass will not be the same shade of orange as the light we see through the glass, because light in the real world is subtractive, and the shadow in such a scene would be a deep, muddy orange, almost brown. But you don't have to calculate light properties or material properties when you illustrate if you understand what the transparency operations do and then choose the operation appropriate for your illustration.

The following definitions of merge modes describe the effect you can expect. Let's say *source* is the top object that takes the transparency effect, the *target* is one or more objects below the transparency object that are overlapped by the transparency object, and the *result* is the color you see in your drawing in the overlapping areas.

- **Normal**   Normal merge mode is the default whenever a new transparency effect is applied to an object. Choosing Normal at 50% opacity usually produces predictable color blends between the source and target objects; for example, a pure yellow object at 50% Normal opacity over a pure red object yields orange as a result in overlapping areas. Similarly and in traditional physical painting, a white source object produces a *tint* result over a pure color object (a pastel color), while a black source object produces a *shade* of the target object's color (if you're shopping for house paints, the salesperson will love this jargon).

- **Add**   The Add(itive) mode applies transparency in a similar fashion to Normal mode, except it whitens and brightens the result—seriously! In English, there's a subtle but distinct different between "plus" and "added to"; similarly, Additive mode moves the combined result of the target and source object colors in a positive direction in brightness value. The artistic result is good for adding subtle shading to composition areas; this is something painters through the centuries could not do without the added step of applying pure white, because inks and pigments use the real-world subtractive color model.

- **Subtract**   This mode ignores the brightness value in the source object and is similar to mixing physical pigments. If you use Subtractive transparency mode on green and red objects and overlap then with a target blue object, the result color will be black.

- **Difference**   Remember color opposites on the color wheel? This is what Difference mode performs; it moves the result color to the difference (on the color wheel) between the source and target colors. For example, a red Difference transparency object over a yellow target object produces green areas. You'll see the difference effect most clearly if you put such an object over an empty area of the drawing page. A red difference object will cast cyan as the result on the page. This is a useful blending mode for creating dramatic lighting effects—for example, you can shine a Difference mode drawing of a shaft of theater spotlight on an object, and get truly wonderful and bizarre lighting effects.

- **Multiply**   Multiply always produces a darker result color from merging the source and target objects. Its effect is similar to wood stain or repeated strokes of a felt marker on paper. Several objects in Multiply mode, when overlapped, can produce black, and this is perhaps the best mode for artists to re-create real-world shadows cast on objects.

- **Divide**   The Divide mode produces only a lighter result color if neither the target nor source object is black or white. Use this mode to bleach and produce highlights in a composition by using a light color for the transparency object such as 10% black.

- **If Lighter**   The source (top transparency) object lightens the underlying object color *only if* the source color/tone is lighter. If the source is darker, there is no visible effect.

- **If Darker**   Similar in effect to Multiply mode, If Darker calculates a new result color if areas in the target object are lighter. If the underlying target object is darker, there's no or very little change. It's particularly interesting to view the result when an If Lighter or an If Darker object is placed above a fountain-filled target object. You will see *clipping,* a hard edge where the fountain fill reaches a specific value where the result color doesn't qualify to display a change.

● **Texturize** This mode will not produce much of a change unless you fill the source object with a bitmap or pattern fill. However, if, for example, you fill the transparency object with a bitmap fill, the result is a shaded and patterned area. This mode removes the hue and saturation from the bitmap fill, leaving only brightness values—in effect, making your target object a shaded version of the original, sort of like merging a grayscale photograph over an object. This is a useful mode when you do not want the target object to influence the result colors with any distinct hues, and you can use this mode to quickly build up texture and simulate real-world complexity in your composition.

● **Hue** The Hue merge mode changes the result color to the hue of the target color, without affecting saturation or brightness in the result. This mode is useful for tinting compositions, and the target object colors are ignored in the result.

● **Saturation** The Saturation merge mode can be used to remove color from the result; it's quite nice at making black-and-white photographs from color images. The best use of Saturation transparency mode is with shades of black as the transparency object's fill, over a color object such as a bitmap photo. You need to make Transparency zero (0) in order to remove all color from an object, photograph, or vector object. The lighter the shade of black, the less saturation in the target object is removed, and as you increase the amount of transparency, the target object becomes tinted instead of containing a rich color. Highly saturated target and source objects will produce no change in the result.

● **Lightness** This is a great mode for brightening the result colors of the bottom object or bitmap because the target object's colors are never changed, just the *lightness* (also called "value" or "brightness"). Try using a bright yellow transparency object at 0 percent Transparency—blacks in the bottom object or photo will be completely removed. Transparency objects that are not bright—such as a deep blue—will only make the resulting object look muddy, so stick to low transparency amounts and bright colors for the transparency object on top.

● **Invert** This merge mode produces the most predictable—and visually interesting— results, if your transparency object is a photo or bitmap painting with lots of different hues and the target object is a shade of black. Invert merge mode produces a result whose original colors become the color *complement* as a result—colors directly opposite their originals on a traditional color wheel. The less opacity you use with the target photo, the more pronounced the colors become. You can simulate a photo negative using Invert mode. If you use a solid color object such as an ellipse over a color object, the target object will still become its color complement, but the areas it lies over will merely blend the inverted target object color with the original color of the bottom object.

- **AND, OR, and XOR**   The AND function includes similarity between the source and target objects; for example, two red ellipses that overlap and that both have the AND transparency merge mode appear not to be transparent at all, but instead display 100% red where they overlap. This is a useful mode when you want only a color result in overlapping areas, because AND creates no change outside of the overlapping result area. The OR operator is an exclusive operator; it excludes stuff: this is a good mode for clipping a color change, thus limiting it only to areas where the target and source objects overlap. You'll see nothing outside the overlapping areas when the target object has the OR operator. XOR is a Boolean math statement, based on something called a *truth table,* where certain conditions must be met to produce a result. However, you might not find a need for this transparency mode unless you use more than two objects in a design area; if either or neither object in an XOR operation is similar, you'll get no result color. This operation works only if there is one differently colored object in the color calculation operation.

> **NOTE**   *Boolean math, invented by George Boole (1815–1864), adds human-understandable language to math operations. You use it all the time when you use CorelDRAW's Shaping docker. When you perform a Trim operation, for example, mathematically (geometrically) the command is expressed as "choose A, but not where B overlaps A."*

- **Red, Green, and Blue**   Each of these merge modes filters out a respective (RGB) channel, and the native color of the source object is ignored. This is a useful transparency mode for color correcting photographs you import to CorelDRAW; for example, if you put a Green transparency mode object over a portrait, and then play with the amount of transparency on the property bar, you can sometimes correct for harsh indoor (particularly cheap fluorescent) lighting.

Creating Multi-Stage Transparencies

You might find you need a transparency object that's more complex than the fountain types offered on the property bar; for example, a lens flare can add a lot of photorealism to an illustration, and this type doesn't appear to be on the property bar. CorelDRAW's Transparency tool's power can be extended by building a multi-stage fountain fill for an object, and then using the Transparency tool in a blend operation that hides certain colors in the fountain fill.

Take a look at the lens flare in Saturn.cdr. To create the effect, you drag shades of black from the Color Palette, and drop them onto the marker connector, as shown next. Remember, darker shades represent transparency, and lighter shades stand for opacity. You might want to reposition the new markers once you've added them; this is done by click-dragging with the Transparency tool. If your drop point for a new marker isn't exactly over the marker connector (the blue dashed line), your cursor will turn into an international "no can do" symbol.

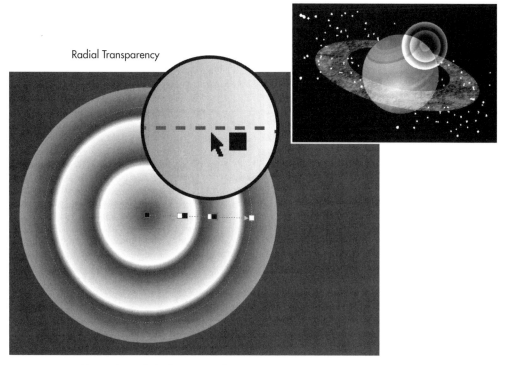

Radial Transparency

Drag color well shades onto marker connector.

Pattern and Texture Transparencies

Pattern and Texture transparencies can add texture to object fill areas below the object, creating intricate detail. The Transparency Type drop-down menu includes Two Color Pattern, Full Color Pattern, and Bitmap Pattern transparency types. With any of these selected for the transparency type, the Starting Transparency slider controls the percentage of transparency applied to brightness values in the chosen bitmap that lie above 126 on a brightness scale of 0–255 (256 shades); the Ending Transparency slider controls the percentage of transparency applied to brightness values in the chosen bitmap that fall below 128.

Figure 22-10 shows Shirt.cdr, a file you should feel free to experiment with, along with the options on the property bar when the Transparency tool is chosen and with the control handles above the target object; you work with scale, rotate, and skew in addition to setting the center point for the transparency exactly as you would rotate and scale an object in CorelDRAW.

FIGURE 22-10 Add both color and a texture to underlying bitmaps and drawings with the Texture Transparency types.

Clearly, CorelDRAW not only provides you with a robust feature set, but it also provides you with enough Hawaiian shirt patterns to last you for several months of vacationing.

Using Transparency Freeze

Freezing a transparency object captures the composite of the object's properties combined with whatever was beneath the object before using the Freeze button on the property bar.

> TIP *Deactivating the Freeze option (without ungrouping it) returns a transparent object to its current and active state. This means if you freeze the object, move it, and then unfreeze it, its interior will display whatever is* currently *under it.*

Using the Bevel Effect

The Effects | Bevel docker provides you with a means to make objects dimensional, but not as completely 3D as the Extrude tool performs. The Bevel docker offers two different types of engraving effect: emboss and soft edge. The emboss effect is an automated routine that creates duplicates of an object, offsets them, and gives them different colors to create the effect of, for example, a seal crimped onto a piece of paper like notary publics do. Although you can manually create this emboss effect, the Bevel docker creates a dynamic, linked group whose color and position can change when you define different light intensities and light angles.

Here are visual examples of the emboss effect. If you choose to use emboss, it's a good idea to create a background for the object, because either the highlight or the shadow object might not be visible against the page background. Usually, a color similar to the background will serve you well for the object color. You can use any fill, including bitmaps and fountain fills, for the object you want to emboss, but the resulting emboss objects will *feature* not the fill, but only solid (uniform) colors.

Original

Two offset duplicates create the effect.

Here you can see the Bevel docker and the options you have while applying the emboss effect.

Here's a rundown of what the options do on the Bevel docker in Emboss mode:

- **Bevel Offset – Distance**   (The To Center option is only available in Soft Edge mode.) This combination num box and spin box is used to set the distance of the duplicate objects from the original. You don't gain anything visually by setting a high value for an object; rather, this box is used to set a relational distance, depending on the size of the object to which you apply the emboss effect. For example, a 4" object will look nice and embossed if you use a 0.09" Distance, but the effect looks a little phony at greater distances. On the other hand, an 8" object will probably not look embossed with a 0.09" Distance setting—however, 0.16" scales the effect proportionately to the object, and the emboss looks good. Use distance as a scaling factor. Also, distance does not auto-scale when you scale the control (parent) object. Therefore, if you need to resize an object, plan to redefine the distance for the emboss effect after you scale the parent object.

- **Shadow Color**   The color of the object has a direct influence on the color of the shadow object behind the control object. For example, if you create an emboss effect with a blue object, the shadow object will be a dark blue, even if you set the color to black. You can neutralize the shadow color by defining the color opposite of the control object; for example, if you have a cyan circle, set the Shadow Color to red, the color complement of cyan. Regardless of what color you choose for the shadow object, the result color will always be duller than the color you define, because—well, it's a *shadow*! Shadow color is unaffected by the Intensity option.

- **Light Color**   This controls the color of the highlight object; it affects neither the control object's color, nor the color or brightness of the shadow object. Light color at full intensity displays the color you choose, and as you decrease intensity, the light color blends with the object color—light color does not depend on any object's color you might have beneath the effect. As light intensity decreases, a bitmap-filled object's highlight color will move from its original color to white.

- **Intensity**   Use this slider to control the contrast of the emboss effect. Although the shadow object's color is not affected by intensity, the highlight object's color is. High values display the highlight object's color most faithfully, while lower Intensity settings dull the highlight color and move its hue toward the control object.

- **Direction**   Use this slider to control the direction that light seems to cast on the emboss object(s). A Direction setting of 0° points the highlight at 3 o'clock, traveling counterclockwise. Therefore, if you need a highlight on an emboss effect at 11 o'clock (a very classic lighting position), you'd set the Direction at about 160°.

- **Altitude**   This option is reserved for the bevel effect, covered shortly.

Creating Soft Edge Bevel Effects

The other mode on the Bevel docker, Soft Edge, performs a lot more calculations than the emboss effect and actually creates a bitmap image, masked by the control object, which can be dynamically adjusted. The Shadow Color, Light Color, Intensity, and Direction options on the docker produce predictable results, much like those you get when using Emboss mode, but because the soft edge effect is generated to bitmap format, the results look more detailed, refined, and almost photorealistic in appearance. In addition to having an Altitude slider in this mode, you have To Center as an available option in the Bevel Offset field. Here's what To Center does and how it works.

All soft edge bevels are produced from the edge of an object traveling toward its center. If, for example, you've created a circle that's 3" across and then type a Distance offset value in the num box in any amount smaller than 1.5", you'll see a dimensional, sloping bevel created inside the circle, with a flat top in the shape of the circle in its center. If, however, you type in a value greater than 1.5", the center of the object will bevel to a point, and the front face of the object is entirely lost. The reason this happens (you might or might not want this visual effect), is that the bevel effect travels toward the interior of the object, and half of the 3" diameter of this circle is 1.5". Just keep in mind the size of the object to which you apply a bevel to gain total control over the effect. If, on the other hand, you intend for the sides of the bevel to come to a point, you don't need to set values in the Distance field; you choose To Center, click Apply, and CorelDRAW creates the maximum width bevel, meeting at a point inside the object. You can create interesting marine creatures such as a starfish by using the Polygon tool to create the silhouette of a starfish, fill the object, and then To Center auto-creates a very lifelike composition.

Here are two very different looks for the bevel effect: at left a Distance has been set for the offset, and at right To Center is chosen.

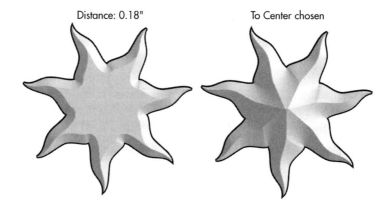

Distance: 0.18"   To Center chosen

Altitude

Altitude determines the angle of the sun illuminating the bevel effect…if the sun were actually *involved* in created the effect. Altitude is a simulation that does something a little different than Shadow Color and Light Color do to increase and decrease the contrast of the effect. At Altitude settings that approach 90°, you lessen the difference in brightness between the darkest and lightest areas in the bevel effect. Think of a coin on the sidewalk at high noon; you can't really see the embossed president, queen, or other famous person on the coin because the bulges and recesses on the coin are fairly evenly lit. It's the same deal with the bevel Altitude setting; smaller Altitude amounts cast the hypothetical sun closer to the hypothetical horizon, and you get a lot more contrast on the bevel. If you want the bevel effect to produce the greatest visual impact with your work, you'll use a moderate Altitude value most of the time.

Using the Drop Shadow Effect

With the Drop Shadow tool and the options available on the property bar when this is the active tool, you can create both shadows and glows, based on the shape of the target object (or group of objects). Although this section walks you through several variations, basically you have three different types of effects at hand when you use the Drop Shadow tool, as shown in Figure 22-11.

- **Flat shadows**   The presets with the prefix "Flat" create the impression that you're viewing an object from the front and that the object is basically lit from the front. These shadow types, also called *drop shadows,* are a popular effect; however, they don't always bring out depth in a composition, because the drop shadow suggests a face-front orientation of a scene—a viewpoint usually reserved for driver's license photos and wanted posters in the post office. However, drop shadows will indeed perk up a web page, because the audience expects a face-front orientation, since we all tend to face the front of our monitors.

- **Perspective shadows**   This effect is sometimes called a *cast shadow.* The effect suggests a shadow casting on the ground and diminishing in size as it travels to a scene's vanishing point. It visually suggests that the audience is looking *into* a scene from a perspective point and is not looking *at* an object placed *on* a scene, as drop shadows tend to do.

Flat (drop) shadow

Perspective (cast) shadow

Glow

FIGURE 22-11   The drop shadow effect can have perspective and can be used to light up a scene, not simply to make things cast shadows.

- **Glows** All effects created with the Drop Shadow tool are dynamically updated bitmaps, and as such they can look soft as shadows do on overcast days; they can also be put into merge modes. Therefore, you take a blurry bitmap, put it in Multiply merge mode, and you have a re-creation of a shadow. However, if you take that same blurry bitmap, give it a light color, and then put it in Normal or Add merge mode, you have a glow effect. This is part of what CorelDRAW does when you use a Glow preset, and you have a lot of manual control for creating a shady or glowing look that perfectly suits a piece of work.

Like other effects in CorelDRAW, drop shadows maintain a dynamic link; any changes to the control object automatically update the shadow. A shadow's look—its position, color, opacity, and feathering—can be customized, plus you can manipulate the angle, stretch, and fade properties of shadows and glows.

Using the Drop Shadow Tool and Property Bar

The Drop Shadow tool is about as hard to use as click-dragging, and after you click-drag to create a custom shadow, you'll see a series of property bar options. The tool is found in the toolbox with other interactive tools.

> **NOTE** *A drop shadow effect is anchored to an object at a specific point. For example, after you click-drag to create a drop shadow, the shadow is apparently anchored to the object by the white marker, the beginning of the effect. However, if you drag to any of the other three sides of an object, the shadow will snap to these other areas. Shadows are anchored because you probably don't want your drop shadow to become detached from your object if you move the object. Losing your shadow is a privilege only to be enjoyed by vampires.*

After an initial click-drag to add a drop shadow to an object, you'll notice the property bar lights up, and you now have a ton of options for refining what amounts to sort of a "default" drop shadow effect. Drop shadows can take one of two states: flat (drop) or perspective (cast). Depending on which state you use, the property bar options will change. Figure 22-12 handsomely illustrates a look at the property bar when applying a flat shadow.

Here's an introduction to shadow-making through a tutorial intended to familiarize you with the property bar options as well as with a little interactive editing. As with most of the effects in CorelDRAW, the onscreen markers for click-dragging to customize a shadow are very much like the markers for the Extrude fountain fill and other tool control handles.

You might be a shadow of your former self after sifting through all the drop shadow options!

Working the Property Bar and Shadow-Making Markers

1. Create an interesting object to which you want to apply a shadow, and finish applying its fill and outline properties. If you deselect it, this is okay—click the object with the Drop Shadow tool to select it.

2. Choose the Drop Shadow tool, and notice that your cursor changes to resemble the Pick tool with a tiny drop shadow icon in its corner. If you don't do anything with the tool, the only option on the property bar is the Preset drop-down list at the moment.

3. Click-drag from roughly the center of the selected object; continue holding down the mouse button so you can see some of the mechanics of this effect. Notice that a preview outline appears that matches your object. This indicates the position of the new shadow once you release the mouse button. Notice also that a white marker has appeared in the center of the object, and that another marker has appeared under the cursor as you drag it. A slider control has also appeared at the midpoint of a dotted guideline joining the two markers.

4. Release the mouse button and boing!—a drop shadow appears. This is a default shadow, colored black, and it has default properties.

5. Drag the slider control on the guideline between the two square-shaped markers toward the center of your original object. This reduces the shadow's opacity, making it appear lighter and allowing the page background color—and any underlying objects—to become more visible.

6. To change the shadow color, click the color selector on the property bar and then select a color. Notice that the color is applied; you can do some wild stage-lighting stuff by choosing a bright color for the shadow, but the opacity of the shadow remains the same.

7. Drag the white marker to the edge of one side of the original object. Notice the shadow changes shape, and the marker snaps to the edge. This action changes a drop shadow to a perspective shadow.

8. Using property bar options, change the default Shadow Feathering value to **4**, and then press ENTER. The shadow edges are now more defined. Increase this value to a setting of **35**, and notice that the shadow edges become blurry; you've gone from a sunny day shadow to an overcast day shadow.

9. Click the Shadow Fade slider control and increase it to **80**. Notice that the shadow now features a graduated color effect, with the darkest point closest to the original object becoming a lighter color as the effect progresses farther away from your object. This is not only a photorealistic touch, but it also helps visually integrate a shadow into a scene containing several objects.

If the Shadow Fade slider is dimmed, it's because you didn't complete step 7 successfully. The Shadow Fade slider is only available when the shadow type is a perspective shadow.

10. Click the Shadow Stretch slider and increase it to **80**. The shadow stretches farther in the direction of the interactive marker, and you've gone from high noon to almost dusk in only one step.

11. Click a blank space on the page to deselect the effect, or choose the Pick tool, and you're done. Take a break and hang out in the shade for a while.

TIP *To launch quickly into the editing state of an existing drop shadow effect while using the Pick tool, click the shadow once to display property bar options, or double-click the shadow to make the Drop Shadow tool the current tool.*

Manually Adjusting a Drop Shadow Effect

After the drop shadow effect is applied, you'll notice the interactive markers that appear around your object. You'll see a combination offset position and color marker joined by a dotted line featuring an Opacity slider. If you're new to interactive controls, this illustration identifies these markers and indicates their functions.

Position marker

Position marker

Opacity slider (80%)

Offset/Color marker (40% black)

Opacity slider (50%)

Offset/Color marker (black)

Shadows as Glow Effects

CorelDRAW's drop shadow effect is not limited to making shadows; if you think about it, a blurry bitmap can also represent a glow effect by using a different merge mode and color.

By default, whenever a new shadow is created, black is automatically the applied color. You can reverse this effect by applying light-colored shadows to dark-colored objects arranged on a dark page background or in front of a darker-colored object. Here you can see a black compound path (the cartoon light bulb) on top of a Radial fountain-filled rectangle (black is the end color and 30% black is the start color at center) with a light-colored shadow effect applied. The result is a credible glow effect; there are also Glow Presets on the property bar when you use the Drop Shadow tool to give you a jumpstart on creating glows.

Background fountain fill rectangle, Radial style

Glow

This chapter has shown a lot of non-special effects; effects that aren't supposed to "wow" your audience, but rather shadows, lens effects, transparency, and bevels speak of a quiet elegance that strikes the viewer on a subliminal level. It's well worth your time to become proficient with these effects for when you need a touch of photorealism in a drawing, something that strikes the audience without hitting them over the head.

This concludes the special effects portion of *The Official Guide,* and if you turn the page, you'll be entering an arena of graphics that look so real, they're picture-perfect. You're going to get into digital imagery and what CorelDRAW and Corel PHOTO-PAINT offer in the way of photo retouching features. Bring along a snapshot of the kids.

PART VIII

The Bitmap Side of Corel
Graphics Suite

CHAPTER 23

Bitmap Boot Camp: Working with Photographs

A time will come when you'll want to set aside the Bézier pen tool and the fountain fill—your layout for a brochure, for example, is all done, and now you want to add a photograph of your product, front page and center. The good news is that CorelDRAW can import just about any bitmap file you have. A photo from your camera, a scan of a photo, a painting you created in PHOTO-PAINT, or an image you snagged off your client's website—you can crop, rotate, and perform enhancements on it right within CorelDRAW. This chapter takes you first through the structure of *pixel-based images* (bitmaps): how you can get them to print well, what you can and cannot do with them, special properties, and the difference between this type of graphic and the one you're more accustomed to: vector artwork. Then you'll work with some photographed and created bitmap images to learn how to do some basic—and some fairly advanced—image editing and enhancing.

Putting a photo into a CorelDRAW document isn't very rewarding unless it's a really *good* photo, and you feel confident it will print well. This chapter delivers the goods on the whats, whys, and whens for bitmap importing, finessing, and integration to make your documents come alive and communicate.

 Download and extract all the files from the Chapter23.zip archive to follow the tutorials in this chapter.

The Properties of a Pixel-Based Image

Many of us take the structure of a pixel-based image for granted, without a lot of concern over its structure. We take a photograph with our megapixel camera, we copy the image to hard disk as a JPEG, we email it, and that's the end of the story.

However, if you want to *do* something with a digital image, such as incorporate it into a flyer, crop it, resize it, or put something else into it within a CorelDRAW composition, this is only the *beginning* of the story of pixel-based images and their manipulation. Without a cursory understanding of how pixel-based images are structured, you won't be able to successfully do as many things as you'd like to with them in CorelDRAW. Therefore, the following sections dig a little into what goes into a pixel-based image, so you can get more out of them as covered in the rest of this chapter.

Pixel Artwork vs. Vector Artwork

Although there are two fundamentally different types of graphics you can work with on a personal computer—vector graphics and pixel graphics—actually 100 percent of what you see onscreen is a *pixel-based graphic.* Your computer monitor has no easy way to display vectors as vectors, so even when you work with paths in CorelDRAW, what you're seeing onscreen is a pixel-based representation that CorelDRAW draws to your screen on-the-fly. This truth is not offered to make your life harder, but rather to get you thinking more about pixels as an art form and as a tool.

Vector artwork, the kind of art you create in CorelDRAW, is *resolution independent,* a term you'll hear a lot, particularly if you're around programmers. Resolution independent means that the art you create in CorelDRAW can be scaled up and down, rotated and distorted every which way, and it still retains focus and its structural integrity. Vector artwork can be boiled down to a direction a path travels in, the width of its outline, its fill color—regardless of how complex you make a drawing, it can be explained and saved to file in math terms. And because math can be divided and multiplied without discarding the values you put into an equation, you understand that scaling a vector drawing doesn't change its core values. For example, $150 \times 2 = 300$ is an equation that results in twice the 150 value, but the 150 value isn't really altered to produce a result of 300.

Pixel-based graphics, on the other hand, are *resolution dependent.* This means that a finite number of pixels goes into what you see onscreen, and it cannot be increased or decreased without making a visible, fundamental change to the structure of such a graphic. Pixel-based images aren't usually as flexible as vector artwork; until you understand the term *resolution,* it's quite possible to irrevocably damage a pixel-based image, throwing it out of focus or adding artifacting (explained in a moment). However, the positives of pixel images outweigh any negatives: while it's very easy to take a snapshot, it's quite hard to draw (using vectors) something that looks exactly like a photograph. Pixel-based images can have depth of field, exposure, a source of scene lighting, and other properties; although many talented artists have created CorelDRAW pieces that look almost like a photograph,

Artifacts and Anti-Aliasing

It's possible to take resolution-dependent bitmap images and make them larger, artificially increasing the size (and the saved file size) of the final image. However, you cannot add *detail* to an existing photograph by enlarging it: when a computer application is commanded to add pixels to an image, it has no real way of telling what color pixels should be added to the photograph. Not CorelDRAW, not Adobe Photoshop—no application (except those phony forensic computers you see on TV shows) can intelligently, artistically, or accurately add, for example, detail to a photo of a mailbox so the address instantly becomes crisp and legible.

What you get when you perform any "make this photo larger" command is "fake resolution"; the program averages pixel colors neighboring the original pixels to create more, similarly colored pixels. This can often lead to *artifacting,* what we commonly describe as "there's some junk in the upper left of this photo near my aunt's face." Artifacting can be introduced to a digital photograph at any stage of photography: your camera didn't write the file correctly, the image became corrupted when you copied it to your hard drive, and/or you tried to enlarge a resolution-dependent image. The cure for the last reason here is, don't resample important images; instead, print a copy of the image at its original size and see how it looks. From there, increase its size, check for visible artifacts in your print, and if there's visible corruption, go back to your original, or seriously consider reshooting the image.

One of the methods CorelDRAW, PHOTO-PAINT, and other programs that can import bitmaps use to lessen and occasionally eliminate visible artifacting from resampling a photo is called *anti-aliasing,* and you have some control over this method, discussed later in this chapter. Anti-aliasing is a math calculation that performs averaging in a resulting photo that's been altered in areas where there is visual ambiguity (some of the pesky pixels are traveling under an alias). For example, suppose you could photograph a checkerboard plane that extends from your feet way out to the horizon. You look down toward your feet and clearly see black squares and white squares. You look at the horizon, and you do not see clear edges of the black and white squares: actually you'll see a lot of gray, as your mind blends black and white together because your eyes don't have photoreceptors fine enough to resolve the very distant black and white squares. Similarly, our computers cannot reconcile black and white areas in a digital image that are smaller than the size of the pixels in the image, so when you resample the image, they create—inaccurately—little black and white squares where they shouldn't be. The inaccuracy means the black and white squares are traveling as an *alias* and presenting themselves falsely.

Anti-aliasing comes to the designer's rescue by *averaging* pixel colors when you resample such a checkerboard photo, or any photo. The anti-aliasing technique examines, in this example, areas that include both a white square and a black one, understands that both colors can't be assigned to only one pixel, and so writes a blend of colors—gray—to the new pixel color value. At left in this illustration, you can see some unwanted patterning toward the horizon—this image was not anti-aliased when it was resampled to produce a larger image. At right, the same image was resampled using anti-aliasing; at 1:1 viewing, you can see the smooth transition as the checkerboard extends into the distance—and the close-up shows the result of good anti-aliasing (some applications anti-alias poorly)—gray is substituted for black and white when it's a tossup for a single pixel color.

Aliased image   Anti-aliased image

many of us cannot invest the time and talent to "make photographs" using CorelDRAW. Fortunately, this chapter shows you the easy way to make your CorelDRAW more photographic in nature: you just import a photograph!

Bitmaps and Pixels

Programmers and users alike are accustomed to calling a pixel-based image a *bitmap.* However, the term "bitmap" is a little like the term "dial phone." Telephones haven't had dials in nearly two decades, and similarly, a bitmap—literally a map of bits of information—is inadequate to describe a pixel-based image, but "bitmap" is used as the term for non-vector graphics in this chapter anyway. We're comfortable with the term, the term is described in the next paragraph, and "bitmap" is shorter to write than "pixel-based image."

Let's say you have onscreen a JPEG fresh off your camera. What are you seeing? Of course, you're probably seeing a friend or relative, but what you're *really* seeing is a finite number of placeholders for color—the number of placeholders for color is so large that your mind integrates the placeholders into a familiar image. That's the "map" part of the term "bitmap"; this map could also be called a "mesh," a "grid," or a "canvas." All the bitmap images you take with a camera or paint in a paint program are composed of information units all lined up in a grid. You don't *see* the grid (or the *map* part of a bitmap); it's only a figurative thing, intangible—it's the *structure* for the visual information. The finer the grid, the less likely you are to see the individual color elements, instead of your mind blending the elements into a photograph. The "bit" part of the term "bitmap" is actually a *byte* of color information: a bit of information can only have two possible values (usually on or off); the graphics that artists work with today have a byte (8 bits) of information per color channel with which to express a color value. The term bitmap was coined in the days when a monitor could truly only display a color or no color; thus the term bitmap, and the term has stuck with us for more than 30 years.

To extend this explanation further, this unit of information lodged in a map is called a *pixel,* short for *pic*ture *el*ement, the smallest unit of color you can see in a bitmap image. A pixel is only a *placeholder for a color value*; it is *not* a unit of measurement. It doesn't even have to be square (digital movie cameras take rectangular-proportioned movie pixels), and it has no fixed size. Other things a pixel is *not* include:

- **A dot**   Occasionally even professionals will lapse into describing the resolution of a digital image in dots per inch. This is okay if they're using the term "dot" as slang to mean a pixel, but this is confusing jargon. Printers print dots of toner and other pigment onto a surface (usually paper); a 1,200 dpi printer, for example, renders 1,200 dots of toner per inch of paper, but it is not rendering 1,200 pixels per inch of toner! In fact, a 1,200 dpi laser printer is incapable of rendering 1,200 pixels per inch (ppi). A pixel is *not* a dot of toner or ink, nor is a dot of ink equal to a pixel—pixels alone have no size.

- **A screen phosphor or LED**   Pixels that make up an image do not correspond 1:1 to whatever the elements on your monitor are made of. With high-quality images, there are many more pixels per inch than there are light units (phosphors, LEDs, and so on) on your screen. This is why CorelDRAW and paint programs such as PHOTO-PAINT and Adobe Photoshop offer zoom tools, so you can get a better look at image areas, mapping small amounts of pixels to your screen, which has a finite number of light-emitting elements. Because resolution is discussed later in this chapter, it's good to know that the most frequently used resolution for web graphics is 96 ppi (pixels per inch). Therefore, if the resolution of an image is also 96 ppi, this means that when you view it at 100 percent viewing resolution, what your screen's light-emitting elements are mapping corresponds 1:1 to the image resolution. This means you're viewing a bitmap graphic exactly as the creator of the bitmap intended it.

- **Any sort of ratio**   The measurement commonly used in bitmap evaluation is pixels per inch, which is a ratio, like mph is a ratio—miles (one unit) per hour (a different unit). A pixel is a unit, but not a ratio, and therefore if someone says they have an image that's 640×480 pixels, they've told you how many pixels are in the image, but *not* its resolution and *not* its size. A pixel is a unit, and needs to be contextualized— for example, 120 pixels per inch, or 300 pixels per centimeter—before the unit becomes meaningful and useful to a printer or designer. If you told friends you were driving your car down the autobahn at "200 miles," they probably wouldn't be impressed, because you haven't contextualized this unit into something meaningful such as a measurement. But "200 miles per hour" tells your friends something—that they probably don't want to ride with you.

Color Depth

In addition to being color value placeholders, pixels also have "depth"—not "depth" as we'd measure a swimming pool, but rather a color "density." For example, GIF images have a maximum color depth of 256 unique values; grayscale images have a brightness depth of 256 shades.

Because 256 unique colors can't truly express the beauty we capture with a digital camera (even dull scenes can contain tens of thousands of unique colors), programmers decided early on in the digital-imaging game to structure high-quality images into components, the most common structure being red, green, and blue, like your computer monitor is based on the RGB color model. We usually call these three components *color channels*: by adding the brightness values of these three channels together, we get the composite view of digital photos and other bitmaps. Channels are a very efficient method for storing bitmap color information—in contrast, GIF images store image colors as explicit color table values, and this is one of the reasons why GIF images are limited to 256 unique colors. By assigning the red, green, and blue color channels in a bitmap image an 8-bit-per-channel color capability, the color capability equals 2^8, meaning the red, green, and blue channels can each have one of 256 possible brightness values with which to contribute color to the RGB composite image. Eight bits per channel times three color channels adds up to 24-bit images—BMP, PNG, TIFF, TGA (Targa), and Photoshop PSD being the most common file formats that can hold this color information. So, 24-bit images have a maximum unique color capability of 16.7 million colors.

However, color depth doesn't stop at 24-bit (8 bits per channel). Although monitors today can only display 24-bit image depth, the camera manufacturers anticipate that this will change soon, with the increasing popularity of high dynamic range (HDR) displays and higher-definition monitors. Today, many of the middle-range digital cameras can write photos to the RAW file format, whose specifics (including file extensions) vary from manufacturer to manufacturer, but happily CorelDRAW can import most digital camera RAW files. RAW files (as covered later in this chapter) are "unprocessed film": they contain exposure settings, f-stops, and other camera data, but they also provide a lot of flexibility and leeway when you import such an image. CorelDRAW has a little utility called Camera RAW Lab where you can color-correct and change image exposure—all after the photo was taken. You can do this because RAW images can contain 16 bits per color channel, to offer a 48-bit image—more than 281 trillion possible colors…indeed this would require a very large crayon box.

Consider it a given that because CorelDRAW can handle such mega-information and has some very good processing tools for imported bitmap images, the compositions you create using bitmaps along with vector designs will print splendidly. Now it's time to discuss image resolution as it relates to outputting your work.

Resolution and Resolution-Dependent Images

As mentioned earlier, resolution is expressed as a fraction, a ratio between units (pixels) and space (inches, usually). As you'll see later in Table 23-1, a few image file types such as PSD and TIFF can store image resolution information, and this is good. For example, let's say you need to inkjet-print a brochure, and the front page needs a photograph. A photograph of insufficient resolution is going to print lousily, pure and simple. However, if the photographer saved the digital photo to PSD, TIFF, PNG, or RAW camera file format (and knows about image resolution), you can import the image and know before you print whether the image needs to be resized (resizing is covered later in this chapter). The rule is that an image's resolution should be in the neighborhood of your printer's resolution. Therefore, let's say that you've imported a photo and you know (by looking at the Bitmap page of Object Properties, covered in detail later in this chapter) that it's 4" wide, 3" tall, and 250 pixels per inch in resolution. Your next move is to check the printer manufacturer's documentation: although manufacturers tend to tap dance around specific printer resolutions, a good working guide is that an inkjet prints about one-third of the stated overall resolution on its box. If the box says the inkjet is a "720 dpi enhanced resolution," disregard the hype about "enhanced" and cut to the chase: a 720 dpi (dots per inch, not pixels per inch) inkjet can render about 240 pixels per inch. Therefore in this example, you can indeed faithfully print this 4"×3" image with no loss in image detail.

There is a way to tell the resolution of image file formats that cannot hold resolution information, so don't worry if you have a bunch of JPEG images you want to use in a composition you need to inkjet-print. As you progress through this chapter, working tutorial files will demonstrate what you want to do and when.

Resolution vs. Image Size

Another digital-image reality that makes many designers pull their hair out is that image resolution is inversely proportional to dimensions: this is another cold, hard fact about bitmap resolution. When you make an image larger in dimensions, its resolution decreases. Viewing resolution and image resolution display the same thing onscreen, but changing *viewing resolution*—zooming in and out of an image—is nondestructive, whereas changing *image resolution* is destructive editing and often irreversible. Here's an example that demonstrates the resolution-dependence properties of bitmaps. Figure 23-1 shows a desktop icon; it's 48×48 pixels and the widely adopted resolution convention is that screen pixels are 96 per inch. At 1:1 viewing resolution, this icon looks fine, but when you zoom into it to 10:1 viewing resolution, it begins to look coarse. The same effect would be visible if you actually were to change the resolution of the image. Bitmap images are resolution dependent; the pixels you capture of a scene with a camera can't be added-to later to increase detail—no application can guess what the extra detail and extra pixels would be. At right in Figure 23-1 you can see an extreme enlargement of the icon, and the pixels are so clearly visible that you can't make out what the design is!

48x48-pixel icon
viewed at 1:1 and
96 ppi resolution

48x48-pixel icon viewed at
10:1 and 96 ppi resolution

48x48-pixel icon viewed at
20:1. Pixels are clearly visible.

FIGURE 23-1 With resolution-dependent bitmaps, the larger the image, the fewer pixels per inch.

The lesson here is that to take advantage of the unique property of bitmap images—that they accurately portray a photographic scene—you need to take a photo that is high resolution— 3,264 pixels×2,448 pixels is average for an 8-megapixel camera, a little larger than 10"×8" at 300 ppi. CorelDRAW can resize an image; for example, this same 8-megapixel image could also be expressed as 20"×15" at 163 ppi without changing any visual information. CorelDRAW can also resample an image, and this is the *destructive* type of editing; you change pixels when you resample, so generally it's a good idea to resize and to resample only as a last resort when adding photos to a CorelDRAW composition.

Importing Bitmaps into a Document

As a CorelDRAW user, you have at your fingertips a vast collection of bitmap import filter selections. Although import commands are discussed in Chapter 3, some of the import options apply specifically to bitmaps and are explained here; you'll find them useful if your work requires photographs and graphics from the Web. Table 23-1 does not list the bitmap types CorelDRAW can import the way that the Files Of Type drop-down list does in the Import dialog. Although it's terrific to have a billion different file types available for import, particularly if you have legacy file formats, you'll probably only use a handful of image types in everyday work. Therefore, the table lists the most common file types first; more exotic and legacy file formats appear toward the bottom of this table. The asterisk after the file extension indicates that a file type can retain resolution information; this is a capability—it doesn't necessarily mean the person who saved the file actually saved resolution information.

If you intend to print a CorelDRAW composition you've created that features a bitmap photo or painting, step 1 is to set up the color management of the document. You can access settings for your document's color profile through Tools | Color Management | Default Settings. Read Chapter 17 for the details on color management: what it does and why you should use it to increase your chances of faithful color output to print and to the monitor. The following steps aren't a tutorial but rather a checklist, a workflow based on your need to bring a copy of a photo into a CorelDRAW composition:

1. After launching CorelDRAW, press CTRL+N (File | New) if you've set up your copy not to show the Create A New Document dialog after launch.

2. Define the Color Settings after you've specified page size, resolution, and other parameters. Your color settings—the color space within which everything on the page "resides"—are not "Oh, yes! I know the answer!" sorts of decisions you make lightly. Generally, you're safe choosing sRGB IEC61996-2.1 because many digital cameras and scanners use this color profile. If, however, after importing a photo, the photo looks dull or lacks contrast, the color space of the photo doesn't match the color settings of your CorelDRAW document. This can be changed later; let's continue the workflow here…

Bitmap Type	File Extension
Adobe Photoshop	PSD*
JPEG and JPEG 2000 bitmaps	JPG*, JP2, JFF, and JTF
Adobe Portable Document File	PDF
TIFF bitmap	TIF*
Portable Network Graphic	PNG*
Targa bitmap	TGA
RAW image file format	CRW, CR2 (Canon); MRW (Minolta); NEF (Nikon); ORF (Olympus); DNG (Adobe); PTX (Pentax); ARW, SRF, SR2 (Sony)
Corel PHOTO-PAINT	CPT*
CompuServe bitmap	GIF
GIF Animation	GIF
Windows bitmap	BMP
Kodak PhotoCD bitmap	PCD*
Painter 5/6	RIFF
Frame Vector Metafile	FMV
WordPerfect Graphic bitmap	WPG
Corel (and Micrografx) Picture Publisher	PPF, PP4, and PP5
Kodak FlashPix Image	FPX
Lotus Pic	PIC
Macintosh PICT	PCT
MACPaint bitmap	MAC
OS/2 bitmap	BMP
PC Paintbrush bitmap	PCX
Scitex CT bitmap	SCT, CT*
Wavelet compressed bitmap	WVL
Windows bitmap	DIB/RLE
Computer Graphics Metafile	CGM
CALS compressed bitmap	CAL

TABLE 23-1   CorelDRAW X5's Importable Bitmap Formats

3. Before importing a photo, choose Tools | Color Management | Default Settings. Check both the "Warn on color profile mismatch" and the "Warn on missing color profile" boxes in both the Open and the Import And Paste areas in Color Management Policies. You're all set to import a photo now.

4. When you choose File | Import (or press CTRL+I), you then have the opportunity to scale an image before placing it on the page. More experienced users might want to simply drag an image file into the workspace when CorelDRAW is not maximized. Using either technique, when you import an image, if it has a color profile that doesn't match your current document—or has no color profile at all—you'll get an alert box where you have the opportunity to choose the color space for the imported image.

Color profile alert

Drag from folder into workspace,
or press CTRL+I (File | Import).

5. Generally, you'll want to choose the same color space as the document's color space. However, if you set up your document incorrectly—for example, your client specified Adobe RGB, you had soap in your ears, and thought they said "sRGB"—import the photo using the Adobe RGB choice from the drop-down list. Then choose Tools | Color Management | Document Settings, and choose Adobe RGB from the RGB drop-down list in the Edit Document Color Settings area. Choose "Convert document colors to new color profiles"—*do not* use "Assign different colors profiles," because this will introduce color-shifting.

Because the method of dragging an image file into the workspace doesn't afford scaling options, you might want to stick with CTRL+I for importing. File | Import also gives you the chance to filter for the file types you seek in a Windows folder, and you have other options in the Import dialog (discussed in Chapter 24). Choose your bitmap format from the Files Of Type menu.

After the Import dialog closes, your cursor will change to an import cursor that has two functions: with it you specify the upper-left corner of your new bitmap using a single-click, which in turn imports the image onto a document page at its original size—whatever dimensions, by whatever its original saved resolution. Pressing ENTER instead of using a mouse click imports the image to the center of the page.

Placing and Modifying an Image

The best way to get the hang of inserting an image into a CorelDRAW composition is by example: open Wally's Wheel's.cdr, and in the tutorial to follow you'll place a picture of an auto and then perform a little manual cropping.

In addition to clicking or pressing ENTER with a cursor that's loaded with an image you import, you can also place and proportionately scale the imported image by click-dragging diagonally. After you specify the size this way, the bitmap is imported and automatically resized to closely fit the defined area with the original *proportions* of the bitmap preserved, but the resolution will not be the original's. As you drag, the cursor changes orientation and the image's bounding box appears, showing the space the new image will occupy. While importing during either operation, the original filename and the image dimensions are displayed beside the cursor. Your goal in the next steps is to place Expensive car.jpg at the top of the 5"×7" riser card layout. As you work through the steps, you'll note that the document's color space isn't the same as the JPEG image, but you already know how to correct this. The native dimensions of the JPEG are also larger than the CorelDRAW page layout, which affords the perfect opportunity to try out this importing and scaling stuff.

NOTE   *You don't have to import large bitmap images to use them in a CorelDRAW composition. Instead, you can link to images externally, and CorelDRAW displays a low-resolution version of the image on the page. After you choose to Import a photo, click the name of the file in the Import dialog box, and then click the drop-down list arrow on the Import button. Choose Import As Externally Linked Image (in Windows 7 and Windows Vista) or enable the Link Bitmap Externally check box (in Windows XP). You can review externally linked photos in your CorelDRAW documents at any time by choosing Window | Dockers | Links And Bookmarks. Camera RAW images cannot be linked externally, and remember that if you change the location of a linked photo or delete it, your document won't print correctly. The purpose of externally linking to large bitmap images is to keep CorelDRAW file sizes down while allowing the original bitmap to be modified—usually optimized for high-resolution PostScript output.*

Putting a Picture into a Car Advertisement

1. Click the Import icon on the standard toolbar or press CTRL+I to import the Expensive car.jpg. Locate it on your hard drive, select the file, and then click Import.

2. You'll now see the attention box that tells you that the Expensive car.jpg is not tagged with the same color space as the Wally's Wheels.cdr file. Click the Convert From Embedded Profile To The Document Profile radio button, and then click OK. Often you'll notice a color difference in the image you view on the page if you choose to ignore the color profile (the first option in this attention box) instead of allowing CorelDRAW to convert it to the document's color space. Another good reason not to ignore a color profile is that if you send this file to a commercial printer with two different color spaces in the document, the commercial printer is not likely to thank you for the time and paper the two of you have wasted. One document requires one color profile for all of its contents.

3. Begin your click as close as possible to the upper-left corner, and then drag down and to the right; don't release the mouse button yet. When you believe you're very close to the right edge of the layout, look at the cursor. If the dimensions it reports are close to 5 inches, release the mouse button. In Figure 23-2, if you can read the cursor, it reports a height and width of 4.997 inches, which is close enough for government work. Move your pointing device up and down on the page just a fractional amount until you're close to 5 inches, and then release the mouse button.

4. If you want this image (or one in your own assignment) to be *exactly* 5" wide, now choose Arrange | Transformations | Size. Click the top left check box below the Proportional check box to set the direction in which the image should be scaled, and then type **5** in the H (horizontal, the width) field, press ENTER, and you've accomplished precision placement and scaling.

5. Save this file to hard disk, and keep it open for the sections to follow.

Bitmap images can't be edited at the pixel level directly in CorelDRAW. For example, if your cousin Flossie's mascara is a little runny in the photo, this is an isolated photo problem area, and you need to use a bitmap-editing application to make the makeup look better. Not to worry, Flossie: you can open PHOTO-PAINT by clicking the Edit bitmap button on the property bar or by right-clicking the bitmap and then choosing to edit it from the context menu. See Chapters 24 and 25 for details on common—and a few not so common—editing techniques using PHOTO-PAINT.

Switching from Resizing to Resampling

If you had right-clicked the Expensive Car.jpg image in the Import dialog earlier and then chosen Properties | Details, Windows would have told you the image is 1,700×1,700 pixels at a resolution of 266 pixels per inch. Any bitmap's resolution can be discovered this way,

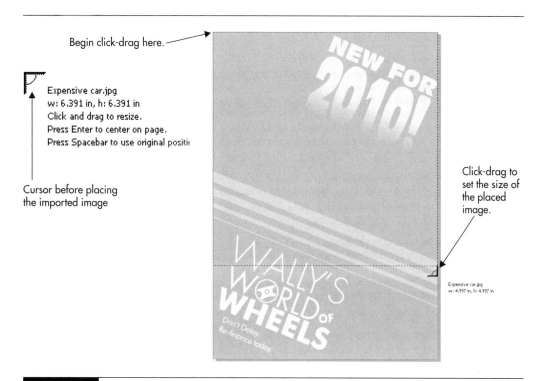

Begin click-drag here.

Expensive car.jpg
w: 6.391 in, h: 6.391 in
Click and drag to resize.
Press Enter to center on page.
Press Spacebar to use original positic

Cursor before placing
the imported image

Click-drag to
set the size of
the placed
image.

Expensive car.jpg
w: 4.997 in, h: 4.997 in

FIGURE 23-2   Import a copy of an image you want to use at a specific size by click-dragging in the document.

within the Import dialog and anywhere in Windows where you can open a folder. However, if you click the image as placed now, the status bar will tell you that Expensive car.jpg on Layer 1 is currently 340 pixels per inch in resolution. The reason is that *image resolution is inversely proportional to image dimensions*—you make one smaller and the other one becomes larger, as discussed earlier. This is a function of resizing; by default, CorelDRAW doesn't change the number of pixels in an imported photo.

However, an imaging service bureau or commercial printer might request that an image placed in a CorelDRAW file be of a specific resolution. A lot of services that make full-color business cards, for example, want 300 ppi images in files, and they often reject art or charge extra for processing fees if an image is of higher resolution. When you change the number of pixels in an image, this is not called resizing, but is instead called *resampling*, and you're altering the visual content of the copy of the image in your CorelDRAW document.

Let's pretend that this auto advertisement needs to be sent to a commercial printer with the image at exactly 300 ppi (pixels per inch; alternatively, dots per inch, dpi). Follow these brief steps to prep this file for proper printing.

Resampling a Photo

1. Select the image with the Pick tool.

2. Choose Bitmaps | Resample.

3. While Identical Values is checked, type **300** in either the Horizontal or the Vertical Resolution field.

4. Check Anti-alias (which makes the reduction of the image smooth and basically undetectable from the original image), check Maintain Aspect Ratio, but do *not* check Maintain Original Size. If you maintained the original size of the image, no resampling would take place; instead resizing would. Compare the Original Image Size and New Image Size in this dialog; this not only provides you with an estimate of how large your saved CorelDRAW file will be, but it's also intellectual reassurance that you're down-sampling the photo and not simply resizing it. Click OK and you're finished. Keep the file open because the layout isn't done. Yet.

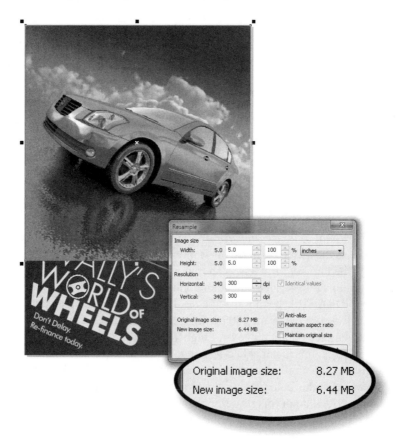

Non-Rectangular Cropping in a Jiffy

This mock advertisement clearly is designed on the diagonal, but the car image—like most bitmap images—is rectangular, somewhat spoiling the look of the ad as it's currently placed. This isn't a big design challenge; it's an opportunity to explore CorelDRAW's cropping features. CorelDRAW offers a Crop tool on the toolbox, which (as discussed in Chapter 25) performs *destructive* editing. No, it doesn't paint a moustache or blacken a front tooth on your portrait photos, but it does *permanently* remove areas of a bitmap (and vector objects) that lie outside of the crop you define. It's useful, but unnecessary for this assignment when you learn how to use the Shape tool.

CorelDRAW considers any placed bitmap image to be an object that has four control nodes, one at each corner of the rectangle. Moreover, these control nodes can be moved (inward because there's nothing outside of the boundary of a bitmap) to change the shape of a bitmap without removing areas of the bitmap—CorelDRAW simply hides them for you. Work through the following steps to hide a triangular area of the placed Expensive Car.jpg image and complete the design.

Cropping with the Shape Tool

1. With the Pick tool, select the image and then press CTRL+PAGE DOWN to put the image behind the text at top.

2. Choose the Shape tool from the toolbox.

3. Click on the image to reveal the control nodes.

4. One approach to removing the slice of the image that's covering Wally's name is to hold CTRL (to constrain the direction in which you'll drag the node) and then to click-drag the left bottom control node way up to about the 5" tick on the vertical ruler so you can see the underlying stripes. Then while holding CTRL, drag the control node down so it meets the bottom of the top diagonal stripe in the design. Then perform the same action on the bottom right control node. Nodes can be nudged: try saying that three times fast! You can use your UP ARROW and DOWN ARROW keys to nudge a selected image control node up or down. If you choose this method, it offers precision and you don't have to hold CTRL. You can also use the super nudge option and hold SHIFT while pressing the UP ARROW and DOWN ARROW keys. By default, if you hold SHIFT, your nudges are twice the value you set.

Shape tool (nondestructive)

Crop tool (destructive)

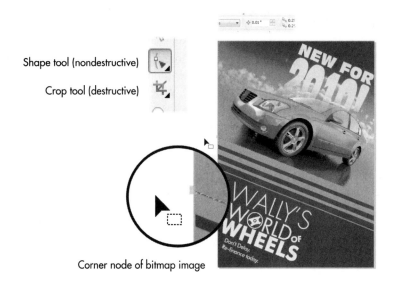

Corner node of bitmap image

> **TIP** *Although nudge distance isn't visible on the property bar when the Shape tool is active, you can choose the Pick tool, deselect any selection (click an empty area of the document window), and set a nudge value that will apply to the Shape tool when you switch back to it.*

Importing Nonstandard Bitmaps

With kind permission from Nicky Elliott, a small version, Monkey Pants Media.psd, of her Monkey Pants Media poster has been provided so you can get hands-on experience importing and performing a minor edit with a bitmap type that CorelDRAW handles well. Adobe Photoshop and Corel PHOTO-PAINT both can write image files that contain layers; you'll see the advantages to using a layered bitmap image shortly, tutorial style. When you choose File | Import and then choose PSD, PHOTO-PAINT's CPT, or even Corel Painter's RIFF file format, any layers in these file types are imported and nested within an entry on a CorelDRAW layer. You can un-nest the layers, move them, and delete them, and one of the most useful properties of image files that are layered is that the file's creator probably did so to include partially transparent areas within the bitmap composition.

Let's say Ms. Elliott wants a change made to the background of the Monkey Pants poster, that she'd prefer a more dramatic treatment than the medium blue solid color. Here's how to import and edit a layered bitmap image.

Working with Layered Bitmaps

1. Create a new document. Standard letter size is fine—the Monkey Pants Media.psd file is 8"×10" at 96 ppi resolution, so it will comfortably fit inside standard letter size at its original 100% size.

2. Click the Import button on the standard toolbar, and then in the Import dialog, scout down Monkey Pants Media.psd on your hard drive. Select it, and then click Import.

3. With the cursor loaded and ready to place a copy of the file, press ENTER to place the file at full size, centered on the page.

4. Choose Tools | Object Manager. Click the + icon to the left of the imported image title to open its nest of layers.

5. Click the Background layer item on the list to select it in the document window. This was a thoughtfully prepared file; the layers were named in Photoshop. In your own work, you might not be so fortunate if the creator of the layered file didn't name the layers. Therefore, always check what's selected in the drawing window before proceeding.

6. You're sure the blue background is selected? Then click the trash icon to delete this layer.

7. Choose the Rectangle tool from the toolbox, and then drag a rectangle of about the size of the Background layer you deleted.

8. On the Object Manager, click-drag the Monkey Pants Media.psd entry to above the Rectangle entry. This puts the remaining two nested layers above the rectangle.

9. Choose the Interactive fill tool from the toolbox. Click to select the rectangle, and then choose Radial as the style of the fill from the property bar.

10. Click the inner color marker on the Radial fountain fill, and then click a bright yellow swatch on the Color Palette. Click the outer color marker, and then click a dramatic deep blue on the Color Palette.

Interactive fill tool

Radial style

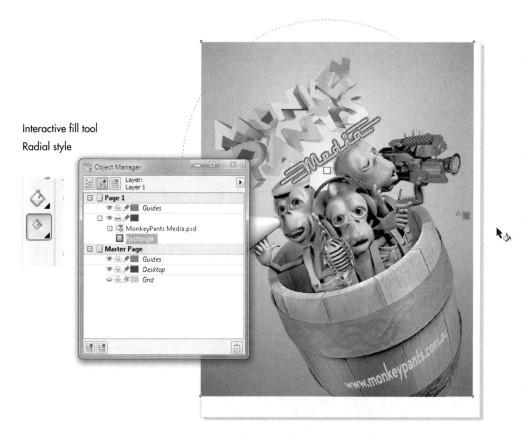

11. The logo layer could use some visual separation from the background. CorelDRAW native effects can be applied to nontransparent areas of imported bitmap layers: choose the Drop Shadow tool from the toolbox, select the logo on the page by clicking on the title "logo" in the Object Manager list, and choose Large Glow from the Presets list on the property bar.

23

Drop
Shadow tool

| FIGURE 23-3 | Combine CorelDRAW objects with layered bitmap file to extensively edit layouts. |

12. Large Glow, at its default settings, will not provide much of an effect. So you *change* the default settings: click the outer color marker, and then choose black from the Shadow color pop-up on the property bar. Then, set the Shadow opacity (also on the property bar) to almost 100% opaque. Finally, set the Shadow feathering to only about 10. Figure 23-3 shows a dramatic transformation of the poster—and because the imported bitmap layers can be edited separately, you can even reposition the Monkey Pants logo on the CorelDRAW page.

Working with RAW Images

Camera RAW is the new generation of high-fidelity imaging; it's affordable, most cameras you *don't* buy at a drugstore can write a RAW file format, and as with any comparatively new technology, there's a small learning curve we'll tackle in this section.

A RAW image is similar to an unprocessed physical piece of camera film; although it contains a lot of data about exposure, light temperature, f-stop, lens, and other conditions, the RAW image does *not* have locked data about pixel colors. RAW offers the ultimate in flexibility—if the light was too low or the wrong temperature, you can adjust for these and other flaws through CorelDRAW's Camera RAW Lab. The Camera RAW Lab appears after you choose to import a RAW camera image; a RAW image cannot be placed in a CorelDRAW composition before it passes through the lab (even if you choose not to do anything to the image). Depending on your camera settings, you'll most likely be working with a 48-bit image, 16 bits per channel; this offers a color space of several trillion unique colors and is part of the reason why RAW images can be adjusted to make dramatic lighting changes while retaining high image fidelity.

Working with the Camera RAW Lab

Working with the Camera RAW Lab in CorelDRAW is an experience you won't want to miss. If you don't have a RAW image handy or if your camera cannot take RAW file format images, a small DNG file is in the zip archive you downloaded for this chapter.

Because no two manufacturers could agree on a file extension, a RAW image could have .CRW, .DNG, or any of over a dozen other extensions. The good news is that CorelDRAW doesn't care about the file extension—you just choose All File Formats from the drop-down list in the Import dialog, and then navigate to the location of a RAW image—in the following example, Catch of The Day.dng. The *better* news is that CorelDRAW can import RAW images from a *three-page list* of manufacturers—just short of photos on a View-Master reel, you're assured that CorelDRAW can import most RAW files.

 The current color space of an open CorelDRAW document is displayed in the Properties tab. Camera RAW has no color space tag, but one is assigned by Camera RAW Lab on its way into the document using the current CorelDRAW document's color space.

Let's dig right into the features and options available to you when you import a RAW image; follow these steps and guidelines to import the image, and then perform minor processing enhancements. There's nothing truly wrong with the image, but this tutorial is instead an opportunity to gain hands-on experience with the Camera RAW Lab features.

 ### Correcting RAW Image Color

1. Choose File | Import, or click the Import button on the standard toolbar.

2. Choose All File Formats, and then choose Catch of The Day.dng from the folder you downloaded the file to. Click Import or press ENTER.

3. The Camera RAW Lab interface appears. First, check the properties of this unprocessed photograph. The Properties tab of the interface tells the day and date of the photo, the camera, whether flash was used, aperture, and ISO-equivalent film speed. If you're familiar at all with cameras, the info shown here will give you a clue to what, if anything, needs adjusting in the image. For example, the photo has a very shallow

depth of field and isn't truly an "out of focus" picture: at ISO 50 at an f-stop of 2.2 and a shutter speed of 1/25th of a second, the Properties tab confirms this. Also, because a flash wasn't used, when you get to the Color tab, you can rule out Flash as a choice from the White Balance options.

4. The Detail tab has a slider for sharpening the image as well as sliders for reducing Luminance Noise and overall Color Noise. This photo doesn't require these enhancements. The Hints area at the bottom of the tab is a handy context-sensitive reminder of what each slider does, and before you take your next RAW image, it's good practice to "get it right in the camera." You'll get less noise in a photo generally if you set your camera to slower ISO speeds. The ISO of 50 in this example image produced very little visible noise (similar to grain in traditional physical film), but an ISO setting of say, 400, for the camera that took this photo would indeed have required noise reduction using the Detail sliders.

5. Click the Color tab; here's where the fun begins. Follow the callout letters in Figure 23-4 to guide you through which features do what.

FIGURE 23-4 Use the Camera RAW Lab to color- and tone-correct high-quality digital images.

- The *A* area is for rotating the RAW image before placing the copy into your CorelDRAW document. RAW camera data can also include portrait and landscape orientation, so you might never need to use these buttons if your camera saved orientation info.

- *B* marks your navigation tools for previewing the image. From left to right you have tools for panning the window (click-drag when your cursor is inside the preview window), zoom in and out, Fit To Window, 100% (1:1) viewing resolution, and finally a slider to zoom your current view in and out.

- *C* marks the Split Pane view (shown in the previous illustration) so you can compare the original image with any corrections you make.

- *D* marks the Color Depth. You'd be ill-advised to change this from 48-bit, because only a high-depth image can be adjusted extensively without taking on banding and color clipping (explained shortly). The only reason you'd choose 24-bit from the selector list is if the image were flawless and you wanted to get down to work by placing it in your document and saving space on your hard disk.

- *E* marks the White Balance selector. You have many choices that influence the color casting of the RAW image. Ideally, you want the placed image to be casting neutral; the grays in the image contain no hues, and the photo looks neither too warm nor too cold. You have selections such as Tungsten, Cloudy, and other lighting conditions that influence the color cast of images. "As Shot" is the default setting, and this image appears to be fine As Shot.

- *F* is the White Balance eyedropper tool, used to define a completely neutral area in the preview window to better set and possibly neutralize color casting. The cursor for this tool gives you an RGB readout of the current area in the preview photo; this is the true color over a pixel, and not the "ideally neutral color." You click an area you believe *should* contain equal amounts of red, green, and blue components (R:64, G:64, B:64, for example), and this action remaps the image to reflect the color casting in the image based on where you clicked. Although it's a useful tool, you might not have a photo that contains a perfectly white or a perfectly neutral gray area; if this is the case, don't use this tool.

- *G* marks color Temperature and Tint, perhaps the least intuitive of RAW digital image properties. The values in the Camera RAW Lab's color Temperature controls run from low at the left of the slider (cools down warm images) to high at right (warms cool images). The temperature controls, specifically values you enter in the numeric field, are *not* degrees of Kelvin; they are correction values for you to only refer to and compare with other settings and other images. However, it *is* correct to *think* of color temperature in general as measured in degrees Kelvin. You might want to "uncorrect" a perfect image to make it warmer or colder. The Tint slider is the color complement of the color Temperature control; a neutral temperature displays a band on the Tint slider from magenta at left to green at right. You always use Tint after you've set Temperature because Tint varies according to temperature.

- *H* is the Saturation control, which is mostly self-explanatory—it's used to compensate for dull photographs (you increase Saturation) or for overly colorful images (you desaturate by dragging to the left with the slider).

- *I* marks the Exposure control. Exposure is not the same as, for example, the brightness/contrast controls on a TV set or the Levels command in image-editing applications. Exposure is the *total light that falls on a scene,* and it's set when you take a picture by setting the ISO value. Therefore, it's always a good idea to double-check the info in the Properties tab: if the ISO is a low value and the picture looks dark or muddy, then Exposure is probably the Color option that needs adjusting.

- *J* marks Brightness, which you should play with only after setting the best Exposure. If you drag Brightness to the right with this image, you'll see that the midtones of the image become brighter, but not the shadow areas. So you use this slider to bring out detail in the midranges in an image without ruining the deeper tones.

- *K* is the Shadow slider, and this option is used only to make deeper areas more pronounced without affecting the midtones and highlights. Shadows might also be called "contrast"; dragging the slider to the right does indeed create a difference between the lighter and darker areas of the overall image.

- *L* marks both the Shadow and Highlights clipping regions. These two buttons— you need to click these buttons—that frame the histogram (*M*), will display a bright red overlay in the preview window in areas where the brightest brights have fallen out of range (they can't be accurately displayed onscreen, and they can't be accurately printed); and deepest shadows will display a green-tinted overlay. If you see a tint in areas, this means that the Shadow, the Exposure, or the Saturation adjustments you've made are too intense. The solution is to choose lesser values for any of these options until the tint disappears in the preview window.

- *M* is the histogram of the current photograph. A *histogram* is a visual representation of how many pixels of what color are located at what brightness in the image. Although there are always exceptions to any rule, and all photos have different brightness content, *usually* a well-toned image will have a lot of color pixels in the mid-region of the histogram—this is where the most visual detail is apparent in digital photographs. If the histogram shows too many pixels—for example, in the lower regions there's a hump in the histogram curve toward the left—it means your image needs less Shadow or more Exposure.

- *N* is the area where you can create Snapshots. When you arrive at a good exposure for an image you want to copy into a page, click the Create Snapshot button, and a thumbnail appears at bottom left. Snapshots are not saved; their purpose is for you to compare snapshots and ultimately to choose one you'll import.

6. Once you've made your adjustments, click OK, and you're then presented with a loaded cursor for placing and scaling the imported image, as discussed earlier in this chapter.

To import more than one digital image at a time, hold SHIFT *while clicking to select contiguous files, or hold* CTRL *while clicking to select noncontiguous files in the Import dialog. As multiple files are imported, the cursor indicates the file information for each image being placed.*

23

An Everyday Bitmap-Oriented Workflow

In addition to CorelDRAW's capabilities to import, resize, resample, and develop RAW images, you also have many of PHOTO-PAINT's effects right within CorelDRAW to filter imported images. And CorelDRAW has an Image Adjustment Lab for enhancing RAW file format images. Once you're finished working on a composition, whether it's vector, bitmap, or a combination of these two elements, you probably want to pop a copy of your work off to a friend or a client. The following sections take you through these four stages of CorelDRAW design work; in the process you'll grow quite comfortable with all this "bitmap stuff" and appreciate CorelDRAW's power to bring different media together for both your import and export needs.

Creating a Catalog Cover

Lux, a fictitious candle manufacturer, needs a new catalog cover for 2010. As to be expected, they have no money to take a new picture for the cover, but they've heard that your copy of CorelDRAW X5 ships with some really cool filters that might put a new spin on an old image. Follow along in the next sections' steps to take a tour of the Image Adjustment Lab, the Bitmap effects CorelDRAW offers, and as a grand finale, you'll breeze through the export options for the JPEG file format so you can send a rough layout to the fictitious client.

Working in the Image Adjustment Lab

For "normal" photographs—photos in JPEG, TIFF, and file formats other than Camera RAW—you have under the Bitmaps menu in CorelDRAW a fairly comprehensive Image Adjustment Lab to make practically every *global* adjustment (but not pixel-editing adjustments) you'll find in PHOTO-PAINT. This makes it very easy to photo-correct imported bitmaps and to integrate them into a composition without ever leaving CorelDRAW; better still, the features are almost identical to those in the Camera RAW Lab.

Let's work through the mock assignment now: first, you'll import and place an image in the layout that's been designed for you.

 ### Adjusting a PNG Image in the Lab

1. Open LUM catalog.cdr. Choose the Object Manager docker (Tools | Object Manager). Click the "put the photo on this layer" title on the Object Manager to make it the current layer (the background layer with the text is locked).

2. Choose File | Import (CTRL+I), and then choose LUM candles.png from the location where you downloaded it. Click Import.

3. Your cursor is loaded with the image now, and it's much larger than the place for it within the layout, so you'll scale the image as you place it. First, make sure Snap To Guidelines is checked on the Snap To list on the standard toolbar. Click an insertion point at the top left of the guides intersection; then drag down until the right edge of the image meets the right guide. You've scaled and placed the image now, as shown in Figure 23-5.

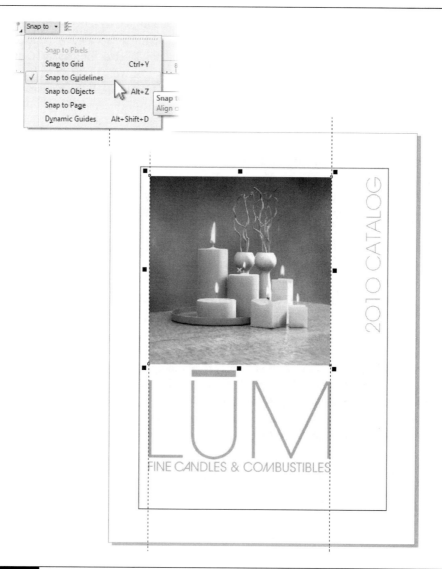

FIGURE 23-5 Scale the imported image as you place it in the design.

4. With the photo selected, choose Bitmaps | Image Adjustment Lab.

5. In Figure 23-6 you'll see a lot of the same navigation controls as you saw in the Camera RAW Lab. However, the Image Adjustment Lab has slightly different features for color and tone adjustments. Always shoot for tone correction for exposure, and then work on the color if necessary.

   - *A* marks Auto Adjust, a one-step routine that adds contrast to an image; let's skip this feature—automated routines don't give "one off" assignments the custom attention they need, and you don't learn anything from automated routines.

   - *B* marks the White Point eyedropper tool, used to define in the preview window the lightest area that should be in the picture. Click in the center of one of the candle flames (presumably the whitest white in the image) to see if the Lab adjusts the other tones and snaps up the image.

FIGURE 23-6   Color- and tone-correction can be performed on photographs with CorelDRAW.

- *C* marks the Black Point eyedropper, which redefines the darkest point in the image based on where you click in the preview window. This step is optional; hover your cursor over the top left of the background in the image. Your cursor will tell you that the background toward the top is almost black with a little red tossed in. Click this point with the eyedropper tool. Your artistic judgment might tell you that the preview pane at right shows a better, snappier image. If you disagree, click the "Reverse the last operation" left-arrow button at bottom left.

- *D* marks the Brightness and Contrast sliders. They basically do what you'd expect; they're like the controls on a television set, but as with a TV set, brightness and contrast don't always make an image better. Skip these controls for this assignment.

- *E* marks the area the professionals use to selectively add contrast and to remove any murkiness the photo might have as a result of too many pixels of similar brightness values neighboring one another in an area of the picture. Leave the Highlights slider alone in this assignment; this brightens the brighter areas in the image without affecting the midtones or shadow areas. However, do drag the Midtones slider up to 2 to open up darker regions to provide image detail without messing up the Shadows region, which is fine as is.

6. Finally, click the Create Snapshot button (*F*). This creates an entry on the Undo docker in case you want to reverse a correction after exiting the lab. Click OK and your adjusted image is now placed in the layout. Keep the file open and Save (press CTRL+S).

Photo Effects

If you need to do something dramatic to a photo, such as making a film negative version (using the Invert style), you have these options:

- Put an object over the photo, and then use lens effects, covered in Chapter 22. You might not get exactly the effect you want with a lens, so the advantage to this method is that the change isn't made directly to the photo—a lens effect can be deleted at any time, restoring the normal appearance of objects beneath it.

- Use the effects on the bottom of the Bitmaps menu, as you'll do in the following tutorial.

Effects you apply via the Bitmaps menu are permanent changes; the bad news is that you can choose to Undo an applied effect *only* right after you've made one. The good news is that all effects are applied only to an image you've imported—your original photo is safely tucked away somewhere on hard disk. Effects filters in CorelDRAW are divided into categories, and you'll be using only two from the Color Transform and Art Strokes categories in this assignment. You should feel free to set aside some time to experiment with the various filters on an image you believe has the potential to look more interesting after a little Distortion or Trace Contour filtering.

It's important to understand that any filter you apply to a photo removes original image information and occasionally supplies altered image information. Therefore, you need to make a creative and qualitative judgment as to whether an image looks "better" after applying one or more filters. There is no such thing as "Instant Art." You need to use your artistic taste when allowing a filter to change the original image's data, and don't dismiss the possibility that an original image might look better and be more appropriate than a filtered one.

Usually, you'd want to reach for the Bitmaps menu filters for two occasions:

- When a photography session isn't possible to provide a new photo for a new catalog or brochure. You or the client have to use an older photo, but you want it to look a little different from last year's photo.

- When a photo is visually boring. It's not a bad photo, just an uninspired photograph whose composition, geometry, and colors are very staid and simple. The LUX candle image isn't a bad image; its problems in this example are that it was used last year, and the geometry in the scene is exceptionally simple and looks like any still photo of a bunch of cylinders.

To use a bitmaps effect, you first need to have an imported bitmap selected. The bitmap has to be either an 8-bit (Grayscale mode, for example) or 24-bit image in either RGB or CMYK color mode. RAW images you import—if they are higher than 24-bit—need to be changed to a *bit depth* the effects can work with. In English, if the effects menus and submenus are dimmed, choose Bitmaps | Mode; then convert the selected image to RGB 24-bit, and life is good. Working with an effect is easy and intuitive: you have different options and sliders depending on the specific effect, but to work an effect, there are four key areas of the dialog that appears when you choose one:

- **Preview** Even at an effect's default settings, you need to click Preview to see what the effect will look like on the page.

- **Reset** Clicking this button removes all changes you've made to the sliders and other controls for all effects.

- **OK** Clicking this applies the effect using the options you've defined and closes the dialog.

- **Controls** To customize an effect, you drag sliders, enter values in num boxes, and/ or drag other controls such as the direction of an effect.

Once you've made changes to the effect's values, you click Preview to update the page preview, and when you're satisfied with the customized effect, you click OK.

Preview Reset Apply Controls Options are unique to each effect.

In the following steps, you're going to kick out all the stops and combine two effects to create a unique stylized version of the candles image. You'll duplicate the image, apply two different filters to the two images, and then use CorelDRAW's transparency effect to combine the two filtered images. You don't *have* to do this in your own work if one effect filter does the job, but these steps show that you *can*.

 ## Filtering a Photo

1. With the Pick tool, click-drag the candles image to the right and then tap the right mouse button before releasing both buttons to drop a copy of it to the right of the original.

2. With the duplicate selected, choose Effects | Adjust | Hue/Saturation/Lightness. Drag the Saturation slider all the way to the left to make a grayscale version of the image, and then click OK to apply. You do this to prepare the duplicate image for a filter effect; this command could also be done in the Image Adjustment Lab.

23

3. Choose Bitmaps | Contour | Find Edges. In the Find Edges box, click the Solid button, click Preview, utter some amazement at how neat the outline version of the image looks, and then click OK to apply the effect.

4. Select the original image. Choose Bitmaps | Art Strokes | Crayon. Drag the Size slider to 20, set the Outline slider to 0, click Preview, and then click OK to apply.

5. With the Pick tool, drag the duplicate over so it's aligned on top of the original. The guides should help snap the duplicate into perfect alignment.

Choose the Transparency tool from the toolbox. Select the top duplicate image and then on the property bar, set the type of transparency to Uniform (from the drop-down list), and then first try the If Lighter operation from the drop-down list. Divide and Texturize operations also produce an interesting effect. It's your call here, and 50% Uniform transparency seems to work best. Figure 23-7 shows the process of laying the Find Edges version of the bitmap over the Crayon filtered image.

Crayon Effect

Remove Saturation; then add Find Edges effect

Find Edges on top, Transparency effect, Uniform, 80% Transparent, If Lighter mode

FIGURE 23-7   Add two different filtered images to create a composite by using Transparency.

Exporting Your Composition to Bitmap Format

One of the terrific things about designing using a computer application is that you can repurpose a good design. A good design such as the front cover of the catalog just discussed can yield several different uses from only one investment in time—and from knowing how to export the design.

Although CorelDRAW is a vector drawing program, it can create a bitmap copy of photographs, a bitmap from photos combined with vectors, and it can export vector art only—text, graphics, anything is fair game. When vectors are copied out of CorelDRAW as bitmaps, a process called *rasterizing* is performed; CorelDRAW examines the vector artwork at the size and resolution you specify and then uses anti-aliasing (unless you specify no anti-aliasing) to create a bitmap that looks as good as what you see onscreen in your CorelDRAW document.

Let's say you want to feature on your website the front cover of the company catalog. This narrows your export choices down to GIF, PNG, and JPEG (see Chapter 28 for more details on web content creation and exporting). Let's briefly run through exporting the composition to JPEG now (exporting bitmaps is covered in detail in Chapter 24).

Saving a Bitmap Copy of Your CorelDRAW Composition

1. In the Object Manager, unlock Layer 1 by clicking the pencil icon to remove the red slash mark. With the Pick tool, drag a marquee from outside the top left of the design to the bottom right. Doing this is simply a good practice for exporting designs: if there had been a hidden object or one outside of your workspace view, CorelDRAW's export filter would not include it in the bitmap version it rendered.

2. Many web browsers expect pictures to be in the sRGB color space. Change the document's color space to sRGB by clicking Tools| Color Management | Document Settings. In this dialog, check "Convert document colors to new color profiles," and choose sRGB IE61966-2.1 in the RGB list.

3. Click the Export button on the property bar.

4. In the Export dialog, choose JPG-JPEG Bitmaps as the Save As Type from the drop-down list. Check the Selected Only check box, type a name in the File Name field, use the directory pane to choose a location for the export, and then click Export.

5. You have the option to select a preset export for JPEGs by choosing from the Preset list at top right, but this doesn't teach you anything. First, set the Color Mode to RGB—JPEGs are increasingly used today for commercial printing, but it's the wrong color mode for the Web and for email attachments.

6. For starters, set the Compression to 80% (the Quality setting is at High). Choose the Hand tool and use your mouse scroll wheel to zoom in or out of the preview window. Using 50% (Medium) compression produces a smaller file—which is reported at the bottom left of the dialog, but this image shows some JPEG artifacting (noise, corruption) at 50% and not very much at 80%.

7. Uncheck the Embed Color Profile box. Doing this saves in this example more than 500 bytes (about half a K) in file size. Also, web browsers today largely "expect" sRGB color profiles, and Adobe RGB is the current color space for the LUX CorelDRAW layout. If you uncheck the Embed Color Profile option, current browsers such as Firefox and Internet Explorer will display the image as expected. Apple Safari does read color profiles, but if it finds none, it defaults to the Web standard of sRGB.

8. Check Optimize to save on a few K of exported image.

9. Choose Pixels as the Units, and then choose 96 as the Resolution for export. The resolution is meaningless for screen documents, but 96 provides you with a benchmark by which you can calculate the absolute height and width of the exported image—in pixels. The layout's original size is a little large for the Web and for the reading pane in mail readers such as MS Outlook; type **700** in the Height field to reduce both the Height and Width of the export.

10. The estimated download time shown at bottom left is calculated based on a hypothetical Internet connection you specify by selecting from the drop-down list toward the bottom center of the dialog. By default, it's set to fast dial-up, which represents an estimated 75 percent (and shrinking) of the United States, but Europe and many other countries are almost entirely on broadband in 2010. ISDN (dial-up) essentially plays to the lowest common denominator—it's the worst speed you can use to estimate how your audience receives your image files. Therefore, 6.2 seconds—and almost certainly less time for most audiences—is acceptable. Click OK and your work is exported to JPEG file format.

Set to RGB

Compression versus quality

Color profile

Pixels are absolute measurements.

Estimated file size/ download time

Fairly low connection speed

11. Close the document *without* saving it. If you save it now, you'll change the document's color space for print output.

If you're feeling a little jazzed after reading this chapter, get a friend to pat you on your back, because you deserve it. You've taken a serious detour in your "CorelDRAW is a drawing program" education and vaulted right into the arena of design professionals who integrate photos and vector artwork on a daily basis. You now know how to scale an image, to check to see whether its resolution is sufficient to pull a good print, to color-correct both RAW images and regular ones, and how to export your work so friends you'd like to send an email attachment to can see it without necessarily owning CorelDRAW—and the composition is web-worthy, to boot.

This is not the complete story of CorelDRAW and bitmaps. You'll want to do things as special as you do with vectors, so Chapter 24 covers more advanced bitmap-editing techniques, converting bitmap art to vector art, and working with transparency to better integrate bitmap and vector objects in a composition. Read on and see how to create exactly the effect you need for tomorrow's assignment at work.

CHAPTER 24

Advanced Photography Techniques with CorelDRAW

Because people seldom photograph an object or a scene with exactly the elements they want in a composition, the field of retouching has thrived since the day a professional had something to sell using a photograph! This is why professionals trim photographs, and so can you by using the CorelDRAW features covered in this chapter. As objects, photographic areas that have been carefully cut out can be composited with other photos and vector shapes to add a whole new dimension to your posters, flyers, and fine art. Additionally, this chapter demonstrates Corel PowerTRACE, part of CorelDRAW; you'll learn how to create a vector copy of a bitmap so you can scale and rotate it, edit it, and never lose details or resolution as bitmap images are prone to do.

NOTE	*Download and extract all the files from the Chapter24.zip archive to follow the tutorials in this chapter.*

Cropping a Placed Photograph

You can perform two types of cropping on placed photos: destructive (permanent) and nondestructive (you can undo what you've done). The Crop tool on the toolbox performs destructive cropping. Unless you press CTRL+Z to undo a crop you don't like, you're stuck with your crop, and no areas exterior to the image remain that you can expose later. Some users prefer this; you'll learn both methods in this section. To crop a photo:

1. Bitmap images—for example, photos, paintings done in Corel Painter, and just about any picture off the Web—need to be imported; you do *not* use File | Open. Choose File | Import, click the Import button on the standard toolbar, or press CTRL+I. In the directory window, scout down the image that you want to place a copy of, and then click Import. Because you're importing ("placing") the image and not opening it, you're always assured that you're not altering your precious original photo.

2. You define the area you want to crop by click-diagonal dragging the Crop tool from one corner to the opposite corner.

3. You can redefine the crop by click-dragging the resulting bounding-box markers. The corner markers scale the proposed crop area proportionately, while the center markers are used to resize the proposed crop area disproportionately.

4. You can rotate the crop box, which is handy if you want an artistic crop or just want to straighten a horizon in the photo. To do this, first click inside the image; doing this puts the crop area into Rotate mode. Then drag a corner double-headed-arrow marker to rotate the crop. This doesn't rotate the photo itself, but rather rotates the crop area.

5. Double-click inside the crop area to finish the crop. Figure 24-1 shows the elements you work with onscreen to crop a bitmap image.

Crop tool

Click-drag

Scale crop box disproportionately

Scale crop box proportionately

Rotate crop box

24

FIGURE 24-1   The Crop tool eliminates the exterior image areas of your defined crop area.

TIP   *To quickly see the resolution of a placed bitmap image, select the bitmap and look at the status bar, which displays the file, its color mode, and its current resolution. The rule is: as a bitmap's dimensions increase, its resolution decreases proportionately.*

Nondestructive Cropping

In a nutshell, if you want to hide an area of a photo and not delete it as you do with the Crop tool, use the Shape tool. Try this out with the Macaw.jpg image by following the steps in the tutorial.

 Using the Shape Tool to Crop

1. Create a new (default-sized) document with landscape orientation. Place the image of the Amazon Macaws in a new document by clicking the Import button on the property bar and then selecting the image from the location you downloaded it to. With the loaded cursor, click-diagonal drag to place the image so it fills most of the page.

2. Choose the Shape tool. Notice that the photo, which is still selected, now has control node markers at each corner. These markers behave and operate exactly like control nodes for vector shapes.

3. Just for the fun of it, click a node to select it, and then drag it toward the center of the image. This is not what the pros call an "expert crop," but you've just learned something that will come in very handy in your future work. When you drag a node inside of the outside dimensions of a placed photo, the two sides that meet at this node hide areas of the photograph. Press CTRL+Z to undo this, and now perform a more practical crop.

4. Click-drag so that you've marquee-selected two neighboring nodes; they can make up a horizontal or vertical edge of the photo. For this experiment it makes no difference.

5. Use the keyboard arrows to nudge the nodes toward the center of the image. Hold SHIFT to super-nudge the nodes if you like. This is how you can nondestructively crop a placed photo; nudge the nodes in the opposite direction now—you've hidden and then unhidden one dimension of the photograph.

6. With two nodes selected, hold CTRL and then drag the nodes toward the center of the photo. The CTRL key constrains movement so the edge you're cropping remains parallel to the dragging page.

Masking Through Nondestructive Cropping

Go to the head of the class if you've already discovered that you can *add* control nodes to a placed photograph with the Shape tool! CorelDRAW "sees" a bitmap as an object that has a fill—specifically, a bitmap fill. Therefore, this object can be shaped and reshaped by adding nodes and also by changing the segment property between nodes. The following sections take you through some advanced bitmap editing to trim around a photograph so it becomes a floating object in a composition.

Trimming Away Unwanted Image Areas

What you'll learn in this section goes way beyond the simple cropping of an image. You're going to trim the background away from an image of a bust of classical composer Johann Sebastian Bach, put a new background behind the bust, and by the end of this section, you'll have designed a concert poster. There are two nondestructive methods for removing the background from a photo's subject, and both techniques are described in this section. The elements of the poster have already been created for you, and by working through the tutorials, you'll see how to make a design with elements in front of and behind each other, just like you do with vector shapes, but using *photographs*.

To begin at the beginning of this poster design (call it an overture), you need to create a new document (portrait orientation, default page size) and then to place the image of Bach—a little smaller than the page size, but he can be scaled at a later time when needed—to use the Shape tool to trim out the background.

Background Removal, Technique 1

1. Click the Import button on the property bar, and then in the Import dialog, locate JS Bach.tif, select him, and then click Import.

2. Your cursor is loaded with the image: click-drag, as shown in Figure 24-2, and then release the mouse when the cursor reports that the height for the placed image will be about 9 inches.

3. Choose the Shape tool. Begin by clicking the top right node of the image, and then click-drag it toward the center of the image until the top and right edges of the image touch the bust of Bach, as shown next. Clearly, you're not going to get where you want to go with only four control nodes, because the geometry of the bust is far from

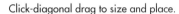
Click-diagonal drag to size and place.

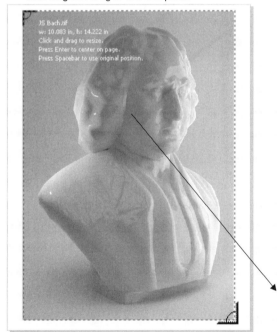

JS Bach.tif
w: 6.34 in, h: 8.942 in

FIGURE 24-2 Scale and place the image by click-diagonal dragging your loaded cursor.

perfectly rectangular. This is okay; you'll add nodes to the outline of the image in the following step.

Click-drag

4. With the Shape tool, click a point on the outline of the photo where there should be a change in direction of the line; Bach's powdered wig near his forehead is a prime area. Now, either double-click the segment, press the keyboard plus (+) key, or click the Add Node button on the property bar to add a node. While you're in the vicinity of Bach's forehead, several additional points will be needed. A quick way to add points in-between existing points is to repeatedly click a point and press the + key.

5. Click-drag points so they visually coincide with the vertices of Bach's wig. It's okay if the lines between the nodes hide areas you want exposed.

6. Click a straight line segment that should curve away from the photo. Then click the Convert To Curve button on the property bar. The segment can now curve; click-drag the segment away from the photo, as shown next, until you can see Bach's locks. You can also right-click a segment and choose To Curve from the pop-up menu.

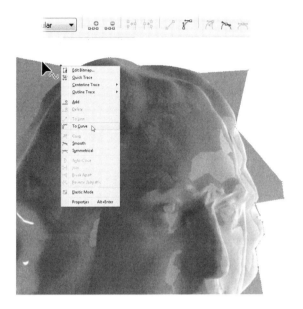

7. That's it; all it takes now is about 10 minutes of your time to work around the profile of the bust, hiding areas and creating curve segments where needed. Yes, it's a lot of work; so is putting on a tuxedo or gown to go and collect an industry award for outstanding design work (*prompt, hint, encouragement!*).

A good thing to do once you've trimmed away the non-essential Bach, because the default color of the page is white, is to put a colored vector shape behind your work to check your edge work. As you can see here, the example looks pretty good; a rectangle was created, filled, and then rotated, and then SHIFT+PAGE DOWN is pressed to put the rectangle to the back of the page's layer.

If you'd like to confirm that the editing you performed is nondestructive, take the Shape tool and marquee-select several control nodes. Then drag them away from the center of the photo, as shown here. Then press CTRL+Z to undo this nondestructive *and unwanted* edit!

Boolean Operations as a Trimming Technique

It takes an equal amount of effort, but it might be easier to visualize the nondestructive photo-trimming process by drawing the outline of the image object you want to isolate and then to use the shaping commands to slice out the area you want to use. If you have Bach trimmed now, you don't have to follow this tutorial, but *do* read the steps, because you might find this technique easier than editing with the control nodes.

 ## Background Removal, Technique 2

1. Using the Pen tool with which you're the most comfortable and experienced, draw a silhouette around the object you want to isolate in the photo, as shown in Figure 24-3. It usually helps if you choose a contrasting outline color as you progress; you right-click, in this example, black on the Color Palette after you've begun tracing. Choosing outline and fill colors *after* you've begun drawing a shape avoids triggering the attention box asking whether all new objects should get a black outline.

2. After you've closed the shape, choose Arrange | Shaping | Shaping to display the docker for performing an Intersect Boolean operation. You could use the property bar shaping buttons to perform this, but the property bar shaping buttons by default leave a copy of the target and source objects after the operation, a minor hassle to clean up later.

3. Select the object you just drew. Choose Intersect from the drop-down selector, and then make sure both of the Leave Original boxes are unchecked. Click Intersect With, click the region of the photograph that is outside of the black outline you just drew, and you're home free, as shown in Figure 24-4.

FIGURE 24-3   Draw an outline that tightly matches the shape of the object you want to trim.

FIGURE 24-4   Use the Intersect shaping command to remove all regions of the photo outside of the shape you drew.

Compositions with Mixed Media

Creating the poster is going to be fun—you're going to go beyond arranging and moving both bitmap and vector objects to laying out a finished art composition. What you'll see in the Concert poster.cdr file are two image objects: the background night image is locked on the bottom layer, and the gold title is an *alpha-channel masked image,* something covered a little later in this chapter.

Work through the following steps to copy your Bach trimming work to the concert poster document (an unlocked layer is active, so duplicating takes only one step). Then you'll add a vector shape to the composition to create an air of elegance…it's a piece of *chorale* sheet music, actually, not an *air.*

Composing a Design Using Vector and Image Shapes

1. Open Concert poster.cdr, and then choose Window | Tile Vertically so you have a view of both your Bach work and the Concert poster.cdr file.

2. Hold CTRL and then drag your trimmed bust of Bach into the Concert poster window, as shown in Figure 24-5. This duplicates your work; it doesn't move it. You can save and then close your Bach image as a CDR file now.

3. Click the Import button on the property bar, and then choose the Bach 4 part Chorale.cdr file from your hard drive. Click Import; your cursor is now loaded with the imported file. You can click anywhere to place it at its original size, but for this example, click-drag beginning about ¾" from the left edge of the page until the legend at the bottom right of the cursor reads about "w: 7.5 in."

FIGURE 24-5 Duplicate your work into the Concert poster.cdr window.

the musical notes selected, click the white color well on the Color Palette.

ose Window | Dockers | Object Manager. Click-drag the title "Group of 100 cts" (the musical notes), and then release the mouse button when the title is w the "JS Bach.tif" object. You should now see the musical notes group of cts on the page *behind* J.S.

s make the music sort of swell behind its composer. Choose the Envelope tool m the Blend group on the toolbox. You're working in Putty mode by default, a od place to start; now, let's customize the envelope for a specific distortion. With le Envelope tool, marquee-select the top and bottom center control nodes; while nolding SHIFT, marquee-select the left and right middle nodes. Then click the Delete Nodes button on the property bar; see top left, Figure 24-6.

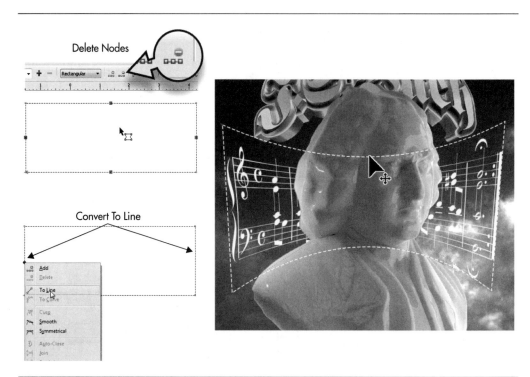

FIGURE 24-6 Shape the music so it appears to extend around the bust toward the audience, as music really does...

7. Click the left side of the Envelope bounding box, and then right-click and choose To Line from the pop-up menu. Then perform the same edit on the right side. The top and bottom default property for Putty mode envelopes is curved segments—they need no editing. See middle left in Figure 24-6.

8. With the Shape tool, one at a time click the control nodes that bound the musical notes, and then drag the top ones up a little and the bottom ones down a little. Then click-drag the bottom line up, and the top line down. Use your artistic eye and Figure 24-6 to guide you. Bach's compositions are stirring; the musical notes should visually reflect this.

9. A time and place for this concert would help sell it; read Chapter 14 if you haven't done so already for good text-composition techniques. As you can see in Figure 24-7, the completed poster looks handsome, and most of its visual success is because you now know how to isolate an important subject from a fairly boring background.

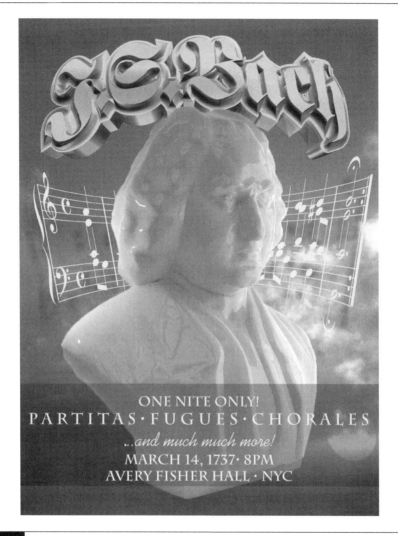

FIGURE 24-7   When you can move image objects around on a page as easily as vector shapes, new design opportunities open up to you.

Working with Alpha Channels and Image Transparency

The following sections explain how some professionals trim subjects out of their image backgrounds, why certain file types are imported with transparency, and what transparency really means in your CorelDRAW work. There are more features than you might imagine for working with bitmaps directly in CorelDRAW; for *exceptionally* tricky image-editing assignments, Chapters 25 and 26 document Corel PHOTO-PAINT.

Using CorelDRAW's Bitmap Color Mask

On the property bar, whenever a bitmap image is selected, you have the Bitmap Color Mask docker button on the property bar. This docker can help mask areas of a placed bitmap, although it's a less robust feature than found in PHOTO-PAINT. Here's the deal: if you have, for example, a scene that has someone who isn't wearing any green, and they're surrounded by green, you can remove the green background by hiding this color value. Whenever you have an image with a background whose color is not remotely similar to colors in the foreground person or object in the photo, the Bitmap Color Mask docker can successfully hide the background, too. What the Bitmap Color Mask docker cannot do is distinguish between subtle variations in differing hues. For example, if you have a maroon background with a pink foreground object you want clipped out, no can do. Maroon contains heavy concentrations of tone in its red color channel, and so does pink, although to a lesser extent. The Bitmap Color Mask docker *looks at colors in channels* in an image; unless you're trying to mask a GIF indexed color image (a file structure that doesn't use color channels, but instead uses a color index), your smartest move is to use PHOTO-PAINT or to manually trim the image using the methods described earlier.

However, lots of professionals receive "object against pure color" photos every day— and now you will, too, to experiment with in the following tutorial. This tutorial shows how to auto-mask images such as Beachball.tif for easy compositing work in CorelDRAW.

 ## Removing a Color from Around a Subject

1. Import the Beach.png image to a new document. This is the background for the composition.

2. Import the Beachball.tif image and then place it anywhere you like for the moment. As shown in Figure 24-8, the green area around the beach ball sort of messes up its integration into the beach scene.

3. With the beach ball image selected, click the Bitmap Color Mask button on the property bar.

4. Click the check box to the left of the first black color swatch. This is the first color you'll mask in the beach ball image.

5. Choose the Color Selector button (Eyedropper tool), and then click over the green area on the beach ball image. Set the Tolerance to about 40%, and then click Apply. The green has become masked—invisible—and you can now use the Pick tool to move and scale the beach ball so it becomes part of the background scene.

FIGURE 24-8 An image without a transparent background can't be successfully melded into a composition.

6. Let's try a little more scene integration by adding a slight shadow behind the ball. This also demonstrates how the image mask allows CorelDRAW effects to be placed behind it. Choose the Drop Shadow tool from the Blend group of tools, and then click-drag down and a little to the right on the beach ball. As you can see in Figure 24-9, the beach ball looks like it's part of the scene. As a little independent experiment (with creative mayhem), try clicking the second check box, and then with the Eyedropper tool, click over a red area of the image and see what disappears. To undo this move, all you need to do is uncheck the red swatch's check box on the docker and then click Apply.

NOTE *Check out Chapter 22 for detailed information on working with the Drop Shadow tool.*

FIGURE 24-9   Use the Tolerance slider on the Bitmap Color Mask docker to increase the mask of the color you chose.

Working with Partial Transparency

Both alpha channel transparency and image layer transparency offer more than simply 100 percent opaque or 100 percent transparent areas. With 24-bit images, you can have 256 levels of opacity in any area of the image, and this leads to some fascinating visual effects you can create. You'll work shortly with an image that has semitransparent areas, but right now it's time to learn how to *build* semitransparent areas into an image that has none but should have them. Bob's Beer, a fictitious micro-brewery, has an image of a bottle in PNG file format that is surrounded by transparency. Let's say Bob wants the bottle to sit in front of a background that has his name repeated far too many times. Visually, his name should partially show through the neck of the bottle where there's only tinted glass and no beer.

The following tutorial shows you how to trim away the top quarter of the bottle, the most transparent part. Then you'll see how to make this area only partially opaque so some of the background shows through. And to top it off, you'll see how to build a shadow that's cast from the bottle onto the "ground" in the composition.

Creating a Photorealistic Glass Effect

1. Open Bob's Background.cdr, and then click the Import button and choose Bob's Beer.png; it's a domestic beer, but you'll import it anyway. Click Import and then with the loaded cursor, click-diagonal drag until the bottle is placed in the image as shown here.

2. With a Pen tool (the Bézier pen works fine in this example), create a shape that fits in the top part of the glass, from the fill line to the bottle's lip, staying slightly inside the neck of the beer bottle so the edge is not part of the trimming operation you'll perform in a moment. You should fill the object after creating it to better see what you're doing in the following steps—any color is fine.

3. Select the shape but not the bottle. Choose Arrange | Shaping | Shaping to display the Shaping docker. Choose Intersect from the selector drop-down list, and then check Leave Original Target Object(s), but don't check Leave Original Source Object(s). Click the Intersect With button, and then click the bottle. The object is

deleted because it's the Source Object, and you didn't choose to leave it. Apparently the bottle has not changed, but there is a perfect cutout duplicate of the top of the bottle resting on top of an unchanged bottle; you're halfway there—you need to trim away part of the bottle using the new intersect object. Switch to the Pick tool now.

4. Click on the top of the bottle to select the product of the Intersect operation in step 3 (don't worry; it's hard to see that it's a separate object). Choose Trim from the Shaping docker's drop-down list, check Leave Original Source Object(s), and uncheck Leave Original Target Object(s). Click the Trim button and then click the bottle, and the beer bottle is now actually two separate pieces. See the following illustration for the docker settings for steps 3 and 4. Now it's on to transparency.

Separate object (not obvious)

5. Select the top part of the shape, and then choose the Interactive Transparency tool from the Blend group of tools on the toolbox. Choose Uniform from the selector drop-down on the property bar, and then drag the Opacity slider on the property bar to about 50%. As you can see here, your editing work resulted in quite a convincing illustration. You can see Bob's logo in the background peeking through semitransparent glass; the background is even tinted a little from the green of the object on top of it.

6. Here's the piece de resistance: with the bottle selected and not the semitransparent piece, choose the Drop Shadow tool. Click toward the bottom of the bottle image to define an anchor for the shadow and then drag up and to the right.

7. Click-drag the end marker of the shadow so the shadow ends closer to the bottle. Then, because the bottle should be casting a deep green (not black) shadow, click the Shadow Color flyout on the property bar, and then from the palette choose a deep green.

8. Well, oops. The area you trimmed in step 4 is not part of the shadow—there's a hole in the shadow where there should be a lighter green, because a shadow cast by green glass through beer would be a little darker than a shadow cast through green glass alone. No problem; you draw a fill object for the missing part of the shadow as shown here, fill the object with green, and then give it about 50 to 60% Uniform transparency.

Blending Photos with Transparency

You'll learn in Chapter 25 how to use PHOTO-PAINT to mask the exterior of an object in a photo. For the moment, let's imagine that the Tree.png file you'll work with in the following steps was created by masking everything except the tree in the photo, and then you saved it as a PNG file with transparency using PHOTO-PAINT.

You know now that an image can have transparent areas, and that you can use CorelDRAW's Transparency tool to make any object on a page partially transparent. The steps that follow show you how to create surreal, completely professional photo-retouching with two images you graft into one another with only one CorelDRAW tool.

Creating a Transition Between Two Images

1. Press CTRL+N to create a new file; accept the default standard letter page size and specify portrait orientation.

2. Import ThumbsUp.jpg. JPEG images do not retain resolution information, so you need to click-drag the loaded cursor after clicking Import to scale the imported image to the 11" height of the page.

24

3. Import Tree.png. PNG files can (in some cases) retain image resolution information, so all you need to do is click the loaded cursor on the page.

4. With the Pick tool, position the tree so its trunk fits over the thumb in the underlying photo.

5. Choose the Transparency tool from the Blend group of tools on the toolbox.

6. Click-drag starting from around the thumbnail area in the underlying photo to just above the trunk on the tree. You should see the amazing transformation between the guy's thumb and the trunk of the tree (see Figure 24-10). If the Start and End points for this Linear transparency aren't perfect, you can adjust the Start and End points with the Transparency tool cursor.

7. Unfortunately, the guy's thumb doesn't taper toward the top like the tree trunk does; some of the thumb is visible, ruining the special effect. Choose the Bezier pen tool from the toolbox, and then draw a closed shape whose right edge matches the contour of the tree trunk's left side. Fill it with the same color as the background of the thumb

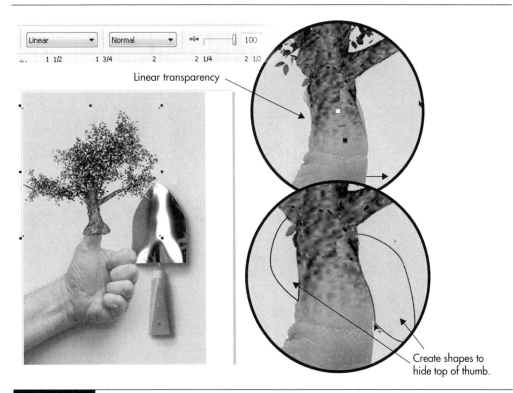

Linear transparency

Create shapes to hide top of thumb.

FIGURE 24-10   Create a blend between two photos to present unique and visually arresting imagery.

photo—choose the Color eyedropper tool from the toolbox, click over the background, and then click the paint bucket cursor on the object you drew.

8. Perform step 7 on the right side of the thumb, after drawing a second object.

9. Remove the outline of both shapes (select them both) by right-clicking the No Fill color well on the Color Palette.

10. With both objects selected, press CTRL+PAGE DOWN to put them behind the tree, yet in front of the thumb photo.

11. Read Chapter 12 on working with text, because this image would make a terrific magazine cover.

Bitmaps to Vector Art: Using PowerTRACE

You can export both vector art and bitmaps to bitmap file format, but once in a while you'll need to go the other way: taking a bitmap and making vector art from it. Many design professionals are faced daily with clients who want to use their logo for a truck sign or a high-resolution print ad, when all they can provide the designer is a really pathetic GIF copy from their web page.

Fortunately, designers don't have to reconstruct logos by hand—Corel PowerTRACE has been reworked in version X5 to become a highly accurate utility that often produces a vector equivalent of a placed bitmap that requires no hand-tweaking afterward. What PowerTRACE does is simple: it creates a vector version of the selected bitmap. *How* PowerTRACE does this is not easy to explain, but if you understand the "how," you'll be better prepared to choose options before making a vector copy of an imported bitmap. In a nutshell, PowerTRACE examines the bitmap based on the criteria you specify in the dialog and then seeks edges in the bitmaps that show a clear and marked difference in color and/or brightness between neighboring pixels. PowerTRACE then creates a vector line at this neighboring region, continues to create a closed path (with the Centerline option chosen, it creates open paths), and fills the path with the closest color match to the pixels inside the area it creates. The following sections take you through the operation of PowerTRACE and offer suggestions on settings and when and why you'd use this handy feature.

Bitmap Conversions for Logo Alterations

Sometimes you'll want to use PowerTRACE to rework an existing logo that's in bitmap format. Suppose SilverSpoon.png, a good, clean graphic, is the logo for a caterer that was bought out yesterday by Phil Greasy, and Phil likes the logo but wants the name changed to…you guessed it. You use settings for PowerTRACE to make a vector conversion of the logo covered in the following section, but this is a prime example of "knowing your fonts" (covered in Chapter 13). A lot of times it's a futile endeavor to trace typography in a logo: it's much easier and provides cleaner results just to recast the text using the same or a similar font.

Pre-Touching: Use PHOTO-PAINT
for Cleanup Before Tracing

The Silver Spoon logo you'll have PowerTRACE convert so you can alter the logo for the new owner is a detailed and complex one. There are four or five areas in the logo that you'll need to assist PowerTRACE with by manually editing the logo before auto-tracing it. Your own artistic eye is hooked up to your brain, and it can discern the edge between the black outline around "Silver" and the black background checkerboard. PowerTRACE, on the other hand, doesn't have eyes and doesn't have a brain (these features are expected in CorelDRAW X475). Therefore, you will make life a lot easier for yourself if you use Corel PHOTO-PAINT to erase the areas—working to the outside of the outline around "Silver"—so there is a gap and

24

so PowerTRACE creates separate objects for the word "Silver" and for the checkerboard background.

This logo is probably the hardest one you'll encounter professionally to use PowerTRACE on for clean-up work and alterations. If you succeed at this fictitious example, your paying gigs will be a charm. These are really quite easy steps, and shortly you'll see how little sweat you have to break to dramatically alter the logo.

Working Between CorelDRAW and PHOTO-PAINT

1. In a new document in CorelDRAW, import the Silver Spoon.png image. Click the loaded cursor to place the bitmap at its original size.

2. Click Edit Bitmap on the property bar. In a moment, PHOTO-PAINT loads with Silver Spoon.png displayed in a document window.

3. Choose the Eraser tool from PHOTO-PAINT's toolbox. On PHOTO-PAINT's property bar, type **10** in the Size field to set the diameter of the Eraser tool. Then set the Feather amount to zero (**0**). Doing this gives you a small, hard tool for erasing areas, exposing the default white background color.

4. The bottom left of the *S,* the dot over the *i,* the upper left of the *l,* the top and bottom left of the *e* where it touches the outline of the spoon, and the bottom and right portions of the *r* all touch what you can see as black background areas. Refer to the illustration here, and carefully erase areas outside of these characters, creating a white gutter between background elements touching the black border around the letters in "Silver".

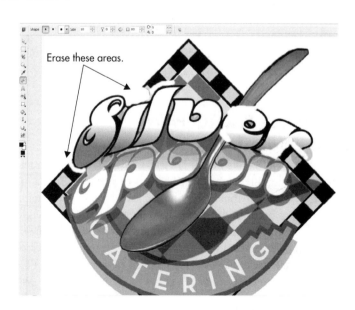

Erase these areas.

5. When you're finished, choose File | Exit or press ALT+F4 to close PHOTO-PAINT. Click Yes to save changes, PHOTO-PAINT closes, and you're returned to CorelDRAW with your edits made to the copy of the logo you imported.

6. With the bitmap selected, click Trace Bitmap, and then choose Outline Trace | High Quality Image. It's not time to trace yet, but it's time to *explore your options* before tracing.

PowerTRACE Options

After you import and select the bitmap, you have the option to Quick Trace the bitmap, or to get more specific about the final traced object's quality and fidelity.

This logo has no dithering and no aliased edges. Therefore, the PowerTRACE can be set for less smoothing and greater precision. As you can see here, the logo has no transparent background, but because you'll trace it, you can automatically delete its white background, a little perk for your client.

- **Trace Type**   You can choose Outline or Centerline from this drop-down. Outline is the method that produces objects based on areas of color similarity in the bitmap. Centerline is a good option when your source bitmap is calligraphy or a technical drawing; this option generates open paths to which you can assign different widths and styles after the trace is placed on the page.

- **Type of Image**   This is a convenience based on what many people call different types of bitmap art. Depending on your choice—from Line Art to High Quality Image—PowerTRACE renders a few objects or hundreds. You can customize a Type Of Image setting by altering other settings, and you can also use an "inappropriate" setting type for your imported image. No two images are alike, and you might be surprised at the hi-fi rendering of a piece of clip art you trace using, for example, the Line Art Type Of Image setting.

- **Colors**   On this tab you can set the number of unique colors PowerTRACE evaluates, from 1 (which will render a stencil of your original) to a varying maximum of unique colors, which you can limit by typing in a value. You can specify the color mode for the trace; you'd choose CMYK, for example, if you needed a trace that could be sent as an EPS file to a commercial printer. Generally, your best bet is the RGB color mode. You can also sort the colors to be used by how frequently they appear in the original bitmap, or by similarity. Additionally, if you intend to replace a color when you edit the traced result, you can do so by clicking a color well and then click Edit.

- **Settings** This tab, shown in Figure 24-11, is used to define how tightly and accurately you want PowerTRACE to render the bitmap as vector object.

  - **Detail** You set the overall complexity of the trace with this slider. Higher values cause PowerTRACE to carefully evaluate the bitmap, while lower Detail settings can produce a stylized, posterized trace with fewer colors and far fewer groups of objects.

  - **Smoothing** This setting controls both the number of nodes along paths and, to a lesser extent, the number of objects the trace yields. A higher smoothing value is good when your bitmap import is a GIF image that contains a lot of noise, dithered colors, and jagged edges.

  - **Corner Smoothness** Use this setting depending on the visual content of your imported bitmap. For example, a photo of a sphere probably doesn't require any corner smoothness. However, a photo of a bird's feather will certainly have a lot of abrupt color and geometry changes—you'd want to use a very low Corner Smoothness setting to accurately represent the sharp turns and corners that make up a feather.

- **Delete Original Image** Upon finalizing the trace, CorelDRAW can delete the image it traced, leaving only the vector objects on the page. This is not usually a good idea—what if you're unhappy with the first trace you perform? Leave this box unchecked.

- **Remove Background** Usually you'll want to check this box. When an imported image such as this logo is floating in a background of white, Remove Background doesn't make the background a huge white rectangle. Optionally, any color can be removed from the final trace by choosing the Specify Color radio button and then using the eyedropper to choose a color from the preview window.

- **Automatically Choose Color** This option chooses the color in the image that is removed from the final trace. This option can be useful as a quick method for separating the foreground areas of interest from a background you want removed, but as with anything "automatic" in a software program, you're best off previewing what's been chosen before clicking OK.

- **Remove Color From Entire Image** If you select this option, every instance of the chosen color will not be traced and the result will be empty areas in your vector version of the bitmap. This result is not always desired, so give this item some thought. If, for example, there's a yellow star on a blue balloon, and the background is also yellow, both the star and the background will not be traced.

- **Merge Adjacent Objects of the Same Color** This option makes one object instead of several if the bitmap contains areas of almost identical color in neighboring regions. If this option is chosen, Remove Object Overlap cannot be used.

- **Remove Object Overlap**   Most of the time, you'll want to leave this box unchecked. If you do choose to enable Remove Object Overlap, there might be visible gaps between the resulting grouped vector shapes, making it hard to put a solid background behind your trace without the background color or texture peeking through. If this option is chosen, the Group Objects by Color option cannot be used.

- **Group Objects by Color**   This is a handy feature that automatically groups identically colored objects after you click OK to make the trace. You can then choose a different color and apply it to the entire group, delete an entire group of objects of identical fill, and not have dozens of objects that can be accidentally moved lying all over the page.

- **Trace Result Details**   This area on the dialog predicts how many objects (Curves), how many Nodes, and how many different Colors will be produced. As a guideline, if the results show more than 200 objects will be created, think twice. It's a large number of objects to edit, and the resulting trace could be a challenge to work with.

Use the features and settings in PowerTRACE to create an optimized group of vector objects based on the bitmap.

Let's put all this knowledge into practice in the next section.

Performing a Trace

You're almost set to click OK and have PowerTRACE convert the Silver Spoon.jpg logo into a set of vector objects.

The original logo's text was cast in Motter Fem font; if you don't own it, this is okay. Install Candid.ttf through the Start menu | Control Panel | Fonts before you begin the tutorial. Candid is not a complete typeface; it's missing punctuation marks and numbers, and it was created after the Candy font by URW. It's very close in look to Motter Fem, and Candy is a great packaging-design font you might seriously consider purchasing for your collection—Candid is an author-cobbled knockoff whose purpose is solely to get you through the techniques in the following steps.

 Reworking a Logo Using Vectors

1. In the PowerTRACE box, set the Detail all the way to the right; a lower setting would ignore details such as the "Catering" text because the text is made up of only a few pixels in character width. Set Smoothing at about 25%; the logo is already fairly smooth and will not benefit from the averaging PowerTRACE would make in defining paths.

2. Set the Corner Smoothness to the far left on the slider (no corner smoothing). You want cusp nodes and sharp corners rendered to keep the checkerboard pieces and serifs on the typefaces sharp. Then, check Remove Background, check "Merge adjacent objects of the same color," and then look at the Trace Result Details Curves field just as a matter of practice.

3. Click the Colors tab and then set the Number Of Colors to **30**—there really aren't more colors than 30 in the image; more colors will create superfluous additional objects. These settings should yield less than 200 separate objects, so click OK.

4. Move the objects away from the bitmap original; you want to keep the original on the page for reference. Ungroup the group of objects (CTRL+U), and then delete what's left of the word "Silver". This will leave a hole in the background in a few places.

5. With the Text tool, type **Greasy**, and then apply Candid from the Font selector drop-down on the property bar.

6. Apply a white fill to the text, and then press ALT+ENTER to display the Object Properties box. Click the Outline tab and then set the outline to **8** points, and check Behind Fill; this makes the apparent outline width 4 points, but areas are filled in within the characters to give the text a bold look.

7. Choose the Envelope tool from the Blend group on the toolbox, and then perform the same steps as you did earlier with the musical notes in the Bach composition. Use the Envelope tool to massage the text to look arced like the original text. If your design looks like Figure 24-12 now, you're in good shape with only a step or two to go.

8. Create rectangles that match the color of the missing checkerboard in the logo, rotate them to the same diamond-shaped orientation as the original logo, position them accordingly for your patchwork, and then send them to the back of the page by pressing SHIFT+PAGE DOWN.

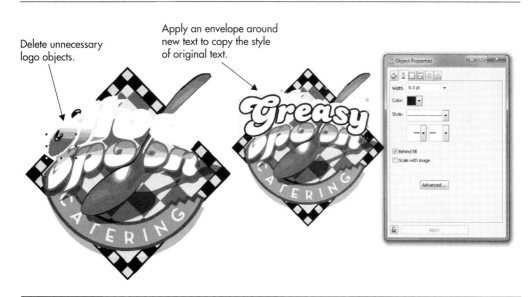

FIGURE 24-12   Replace the text in the original design using a similar font choice.

9. With the Shape tool, edit the characters in the word "catering" to make them look more refined. At small image sizes, CorelDRAW does its best to render approximations of small text, but they still often need a little human intervention!

Create background replacement pieces.

Clean up remaining text where necessary.

10. You can embellish the revised logo by adding a drop shadow to the new owner's name, as it appears in the original logo, and you can smooth out the posterized edges on the spoon by overlaying an object that uses a fountain fill of the same colors. But as you can see here, the new logo is pretty faithful to the original, and with the help of PowerTRACE it took ten steps. Think of how many steps and lost nights of sleep you'd have without an auto-tracing utility.

TIP *To get superfluous objects out of a finished PowerTRACE very quickly, use Edit | Find And Replace | Find Objects, and set the criteria for the search to specific unwanted colors. Then you can delete all the selected objects at once.*

PowerTRACE for Traditional Artists

Lots of different types of users are attracted to CorelDRAW, and logo and other graphics designers are one category of visual communicators. CorelDRAW's tracing feature will also appeal to artists who came to the digital world of illustration after years of work with physical pens, pencils, and inks.

If you have a scanner, and have, for example, a pen-and-ink cartoon, PowerTRACE makes child's play out of re-creating your cartoon as scalable vector art, to which you can apply color fills with a smoothness and precision that enhance your cartoons and can elevate them to the status of Fine Art. Seriously!

Cartoon sneaker drawing.png is a fairly high-resolution scan to get you started with a specific workflow you can adopt to use with scans of your own drawings. One important issue is removing pencil or other marks on the physical paper before you scan; use a kneaded eraser, and even if the paper doesn't come completely clean, the following steps show you a novel way to use PowerTRACE to remove stray marks.

Here's how to create a digital cartoon suitable for exporting as either vector or bitmap art to any size you need; this is a perk you don't have when working with only physical tools.

 Digi-tooning

1. In a new document, landscape orientation, click the Import button on the standard toolbar, and then choose Cartoon sneaker drawing.png. Place it by click-dragging the loaded cursor so it fills the page.

2. Click Trace Bitmap, and then choose Outline Trace | Line Art. You'll receive an attention box that the bitmap size is too large, and that if you choose not to resize the bitmap, the trace process might be on the slow side. This is your artistic call: if you want the pen strokes to look extremely faithful to the author's original cartoon, click Keep Original Size. If you're in a hurry, click Reduce Bitmap.

3. In the PowerTRACE window, choose a medium amount of Detail, about 25% Smoothing, no Corner Smoothing, check Remove Background, and check "Merge adjacent objects of the same color."

4. Click the Colors tab. Set the number of colors to **2**. Doing this will generate almost entirely black objects with the exception of one or two areas that are totally enclosed, which should produce a white fill inside a black object. Click OK, and you'll see that the pencil marks which are not entirely a black color disappear from the trace.

5. Delete the bitmap; you'll need to move the grouped objects first.

6. Choose Tools | Object Manager. Create a new layer and then drag its title on the list to below Layer 1. You can rename these layers "Coloring" and "Trace" by clicking to select the name, and then click a second time to open the title for editing—type anything you like in the field. Lock the tracing layer.

7. With any Pen tool you're most comfortable with for creating free-form shapes, create objects that represent the different areas of the cartoon you'd like to color in. For example, the treads of the sneaker would look good in several different shades of warm gray. The solution would be to use the Mesh fill on this object you draw—see Chapter 15 for thorough documentation of object fills. The top of the sneaker could be an interesting Linear fountain fill, traversing from deep orange at bottom to a bright yellow at top. Another great thing about coloring your work digitally is that you never have to decide on a final color.

8. You continue this process until you've "colored inside the lines" and filled as much of the drawing as you see artistically fit. Figure 24-13 shows a logo mockup for a children's footwear store. Clearly the drawing has an organic sense about it, the opposite of the sterile and flawless "computer art" we see occasionally, and yet this is CorelDRAW computer art, with a little ingenuity added to make a symbiosis between the physical and traditional elements.

You can take a look at how this drawing was completed if you open Sneaky kids finished.cdr.

FIGURE 24-13   The best way to execute a hand-drawn look with CorelDRAW is to hand-draw a picture, scan it, and then PowerTRACE it!

This chapter has shown you how to work with bitmaps in almost the same way as you work with vector art in CorelDRAW. Both vectors and bitmaps can happily coexist in a single document. You can shuffle and rearrange objects as if they were made of the same digital materials, and you do need bitmaps in your work when you're trying to convey any sense of photorealism. Your next stop, in Chapter 25, is to get some hands-on education with PHOTO-PAINT and working directly on bitmap photographs and illustrations. You'll see shortly that editing bitmaps and drawing with vectors can be a seamless creative process when you put the power of the Corel Graphics Suite to its best use.

CHAPTER 25

An Introduction to PHOTO-PAINT

Photography tells a different story than the vector graphics you create in CorelDRAW; while vector drawings can look crisp, powerful, and brilliant in coloring, photographs typically tell more of a human story, with soft tones, an intricate latticework of highlights and shadows, and all the photorealistic qualities that portray the world as we're accustomed to seeing it. Understandably, the tools you use to edit a digital photo or other bitmap image are different from those you use to edit paths in CorelDRAW. And this is where PHOTO-PAINT enters the creative scene.

This chapter introduces you to the fundamentals of bitmap images; how you measure bitmaps, how to crop them to suit a specific output need, and ultimately how to make your original photo look better than it came off the camera.

> **NOTE** *Download and extract all the files from the Chapter25.zip archive to follow the tutorials in this chapter.*

The Building Block of Digital Photos: The Pixel

The term "pixel" is funny-sounding, and we use it occasionally in a humorous context, but seldom is an explanation or definition of a pixel provided in a way that is useful when you need to alter a digital photograph. A *pixel*—an abbreviation for *pic*ture *el*ement—is the smallest recognizable unit of color in a digital photograph. It is *not* a linear unit of measurement, a pixel doesn't have to be square in proportions, and it's not restricted to having any specific color. Now that what a pixel *isn't* has been covered, read on to learn what a pixel *is* and how understanding its properties will help you work with PHOTO-PAINT's tools and features to make photo-retouching go as quickly as your CorelDRAW work.

Pixels and Resolution

A pixel is a *unit of color*; as such, it has no fixed size we can measure the same way as you'd measure the length of a 2-by-4 (which is usually 2"×4"). If you were to discuss a pixel with a friend or coworker, it would be hard to do without any context, because these units of color cannot exist unless they're within a background, usually called the *paper* or the *canvas*. The *paper* in PHOTO-PAINT is an imaginary grid into which you assign units of colors with the Paint tool or the Fill tool. When you open a digital photograph, the "paper" in PHOTO-PAINT is predefined by the presets of the digital camera and software. The resolution of your photographs is then fixed by that combination, but can be changed later.

> **NOTE** *The term "bitmap" was derived from the imaginary grid on an image's canvas—a map—and the amount of color information placed on this map was expressed as a bit of digital information. Usually, more than one bit of information is held by a pixel; more often a pixel holds a byte of information (8×a single bit), but somehow the term "bitmap" stuck as one of the names for pixel-based images.*

Resolution is expressed as a fraction, a ratio: *pixels per inch* expresses image resolution in the same way that miles per hour expresses speed. We often call this resolution *dpi* (dots per inch) due to the visual similarity of dots of ink on a printed page and the pixels of color we see on a monitor. Bitmap images are also called *resolution-dependent* images because once a photo has been taken or a paper size defined for a PHOTO-PAINT painting, you cannot change the resolution without distorting the visual content of the picture. Here's an example that shows the use of resolution when you press CTRL+N or choose File | New.

1. In the Create a New Image dialog, you're offered a Preset Destination of PHOTO-PAINT's default size, which as you can see here is 5 inches in Width by 7 inches in Height. However, the print size is not a *complete* description of how large the image will be in *other* important measurements, such as pixels. How many *pixels* will be created per inch? Pixels are the units of color for the document, so without knowing the resolution, the size of the paper is as meaningful as how many grapefruits per inch will fit on the page! Fortunately, below the Height and Width fields, you're offered the Resolution, set to the default of 72 dpi.

2. Aha! Now the number of pixels in the new document can be Discovered. This can be important for website work, because we always presume a fixed screen resolution with the audience, and therefore images are always measured in the absolute number of pixels in width and height for graphics. In this example, 504 pixels wide might make a good logo on the top page of a website; the majority of people who visit websites run a screen resolution of 1024×768 or higher, so this default paper size is about half the width of an audience's monitor.

5"x72 dpi = 360 pixels

7"x72 dpi = 504 pixels

Image Resolution

Any PHOTO-PAINT document's resolution can be great for web graphics but not so good for printing. The web display and print quality differ because of the finite number of pixels in the resolution-dependent, bitmap image. Figure 25-1 shows at left a CorelDRAW illustration of a child's paint box. In this book the drawing looks crisp around the edges, and smooth in its transitions from neighboring tones. It was a graphic suitable for printing as a bitmap because it was exported at a high resolution (300 dots per inch) for printing in this book. However, at right is an illustration of the same paint box, with the imaginary bitmap grid shown, but it was exported at desktop icon size (about 48×48 pixels), and the loss of image detail is evident at its resolution of 72 pixels per inch.

Resolution, Pixel Count, and Printing

It's a frequently asked question whose answer is imprecise: what is the resolution I need for a photograph to make a good print?

Scanning a physical photograph doesn't provide the best sampling of color pixels to produce a terrific photograph, but it does ensure that you have a sufficient number of pixels (an image's *pixel count*) to print the scanned photo.

The most direct way to acquire a photo and manipulate it in PHOTO-PAINT is by using a digital camera. Today's digital cameras are capable of taking full-frame pictures that can be printed to inkjets printers at 12"×18" in high quality. Digital cameras measure the number of pixels in width and height of the picture's frame in megapixels (MP): a million pixels

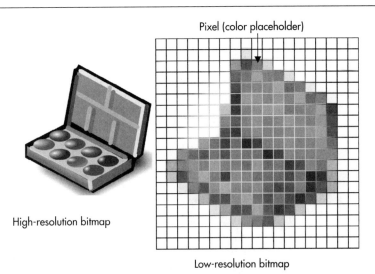

Pixel (color placeholder)

High-resolution bitmap

Low-resolution bitmap

FIGURE 25-1 The number of pixels in a bitmap, combined with the image's resolution, determines whether an image is suitable for printing.

equal a megapixel. For example, the Nikon D90 can take 12.3 MP—its sensor array captures 4,288 pixels along one dimension and 2,848 pixels along the other. Thus, 4,288×2,848 = 12.2 (plus a fractional amount) megapixels.

Depending on the make and model of your digital camera (price plays a deciding factor here), you can take images that vary in maximum print size. The following table provides the maximum printable dimensions for different megapixel-capable cameras:

Camera	Max. Print Size
12.3 MP	12"h×18"w
10.1 MP	10.8"h×16.2"w
9 MP	10.2"h×15.3"w
6 MP	8.3"h×12.5"w

These are not hard-and-fast dimensions, but for two reasons are guidelines for print output:

- The dots that inkjet printers render are imprecise. They are more like splats than dots because the print head sprays color onto the page.

- There is some flexibility when printing to home inkjet printers because *image dimensions are inversely proportional to image resolution.*

Manufacturers of inkjet printers, makers of inks, and other printing experts agree that the ideal resolution for printing—720 dots per inch—requires about 1/3 this number, in pixels per inch, for the image to be printed. The math goes like this: most affordable inkjet printers offer a high-quality resolution of about 720 dpi. The documentation might claim that the printer offers "enhanced resolution of 1,440 dpi," but usually this enhancement is only rendered in one direction, height or width, depending on your print layout. The true resolution is always the lower number when two are offered in the inkjet printer's documentation. Thus, 720 / 3 is 240 (dpi).

NOTE *A* pixel *is not the same unit of color measurement as a printed* dot. *Dots per inch (dpi) is the measurement of the fixed resolution of an image as printed to a physical page, and a dot on a page can be physically measured if you have a very small ruler. The resolution of an image as measured on your monitor is expressed in pixels per inch (ppi), and as you'll learn in this chapter, the dimensions of a bitmap image can be changed by changing the resolution. However, many software manufacturers, including Corel Corp., use ppi and dpi interchangeably. Similarly, the term "dpi" is used in this chapter to express pixels per inch to avoid the discrepancy between terminology used in digital photography and the labels of certain options in PHOTO-PAINT's dialog boxes.*

The good news is that you can change the resolution of an image, thereby changing its real-world dimensions, without changing the pixel count—which tends to sharpen an image when it's made smaller, but blurs it when enlarged. For example, a photo that is 3"×3" at 300 pixels per inch has *exactly the same number of pixels* as the image at 6"×6" at a resolution of 150 ppi. Both images have the same number of pixels, but the print dimensions and resolution have been changed.

Let's walk through an example on how to determine a photo's resolution, and then adjust it for printing.

Resizing a Photograph

1. In PHOTO-PAINT open CRW_6115.jpg, a photo that has been (mal)adjusted to demonstrate a technique in this chapter.

2. Let's say that you need to print this photo at inkjet high quality. This means at least 240 dots per inch (dpi) are required. To check the resolution of the current foreground document, use the Object Pick tool to right-click the document, and then choose Document Properties from the context menu.

> **TIP** *To display rulers around the edges of a document, press CTRL+SHIFT+R (View | Rulers). To hide rulers, press CTRL+SHIFT+R again to toggle them off. If the rulers don't display the units you need, right-click either ruler and then choose Ruler Setup from the context menu.*

3. Well, oops. This photo is a nice 8"×11", but it's of insufficient resolution to print at the required 240 dpi, as shown in Figure 25-2. It *can* print with high quality and great image fidelity, but the physical output dimensions need to be decreased to *increase* the resolution.

4. Right-click the photo and then choose Resample from the context menu. The Resample (Image menu item) box does more than *resample* an image; it can also *resize* it, and the two terms are very different. *Resize* is the action of decreasing or increasing image resolution, affecting image dimensions inversely, and the result is an image that has the same number of pixels. *Resampling* (covered in this chapter) involves changing the number of pixels in the image. Original pixel colors are moved around the grid, some are duplicated, some removed, and the resulting color pixels are a new color based on an average of neighboring original color pixels. Resampling changes original image data and occasionally blurs or creates unwanted harsh edges in image areas.

5. Check the Maintain Original Size box, make sure the Maintain Aspect Ratio box is checked, and then type **7** in the Height field. Because the photo was doctored for this example, the photo is now a perfect 7"×5", smaller than its original dimensions. As you can see, as the dimensions decreased, the resolution increased and is now more

FIGURE 25-2 Pictures that need to be printed demand a higher resolution than 144 dots per inch.

than adequate in resolution for inkjet printing. Save the file if you like owls, and then print it to see what image resolution does for digital images: it *improves* them.

Maintain Original Size keeps file size and pixel count the same.

Scanning Photos into PHOTO-PAINT

You might want to acquire an image by scanning instead of using a digital camera for two common reasons:

- The picture wasn't originally taken with a digital camera. There were very few digital cameras in 1924, so your great grandmother's photo probably exists only as a print, or if you're extremely lucky, as a film negative.

- The picture is a drawing. You want to use Corel PowerTRACE to clean up a logo or other graphic.

In either event, scanning images is very simple using PHOTO-PAINT as the host for the resulting bitmap. Follow these steps:

1. Make sure the scanner is plugged in, turned on, and connected to your computer directly or through a network. Don't laugh; these are the first things the manufacturer's tech support asks you at $5 a minute.

2. Make sure your computer recognizes the scanner. Your scanner came with an installation disk that has drivers Windows needs to read to be able to create a handshake between the two pieces of hardware. Go to the manufacturer's website, and download and then install the most current drivers if you put the install disk in a safe place you've forgotten.

3. Make sure the imaging surface (the platen) on the scanner is clean. Place your image on the platen, making sure the image isn't crooked within the rectangular edges of the platen, and then launch PHOTO-PAINT.

4. Choose File | Acquire Image | Select Source. Choose your device from the list and then click Select. If you have several devices hooked up to your computer via USB, Firewire, or other connection protocol, choose your scanner. It's possible that an entry that begins with "WIA" (Windows Interface Application) is a scanning choice. Don't choose the WIA connection if you can make a different choice; WIA is a generic driver and as such can only access the most basic of features on your scanner.

5. Choose File | Acquire Image | Acquire. The UI for your scanner will appear on top of PHOTO-PAINT's UI. Different scanners have different interfaces, but the common elements are a preview window in which you can crop the image you want scanned to a bitmap file, and dimensions and resolution fields. Usually, you click the Preview button to refresh the preview, updating your view to the scanner's current contents on its platen.

6. Choose your color mode for scanning. RGB is generally the best choice because you can always convert an acquired image to grayscale or other color mode directly in PHOTO-PAINT. Only choose Grayscale if you're scanning a black-and-white photo—aged photos that look like a black-and-white photo can contain valuable image data in sepia areas, so color-scan heirloom photos. If given the option to scan in "bitmap," "fax," or "1 bit per pixel," *don't*. This mode should be reserved for documents, faxes, and other material that requires absolutely no image fidelity.

7. Use the interface controls to drag an area of the platen that contains your document. Don't crop too closely to what you want scanned.

8. Set the scanning percentage to 1:1 (100%) so that a scanned inch actually equals an inch at the resolution you'll set in step 10.

9. Check the height and width of the highlighted, cropped area on the platen. Many scanners do not offer onscreen rulers; height and width fields should be onscreen, as shown in Figure 25-3. If you need to increase the dimensions, adjust the value in the Percentage field.

10. Set the resolution of the scan. As mentioned earlier in this chapter, if your intended output is 1:1 scale and the printer is a personal inkjet, set the scanning resolution to 240 ppi (often labeled "dpi"). However, if your scan is destined for a desktop publishing document done at a commercial printer, set the resolution to *at least* 266 ppi. Many commercials printers will ask for 300 ppi.

11. Click Scan and wait a little as the samples of the image are streamed to your computer.

12. When the scan is completed, your scanner's interface disappears and "Untitled-1.cpt" appears in PHOTO-PAINT's workspace. Save the image to hard disk (CTRL+S); in the Save an Image to Disk dialog, name the file and choose a file type from the Save As Type drop-down list. PHOTO-PAINT's native *.CPT file format is fine, except in business situations where you need to share documents. The CPT file format can only be opened on CorelDRAW and PHOTO-PAINT. TIFF and PNG file formats are almost universally understood by applications other than Corel's—the TIFF format can retain image resolution information, PNG as written by PHOTO-PAINT saves files at the default screen resolution of 72 ppi, but the files are often smaller than uncompressed TIFFs. Be careful when choosing to save a picture as a JPEG— it compresses images by discarding visual detail it thinks is unimportant (but you might not).

FIGURE 25-3 A good size for a scanned image you want to print or retouch should rival the saved file size of photos taken with digital cameras, anywhere from 6MB to 20MB.

NOTE *Some in the imaging community disagree about whether screen resolution should be measured at 72 pixels per inch or 96, the standard that Microsoft put forth with Windows 95. The answer is that when you're measuring pixels for screen display,* resolution *makes absolutely no difference. Screen resolution, regardless of how you measure it, is of a fixed size, so a 300-pixel-wide bitmap might look larger or smaller depending on the screen resolution you use for display, but nothing changes the number of pixels in width, nor the total pixel count of a bitmap when you display it on your monitor.*

If you have an older scanner whose drivers do not work with Vista or Windows 7, check out VueScan, a stand-alone scanning software at www.hamrick.com. It runs as an application separate from Windows and separate from PHOTO-PAINT. It will usually restore the use of a scanner you bought even two decades ago that you couldn't get to work with your new computer.

Resampling and Resizing Photos

At times you absolutely *have* to upscale a photo; you might not have a better image, and you can't retake the scene or portrait. When you increase the number of pixels in a photo, you're not increasing image detail—all the details in the scene were captured when you took the photo. PHOTO-PAINT adds pixels by duplicating existing pixel colors and then averaging the colors a little to make a smooth photo transition between neighboring pixels in the resampled photo *if* you leave Anti-alias checked in the Resample box.

How much larger you can make a photo before the individual pixels become apparent depends a lot on the visual content of the photo. Pictures of intricate machinery and images of lots of different-colored small objects such as leaves do not "upsample" nearly as well as, say, a photo of soft clouds on an overcast day. If you need to make a photo 150% of its original size, usually you can get away with this with no additional steps. However, if, for example, you need to print a picture from the Web that's only 300 pixels wide, you have two things going for you in this endeavor:

- Inkjet printers tend to smooth out small rough areas in a digital image, because ink spreads on the printed page, blending flaws together. Don't count on this factor; it's an assistant, but a small one.

- PHOTO-PAINT can sharpen edges in the resampled photo while keeping large areas of similar colors smooth in appearance.

TIP   *PHOTO-PAINT has several sharpening filters under Effects | Sharpen. PHOTO-PAINT's Help system provides a good general explanation of the sharpen filters; launch any of them and then click Help in the filter box. Generally, when in doubt, choose Unsharp Mask to add some crispness to resampled photos. Good base point settings to work from and then tune are Percentage: 100, Radius: 1 to 3, and Threshold: 10. They provide very good sharpening without an overwhelming number of options you need to learn. Click the Preview button in filter boxes to see what the filter will look like before applying it.*

Figure 25-4 shows a small JPEG photograph; let's pretend for the purposes of working through a tutorial that you own this condo and want to time-share it. And you want to print postcard-size images to hand out in addition to your website's image.

350 pixels wide   Zoom to 800%

FIGURE 25-4 Unless some corrective steps are taken, this small photo would print with huge, clearly visible color pixels.

 The Zoom tool (Z) lets you get in very close to an image area to view and edit. However, if you're not familiar with resolution-dependent bitmap editing, a zoomed-in view of a photo might look coarse, and your instinct might be to soften the image. Periodically check the document title bar: after the name of the file, there's an "@" symbol followed by your current viewing resolution. If the zoom factor is greater than 100%, this document is not displaying as your audience will see it. To quickly zoom a document to 1:1, 100% viewing resolution, double-click the Zoom tool on the toolbox.

The following steps are a worst-case scenario—you will almost certainly be able to enlarge photos to become printworthy by resampling up to 150% or so, and not with the *gross* sort of enlargement and image corrections featured in these steps. However, as you'll soon see, the High Pass effect you'll use does indeed enhance a copy of the small JPEG photo to a usable state.

Making a Thumbnail Image Suitable for Printing

1. Open Hollywood-5203.jpg in PHOTO-PAINT. With the Object Pick tool, right-click over the image, and then choose Resample from the context menu.

2. In the Width field, type **7**, and then click an insertion point in the Resolution | Horizontal field. Make sure the Maintain Aspect Ratio and Anti-alias check boxes are checked, and then type **240** in the box. Click OK to resample the photo.

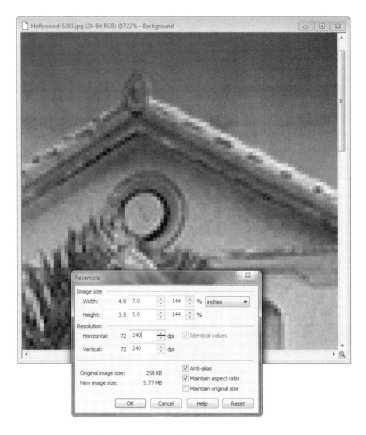

3. At 100% viewing resolution, clearly the photo needs a little edge-sharpening without sharpening the larger smooth areas of the photo. Press CTRL+F7 if the Objects docker isn't docked to the window or isn't visible. You're going to duplicate this image and put the copy on top of the original. This is an unusual thing to do, and *to be able to do,* but PHOTO-PAINT has advanced image-editing features that let you change and merge image areas (called *objects*) so the pixels in objects can have different colors but are identically aligned to the imaginary grid in the document.

4. With the Object Pick tool, drag the thumbnail labeled "Background" to on top of the New Object button on the Object docker, and then release the mouse button. Doing this duplicates the image, creating the new object directly on top of the original.

Drag Background thumbnail on top of New Object button.

Result is a duplicated object.

5. Click the Object 1 thumbnail on the Objects list to select it—you want to edit this, not the Background object.

6. Choose Effects | Sharpen | High Pass. Wherever sharp transitions between pixel colors appear in the photo, edge details are retained and strengthened. Wherever there is little color difference between neighboring pixels (called *low-frequency* areas), the visual information is filtered out, leaving a neutral gray. The higher the Percentage you specify (use 100 in this example), the less original color is retained. The greater the Radius (use about 12 in this example), the greater the distance this filter examines from neighboring pixels to filter out areas of little detail difference. Click OK to apply these settings.

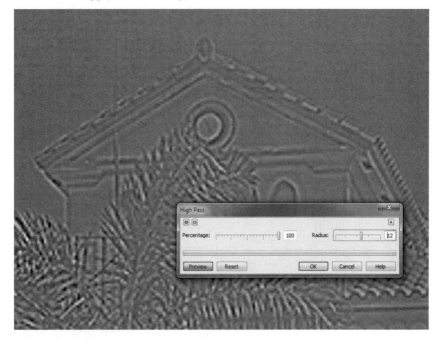

7. Beyond the strong edges in Object 1, this object doesn't look as though it will contribute a lot to enhancing this enlarged image, but the correct answer is, "Yes, it will!" Merge modes are covered in the transparency section of Chapter 22, but for now, here's a simple explanation of why Overlay mode will turn this largely gray object into a perfect "lens" to sharpen the underlying Background photo. The brightness values in a photo (the tones, not the colors) are usually calculated on a scale from 0 to 255, 255 representing the brightest area (pure white has a brightness of 255). Overlay merge mode can be thought of as a filter: Overlay mode objects that have a brightness over 128 lighten (bleach, screen) objects under them, while brightness pixel values under 128 darken (multiply) the underlying pixels. The High Pass filter made most of the pixels in this object neutral gray—which has no effect in Overlay mode on the underlying pixels. However, the *edge details* in Object 1 are darker and lighter than the underlying, corresponding Background areas. Choose Overlay from the Merge Mode drop-down list.

8. Objects do not have to be 100% opaque. This Overlay mode object contributes a little too strongly to the overall picture; click the Transparency combo box at the top right of the Object docker to reveal the slider, and then drag the slider left to about 29%, or whatever value looks best in the document window.

9. You can choose to save this file right now as a PHOTO-PAINT (CPT) or Adobe Photoshop (PSD) document, and the objects will retain their order using these special image file formats. And you can now print the composition. However, if you'd like to standardize the image so it can be saved to practically any file format (PNG, JPEG, TIFF, and others) and thus shared with most other computer users, then with the Object Pick tool, right-click either object on the Object docker, and then choose Combine | Combine All Objects With Background.

As you can see in comparison in Figure 25-5, without the High Pass copy of the image in Overlay mode, at left the pixels dominate the image in visual importance. At right, however, with the duplicate object you filtered and merged with the original, it's a fairly photogenic image…given that you enlarged it to almost *23 times* its original file size!

Automation: Recording Your Cropping and Resampling

It's almost a foregone conclusion that if you work at a small to medium business, you have dozens if not hundreds of photos that need some sort of alterations and uniformity so they'll

Without High Pass object   High Pass object in Overlay mode

FIGURE 25-5   Use PHOTO-PAINT filters and objects to selectively strengthen and smooth image areas.

look consistent in size when you make a catalog or web page. Cropping is a separate process from resizing photos in PHOTO-PAINT, but the good news is that if your photos are even remotely similar in subject matter, you can record your cropping and resampling moves, and then play this recorded script back on an entire folder of images. The result: no errors, no recalculations, and you might have a free hand to eat your sandwich as you work through lunch.

Evaluating a Crop Area for a Collection of Photos

PHOTO-PAINT's Crop tool does only one thing, perfectly well: it eliminates areas of a picture outside the crop rectangle you drag before double-clicking or pressing ENTER to finalize the crop. You are free before finalizing to reposition, reset, and move the crop rectangle. The Crop tool resizes an image area: it does *not* resample the area you want to remain in the document. Therefore, if you want to enlarge or decrease the number of pixels in the finished version, the additional step of resampling must be performed *before* saving a copy of the photo.

The imaginary company in the tutorial that follows specializes in exotic minerals—no common quartz or hematite to be found on their website—and the photographer took seven pictures whose visual content is more or less in the same position from photo to photo. Your mission is to crop out the bottom pedestal and place card in all the photos to favor the mineral itself, and to reduce the size of all the pictures, all sized to exactly the same dimensions, so the collection of minerals can be featured on a web page. Because Windows 7 (and XP) can display large thumbnails of common image file formats such as PNG, it's easy to preview the contents of an entire folder of images, to better see which individual photo needs the most height or width to then apply a suitable crop for all the images.

Figure 25-6 is a view of the folder of mineral pictures as seen from the File | Open box in PHOTO-PAINT, with Extra Large Icons chosen in the dialog. The overlay of the dotted line shows that the Fliakite.png image requires the greatest width of all the files—this is something you can detect by eye. Therefore, when you begin the tutorial, you'll begin by choosing Fliakite.png as the image you'll record your cropping and resampling edits on.

25

FIGURE 25-6 Out of the many images you need to resample and crop, choose the one that requires the loosest cropping as the basis for your automation recording.

Recording Your Edits

The following steps guide you simultaneously through recording and editing the resampling and cropping process. Playing the saved recording back on a folder is very simple and covered in a following section. If you have a real-world need to crop and resample scores of images, and your boss or client wanted them yesterday, you're going to have your solution and the images completed sooner than anyone might imagine! Locate the images you downloaded at the beginning of this chapter: put only the mineral PNG files in a unique folder.

1. Choose Windows | Dockers | Recorder (CTRL+F3).

2. Choose File | Open (CTRL+O) and then open Fliakite.png from the folder to which you copied the seven PNG files.

3. Click the red button at the bottom of the Recorder docker; you're recording now. Choose the Crop tool from the toolbar.

4. Drag a rectangle around the top of the image, excluding the glass pedestal from your crop.

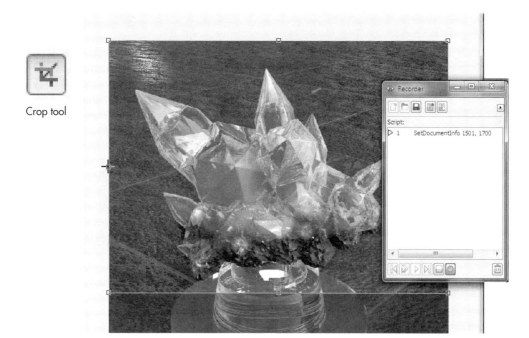

Crop tool

5. Press ENTER to finalize the crop (double-clicking inside the document does the same thing).

6. Press O (Object Pick tool), and then right-click over the image and choose Resample.

7. Allowing for three or possibly four thumbnails across a conservatively sized web page of 800 pixels wide means the width to resample this image should be about 200 pixels. Choose Pixels from the Image Size units drop-down list, and then type **200** in the Width field. When you move your cursor to a different field, the Height will scale down in proportion.

8. Because you're not measuring in real-world units but instead in numbers of pixels, you don't have to specify 72 or 96 dpi for the resampled image. On the Web, a screen pixel is an absolute, unchangeable size. Additionally, if you change the dpi setting now, you'll need to go back and specify the Width to 200 a second time, because you will have changed the resolution value. Click OK to apply.

9. Double-click the Zoom tool to move your view to 100%. The resampled image could use just a touch of Effect | Sharpen | Sharpen, a good choice for extremely small images. Set the Edge Level to about 26%; this is the degree of sharpening with emphasis on neighboring pixels that have dissimilar colors. Set the Threshold to 0 (zero)—the lower the value, the more pronounced the sharpening effect.

10. Click the Stop button on the Recorder docker.

11. Click the Save button on the Recorder docker, name the script, and let PHOTO-PAINT save the script to the default location, because you'll never find it again if you create a custom location.

NOTE *The Save icon on the Recorder and other dockers represents a floppy disk. Floppy disks were used to store digital media before DVDs, CDs, air travel, and horses were invented.*

12. You can close the Fliakite file without saving changes. In the following section, you'll run the recorded script on this image and save it, so your unfinished work will be automatically done for you.

The Fun Part: Playing Back Your Script

The following steps will seem anticlimactic; the bulk of the work you have ahead of you is accomplished merely by filling out a few fields in the File | Batch Process box and clicking Play.

1. Choose File | Batch Process.

2. Click Add File. Navigate the dialog to where you stored the mineral images. Select all of them: click one file to place your cursor inside the file box, press CTRL+A to select all, and then click Import.

3. Click Add Script. Look at the path to where PHOTO-PAINT default-saves scripts at the top of the box. The location is under your User Account | Appdata | Roaming | Corel if you lose a file in the future. Click the name of the script you saved in the previous tutorial, and then click Open.

4. In the Options area, click the On Completion drop-down list, and then choose Save As New Type. You'll probably want the JPEG file type for the resampled photos if this is a website display.

5. The Save To Folder option is an important choice if you want to find the processed images later! Because you'll be saving to JPEG, it's okay to save the processed images to the same folder as the originals, which are in the PNG file format and will not be overwritten by the batch process.

6. Click the Save As Type drop-down list, and then choose JPG - JPEG Bitmaps.

7. Click Play. Done!

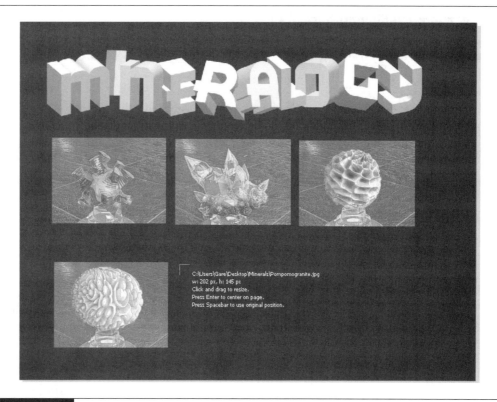

FIGURE 25-7 Standardize scores of image files in minutes by using PHOTO-PAINT's Recorder and Batch Processing features.

Figure 25-7 is back in CorelDRAW, where the Extrude tool was used for a fancy website banner. As you can see here, when you select the multiple files for import into CorelDRAW from the destination folder to which you saved your batch processing, you can simply click the page to place the images, one at a time, at 100% their size, and in no time you either look like a miracle worker to your boss, or if you're self-employed, you can look in your bathroom mirror and say, "Darn, I'm good!" (this is a PG book).

 You may not need to use the Zoom tool very often to change your view if your mouse has a scroll wheel. With the Object Pick tool as your current tool, spinning toward you with the wheel zooms your view out, and pushing away zooms you into the current document window.

Flipping Images...with a Twist

Before moving on to Chapter 26 and more advanced image-editing techniques, let's cover one more common imaging need, and a problem that occurs when you try to accomplish something seemingly as simple as mirroring a photograph. This is going to be your first step into the league of the pros: invisible image-retouching.

Photos of many objects in the real world and portrait photos of people are bilaterally symmetrical—when you look in the mirror, you recognize yourself because even though your image is horizontally flipped, the right and left sides of your face look pretty much the same. This reality usually allows you to flip a photograph when you need, for example, your subject looking to the right instead of to the left. The fly in the ointment, however, is when your subject is wearing a garment that has text on it; similarly, when a building in the background has text, or there's only one shirt pocket on a garment—these flipped images will have something in them that clearly looks wrong to the audience.

The following steps venture into the area of PHOTO-PAINT objects: how you can lift an area, copy it to a new object, and then flip the background but not the new object, which in this example is the text on a child's T-shirt. Retouching is not this simple—you will have a little edgework to clean up before considering the task completed—but with a little guidance, you'll learn a technique now that can be applied to a number of different retouching needs down the road:

1. Open Two Kids.tif in PHOTO-PAINT. On the Object docker, you need to convert this "normal" bitmap image into an object-capable one so that objects can be flipped independently of one another. Click the Create Object From Background icon at the right of the thumbnail, as shown in Figure 25-8, and the name of the item now changes to "Object 1." This step can also be performed by choosing Object | Create | From Background on the main menu.

2. Choose the Freehand Mask tool from the toolbox; if it's not visible, click-drag the second-from-top icon on the toolbox (usually the Rectangle Mask tool) to reveal the entire group of masking tools, and then choose the Freehand Mask tool.

3. On the property bar, set the Feathering value to about **6** pixels. Feathering softens a selection, so inside and outside the edge of a selection mask, pixels are *partially* selected. This might sound strange to have an area partially selected (like an egg being partially broken), but the effect ensures smooth and seamless retouching work.

4. Drag around the word "Julian" on Julian's T-shirt to select it; double-click when you're done, and the image area is now available for editing. If you don't include all of the name on your first try, click the Additive Mode button on the property bar, and use the Freehand Mask tool to add to the existing mask.

25

Click to turn a Background
into an object.

FIGURE 25-8	Once a photo is an object, you can perform many PHOTO-PAINT feats not possible with a standard JPEG or other image file.

5. Right-click inside the dashed indicator lines for the mask area, and then choose Object: Copy Selection from the context menu. On the Object docker, you'll now see a new thumbnail at the top of the list of objects, titled "Object 2"; see Figure 25-9.

> **TIP** *Pressing CTRL+R removes a mask in a document window. This is equivalent to a Select | None command in other programs. To hide the marquee lines running around a masked area of an object—and you're only hiding, you're not deselecting but only hiding an onscreen element—press CTRL+H to alternately Hide and Restore the marquee.*

6. Click the Object 1 entry on the Objects list to make it the current editing object. Then, choose Object | Flip Horizontally. And yes, it will look strange to have "Julian" floating above the other kid's chest!

7. Click the Object 2 entry on the Objects docker, choose Lightness from the Merge Mode drop-down list—a good mode for making underlying areas fade away only if the top affecting object has lighter corresponding pixels—and then move the object over Julian's chest at image left with the Object Pick tool.

Feather amount

FIGURE 25-9   Copy the image area that you don't want to flip to a new object in the document.

8. Evaluate the composition for a moment. What needs to be done now is to remove some of the backwards text on Object 1 to keep it from showing through. A straight paint color won't do the job, because the image area has varying tones of color from the texture of the T-shirt. Choose the Clone tool from the group that contains the Red-Eye Removal tool.

9. The Clone tool picks up an image area you define by right-clicking and then applies the image area to a different area when you drag, based on the diameter and feather amount (*softness* or soft-edge in other bitmap programs) you set for the tool. On the property bar, choose Medium Soft Clone from the drop-down list.

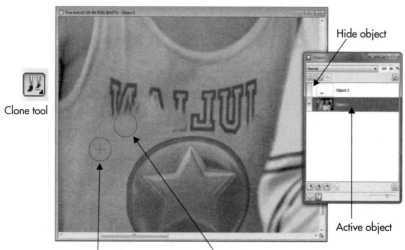

Clone tool

Hide object

Active object

Right-click to set sample point... then stroke over area to be retouched.

FIGURE 25-10 Use the Clone tool to visually integrate the areas in Objects 2 and 1.

10. Hide Object 2 by clicking the visibility (the eye) icon to the left of its thumbnail.

11. Right-click with the Clone tool just below the name on Julian's T-shirt. You're choosing a sampling area that's close in tone and color to the area you want to hide.

12. Drag, ever-so-slowly, slightly, and carefully over the backward lettering on the T-shirt, to get a feel for the Clone tool. When you release the mouse button, the sampling point for the Clone tool snaps back to its original position. Therefore, release the mouse button when you see that the traveling sampling point is getting mighty close to an undesired area for sampling. Work from the outside inward, resampling frequently to match the original tones of the light shirt. Periodically, unhide Object 2 to see how much work you need to do, and what areas are not necessary to clone away.

Eraser tool

Lightness merge mode

FIGURE 25-11 Erase areas whose tone and color don't match the edges of the object.

13. When you think you're finished cloning, restore the visibility of Object 2. You might be done, but you might want to refine the edges of Object 2 with the Eraser tool. If so…

14. Choose the Eraser tool, and then on the property bar, choose a soft tip from the Presets drop-down list, and set the size to about 35 pixels in diameter.

15. Zoom into the editing area, and then drag over any areas whose brightness doesn't match the edge of the object. Figure 25-11 shows the work in progress, and the illusion looks pretty convincing.

16. Optionally, you can standardize this image's data by combining all objects—as you did in the Hollywood condo example. Right-click over either object title on the Object docker, and then choose Combine | Combine All Objects With Background.

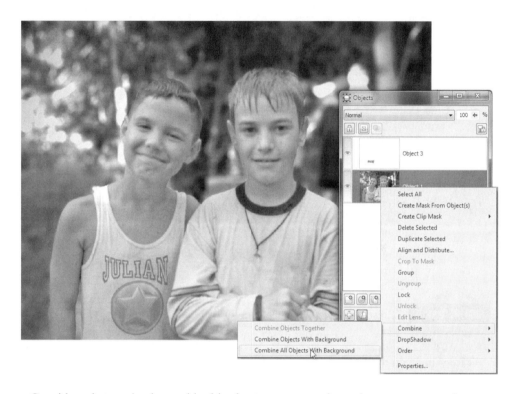

Consider what you've learned in this chapter: you now know how to repeat actions on an entire folder of images, you can scale, crop, and flip pictures, and you have a basic handle on all the sophisticated editing you can perform using transparency, objects, and merge modes. But the biggest payoff is an ironic one: a good photo retoucher's work should go unnoticed!

Now bring what you've learned into Chapter 26, for more invisible mending and a technique or two that will definitely get your work noticed. Special effects and advanced retouching techniques lie ahead.

CHAPTER 26

PHOTO-PAINT Effects
and Advanced Editing

C hapter 25 got you off the ground with some basic photo-editing techniques; this chapter approaches a lot more ambitious editing of images, yet stays within the realm of common tasks for professionals you've seen and would like to re-create. Removing backgrounds, combining areas of different photos into a seamless composition, and creating animated GIFs are on the menu today. Along the way, you'll discover and learn to use some of the most important tools and features in PHOTO-PAINT, and by the end of this chapter, you'll be able to do a lot more than simply re-create the images in the following tutorials. You'll make the techniques, and anything you work on in the future, truly *your own*.

> **NOTE** *Download and extract all the files from the Chapter26.zip archive to follow the tutorials in this chapter. This folder has a Gallery subfolder with finished examples of the tutorial files for this chapter.*

Turning a Snapshot into a Photograph

If you've ever worked in a large manufacturing company as a designer, you already know that whoever takes the picture of a new product has tunnel vision: they pay attention to focus, and perhaps even lighting the product—but pay no attention to a cluttered, inappropriate background! And your boss is no help because he's conditioned by watching YouTube to think that, "Oh, you can just Photoshop this, can't you? Takes two secs!"

Nope: you own Corel PHOTO-PAINT and you're going to learn how to PHOTO-PAINT this sorry photograph into something that looks terrific in that brochure that was due yesterday.

Objects and the Path Tool

Open Labeling machine.cpt in PHOTO-PAINT now: clearly, all that's missing is a coffee cup and a deck of playing cards to *totally* ruin the visual importance of the Market Up® 8500 labeling machine. When photographing product, you either highlight it within a compatible setting (in this example, perhaps next to retail packages or a shopping cart), or you go very minimalist and shoot against a pastel seamless paper. The purpose of this section is to show how you use PHOTO-PAINT to lift only the labeling machine off the background, and then replace the background with something stylish yet neutral in content so the machine is the hero of the photo.

Because the silhouette of a machine, or a box, or anything with clearly defined geometry is a hard edge, the best and quickest tool to use in PHOTO-PAINT for extracting the image area is the Path tool. The Path tool operates almost identically to the Bezier pen tool in CorelDRAW. When you use the tool, the property bar has options that you'll feel right at home with, and paths you draw have special properties in this bitmap-editing program. Paths you create can:

- **Stroke a Path**   Once a path is selected, you can choose any of the brush tools (Paint, Effect, Image Sprayer, and even the Eraser tool), and then choose Object | Edit Path | Brushstroke from Path. If you're new to PHOTO-PAINT, this action is fraught with peril, so don't just leap into using this command. You probably want to create a new object upon which to stroke the path before doing anything permanent to a photo: choose Window | Dockers | Objects, and then click the New Object button. Also make sure that the size of the brush and the preset for the brush along with the color (if any) is the one you want. By stroking a path onto an object—paths do not belong to any specific object—you're free to experiment and can delete the object if you mess up.

TIP   *In addition to the Objects Docker button you'll use in this chapter's tutorials, the New Object command is also in the Object | Create main menu.*

- **Mask from Path**   This is the command you'll use in the steps to follow. You can make a *mask*—a selected area of an object or the background of a photo—based on the shape of a path. The mask allows edits only within the interior of the shape; you can fill (see the next item here) and also delete the interior of an object, leaving transparency. If you want to work on the exterior areas defined by a mask, press CTRL+SHIFT+I to invert the areas so the exterior is subject to changes while the interior of the object is protected from changes.

- **Fill a Path**   You can fill the interior of a path by first defining a mask based on the shape of the path; to do this, with the Path tool selected on the toolbox (so you can see options on the property bar), click the Mask From Path button, and then mosey on over to Edit | Fill. In the Edit Fill & Transparency box, click the type of fill you want, and then click Edit to use and customize the presets available.

TIP   *Regardless of how you create a mask, to remove it, the keyboard shortcut is CTRL+R.*

Here's the game plan: in the following steps, you convert the image background to an object. Then use the Path tool to work around the edge of the labeling machine, closing the path around the machine; create a mask from the path; use the Object | Create | Object: Copy (or Cut) Selection; and then delete the original background. Let's begin.

 ## Using Paths as Masks

1. Open Labeling machine.cpt in PHOTO-PAINT. Then choose Window | Dockers | Objects (CTRL+F7 is the shortcut).

2. Click the Background icon to the right of the Background item on the Objects docker list. This is a shortcut to Object | Create | From Background, and the title of the image is now "Object 1."

3. Drag the document window edge outward a little. You'll notice a white area surrounding the image—this is the background to the document, and Object 1 is now floating above it. If you like, increase the size of the thumbnail for Object 1 by dragging the slider to the bottom right of the Objects docker to the right.

Document Background   Entire photo is a floating object.   Click to turn a Background into an object.

Thumbnail size

4. Press ALT+F10 to display the Paths docker. You're going to draw a path around the labeling machine now.

5. Choose the Path tool from the group of shape tools in the toolbox. Before you begin, if you're not experienced with CorelDRAW's Shape and Bezier tools, the Path tool is used both to draw paths and to edit them. Figure 26-1 shows what the property bar in PHOTO-PAINT looks like when the Path tool is active. The callouts in this figure pertain only to this chapter's example. The other tools have familiar icons that perform the same functions as those on the property bar in CorelDRAW when the pen tools are used.

Shape   Bezier   Freehand   Mask From Path

Path
tool

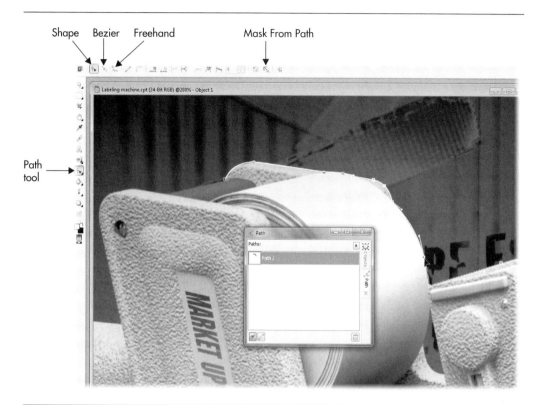

26

FIGURE 26-1   The features on the property bar when the Path tool is chosen help refine the paths you create.

6. Traveling clockwise, click to place a control point toward the top left of the outline of the labeling machine; you can start anywhere you like along the edge, but this tutorial would become a little oblique if we didn't use a common reference point.

7. The next node to be placed is at the end of a curve: to build a curved path between node 1 and node 2, click-drag after you define the point, exactly as you would using the Bezier tool in CorelDRAW.

8. At some point you might need to zoom or pan your view of the document. If you choose to press H as a shortcut to the Pan tool, then press ENTER to return to the last-used tool; there's a good chance you won't be able to extend the path you're drawing because you've switched tools. Make sure to click the last node on your path—the cursor features a "+" sign, which means it's good to extend the path now. The illustration here shows the three cursor states for the Path tool. As you pan your view and change tools, do not try to extend the path when your cursor looks like the

"create node" cursor. If you use the document scroll bars for changing your view, you haven't switched tools and you're cool to continue drawing the path.

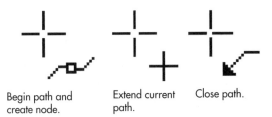

Begin path and
create node.

Extend current
path.

Close path.

9. Draw a tight path all the way around the outline of the labeling machine, and finally click at your start point to close the path. Right now is a good time to zoom into various areas to make sure the path is faithful to the edge of the machine. If there's a misplaced node or curve segment, with the Path tool selected, choose the Shape tool on the property bar, click the node and move it, or click the node to display its control handles and then drag a control handle to steer the curve segment so it fits the edge of the machine.

10. Click the Mask From Path button on the property bar. The interior of your path is now selected.

11. Choose Object | Create | Object: Copy Selection (CTRL+UP ARROW). Usually, when beginning a new program, it's better to duplicate something by copying it than cutting it (the author used CTRL+SHIFT+UP ARROW in these figures).

12. On the Objects docker, click the Background entry—the image without the machine—to make sure it's the chosen object (the title will be highlighted in a foreground Windows color), and then click the Delete button (the old-fashioned metal trash can). Now you have only the labeling machine as an object in the document, and it's surrounded by a checkerboard pattern indicating that there are no pixels surrounding it.

13. Take a break, keep the document open, and press CTRL+S to save your work up to this point.

You can name an entry on the Objects docker anything you like; you don't have to accept the default name of "Object n." To rename an entry, click the name, then click again to open the name for editing, and then type anything you please.

Replacing the Background

Because the labeling machine is supposed to be the primary focus of the image, a new background can be quite simple—you just add a hint of detail to make the overall scene look consistent in its photorealism. In the next steps, you'll add a gradient to a new object behind the machine, distort the object a little to add perspective, and apply a little texture to keep the fountain fill object from looking too perfect. Here's how to set up and edit a new background for the scene.

Putting a Background Behind an Object

1. Hide or delete the path in the document by clicking either the Show/Hide Path button at the bottom of the Paths docker, or click the Delete button.

2. On the Objects docker, click the New Object button. A new entry appears on the docker, labeled "Object 2," and it appears above the labeling machine in the order of objects in the document.

3. Drag the title "Object 2" to below "Object 1" on the Objects docker. You'll see the little hand turn into a little clenched hand as you perform this action.

Drag Object 2 down below Object 1.

New Object

4. Click the "Object 2" title to make sure it's the current editing layer. Choose the Interactive fill tool from the toolbox, and then drag from top to bottom in the document window.

5. Right now, you might not have the fountain fill traveling from the ideal color to an ideal color. The Interactive fill tool uses the current foreground and background colors on the toolbox to create a Linear fountain fill. Double-click the top color marker (node), and then in the Node Color dialog, choose R: 166, G: 166, and B: 166. Click OK to apply the color. Double-click the bottom node marker, and set its color to R: 204, G: 204, and B: 204. Click OK to apply the color and close the box.

Interactive
fill tool

Foreground
color

Background
color

Drag top to bottom, and
then double-click a marker.

6. Eventually in this tutorial, you'll use the Mesh Warp effect to bend the background to suggest a floor in the composition. To do this, you first need to shrink Object 3 a little so you'll be able to drag the handles of the Mesh Warp past the edges of the object. Choose the Object Pick tool, click the Scale button, and then click the Maintain Ratio button so the object scales proportionately. Zoom out of the document if you can't see the four handles at each corner of the object (you can scroll toward you with the mouse wheel to do this); drag a corner control handle toward the center of the object until the object is just a little wider than the labeling machine, and then drag toward

the center of the object to move it back so it's centered relative to the document window.

7. Choose Effects | Texture | Canvas. In the Canvas dialog, set the Transparency to about 66% so the fountain fill isn't completely hidden by the effect, and then set the Emboss value to about 115% for a visible yet not overwhelming effect; see Figure 26-2. Click OK to apply the texture.

8. Choose Effects | Distort | Mesh Warp. In the Mesh Warp box, at the default Gridlines frequency of 4, you have nine intersections within the warp lines that you drag to reshape the selected object. The idea is to mold the canvas object, as shown in Figure 26-3, so that its bottom sweeps toward the audience, creating the illusion that the labeling machine is resting on a plane that sweeps up and back off the top of the

FIGURE 26-2   Apply a subtle texture effect to the fountain fill to add visual "business" to the background object.

document window. First, drag the bottom right intersection to the right; doing this warps the middle right intersection in an unpleasant way, bulging the right side too much. Drag the middle right intersection to the left until the right vertical warp line describes an arc toward the bottom. Then drag the top right intersection to further smoothen the arc the right vertical mesh line describes.

9. Perform step 8 on the left vertical mesh line, mirroring it in its direction. Click OK to apply the effect.

10. With the Object Pick tool, click the Scale button on the property bar, and then increase the size of the object until you cannot see the background in the composition.

11. Save. Keep the file open.

Drag at
intersections.

FIGURE 26-3   Use the intersections of Mesh Warp by dragging them to reshape an object.

Adding a Shadow

What's missing now is a visual element that binds the machine to its new background: a
drop shadow. Frequently, a shadow can be painted into a composition, and you really need
only to suggest the shape of the shadow—audiences anticipate the presence of a drop
shadow, but usually don't notice whether the shape is authentic.

In the following steps, you'll add an object between the background and machine
objects, do a little painting to represent the shadow, blur it to make it look more believable,
and then use the Multiply merge mode before combining all the objects to make your blurry
painted shadow look more dense in the composition.

Painting Detail into the Picture

1. Click the Object 2 title on the Objects docker, and then click the New Object button.
   Doing this forces PHOTO-PAINT to create a new object directly above the current
   object, sparing you the need to reorder objects by dragging their entries on the docker.

2. Choose the Paint tool on the toolbox. On the property bar, choose the Art Brush category thumbnail, and to its right, choose Loaded Cover from the drop-down list; the diameter of the brush is set to 46 pixels, and this is a good size for the next steps. It doesn't make a lot of difference which brush you choose, because you'll soon blur your strokes, but this particular variation is nice because it adds a little grain when you use it.

3. Double-click the Foreground color icon on the toolbox to display the foreground color mixer. Choose black and then click OK.

4. Make a few strokes beneath the machine, as shown in this illustration. Notice how your strokes appear to go behind the labeling machine because it's the top object, above your strokes and the background object.

5. Click the Merge Mode drop-down list while the shadow object is the current editing object, and then choose Multiply. Then drag the Opacity slider down to about 75%.

6. Choose Effects | Blur | Gaussian Blur; there are several effects to apply a blur to an object, but Gaussian produces the most intense and pronounced. You'll see that Gaussian Blur leaves what looks like a diffuse shadow beneath the labeling machine. Set the Radius for Gaussian Blur to about 35 pixels, and then click OK to apply it. Press CTRL+S to save your work one final time.

7. You can consider your retouching work finished, or you can "standardize" the CPT file so a copy can be shared as a JPEG image. PHOTO-PAINT object files can't be shared with friends and clients who don't own PHOTO-PAINT. On the Objects docker, right-click over any of the object titles, and then choose Combine | Combine All Objects With Background.

8. Choose File | Save As, click the Save As Type drop-down list, and pick JPG-JPEG Bitmaps. Choose a file location, and then click OK. In the Export as JPEG dialog, click the Quality drop-down list, choose Highest, and then click OK. Then email your work to your fictitious client, and they'll be astounded and send you a large, fictitious check. Take it to a fictitious bank and cash it right away.

Creating a Fantasy Composition

It would be hard to miss some of the extraordinary ads on the Web that feature smaller-than-life people in unusual settings: swimmers in a drinking glass, ant-sized folks exploring a kitchen drawer—you get the picture. This section takes you through the steps involved in

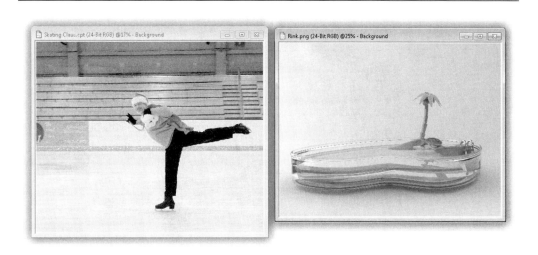

FIGURE 26-4   Santa Claus in the tropics is a novel idea for a PHOTO-PAINT composition.

getting a fellow ice-skating into a scene of a miniature turtle pond; he won't care that the water might not be frozen, it's all in good fun, and you'll use PHOTO-PAINT's features to make it a *believable* fantasy. Figure 26-4 shows the two images you'll visually integrate.

Using the Brush Mask Tool

Shortly, you'll use PHOTO-PAINT's Cutout Lab to assist you in trimming the skating fellow from his skating rink background. However, it will give you a better idea of how much the gentleman needs scaling down if you first remove most of the background manually—it also gives you the opportunity to experience the Brush Mask tool in PHOTO-PAINT. The Brush Mask is an intuitive and easy-to-use selection tool; wherever you stroke in an image becomes subject to editing, while the exterior areas are not available for editing. In the steps to follow, the editing is simple—you'll move the selected area, the skater, to a new object in the image, and then drag him over to the turtle pond image.

Stroking to Select an Area

1. Open Skating Claus.cpt and Rink.png. Arrange the windows so both are in full view; you'll want to zoom out of both images and resize the documents to fit them both within PHOTO-PAINT's workspace.

2. Click the title bar of the skater image to make it the foreground document, and then choose the Brush Mask tool from the mask tools group just below the Object Pick tool on the toolbox.

Brush Mask
tool (B)

FIGURE 26-5   Every area you stroke over can be selected.

3. Click the Nib Shape drop-down list, and then click the 100-pixel-diameter hard nib. Then increase the size of the nib by typing **133** in the Nib Size box, or you can use the elevator buttons to the right of the box to enlarge the nib size.

4. Stroke around the image so the skater is entirely selected. If you've gone a little too far, click the Subtractive mode button on the property bar, and stroke over the areas of excess in your selection. Figure 26-5 shows you what your screen should look like.

5. Right-click inside the selection border, and then choose Object: Copy Selection. Note that the toolbox has automatically chosen the Object Pick tool for you now. Also, the marquee lines have disappeared, and selection box handles now are at the edges of the new object.

6. With the Object Pick tool cursor, drag the object from the Skating Claus.cpt document window into the Rink.png image window.

26

7. Close the Skating Claus.cpt document without saving it.

8. Save the Rink.png file as **Rink FINAL** in PHOTO-PAINT's native CPT file format. Keep the image open in PHOTO-PAINT. Use the Object Pick tool to increase the window's size, and then use the mouse scroll wheel to zoom out so you can see all of the fellow in the composition.

NOTE   *If you are uncertain about the exact areas you've selected with the Brush Mask tool, you can preview the area by using the Mask | Mask Overlay view of your work. By default, the red tint is covering areas that are not selected by your Brush Mask work.*

Working in the Cutout Lab

PHOTO-PAINT's Cutout Lab is sort of an advanced Mask tool; it provides you with a complete workspace for tracing around the edge of an area you want to integrate with other document objects. However, unlike the other mask tools, the Cutout Lab automatically refines edges that are fuzzy, such as the soft edges of our Santa's cap and back, as well as producing crisp edges in clearly defined areas. In the steps to follow, you'll enter the lab and cook up a beautifully refined selection of Santa for the composition.

Cutting a Complex Selection

1. If you don't have the Objects docker open right now, press CTRL+F7.

2. Click the Object 1 entry on the Objects docker list, and then choose Image | Cutout Lab. You can quickly navigate your way around your view by using the scroll wheel on your mouse to zoom in (push the wheel away from you) and to zoom out (pull the

wheel toward you). You can also use the shortcut key H to access the Hand tool, and then press the SPACEBAR to return cursor use.

3. Zoom into Santa's hat. Choose the Highlighter tool, set the Nib Size to 13 pixels in this example, and then choose Black Matte for the moment from the Background drop-down list so you can clearly see the edge of the object.

4. This is the key technique for telling PHOTO-PAINT where to refine the edge of the selection you create: you *straddle* the edge of your subject—you want to leave a little of the Highlighter *both inside and outside* the area you define as the edge of your object. Then PHOTO-PAINT will later work on the edge for you, producing refined edges in both soft and sharply contrasting areas where you've stroked. Work counterclockwise in this example: start at the cap, stroke along the edge, and if you make a mistake, click the Eraser tool and erase the stroke, and then continue with the Highlighter tool. Figure 26-6 shows the work in progress.

FIGURE 26-6 Use the Highlighter tool to trace an outline of the intended selection.

5. Continue tracing at the edge of Santa until you've completely outlined him in Highlighter color. When you get to the ropes that Santa's holding his bag by, completely highlight them. Also, when you arrive at the point where the skate meets a boot, highlight around the negative space—the area through which you can see the background.

6. Click the Background button and then choose None, so you can clearly see Santa's trousers separated from the background. Click the Inside Fill tool, and then click *inside* your highlighter boundary. This tells PHOTO-PAINT to leave everything that's default blue alone.

Change Background to None.

Click the Preview button.

7. Click Preview. Your Cutout Lab should look like the following illustration. If some area is *grossly* missing, you need to choose the Highlighter tool again. The moment you click-drag in the window the preview goes away, and you're left with your current highlighting work. You will need to fill the highlighted areas again if you do this, and then click Preview. Let's assume you took your time, and after clicking Preview, the Cutout Lab did pretty well, as shown in the illustration. Your next step is to zoom into the edges and check for any areas that need refining. First, check out the ropes to his sack that Santa is holding.

8. Learn to leverage the power of the Background drop-down list. First, change the Background to Gray so you can clearly see contrast around the ropes. If areas outside the ropes need removing, click the Remove Detail tool, and use it as you would an eraser or a brush tool. Stroke around the areas that shouldn't show, and the tool gently and smoothly hides these areas. If you're missing an area of the rope, click the Add Detail tool, and stroke over the missing areas. You might need to unhide areas and then hide them again, working with the Add and Remove Detail tools.

9. When you arrive at the hat area, switch to Black as the Background color: always use a Background that provides color contrast with the edge of your subject, as shown next.

10. Pan around the entire silhouette of Santa, and *only* when you've corrected all the edge work, click OK, and Cutout Lab makes a *permanent* change to the object, and only Edit | Undo can restore the object.

11. Press CTRL+S; keep the file open.

Final Edits

Although you have a pretty good view in Cutout Lab of how the edge work looks compared in the Gray, Black, and other Background views, the proof is in the pudding. You need to check and perhaps correct a few areas now that you can see Santa against the turtle pond picture. Santa also needs to be scaled down almost by half his current dimensions, but there's an important reason to do this *last*. When you erase part of an object—by using the Cutout Lab, the Eraser tool, or other device—you aren't changing the resolution of the object. However, when you *scale* an object, you're removing pixels from or adding them to the entire object, pixel colors will shift as part of any bitmap scaling, and frequently the editing becomes obvious if you later try to edit a scaled object.

So first in the following tutorial, you'll erase any stray areas that weren't removed in Cutout Lab, and *then* scale Santa to fit in his new skating rink as a final edit.

Erasing and Scaling the Object

1. Choose the Eraser tool from the toolbox. In this example, the default soft 10-pixel-diameter tip works well. When you erase in an image that is a background only image (such as a JPEG), you erase to the current background color. However, when you erase object areas, they erase to transparent.

2. Zoom into the skate area, where the color of the skate is nearly the same as the ice in the original photo—probably the Cutout Lab didn't catch an area or two.

3. Take your time; erasures are destructive—permanent! Slowly stroke around the outside edge of the skate, as shown here, if this proves to be an unwanted area.

4. Work this way: zoom in or out of the object using the mouse wheel. As you erase and finish an area, press H to toggle to the Hand tool and move your view. If an area needs attention, press the SPACEBAR to return to the last-used tool (the Eraser), do your work, and then press the SPACEBAR again to access the Hand tool. Work your view around the perimeter of Santa, and then press CTRL+S when you're done.

5. Scaling an object proportionately can be done one of two ways: by using the percentage spin boxes when Scale Transform (and Maintain Ratio) are active on the property bar, or by directly click-dragging the object control handles. When you click the down button for Scale percentage, you get live feedback, but the exact amount of scaling needs to be determined by watching what's happening in the document. Santa is currently a little more than 20" tall, and he needs to be about 12", which is about 60% of the original height. You *could* type 60 in the percentage box, but this value can't really be discovered, so let's use the interactive control handles surrounding Santa instead for immediate visual feedback. With the Object Pick tool chosen, zoom out so you can see all of Santa, and then drag the document window edges away from the document center to reveal all the control handles around the object.

6. Click either Move or the Scale transform buttons on the property bar, and then, holding SHIFT to scale from the center inward, drag a corner control handle until you judge that Santa is comfortably scaled to fit into the composition. If necessary, begin by pressing CTRL+SHIFT+R to display rulers, and then stop shrinking Santa when you see that he's about 12" tall.

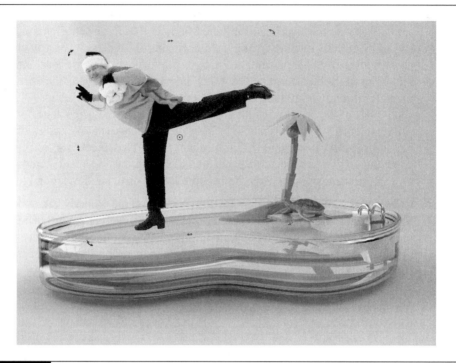

Use the Transform controls on the property bar for moving, scaling, and rotating an object.

7. You might feel Santa needs a little rotating counterclockwise to look more appropriate—*balanced*, literally and compositionally—within the document. Click the object with the Object Pick tool while Santa is selected to put the object into Rotate/Skew mode, and then drag a corner rotation handle just a little in a counterclockwise direction. Figure 26-7 shows the composition nearing completion.

8. Press CTRL+S, and leave the document open.

Adding a Reflection

Santa Claus hasn't quite come to town in the composition—notice that the turtle is casting a reflection, and Mr. Claus should, too. Fortunately, Santa was photographed at about the same camera height as that used with the rest of the scene, so a copy of the object can be successfully mirrored and superimposed below him. The next tutorial shows how to disproportionately scale a copy of the object and to mirror it horizontally using only the object control handles. Then you'll add transparency so the copy fades out at the bottom of the composition, and finally you'll learn how to blur the copy a little so it looks appropriate but is a little hard for the audience to closely examine for trickery.

Putting someone *in* a scene and not simply on top of one is the distinction between photo retouching and just another humorous picture. Here's how to add a reflection that serves as a binding element to tie all the components of the composition seamlessly together:

Santa Needs to Do Some Personal Reflecting

1. The fastest way to duplicate an object so it occupies the same position in a document is to drag its title on the Objects docker to on top of the New Object button. Click the Santa object entry on the docker so it's the currently selected object, and then drag so that the new object is the top entry on the Objects docker now. Then click the bottom object entry—labeled "Background"—to make it the current active object.

New Object button

2. With the Object Pick tool, click the duplicate Santa in the document window to make sure you can see the object control handles. Then click-drag the top center handle so Santa mirrors his original horizontally with disproportionate scaling— exactly as you perform in CorelDRAW, going way past the object's original bottom point, and releasing the mouse button when Santa's original top point lies a little below his right skate blade.

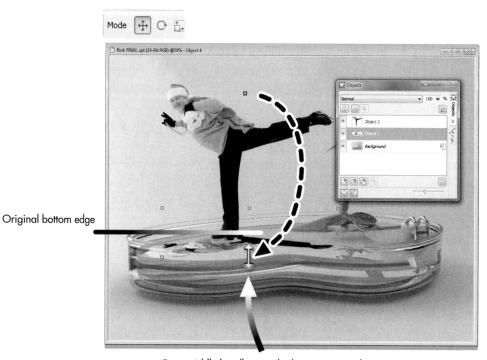

Original bottom edge

Drag middle handle to scale disproportionately.

3. If necessary, with the Object Pick tool, move the duplicate down so both of Santa's ankles are in about the same location in the composition.

4. Choose the Object Transparency tool from the effects tool group on the toolbox.

5. Beginning at Santa's ankle region, click-drag down to about the duplicate's head area. By default, you've created a Linear style transparency, with opaque regions traveling to transparent regions from top to bottom, almost exactly the way you'd see a real reflection when viewed in perspective.

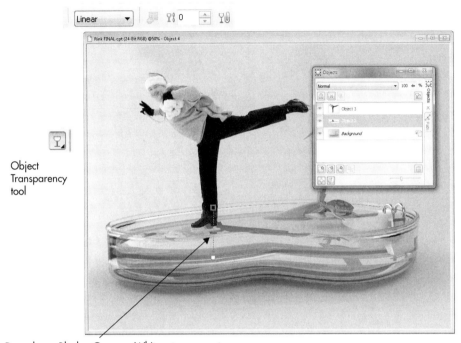

Object Transparency tool

Drag down. Black = Opaque; White = transparent

6. Choose Effects | Blur | Motion Blur. This type of PHOTO-PAINT blur filter comes in handy in a variety of design situations because it can emphasize the direction of a blur, which can often lend a more photorealistic quality to blurry areas than Gaussian blur does. Set the Direction to about 34 degrees, adding much more horizontal blurring than vertical in this example. Then set the Distance to about 35 pixels—Distance is relative to the overall size of your images when doing editing outside of this tutorial.

Click the Sample Nearest Edge Pixel option so transparent areas outside of this object take the Motion Blur effect using the nontransparent object pixels toward its edge. Finally, click Preview and if the document looks good, click OK to apply the effect.

7. You'll have a little cleanup work to do with Object 1 in the document, because the ankle area is not only visible, but it's also blurred now. With the Eraser tool, stroke over areas outside of Object 2's leg area that are visible.

8. You can choose File | Save As, and choose the JPEG file format now so the completed composition can be shared as an email attachment.

In the Gallery folder, in the ZIP file you downloaded, is the completed version of the preceding tutorials. Compare your version with the author's, and then have a good laugh because you did much better than he did!

Performing Subtle Image Edits

Many times you won't need to use the full power of PHOTO-PAINT to make a less-than-perfect image perfect. Your artistic judgment can combine the shades of gray in life with degrees of subtlety to "nudge" a picture to the sublime. Leyka_3856.cpt, shown in Figure 26-8, is a near prizewinner. Open this image in PHOTO-PAINT now, and look carefully at the photo before looking at Figure 26-8 to see what's wrong with it.

Most of what you'll learn in this section has very little to do with PHOTO-PAINT and everything to do with your own *ingenuity.* How can the rain droplets in the photo be deemphasized, and how can that bright orange window sticker be removed from an otherwise charming family photo? The overall solution is to add the Motion Blur effect to the offending area; blurring image areas is not always the best, most aesthetically acceptable means of enhancing a photo, but it's appropriate here for at least a couple of reasons:

- Leyka's hair in this photo is blowing, and yet we see no open window, so we presume an open car window is behind the camera on the other side of the car. Therefore, if you blur the window behind Leyka with Motion Blur, not only are the raindrops blurred, but you've also added a sense of motion to the entire scene, and the blurred window helps explain why Leyka's hair is wafting about.

Water droplets make window look dirty.

Window sticker detracts from scene.

FIGURE 26-8   Even when a background area is small, it can tarnish the entire photo.

- You establish a narrower simulated depth of field by selectively blurring a background element. Depth of field is extremely hard to fake, even with a third-party plug-in for such an effect, so you're not actually creating depth of field that wasn't originally done with the lens aperture, but rather suggesting it. You move the point of interest to the little girl when you remove visual interest from the background.

You'll work systematically in the sections to follow, and get some hands-on practice with the different tools in PHOTO-PAINT. And you'll see that the approach covered here really is the key to first judging what needs to be done, and then choosing the PHOTO-PAINT that gets you to the finish line.

Cloning Away the Background Window Sticker

You want to remove the orange-on-white window sticker before blurring the overall window area, because if it remains, you'll end up with an orange streak that calls almost as much attention to it as in its current state. This is a job for the Clone tool (press C); the interesting thing about the next steps is that you don't have to be terrifically accurate with your Clone tool stroking work. Your goal is to remove the colors you see in the sticker—no one is going to be able to see "mistakes" in the final motion-burred area as long as you remove and replace the orange sticker with the fairly blue tones of the droplets on the window. Consider geometry and color as two separate issues when working in PHOTO-PAINT; this program has features to address geometry without affecting color, and vice versa.

Here's how to use the Clone tool to remove the sticker.

Replacing Color with the Clone Tool

1. Zoom into the area of the orange-and-white window sticker.

2. Choose the Clone tool from the group of image repair tools on the toolbox; click-hold to reveal the flyout group, the eighth from the top where the Object Pick tool begins the tools.

3. On the property bar, choose Large Soft Clone from the Brush Type drop-down list. This brush has a good size for the job ahead of you, and a nice feathered edge, but it also is partially transparent, and you need a 100% opaque brush.

4. Set the Transparency to 0.

5. Right-click way above the orange sticker, on the water droplets on the window to set a traveling source point for the Clone tool.

6. Stroke over the orange area, until all of it is replaced with water droplets. Note that you can inadvertently create a "hall of mirrors" effect, an unwanted one, if your source brush travels into an area you've just cloned over. Avoid this resampling when you arrive at an area that's already been cloned. Right-click on or near the

original area you sampled to reset the traveling sample area, and then finish up the work.

Masking an Area with the Brush Mask Tool

Because you can select an area while protecting other image areas from editing, you're presented with a seemingly contrary pair of terms to describe editable and non-editable image areas when you use the Brush Mask tool with Mask Overlay turned on. The Brush Mask is a terrific and intuitive way to select feathered areas of an image so no hard edges are visible, and that's what you'll do with the car window in the following steps. But first, to be totally clear on what is selected in an image and what's not:

- When you stroke with the Brush Mask tool in its default mode, everything inside the marquee (the "marching ants" you see in the document) is subject to change—selected.

● When you turn on Mask | Mask Overlay, you get a lot more intuitive visual feedback than the animated marquee. You see a tint over the image that indicates protected, masked areas, the exact *inverse* of what you selected. You're painting a mask, and not a selection area.

Although Mask Overlay was originally designed as a preview and touchup view of your work, you can also work in this mode from start to finish when defining an area you want to retouch in a photo. If you keep in mind that when you stroke in Mask Overlay you're protecting areas, you might just come to love using the Brush Mask tool in this special tint view mode.

Here is how to select the car window area and copy it as a new object that you'll soon edit to make the audience focus on Leyka and not on the backlit raindrops.

Stroking to Define an Image Area for Editing

1. Choose the Brush Mask tool (press B or click-hold the mask tool group to reveal the flyout), and let's try selecting an area in standard marquee mode just to make a coarse selection you'll refine later in Overlay mode.

2. Choose the 100-pixel-diameter feathered nib—not the hard-edge guy—from the Nib Shape flyout list. At the edge of where you'll stroke, the amount of selection will be 100% at the center of the nib, decreasing to 0% selection (or 100% masking) at the outside of the nib selection edge. This choice of brush nib results in a feathered selection edge, making retouching work invisible when blended against other objects and masked areas.

3. Start at the inside edge of the window, and then click-drag up, down, and across to define all four sides of the window. When you get to Leyka's wafting hair, click-drag to straddle the edge, leaving some of the marquee inside her hair. Release the mouse button, but do not continue.

4. Click the Additive Mode button on the property bar. By default, the Normal Mode brush style is always chosen, and if you were to continue stroking after releasing the mouse button, you'd *lose* your first defining stroke. In Additive mode, you fill in whatever you've missed in the interior of your selection.

5. Choose Mask | Mask Overlay. Remember: the tinted areas are non-editable, and the area you see without the tinted overlay is selected—you are simply not seeing the selection marquee in Overlay mode.

6. Use the Additive mode to add image areas to be selected, and use Subtractive mode to mask (apply tint) to areas you don't want selected. You are unmasking in Additive mode, and masking in Subtractive mode. Choose a different diameter Nip Shape at any time to really make a good selection that's soft along the edges; 50 pixels is a

good alternative brush diameter for stroking along the edges of Leyka's hair. The brighter areas directly in front of the window should be exposed to editing— selected—while her golden locks closest to her right cheek should be masked— protected from editing.

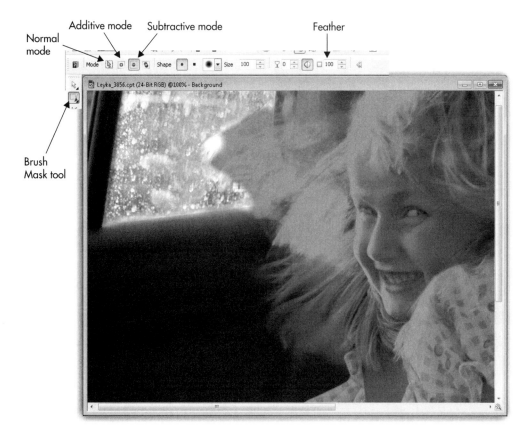

7. When you think you're ready to make a perfect copy object from your selection, right-click and choose Object: Copy Selection from the context pop-up menu.

8. Press CTRL+S to save your work up to this point, and keep the file open.

Don't click the Object Pick tool on the document now, because you'll inadvertently move the new object in the picture. Because Object 1 (its default name) is directly over the original area, it's not obvious that you have a Background and an object on top of it. Press CTRL+F7—a good keyboard shortcut to commit to memory—to view the Objects docker list of document elements. You can see in Figure 26-9 that if you just hover and don't click over the active object, a tooltip tells you that your cursor is over an object, and the Objects docker confirms this. Now it's on to visually deemphasizing the object by blurring it.

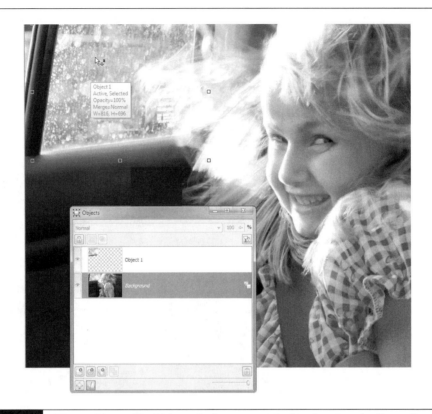

FIGURE 26-9 Use tooltips or the Objects docker to see whether there's a duplicate directly over the Background.

Creative Blurring

It's easy and usually embarrassing to take a blurry photo, but in this example, the degradation of the window area in the background will *improve* the overall picture. By applying Motion Blur to the object, you'll remove detail, improve the hue of the object to complement Leyka, and add a little motion to the outside view from the auto, suggesting that the auto is indeed in motion.

Here are the short and simple steps to finishing the editing of this photograph.

Using Motion Blur

1. With Object 1 chosen as the editable object in the Objects docker, choose Effects | Blur | Motion Blur.

FIGURE 26-10 Set the Direction to match the horizontal angle of the object, the direction in which the car is traveling.

2. Drag the Direction icon to a value of nearly 0 degrees, or type **0** in the num box. You have some leeway here with Distance; depending on your own artistic taste, you can drag the Distance slider anywhere between 65 and 140 pixels. Try previewing at 65 first; drag the slider and then click Preview. Try some more powerful distance settings, and when you're pleased with the effect, click OK to apply the blur. See Figure 26-10.

3. The Motion blur will leave a gap between Object 1 and the Background at high distance settings. If you detect a gap, choose the Object Pick tool, and then drag a corner control handle on Object 1, scale it up a little, and then use the Object Pick tool to adjust its position, as shown in Figure 26-11.

4. Save a copy to JPEG file format so you can email the finished piece.

The tutorial in this section demonstrated one of the most powerful tools when using PHOTO-PAINT: your *ingenuity*! There's a lot of wonderful stuff under the hood in PHOTO-PAINT, and to get the best results, adopt a personal workflow: first, you detect a problem, then you invent a solution, and finally, you choose the appropriate tool.

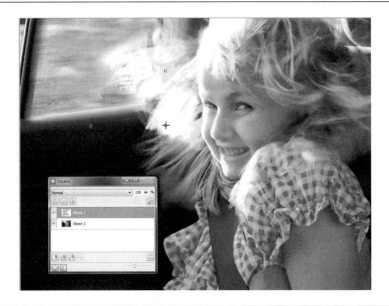

FIGURE 26-11   The object is already significantly blurred, so scaling it won't produce any more visible degradation.

Creating an Animated GIF

No tour of PHOTO-PAINT would be complete without a tutorial on how to build an animated GIF. Although GIF files are giving way to Flash and other video file formats, GIFs are universally supported by Internet browsers—they don't require your audience to go fetch a browser plug-in. GIF animations can make terrific banner ads for websites, and the following sections take you through some CorelDRAW and PHOTO-PAINT moves to create a sample animation.

Playing with a Paper Airplane

When you design an animation, you follow a checklist as you do in gathering resources for any composition. The example in this section is a paper airplane, which has already been drawn for you as a CDR file. Let's pretend that a travel agent wants you to put a web banner on their site advertising that children under 12 fly free this month only, or some similar offer. The concept is to fly a paper airplane across a sky, with a tag attached that spells out the offer.

The sky photo has been provided for you in the ZIP archive for this chapter, but the paper airplane CorelDRAW illustration is blank—it needs something written on the tag—so it's off to CorelDRAW to begin the next tutorial. The tag is intentionally blank: feel free to work with the file, take it apart and learn from it, and use it as a part of your own composition with a different slogan written on it. Let's begin.

Adding Text and Exporting a CorelDRAW Drawing

1. Open Paper Airplane in CorelDRAW, and then zoom into the tag area.

2. With the Text tool, type **Kids Fly Free** (or whatever you like) over the tag area. You can put a line break after "Kids" to avoid running over the tag's hole in this area.

3. With the text selected with the Pick tool, choose a contrasting color for the text, such as bright yellow, by clicking the color well on the Color Palette.

4. On the property bar, choose a lighthearted typeface such as Comic Sans MS, bold. Scale the text up or down so it nearly fits inside the tag area.

5. Choose the Envelope tool from the effects group of tools on the toolbox, and then distort the text a little, as shown in Figure 26-12. The drawing is at an angle to an imaginary camera, so the text shouldn't be perfectly parallel to the screen.

6. Select all the objects (press CTRL+A) and then click the Export button on the standard toolbar. In the Export dialog, choose PNG-Portable Network Graphics (*.PNG) from the Save As Type drop-down list. Make **Paper Airplane.png** the name for the file, choose a hard drive location for the bitmap file, and then click OK.

7. In the Export dialog, make sure the export Resolution is 96 dpi—if the Transformation area is not visible, click the down arrow to expand your view—or the airplane will be far too large for the GIF animation (see the following Note). Check the Transparency check box if it's not checked, and finally, look to see if the export file width is 513 pixels—choose Pixels as the Transformation | Units if it's not set this way.

FIGURE 26-12   Don't export with the text you've added looking too perfect!

26

Click OK to export and after CorelDRAW makes a bitmap copy of the illustration, you're finished and can close CorelDRAW and launch PHOTO-PAINT.

NOTE *You didn't have to set a lot of options in the Export dialog, because the CorelDRAW file was carefully set up and the airplane scaled to a predetermined size that made the tutorial work easily. When exporting drawings to be used as bitmap versions in PHOTO-PAINT, you begin your drawing with a new file in CorelDRAW whose resolution is 96 dpi, the same as your screen and the same resolution as graphics you see in your Internet browser. In the Create a New Document dialog, type **96** in the Rendering Resolution field and you're good to go. Then set the Units in CorelDRAW to Pixels by choosing from the Units drop-down on the property bar. Keep in mind that GIF animations have to have small dimensions. For example, the airplane is about 500 pixels wide because the composition you'll make is about that width. When you draw a foreground object, you keep it to the width you want it to be, measured in pixels, for your final composition. Then, exporting the drawing to the correct pixel width and height is a simple and nearly automatic process. Measuring is a pain, so when you set up your document for web export, it's a pain you have only once when you begin a new drawing.*

Animation: Defining Frames and Basic Setup

You'll move procedurally, and this means "not at breakneck speed" through the next sections, because unlike with Flash movies (covered in Chapter 28), you need to build each frame of a GIF animation one at a time—PHOTO-PAINT doesn't perform "tweening" to auto-create intermediate animation frames. First on your "To Do" list is to import the Background image, Sky.jpg, and to turn the document into a movie. Then you'll open, and keep open, the imported paper airplane file, and then copy it several times into the movie document. By changing the airplane file's position in each frame you add to the movie via the Movie docker, you create an animation of the airplane traveling from left to right, thus creating an *animation cycle* that will play indefinitely on a web page. You'll create six frames of animation as the airplane travels from camera left to an exit at camera right, and it will pause in the middle of the frame so audiences can clearly read the text.

Let's get moving!

Building a GIF Animation: Part 1

1. In PHOTO-PAINT, press CTRL+O and then choose Sky.jpg from your hard drive.

2. Choose Movie | Create From Document. Open the Movie docker by choosing Window | Dockers | Movie. Note that currently one frame is on the Movie docker list, and it's set to a 200 millisecond (ms) duration. Duration can be changed, and you'll do so a little later; a millisecond is a tenth of a second, about the duration of a 1/16th note in music (at an average tempo of 60 beats per minute), also evaluated as the minimum time it takes for a human to recognize a picture.

3. Open Paper Airplane.png. Because you exported this PNG file with Transparency, it's floating against a transparent background and is easy to animate against the sky image.

4. Click the title bar of what PHOTO-PAINT is now calling Sky.AVI to make it the foreground document. Click the Insert Frame button at the lower left. In the Insert Frames dialog, type **5** in the Inset Frames box, click After, Frame 1 (this is not critical, but just a good practice), and click the Copy Current Frame button, and then click OK.

5. Let Figure 26-13 be your visual reference for the rest of this chapter. What you're going to do is to create frames, and they exist in time as the airplane animates across the screen. The Objects docker isn't going to be of help—it won't show you what's going on in the document at any point in time—but the Movie docker will. First, click the First Frame button on the Movie docker. Your document is now at the first point in time for the GIF animation you'll build, and at this time there's nothing in the foreground. CTRL+click-drag the airplane in the Paper Airplane window into the Sky.avi window to copy (not move) the airplane object to on top of the sky. You have not really added the airplane to a "normal" document—it's a movie document and although the Objects docker shows the airplane object, it exists only in Frame 1 *in time,* not in any other frames.

First Frame Previous Frame
Stop Next Frame
Play Last Frame

Insert Frame Overlay
Insert From File

FIGURE 26-13   The Movie docker features DVD player–like controls for advancing and rewinding to the exact frame you want to build or edit.

6. Drag the window edges away from the center of the document so you can see white surrounding the composition, and can move Object 1, the airplane, to put it in position for an entrance, camera left.

7. With the Object Pick tool, move the airplane mostly out of frame, just so its nose is sticking out. Your four-arrowhead cursor should be slightly in the white border area as you move the airplane out of frame, and vertically centered.

8. You're going to turn Frame 1 now into an honest-to-gosh movie frame that features the nose of the airplane for a duration of 200 ms—a fifth of a second. Right-click over the Object 1 title on the Objects docker, and then choose Combine | Combine All Objects With Background. The Objects docker now shows only the Background in the Sky.avi file, and evidently you cannot move the airplane more to the right for

Frame 2. Fortunately, that's not how you animate a GIF file—this is why you have five more frames on the Movie docker. Yes, Frame 1 has the nose of an airplane, so the background sky has been altered, *but only in Frame 1.* Frame 2 *has* no airplane; let's add one now.

9. Click the Next Frame button on the Movie docker; you'll see that the nose of the airplane isn't in this frame, because at Frame 2 in time, it's not there. CTRL+click-drag the airplane from the Paper Airplane.png document window into the Sky.avi window.

10. It's not critical here, but when you want to move objects in time in PHOTO-PAINT, use the Overlay feature on the Movie docker to display a combination of the frame and the next frame at once in the document window. In traditional animation, this is known as "onion skinning."

26

Frame 1

Frame 2

Frame 1 overlaid on Frame 2

11. First click the Overlay button on the Movie docker to activate the slicer. Click the First Frame button, and automatically Frames 1 and 2 are bracketed, and you see a blend of both frames in the document window. Drag the Overlay Amount slider to adjust how much of Frame 1 intrudes on Frame 2.

12. Using the Pick tool, drag the airplane to the left until it more or less aligns vertically with the nose of the plane in overlaid Frame 1. You can progress the plane to camera right so you can almost see the tail of the plane, but not the message tag.

13. When you think the airplane has moved enough to suit Frame 2, do what you did in step 8: flatten the copy of the airplane against the copy of the sky.

Take a well-deserved break, but don't save the file and don't close it. This movie file is a special file format that cannot be saved as a CPT file. It's PHOTO-PAINT's presumption that when you save the file, you're saving a movie…but the movie's *not finished* yet. This *tutorial* is, but there's much more ahead.

Instead of using the Next Frame and Previous Frame buttons on the Movie docker, you can double-click the frame title (or the thumbnail) to go to a specific frame.

It's a good idea just before combining the plane object with any Background frame to look at which frame is the current one. You can easily see this on the bottom of the document window. In fact, the document window has advance and rewind controls you can use instead of the Movie docker buttons. Remember, an object doesn't belong to any frame. It's a floating element within the context of the animation and only "belongs" to a frame after you choose Combine | Combine Objects With Background—accessed by right-clicking the thumbnail on the Objects docker, by right-clicking in the document window, or via the Object main menu.

Finishing the Animation

You have four frames remaining that don't contain the plane. You don't need a repetition of the preceding tutorial steps to finish animating the plane: use the Next Frame button to advance to the next missing-plane frame, CTRL+click-drag a new copy in from the PNG document, position it, and then combine the plane with the frame's Background. The last frame, Frame 6, should show only the extreme tail of the plane's message tag. Once you've done that, it's fun to click Play and see what you've whipped up!

26

The following steps take you through timing; as mentioned earlier, the frame where you get a good view of the message you typed on the tag needs to have a longer view duration. Follow these steps to put the finishing touches on the animation, and then you'll see how to export it to GIF file format.

Exporting an Animation

1. Now that the frames all have content in them and no objects are in the composition—only Backgrounds—go to the frame that's centered with the text easy to read, probably Frame 3 or 4. Double-click an entry on the Movie docker.

2. Click the "200 ms" title for this frame to select it for editing; then type in **800**. Press ENTER, PHOTO-PAINT automatically adds "ms" at the end, and you're all set. Four-fifths of a second is plenty of time for the audience to see the message. Also, this GIF will continuously loop (coming up next), adding more time for the "sell" sandwiched in-between the light entertainment.

3. Choose File | Save GIF - GIF Animation (*.gif) as the file format from the Save As Type drop-down list. Choose a file location, give the file an appropriate name, and then click OK to enter a couple more dialogs where you specify color depth and the means by which certain colors are averaged to produce a relatively small file size.

4. In the Convert to Palette dialog, set the type of dithering and color palette used in your animation frames. You'll see that many options are dimmed on the Options tab and on the other tabs. This is because you're exporting a special animated file and not a still image. GIFs can be stills or animations. You're best off with either Uniform colors or Image Palette as the Palette choice; GIFs have a maximum of 256 unique colors, and these palettes help preserve the delicate shading of the cloud photo and some of the fountain fills used in the CorelDRAW airplane drawing.

5. Jarvis, Stucki, and Floyd-Steinberg are all types of diffusion dithering. They evaluate the most predominant colors in the animation and attempt to represent these colors accurately, while letting less frequent colors degrade by scattering similarly colored pixels around in the frame to represent, to "fake," the colors the process will eliminate. The other choices are Ordered dithering, which looks like a pattern weave and is usually inappropriate for photographic GIF animations, and None (don't use this unless your animation uses uniform-colored geometric shapes). When no dithering is used on photographic images, the result looks like a bad poster print made by silk-screening. Click OK to proceed to the next and final dialog.

6. In the GIF89 (that's its proper name) Animation Options dialog, choose Automatic for the Page Size, because we intended all along for this slightly larger than usual GIF animation to be presented as the frame size of the sky image. You could make the dimensions smaller by unchecking the Automatic box and typing in custom values in your work to make an animation smaller in both file size and dimensions. In Color Options, PHOTO-PAINT calculates in this example animation that only 236 of the 256 possible colors are necessary, saving a little on the file size of the animation, and the evaluation is based on the Dithering and Palette preferences you set in the previous dialog. You can decrease the number by using the spin controls or by typing in a value; then click Preview to see if fewer colors are acceptable, or if they make your animation look hideous. You can also try Adaptive Palette; with this example animation, Adaptive removes a lot of the visual dithering in the finished animation file.

7. Click the Loop Frames check box to make the animation start over again after the last frame. You can choose Forever, or set the number of times the animation loops. It's usually a good idea to set it to Forever; if visitors to your web page are distracted, for example, and your animation plays only five times before stopping, your audience misses the show unless they know how to reload a web page—but probably won't bother.

8. Check the Save Difference Between Frames Only box for sure! This helps reduce the saved file size, because only the pixels that change from frame to frame are rewritten with each successive frame.

9. Nothing on the Frame Settings tab applies to this example animation, but here is what you might want to choose from in your own animation work: Transparency is actually assigned to a single color in your animation, and this option makes that color invisible. This is great for composing a web page with a colored background you want to "float" an animation against, but the paper airplane doesn't need this option because we want the entire background area visible. In the Palette area, Use Local and Use Global are a strategy for making your animation a little higher in quality at the same or slightly smaller file size. "Global" means that one palette is used to dither down colors in the entire animation, while "Local" means that the PHOTO-PAINT rendering engine examines each frame for the most predominant colors while dithering down. Frame Delay is your last chance to speed up or slow down frames, and the How To Dispose list box is an option for clearing a single frame before the following frame loads. Dispose options are only relevant for experienced users who want to do something tricky or startling with how an animation plays. Your airplane animation doesn't fit into this category of special effects. You've created a highly interesting animation, so let's leave the options at that. Click OK, and then drag the GIF file into an Internet browser window to watch it play!

Kids fly Free.gif is the completed animation file in the Gallery folder in the ZIP archive you downloaded.

You owe yourself a big congratulations for getting through this chapter. Imagine: you now not only have quite a few advanced image-retouching tricks tucked under your belt, but you now know how to make a visually rich GIF animation with a moving object that loops continuously. This is a *lot* better than learning how to make a GIF animation that blinks on and off static text like "My First Website 101." Now that you know how to make, save, and change movie frames, you have weeks if not years to experiment with new ideas and different animation objects of your own. And you can save an animation to AVI and QuickTime in addition to GIF file format—you can choose these from the Save As Type drop-down list when you choose File | Save and Save As. AVI and QuickTime files are a lot larger to save to disk, but the animation quality is also much, much better, because these animation file types are not limited to 256 maximum unique colors.

Chapter 27 moves from the screen to the printed page. Come learn how to ensure the best possible render to a home printer and a commercial printer with CorelDRAW's features.

PART IX

Thinking Outside of the (Tool) Box

CHAPTER 27

Printing: Professional Output

P rint is *not* dead! It's alive and well, thank you, in almost every enterprise, and outputting your work so your clients can hold it in their hands is just as much an art as designing a piece in CorelDRAW. This chapter takes you through *professional* output—CorelDRAW's features that extend *beyond* the now-familiar File | Print command—and what it takes from CorelDRAW and you to make every dot of ink on a page look exactly like every pixel you designed on the screen.

CorelDRAW's print engine is organized into several well-defined and easy to understand areas for setting printer hardware parameters, previewing your print selection, and using various other options to enhance your finished printed work. In this chapter, you'll learn to set options from beginner to advanced levels in these areas.

Printing a Document to a Personal Printer

Let's suppose that you want to print a "one off," perhaps to show to your boss or coworkers as a proof of concept, or for personal pleasure, or to see if everything is arranged on the page correctly before packing off a copy to a commercial press. If your artwork is black and white (you used no color, but only shades of black in the design), you'll probably print to a laser printer. Laser printers don't really have any color-critical settings, so you're probably as ready to go as you'd be if you were printing a text document. If you're printing to an inkjet, most of today's inkjet circuitry does an automatic conversion from RGB color space and the color ink space (usually CMYK, although many affordable printers use six inks), and again, you really don't have to jump through any hoops if you've designed a document that uses RGB, LAB, or CMYK color spaces to define the colors you filled objects with.

Here's a tutorial that covers the basics for outputting your work to a personal printer. Before you begin, make sure on the Object Manager docker that the layers you want to print are visible and that printing is enabled for the layers; a tiny red international "no" appears on layer properties that are disabled—you click the "no" symbol to enable the layer property.

Printing Single- and Multiple-Page Documents

1. Open the document you want to print, and then choose File | Print (CTRL+P), or click the Print button on the standard toolbar. Any of these actions opens the Print dialog, shown next. Pay attention to the orientation of the page with respect to the *orientation of the paper* as it will print. The Page drop-down offers to match the orientation of the page, or to use the printer default orientation settings. Changing the orientation doesn't change your document, but only the way it prints.

Quick Preview button   Quick Preview

2. In the General tab, choose your printer from the Printer drop-down menu, and then click Preferences to set any printer properties such as the print material page size, orientation, and so on. Keep in mind that any special features specific to your printer might override any CorelDRAW-specific features, in particular, color management (discussed later in this chapter). In general, it's *not* a good idea to have a color management feature enabled on your printer when CorelDRAW color manages the document. Two color-management systems will contend with each other, and what you see onscreen will *not* be what you get in your print.

3. Click the Quick Preview button to expand the dialog to show a preview window if you'd like to check the document for position on the printable page. A dashed line appears in the preview window, indicating document areas that are close to or that go over the printable page margin. If you see this, you might want to cancel the print operation and rework your page. Alternatively, you can click the Layout tab and then check Fit To Page, although doing this scales the objects in your document (so forget about the CD label you want to print fitting perfectly on a physical CD).

4. If you have more than one document open in CorelDRAW, you can choose which document to print by clicking the Documents radio button in the Print Range area; make certain that all documents you want to print have the same portrait or landscape orientation before printing, or you're inviting a headache. In a multi-page CorelDRAW document, choose the page(s) you want to print from the Print Range area, and then enter the print quantity in the Number Of Copies box. See the following Tip.

5. Before you click Print, check to see whether any issues are on the Issues tab. If the tab reads "No Issues," proceed to step 6 and collect $200. However, if there's an issue, you should address it (or them) first. Issues come in two varieties: showstoppers, indicated by a triangular traffic sign with an exclamation mark, and trivial stuff, indicated by an info (*i*) icon. A common example of trivial stuff is printing blank pages; the Issues tab will inform you, and you can easily correct this by changing the Pages value in the Print Range area of the General tab. Showstoppers require careful reading of the explanation provided on the Issues tab; the remarks and explanations are quite clear—such as attempting to print a low-resolution image to a high-resolution printer. Your best bet is to cancel the print and to read the rest of this chapter…and save paper and ink. Here's what the issues icons look like:

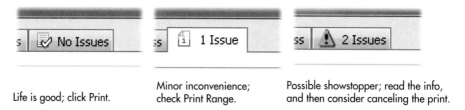

Life is good; click Print.

Minor inconvenience; check Print Range.

Possible showstopper; read the info, and then consider canceling the print.

6. Click Print, go get your favorite refreshment, wait a moment, and then get your print.

> **TIP** *To print contiguous (consecutive) pages of a document, in the Print Range area's Pages box, enter the page numbers separated by a hyphen (for example, type* **6-8** *to print pages 6, 7, and 8). To print noncontiguous pages, for example, pages 6, 8, and 16, type commas between specific page numbers:* **6, 8, 16** *in this example. You can also combine these two conventions to print both contiguous and noncontiguous pages by separating each entry by a comma. For example, entering* **6-8, 10-13, 16** *will print pages 6, 7, 8, 10, 11, 12, 13, and 16.*

The Quick Preview deserves a little more coverage here. After clicking the Quick Preview button, you're shown a preview window and page-browsing controls (see Figure 27-1). While you're previewing, a right-click offers invaluable commands from the pop-up menu to Show Image, Preview Color, Preview Separations, and to toggle the view of rulers. When you want to print a multi-page CorelDRAW file, you can quickly turn pages in Quick Preview to make sure you're printing within page boundaries and that all the pages contain what you want to print. To print the preview page at the current settings, choose Print This Sheet Now from the pop-up menu.

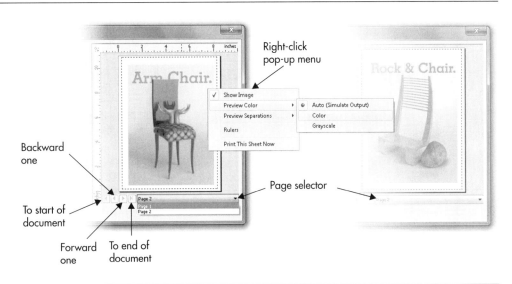

Right-click pop-up menu

Backward one

To start of document

Forward one

To end of document

Page selector

FIGURE 27-1 Use the buttons on the bottom of the dialog to more easily choose what pages you'd like to print.

Setting Print Options

The tabbed areas of the Print dialog more or less follow from left to right a progression from personal printing options to more ambitious endeavors such as printing separations for process *color composite* (commercial) printing. Some of the areas on the tabs are device dependent and appear only after CorelDRAW evaluates your printer's capabilities; Use PPD (PostScript Printer Description), for example, is dimmed on the General tab until you've chosen a printer that is PostScript capable. This is why selecting your printing device must be your first step in printing from CorelDRAW. Depending on the printer defined, you'll see tabbed areas for General, Layout, Separations, Prepress, PostScript, Misc, and Issues.

Setting General Options

The General tab of the Print dialog, shown in Figure 27-2, offers control over some of the most common printing options.

FIGURE 27-2   Use the General tab of the Print dialog to set the most basic printing options.

Here's a description of what each option in the General tab controls:

- **Destination**   This area represents the feedback provided by the printer driver used for your selected printer showing the Printer name, Status, Location (local port, or on a network), and Comment information. Direct, network, or spooler printers are indicated according to their connection status. If CorelDRAW cannot find a printer connected directly or remotely (through a network) to your computer, you'll need to pay a visit to the Windows Start menu | Devices and Printers, and then choose to Add A Printer. The good news is that this is a wizard-style process and that Windows ships with just about every conceivable print driver for popular makes and models. You might be prompted for a specific print driver, so it's a good idea to have the manufacturer's disk handy or to download the latest drivers from their website. Clicking the Preferences button provides control over printer-specific properties and output material sizes. Choosing Use PPD lets you assign a PostScript Printer Description file; checking this box displays the Open PPD dialog, where you locate and then select an appropriate PPD file. Unless you're already familiar with what Print To File does, don't check this box in your everyday printing; see "Saving a Print File" later in this chapter.

- **Print Range**   This area contains options to select pages from the file you have maximized in the drawing window—or from *any* document you have open in CorelDRAW; it can be minimized, and you can print it as long as it's open. Choose Current Page to print the page currently in view in your CorelDRAW document, or enter specific page numbers in the Pages box. If you go into the Print command with one or more objects selected in your document, the Selection option becomes available, so you can print *only* your selection; this is quite handy for printing only a part of your document without rearranging or hiding objects, or for changing your document before printing. If you have more than one document open, choosing the Documents option displays a list of the open documents, so you can choose which document to print. Choose Even and/or Odd from the drop-down menu to print only certain pages. By default, both Even and Odd pages are printed.

● **Copies**   This area has two options for setting the Number Of Copies to print either collated or not. When Collate is chosen, a picture appears indicating the effect of collating. Collating is a great timesaver when you want to publish a multi-page presentation and don't need the hassle of reordering pages as they come out of the printer.

Using Print Styles

Print styles remove the repetitive task of setting up the same (or similar) printing parameters by letting you choose to save all the selected options in the Print dialog in one tidy print style file. If your printing options have already been saved as a style, open the Print Style drop-down menu on the General tab of the Print dialog, and choose the style from the list.

To create a style that includes all the settings you have currently selected, follow these steps:

1. On the General tab, click Save As to open the Save Settings As dialog, shown here. As you can see, this dialog includes a Settings To Include tree directory listing the categorized print options and check boxes according to current settings.

2. Click to select the options you want to save with your new style, enter a unique name for your style, and then click Save to store the settings, after which they are available from the Print Style drop-down list.

Saving a Print File

Print To File goes back to the days of DOS, and today you'd be hard-pressed to use this option more than twice in your career. However, Print To File is supported in CorelDRAW, and you might want to generate this huge, text-based PostScript file for a couple of reasons:

- If you're handing the document over to a third party to print because you don't have a specific printer hooked up to your computer, and you don't want them editing the document in any way. Print To File files are text-based printing instructions; they contain no graphics as graphics, so they are nearly impossible to edit using a graphics application.

- If (and this is a *big* "if") someone has specifically requested a Print To File document because they like the intellectual challenge of decoding the PostScript printing instructions to reconstruct the graphic using Ghostscript or a similar PostScript deciphering program.

Throughout the history of PC printing, printing to file has served a valuable purpose. It enables someone who doesn't own CorelDRAW to print your CorelDRAW file; a dozen years ago, high-resolution printers such as Linotronic image-setting devices were the only game in town when you wanted coffee table–book printing quality. If a service bureau that owned the device didn't own CorelDRAW, you printed to file. Today there are alternatives to making a CorelDRAW document portable for a service bureau to render, but if Print To File is a client's mandate, here are the steps to use:

1. Choose the Print To File check box in the General tab of the Print dialog, and then choose from four options in the adjacent flyout menu. Choose For Mac if the file is to be printed from a Macintosh system. Choose Single File (the default), Pages To Separate Files, or Plates To Separate Files to set how the files are prepared. Single File creates one, usually huge, print file for the entire printout. Pages To Separate Files creates separate files for each page. The Plates To Separate Files option creates a single file to represent each page *and* each of the color separations you've chosen to print if your printing destination is to CMYK process color printing.

2. Click Print to start creating the print files, and the Print To File dialog will open, where you choose a destination for the PRN file.

NOTE | *Even if you've specified a PRN file type in the Save As Type drop-down list, a file with the extension .PS (example: MyFile.ps) will be generated if you've designated a PostScript printer as your default computer. However, if your computer's printer is non-PostScript—and inkjet printers are non-PostScript—the file extension written will be .PRN as expected.*

You then copy the PRN file to removable media, and take it to the party who will print the file; alternatively, many service bureaus offer FTP (file transfer protocol) upload sites for getting files to them. Traditionally, before artists use Print To File, they have a target device's print driver installed—this is done just like you install a printer in Windows, except you're only installing a *device driver* and *not* the physical printer itself. Service bureaus like to provide you with their print drivers because if you write a Print To File using an incompatible driver, you're left with a job the service bureau can't print, and you've wasted time and hard disk space.

Also, if the CorelDRAW file you print to file contains fonts, you either need to convert all text to curves (which significantly increases the saved PRN file's size), or you need to include the typefaces on the disk you give to the service bureau, which is a thorny legal issue. Users give service bureaus digital typefaces all the time, but according to most font licenses, this isn't legal. On the other hand, you cannot depend on a service bureau or commercial press house to have exactly the same font as the one you used—if a high-resolution printer reads a Print To File and cannot find the typeface on its operating system, chances are you'll get a beautiful high-resolution print that uses Courier instead of your typeface.

In short, before you send out work for printing:

- Find a service bureau that owns CorelDRAW and save yourself some headaches.

- Failing that, find a service bureau that accepts Acrobat PDF documents (more on this later in this chapter).

- Export a copy of your CorelDRAW to Illustrator file format. It might not export perfectly, and certain CorelDRAW-specific effects will not translate, but Windows and especially Macintosh service bureaus are likely to own a copy of Illustrator.

- Use Print To File.

Using the Color Tab Settings

In version X5, users of previous versions will find additional options for printing that have been moved from other tabs to streamline the printing process. The following sections document color-related operations.

Print Composite/Print Separations

At the top of this tab is the area where you choose to print color separations (covered later in this chapter) or to print a composite—which is the standard way most users print color documents to a home inkjet printer. If you choose separations, the Print Composite tab in the Print box changes to Print Separations options and vice versa.

Document/Proof Settings

Clicking either of these buttons determines whether your print uses your current document color settings—found under Tools | Color Management—or disregards color settings you've made in the file, by using the settings you pick in the Print box here.

Color Conversions Performed By

This drop-down list provides you a way to convert the color space of the document using CorelDRAW's features or lets your printer handle the conversion from your monitor's color space to the slightly smaller and duller color space of physical pigments. If you're undecided, it's a safe bet to let CorelDRAW handle the conversion if your printer is an inkjet and not a PostScript printer. If you choose Device Independent PostScript File, it will display on the Color tab. However, this is not a Color Conversion option—the option is missing on the tab—if you've defined another printer, even a PostScript printer. Basically you have two options: use CorelDRAW's engine, or use the printer's print driver.

Output Colors As

When you're printing to a personal, non-PostScript device such as an inkjet, your options are only RGB and Grayscale, which is fair enough: laser printers can only reproduce grayscale halftones, and inkjets usually use the RGB color space to then convert colors to the color space of CMYK. When a PostScript device is defined, your options are:

- **Native**   CorelDRAW handles the reconciliation between any different color models you've used when filling objects and the colors in any imported bitmaps image.

- **RGB**   The file is sent to the printer using the RGB color model. This is an appropriate option to use when you're printing a composite image (not separations) and you're lucky enough to own a color PostScript printer.

- **CMYK**   This is a good mode to use when you want to proof your work and get a good idea of what your colors will print like when sending a file to a commercial printer (composite printing). Similarly, if you're printing separations, CorelDRAW forces all colors in your document into the CMYK color space using the rendering intent you've selected (covered next).

- **Grayscale**   Choosing this mode sends all color information to the printer as percentages of black. When choosing this option, you will also see a Convert Spot Colors To Grayscale option, something you might not want to choose if you want a plate to print of your spot colors.

- **Convert Spot Colors to CMYK**   If for some reason your budget doesn't allow a spot color, clicking this check box will force any spot color plates to be rendered as CMYK process color equivalents. Forget about color fidelity and accuracy, but the option is available.

Correct Colors Using

When printing to a non-PostScript device, you have the option to choose to correct colors to the color profile of a specific printer, or to choose from the list of available ICC color profiles installed on your computer.

You might be surprised at the lush colors you'll render to a home inkjet printer by choosing sRGB IE6C 1966-2.1 as the color correction option instead of relying on your printer's color correction. sRGB is a widely used color space for today's consumer-level scanners and printing devices.

When you've defined a PostScript printer as your target device, you can choose from several presets defined from many different image-setting manufacturers, or choose a predefined color space, the same ones as if you were using a non-PostScript printer.

Rendering Intent

You have four options for how CorelDRAW handles the conversion of color space to another. In a nutshell:

- Perceptual and Relative produce the best color conversions for digital photographs.

- Saturation preserves highly saturated color areas, at the expense of rendering photos like comic book art. Use this conversion type for business graphics such as charts and detergent labels.

- Absolute Colormetric maintains the original white point of the composition, but shifts hues in photographs in an unrealistic way.

Choosing a Layout

Options on the Layout tab give you the control to set how the page is laid out on the printing material you've loaded into your rendering device. Although the options are set to defaults for the most common print tasks, you can customize options in each area.

Setting Image Position and Size

Image Position And Size options control the position of the layout of each page. These settings will override settings you've defined in Printer Properties (your system's printing preferences, which aren't related to CorelDRAW). The following options are available:

- **As In Document**   This option (the default) leaves the current layout unchanged.

- **Fit To Page**   Choose this to enlarge or reduce your page layout to fit exactly within the printable area for your selected output material size. Understand that choosing this option immediately ruins as a print any precise measurements you've created in your file. For example, if you've labored on a fancy spine design for a presentation booklet that's 12" high, CorelDRAW will scale the design for print to the maximum dimension of your media, such as an 8½×11" sheet of paper. If you run into this problem, hang on and check out the Print Tiled Pages option covered shortly.

- **Reposition Images To**   Choose this option to change the position of images as they print relative to how they're arranged on your CorelDRAW page. By default, images are automatically positioned to Center Of Page on your printing material. However, you can align images to the top, left, right, and bottom corners of the printing material page size—a very convenient way to save paper and to make trimming a printed piece easier. Using this option, you can also individually specify the position of images on each page of a multi-page document differently by choosing a document page number from the Settings For Page menu. Use the Position, Size, and Scale Factor boxes to enter specific values. Unlocking the horizontal/vertical lock by clicking the nearby lock icon gives you the opportunity to set the horizontal and/or vertical Scale Factor separately for non-proportional scaling, although you might not want a distorted print.

- **Imposition Layout**   *Imposition* is the orientation and position of multiple pages to create a book signature—pages are ordered and rotated so that a commercial press can print a large page, and then the pages can be trimmed and bound so the book looks like a finished product. If you intend to print to high-resolution output, this option must be set exactly according to the specifications given to you by the printing service or other vendor you are using. It's always wise to talk with press operators (or their boss) before an expensive print job, because the owners of the press know the characteristics of it better than you do. Clicking the Edit button opens a preview feature, where you can customize the imposition requirements; you can rotate pages, move gutters, and even reorder pages at the last minute. However, Imposition Layout is also an important feature even if you're at home printing a single copy of a booklet from your inkjet printer. Next you can see a layout defined from a four-page CorelDRAW document; a template was *not* used to set up the file, and yet by choosing from the Imposition Layout drop-down, you ensure that the pages will indeed be printed in book fashion.

Tiling Your Printed Document

Often you'll need to print a piece that is much larger than the maximum output size of a personal printer: a bake sale banner, for example, or other display that exceeds even the output dimensions of today's wide-format inkjet printers. This need calls for using the Print Tiled Pages option. After printing, get a utility blade, a metal ruler, some adhesive, and a cutting surface, and you're in business. The options for setting how each tile is printed are as follows:

- **Print Tiled Pages**   Choose this option to print pages in portions. Once selected, the # (Number) Of Tiles, Tiling Marks (you want to use Tile Overlap if you use this, to avoid showing the marks in your finished project), and Tile Overlap options are available. The # Of Tiles option lets you print your document in vertical or horizontal tiles, up to 24 portions for each. Setting the Tile Overlap option gives you control over how much image portion is repeated around the edges of each tile, based on unit measure or a percentage of the original page width. By default, Tile Overlap is set to 0 inches.

- **Tiling Marks**   Choose this to have crop-style marks print around your tiles, making it easier to realign the tile pages when you put the tiles together.

- **Tile Overlap**   This option adds an extra printed portion around each tile to make it easier to align the tiles for your large sign. Overlap can be set from 0 through 2.125 inches.

- **% of Page Width**   Use this to specify the tile overlap as a percentage of the page size between 0 and 25 percent.

- **Bleed Limit**   Choosing this check box lets you use a portion of the area surrounding your document page. For example, if certain objects overlap the page border of a document, this option lets you print a portion outside the limits of the page. Bleed Limit can be set within a range of 0 to 40 inches, the default of which is a standard 0.125 inch.

The illustration here shows dashed lines (which would not be in the finished banner) where the single sheets tile in the bake sale banner, only one of scores of needs for tiling a print when your budget prohibits extra-extra-large-format prints.

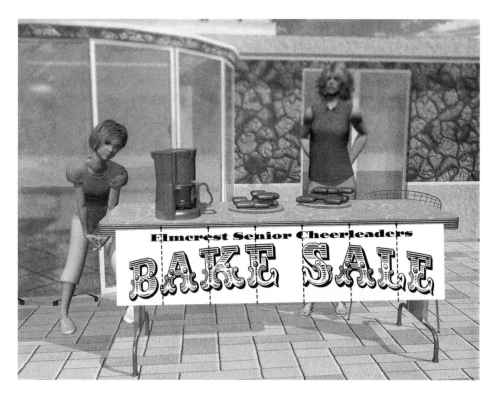

Printing Separations

If you know what color separations are and you work at a commercial printer, this next section is for you. If you *hire* a commercial printer when you have a color job and only have a working understanding of process color and separations, read on to learn a little more, but *don't* provide a commercial press operator with your own color separations! CorelDRAW creates terrific color separation work, but you really need to output to a high-resolution (expensive, you don't buy them at a department store) image-setting device that can render to film or another reproduction medium. You need to know as much about the printing characteristics of a printer as you do about color separations to prepare your own job for printing presses—for example, trapping margin of error, undercolor removal, ink characteristics, and other factors. You probably wouldn't practice brain surgery on yourself—similarly, don't do your own separations ("seps") if you're inexperienced in the field of standard web-offset printing.

If you're a silk screener or know a commercial press inside-out, when Print Separations is selected in the Color tab of the Print dialog, you have control over how each ink color prints; see Figure 27-3.

FIGURE 27-3   Use the Separations tab options to specify ink colors and trapping preferences.

Choosing Separation Options

If you've first chosen Print Separations on the Color tab, you'll now see the Separations tab in the dialog. Here is the rundown on your color separation options as shown in the dialog in Figure 27-3:

- **Print Separations in Color** This option is available only if the printer you've defined is a color printer such as a personal inkjet, which prints a simulation of a coated printing plate, each plate reproduced in its respective color. This option is sometimes used for printing progressive proofs, checking registration, and checking color accuracy. Understand that if you use this option on a personal inkjet printer, you'll print several pages, each containing a single color; this could use a lot of ink, particularly if your CorelDRAW is dense with colored objects! Printing separations in color results in a good test for separations, but it's nothing you would want to frame and hang in the den later.

- **Convert Spot Colors To** This option has been moved to the Color tab in version X5. Choosing this option is often a wise choice in non-color-critical printing, when you can't afford to print a fifth plate using a spot color. This option converts non-CMYK colors such as fixed-palette, spot-ink colored objects to the closest process color equivalent when printing. You can usually get away with this if your spot color *is not* a special ink, such as a metallic. Letting CorelDRAW convert a metallic, fluorescent, or other specialty spot ink to process will dull the final print job; the results will look amateurish at best.

- **Show Empty Plates** While unchecked (the default), this option causes pages without any objects to be skipped during printing to avoid printing blank pages. To include the blank pages, check this option. This can save you time, for example, if you have a spot color on only one page but not on others in a multi-page document.

Frequency and Angle and Overprint Options

When separations are selected to print, the ink colors used in your document are listed at the bottom of the Separations tab. Each ink includes options for choosing if and how they will be printed. You'll see a series of columns that show how each ink color is set to print, with its color reference, ink color name, screen frequency, screen angle, and overprint options. The inks will ultimately print in order from top to bottom as you see them on the list.

First, *don't* change the frequency or line angle unless you're a professional—the default values are standard among the printing community. To change the Frequency and/or Angle of a specific ink color, first check the Use Advanced Settings check box, then click directly on the value, and then enter a new value. To change overprinting properties of a specific ink color, click directly on the Overprint symbols for text and/or graphic objects to toggle their state. As a visual reminder the Overprint symbols turn darker when set to overprint. The following list explains what each of these options controls:

- **Order** Use the selector for each ink to set the order in which separations are printed based on the number of available ink colors.

- **Frequency** This option sets the output resolution in lines per inch (lpi); high-resolution image setters that speak PostScript organize dots for printing into lines. A typical line frequency for high-quality printing is 133 lpi, which results in color process prints of 2,500 dots per inch and higher. In comparison, a home laser printer, the 1,200 dpi variety, is only capable of rendering 80 lines per inch—you would not get magazine-quality prints using 80 lpi for color separations. Screen frequency values are automatically set to the default values of the image setter or printer selected on the General tab. Screen frequency values are also controlled by settings in the Advanced Separations Settings dialog.

- **Angle** This option sets the angle at which the rows of resolution dots align. When separating process color inks, the following standard default screen angles are set automatically: Cyan = 15°, Magenta = 75°, Yellow = 0°, and Black = 45°. When separating fixed palette ink colors such as Pantone, TOYO, DIC, and so on, all colors are set to the default 45° value. You occasionally need to check the Issues tab when custom inks are used for spot-color plates to ensure that the spot plate is not at the same or even similar angle to the process plate screen angles. Change the angle if necessary; an incompatible spot-color screen angle can result in moiré patterning in your print, an effect similar to laying a screen window on top of another one at a certain angle.

- **Overprint** Click directly on the symbols for text (the *A* symbol) and/or objects (the page symbol) to set whether text and/or objects for each ink are printed. Both states toggle on or off when clicked, and a gray overscore above the icons confirms your alterations.

NOTE *If you've used even one spot-ink color in your document—or perhaps more than just one—these inks will separate at the default 45°. Consult with your print vendor for the correct screening angles for overlapping fixed-palette, spot-ink colors.*

The Use Advanced Settings option is always dimmed unless you have a PostScript printer selected. When it's enabled, advanced settings will override settings in the Separations tab. Clicking the Advanced button displays the Advanced Separations Settings dialog, shown next.

Here's what the options in this dialog control:

- **Screening Technology**   This selector drop-down contains scripts for specific printing technologies such as Agfa and Linotronic image-setting devices. When Standard Defaults is used as the Screening Technology, other options are set according to settings for your specific printer driver, accessed through Properties on the General tab.

- **Resolution**   This displays the output resolution of your printed material, the default value of which is set according to the Screening Technology selected. A service bureau or your print vendor will know the specifics.

- **Basic Screen**   This option sets the resolution as measured in lines per inch of the screens rendered in your output material. Check with your print vendor for the exact setting needed. If you need to adjust this value, various choices will appear depending upon which Screening Technology and image setter Resolution is currently selected. The options shown in the Basic Screen section will also be available back in the Separations main tab.

- **Halftone Type**   The Halftone Type selector is used to set the shape of the actual dots that compose the screens in the final output. Using this drop-down menu, you can choose to use such shapes as the Default (Dot), Line, Diamond, Elliptical, Euclidean, Lines, Grid, Microwaves, Rhomboid, and Star. If you're just getting into commercial printing, anything other than a dot halftone shape is used either because the print press pulls better prints, or because you really know what you're doing and want to create an effect in the finished print job. Microwaves, for example, is a special effect that sounds interesting, but you would need to have already seen the effect on a printed sample before choosing it, and then you would do a short run to see whether the example produces the same effect in your own piece. On the other hand, Elliptical and Star shapes can be used to sharpen the output of a print, and therefore are more of an enhancer than an effect.

Setting Trapping Options

Trapping involves either spreading or overprinting portions of colored objects to avoid printing inaccuracies, the most common one being paper white showing at the edge between two color objects. *Overprinting* causes one ink color to print over another, resulting in two layers of ink—it's a technique used to work around imprecise ink alignment. You can set the overprinting of fills and outlines applied to objects directly in your document; you cancel out of the Print dialog and return to the open document. Then with the Pick tool, right-click one or more objects, and choose Overprint Fill or Overprint Outline from the pop-up menu options.

Overprinting can be set in three ways: directly in your document for each object, in the Separations tab using either fill or outline ink overprinting options, or using automated trapping. Where options have been set manually in your document or for each ink color, overprinting operates on a three-level hierarchy, which creates a condition where one overprinting setting overrides another one, as follows:

1. When printing, the objects in the drawing are first examined for any selected fill and/ or outline overprinting properties. Applying overprint properties directly to an object in a drawing overrides all other overprinting functions.

2. Next, ink color overprinting options are examined. If an ink color is set to overprint and no object fill or outline overprint properties are applied, the ink color overprints the objects beneath it.

3. Finally, the trapping options you have chosen in the Separations tab of the Print dialog are examined. If no overprint options are set, then automatic trapping will be applied if either Auto-spreading or Fixed Width is selected.

Automatic trapping and overprinting options in the Separations tab have the following effects on how colors in your document are printed:

- **Preserve Document Overprints** This option preserves the overprint options applied directly to your drawing objects, regardless of the settings selected elsewhere. Your other option (on the drop-down list), Ignore, lets you work with the settings in the Separations tab, and any custom overprinting you've applied directly to objects in your document is ignored.

- **Always Overprint Black** When this option is selected, all objects that have color tints between 95 and 100 percent black will overprint underlying ink colors. Usually, you want black to overprint; black is the key plate for all the fine details, particularly necessary if you're using a bitmap image in part of your design.

- **Auto-spreading**   This option causes CorelDRAW's print engine automatically to create an overprinting outline of identical ink color around objects where they overlap other ink colors. When the option is selected, you can set the Maximum width of the spread within a range of 0 to 10 points (0.5 point is the default, a little wider than a hairline). Automatic width values vary according to the difference between the color being overprinted and the underlying color. Choose Fixed Width to set the Auto-spreading width of the outline to a constant width regardless of this color difference. When Auto-spreading is selected, choosing the Text Above option makes CorelDRAW ignore text sizes below a certain size; small text is often distorted by the spread effect. Choose a size between 0 and 200 points; the default is 18 points.

In-RIP Trapping Settings

If your output device is equipped with its own In-RIP trapping software, you can use this option. The term *RIP* stands for *raster image processor,* the process of converting mathematical chunks of information to a map of where dots of ink go on the page to represent what you see onscreen. Many high-end image setters are equipped with internal software with which certain In-RIP trapping makes the whole trapping process faster and more efficient.

This option is dimmed unless the output device defined on the General tab is PostScript compatible, PostScript 3 is selected in the Compatibility area of the PostScript tab, and Print Separations is *disabled* in the Color tab. With the feature enabled, choose the In-RIP Trapping option, and then click the Settings button to open the In-RIP Trapping Settings dialog, shown in Figure 27-4.

Here you'll find an ink listing similar to the one in the Separations tab, plus other options for setting these items:

- **Neutral Density**   This is a value based upon the relative darkness of each process ink, ranging from 0.001 to 10.000. Trapping software derives neutral density for spot colors based upon their CMYK equivalents. Default values often work, or the value can be set according to advice from your print vendor. Most third-party ink swatches list the neutral density values for each ink color.

- **Type**   You choose the Type for an individual ink by clicking its type in the top list to reveal an options drop-down. Although Neutral Density is the default for Image Trap Placement, this option becomes available when you have a specialty ink defined for a spot plate, such as a spot varnish. You can choose from Neutral Density, Transparent, Opaque, or Opaque Ignore. Opaque is often used for heavy nontransparent inks such as metallic inks, to prevent the trapping of underlying colors while still allowing trapping along the ink's edges. Opaque Ignore is used for heavy nontransparent inks to prevent trapping of underlying color *and* along the ink's edges.

FIGURE 27-4 If your output device is equipped with In-RIP trapping, these options are available.

- **Trap Width** This option controls the overlap of adjacent colored objects into each other. The slightly overlapping colors prevent the appearance of white gaps due to misregistration when printing. The default Trap Width is 0.25 point. A larger number will accommodate larger printing errors due to older machinery.

- **Black Trap Width** This option controls the distance that inks spread into solid black, or the distance between black ink edges and underlying inks. It is used when the amount of black ink reaches the percentage specified in the Black Limit field (in the Thresholds area).

- **Trap Color Reduction** Use this option to prevent certain butt-aligned colors (areas on different plates that meet one another) from creating a trap that is darker than both colors combined. Values smaller than 100 percent lighten the color of the trap.

- **Step Limit** This option controls the degree to which components of butt-aligned color must vary before a trap is created, usually set between 8 and 20 percent. Lower percentages increase sensitivity to color differences and create larger traps.

- **Black Limit** This value controls the minimum amount of black ink required before the value entered in the Black Trap Width field is applied.

- **Black Density Limit**   This option controls the neutral density value at, or above, the value at which the In-RIP feature considers it solid black. To treat a dark spot-color as black, enter its Neutral Density value in this field.

- **Sliding Trap Limit**   This value sets the percentage difference between the neutral density of butt-aligned colors at which the trap is moved from the darker side of the color edge toward the centerline. Use this option when colors have similar neutral densities, to prevent abrupt shifts in trap color along a fountain fill edge, for example.

- **Trap Objects to Images**   Choosing this option lets you create traps between vectors and bitmaps.

- **Image Trap Placement**   This option sets where the trap falls when trapping vector objects to bitmap objects to either Neutral Density, Spread, Choke, or Centerline in this option's drop-down list. Neutral Density applies the same trapping rules used elsewhere in the printed document. Using this option to trap a vector to a bitmap can cause uneven edges because the trap moves from one side of the edge to the other. Spread produces a trap in areas where bitmaps meet vector objects. Choke causes vector objects to overlap the bitmap (the bitmap is choked). Centerline creates a trap that straddles the edge between vectors and bitmaps. Trap Objects To Images must be checked for Image Trap Placement to have any effect.

- **Internal Image Trapping**   This option creates traps *within* the area of a bitmap, which is useful when very high contrast and posterized images are part of a design.

- **Trap Black-And-White Images**   Choosing this option performs trapping between vectors and black-and-white (monochrome) bitmaps.

Setting Prepress Options

The term *prepress* is used to describe the preparing of film for various printing processes. Choosing the Prepress tab displays all options controlling how your printing material will be produced, and which information is included on the page, as shown in Figure 27-5.

Here's what the options in the Prepress tab offer:

- **Paper/Film Settings**   These two options specify negative/positive printing and on which side of the film the light-sensitive emulsion layer appears. Choose Invert to cause your output to print as a negative; choose Mirror to cause the image to print backward. Ask the press operator or service bureau which way their image setter is set up for film.

- **Print File Information**   A Job Name/Slug Line text box is printed on each separation, to better visually identify each printed sheet. The path and filename of your document is used by default, but you can enter your own information. Choose Print Page Numbers

FIGURE 27-5   Use these options to control how your output is produced and to add prepress information and markings.

to print page numbers as defined in your CorelDRAW document; choose Position Within Page to print this information *inside* the page boundaries—outside is the default.

- **Crop/Fold Marks**   Crop marks help locate your document's page corners; fold marks indicate folds for a specific layout. Choose Crop/Fold Marks to print these markings. While this is selected, you can also choose Exterior Only to cause the marks to print only outside the page boundaries on your printing material, which produces a more polished final presentation. Both options are selected by default.

- **Registration Marks and Styles**   Registration marks help to align each separation plate; the film print is used to make the plate, and the plates need to be precisely aligned when your piece is printed, or you get a "Sunday Funny Pages" finished output. Choosing Print Registration Marks (selected by default) includes these marks on your output. Use the Style selector to specify a mark shape; the selector includes a preview of both positive and negative versions.

- **Calibration Bars and Densitometer Scales**   These two options enable you to include color calibration bars and densitometer scales outside the page boundaries of your printed material. Calibration bars are useful for evaluating color density accuracy by printing a selection of grayscale shades that may be used for measuring the density—or blackness value—of film or paper output.

- **Bitmap Downsampling** Unless you've imported a bitmap image whose resolution as placed in a document exceeds the maximum output resolution of the printing device, it's *not* necessary to check either the Color & Grayscale or the Monochrome check boxes. This feature is provided as a time-saver: for example, if an image is greater than 300 dpi and your output device is only *capable* of a maximum of 300 dpi, time is wasted as excess data is spooled to the printer … and then discarded.

- **Marks to Objects** Choosing this option places the currently selected prepress marks around the bounding box containing the objects on each page. These appear regardless of whether the Crop/Fold Marks option is selected to print.

Choosing PostScript Options

None of the preceding information on separations and advanced trapping features will be meaningful if your chosen output is not to a PostScript device. If you don't currently see the PostScript tab, shown in Figure 27-6, you need to define a different print driver on the General tab. PostScript options offer control over a specific type of page description language, Level 2, Level 3, the type of device, compatibility, and features covered next.

FIGURE 27-6   These options become available if your selected printer is PostScript compatible.

You set the following options on the PostScript tab:

- **Compatibility** In most cases, the printer and the PPD (PostScript Printer Description) file you choose are automatically set with the Compatibility option, which determines which PostScript features the output device is capable of handling. Older printers may be limited to PostScript Level 1 or 2 technology; most new models are compatible with Level 3. If you're unsure which to choose, check out the manufacturer's FAQ area on their website or the physical printer documentation.

- **Conform to DSC** Document Structuring Convention (DSC) is a special file format for PostScript documents. It includes a number of comments that provide information for *postprocessors*. Postprocessors can shuffle the order of pages, print two or more pages on a side, and perform other tasks often needlessly performed by humans.

- **Bitmaps** Selecting Level 2 or 3 PostScript-compatible printers offers you the Compression Type option of Use JPEG to reduce printing time if you have bitmap images in your document. When this option is selected, the JPEG Quality slider is available for setting the quality of the bitmaps being printed. Keep in mind that JPEG is a *lossy* compression standard; some of the original image information is discarded, quality is compromised, and at high compression settings, a photograph can take on visual noise.

- **Maintain OPI Links** This option preserves links to server-based bitmap images, provided you have imported temporary low-resolution versions using the Open Prepress Interface (OPI) option when you created your CorelDRAW document. Using OPI, you can store high-resolution bitmap images in a printer's memory, and work temporarily with an imported low-resolution version. When your document is printed, the lower-resolution version is swapped with the higher-resolution version. By default, this option is selected.

- **Resolve DCS Links** Desktop Color Separation (DCS) technology is similar to OPI; you use placeholders in your document that have links to digitally separated images for use in process or multi-ink printing. When this option is enabled, the linked images automatically replace the placeholder images at print time. By default, this option is selected. If this option is not selected, a prompt will appear while the document is being printed, so you can relink the files manually through directory boxes.

- **Fonts** PostScript printing devices can print Type 1, True Type, and OpenType fonts. Type 1 fonts are often preferred because the font data is written in PostScript language. OpenType fonts, when a typographer creates them, can be coded to Bézier curves (in which case programs recognize them as PostScript encoded) *or* to Quadratic B-Splines—which are usually interpreted by an application as True Type

27

in structure. A good reason to lean toward Type 1 fonts when you output to PostScript is that there is no ambiguity to the structure of a Type 1 font. CorelDRAW's options let you control which fonts are used during printing. It's more reliable to download the fonts to the printing device; this speeds printing and produces better-looking text. To enable this feature, select Download Type 1 Fonts. If this option is disabled, fonts are printed as curves, which can take a lot of printing time when you have a lot of text on a page. When you select the Download Type 1 Fonts option, the Convert True Type To Type 1 option becomes available (and selected by default).

- **PDF Marks** If your document is being prepared for printing as a composite to an Adobe PDF distiller, these options become available. You can specify how your PDF file initially displays when viewed in Adobe Acrobat Reader or in a third-party reader by using options in the On Start, Display selector. Choose Page Only, Full Screen, or Thumbnail view. You can also choose whether to Include Hyperlinks and/ or Include Bookmarks in the resulting PDF file. If you're preparing a PDF to send to a service bureau for high-resolution output, don't use hyperlinks; they mess up the appearance of your printed piece, and let's get real—how does your intended audience click on a piece of paper to visit a website?

- **Auto Increase Flatness** This option lets you simplify the printing of curves by decreasing the number of straight vector lines that describe the curve. This option can be used as a last resort if you run into problems printing highly complex shapes in your CorelDRAW document, usually a printer memory problem, as in *not enough* memory.

- **Auto Increase Fountain Steps** This option makes the print engine examine your document for opportunities to increase the number of fountain steps in an effort to avoid fountain fill banding. *Banding* is the visible effect of not having enough sequential steps in a fountain fill; you see bands of gradually changing color instead of a smooth transition from one object area to another. Increasing the number of steps that describe a fountain fill will cause fountain fills to appear smoother, but it will also increase printing complexity and output time.

- **Optimize Fountain Fills** This option works in reverse of the previous option by setting the print engine to *decrease* the number of fountain steps set for objects in your document to the number of steps your printer is capable of reproducing.

CorelDRAW's Printing Issues Tab

The process of verifying that every last detail in your document will print as expected is often called *preflight,* and the good news is that the Issues tab is your flight attendant. CorelDRAW examines the contents of your document and the printing options you've selected and then compares them with the capabilities of your selected printer and your

FIGURE 27-7   If CorelDRAW anticipates printing problems, they'll be explained in this dialog.

selected output material. Printing snafus are found automatically and flagged by warning symbols, as shown in the earlier illustration in this chapter about issues icons. Figure 27-7 is the Issues tab, which is divided into two sections; with Print Preview turned on, it's both documented and visually obvious what this proposed print has going against it.

The top half of the Issues dialog lists the preflight issues detected with a brief explanation. The bottom half explains the causes, identifies the exact problems, and offers suggestions and recommendations for correcting them.

The Issues feature will not prevent you from printing your document. If you want, you can deactivate the feature by selecting the found issue in the upper portion of the tab and choosing "Don't check for this issue in the future" at the bottom of the tab. This disables the detection of the issue in the Preflight Settings dialog. Clicking the Settings button opens this dialog, which also lets you save and load current settings for future use.

Previewing Your Printed Document

CorelDRAW's Print Preview feature provides a very good way of viewing your document and performing minor touchups, and it's fully integrated with CorelDRAW's print engine. To open the Print Preview feature, click the Print Preview button from within the Print dialog. Print Preview also is available in the File menu.

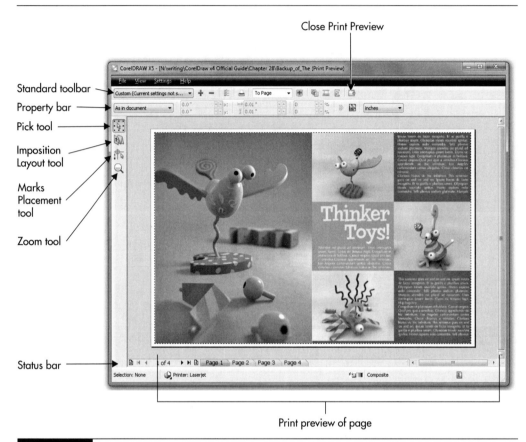

Close Print Preview

Standard toolbar

Property bar

Pick tool

Imposition Layout tool

Marks Placement tool

Zoom tool

Status bar

Print preview of page

FIGURE 27-8   Print Preview is a program within a program, with its own interface, tools, shortcuts, and commands.

Print Preview (see Figure 27-8) is a separate application window and includes its own command menus, toolbars, property bar, status bar, and toolbox. When Print Preview is open, CorelDRAW is still open in the background. The Print Preview utility provides a higher level of control over the finished print than preferences you set in the File | Print dialog.

Browsing and Viewing Previews

The first thing you'll want to do in Print Preview is to examine how your printed pages will look. Across the bottom of the Print Preview window, you'll find page controls, shown next, so you can browse each printed page. Use the arrow buttons to move forward or backward in the sequence, or click a page tab to display a specific page. As you do this, you'll discover each printed page is represented—including individual ink separation pages for each page in your document when you're printing separations.

You can view your pages in a number of different ways based on output mode, color, and object type. To change view modes, choose one of the following from the View menu:

- **Show Image** Choosing this lets you hide the display of page contents to speed screen redraw times when you've got a lot of objects on a specific page.

- **Preview Colors** Choose this to access three basic previewing states. Auto (Simulate Output) shows each page's color according to your selected options and your printer's capabilities. If your chosen printer driver does not print in color, you'll see only grayscale color on your pages. To override this, choose either Color or Grayscale, which forces a specific view.

- **Preview Separations** Choose Preview Separations to access three basic states. Auto (Simulate Output) displays separations according to your printer driver and selected print options. If Separations are not selected to print, only a composite is shown, and vice versa. You can override this by choosing either Composite or Separations to force a specific separation display state. Overprints do not display accurately in Print Preview, and trapping cannot be seen.

- **Printable Area** This varies from printer to printer; the *printable area* is the physical area that the printer can render onto a page. Choose this option (selected by default) to show a dotted line representing the maximum extent to which the printer can render.

- **Render PostScript Fills** Use this option to have PostScript fills display as they will print. Deactivating this option can free up system resources when viewing documents where you used a lot of PostScript-filled objects.

- **Show Current Tile** This option highlights individual tiles as you hover your cursor over them when previewing, and it's useful when printing large documents in sections onto small output material (called *tile printing,* covered earlier in this chapter). To use tile printing from within Print Preview, choose Settings | Layout to open the Print Options dialog to the Layout tab, and then click to activate the Print Tiled Pages option.

TIP *To get to Print Options without leaving Print Preview, press CTRL+E to bring up the General tab, and then click your way to the tab you seek.*

Print Preview Tools and the Property Bar

The key to using Print Preview to its fullest is learning where all the options are, what each tool does, and what print properties are available while using each. Four tools are on the toolbox—the Pick tool, Imposition Layout tool, Marks Placement tool, and the Zoom tool— each of which is discussed in the sections to follow. The standard toolbar, shown next, contains printing options, viewing options, and shortcuts you can use to open print-related dialogs.

First is the Print Style selector, which is used to choose all printing options according to a saved set of print parameters. As with other CorelDRAW Preset features, you can select, save, delete, or modify print styles in the selector. Choose an existing Print Style, use the current unsaved settings on the current print job, or choose Browse to show the Open dialog so you can work with a saved Print Style. To delete a selected Print Style, click the Delete Print Style (–) button. To save a Print Style, click the Save Print Style As (+) button (or use the F12 shortcut) to open the Save Settings As dialog. Use the Settings To Include options to specify which print options to save with your new style, and click Save to add the Print Style to the selector.

The remaining options in the standard toolbar have the following functions, many of which are covered earlier in this chapter:

- **Print Options** This button opens the Print Options dialog.

- **Print** This button immediately sends the document to the printer using the current options. Use CTRL+T as a shortcut; CTRL+P works, too, as a common Windows command for applications that can print.

- **Zoom** Select a predefined zoom level from the list to change the view magnification level.

- **Full Screen Preview** This button is self-explanatory. Press ESC to return to Print Preview. You can also use CTRL+U as a shortcut.

- **Enable Color Separations**   This button sends the printing of color separations to the output device using color selected in the Separations tab of the Print Options dialog.

- **Invert**   This button inverts the printed image to print in reverse. This is for film using an image-setting device, but can also provide an amusing special effect (and use a lot of ink!).

- **Mirror**   This button flips the printed document to print backward to set emulsion orientation on image-setting devices. You can also use this to print to T-shirt transfers.

- **Close Print Preview**   Pressing this button (or using the ALT+C shortcut) returns you to the current CorelDRAW document.

Pick Tool Property Bar Options

The Pick tool in Print Preview is used in much the same way it's used in the drawing window; with it you select and move (by click-dragging) the contents of the current page. While the Pick tool and objects on a page are selected, the property bar features a variety of printing options, shortcuts, position settings, and tool settings, as shown here:

Many of these options are for positioning and scaling the contents or whole pages in relation to the printed output page size that your printer is currently set to use. Click-dragging the object control handles lets you scale the objects interactively.

Imposition Layout Tool Property Bar Options

The Imposition Layout tool provides control over the print layout. Only certain image setters are capable of printing multiple pages in signature formats, so it's best to check with the person doing your print job before making changes using the imposition options.

When the Imposition Layout tool is selected, the preview is changed to display imposition-specific properties. This tool has four separate editing states, each of which is chosen on the Edit Settings selector. Options accessible on the property bar while Edit Basic Settings is selected, shown next, give you control over imposition layout options. Choosing Edit Page Placements, Edit Gutters & Finishing, or Edit Margins from this selector displays a set of imposition options for each state.

Marks Placement Tool Property Bar Options

The Marks Placement tool lets you alter the position of crop and fold marks, registration marks, color calibration bars, printing information, and Densitometer (density scale) positions. When the Marks Placement tool is selected, the property bar features options for positioning and printing certain mark types, as shown in Figure 27-9.

To position crop and fold marks, click-drag the top, bottom, or sides of the rectangle defining their position, or enter values in the property bar boxes. To change the position of other marks you have selected to print with your document page, choose the Marks Placement tool, and drag directly on the marks.

Zoom Tool Property Bar Options

The Zoom tool in the Print Preview window is used much the same way as the Zoom tool in CorelDRAW, so you can increase or decrease the view of your Print Preview. Many of the

FIGURE 27-9   While the Marks Placement tool is selected, the property bar features these options.

functions of the Zoom tool are performed interactively or by using hot keys. While the Zoom tool is selected, the property bar features all Zoom options and magnification commands, as shown here:

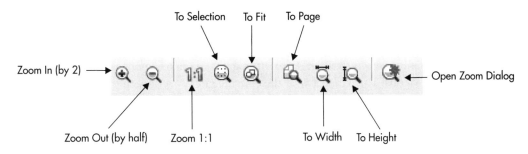

You can also change Zoom settings by choosing View | Zoom (CTRL+Z) to open the Zoom dialog to choose among all Zoom tool functions. Use shortcuts to change your view magnification while using Print Preview's Zoom tool: Zoom Out using F3, Zoom To Page using SHIFT+F4, Zoom To Selection using SHIFT+F2, and Zoom To Fit using F4.

   Print Preview doesn't have an Undo command; to reset options quickly, click the Print Styles selector and then choose CorelDRAW Defaults. All crop marks vanish, imposition settings revert, and any repositioned object reverts.

Setting Printing Preferences

Once you're familiar with the ocean of printing options, what your output device is capable of, and what you want from a specific print job, Printing Preferences can be your one-stop shop for most of the items covered in this chapter. Choose Settings | Printing Preferences (CTRL+F is the shortcut) while in the Print Preview window to open the Printing Preferences

FIGURE 27-10 The Printing Preferences dialog offers comprehensive control over output settings.

dialog, shown in Figure 27-10. Preferences are subdivided into General, Driver Compatibility, and Preflight options. To change any of the options, click a Setting title; a drop-down selector appears, and then you make your change.

General Printing Preferences

Options in the General tab provide control over fonts, crop mark color, driver banding, and so on, and they set the parameters for potential preflight issues or warning dialogs that appear before and during printing. These options are set by default to the highest fault tolerance for most printing jobs; 99 percent of the time your prints will come out fine if you don't change the settings. Here's a list explaining the most common states:

- **Spot Color Separations Warning** This option lets you control the warning state while printing color separations. The warning can be set to appear if more than one, two, three, or any spot colors are used in the document being printed.

- **Preview Color Default** This option sets the initial color display of your printed document when the Print Preview window is first opened. Choose Auto (Simulate Output), Color, or Grayscale.

- **Preview Separations Default**   This option sets the initial color display of your separations when the Print Preview window is first opened. Choose Auto (Simulate Output) or Composite.

- **Preview Image Default**   This controls whether your document image is automatically set to show when the Print Preview window first opens. Choose On At Startup (the default) or Off At Startup.

- **Overprint Black Threshold (PS)**   During overprinting, CorelDRAW X5 sets a default value for overprinting black objects only if they contain a uniform fill of 95 percent or more black. The Overprint Black Threshold setting can be changed using this option, so you can further customize the global overprinting function. The threshold limit can be set between 0 and 100 percent black.

- **Send Large Bitmaps in Chunks**   This option works in combination with the Bitmap Output Threshold setting and can be set to Yes, If Larger Than Threshold (referring to the Bitmap Output Threshold value), or No.

- **Bitmap Output Threshold (K)**   When printing to non-PostScript printers, this option lets you set a limit on the size of bitmaps, as measured in kilobytes, sent to the printing device. By default, this value is set to the maximum, but you can set it to specific values within a range of 0 to 4,096 (the default). This is a good option to change if your non-PostScript printer doesn't have a lot of memory and you're pulling prints that are unfinished due to lack of RAM for processing the image.

- **Bitmap Chunk Overlap Pixels**   If a printing device has insufficient memory or another technical problem processing very large bitmap images, you can have CorelDRAW tile sections of such a bitmap. The overlap value is used to prevent seams from showing between "chunks" of the large image. When you're printing to non-PostScript printers, this option lets you define the number of overlap pixels within a range of 0 to 48 pixels. The default is 32 pixels.

- **Bitmap Font Limit (PS)**   Usually, font sizes set below the Bitmap Font Size Threshold preference are converted to bitmap and stored in a PostScript printer's internal memory. This can be a time-consuming operation that usually increases the time your document takes to print. You can limit the number of fonts to which this occurs, forcing the printer to store only a given number of fonts per document. The default setting here is 8, but it can be set anywhere within a range of 0 to 100. Unless your document is a specimen sheet of all the fonts you have installed, 8 is a good number to set this option to.

- **Bitmap Font Size Threshold (PS)**   Most of the time CorelDRAW converts very small sizes of text to bitmap format when printing to PostScript printers, such as 4-point legal type on a bottle label. This option lets you control how this is done, based on the size of the font's characters. The default Bitmap Font Size Threshold is 75 pixels, but it can be set within a range of 0 to 1,000 pixels. The actual point size converted to bitmap varies according to the resolution used when printing a document. The threshold limit will determine exactly which font sizes are affected. For example, the equivalent font size of 75 pixels when printing to a printer resolution of 300 dpi is roughly 18 points, while at 600 dpi it's about 9 points. The higher the resolution, the lower the point size affected. A number of provisions determine whether these controls apply, including whether the font has been scaled or skewed, and whether envelope effects, fountain or texture fills, or print scaling options such as Fit To Page have been chosen.

- **Small Fonts** This controls a warning that appears if the document you're printing includes fonts below a 7-point size threshold by default. The Small Fonts warning option can be set between 3 and 18 points. Resolution plays an important part in rendering small point size typefaces, as does the design of the characters within the font. For example, a 1,200 dpi laser printer can render 4-point Helvetica quite legibly, less so with a serif typeface such as Times Roman because the serifs at this size are about equal to insect parts. Choose a simple sans serif font for extremely small font sizes. Do not expect a perfect rendering of a very small typeface, because the dots of ink or toner cartridge can render only a finite number of dots to represent very small text.

- **Image Resolution Too Low** By default, this value is set to 96 ppi, alerting you if bitmaps have a resolution below this value. This is probably too low for even today's personal inkjets; it's recommended that you increase this value to at least 225 ppi.

- **Composite Crop Marks (PS)** This is a useful feature for setting the pen color of crop marks either to Output In Black Only or to Output On All Plates—in process (CMYK) color, making the crop marks print to every color plate during process color separation printing.

- **PostScript 2 Stroke Adjust (PS)** The PostScript Level 2 language has a provision particularly useful for graphics programs such as CorelDRAW. Stroke Adjust produces strokes of uniform thickness to compensate for uneven line widths due to the conversion of *vector* artwork to *raster* printed graphics, which is what all printers do. The PostScript 2 Stroke Adjust option *should not* be used for older printers that are not compatible with PostScript Level 2 or Level 3 technology. Most recently manufactured printing devices are at least PostScript Level 2 compatible. If you are not sure what level your printing device is, leave this setting off or consult the docs that came with the device.

- **Many Fonts** This controls a warning that appears if the document you're printing includes more than ten different fonts. If you're new to CorelDRAW and are experimenting with all the cool fonts that came on the CD, your file can easily exceed this limit. If your printer's memory and/or your system resources are capable of handling large numbers of different fonts, consider increasing this value. The Many Fonts warning option can be set within a range of 1 to 50 fonts. Tangentially related to this option is a creative design issue: very few professionals use more than ten different typefaces in a design; five can express an idea using text quite well in most situations.

- **Render to Bitmap Resolution**   This option by default is set to Automatic, which causes bitmaps to be output at the same resolution as vector objects and text in your document. To specify the resolution of bitmaps to be printed at lower or higher resolutions than the rest of the document, choose specific settings within a range of 150 to 600 dpi.

Driver Compatibility

The Driver Compatibility area, shown in Figure 27-11, provides control over specific driver features for *non-PostScript* printers. Choose a Printer from the drop-down menu, and then choose specific options in the dialog to make changes. Clicking Apply saves and associates your changes with the selected driver.

Printing Issues Warning Options

You can customize issues found by CorelDRAW's built-in preflight feature using options in the Preflight page of the Printing Preferences dialog (CTRL+F), which can be accessed only from within Print Preview by choosing Settings | Printing Preferences and clicking Preflight in the tree directory, as shown in Figure 27-12.

FIGURE 27-11   Use the Driver Compatibility options to specify how non-PostScript printers handle specific object types.

Preflight options let you control how and when detected printing issues appear.

This is a comprehensive list covering specific issues ranging from mismatched layout sizes to spot colors with similar names. Use the check box options in the list to activate or deactivate each option, or use the "Don't check for this issue in the future" option, located at the bottom of the Issues tab of the Print Options dialog when an issue is discovered.

Corel's Duplexing Wizard

You can create booklets and other double-sided printed documents on your personal printer by using the Duplexing Wizard. You can access this feature independently of CorelDRAW by choosing Start | All Programs | Corel Graphics Suite | Duplexing Wizard, or by pressing CTRL+D while in Print Preview.

This wizard is fairly self-explanatory and straightforward to use. When a driver is set to use the duplex printing feature, the Manual Double-Sided Printing dialog displays when CorelDRAW's print engine starts to print, asking whether you want to print on both sides of a printed page. For specific page-insertion directions, you'll find an option that will print an instruction sheet to show you which way you should reinsert the sheet of paper after printing the first side.

The Duplexing Wizard is not intended for use with a PostScript printer.

Using the Collect for Output Wizard

CorelDRAW provides a wizard that collects all the information, fonts, and files required to display and print your documents correctly if you don't own an image setter or other high-end output device and need to send your document to press.

Corel has a service bureau affiliate program, and service bureaus approved by Corel can provide you with a profile to prepare your document with the Collect for Output Wizard. This profile can also contain special instructions that a service bureau needs you to follow before sending your files. Check with your vendor to see whether it is a Corel Approved Service Bureau (CASB). If it's not, and your printing need is a do-or-die situation, it's easy to use File | Export. Choose PDF-Adobe Portable Document Format (*.PDF) from the Export Save As Type drop-down list, and then choose Prepress from the PDF Preset drop-down list in the PDF Settings dialog box. The PDF file is usually accepted by commercial press places and the results can be quite good.

To launch the wizard, choose File | Collect for Output. From there, the wizard guides you through a series of question-and-answer pages that gather the information you need to upload or put on a disk to deliver to a printer or service bureau. When you finish the process, all necessary files are copied to a folder you define, and optional documents specifying your required output are included, depending on your wizard option choices. Figure 27-13 shows the succession of wizard dialogs from the beginning to the end of the process. At the end, CorelDRAW offers a final screen with a summary; click Finish.

FIGURE 27-13   In five steps your files are prepared for sending to a service bureau.

Print Merge

Print Merge gives you the design and business opportunities to merge database information with specific fields of your CorelDRAW documents at print time, to print personalized documents with only a click or two. If you create mailing labels, short runs targeted at a specific audience, and marketing documents, this feature will be invaluable. By creating special fields, you can merge specific database information into your document and set properties such as color, font style, and so on. This feature also lets you use ODBC Data Sources from database management systems that use Structured Query Language (SQL) as a standard.

Follow these steps when you need to create a Print Merge:

1. Choose File | Print Merge | Create/Load Merge Fields. Choosing this command opens the Print Merge Wizard, and you either create a database from scratch or choose an existing one.

2. If you need to create a custom merge document, choose the Create New Text option and then click Next. Create fields for your custom database by entering unique names in the Text Field and/or Numeric Field, shown in Figure 27-14, and then click the Add button. As you build your field list, you can change the order of the fields by clicking to highlight a field in the Field Name list, and then clicking the Move Up

FIGURE 27-14   Create your custom database fields by typing in the Text and/or Numeric Field box and then click Add.

and Move Down buttons. You can also edit the fields you've created by using the Rename and Delete buttons to change or remove a selected field. Choose the Incremental Field Data option while a field is selected in the list to number each entry in the field automatically. If you need numeric data, enter the value in the Numeric Field; when this option is used, new fields display, letting you specify the numeric sequence of your data and formatting. You can also choose the "Continually increment the numeric field" box to save time making your field entries. Once your list is created, click Next to proceed.

3. The next page of the wizard, shown in Figure 27-15, gets you right into building your database by entering values to build sets of field entries. To begin a new entry, click the New button, and then fill in the fields with the appropriate data; click the spreadsheet-like box to highlight it, and then type your entry. You can quickly revise an entire field by highlighting it and then pressing DELETE or BACKSPACE. To delete an entire record, make sure it is the only one with a check to the left of it, and then click the Delete button. Browse your database entries using the navigation buttons, or search for specific entries by clicking the Find button. Once your database is complete, click Next to proceed.

27

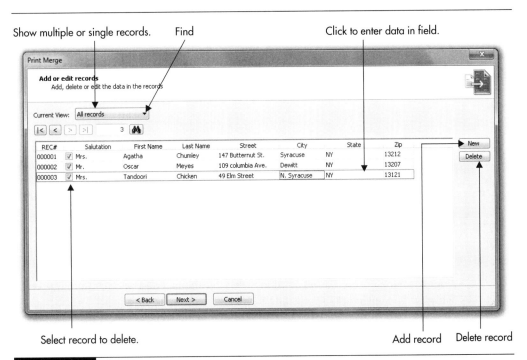

FIGURE 27-15 Use this page of the wizard to begin building your field entry sets.

4. The final wizard page is where you save your database to reuse and update in the future. Choose the Save Data Settings As box, and then browse your hard drive for a location to save the file in Windows Rich Text Format, Plain Text, or File With A Comma Used As A Delimiter (CSV Files). You probably also want to save the incremental field data to make looking up a record easier in the future. Click Finish to exit the wizard and automatically open the Print Merge toolbar, shown here. If you are still running Windows XP, you must navigate to a folder to be able to save your database. You'll receive an error telling you that CorelDRAW failed to save the print merge data if you don't "spell out" the save path for CorelDRAW.

5. By default, the toolbar opens with your newly created database open and the individual fields it includes listed in the Field selector. To load your fields from a different database, click the Create/Load Print Merge Fields button to relaunch the Print Merge Wizard.

6. By inserting fields, you're creating a link from entries in your database to insertion points in your document. To insert a field into your document, make a selection from the Field selector, and then click the Insert button. Use the cursor to define an insertion point in your document with a single click. As you insert a field, a code appears in your document with the name of the field bracketed, such as <Street Address>. Repeat your insertion procedure for each field you want to include in your print merge operation.

7. The print merge fields can be formatted as artistic text, so you can apply any properties associated with artistic text to the field text to format it as you would like it to appear when printed. This includes color, alignment, font, size, style, and so on. Fields can be inserted as stand-alone text objects, inserted into paragraph text, or simply typed using the same code format.

8. Once your fields have been placed and formatted, the print merge document is all set up, and you might want to click the Merge To New Document button to proof the different pages with the data entered. When it comes to merging your printed document with the Print Merge feature, use the Print button on the Print Merge toolbar. If you simply press CTRL+P, CorelDRAW will prompt you to choose to Perform Print Merge, or to Print As A Template. Alternatively, choose File | Print Merge | Perform Merge. Doing so immediately opens the Print dialog, where you proceed with printing using your print option selections.

9. Finally, if you want to import text from a file or ODBC database, you must do this by first opening up a new document, or by closing a merge document, reopening it, and choosing File | Print Merge | Create | Load Merge Fields.

This chapter has shown you where the print options are for both PostScript and non-PostScript output, how to check for errors and correct them before you send your CorelDRAW file to an output device, and how to make your work portable so someone with more expensive equipment than mere mortals own can print your work to magazine quality. But this is only half the story of CorelDRAW output. Take a trip to the following chapter, where output for the Web is explored; you'll want companion pieces up on your website in addition to printed material. Regardless of whether you put dots of ink on a page or broadcast pixels to a screen 10,000 miles away, today it's called *publishing* your work.

27

CHAPTER 28

Basic HTML Page Layout
and Publishing

Whether it's for personal pleasure or selling your wares, the Web connects your ideas with your business and social contacts. It's far less expensive than other publication media such as television and print, and the really great thing about it is that it's *hot*. You don't have to be a rocket scientist to get media up on your website using CorelDRAW, and once you've designed a piece for print, it's practically ready to go on the Web. Create once, publish many times!

In this chapter you learn about the many tools and features at your disposal in CorelDRAW for optimizing your work for the Web, and about how to create special web graphics such as rollover buttons that turn your art into *interactive* art.

> **NOTE** *Download and extract all the files from the Chapter28.zip archive to follow the tutorials in this chapter.*

Web Page Navigation Buttons and Hotspots

What makes the Web a *web* are the links that connect pages to other pages. The World Wide Web is engineered by connecting *this* bit of this page to that bit of *that* page on the same site—or on any other website in the world. The engine that performs all this interconnecting magic is actually the text-based *hyperlink*. Although text-based hyperlinks are the foundation of the Web, text links by themselves aren't very visually attractive, and the links themselves often are just a bunch of letters and numbers that mean something to a computer, but mean nothing to a human.

However, if you put a graphic *face* on a link—perhaps one that changes as a visitor hovers over or clicks it—you have a web page that speaks well of your artistic skills. You also get a chance to provide nonverbal communication, the sort that plays to a worldwide audience, many of whom might not speak your native tongue. With a graphic, you can clearly point out that Area X is a link and not part of your text message. Using a graphic also gives you the opportunity to provide a visual clue about where the link goes. How about the humble shopping cart icon? A great many people in this world now know that clicking a shopping cart button takes them to a page that has something to do with buying something. That's a pretty all-encompassing message using only a few pixels.

Creating and applying attractive, well-thought-out navigational aids to a web page are a must in the competitive online marketplace. The following sections take a look at how you can combine CorelDRAW's tools with your input and ingenuity to create web pages worth a thousand words.

CorelDRAW's Internet Toolbar

You'll find that several web tools and resources are located throughout CorelDRAW, but the *central* location for many of these resources is the Internet toolbar. Here's a look at the toolbar; you choose Window | Toolbars | Internet, or right-click any visible toolbar and then choose Internet from the pop-up menu. The buttons on this toolbar are dimmed unless you have an object or two on the current drawing page; now is a good time to create a few button-shaped graphics for tutorial steps you can follow a little later.

From the Internet toolbar, you can apply web-specific properties to objects, such as hyperlinks, rollover effects, and image maps. *Hyperlinks* are links to existing web pages (or to bookmark links applied to objects in your CorelDRAW document). *Rollovers* are objects that can change their appearance and perform an event in response to a user's cursor action over the object. *Image maps* are objects that have one or more linked areas to web page destinations. Rollovers are unique object types (that this chapter shows you how to make); however, hyperlinks can be applied to *any* single object or to specific characters in a paragraph text object.

CAUTION   *Arial, Verdana, Times New Roman, and several other typefaces are web compatible; when CorelDRAW exports these fonts—when you use them as paragraph text on a page—they will appear as editable text in the audience's browser. Be sure to click the Make Text Web Compatible button before exporting your HTML; otherwise CorelDRAW will export the text as a bitmap graphic, as you'll see when you get to the Images tab while exporting. See "Web Text Options" later in this chapter.*

The Internet toolbar provides a convenient hub for applying nearly all web object properties. Many of these properties can also be found and applied elsewhere in CorelDRAW, but it's more convenient to use the toolbar. Making your graphics actually perform the duties you've assigned to them (by applying web properties) requires that a matching piece of HTML code is added to the web page HTML. CorelDRAW will write this code for you when you export your Corel document. You *will* need to provide the HTML along with the graphic to your client or to the webmaster to make the interactive graphics you've created do what they're supposed to do. In the sections to follow, you'll learn what options are available, and where to find them.

Creating Rollover Buttons

Almost any object you draw can be made into a rollover that reacts to cursor actions, so you can liven up your published document with simple animated effects and hyperlinks. *Cursor actions* are events such as when a user holds or passes a cursor over the object, or clicks the object by using a mouse.

When you're creating rollovers, three basic states can be defined: Normal, Over, and Down. The *Normal state* sets how an object appears in its "static" state—when the cursor is not over or clicked on the object on the web page. The *Over state* sets the appearance of the object whenever a cursor is over it. The *Down state* reveals the object in the rollover group when the user's cursor is above the object and has clicked their mouse button. By varying what the graphic looks like in these states, you can create interesting visual effects and give your users meaningful feedback related to their cursor movement.

This is fun stuff and deserves a tutorial. The following steps show how to make a region interactive when an object (or group of objects) is displayed on a web page. Although the button will react to cursor actions when you've completed the tutorial, the actions will not link to anything; linking a button is covered later in this chapter—let's concentrate on the *art* for the button first. Let's suppose you want a button that tells the visitor that something is for sale: a button with a $ symbol plays in several countries, or use a currency symbol of your preference in this example. To continue the concept here, the action a visitor would take would be to click to buy the item; therefore, when visitors hover their cursor over and/or click the button, the button should change to a different look. In this example the button will change its text from a $ symbol to an official-looking "SOLD" message. Yep, as ambitious as this might sound, all you need to do is to follow these steps…

Creating Different Looks for Rollover States

1. Create a button object, make it as fancy as you like (Effects | Emboss works well), but keep the size of the button to approximately the size you'd want it on your web page—under an inch is fine for this example. Then with the Text tool, type **$** and give the symbol a fill color that contrasts with the button color.

2. Select all the objects (CTRL+A), and then click the Create Rollover button on the toolbar to let CorelDRAW know this is going to be a rollover button once you've finished, as shown here.

Several objects selected

Less than 1"

3. With the object now defined as a rollover object, all the states on the Active Rollover State selector display the same group of objects you selected…and it's time to create a change now. Click the Edit Rollover button to enter the editing state, as shown here, and then choose Over from the selector list.

Choose state

4. Edit your button; in the next illustration the embossed circle has actually been replaced with a polygon object. You *can* replace objects, change the fill, do just about anything you like because this editing state is not a "normal" page view in CorelDRAW's drawing window. Some tricky stuff is going on behind the scenes, and if you choose to delete a shape and replace it now, you haven't really deleted it. You remove an object from a state's *view,* in this case from the Over state, but in the Normal state all your original objects are still there. Similarly, delete the $ and then with the Text tool, type **SOLD** in an interesting font.

28

Replacement objects

5. For the sake of testing all these features, let's suppose that the Over state, the SOLD button, is also good for the Down state, the state that occurs when the visitor clicks the button. By default, the Normal state was assigned to all three available states when you first made the collection of objects a rollover button. First, click the Active Rollover State selector and choose Down; a view of the Normal state objects appears.

6. Trash the contents of the Down state by clicking the Deletes Rollover State trashcan button.

7. Choose Over from the selector, and then click the Duplicates State button. The Over state now duplicates the following unassigned state (Down).

8. Mission accomplished! Click the Finish Editing Rollover button (shown here), and save this file to CDR file format.

9. Oh, yeah, you want to see your creation *in action*! CorelDRAW will preview your interactive button right on the drawing page. Click the Live Preview Of Rollovers button; before you move your cursor over the button, it should look like it did when you set it to Normal—your original group of objects. Move your cursor over the button, and it should show the Over state, as it will in the Down state (when you click the button) because you duplicated Over to Down in the tutorial. After previewing the effect, click the Live Preview Of Rollovers icon again to deactivate the live preview, because live drawings can get a little disconcerting.

Look at rollover.cdr and take it apart to better see the wealth of creative possibilities in your own work. This setup has three different states, and when you click the button, it changes shape and sort of squishes away from you. Just about any edit you can perform on objects, including totally replacing them, can be used in a Rollover button.

The Internet toolbar also has other rollover-related commands to objects, as follows:

- **Edit Rollover**   This was covered earlier, but you should know that even after you think you're finished, rollovers can be edited a week or a year from now.

- **Extract All Objects From Rollover**   This is a *destructive* edit! Think about this command twice before you undo all your rollover work. Depending on the replacement objects you've built into a rollover, use this button to view and edit everything CorelDRAW has hidden while the document was a rollover. The objects will be stacked on top of each other, so you will have to change the stack order or drag them apart to see them.

Rollover buttons can't be edited while the Live Preview Of Rollovers option is on. To edit any button, first disable this option by clicking the button. You can turn on Live Preview again when you finish editing the button.

- **Duplicates State**   Covered briefly in the tutorial, this button is used to copy the Normal state to Over and Down states if you have deleted them using the command button, discussed next.

- **Deletes Rollover State**   This deserves a little more quality time: while editing any rollover state, you can delete the object(s) representing it by clicking this button. After a state has been deleted, there will be no object to represent it, so the rollover state will appear blank. If needed, use the Duplicates State button to create an exact copy of the Normal state back into a blank state to avoid the need to re-create the object(s) used for this state. If you've deleted a state, be sure to set the Active Rollover State list back to Normal, or your button will be blank during an action when it's put up on a web page.

You've just created a three-step rollover button! It is an interesting graphic effect, and sometimes you might want to use it just the way it is—a sort of graphic hide-and-seek game. Most of the time, however, you'll want something additional to happen; you want the action of clicking the link to activate a hyperlink, and the user to be taken to the link's destination. The destination can be a bookmark location on the current page, like the top or bottom of the page, or the destination might be another web page or URL location altogether. How to make the rollover or any other element do something is presented in the following section.

Setting Internet Object Behavior

While any individual object or rollover state is selected, you can set its behavior as a web object to either a URL or an Internet bookmark using options in the Behavior selector on the Internet toolbar, shown here.

Adding URL Behavior

You can apply hyperlinks to any object using this option. For example, Corel's URL is http://www.corel.com. Internet addresses must be preceded with the correct Internet protocol prefix (such as *http://, https://,* or *ftp://*). For example, if you're linking to www.corel.com, the format must be http://www.corel.com. You can also use a "mailto" protocol to link to an email address, such as by entering **mailto:*someone@somewhere.com***. This is a great way to get, for example, a potential client to write to you. By default, the *http://* protocol is automatically added to precede your URL, but you can edit it as needed.

To set a URL as the behavior for your web object, click to select the object, and use the Behavior selector on the Internet toolbar to specify the URL. With this option selected, type the actual URL in the Internet Address box, pressing ENTER to apply the address link. Once a

URL has been applied, the Internet toolbar displays other options. Here are the URL-specific things you can define:

- **Target Frame** Use this option to specify an optional browser window location for the new page to open into. Unless you specify differently using this drop-down, the page that is called by the assigned URL address will open in the current browser window, replacing the page that contained the link. This produces the same results as the Default [None] setting in the Target Frame list. Choosing the _blank option from the list causes a new web browser window to open to display the linked page.

If your web page uses frames for its display, you can specify where in the frameset the new content will open. Choosing _self opens the new URL to the same frame where the web object is located. The _top option opens the new URL in the full body of the window, and all frames are replaced with a single frame containing the new document. The _parent option opens the new document in the current frame's Parent frameset. You can also enter custom frame names by typing them in the Target Frame combo box.

> **NOTE** *Frame-based web pages cannot be searched by most search engines such as Google, and onscreen readers for the visually impaired cannot read the contents of frames. Think very carefully if you choose a frame-based web document, and consider the audience you might lose and annoy.*

- **ALT Comments** This option is covered in more detail later in this chapter. Briefly, *use* the comments. If you don't, your visitors who have graphics turned off in their browser won't know what your message is.

- **Hotspots** A hotspot in a graphic can be a great way to create one graphic and yet tag several different areas to different links. Once you've entered a link for an object, click this icon to choose whether an object's shape or its bounding box will define the clickable area. Choose either Object Shape or Bounding Box Of Object in the selector, as shown. You can choose the Cross-hatch and Background colors if the currently set colors are difficult to distinguish from other colors in your document. These don't show on your published web page; they're only a visual convenience while you work in CorelDRAW.

- **Show Hotspot** This option in the middle of the toolbar can be toggled on or off, and it can activate or deactivate the display of the crosshatch pattern, which indicates hotspots applied to web objects, shown here.

Adding Bookmark Behavior

Assigning a bookmark to a graphic object is a method you can use to provide a convenient way for users to navigate between web pages on your site. For example, you could use a bookmark if you wanted your audience to be able to click a button or other link and return to the first page of your site from another page in your site. This is a two-step process. In the first part of the process, you define a fixed location to which one or more URL links can point. The fixed location is an anchor or bookmarked object. The second step in the process would be to create a button or text link elsewhere that points to the object's bookmark. Let's walk through the process.

Creating Bookmark Links

1. Select an object that you want to serve as the anchor or bookmark, for example, a graphic at the top of the page. The object that is bookmarked *must be a graphic, not text.*

2. From the Behavior drop-down list in the Internet toolbar choose Bookmark.

3. In the Internet Bookmark box enter a descriptive name for the bookmark, such as "home_page" or "page_4_bottom" and press ENTER, as shown in Figure 28-1.

4. Select another object or button or piece of paragraph text on the same page or on another page in your document. This is the object that when clicked will take your user to the object you previously bookmarked.

5. From the Behavior drop-down list in the Internet toolbar, choose Link.

6. From the Internet Address drop-down list, choose the Bookmark name you gave to the object in step 3. For example, if "Home page" was the bookmark name you used, you would see an entry like this: _PAGE1#Home page, as shown in Figure 28-2.

FIGURE 28-1 A bookmark object can be on any page of a multi-page document you want to publish as a website.

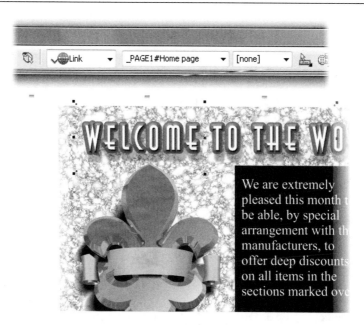

FIGURE 28-2   Use the target for the Bookmark you find on the Internet Address drop-down selector.

You can also enter a fully qualified URL in the Internet Address field to link to the bookmark. The URL would take the form of the web page's address, followed by a pound (#) sign and then the bookmark name. For example, a website's home page is usually named index.html. So a bookmark named "picture" on the index.html page would be typed in as http://www.mysite/index.html#picture.

 If you are not familiar with how to write valid HTML hyperlinks and link anchor names or IDs (called bookmarks *in CorelDRAW), consult your favorite HTML manual or the World Wide Web Consortium (W3C) page on Links and Anchors at http://www.w3.org/TR/html4/struct/links.html#h-12.2.1.*

Web Properties and the Object Properties Docker

You can use the Object Properties docker, shown in Figure 28-3, as an alternative to using the Internet toolbar. While you can apply many of the same settings from here, rollovers cannot be created from this docker. To open the Object Properties docker to display web object properties for a selected object, choose Window | Dockers | Properties, or more simply press ALT+ENTER. With the Object Properties docker open, click the Internet (globe icon) tab.

28

Behavior

Internet Address (URL)

Target Frame

ALT Comments

Hotspot Shape

Hotspot Options

FIGURE 28-3 The Object Properties docker provides an alternative way of applying common Internet properties to objects.

Using the Links and Bookmarks Docker

Use the Links and Bookmarks docker to view, name, and apply preexisting bookmarks to objects. To open the docker, shown in Figure 28-4, choose Window | Dockers | Links and Bookmarks.

Purely for convenience, this docker automatically lists the currently applied bookmarks and includes commands for linking, selecting, and deleting existing bookmark links. The bookmarks can be created only by using the Bookmarks option from the Behavior selector in the Internet toolbar. You will find this docker most useful if you are trying to find a particular bookmarked graphic in a multi-page document that contains a lot of bookmarked items.

To find a bookmark in your document, open the Links and Bookmarks docker, and then double-click an entry in the Name column. You're automatically taken to the page, and the bookmarked object is selected.

To create a link to a bookmark, first select the object to which you want to link a bookmark, click the New Link button, and then type the name in the open field on the Name list.

FIGURE 28-4   The Links and Bookmarks docker provides a convenient way for you to manage bookmarks applied to objects.

Applying a Page Background

If the background of your web page design calls for something other than white, you'll need to apply a unique background color or tiling background pattern. Page background is applied using the Page Setup pane of the Options dialog (CTRL+J), shown in Figure 28-5. To access this dialog quickly, click to expand the listing under Document, and then click Background in the tree directory to view the available options.

Although it might seem logical to create a separate background object for your page and to apply your background properties to it, this can cause problems when it comes time to export your page. The Background should be chosen in this dialog as No Background (the default), a Solid color, or a saved Bitmap.

Choose Solid to access the color selector for choosing a uniform color. Choose Bitmap and click the Browse button to select a bitmap image as the tiling background.

While Bitmap is selected and a bitmap file has been specified, the Source and Bitmap Size options in the dialog become available. The Source option lets you link to and embed the bitmap with your document, but it has no bearing on how exported web pages are created. The Bitmap Size options let you use either Default Size (the inherent size of the original bitmap) or a Custom Size as the size. By default, the Print And Export Background option is selected, which should remain so to be included as one of your web page elements.

FIGURE 28-5   Use these options to apply color or tiling bitmap backgrounds to your web document pages.

Publishing Web Documents

The Publish To The Web command is used to export your CorelDRAW document to web page file format. To access this command, choose File | Export HTML or click the Export HTML button in the Internet toolbar. Doing either opens the same Export HTML dialog, shown in Figure 28-6, which has options for you to set exactly how your web page content will be exported. The tabbed dialog looks like and is arranged similarly to CorelDRAW's Print Options dialog.

You'll find everything you need to save your web page and images. You can also use options to upload your page and the image content to a web server. The dialog itself is divided into six option areas ranging from General to Issues. You can also view a detailed Summary of the exported content and any web export preflight issues that CorelDRAW detects. Use the Browser Preview button to check the appearance of your web page; by default, CorelDRAW launches Internet Explorer for previews. The sections that follow provide a close look at all the options available.

Setting General Options

Use the General tab to set options such as the destination folder for your exported files. You can specify a separate subfolder for your graphics, or remove the default subfolder name

FIGURE 28-6   You can use these options for total control over how your page content will be exported.

(images\) to have the graphics saved in the same folder as your HTML document. To give the graphics subfolder the same name as the HTML document, select "Use HTML name for image sub-folder."

As for the HTML Layout Method area, the best choice for the majority of users is the HTML Table (Most Compatible) method. If you're using the export filter to export the HTML code only for an image map (rather than for an entire web page), you should select Single Image With Image Map.

Examining Web Page Details

The Details tab, shown next, provides information regarding exactly what you selected for export and what the exported file(s) will be named. If you want, you can apply unique page titles and/or HTML filenames to your exported web pages by clicking the existing fields and typing in the current names.

Reviewing Web Images

The Images tab, shown in Figure 28-7, provides a detailed list of the images that will be exported and their default filenames. For a thumbnail preview of each image, click the Image Name. To change the type of format to which an image is exported, click the field adjacent to the Image Name under the Type heading.

To change the settings used for each type of exported image, click and then choose from the Type drop-down list. This dialog is where you choose an export format for GIFs, JPEGs, and PNGs.

Setting Advanced HTML Options

The Advanced tab provides options for maintaining links you may have made to external files, including JavaScript in your HTML output, and for adding cascading style sheets (CSS) information in your web page. If you're using rollovers, be sure to choose the JavaScript option.

FIGURE 28-7 Use the Images tab to locate a bitmap and to change the type of file CorelDRAW exports.

Browsing the Web Page Export Summary

The Summary tab, shown in Figure 28-8, provides information on the total size of your web page and on how long it will take users to download your page at various modem speeds. The information is then itemized for each HTML page and image, so you can see if something in particular (such as a large image) might cause an unnecessarily long download time.

Preflight Web Issues

The Issues tab, shown in Figure 28-9—where an object that's off the web page has been flagged—detects and displays potential HTML export problems by using a series of preflight conditions. Preflight issues are found and displayed according to the options set throughout the Publish to the Web dialog, most commonly regarding issues surrounding color model use, text compatibility issues, and image size and resolution. The top portion of the Issues tab lists any found issues, while the bottom portion offers suggestions for correcting the problems. Images should be RGB for web images.

28

		Download Time (secs)			
	File Sizes	14.4k	28.8k	33.6k	56k
Total file:	6.22 KB	3 s	1 s	1 s	0 s	0
File list					
images/hex4.gif	51 bytes	0 s	0 s	0 s	0 s	0
images/side.jpg	12.7 KB	7 s	3 s	3 s	1 s	0
images/burst.jpg	12.2 KB	6 s	3 s	2 s	1 s	0
images/text.jpg	1.76 KB	1 s	0 s	0 s	0 s	0
VIP website.htm	2.28 KB	1 s	0 s	0 s	0 s	0

FIGURE 28-8 The information in this page helps you to measure download times against connection speeds for each of your web pages.

Use this page to troubleshoot problems and to resolve them before exporting.

To change the issues the preflight feature detects, click the Settings button to open the Preflight Settings dialog, and then click to expand the tree directory under Issues To Check For, shown here. You can also use options in this dialog to Add (+) saved preflight issue sets or to Delete (–) existing issue sets in the list. HTML preflight rules are a function only of the web document HTML that you are exporting. If you have, for example, more than three issues flagged, it's often a good idea to make a mental note of the problems, cancel out of the Export HTML dialog, and then manually correct the issues in your drawing.

Setting Web Publishing Preferences

CorelDRAW gives you complete control over your web-publishing preferences by enabling you to set Export HTML options. These options let you predetermine many of the settings used when your documents are exported to HTML format, as described earlier. To access these options, open the Options dialog (CTRL+J), click to expand the tree directory under Document, and click Export HTML, shown next.

When this Options page is selected, you'll see three options for setting conditions under which object position and white space are handled when your web page is exported:

- **Position Tolerance**   Here you can specify the number of pixels that text objects can be nudged to avoid creating very short rows or narrow columns when the page is converted to HTML during export. Position Tolerance can be set within a range of 0 (the default) to 100. Increasing this value adds extra space.

- **Image White Space**   Here you specify the number of pixels an empty cell may contain before being merged with an adjacent cell to avoid unnecessary splitting of graphic images.

- **Position White Space**   This option controls the amount of white space to be added to simplify your exported HTML document. By default, the white space is set to 4 pixels.

- **Image Map Type**   Choosing Client for the Image Map Type is best because client image maps provide faster interaction with your user than server image maps do. Only use Server if your provider specifically requests it.

28

Exporting Images for the Web

Although you can specify PNG, GIF, and JPEG file formats for images in your HTML page, you don't have access to nearly the variety of compression types or transparency options unless you pass your images through File | Export for Web. This is a process separate from Export HTML, and to get images that feature transparency so they "float" against a page background, follow this procedure:

1. Export your HTML document and allow images to be exported to the Images folder CorelDRAW creates.

2. Export images you'd like to treat as special elements—such as PNGs and GIFs with transparent backgrounds—using File | Export for Web.

3. Save these files and then replace the ones in the Images folder with your new files, using the same filenames as the ones in the Images folder.

Create a graphic you'd like to appear on a web page against a background, and follow these steps to learn how to export the graphic with transparency.

Exporting a Graphic with Transparency

1. Select the graphic on the page with the Pick tool. If the graphic has a background, don't select the background and you'll save a step.

2. Choose File | Export for Web.

3. In the Export for Web dialog, choose GIF from the Format drop-down list.

4. Click the eyedropper tool to select it, and then click over the background in the GIF preview pane, not the one marked "Original" at its bottom. You can arrange the preview panes to top and bottom, left and right, or other multiple views by clicking the buttons in the upper left of this dialog.

5. Click the Makes The Selected Color Transparent button; in a moment, you'll see the preview of the graphic with a checkerboard background indicating the transparent areas of your intended export.

6. Because GIF images can drop out only one color and not a range of colors, if the background of your document isn't black, consider using one of the Matte colors, selected from the Matte mini-palette. If, for example, your web page is solid blue, choose solid blue. Doing this has nothing to do with the color you selected to drop out as the background color, but instead has to do with fringing. You choose a compatible background color from the Matte colors to disguise aliased edges around your graphic.

7. Set the unique number of colors for the export. By default, it's 256, but to save transfer time, many simple graphics can look fine using 128 or even 32 colors. You specify the number of colors from the Number Of Colors drop-down below the preview of the Color Palette, or you can type a value into the box.

8. If you need to resize the graphic, use the Percentage boxes in the Transformation field of this dialog. But *think twice about this*: your HTML page *won't display the image properly* if you're replacing, for example, a 400×300-pixel GIF that CorelDRAW just exported to the Images folder with a new graphic that's 375×285 pixels.

9. Click Save As, and after you're done, replace the original exported image with this one, renaming the file to match the original filename. See Figure 28-10 for the location of the features used in this tutorial.

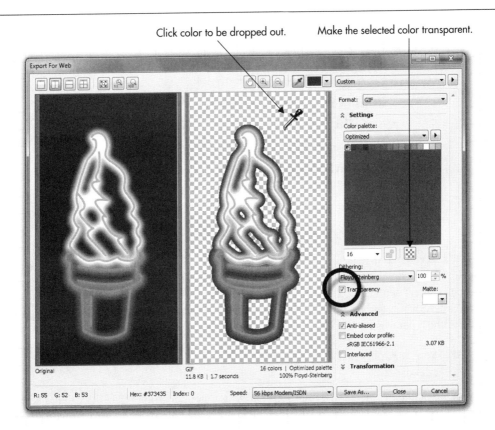

FIGURE 28-10   Export at the file size and with the options you need with the Export for Web dialog.

Swapping graphics into an HTML page has to be done with precision. The filename, the file type, and image dimensions have to be identical, because the image dimensions are written into the HTML code. And very few artists want to backwards-correct an HTML document!

Web Text Options

Fonts that you use when designing a web page will not always show up on a visitor's web browser: web browsers such as Internet Explorer, Mozilla Firefox, and Apple's Safari are almost completely dependent on which typefaces are installed on the visitor's computer. There is no true "default" font for the Web, but over the years, Microsoft has quietly provided your system—and tens of millions of others—with system fonts that you basically can be assured reside on more than 90 percent of all computers used to surf the Web. Here are the current "web safe" typefaces:

Arial is a web-safe font.

Comic Sans MS is a web-safe font.

Courier New is a web-safe font.

Georgia is a web-safe font.

Impact is a web-safe font.

Lucida Sans is a web-safe font.

Palatino Linotype is a web-safe font.

Tahoma is a web-safe font.

Times New Roman is a web-safe font.

Trebuchet is a web-safe font.

Verdana is a web-safe font.

It's considered discourteous on the Web to post long sections of text as bitmap graphics: visitors can't copy or bookmark the text, and it violates the rules of accessibility—text-to-speech readers can't decipher text-as-graphics, and indexing services will ignore what to you might be valuable information. Therefore, when you create paragraph text for a web page, use one of the typefaces listed in the previous illustration, for at least two more important reasons:

- Your web page will load more slowly with text displayed as a graphic instead of as editable text.

- Small text, such as 10 point, probably will not be legible. Consider that a screen pixel is approximately 1/72 inch, and a typographic point is approximately equal in size to one pixel. Therefore, 10-point text has to be rendered to screen using only 10 pixels in height. That's the size of the font previews on CorelDRAW's Fonts drop-down list, and many of the fancier fonts are not legible at this size as bitmap renders.

Needs to be a bitmap graphic

Needs to be a
bitmap graphic

Paragraph text
can be Tahoma.

Needs to be a
bitmap graphic

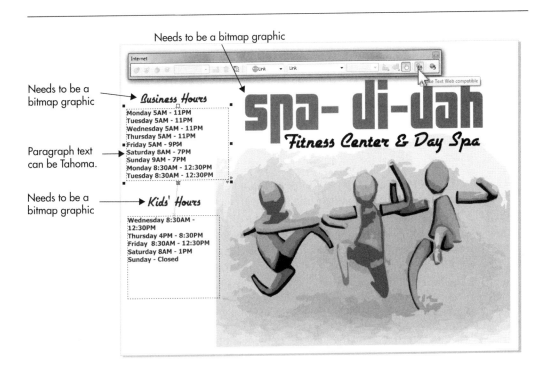

28

FIGURE 28-11   Text that uses distinctive typefaces has to be exported as bitmaps to retain its look on the Web.

Figure 28-11 is an example of a web page layout, and as you can see, the text for the business hours is small and formatted as paragraph text. This text needs to be exported as text and not as a bitmap. On the other hand, the name of the fictitious spa, and the elegant headlines above business hours can be exported as bitmap graphics, especially if the designer wants to retain the style of the typeface.

Follow these steps with any web page layout you have that contains text, to learn how to make the document conform to web standards for text.

Formatting Text for the Web

1. Format any text you want to be editable text on the web page using the fonts enumerated earlier.

2. The first thing to do is to check to see that any text you want displayed as text on the web page is paragraph text. Select any text in question with the Pick tool, and then choose Text from the menu. If the command Convert To Paragraph Text is available, choose this command. If it's not available, the text is already paragraph text, and it's easy to spot on the page because a nonprinting frame is around paragraph text.

3. Conversely, any headlines or other ornate large, short text entries should be artistic text. With the Pick tool, select any text that's paragraph text but needs to be artistic text, and then choose Text | Convert to Artistic Text.

4. Choose Window | Toolbars | Internet. Select a paragraph text block, and then click the Make Text Web Compatible button. Do this again for any remaining paragraph text blocks.

5. If there is nothing left to link on your web page, click Export HTML.

You will not see paragraph text change in any way on your CorelDRAW page; the Make Text Web Compatible button is a toggle—you can select tagged text and then turn off its web compatibility, and this compatibility is just an instruction on how CorelDRAW writes the HTML. You need to look at the finished HTML page in a web browser—*on a computer other than your own*—to truly see how the web-compatible paragraph text looks. Because web browsers examine your installed fonts, you have no other way to see the text as the rest of the world will see it unless you go through the unpleasant process of temporarily uninstalling several typefaces from your own computer.

Use ALT Tags

The ALT Comments button on the Internet toolbar is used to provide descriptive information—popularly known as *ALT tags*—about a graphic for those in your web audience who either are surfing with graphics disabled (it's a fast way to perform text searches), or have a visual impairment. It's good "netiquette" to label graphics on a web page with an ALT tag, particularly if your logo is a graphic and it's the only time it's seen on a web page. Applying ALT tags takes only a second, and here's an example: the fictitious SPA-Di-Dah Health Club's logo is a special typeface and therefore has to go out to the Web as a bitmap graphic. Here, the logo is selected, the ALT Comments button is clicked, and a description of the graphic is typed in.

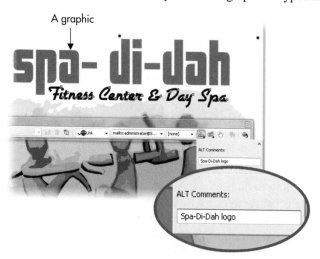

SVG: Export as Vector Objects

Scalable Vector Graphics (SVG) are web objects CorelDRAW can both import and export. Since 1999, the SVG file format has been under development by the World Wide Web Consortium (W3C). SVG is based on the text-based Extended Markup Language (XML) for describing 2D vector graphics. All current web browsers except Internet Explorer can directly render an SVG web page element to screen; IE 9 is expected to adopt this capability.

One of the most useful properties of an SVG graphic is that it is scalable, with no loss of image detail. This means that you can post a graphic, for example, of directions as a map, and if the SVG file is coded properly into a page, a visitor to your site can enlarge or decrease the size of the map to exactly find a location. Also, SVG files are very small because they are text based, and if a friend or client doesn't own CorelDRAW, SVG is an ideal medium for sharing graphics, a good alternative to the PDF file format.

Open Map.cdr in CorelDRAW now, and follow these steps to see how to export a graphic to the Scalable Vector Graphics file format.

Exporting Vectors as Vectors for the Web

1. Select the graphic with the Pick tool, or press CTRL+A to Select All.

2. Choose File | Export (or click the Export button on the standard toolbar). Choose SVG Scalable Vector Graphics (*.SVG), pick a filename and location, and then click Export.

3. Choose Unicode UTF 8 as the encoding method. This produces a smaller file than UTF 16 because it encodes words to 8 bits, eliminating some multilingual parameters used in non-Latin text.

4. In the Export Text area, you can choose to export any text in the selected objects as text or as curves. If you chose UTF 8, you should export as curves if you've used non-Latin characters such as those available in fonts such as Arial and Georgia—Chinese and Greek glyphs are present in Unicode fonts.

5. In the Styling Options list box, you can choose to embed a style sheet (a cascading style sheet, CSS) internally or externally with the exported SVG file. If you choose an external style sheet, it's linked to the graphic and can help a webmaster embed the graphic in a web page. You can also make the SVG part of a rollover button if you check the Link Externally box in the JavaScript area.

6. Choose to embed fonts if you're using a typeface that's not web compatible.

7. You can create smooth fountain fill steps by increasing the value using the Fountain Steps box. Doing this increases the saved file size, however.

8. Choose the dimensions at which you want the SVG graphic to display in a browser window. It makes no sense, in this example, to make it a small graphic, so a width of 900 pixels is chosen.

9. Export Bitmap is only a relevant field in this export box if objects you've selected cannot be interpreted as vectors. Choose this option if you've used drop shadows, mesh fills, texture fills, and any effect such as lens effects. You can embed or export the bitmaps-linked files. Embedding the bitmaps makes the SVG file much larger; if you choose to do this, JPEG—a highly compressed image file type—is probably a smarter choice than PNG.

10. Click OK to export the SVG file. If you have Firefox, Safari, Opera, or an Internet browser other the Internet Explorer, try dragging the SVG file into an open browser window to see the results.

Flash and Web Pages

Flash is an openly published media standard, owned by Adobe Systems, that is yet another web-worthy vector file format. If you bought the physical DVD installation of CorelDRAW X5, you have a copy of SwishMiniMax v2.0, and you can make incredibly small animation files by working between CorelDRAW and SwishMiniMax. If you bought the download version of X5, you didn't get the animation application, but you can still export non-animating SWF (Flash) vector graphics you can put on the Web. In either case, animation is an exciting part of the Web, and the tutorial that follows guides you through some basic steps on using the Swish animation program.

Exploring SWF Files

CorelDRAW can add some fill and outline properties to objects that the Flash file format doesn't support. As with SVG files, if a Flash file can't write a vector, a bitmap copy of the graphic is included in the exported file. Exporting bitmaps within a Flash file sort of defeats the purpose of this compact vector-enabled file type, so reviewing what can export as vector objects, and what cannot, is a good idea here.

Objects and Fills that Flash Supports

You can create certain shapes and fills in CorelDRAW that Flash animation can't handle, and you're warned of this before you export an animation. The good news is that everything that Flash can handle, CorelDRAW can create. The following list describes what you should and shouldn't use when making a scene for animation:

- **Outline Properties**   Standard Flash export supports outline width and color, but only rounded line caps and joins for the Flash standard previous to version 8; CorelDRAW's export filter doesn't do 8, so press ALT+ENTER, click the Outline tab, and then click Advanced before exporting any outlines, and change the connections to round. Flash does not support dashed lines, arrowheads, or artistic media strokes. However, if your design calls for a fancy outline stroke, you can convert the line to a shape by choosing Arrange | Break Artistic Media Apart, and then delete the parent stroke choosing when an outline is selected. The Export dialog also offers to convert only dashed outlines to be compatible with Flash.

- **Fill Properties**   Flash will render Uniform color fills, plus Linear and Radial fountain fills. A gradient can contain up to eight color transitions (color stops).

- **Transparency**   If you apply transparency to a gradient-filled shape, you are limited to the Uniform transparency type. However, when a shape is filled with a flat (solid) color, you can use Linear and Radial transparency types.

- **Text**   You can use any typeface you have installed. However, if you want fancy text animations, it's best to type your text directly in SwishMiniMax instead of in your design. SwishMiniMax reads imported vector text as one solid block of graphic and can't animate individual characters as a single object.

28

- **Bitmaps** Photos and digital paintings can be exported to a Flash animation, but they cannot be as efficiently compressed as vector shapes. It's a good idea to make a copy of high-resolution images at the size you intend to use, in JPEG file format.

- **Effects** All effects—contours, blends, and envelopes—applied to shapes can be exported; using these effects is a good workaround to certain types of fountain fills that don't work as a flash vector object.

Exporting a Static Flash Vector Design

Open Solutions Graphic.cdr in CorelDRAW now. This design has been created in a tricky sort of way to make an interesting animation, but first let's check out how to export a static, nonmoving Flash file from CorelDRAW. Here's the procedure and your options.

 ## Making a Single-Frame Flash File

1. Select all the objects using the diagonal-drag, marquee technique around the objects. They are on different layers, so CTRL+A doesn't work here.

2. Click the Export button on the standard toolbar, and then choose SWF - Macromedia Flash (.SWF) from the Save As Type drop-down list. Choose a location for the saved file and name it, and then click Export.

3. On the General tab, bitmap settings are only relevant when objects have fills that the export engine cannot recognize. In your own exporting adventures, use JPG Compression of 0 or 10 percent to preserve the appearance of vector objects that have texture or other non-acceptable fills.

4. Click Objects in the Bounding Box Size area; you have the objects already selected in step 1, so this option is the smart one.

5. Check Convert Dashed Outlines just as a matter of practice. Use Default Fountain Steps is a handy option if your objects have only subtle fills or fewer than 8 color transitions. Unchecking this box can create larger files, but unchecking this box might cause visible banding when you look at the Flash file.

6. The HTML tab really contains only one item of interest: Image Size. If you want to export this graphic at any size, select the size using the spin boxes or by typing a specific value here.

7. If the Issues tab reports that non-RGB colors are in the selection, ignore it. Click OK to export the graphic as a flash media object.

8. Internet Explorer needs the help of a JavaScript to display a Flash file directly in a web browser window, but if you have a copy of Firefox, you can drag the SWF file into its browser pane, and you'll see the graphic full screen. Also, Adobe's Flash

Player 10 will display the file if you've downloaded the player; chances are good that some application has already fetched it for you and made the file association. Double-clicking the file icon might bring up Flash Player.

NOTE *CorelDRAW X5's Flash Export options aren't correct on the HTML tab. No Play or Loop options are exported for files that contain no animation. This is why you should read on and learn about SwishMiniMax, which does indeed use sound and full vector animation when it creates an SWF file.*

Exporting SWFs to SwishMiniMax

The documentation for SwishMiniMax 2 will tell you that WMF (Windows Metafile) and SWF files are accepted for import as vector-based media. Unfortunately, the WMF file format is quite limited in translating your handsome CorelDRAW artwork, but SWF files do, indeed, translate your CorelDRAW drawings with quite high fidelity. SwishMiniMax thinks all SWF files are vector *movies,* but that's okay; you're not going to tell SwishMiniMax a word, and your SWF imports will look splendid. The following sections walk you through an example scenario: Solutions, Inc., a fictitious company, wants an animated logo—the block with the three pegs in the Solutions Graphic.cdr file. What do you say you knock their socks off and deliver an animated logo, animated text, and music playing during the animation?

Building the Architecture of Animated Graphics

Open the Object Manager now to get a better look at the trickery beneath this graphic (Tools | Object Manager). Figure 28-12 shows the composition taken apart: if you move any of the objects marked yellow, orange, or magenta, you'll see that they appear to fit through the holes in the brick object. The reason this illusion works is that on the top layer in this

FIGURE 28-12   Stage a composition with carefully designed objects on layers to create the illusion that objects pass through a hole in other shapes.

drawing is a mask that *hides* the bottom of the brick object; thus, you can duplicate this 2D illusion—making a composition move in "3D" if you build a similar mask group of shapes in compositions of your own that you want to animate.

Move the Composition to SwishMiniMax

As mentioned earlier, SwishMiniMax will accept CorelDRAW-exported SWF files. The next trick is to export the drawing as six separate objects: the three pegs, the brick, the mask group, and the shadow for the pegs on the brick. Create a new folder on your hard disk for these project files. Additionally, put the Solutions.mp3 file you downloaded in this new folder—it's the music for this big-time animation.

Select one object at a time, click the Export button on the standard toolbar, and then choose SWF as the File Of Type when you export—make certain Selected Only is checked. Give each export a name you'll remember; SwishMiniMax understands layers and it's quite easy to order all six shapes, but you need to select an object before exporting, as shown here, or you'll wind up exporting the entire page of objects.

A Taxi-Driver's Tour of SwishMiniMax

The Official Guide cannot possibly comprehensively document SwishMiniMax's features; the following sections you'll work through, however, will give you a base education on its animation options. By just following the steps, you'll learn how to build a basic, finished animation, and use variations on the steps later to build a handsome Flash movie of your own.

Setting Up Your SwishMiniMax Stage

A number of terms might be new to you after opening SwishMiniMax; there are equivalents in CorelDRAW, but some terms have no equivalents, and they'll be described as you need to use the features in the tutorials. Two items are of immediate importance, though:

- **The Stage**   Flash movies can have different scenes—scenes are out of the scope of this book to describe—and every scene has a *stage*. For the purposes of this tutorial, a stage is the drawing window, into which you import and create actors.

- **Actors**   You put several automatable elements on the page (the stage), but the most common one is an actor. Actors in this example are objects: text objects, a background you'll manually add, and the music MP3 file.

- **Frame Rate**   Digital video usually is measured in frames per second (fps). This frame rate has very little to do with how fast an animation plays, but instead controls *how smoothly* or jittery a video plays back. If you remember the (relatively!) old NASA footage of spacewalks, the video was at a frame rate of anywhere from 8 to 10 fps. And although the footage was breathtaking, it looks a little on the Keystone Cops side. By default, SwishMiniMax offers you a new video project at 25 fps, which is a good, all-purpose frame rate. If there's not a lot of dramatic action in a video, you can customize a project to play at 20 or even 12 frames per second. How fast an object moves in an animation depends on how many frames there are between keyframes—you'll work with keyframes in the examples to follow.

Let's open SwishMiniMax now, define the size and frame rate, and create and import an object or two.

Beginning an Animation

1. Click the SwishMiniMax icon to launch it, or use the Windows Start menu to launch it. The very first screen is a wizard, where you pick a default template. Choose the Default template and then click OK.

2. Choose File | Save As, and then save your project to the folder you created with the Flash objects in it.

3. On the Properties panel, click Movie Properties.

4. Here's the deal: animations can be any time length you like, but this animation will have a soundtrack, which is 4 seconds long. This 4 seconds is something you can't change, so the concept is to make a 4-second-long animation so both the video and the audio end at the same time. To be on the lazy side here, type **30** in the Frame Rate box (30 frames per second × 4 seconds = 120 frames). Now you know how

long you have to animate on SwishMiniMax's timeline to make a perfect little flash video that loops continuously while staying in synch with the audio.

5. As you can see, the Width and Height are predetermined by the Default template, and this is fine: 560 pixels wide × 410 pixels high will work because the Solutions graphic.cdr file was carefully measured beforehand to scale to these dimensions. Usually, it's a good idea to preplan this way in your own work, but it's not a showstopper because the SWF files you exported are vector objects, and vector objects can be scaled in SwishMiniMax smoothly, exactly like in CorelDRAW. Click OK to apply the frame rate and close the box.

6. Unless you like black or transparent, this scene could use a background. Let's make it a circular gradient background, going from a white interior to black at the outside edges. Choose the Rectangle tool from the toolbox, and then drag from upper left to bottom right in the scene window. It's okay if you go outside the frame a little: Flash files truncate any object area outside of the stage.

7. On the Properties panel, click the Fill drop-down list and choose Gradient. Now click the Gradient Type button and choose the Radial button.

8. To invert the gradient, drag the white marker from its position on the right, nearly over to the black marker at left. Then move the black marker to the far right. Finally, move the white marker to far left. You're more prone to accidentally delete a marker if you put two in the same position—that's why you took the extra step here.

9. It's time to bring the brick—the backmost imported actor—to the stage. Choose File | Import to Stage | Animation. Choose Brick.swf (or whatever you named the brick) from the directory list and then click Open.

10. In the Import dialog, Animated Movie Clip is the only button that needs to be clicked—SwishMiniMax doesn't know the file isn't an animation, and you're not going to tell it. Click Import, save the file again, and take a break for a moment. Your screen should look like the one in Figure 28-13.

Timeline

Order of objects in scene

FIGURE 28-13   The brick imported object is in the scene, on top of the background
you created.

Finishing the Imports

Procedurally, it's a good idea to have all your actors in the scene before animating them.
Once you become familiar with SwishMiniMax, you might want to bring your actors to the
scene all at once—you can do this by multiple-selecting SWF files in the Import box. But
for now, let's keep it simple and keep the actors in the proper order for the animation. One at
a time, import the yellow, the orange, and the magenta pegs, then import the mask, and
finally import the shadow object. You should have no problem aligning them. With
SwishMiniMax's Selector tool (it's the same as CorelDRAW's Pick tool), first select the
name of an actor from the Outline list, place the Selector tool in the scene window, and after

it turns into a four-headed "move" cursor, move the objects. Then import the MP3 file as an actor to the scene: File | Import to Stage | Sound. Then press CTRL+S!

How to Move an Actor

This section will be the most demanding for users who have never worked with a timeline or a video application. Here is the strategy, and then you'll actually work through the procedure as tutorial steps:

- The concept is to make first the left peg, then the middle, and finally the right magenta peg come out of the holes. So first, position all the pegs in a retracted state.

- These peg actors are in the scene, but not on the stage yet. This is admittedly a confusing screen convention, but it's the way Flash animates things. So after the pegs are in their first frame position, on its track on the timeline, right-click the first frame, and then choose Place from the pop-up menu. You've placed the actor (the peg) in its initial position.

- You want to move the peg up and to the left over time, so you right-click anywhere to the right of the little Place icon on its track (the traffic light icon), and then choose Move from the right-click menu.

- You now move the actor: you click the last segment of the Move segment on the track—the diamond dot at the right end of the arrow—and then you put your Selector tool in the window and move the object. You'll see a preview line over the object in the scene window indicating its movement.

- If you want to change this movement at the beginning or end, you need to click either the Place icon at the beginning, or you need to be at the diamond marker at the end of the Move segment. At any point in between, you cannot move the actor.

- To move where the movement starts, you drag the Move marker on the track in the timeline.

- To make an object move slower or faster along the path you've created, you need to increase or decrease the number of frames for the transition. To do this, click-drag either the head or the tail of the Move marker. You know your cursor is in position when the cursor changes to a double-headed arrow with a brace between the arrows.

So much for explanations: the best way to get results is by actually *doing* these moves.

Creating Animation

1. Begin by selecting the orange round peg at left. On its track on the timeline, right-click the first frame, and then choose Place from the pop-up menu.

2. Click Frame 2 on the track in the timeline. Right-click and then choose Move. By default, this puts a 10-frame movement segment on the track, which is too frenetic for a 30 fps animation, but you'll correct that in a moment.

3. Click the end of the Move event, at the diamond dot.

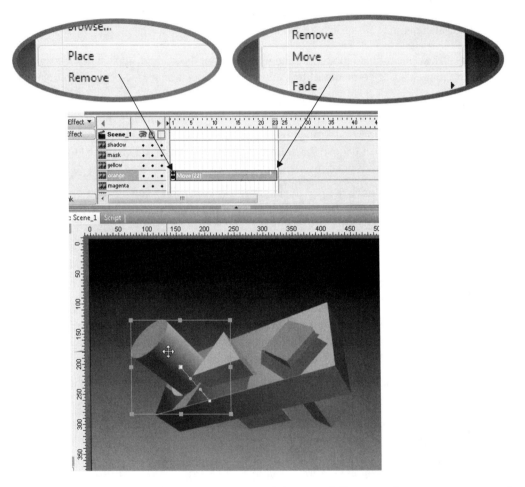

4. Put your cursor in the scene window, and then carefully move the orange peg up and left so it sticks out of the brick.

5. Click the tail of the Move event on the track, and then drag it out to about Frame 20. The Move event marker should tell you how many frames you have the move specified for in parentheses.

6. As a reward for getting this far, click the Play button below the main menu bar. Then click the Stop button and get back to work!

7. Repeat step 1 with the yellow and magenta animation tracks.

8. For the yellow peg, click over Frame 3, and then right-click and choose Move from the menu. Click the last frame of the Move event, and then move the yellow peg in the scene, as you did with the orange peg in step 4.

9. Drag the track out to about 20 frames in duration so that Move ends at about Frame 39.

10. Do the Magenta peg's animation now. Start the Move at Frame 30, and end it at about Frame 58.

11. File | Save. Keep it open.

Gosh: all the action is over with at Frame 60, and we have a whole 60 frames to spare. This is by design! In the sections to follow, you'll add a fancy animated piece of text, and then add the music to make a perfectly timed Flash video.

Applying a Canned Effect

In addition to the Place and Move commands on the pop-up menu, this menu is also a handy shortcut to accessing canned scripts that auto-animate object properties. The shadow object is a perfect example of an element that's in need of a certain scripted effect. It would be too time-consuming to animate the movement of the shadow so it's in synch with the movement of the pegs apparently casting the shadow—what will work almost as well is to fade it in. Here's how to script an event using a SwishMiniMax preset.

Using the Fade in Preset

1. The precise entry point and duration of the shadow object fading in is based on your artistic taste, or on having had experience in traditional animation. Click the shadow object in the Outline panel first.

2. Click at about Frame 15 on the shadow's track on the timeline to move the current time to Frame 15.

3. Right-click over Frame 30, and then on the pop-up menu, choose Fade | Fade In. Because this object is making its stage appearance by fading in, the Place marker is not needed for this track. Play the movie back now to see how you're doing, and to amaze anyone watching over your shoulder.

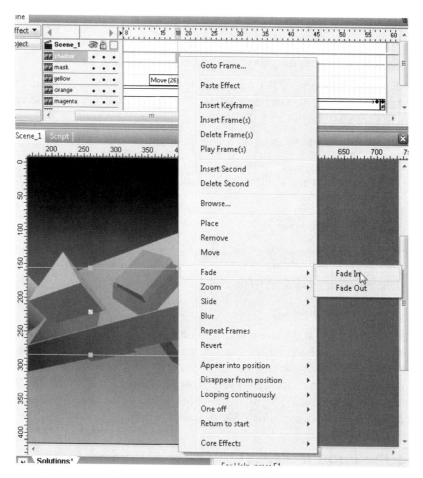

Adding and Animating Text

Here's the part where not using CorelDRAW text as a graphic begins to make sense. You can access any installed system font in SwishMiniMax via the Text tool and the Properties panel. Let's cut to the chase now and add text, and then animate it. No one knows this is Solutions, Inc.'s logo. Yet.

Text as Flash Actor

1. Choose the Text tool from the toolbox.

2. Move the current time to Frame 54 on the timeline.

3. Marquee-drag a text box below the design in the scene window. It's perfectly okay if objects overlap in a Flash composition, and it's okay to drag a large defined area. "Large" is easier to correct later than making a box that's too small for your text— then you have to resize the box.

4. Type **Solutions, Inc.** in the open text field in the scene window.

5. Choose a typeface in the Properties panel, then choose a point size, choose center alignment from the Text Justification drop-down, and finally, click The Color Of The Text button to reveal the palette of web-compatible colors. Choose a bright gold.

The Color Of The Text button

6. File | Save. Now, with the Selector tool, right-click over Frame 54 on the text track in the timeline, and hover over Appear Into Position. Don't freak out over the arm's length of preset animation scripts here. Save some for future use, and choose any of the presets that end in the word "in," such as Burn In, Blur In, or Flip And Shrink In. Make this action about 20 frames long.

7. File | Save.

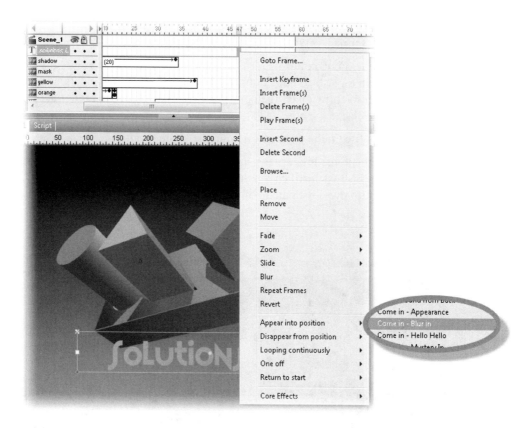

Adding the Finishing Touches

Because you added the MP3 file as an actor to this project, it's placed on the timeline, and if you locate it for a moment, you'll see a faint red stripe on its track, which tells you in absolute frame count (at 30 fps) where it ends, which is at Frame 120. Now ensure that the longest-duration actor in the scene stays on stage until the music is over. This forces the Flash video you'll export shortly to keep the audio in synch with the video, and the other placed actors will inherit this duration because they've appeared and have no cue to disappear until the animation loops back to Frame 1.

Setting an Overall Flash Video Duration

1. The text entered the scene last, so it's a good candidate for the Place command. Make the current time 120 frames by clicking the timeline.

2. Right-click over Frame 128 on the Solutions, Inc. track. It's just a little after the end of the MP3 music.

3. Choose Place. Done! It's time to go live with this hot piece of motion picture entertainment!

4. Press CTRL+E (File | Export…SWF).

5. Choose a name and location for the saved Flash file, click Save, and then save one last time in SwishMiniMax; then you can close the program.

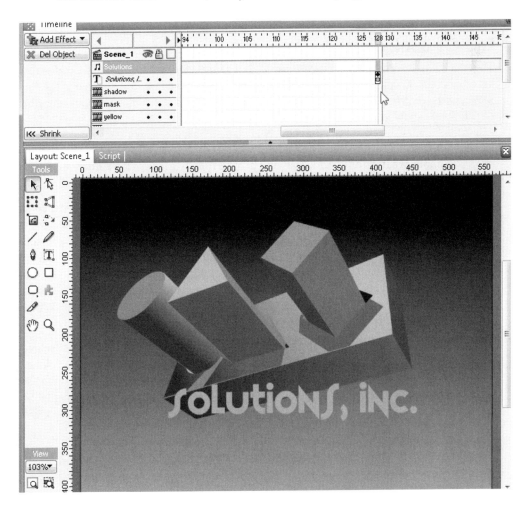

Gather as many friends as possible, and then seat them around your monitor. Get popcorn, and break out the non-alcoholic sparkling grape juice. What you've just exported is only 68K (some *typefaces* are larger and not as entertaining), yet it has music and plays for 4 seconds at any size dimensions you set up a web page for to place this media. If you have Firefox or any Internet browser other than IE Explorer, just drag the file icon into an open browser window to play it. Alternatively, you probably have Adobe Flash Player 10 installed—an application or your browser might have installed it for you. If the icon is a page with a big "f" on it, it's associated with Adobe's Flash Player, and all you need to is double-click the icon to play it.

The End-Of-Book Special

The preceding tutorial is by no means the end of this chapter or *The Official Guide.* You have some serious playtime ahead of you! In the ZIP archive you downloaded is the finished SWI SwishMiniMax file you can load in SwishMiniMax to verify that you did everything like the steps showed, plus:

- Several other "ambient" MP3 sound files for your use in the future. These are completely free for commercial and private use, created by the author, so there are no sticky encumbrances with royalty-free online music or commercial restrictions.

- A full-frame animation of the Solutions, Inc. logo. This SWF file was created as a movie from a 3D modeling and rendering program. Full-frame animations are larger than vector animations because every frame is totally different from the previous one. If you have a movie you'd like to turn into a Flash file with SwishMiniMax, give this experiment a go with Solutions 3D.swf first. All you need to do is follow the steps in this chapter with SwishMiniMax, but import the Solutions 3D.swf as an animated movie clip, exactly as you did with the CorelDRAW exported SWF still vector images.

- The finished SWF files can be found in the Gallery subfolder of the ZIP archive, for viewing and examining. Figure 28-14 shows two different versions of the Solutions, Inc. assignment. If you don't have the typeface Variex installed on your computer, SwishMiniMax will inform you that the typeface the author used is unavailable. This is okay—let SwishMiniMax substitute a font, probably Arial, and you can choose a different typeface as you experiment with the file.

As far as embedding Flash files to play in an HTML document you've exported from CorelDRAW, SwishMiniMax provides the HTML code snippet if you choose File | Export | SWF+HTML. However, you *do* need to know a little about HTML code to manually insert the code so the movie plays on your CorelDRAW exported web page. Alternatively, if you really want moving content on your website, consider a free HTML editor such as the one

FIGURE 28-14   Flash files can contain static vector objects and also can contain complete full-frame animations.

offered by Coffee Cup software. You can import your CorelDRAW exported file, and perform a little embedding with the WYSIWYG editor.

The last word in animation is that as a designer, it's probably best to turn your work over to a webmaster or other expert in HTML coding, and to ask them to embed your work on an HTML page. You've learned a lot in this chapter; don't overdo it!

This chapter has shown you how to take just about any media on a CorelDRAW page, be it a drawing, a photo, or text, and make your design compatible as a web page. With links, your web page connects you to a community and keeps you connected with business associates, friends, and potential customers you haven't even met yet.

INDEX

More than you thought possible

Power up your designs with **CorelDRAW® Graphics Suite X5**! This versatile graphics suite offers an all-in-one solution for illustration, layout, tracing, photo editing, Web graphics and animation. Designed for professional and aspiring designers alike, CorelDRAW Graphics Suite is used to create many of the things you see around you every day—from distinctive logos and signs, to Web graphics and animations, billboards, car wraps and more.

The quick, intuitive workflow, accurate color control and powerful design tools help you turn creative ideas into professional results. Start smoothly, learn quickly and create with confidence with built-in learning tools, high-value content and compelling video tutorials. Get super results without super effort—do more than you thought possible!

More efficient content management

Speed up your workflow with a new built-in content organizer—Corel® CONNECT helps you find graphics, templates, fonts and images quickly on your computer. Save valuable time by instantly accessing your selected content, which is stored in the tray synchronized between CorelDRAW® and Corel® PHOTO-PAINT™.

Enrich your designs with high-value digital content
Create more impactful designs with over 1,000 professional fonts, including the Helvetica® and Frutiger® fonts, new to CorelDRAW. Meanwhile, **enhanced** clipart, royalty-free photos and **enhanced** vehicle templates boost creativity. Give your work a professional finish without spending extra time and money—you'll find everything you need here!

More confidence in your creations

Create eye-catching Web graphics with efficient new Web tools— Design Web graphics more effectively than ever with a new Pixels mode that lets you preview how content will display online. Plus, a new integrated Web animation tool lets you open and animate graphics and designs created in CorelDRAW. Optimize your settings to achieve the highest graphics quality with a new Export for Web dialog box.

Boost your creativity and productivity with enhanced drawing tools—Benefit from new features that include the option to lock toolbars in place, more printing options, and improvements to the Eyedropper, Mesh Fill and other popular tools. Plus, the enhanced Corel PHOTO-PAINT lets you get more creative with exciting photo effects, such as Vibrance, Grayscale and Photo Filter.

More learning tools for design growth

Increase your design knowledge with engaging learning materials—Start smoothly and learn quickly with new and updated video tutorials, built-in tool tips and a visually rich, online guidebook that contains new articles from experts. The box version comes with a hard cover, full-color, printed guidebook.

More ways to share your designs

Control color consistency with a powerful new color management engine—Match the colors you see on screen across printed materials and Web graphics. A new color management engine enhances color consistency across all media and introduces support for new color profiles from PANTONE®. Minimize your ecological footprint and reduce costly reprints by knowing that your colors are accurate before you print.

The completely redesigned color management engine accurately preserves colors during file import and export.

Eliminate any barriers to file sharing with market-leading file compatibility—Import and export files quickly and easily with dozens of supported file formats, including PDF, JPG, PNG, EPS, AI, TIFF, PSD, DOCX and many more. CorelDRAW Graphics Suite X5 ranks among the most compatible graphics software in the market.

More speed and efficiency

Complete your tasks faster than ever with powerful performance enhancements—Maximize your computer's power with new multi-core processing that makes your tools more responsive than ever. Plus, take advantage of newly integrated Microsoft® Visual Studio® for Applications (VSTA) technology, which offers more options for automating time-consuming tasks, as well as add-in solutions that enhance the existing functionality of CorelDRAW.

Work in the latest Windows® environment with optimization for Microsoft® Windows® 7—Enjoy a hands-on experience with new touch-screen support for Windows 7 that lets you pan, zoom and scroll with your fingertips. This latest version is optimized for Windows 7, and also supports Windows Vista® and Windows® XP.

The box version of CorelDRAW Graphics Suite X5 comes with a hard cover, full-color, printed guidebook.

What's included:

- **CorelDRAW® X5**
  Intuitive vector-illustration and page-layout applicat

- **Corel® PHOTO-PAINT™ X5**
  Professional photo-editing application

- **Corel® PowerTRACE™ X5**
  Accurate bitmap-to-vector tracing tool

- **Corel CAPTURE™ X5**
  One-click screen-capture tool

- **Corel® CONNECT**
  Built-in content organizer

- **SWiSH miniMax™ 2**
  Easy Web graphics animation tool

- **PhotoZoom Pro 2**
  Plug-in that preserves photo quality when enlarging digital images in Corel® PHOTO-PAINT™

- 10,000 high-quality clipart and digital images

- 1,000 professional, high-resolution digital photos

- 1,000 OpenType® fonts, including Windows® Glyph List 4 (WGL4) and engraving fonts

- 350 professionally designed templates

- 2,000 vehicle templates

- Full color, hard cover, printed guidebook

- 2 hours of training videos on DVD

Do more than you thought possible with

CorelDRAW®
GRAPHICS SUITE X5

For more information,
please contact your local reseller or visit
www.corel.com/coreldraw
Try it for free!